D0531886

Data Structures

RICK DECKER

Hamilton College
Clinton, New York

PRENTICE HALL, Englewood Cliffs, New Jersey 07632

Library of Congress Cataloging-in-Publication Data

Decker, Rick
Data structures / Rick Decker.
p. cm.
Includes index.
ISBN 0-13-198813-1
1. Data structures (Computer science) I. Title.
QA76.9.D35D43. 1989
005.7'3—dc19 88-37633
CIP#

Editorial/production supervision and
interior design: David Ershun
Cover design: Diane Saxe
Cover art: Thomas Cole: *The Voyage of Life: Youth*, 1840. Oil on canvas, 52½ × 78½ inches. *Credit:* The Munson Williams Proctor Institute Museum of Art, Utica, New York.
Manufacturing buyer: Mary Noonan

A Division of Simon & Schuster
Englewood Cliffs, New Jersey 07632

Printed in the United States of America

10 9 8 7 6 5 4 3

ISBN 0-13-198813-1

PRENTICE-HALL INTERNATIONAL (UK) LIMITED, *London*
PRENTICE-HALL OF AUSTRALIA PTY. LIMITED, *Sydney*
PRENTICE-HALL CANADA INC., *Toronto*
PRENTICE-HALL HISPANOAMERICANA, S.A., *Mexico*
PRENTICE-HALL OF INDIA PRIVATE LIMITED, *New Delhi*
PRENTICE-HALL OF JAPAN INC., *Tokyo*
SIMON & SCHUSTER ASIA PTE. LTD., *Singapore*
EDITORIA PRENTICE-HALL DO BRASIL LTDA., *Rio de Janeiro*

for Barb

Contents

Preface

The overwhelming majority of authors have very little to say.
If we suppose, rather charitably, that in a typical book of fifteen chapters
there are only eight passages worthy of quotation, then simple
mathematics will convince us that in short order there will be no original
quotations left for chapter headings. The implication is obvious. ...

ARMAND BLAGUE, *How to Write*

Over the years, I've had a number of students who have said, in one form or another,"I want to be a computer scientist because I really like programming and am very good at it." Of course, computer scientists, both novices and seasoned veterans, are often called upon to write programs, but to equate computer science with programming is to confuse the product with the process. Being an excellent draftsman who can faithfully represent a scene on paper is no guarantee that your works will eventually hang in the Metropolitan Museum. It's a step in the right direction, but an artist must also have an intimate familiarity with the more general principles of composition, persepctive, color, and so on.

In essence, programming is little more than the efficient management of a particular kind of large intellectual process, and the guidelines for good programming are nothing but the application of commonsense principles that apply to any complex creative task. It goes without saying, however, that before you can think efficiently you must have something to think *about*, which for our purposes means that in order to write good programs, you must have an idea about how information may be represented in a program.

Computer science is a young discipline, but it has developed enough over the past few decades that there is a growing consensus about what should constitute the core data structures. In this book, I tried to capture this core by providing what might be called the "classic" data structures, the most commonly applied methods for representing information in a computer program, along with the algorithms for manipulating this information. In terms of something to think *about* when thinking about programming, you have here a collection of tools that should be part of the working knowledge of any programmer.

This book is not about programming, however. Computer science is a science and, in common with other sciences, consists in the main of seeking a theoretical framework that can be used to describe the behavior of the objects it studies—in our case, computers and their programs. One of the themes that determined the form of the book is to provide a broad view of what a data structure really is. I have taken the approach that data structures are not just a collection of ad hoc declarations and procedure definitions, but, rather, that any data structure is a particular instance of an *abstract data type*, which consists of (1) a set of objects, with (2) a common logical structure defined for each of the objects, along with (3) a collection of structure-preserving operations on the objects.

I chose to define the structure of an abstract data type by specifying a *structural relation* on each set of positions. Doing so provides a natural progression of the chapters, where each new abstract data type is introduced by removing some of the structural restrictions from a prior type. Thus, we begin with lists, whose structure is defined by a linear order, and progress to trees by removing the requirement that each position have a unique successor, then to directed graphs by removing the requirement of unique predecessor, then to sets by removing all restrictions on the structural relation. Throughout this process, we see that each new abstract data type still can be described by the threefold view of a collection of sets with a structural relation and a collection of operations on those sets.

THE AUDIENCE

Though I did not set out to tailor this book to any preexisting curriculum, it turned out that it covers essentially all of CS2 and part of CS7, as described in the ACM *Curriculum '78*, and a subset of the union of CS2 and CO2, set forth in Norman Gibbs's and Alan Tucker's 1985 *Model Curriculum for a Liberal Arts Degree in Computer Science*. The material contained here should be covered early in any computer science curriculum, and I wrote this book for an audience of first- and second-year students in computer science who were familiar with a high-level language such as Pascal. A course in discrete mathematics is desirable as a pre- or corequisite for this material, but the relevant mathematical background in relations, probability, and other topics is summarized in the appendixes for those who need it.

THE CONTENTS

My intent was to write a book that could be used as the basis for a semester-length course in data structures or advanced programming. Realizing that the subject matter of this book comes at an early stage in the education of a computer scientist, I included a number of mentions, necessarily brief, of some of the interesting topics that await the student down the road. Most of the canonical sorting algorithms are covered, along with mentions of computational complexity, compiler design, unsolvable problems, NP-completeness and the fundamental paradigms for algorithms.

Chapters 1 and 2 form the introduction of the text. Chapter 1 covers the necessary preliminaries, such as program design, the definition of an abstract data type, a review of Pascal-based pseudocode and pointers, big-O estimates, and the notion of time and space estimates. Appendix A, on relations, provides a more detailed study of the material of Chapter 1. Chapter 2 is typical of subsequent chapters, in that we introduce an abstract data type, STRING, describe how it may be implemented, compare the implementations, and provide extensive application, in this case the Boyer-Moore string-matching algorithm.

In Chapters 3 and 4 we continue the investigation of linear data structures. Chapter 3 covers lists, along with related list-like structures such as doubly linked lists, sorted lists, and braids, and concludes with a discussion of memory management. Chapter 4 covers the rest of standard linear structures, stacks and queues, motivating these by applications to manipulate postfix expressions. Since a considerable amount of queue applications involve simulation, Appendix C would be appropriate at this point.

Chapter 5 provides a segue into nonlinear structures by providing an introduction to recursion and recursively defined data structures. Timing estimates for recursive algorithms are covered in depth, along with an introduction to LISP. Appendix B covers logs and exponentials, induction, and elementary combinatorics, and would be appropriate supplementary material at this stage.

Chapters 6 and 7 cover trees. Chapter 6 provides the necessary background on binary trees and their implementations, traversal algorithms, treesort and heapsort, and discusses minimal-length codes and tries. Chapter 7, which could be omitted if necessary, covers two extensions of binary search trees, namely AVL trees and B-trees.

Chapter 8 could also be optional. It covers graphs and digraphs, along with a representative sample of graph algorithms for traversal, spanning trees, minimal-cost paths, minimal spanning trees, and an introduction to complexity theory through the Traveling Salesperson Problem.

Chapter 9, on sets, describes bit vector and list implementations of sets, as well as dictionaries, and provides a comprehensive introduction to hashing. The last section of Chapter 9 discusses the UNION-FIND data structure, and could be omitted, if worse came to worse.

In Chapter 10 we consider a problem of regenerating text from a large sample and trace the development of programs to solve this problem, using a real computer/compiler system to show how time and space constraints arise in practice from choices of data structure.

ACKNOWLEDGMENTS

Stephen King will probably make more money from his next book than I'll see in the rest of my life. It's worth every penny, folks: writing is just plain hard work. A lot of people deserve praise for seeing this book of mine through to completion. Thanks go to my colleagues for reading advance copies, especially to Peter Allen of Columbia University, Brian Kernaghan of AT&T/Bell Labs, and Seymour Pollack of Washington University for their review of the manuscript; to my students for catching the countless errors in the earlier versions; to Eloise Starkweather for producing a cover that knocked my socks off; to the nice folks at Prentice Hall for being so tolerant of my first effort with them; and especially to my family and friends, none of whom will ever read *Data Structures*, but all of whom were supportive and understanding when I came dragging in after a long day's work.

PART 1
Introduction

1

Preliminaries

When making haggis, the easiest part is obtaining the ingredients.
Anyone can get a sheep's stomach and a quantity of oatmeal,
but the real trick is knowing how to combine them.

Roberta Campbell, *The Cuisine of Scotland*

The discipline of computer science is concerned with the study of problem solving with computers. Notice that we did not say that computer science *consists* of problem solving with computers, any more than mathematics consists of solving equations or music consists of producing notes. It is not enough to be able to answer the question, "How do we solve a particular problem with the help of a computer?" If it were, the study of computer science could stop after one or two introductory programming courses. Instead, the proper subject matter includes questions like

1. What are the possible different ways to solve a problem?
2. How are the solutions for a particular problem related?
3. What technique is best for a particular problem?
4. What do we mean by a "best" solution for a problem?
5. In what ways are solutions for different problems related?
6. How do we verify that we have a solution for a problem?
7. What problems can, and cannot, be solved with a computer?

Although all of these questions contain the word *problem*, they all seek answers in a context that is broader than simply solving a particular problem. In fact, all of these questions, and all of the questions of computer science, are different aspects of the same fundamental question:

> What *general principles* underlie the notion of problem solving with computers?

In this text, we will concern ourselves primarily with those aspects of this fundamental question that deal with the structure of the data in a program and, to a lesser extent, with the techniques of manipulating that data.

1.1 PROGRAM DESIGN: ALGORITHMS AND DATA STRUCTURES

We can view the subject matter of computer science as the result of the process of generalizing from specific problem-solving instances, which is to say that computer science seeks to find properties common to many instances of problem solving. Program design—the writing of programs to solve a problem—proceeds in the opposite direction: from a vague notion of what needs to be done, to the writing of a program in a specific language for a specific computer. The aim of program design is captured in the most appropriate title yet invented for a book on computer science, Nicholas Wirth's *Algorithms + Data Structures = Programs*. Wirth, the developer of the Pascal language, chose his title to point out the twofold nature of a computer program: that a program consists of an algorithm describing how to manipulate information with a computer, along with a data structure that provides a logical basis for organization of that information in the computer. These two aspects of a program are intimately intertwined: Making a decision about one of the aspects often profoundly affects the other.

Algorithms

An **algorithm** is a finite list of unambiguous instructions that can be performed on a computer in such a way that the process is guaranteed to halt in a finite amount of time. "Add up the integers from 1 to 100" almost qualifies as an algorithm, except that the single instruction it uses is ambiguous—it does not provide sufficient detail for us to decide how to perform the required operation. The instruction does provide us with a useful starting point, however: Reading it, we have a clear idea of what problem we have to solve. Indeed, just getting to the point where we know what the problem is can often represent the major part of a programming task. Knowing the problem, we can now try to refine the problem into a suitable algorithm.

This simple addition problem occupies a hallowed place in mathematical folklore, and will serve as a good example of a situation in which there is more than one algorithm to solve a given problem. Karl Frederich Gauss was born in Germany in 1777, and grew to be, if not the best, then certainly one of the best mathematicians who ever lived. The story goes* that when Gauss was a boy in what would be the eighteenth-

*This story has about the same amount of truth to it as the tale of George Washington and the cherry tree, and has survived for about the same reasons.

century German equivalent of present-day American elementary school, his teacher, J. G. Büttner, gave the class the problem of adding the numbers from 1 to 100 (presumably to give himself an extended break from lecturing). The students bent over their slates and in less than a minute young Gauss came to the teacher's desk, laid down his slate, and said "*Ligget se*," which means "There 'tis." Herr Büttner, incredulous, looked at Gauss's answer and found that it was indeed correct.

Gauss's success came from what we would describe as a clever choice of algorithm. It is reasonable to guess that his classmates had all hit upon a variant of the same algorithm, which we would describe in modern terms as:

```
function BusyWork(n : integer) : integer;
{Add the integers from 1 to n.}
   var
      i, sum : integer;
begin
   sum := 0;
   for i := 1 to n do
      sum := sum + i;
   BusyWork := sum
end;
```

Gauss, on the other hand, is said to have argued as follows: "*Wenn ich die Summe im Geist ausschreibe, dann habe ich '1 + 2 + 3 + . . . + 100.' Nun, angenommen ich addiere diese Zahlen paarweise: 1 + 100 = 101, 2 + 99 = 101 (aha!), 3 + 98 = 101, und so weiter. Alle diese Paare ergeben eine Summe von 101 und es gibt 50 Paare, so muss die Summe 50 × 101 = 5050 sein. Ich bin fertig*." You don't need to understand German to make sense of Gauss's argument; he mentally added the numbers in a different order, breaking them into 50 pairs, each of which summed to 101. In other words, Gauss's algorithm would take the form

```
function BetterSum(n : integer) : integer;
{Add the integers from 1 to n.}
begin
   BetterSum := (1 + n) * n / 2      {multiply sum of each pair by the number of pairs}
end;
```

Comparing the two algorithms, we see that not only is Gauss's algorithm more esthetically pleasing, but it is also better in a way that we can measure. The obvious algorithm required 100 additions, along with the overhead inherent in the **for** statement, whereas Gauss's algorithm required only one multiplication. Although this would make no noticeable difference if the algorithms were run on fast modern computers, it would make a significant difference if the "computer" was a seven-year-old child. (We are actually cheating a little here, since multiplication takes more time than addition. We can explain this away, however, if we restrict our attention to numbers that are fairly small. In this case, multiplication typically takes about three to ten times as long as addition on most computers, so we still come out way ahead.) This provides a partial answer to one of the questions we mentioned earlier: We can say that one algorithm to solve a problem is "better" than another if it requires less time to execute.

We don't need to stop here, though. It takes but a little thought to convince yourself that Gauss's algorithm would also be applicable to adding the numbers from 1 to 200 (quick, what's the answer?), so from there to adding the numbers from 1 to n, for any $n \geq 1$, is not hard at all. Having done that, it is easy to convince yourself that the algorithm will work equally well to find the sum of the integers from n to m, for any $n \leq m$. In fact, the algorithm could be used to find the sum 3 + 11 + 19 + 27 + 35 + 43 + 51, or any **arithmetic series** of numbers in which the difference between any consecutive terms is the same (8, in the preceding sum, for instance). Finally, notice that we need not restrict ourselves to integers; Gauss's algorithm can be generalized to find the sum of any arithmetic series of real numbers. The moral of this little digression is that we should never try to solve a particular problem if we can solve a more general one with just a little more work. In this case, we have gone from an efficient algorithm for one problem to one that solves an *infinite* collection of related problems.

Data Structures

The data structures used in a program reflect the programmer's decision on the means of representing information in a program, just as the algorithm reflects the decision on how to manipulate the information. When we refer to a **data structure**, we mean the way information is logically organized in a program, subject to the constraints given by the language chosen for the program. For example, suppose you were writing a bridge-playing program. Thinking about the problem, it seems that there should be some way of representing the contents of a hand. This, in turn, implies that a choice must be made about how to represent the fifty-two cards in the deck. Concentrating on just this part of the problem—how to represent the cards and the hands—we can come up with a number of possible data structures.

If we had decided to write the program in standard Pascal, for instance, we would have available a number of **data types** from which to build our data structure, where by *data type* we mean the representations for information that are predefined as features of the particular language in question. The difference between data structures and data types lies primarily in their complexity—typically, a data structure is constructed out of the available data types in a language. For example, almost all programming languages contain an *integer* data type (which, by the way, is never what a mathematician means when he or she uses the word "integer." Why?), and many allow the use of arrays.

Since Pascal allows user-defined ordinals, arrays, and records as data types, we might decide on the following data structure:

```
type
{ Data Structure #1 for bridge hands }
    SuitType = (club, diamond, heart, spade);
    ValueType = (two, three, four, five, six, seven,
                 eight, nine, ten, jack, queen, king,ace);
    Card = record
               suit : SuitType;
               value : ValueType
           end;
    Hand = array [1 .. 13] of Card;
```

This has the advantage that it mirrors exactly the situation being modeled, but it depends upon Pascal's user-defined ordinal type to declare the possible values for *SuitType* and *ValueType*. If we had decided, for reasons of either familiarity or availability, to use a language without user-defined ordinals, we would have to encode the possible card values in another way that was compatible with the available types in that language.

Since, as we mentioned, virtually every programming language includes integers as an available type, it would be a safe bet to code the cards by the numbers 2 through 53. In this representation the 2 of clubs would have the code 2, the 3 of clubs would have code 3, the ace of clubs would have code 14, and so on, as in Figure 1.1.

A look at Figure 1.1 will explain the choice of using codes 2 through 53, rather than the apparently more natural choice 1 . . . 52. For the non-facecards, the translation from code to card value is simply given by *value* = *code* **mod** 13. This coding has the further advantage that it reflects the order of the cards in the rules of bridge: Any club is less in value than any diamond, which is less in value than any heart, which is less in value than any spade, while within suits the order is 2, 3, 4, 5, 6, 7, 8, 9, 10, jack, queen, king, ace. We could then write substantially the same data structure as before by the declaration

```
type
{ Data Structure #2 for bridge hands }
    CardCode = 2 .. 53;
    Hand = array [1 .. 13] of CardCode;
```

	2	3	4	5	6	7	8	9	10	J	Q	K	A
♣	2	3	4	5	6	7	8	9	10	11	12	13	14
♦	15	16	17	18	19	20	21	22	23	24	25	26	27
♥	28	29	30	31	32	33	34	35	36	37	38	39	40
♠	41	42	43	44	45	46	47	48	49	50	51	52	53

Figure 1.1 Possible numeric codes for cards in bridge.

This by no means exhausts the possible data structures we could choose for this program. Another, less obvious, possibility might be to use a bit vector to represent the subset of cards in the deck that were in a hand. A **bit vector** is simply an array of zeroes and ones, and is frequently used as a compact representation for a set, as we will see in Chapter 9. In this data structure we would code the card values as above, and consider the card with code c to be in the hand represented by the bit vector v if the element $v[c]$ was equal to one, so that a hand would contain the jack of diamonds if and only if we had $v[24] = 1$. This data structure, which we will refer to as Data Structure #3, would then be defined by the declaration

```
type
{ Data Structure # 3 for bridge hands }
   Hand = array [2 .. 53] of boolean;
```

where the data type *boolean* consists of only the values *true* and *false*, which could be regarded as the single binary digits 1 and 0, respectively.

We saw that it was possible to compare the relative merits of algorithms by considering the number of steps they took to run. Now, is there some way of assessing the merits of two data structures? Glancing down this paragraph, you will likely conclude that since we are not at the end of this section, it is reasonable to assume that there must indeed be a way to compare data structures. In fact, for this example, there are at least two different measures we can use. First, we need to know a bit (no pun intended) about the way a computer stores information in memory. Many, though not all, computers are **byte-addressable**, which means that a **byte** of 8 binary digits is the smallest piece of information that can be directly accessed. In such computers, an integer is typically stored in 2 or 4 consecutive bytes in memory, that is, in 16 or 32 binary digits. Assuming that an integer requires two bytes of memory, the array of 13 integers in Data Structure #2 would require 26 bytes of memory. In many computers, bit vectors are *packed* by storing 8 elements in a single byte. In such machines, a bit vector requires only as many bytes as it has groups of 8 elements, plus one more if there are leftover bits beyond a multiple of 8. In Data Structure #3, there are 52 bits, which works out to 6 groups of 8 plus one leftover group of 4 bits, so the bit vector could be packed into 7 bytes of memory, only 27 percent as much space as was required by Data Structure #2. This could be significant if we saw that our bridge-playing program was going to have to store, say, 10,000 hands in memory.

We mentioned earlier that there is an intimate connection between the way information is represented in a program and the nature of the algorithms that manipulate this information. Not only can we compare these data structures by the space they require, but we can also compare data structures by the time it takes for the algorithms to process this information. Suppose, for instance, that we saw that our program was going to do a lot of checking to see whether a particular card was in a hand. Given a code, c, for a card, and a hand, h, the algorithm for Data Structure #2 would have to inspect each of the values $h[1], h[2], \ldots, h[13]$ to see if any one of them was equal to c, while the algorithm for Data Structure #3 would need only one comparison, to see whether the bit vector entry $v[c]$ was equal to 1. Assuming that comparisons of integers and comparisons using bit vectors took the same amount of time, Data Structure #3 would represent a thirteenfold saving of time for the card-checking algorithm. It is worth stressing the connection between data structures and algorithms once again—in our examples the card-checking algorithms had the same results, but, because of the different data structures involved, they had to be written in entirely different ways.

Both of these data structures exhibit the same desirable feature we saw with Gauss's algorithm: generality. With slight modification, we could use these data structures to model such card games as poker (just change the size of the hands to five or seven), pinochle (change the size of the hands, the cards in the deck, and the code for the cards to reflect a different order), euchre, hearts, fish, skat, and so on.

We have just scratched the surface of program design. Although the primary goal of the programming process is to produce a correct program that is immune to most, if not all, errors of input, there are important secondary goals along the way. A good program not only works correctly, but also exhibits features such as generality, modularity (it is better to produce a "package" of related data structures and algorithms that can be used with little or no change for similar problems), and information-hiding (the user of the package should not need to be concerned with implementation details like how large the arrays are). In many respects, programming is still an art rather than a science; we do not yet have any well-defined process that will allow us to pass in a mechanical way from a vaguely worded English description of a problem to a program that will solve that problem. A knowledge of abstract data types, however, will provide powerful help in going from a problem statement to a finished program.

1.2 ABSTRACT DATA TYPES: THE THREEFOLD WAY

The study of abstract data types stems from the realization that there is a well-defined middle ground between problem statements and implemented programs. This middle ground is more concrete than the realm of problem statements, but more abstract than that of finished programs. Just as biologists identify certain common properties among animals to group them into genus categories—cat-like, dog-like, bear-like—computer scientists classify data structures into categories such as linear, hierarchical (or branched), and network (or web-like) structures. Once we understand what these categories are, the properties they have in common, and how to implement them efficiently, much of the work of program design is done for us. For example, if we know about the linear abstract data type LIST, then it should make little difference whether the problem we seek to solve involves employee records, patients waiting in a doctor's office, or multiple precision arithmetic, since all of these can be viewed as instances in which the information is organized in a linear order.

All of the abstract data types are derived from a single classification scheme, describing what the objects of the abstract data type look like and what we wish to do with them. As a start, we can say that an **abstract data type**, which we will abbreviate as **ADT**, consists of

1. Two sets of underlying objects: a set, ATOM, and a set POSITION where, intuitively speaking, we will place the atoms.
2. Another set, E, of **elements** of the ADT, such that each member of E is a triple, (P, R, v), where:
   a. P is a finite subset of POSITION.
   b. R is a relation on P, which provides the structure of P (about which we will say more shortly) and where the relations R have the same properties for all elements of E.
   c. v is a function from P to ATOM, called the *evaluation function.*
3. A collection of **operations** that can be performed on those elements.

For example, we could define the abstract data type BRIDGE_HAND as follows:

1. The underlying set of atoms consists of 52 cards. The underlying set of positions consists of 13 elements, corresponding to the 13 possible positions in a bridge hand.
2. An element of BRIDGE_HAND consists of a set of 1 to 13 positions for cards, with no assumption about structure within elements (reflecting the fact that a bridge hand is the same no matter how the cards within it are rearranged — that is, that the only important part of the *structure* of a bridge hand is how many cards it contains). The evaluation function, v, for a hand allows us to say, for instance, that the card in position p is the three of clubs.
3. The operations defined on BRIDGE_HAND might include the following:

   procedure Create(**var** newHand : Hand), which serves to bring a new player into the game with an empty *newHand.*

   procedure PickUp(thisCard : Card ; **var** thisHand : Hand), which has the effect of adding *thisCard* to *thisHand.*

   procedure PutDown(thisCard : Card ; **var** thisHand : Hand), which removes *thisCard* from *thisHand.*

   function Seek(thisCard : Card ; thisHand : Hand) : boolean, which returns *true* if and only if *thisCard* is contained in *thisHand.*

There are a number of other operations we could define for this ADT, but the pattern should be clear. It would not be worth our efforts to pursue this ADT any further because, as you will see, it is just a specific instance of the SET abstract data type. Notice that this definition of the abstract data type BRIDGE_HAND makes no mention of implementation. An abstract data type is just what its name implies: an abstraction of the features common to any implementation of the ADT as part of a program. We cannot emphasize too strongly that an ADT consists of elements and operations on these elements. When the ADT is implemented, the elements become instances of a data structure, and the operations become algorithms.

It is very important to point out the difference between the position of an atom in an element of an ADT, and the atom itself. The whole reason for such a complicated, multitiered definition of an ADT is to isolate the notion of position from that of the atom that is found in that position. In BRIDGE__HAND, for instance, any two-card hands may be thought of as having the same *structure*, namely the set of positions $P = \{a, b\}$, with no assumption that a is "before" or "after" b. In other words, we may think of the positions as "slots" into which we may place atoms. The difference between the hands {7 diamond, Q club}, and {K heart, 3 spade} lies only in the evaluation functions from POSITION to card values (i.e., the set ATOM). In the first instance, the evaluation function is defined to be $v_1(a) = 7$ diamond, $v_1(b) =$ Q club, while in the second instance we have the evaluation function $v_2(a) =$ K heart, $v_2(b) = 3$ spades, meaning that there is a seven of diamonds in position a, and a queen of clubs in position b, as indicated in Figure 1.2.

Relations

The only part of the definition of an ADT that is not clear at this point is (we hope) what exactly we mean by the "structure" of an element of the ADT. The most general way to define the structure of an element is to say that the subset P of POSITION that makes up an element has a relation, called a **structural relation**, defined on it, with the provision that the structural relations for each element have exactly the same properties. We will give a brief review of relations here; for a more detailed discussion, see Appendix A.

A relation on a set, P, is nothing more than a function, R, which takes in two objects from P and returns either *true* or *false*. If $R(x, y) = true$, for x and y in P, we say that **x and y are related by R**, and write "$x\ R\ y$." Otherwise we say that x and y are not related by R. A commonly known relation is "less than," defined on any subset of the integers, written "<." We would say that 3 and 277 are related by "less than," and we would write "3 < 277." Note that order is important here: It is correct to say "3 < 277," but it is incorrect to say "277 < 3." Certain properties of relations appear so frequently that they are singled out by name. In the following descriptions, assume that R

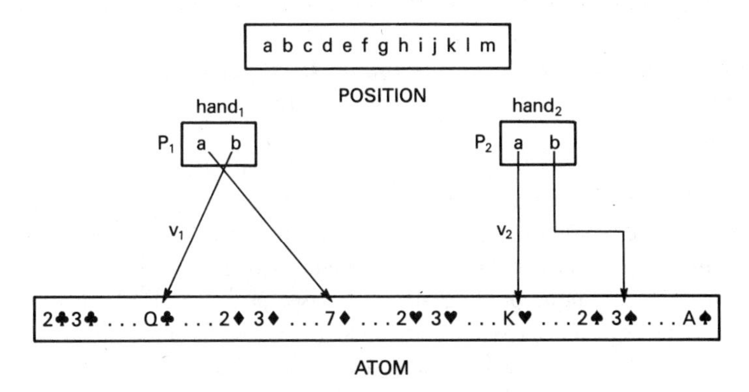

Figure 1.2 Two elements of the BRIDGE__HAND abstract data type.

is a relation on a set P, and that a, b, and c are elements of P. The relation R has the following properties:

1. **Reflexive**, if $a\ R\ a$, for all a.
2. **Symmetric**, if $a\ R\ b$ implies that $b\ R\ a$, for all possible a, b.
3. **Antisymmetric**, if $a\ R\ b$ and $b\ R\ a$ implies that $a = b$, for all a, b.
4. **Transitive**, if $a\ R\ b$ and $b\ R\ c$ implies that $a\ R\ c$, for all a, b, c.
5. **A chain**, if either $a\ R\ b$ or $b\ R\ a$, for all possible a, b.

For example, the relation "less than or equal to," on the integers, written as "≤," satisfies all the listed properties except symmetry, whereas "<" is neither reflexive, symmetric, nor a chain.

We can generalize the relation "≤" by identifying by name any relation that has the same properties as "≤." We say that a relation, R, is a **linear order** (also known as a *total order*) if it is reflexive, antisymmetric, transitive, and a chain. Linear orders are important because, just as with "≤" on the integers, they guarantee that, for finite sets, each element in the set has at most one element immediately following it. In more precise terms, suppose that R is a relation defined on a finite set P; we define an **immediate successor** (under the relation R) of an element p of P to be an element $succ \neq p$ of P, with the properties

1. $p\ R\ succ$ (that is, *succ* comes "after" p in the order imposed by R).
2. For any $q \neq p$ in P for which $p\ R\ q$, it is the case that $succ\ R\ q$ or $succ = q$ (that is, any element "after" p also must be "after" the successor, or be the successor itself).

Even if R is a linear order on a set P, there is no guarantee that each element of P must have a successor under R. If, for example, we took P to be the set $\{0, 1, 2, 3\}$, and R to be "≤," we see that 3 has no successor under "≤." In addition, if P consisted of all the real numbers, and R was "≤," the number 3 (or any other number, for that matter) would have no successor. What we can claim, however (and we prove in Appendix A), is that if R is a linear order on a *finite* set P, then every element has at most one immediate successor under R and, further, there is only one element that has no immediate successor.

This property of unique successor can be recast in almost exactly the same form if we define the **immediate predecessor** of an element, p, under a relation to be an element that comes "immediately before" p. It is not difficult to parrot the definition and argument for successor to show that under a linear order relation on a finite set, every element has a unique predecessor, if it has a predecessor at all. Assuming these properties of linear orders, it is not hard to see that the name *linear* order is derived from the fact that we can give a familiar structure to a linearly ordered set, thinking of it as a chain of elements, like birds on a wire.

In what will come, we will frequently use a graphic representation to describe a relation on a set. In doing so, we will use labeled boxes to denote elements of the set, and an arrow from box x to box y will indicate the relation $x\ R\ y$ between those elements. In Figure 1.3, for instance, we have indicated the linear order R on the set $P = \{a, b, c, d\}$ for which $a\ R\ b\ R\ c\ R\ d$. We will frequently indicate just the immediate successor relations, as we have done in Figure 1.3(b), rather than showing all relations, as in Figure 1.3(a).

The successor relation provides us with enough information to reconstruct the entire relation, if we know its properties. In the example of Figure 1.3(b), knowing that the relation was a linear order, we would know that it was reflexive and transitive, so we would add arrows from each box to itself (mirroring our knowledge that $x\ R\ x$, for all x in P), and we would add any arrows, such as the one from box d to box b, which transitivity would require (since the original diagram indicated that the relations $b\ R\ c$ and $c\ R\ d$ held). In technical terms, what we have done is to fill in the remaining arrows by taking the **reflexive closure** and the **transitive closure** of the relation of Figure 1.3(b) to produce the relation of Figure 1.3(a). Although we will not prove it here, it is true that the relations we will deal with can always be reconstructed in this fashion.

Earlier, we indicated that we would use relations to describe the structure of the elements of an abstract data type. We can now see how this will take place. The abstract data type LIST, for instance, has as its elements lists $L = (a_1 a_2 \ldots a_n)$, where the objects, a_i, in each list are members of an underlying set, ATOM, of atoms. In a list, the order of elements is important, so, for example, we would consider the lists $(a\ b\ c)$, and $(b\ a\ c)$ to be different. In a list, it should also be the case that we could identify the successor and the predecessor, if they existed, of any object in the list.

With these criteria in mind, it is easy to see how we might consider a list as an instance of our definition of an ADT. We take the underlying set of atoms to be whatever we wish, and let the positions be represented by the integers 1, 2, 3, ... Then, an element of LIST consists of a subset of the integers, with structural relation "$\leq$." In fact, since any set of n integers with relation "$\leq$" is essentially the same as the set $\{1, 2, \ldots, n\}$, we can take such sets as the position subsets, and notice that the representation $L = (a_1 a_2 \ldots a_n)$ describes not only the contents of the list, but also the positions of the atoms in the lists (which are just the subscripts). In this representation, the evaluation function, v, is particularly easy to describe; it is just $v(i) = a_i$. Notice that this linear order that defines the structure *does not have anything to do* with any order that

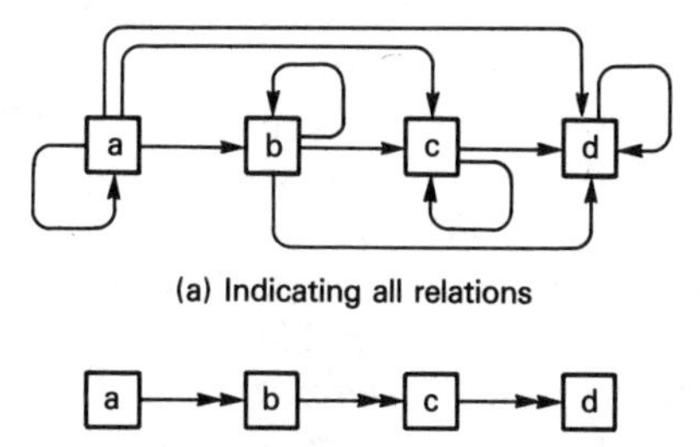

Figure 1.3 Graphic representation of a linear order relation.

might exist among the elements of ATOM. If ATOM was the set of integers, and L was the list (4 22 16 19), the atom 22 would be structurally "before" the atom 16, regardless of the fact that the atoms themselves had an order in which 22 is greater than 16. Notice, finally, that each list in the abstract data type LIST has its own linear order, mirroring the fact that each list has its own first, second, . . . element.

We warned you earlier that it would take a while to get used to this definition of abstract data types. It might help to think of an ADT as a set of custodial rules for placing chairs in a room, along with instructions for manipulating the chairs (and the people sitting in them). A typical "abstract custodial type" (ACT for short), then, might be defined as follows:

1. (Base objects) The **SEMINAR** "ACT" has ATOM, consisting of all possible people, and POSITION, consisting of all possible chairs.
2. (Structure) A SEMINAR consists of a finite set of chairs, arranged in a circle, with each chair occupied by a person. At any time the seminar isn't empty, there is a special chair, called the **current** chair.
3. (Operations) The operations on a SEMINAR consist of:

   CREATE a new seminar with no chairs.

   ENROLL a chair (and its occupant) immediately to the right of the current chair, if any.

   EXPEL a chair (and its occupant) from the seminar.

   CHANGE the current chair to be the one immediately to the right of the current chair (allowing someone else to speak, if you will).

   UPDATE the current chair, by replacing its occupant by someone else.

   POLL the current chair, by returning the name of its occupant.

With this definition, we include all possible sizes of seminars and all possible occupants. The important thing is that any seminar has the same logical structure and the same operations defined on it. This somewhat frivolous definition of an abstract custodial type is general enough to include any arrangement of chairs: to define the ACT **LECTURE HALL**, all we would have to do is change the structure (to seats arranged in rows, for instance) and the operations (allowing us to poll the occupant of seat n in row m, for instance). This is exactly what we are trying to do with our framework for ADTs — provide a way of looking at data that is flexible enough so that we can use the same basic scheme for all arrangements of information.

In subsequent chapters, we will adopt the program of beginning with a linear order as the structural relation, and gradually weakening the properties of the structural relation to produce less restricted structures on the elements of the ADTs. From linear structures, we will remove the chain condition to produce **hierarchical** structures, such as the family tree in Figure 1.4; and from the hierarchical structures we will further remove properties to produce **network** structures, such as the diagram in Figure 1.5; and eventually we will arrive at the abstract data type SET, which has no structural relation at all on its elements.

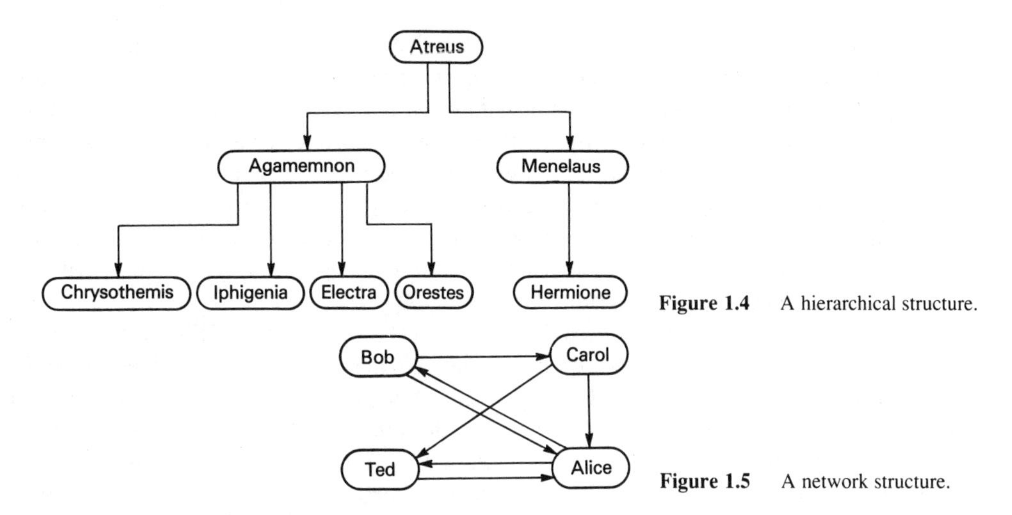

Figure 1.4 A hierarchical structure.

Figure 1.5 A network structure.

1.3 PSEUDOCODE AND POINTERS

The programs in this text will be written in Pascal, sort of. By this we mean that the syntax of the programs will be that of Pascal, but we will occasionally use English descriptions of some of the steps to avoid obscuring the sense of a program with too many small details. Such a "meta-language" is called **pseudocode**, and it represents a compromise between natural languages, like English, and programming languages like Pascal. In essence, if a statement or group of statements is simple enough to be described unambiguously by an English phrase, we will often do so in order to make the program easier to read. This course of action is particularly appropriate when we are writing algorithms at the level of abstract data types, since when we are talking about an abstract data type we specifically wish to avoid making any choice about how the ADT will be implemented. As an example, suppose we were dealing with the LIST abstract data type, for which the structure of each element was that of a (finite) linearly ordered set. We could define the function **First**, which, given an element E of the abstract data type, returned the "first" position in that element, as follows:

```
function First(E : Element) : POSITION;
{Returns the "first" position in an element E = (P ,R , v ), where R is a linear order }
   var x, y : POSITION;
begin
   y := some position in P;
   P := P - [y];                         {remove position y from P}
   while P is not empty do begin
      x := some position in P;
      if x R y then                      {if x is "earlier" than y in position}
         y := x;                         {set y equal to that "earlier" position}
      P := P - [x]                       {and in any case remove x from P}
   end;
   First := y
end;
```

In this example we have no need to describe how the ADT will be implemented in terms of the data types available to us in whatever language we eventually choose. We may eventually decide to implement this linearly ordered abstract data type using arrays in FORTRAN or linked lists in Pascal; at the abstract level the choice is immaterial. What is important is that this pseudocode algorithm is written so that we could easily translate it to whatever language we eventually choose. To see what we mean by this, think of your favorite programming language. However we may decide to represent the elements of this ADT, it should not be hard to imagine how you would write the code to replace the statement **while** P is not empty **do**.

In writing algorithms in pseudocode we must strike a rather delicate balance. On one hand, we need to include enough detail so that the English phrases could be translated into a programming language without a great deal of thought on our part about exactly how to do the translation; on the other hand, we want to eliminate as much of the nuts and bolts as we can, so as not to obscure the sense of what the algorithm does. This is why we called pseudocode a "meta-language." We can't implement pseudocode directly on a computer, since no one has yet written a compiler to translate English phrases into machine language. Such a compiler may be written someday; it is not completely out of the question, and it would certainly simplify things for programmers. In the meantime, nothing prohibits us from pretending that we have such a tool available, especially if such a fiction smooths the way toward understanding the algorithms we encounter.

Pointers

Pointer variables are included in some, but not all, high-level languages. For that reason, and since they are a useful feature of our pseudocode, we include a brief discussion of their use here. Unlike all the other variable types in our pseudocode, pointers permit *indirect* access to the memory of the computer. For instance, if *total* was an integer-type variable, then any reference to *total* would be a reference to an integer stored in some fixed location in the memory of the computer. On the other hand, if we had the following pointer declarations

```
type
    CellRef = ^integer;
var
    first, last : CellRef;
```

then *first* and *last* would be variables that contained not integers, but *addresses* of locations in memory in which integers could be stored. During the course of execution, the variable *first* might contain the value 13376. This would not be interpreted as an integer, but, rather, would imply that there was an integer stored in location 13376 in the memory of the computer (since we can imagine the memory arranged as a very long array).

This notion of indirect access is a bit complicated, so perhaps we should explain with an extended metaphor. Imagine the memory of a computer as an array of post

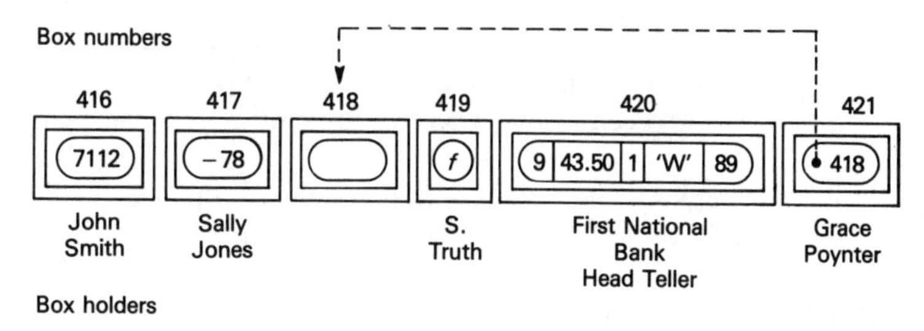

Figure 1.6 Post office model of pointers.

office boxes, with variables corresponding to people's names. *JohnSmith* and *SallyJones* might be integer-people with ordinary-sized boxes, *SojournerTruth* might be a boolean-person with a very small box, and *FirstNationalBankHeadTeller* might be a record-person with a large drawer, arranged in different-sized cells. The postmaster (i.e., the compiler) would know that any reference to *JohnSmith* would be a reference to the contents of John Smith's post office box. The fact that John Smith's box number was actually 416 would be immaterial to anyone except the postmaster and, in fact, would be hidden from the general public. If Grace Poynter declared herself to be a pointer-to-integer-person, the postmaster would assign her a box suitable in size to hold a box number, and any reference to *GracePoynter* would thereafter be understood to be a reference to a slip of paper on which was written the box number of an integer-sized box. In Figure 1.6, we depict this situation for a very small post office. Notice in this diagram that *SallyJones* contains the integer −78, *SojournerTruth* contains the value *false*, and *GracePoynter* contains the *address* of a box (418, at present) into which an integer may be stored. Don't be misled by the fact that Grace Poynter's box appears to be an integer-type box. It is not. It is a box for addresses; the postmaster knows this and will treat it accordingly.

Returning to the declarations, then, it might be that *first* would contain the value 13376. The integer in location 13376 would be available under the pointer reference *first^*. Notice the difference between a pointer variable and the value referenced by that pointer: *first* refers to a location in memory, whereas *first^*, with a caret following, is an integer. In our analogy, *JohnSmith* always refers to the contents of box 416, while *Grace Poynter^* (notice the caret) may refer to the contents of many different integer-sized boxes throughout its history. For this reason, we refer to pointer variables as **dynamic variables**, since the locations they reference may change during execution.

Because of their special nature, it should come as no surprise that pointer variables are handled specially in a program. The only operations on pointers allowed in Pascal (and hence in our Pascal-derived pseudocode) are

1. Assignment, such as first := last, between two pointers.
2. Comparison for equality or inequality, as in **if** first = last **then** . . . .
3. Creation, by the predefined procedure *New*. For example, the call New(first) would set *first* equal to the address of a free location in memory of a size suitable to whatever *first* is declared to point to (an integer, in our example).

4. Destruction, by the procedure *Dispose*. Calling Dispose(first) would free the location pointed to by *first*, and make any subsequent reference to *first^* illegal until *first* had again been given something to point to by assignment or *New*.

For our purposes, no reference to the value of a pointer variable will be allowed. In other words, it would be an error to write any of the following statements

```
if first > 13000 then writeln('large address');
write(first);
first := first + 20;
```

although all these statements would be perfectly legal if we had written *first^*, instead of *first*, because then we would be comparing, printing, and performing arithmetic on integers. (Some languages, such as C, allow reference to pointer values.) There is, however, one exception to the rule about no direct reference to pointers. There is one special constant pointer value, called **nil**, to which we can always refer. This pointer is almost invariably used as a flag or sentinel value for a special state of affairs, as we will demonstrate shortly. The value **nil** does not point to any location in memory (in the post office analogy, we could consider **nil** to be the number, zero, of a nonexistent box), and so it is an error to use the caret to access the value stored via any pointer that has the **nil** value.

The most common use of pointers is as pointers to records. These records have one or more fields which are themselves pointers to records. Doing this allows us to have a collection of records that are logically linked by pointers, even though the records themselves may be scattered throughout the memory of the computer. A typical instance would be declared by

```
type
   Link = ^Cell;
   Cell = record
             key : integer;
             nextCell : Link
          end;
```

Notice that there is a circularity in this declaration: *Link* is declared to be a pointer to a location in memory in which a value of type *Cell* can be stored, despite the fact that at the time *Link* is defined, the type *Cell* is unknown to the compiler. Reversing the order of the two declarations would lead to the same problem, so we resolve the confusion by insisting that a pointer type to a record that contains a field of that type must occur first—that is, in the order given in the example—and by relying on the fact that any correct Pascal compiler will be written so as to take this convention into account. In Pascal (but not in C, for instance), the decision to refer to a pointer before the compiler knows what it points to is based on the fact that all pointers have the same size, regardless of the sizes of the objects to which they refer, so the compiler can allocate space for a pointer before knowing its reference.

Bear in mind that if p is a pointer variable of type *Link*, then *p^* points to a record with two fields, *p^.key*, which is an integer, and *p^.nextCell*, which is another pointer (to a cell), as follows:

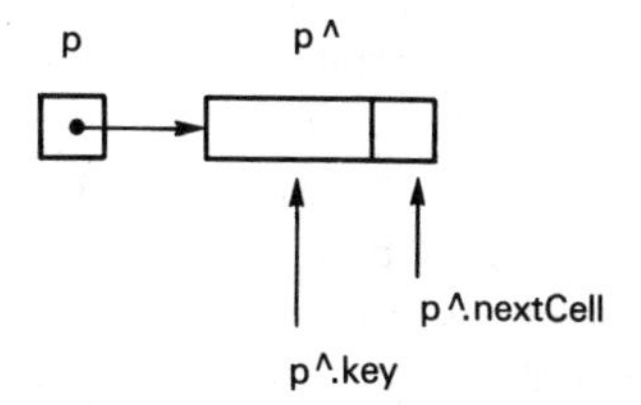

Suppose that, having made the foregoing declarations, we were to continue with these lines of code:

```
var
    header : Link;
begin
    New(header);
    header^.key := 209;
    New(header^.nextCell);
    header^.nextCell^.key := 820;
    header^.nextCell^.nextCell := nil;
```

The effects of this program segment are as follows:

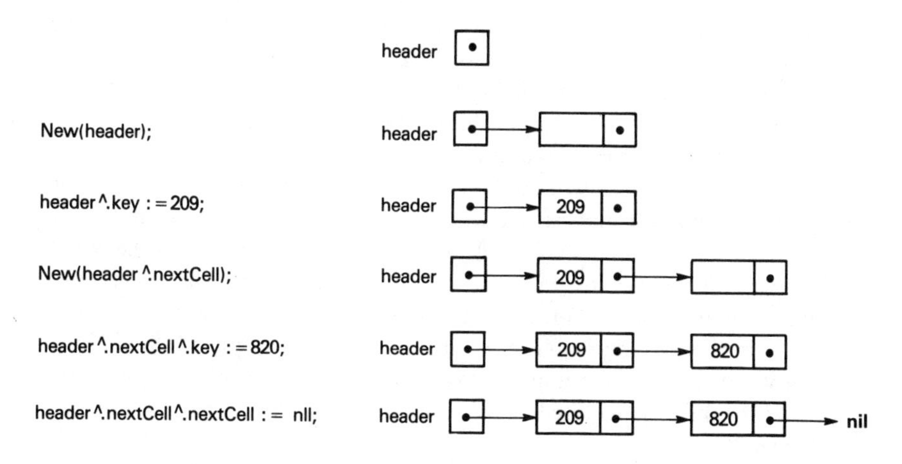

The first statement establishes an uninitialized record of type *Cell*, which is pointed to by the variable *header*, and the second statement stores the value 209 in the *key* field of that record. The third statement allocates storage for another record of type *Cell*, which is pointed to by the field *nextCell* of the original record, and the fourth statement places the value 820 in the *key* field of the newly created record. Finally, the last statement sets the *nextCell* field of the last record to the sentinel value **nil**.

1.4 COMPLEXITY MEASURES

You have already seen several examples in which we considered the question of whether one data structure or algorithm was "better" than another. We saw that Gauss's summation algorithm was preferable to the obvious technique because it took less time to run, and that the bit vector representation of a bridge hand was preferable to the array of card values because it took less storage space. When we are faced with the problem of writing a program, we must be aware that we are dealing with two scarce resources: time and space. It is worthless to write a program that takes, say, twenty years of computer time to solve a problem, just as it makes no sense to choose a data structure that requires more memory than the computer has available. The study of the **computational complexity** of programs seeks to find general principles governing the use of these resources. This is a vast, fascinating, and as yet not completely explored aspect of computer science, one to which we will refer throughout this book. We will begin by concentrating on the time complexity of an algorithm, recognizing that the choice of data structure can often profoundly affect the running time of a program.

For many programs, the running time depends largely on the *size* of the input in the sense that multiplying two 10-digit numbers will likely take less time than multiplying 100 10-digit numbers (number of inputs) or multiplying two 100-digit numbers (length of inputs) with the same program. Because we can't guarantee what kind of computer or compiler we will use to run the program, it is customary to talk of the running time, $T(n)$, of a particular algorithm as a function just of n, the size of the input.

To use the example of multiplication, we might have a program that multiplies two n-digit numbers and find that it takes $117.65n^2$ milliseconds on a microcomputer but only $5.08n^2$ milliseconds on a fast mainframe computer. Rather than having to redo our timing estimates for every possible computer, we will simply say that the program we are investigating has a running time *proportional to* n^2, recognizing that the contributions from the particular machine–compiler combination only change the running time by a constant multiple, as a rule.

Furthermore, we will factor out as much of the contribution of the input as we can by restricting our estimates to a *worst-case* analysis. By this we recognize that not only is the size of the input significant in the running time, but so is the nature of the input; but we will choose to ignore all but those inputs for which the program takes the longest time possible. For example, it is not difficult to imagine that our unspecified multiplication program might take much longer to multiply 5548716225 by 8848710094 than it would take to multiply 5000000000 by 8000000000, but in estimating an upper bound for the time required, we will consider only the worst instances of problems of a given size.

Big-O

We are then in the position of trying to analyze a function $T(n)$ in such a manner that (1) we will not concern ourselves with constant multiples and (2) we will be concerned only with the largest (i.e., worst-case) estimates that are still "good" in some sense. This kind of analysis is sufficiently common that mathematicians have developed terminology to make our task easier as well as more precise.

Definition. If $f(n)$ and $g(n)$ are two functions of n whose values are always positive, we say that $f(n) = O(g(n))$, which is said "f of n is big-O of g of n," or simply "f is big-O of g," if there is some number c greater than zero for which $f(n) \leq c\ g(n)$ for all n greater than some fixed number N (i.e., for all n sufficiently large).

For instance, we can say that $n^2 + 4n = O(n^2)$ because $n^2 + 4n$ is less than or equal to $2n^2$ for all n greater than 4 (so in this case c is 2 and N is 4). We can get some idea of the choice for c and N by arguing as follows. We first guess that $n^2 + 4n = O(n^2)$ and we see that the contribution of $4n$ will make $n^2 + 4n$ grow faster than $1n^2$, so we try $2n^2$, using the constant $c = 2$. We now try some values for n to see whether $2n^2$ eventually gets larger than $n^2 + 4n$.

n	$n^2 + 4n$	$2n^2$
1	5	2 (smaller)
2	12	8 (smaller)
3	21	18 (smaller)
4	32	32 (equal)
5	45	50 (larger)
6	60	72 (larger)

The table seems to indicate that $n^2 + 4n \leq 2n^2$ for all $n > 4$, and indeed we could prove that with a little more algebraic manipulation. Thus we see that $c = 2$ and $N = 4$ in the definition, and we have thus established the result $n^2 + 4n = O(n^2)$.

Notice how this choice of c effectively "cancels out " any constant multiples due to choice of machine since, using the timing above, we can say that both $117.65\,n^2$ and $5.08\,n^2$ are $O(n^2)$. Notice also that this notation allows us to consider just the worst-case situations, since if we had an algorithm that took n^2 time if n was evenly divisible by 10, and $2n$ time otherwise, we would still claim that the algorithm was $O(n^2)$, rather than $O(n)$.

Notice that this process of finding upper bounds on time complexity is only as good as our cleverness in evaluating time complexity. Suppose, for instance, we had an algorithm that, unknown to us, actually had timing function $T(n) = n^2 + 4n$. In this case, we would be correct if we said $T(n) = O(n^2)$ or $T(n) = O(n^{43})$ (why?). Both estimates are correct, but clearly the first is in some sense "more" correct than the second. Not uncommonly, the analysis of some algorithm is so complicated that we simply don't know whether the big-O estimate we've found is the best possible, in the sense of providing the *least* upper bound on the running time.

(As a brief digression, you might rightly ask why we concentrate on worst-case estimates. Might not the behavior of an algorithm be better expressed in terms of the *average* running times over all possible inputs? As it happens, we can do just that in some cases, but far more often than not the average behavior is very difficult to calculate. Mathematicians and computer scientists, just like other folks, tend to shy away from the really hard stuff when there is a simpler way that's almost as good. Admittedly, there are instances when average-time estimates are very instructive; it's just that to do a proper job of average-case analysis would require an introduction to probability theory, which would take us too far afield at this time. On another subject, big-O notation provides what is probably your first exposure to industrial-strength jargon: If a function is constant or never gets beyond a fixed upper bound, you can refer to it as $O(1)$, so you could say of a particularly easy course that the homework assignments are always $O(1)$.)

Big-O notation looks forbidding at first, but there is less here than meets the eye. It is easiest to think of the statement "$f(n) = O(g(n))$" as saying "f eventually grows no faster than (a multiple of) g." For example, polynomials like n^2 or n^{2000} are always beaten eventually by exponential functions like 2^n, no matter what the constants are. This is often a surprise the first time it is encountered. Comparing the values of n^{2000} with 2^n, for instance, we find that there is no contest at all, at least for small values of n. When $n = 3$ we have 3^{2000} (a number with 955 digits) for the polynomial, versus 8 (a number with 1 digit) for the exponential. Nevertheless, the exponential function eventually grows faster than the polynomial, and in fact, if we try enough values for n, we can discover that we have $n^{2000} < 2^n$ for all values of n greater than 29,718, so we can say that $n^{2000} = O(2^n)$. In a similar way, logarithmic functions are always eventually beaten by positive powers, so $log(n)$ will eventually be less than, say, $n^{1/2000}$. Notice, too, that the relation "=O( )" among functions is not symmetric. Although it is true that $n^2 = O(n^{20})$, it is certainly not the case that $n^{20} = O(n^2)$.

Order Arithmetic

We would like to be able to develop a collection of rules for big-O that allow us to compute upper bounds of functions by combining big-O estimates of their parts. Throughout, we will keep to the assumption that we made earlier, namely that all functions we deal with are positive-valued. The first rule follows directly from the definition and tells us what we already know: that big-O ignores constant multiples.

Rule 1. For any k and any function f, $k\,f(n) = O(f(n))$.

The next thing to observe about big-O notation is that it is transitive, in the following sense:

Rule 2. If $f(n) = O(g(n))$ and $g(n) = O(h(n))$, then $f(n) = O(h(n))$.

To prove this, we first see that $f(n) = O(g(n))$ implies that there are constants c_1 and N_1 such that $f(n) \le c_1 g(n)$ for all $n > N_1$, and similarly that $g(n) = O(h(n))$ implies that there are constants c_2 and N_2 such that $g(n) \le c_2 h(n)$ for all $n > N_2$. Suppose we define N_3 to be the maximum of N_1 and N_2. For all $n > N_3$ we will have

$f(n) \le c_1 g(n)$ and $g(n) \le c_2 h(n)$, and substituting for $g(n)$ we have $f(n) \le c_1 (c_2 h(n))$. In other words, if we let $c_3 = c_1 c_2$, then for all $n > N_3$ we will have $f(n) \le c_3 h(n)$, which is simply the definition that $f(n) = O(h(n))$.

We will frequently find ourselves in the position of knowing something like $f(n) = O(n^2)$ and $g(n) = O(n^3)$. What does this permit us to say about the function $f(n) + g(n)$? Well, since f is eventually dominated by some multiple of n^2, and a multiple of n^2 is certainly less than n^3 for n large enough, we know that $f(n)$ will eventually be no larger than n^3. This means that f and g together will eventually be bounded above by some multiple of n^3, so we can say $f(n) + g(n) = O(n^3)$. In fact, if we define $\max\{f(n), g(n)\}$ to be the function whose value at n is the larger of $f(n)$ and $g(n)$, then we can prove the following rule in much the same way as we proved Rule 2.

Rule 3. $f(n) + g(n) = O(\max\{f(n), g(n)\})$.

Since big-O changes addition to maximum, you might think that it has some unexpected action on multiplication. Not so, as you could see by using the techniques of the proof of Rule 2. We have as our last rule the following:

Rule 4. If $f_1(n) = O(g_1(n))$ and $f_2(n) = O(g_2(n))$, then $f_1(n) f_2(n) = O(g_1(n)\, g_2(n))$.

We can now use these rules to compute big-O estimates without having to find explicit c and N values. For example, suppose we wished to find an estimate for $8n \log n + 4n^{3/2}$. We could argue as follows:

1. $\log n = O(n^{1/2})$, since logs are beaten by any positive powers (and we're thinking ahead a bit here).
2. $n \log n = O(n\, n^{1/2}) = O(n^{3/2})$, by Rule 4 (which is why we thought ahead in step 1).
3. $8n \log n = O(n^{3/2})$, by Rule 1.
4. $4n^{3/2} = O(n^{3/2})$, again by Rule 1.
5. $8n \log n + 4n^{3/2} = O(\max\{8n \log n, 4n^{3/2}\})$ by Rule 3.
6. $8n \log n + 4n^{3/2} = O(\max\{n^{3/2}, n^{3/2}\}) = O(n^{3/2})$, by Rule 2.

You still might think that there is something vaguely unsatisfactory about ignoring constant multiples in our timing estimates, something mathematically not quite right. In a sense such an objection is well founded. Suppose, for instance, that you had two programs to accomplish a given task, one that took $100n^2$ milliseconds to process an input of size n and another that took 2^n milliseconds. Which one is better? What we've seen so far would lead us to say that the $O(n^2)$ algorithm should certainly be preferred over the $O(2^n)$ one.

It turns out that we can't answer that question as stated. If you try some sample values for N, you'll see that 2^n is less than or equal to $100n^2$ as long as $n \le 14$, so as long as you restrict yourself to running inputs of size 14 or less, the exponential algorithm beats the quadratic, even though in the long run the exponential one takes much more time. An old maxim among the people who employ computer scientists (though not necessarily among computer scientists themselves) runs "theory is fine, but there's nothing better than results." In fact, in many cases it is simply not worth the effort of developing and running a very complicated (though sophisticated) algorithm when there is a simple one already in the program library that is nearly as good or even better on the inputs you'll be using. Your choice will be dictated to a large extent by the reason for developing your program.

Timing Functions

Now that we have the machinery to analyze the running time of algorithms, it is time to see how this analysis works in practice. First, notice that we said "the running time of *algorithms*," not the running time of programs. Earlier in this section we mentioned that the running time of a program depends not only on the size and the nature of the input, but also on such features as the computer the program runs on and the efficiency of the code produced by the compiler. The emphasis on big-O notation allows us to "factor out" the contributions that are beyond our control, such as the speed of the computer, and concentrate on the behavior of the algorithm behind the program. In general, an algorithm that has time complexity $O(n^2)$ will run as a program in time $O(n^2)$, no matter what language or machine is chosen for the implementation of the algorithm. Given an input of size n, whether the algorithm takes $117.65n^2$ milliseconds in BASIC on an IBM PC or $0.28n^2$ milliseconds in FORTRAN on a Cray X-MP is of little importance to us. What is important is that, no matter how fast the computers chosen for the implementation, a program based on a $O(n^2)$ algorithm will, for large enough n, eventually run faster than an implementation of a $O(n^3)$ algorithm.

To analyze an algorithm, we make the simplifying assumption that each statement, except perhaps for procedure and function calls, takes the same unit amount of time. This will not affect the timing analysis since we are only interested in big-O estimates and so are ignoring constant multiples. As an example, if multiplication takes five times as long as addition when implemented on a computer, we are off in our timing estimate by no more than a factor of five if we treat them as equal in the algorithm, and the multiple of five will be absorbed in our big-O estimate anyway.

The only statements in a pseudocode algorithm that can result in a non-unit contribution to the running time are transfers of control, such as **if** statements, loops, and procedure and function calls. We will concentrate on simple transfers of controls here, and will defer detailed analysis of procedure calls until Chapter 5. If it were not for transfers of control, an algorithm would have time complexity equal to the number of statements in the algorithm, and so would run in constant time, independent of the size of the input. It is only when some statements are to be executed more than once that we may have time complexity larger than $O(1)$.

There are two more simplifying assumptions we will make in the timing analysis of an algorithm:

1. Unless there is compelling reason to the contrary, we will always assume that an **if** statement takes time equal to the larger of its two branches (in order to obtain worst-case timing estimates).
2. Unless there is compelling reason to the contrary, we will always assume that the statements within a loop will be executed as many times as the maximum permitted by the loop control.

Example 1.

Consider the following routine

```
procedure LinearSearch(n, key : integer ; a : NumberArray ;
        var where : integer);
{Searches an array with n elements for any element with value equal to key.}
{Returns the last location where key is found in variable where, or zero if not found.}
    var
        index : integer;
begin
    where := 0;
    for index := 1 to n do
        if a[index] = key then
            where := index
end;
```

In this algorithm, the **for** loop is always executed n times. The body of the loop consists of a single **if** statement, which causes at most one statement to be executed each time it is encountered. In essence, then, we have the following timing schematic for this algorithm:

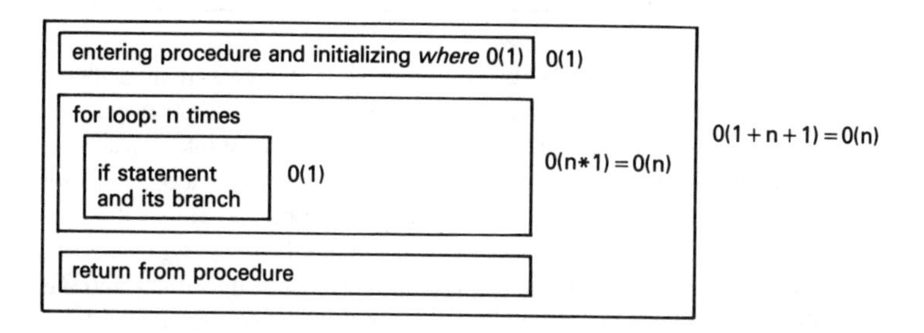

We have included timing for operations, such as entering and leaving the procedure, that are not explicitly written as part of the routine. In the future we will omit these from our timing analysis, since they contribute only a constant amount of additional time, and so will not appear in the big-O estimate. Notice that we have made use of the rules for evaluating big-O expressions.

Example 2.

In this example, we consider a routine with nested loops.

```
function SumProd(n : integer) : integer;
   var
      result, k, i : integer;
begin
   result := 0;
   for k := 1 to n do
      for i := 1 to k do
         result := result + k * i;
   SumProd := result
end;
```

To analyze the time complexity of this algorithm, we make use of assumption 2, and assume that the inner loop is executed the maximum number of times possible. Since the inner loop iterates k times each time it is entered, and k in the outer loop can be as large as n, we make the simplifying assumption that the inner loop iterates n times each time it is entered. You might well object that this overestimates the number of times the inner loop iterates, because there is only one instance when the inner loop actually iterates n times. You would be right, but we will show that this overestimate has no effect on the final timing estimate. Under our assumptions, we have the following timing schematic:

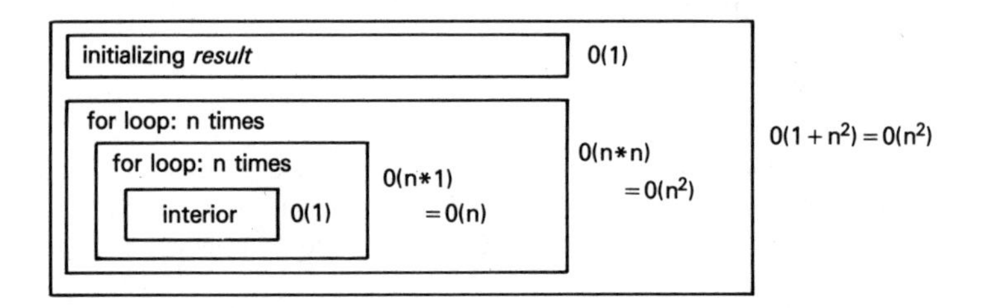

We mentioned the objection that we are overestimating the contribution of the inner loop, the one controlled by the index variable i. Suppose we took into account the fact that the first time the inner loop is encountered it iterates once, the second time it iterates twice, and so on. In that case, as k varies in the outer loop, it causes the inner loop to take time $O(k)$. Since k in the outer loop takes on the values 1, 2, . . . , n, the amount of time contributed by the outer and inner loops is $O(1 + 2 + \ldots + n)$. This, of course, is just the sum we saw in the discussion of Gauss's algorithm, and we can use Gauss's technique to evaluate it. The pairs of outer terms all sum to $n + 1$, and there are $n/2$ such pairs, so the sum $1 + 2 + \ldots + n$ is equal to $n(n + 1)/2$ which is $O(n^2)$, the same result we obtained from our simplifying assumption that the inner loop is always iterated n times.

Whenever we are dealing with nested loops, as long as each inner loop is iterated a number of times that is a linear function of the number of times the next outer loop is iterated, we do not alter our big-O estimate by assuming that the inner loop iterates as often as the outer loop does.

This result can be generalized to any depth of nesting. In fact, you may have seen generalizations of Gauss's identity for sums of powers other than the first power, some of which are given in Figure 1.7.

$$\sum_{i=1}^{n} i = \frac{n(n+1)}{2}$$

$$\sum_{i=1}^{n} i^2 = \frac{n(n+1)(2n+1)}{6}$$

$$\sum_{i=1}^{n} i^3 = \frac{n^2(n+1)^2}{4}$$

Figure 1.7 Formulas for sums of powers.

As an example of the use of these identities, consider the following program segment, consisting of three nested loops.

```
for i := 1 to n do
   for j := 1 to i do
      for k := 1 to i do
         something that is O(1);
```

Our simplifying assumption applies here, so we know that this segment of pseudocode will contribute $O(n \times n \times n) = O(n^3)$ to the timing. To be more precise (at the cost of slightly more involved calculations), we see that for each value of i in the outer loop, the two inner loops together will contribute i^2 to the timing. As i takes on the values $1, 2, \ldots, n$, then, the entire segment will contribute $1^2 + 2^2 + \ldots + n^2$, which is just the second identity above. Thus, a more accurate timing estimate for this segment would be $T(n) = n(n+1)(2n+1)/6$, which is still $O(n^3)$.

Example 3.

Finally, consider a program segment with a **multiplicative loop**, one that is nested within another loop, but whose iterations are not a linear function of the control variable of the outer loop. This is an instance of "compelling reasons to the contrary," so, as you will see, we will not be able to assume that the inner loop will iterate as often as the outer loop.

```
m := 1;
for i := 1 to n do begin
   m := m * 2;
   for j := 1 to m do
      {something that is O(1)}
end;
```

In this case, as the outer loop control takes on the values 1, 2, 3, . . . , the inner loop iterates 2, 4, 8, . . . times, giving us a running time of $O(2 + 4 + \ldots + 2^n)$. This is a **geometric series**, in which each term is a constant multiple of the preceding one. It happens that for such a series with n terms, first term s and constant multiple r (both of which are 2 in this case), the value of the series is

$$s\frac{r^n - 1}{r - 1}$$

so that we have a running time of $O(2(2^n - 1)/(2 - 1)) = O(2^{n+1})$, rather than the $O(n^2)$ that we would expect in a nonmultiplicative loop.

1.5 SUMMARY

An abstract data type is an abstraction of the means of organizing data in a program, in much the same way that a pseudocode algorithm is an abstraction of the statements executed in a program. The use of abstract data types provides a middle ground between an informal description of the logical arrangement of information, and the data structures used for the storage of information in a program. An abstract data type consists of three aspects: (1) an underlying set, ATOM, and a set, POSITION, of possible positions into which to place the atoms; (2) a collection of elements with a common internal structure; and (3) a collection of structure-preserving operations on these elements.

The structural relations on the elements of a given ADT all share the same properties, some of which may be reflexivity, symmetry, antisymmetry, transitivity, and the chain condition. An example of a structural relation is the linear order, which is reflexive, antisymmetric, transitive, and a chain. Such a relation is used in the LIST ADT to reflect the notion that a list has a first, second, third, . . . , last element.

Any ADT may be implemented in several ways, depending on the choice of the data structure chosen in a program. The choice of data structure often influences the utilization of the resources of running time and storage space in a program, as well as being dictated by considerations such as ease of programming and the availability of data structures in a programming language. At least in some simple cases, it is possible to analyze the running time and memory requirements of an algorithm. Big-O notation provides a means of determining the **asymptotic** (i.e., long-range) behavior of an algorithm as a function of the size of the input. Although asymptotic estimates of the behavior of an algorithm provide some indication of the complexity of an algorithm, it is important to pay attention not only to the asymptotic behavior of an algorithm, but also to considerations such as ease of implementation, behavior of the algorithm on inputs that are expected in actual practice, and readability and maintainability of the program itself.

1.6 EXERCISES

1. Implement Gauss's algorithm to find the sum of an arithmetic series as

   function SumArithmeticSeries(start, difference, terms : integer) : integer;

   where *start* is the lowest value in the series, *difference* is the difference between successive terms, and *terms* is the number of terms in the series.
2. Using the numeric codes 2 . . . 53 for the cards in a bridge deck, find algorithms to translate from *code* to (*suit, value*) and back again.
3. In the bit vector representation of a bridge hand given in the text, what hand would be represented by the bit vector that contained, from positions 2 to 53, the values

   00000010 01000000 00111001 11000100 00000001 00000010 0110?

4. Suppose you wanted to implement bit vectors on a computer that did not pack boolean values one to a bit but, rather, required a 16-bit word for each variable. In such a case, you would have to write your own packing and unpacking routines if you wished to provide efficient storage. In order to store a packed bit vector with n bits, you would require n **div** 16 words, plus one more word if n was not a multiple of 16. Assuming you had already written a packing routine, show how you would write an inspection function which would return the value of bit k in the packed array V. You may assume that you have available a function *BitTest(n, w)* : integer, which returns the value of the nth bit in the word w.
5. Fill in the following table by placing a check in each cell for which the given relation, on the set $P = \{2, 3, 4, 5, 6\}$, has the indicated property.

	<	≤	=	Divides	Has no factor in common with
Reflexive					
Symmetric					
Antisymmetric					
Transitive					
Chain					

6. Terry Winograd developed a program called SHRDLU that was intended to model a simple "world" consisting of children's blocks of various shapes and colors. Among other things, SHRDLU was designed to simulate manipulation of the blocks by picking them up and placing them elsewhere. Give a specification of the abstract data type BLOCKS, keeping in mind such properties as color, shape, "on top of," and so on.

7. Show that if S is a finite set with a linear order relation R, then

(a) Every element of S has at most one immediate successor.

(b) There is exactly one **maximum** element, namely an element that has no immediate successor.

(c) If the set S is not finite, (b) is not necessarily true .

8. Provide (P, R, v) definitions for the structure of the following ADTs, being especially careful to describe the structural relation R precisely. If you wish, you may describe R in terms of (immediate) successors and predecessors.

(a) SET, under the usual interpretation of the word.

(b) BAG, also called **multiset**, which is similar to SET, except that atoms are allowed to occur more than once in each element. In other words, {a, a, b, c, c, c} is a legal bag, but would not be a legal set.

(c) RING, which has the circular structure of the SEMINAR example in the text. This is commonly used to handle jobs on several terminals that are waiting to use a single central computer.

9. **(a)–(c)** Provide implementations of the structures of Exercise 8.

10. **(a)–(c)** Describe a reasonable collection of operations on the structures of Exercise 8.

11. Pascal does not allow the values of pointer variables to be manipulated directly. In other words, address arithmetic is not allowed in Pascal. Give two reasons that this might be so, in terms of the potential for accidental or deliberate damage.

12. Suppose we have the following declarations:

```
type
   Link = ^Cell;
   Cell = record
               key : integer;
               nextCell : Link
          end;

function Insert(x : integer ; var p : Link);
   var q : Link;
begin
   q := p^.nextCell;
   New(p^.nextCell);
   p^.nextCell^.nextCell := q;
   p^.nextCell^.key := p^.key;
   p^.key := x
end;
```

What would be the result of **Insert**(1002, p), applied to the following data?

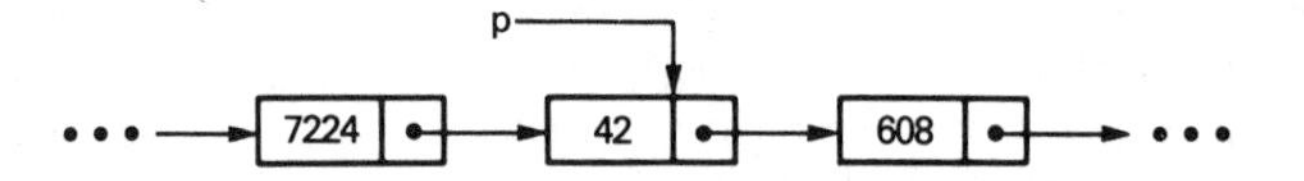

13. Prove the following assertions by finding suitable values for c and N in the definition of big-O.

(a) $n^3 + n^2 + n + 1 = O(n^3)$.

(b) $(3n^3 + 9n^2 - 24)/(n + 1) = O(n^2)$.

(c) $\sum_{i=1}^{n} i^k = O(n^{k+1})$.

14. We could show that $\sqrt{8n^2+20} = O(n)$ by setting $c = 3$ in the definition of big-O. How large does n have to be before $\sqrt{8n^2+20} < 3n$?

15. Find the best big-O estimates you can for the following functions, without finding c and N.

(a) $f(n) = (8n^5 - 25n^3 + 7n)/(4n^2 - 1)$.

(b) $f(n) = \begin{cases} 4n^2, & \text{if } n \text{ is even.} \\ 3n+4, & \text{if } n \text{ is odd.} \end{cases}$

(c) $f(n) = 3^n - 2^{n+2}$.

16. For two functions, $f(n)$, and $g(n)$, define the relation "$\leftarrow$" by $f(n) \leftarrow g(n)$ if $f(n) = O(g(n))$. Arrange the following functions in "$\leftarrow$" order: n^2, 2^n, $\log n$, $n \log n$, 3^n, $(\log n)^2$, n, $n/\log n$, $n(\log n)^2$.

17. What is wrong with the following statement?

Algorithm A and Algorithm B both have the same result, but accomplish that result in different ways. On inputs of size n, Algorithm A runs in time $O(n^2)$, while Algorithm B runs in time $O(2^n)$. If $n = 20$, $n^2 = 400$, while $2^n = 1{,}048{,}576$, so for inputs of size 20, Algorithm A will be approximately 2,621 times as fast as Algorithm B.

18. Provide big-O timing estimates for the following algorithms:

(a)

```
function Max(a : ArrayOfIntegers) : integer;
{Finds the largest element in an array, a, of n elements}
   var largest, i : integer;
begin
   largest := 0;
   for i := 1 to n do
      if a[i] > largest then
         largest := a[i];
   Max := largest
end;
```

(b)
```
procedure SelectionSort(a : ArrayOfIntegers ; var b : ArrayOfIntegers);
{Takes an array, a, of integers of size n, and produces an array, b, which}
{consists of the elements of a arranged from smallest to largest.}
    var smallest, where, i, j : integer;
  begin
    for i := 1 to n do begin
      dummy := {some integer larger than anything in it };
      smallest := dummy;
      for j := 1 to n do
        if a[j] < smallest then begin
          smallest := a[j];
          where := j
        end;
      a[where] := dummy;
      b[i] := smallest
    end
  end;
```

19. Consider the following two algorithms

```
function Expo1(x, n : integer) : integer;
{  Returns the result of raising x to the power n.}
{  Requires that n be nonnegative. }
  var i, result : integer;
begin
  result := 1;
  for i := 1 to n do
    result := result * x;
  Expo1 := result
end;

function Expo2(x, n : integer) : integer;
{  Does the same as Expo1. }
  var result : integer;
begin
  result := 1;
  while n > 0 do begin
    if odd(n) then
      result := result * x;
    x := x * x;
    n := n div 2
  end;
  Expo2 := result
end;
```

(a) Provide an example that *Expo2* does the same thing as *Expo1* by tracing the action of *Expo2*(2, 13).

(b) Find estimates of the running time of the two algorithms. Which is better?

20. Show that in Example 2, the function *SumProd* satisfies

$$SumProd(n) = n(n+1)(n+2)(2n+1)/12.$$

21. Suppose S is a statement that takes time $O(1)$. We have seen that

```
for i := 1 to n do
    S;
```

takes time n, and that

```
for i := 1 to n do
    for j := 1 to i do
        S;
```

takes time $n(n+1)/2$.

(a) Find the best timing function you can (in the sense that an answer like $n(n+1)/2$ is to be preferred over $O(n^2)$ for the segment

```
for i := 1 to n do
    for j := 1 to i do
        for k := 1 to j do
            S;
```

(b) Generalize your answer to part (a) for the case of k nested loops, as

```
for i1 := 1 to n do
    for i2 := 1 to i1 do
        for i3 := 1 to i2 do
                .
                .
                .
                for ik := 1 to ik-1 do
                    S;
```

2

Strings

Writing consists of nothing but arranging letters to form words, arranging words to form sentences, arranging sentences to form paragraphs, all the while inserting, removing and rearranging smaller units to make larger ones.

Armand Blague, *How to Write*

Most people with a background in programming are familiar with strings, since almost all common programming languages include character strings among their predefined data types. This chapter will be a warm-up to get you used to the study of abstract data types through this familiar example. We will follow the course of action that we will use throughout most of this text by first defining the ADT, then describing how to implement the ADT using the simple data structures available in most programming languages, and finally exploring some problems for which the ADT is particularly useful.

2.1 THE ABSTRACT DATA TYPE STRING

A **string** is a collection of characters written in order as, for example, 'Alan Turing'. In all programming languages in which strings are defined, the underlying set of characters contains not only the letters of the alphabet, but also nonalphabetic characters such as '7' and '+'. We will follow the notation used in most languages by enclosing strings in single quotes, so, for example, we can write the strings 'AARDVARK' and '%*blort!!'. Notice that we said that the order of characters was important: Although 'TEACHER' and 'CHEATER' contain the same characters, your author, in particular, would consider them to be unequal (from several points of view). Consider also the string '1667': Although it looks like an integer, it is a different animal entirely—it is a string consisting of the four characters '1', '6', '6', and '7', and, as a string, has no more numeric meaning than 'AARDVARK'. This confusion, which brings grief to countless beginning programmers, is a topic that we will investigate in more detail in the exercises. Finally, we will abuse notation slightly and will speak of a *character* and a *string consisting of a single character* interchangeably, although strictly speaking they are of different types.

As with any abstract data type, a precise definition of STRING requires describing both the elements of the ADT, and the operations that we can perform on these elements. In terms of the (P, R, v) notation, a string S of n characters could be viewed as the triple (P, R, v), with P being any set of n elements, R a linear order on P, and v a function that maps the ith position onto the character that we wish to occupy position i. Since any linearly ordered set with n elements is essentially identical to the set of integers $P = \{1, 2, \ldots, n\}$ with the linear order $R =$ "$\leq$" (identical in the sense that any linearly ordered set could have its elements renamed by integers and would then be indistinguishable from P in all its order-related properties), we could equally well think of a string this way, and then observe that the evaluation function v is defined by making $v(i) = c_i$.

We could then view the elements of the abstract data type STRING simply as sequences, $(c_1, c_2, \ldots, c_n)$, where each c_i is a character. For example, the string 'BAZ' would be denoted by the sequence (c_1, c_2, c_3), with c_1 = 'B', c_2 = 'A', and C_3 = 'Z'. In this case, it would make no sense to refer to c_i for any $i > 3$, just as it would make no sense to refer to the tenth character of the word "book." We allow the case where n is equal to zero; in this instance the string is called the **empty string**, and there are no elements in the sequence. Unless otherwise noted, we will assume throughout that the underlying set of objects in the sequence will be a set of characters, although strictly speaking we could choose any underlying set we wished, and talk, for instance, about strings of integers.

Now that we know what the elements of STRING are, we must also describe the operations that act on the elements of the ADT. In any such description there is considerable freedom of choice, so we include the operations we would like to have available for applications, and leave out those that do not seem "natural" in the ADT. For instance, in all likelihood we would exclude arithmetic operations on strings. We will adopt the strategy of listing a collection of operations as "primitive" and then including other useful operations that could be defined in terms of the primitives.

The STRING ADT includes the following five primitive operations:

1. **Create**(**var** S : STRING), which sets S equal to the empty string. This operation may also be used to clear an existing string, making it the empty string.
2. **Length**(S : STRING) : integer, a function that takes a string $S = (c_1, c_2, \ldots, c_n)$, as input and returns the length, n, of S.
3. **Retrieve**(S : STRING ; i : integer) : character, a function that returns the ith character, c_i, from the string $S = (c_1, c_2, \ldots, c_n)$. This definition assumes the **precondition** that $1 \leq i \leq n$, namely that there *is* an ith character in S, and the operation returns an error message or takes appropriate action otherwise.

4. **Append**(**var** S : STRING ; c : character) changes S by placing the character c after the last element of S. Formally, if S was the empty string prior to the call to *Append,* S will be the string consisting of the single character c after the call, and if $S = (c_1, c_2, \ldots, c_n)$, with $n > 0$ before the call, then after the call to *Append* we will have $S = (c'_1, c'_2, \ldots, c'_n, c'_{n+1})$, where $c'_i = c_i$, for $i = 1, \ldots, n$, and $c'_{n+1} = c$. It might appear that there is no reason to prefer appending a character to the tail over appending a character to the head, but one of the exercises demonstrates that there is indeed a reason.
5. **Delete**(**var** S : STRING), the "opposite" of *Append,* removes the first character from the string S. As with *Retrieve,* there is a precondition, namely that S not be the empty string. If $S = (c_1, c_2, \ldots, c_n)$, with $n > 0$, before the call, then after the call we will have $S = (c'_1, c'_2, \ldots, c'_{n-1})$, with $c'_i = c_{i+1}$, for $i = 1, \ldots, n - 1$.

Along with these five primitives, there are several other operations that are commonly used with the STRING ADT. We will include these in our definition of STRING and will show how one of them may be written in terms of the primitives. The descriptions of the other operations in terms of primitives we leave as exercises.

6. **Substring**(source : STRING ; start, size : integer ; **var** sub : STRING), is a generalization of *Retrieve* in that it sets *sub* equal to that part of *source* which begins in position *start* and is of length *size* characters. For example, the call *Substring*('ABCDE', 2, 3, *sub*) would result in *sub* being set to the string 'BCD'. There is a somewhat complicated precondition for this procedure, depending upon the length of *source,* and the values of *start* and *size.* We leave the determination of this precondition as an exercise.
7. **Concat**(**var** first : STRING ; last : STRING), is a generalization of the procedure *Append,* but instead of attaching a single character to the tail of a string, *Concat* attaches all of *last* to the tail of the string *first.* For example, if *first* was the string 'DOG', then *Concat(first,* 'FOOD') would cause *first* to be set equal to the string 'DOGFOOD'. To be more formal, if *first* is empty, then it is set equal to the string *last*; similarly, if *last* is empty, then *first* is returned unchanged. If, on the other hand, $first = (c_1, c_2, \ldots, c_n)$ and $last = (d_1, d_2, \ldots, d_m)$, with $n, m > 0$, then, after performing the operation, we have $first = (f_1, f_2, \ldots, f_{n+m})$, with $f_i = c_i$, for $i = 1, \ldots, n$, and $f_i = d_{i-n}$, for $i = n+1, \ldots, n+m$.
8. **Insert**(**var** source : STRING ; p : integer ; inner : STRING), is a further generalization of *Append,* which places *inner* into *source,* between positions p and $p+1$. If $p = 0$, *inner* is inserted before the first character of *source.* The precondition for this operation is that p is a legal location in *source,* that is, that $0 \leq p \leq Length(source)$. For example, if we had *source* = 'ABCDEFGH', then *Insert(source,* 3, 'XYZ') would result in *source* being set to 'ABCXYZDEFGH'. Notice that if p = *Length(source),* then a call to *Insert(source, p, inner)* has the same effect as *Concat(source, inner).*
9. **Remove**(**var** source : STRING ; start, size : integer), generalizes *Delete,* removing from *source* the substring of length *size,* which begins in position *start.* The precondition for this operation is the same as for *Substring.*

10. **Find**(source, target : STRING) : integer, returns the position in the string *source* of the first instance of the substring *target*, if it is found, and returns the value zero otherwise. For example, *Find*('ABCDBC', 'BC') would return the value 2, and *Find*('ABCD', 'BA') would return zero. In other words, if *target* was the empty string, *Find* would return zero regardless of what *source* was, and otherwise if $source = (c_1, c_2, \ldots, c_n)$, and $target = (d_1, d_2, \ldots, d_m)$, with $m > 0$, then *Find(source, target)* would return the least integer p for which $c_{p+i-1} = d_i$, for $i = 1, \ldots, m$, or would return zero if no such p existed.
11. **Copy**(**var** destination : STRING ; source : STRING), sets the string *destination* equal in length and contents to the string *source*.
12. **Equal**(S, T : STRING) : boolean, is a function that returns *true* if S and T are identical strings, and returns *false* otherwise. In other words, *Equal* returns *true* if and only if either S and T are both empty, or $S = (c_1, c_2, \ldots, c_n)$ and $T = (d_1, d_2, \ldots, d_m)$, with $n = m > 0$, and $c_i = d_i$, for $i = 1, \ldots, n$.

Finally, it is almost always the case that the underlying set, ATOM, of characters in the STRING ADT itself has a linear order relation defined on it, so that it makes sense to say that some object is "before" or "less than" another. In particular, the order for sets of characters is usually taken to be an extension of alphabetic order. This order for characters depends on the machine on which a program is run, and differs from manufacturer to manufacturer. The most common orders for printable characters (that is, excluding characters that represent line feeds, carriage returns, bells, tabs, and the like) are:

ASCII (American Standard Code for Information Interchange) order: (space) ! " # $ % ' ( ) * + , – . / 0 1 2 3 4 5 6 7 8 9 : ; < = > ? @ A B C D E F G H I J K L M N O P Q R S T U V W X Y Z [\ ] ^ _ ` a b c d e f g h i j k l m n o p q r s t u v w x y z { | } ~

EBCDIC (Extended Binary Coded Decimal Interchange Code) order: (space) ¢ . < (+ | & ! $ *) ; ¬ – / ^ , % _ > ? : # @ ' = " a b c d e f g h i j k l m n o p q r s t u v w x y z \ { } [ ] A B C D E F G H I J K L M N O P Q R S T U V W X Y Z 0 1 2 3 4 5 6 7 8 9

Because the underlying characters can be ordered (so we can say, for instance, that the character '+' is "less than" the character 'A' in either of the above orders), it is possible to extend this to an ordering on character strings. This **lexicographic order** is similar to that used in dictionaries and telephone books: We define the lexicographic order "$<_L$" on strings as an extension of the order "$<_C$" on characters as follows:

1. The empty string is less than any nonempty string.
2. If S = $(c_1, c_2, \ldots, c_n)$ and T = $(d_1, d_2, \ldots, d_m)$, then $S <_L T$ if
   (a) there is a number p, with $0 \le p \le \min(n, m)$, such that $c_i = d_i$, for all $0 \le i \le p$ (so the first p characters of S and T match).
   (b) either $c_{p+1} <_C d_{p+1}$ (the first nonmatching character of S is "less than" the corresponding character of T) or $p = n$ (i.e., S completely matches the first n characters of T, but T is longer than S).

For example, using either of the foregoing orders for characters, we see that 'A' $<_L$ 'Z', 'BRAINS' $<_L$ 'BRAWN', and 'HOT' $<_L$ 'HOTTENTOT'. In case there is a linear order on the underlying set of a STRING type, we can define the string order function **Less** (X, Y : STRING) : boolean, to reflect this lexicographic order, by returning *true* if X $<_L$ Y, and *false* otherwise.

We separated the operations on the STRING abstract data type into *primitives* and *nonprimitives* in order to emphasize the fact that the primitive operations were a minimal set of operations necessary, in the sense that the other operations could be defined in terms of the primitives. As you will see, this is a somewhat artificial division, since once a choice has been made for the implementation of an ADT, it is often easier to define a nonprimitive operation directly than to define it in terms of primitives. Nevertheless, it is a worthwhile exercise to define an operation in terms of primitives, if only to make the definition of an ADT as independent of the choice of implementation as possible.

For example, consider the operation *Insert*. We will define this procedure in terms of the primitives. The algorithm is simple to understand: We build the output string *result* by appending to it, in order, (1) the characters of *source* up to the insertion point, followed by (2) all the characters from *inner*, followed by (3) all the characters from *source* after the insertion point.

```
procedure Insert(var source : STRING ; p : integer ; inner : STRING);
   {Inserts string inner between positions p and p+1 in string source }
   var
      result : STRING;
      i : integer;
begin
   if (p < 0) or (p > Length(source)) then
      writeln('illegal position in Insert')
   else begin
      Create(result);
      for i := 1 to p do                         {append front of source to result }
         Append(result, Retrieve(source, i));
      for i := 1 to Length(Inner) do              {append inner to result}
         Append(result, Retrieve(inner, i));
      for  i := p + 1 to Length(source)  do       {append rest of source to result }
         Append(result, Retrieve(source, i));

      Create(source);                             {clear source }
      for i := 1 to Length(result)  do            {copy result into source }
         Append(Source, Retrieve(result, i))
   end
end;
```

2.2 ARRAY IMPLEMENTATIONS OF STRING

The simplest implementation of the STRING ADT mirrors directly the definition given in Section. 2.1. We represent each string by two pieces of information: (1) an integer representing the length of the string, along with (2) an array of characters containing the contents of the string. This has the disadvantage that in many programming languages (such as FORTRAN77, COBOL, Pascal, and BASIC) the size of an array must be fixed at the time of writing the program. Arrays in these languages are **static arrays** in the sense that their sizes cannot be altered while the program is running.

Some implementations of programming languages, for example, represent each character by a byte of 8 binary digits, and represent each string by an array of 256 bytes, $b_0, b_1, \ldots, b_{255}$. Now, there are 256 different numbers that can be expressed with 8 binary digits, which is more than sufficient to encode all the characters in the underlying set. The clever part of this implementation comes from interpreting the bytes in two senses: bytes b_1 through b_{255} are numeric codes for characters, and byte b_0 is interpreted by the compiler to be the length of the string. In the ASCII encoding, for instance, the character 'A' has numeric code 65, 'B' is represented by 66, and so on, so the string 'CAB' would be represented by the sequence of 256 numbers beginning with 3, 67, 65, 66, ... The first number indicates that the string has length 3, the next 3 numbers are the ASCII codes for the characters in the string, and the last 252 numbers would not correspond to anything meaningful, since the string consists of only three characters. We see that for this implementation a string could have any length from 0 to 255 (since 255 is the largest integer that can be represented by one byte) but is always represented by 256 bytes, regardless of the actual length of the string.

This particular choice of implementation is in no way to be regarded as engraved in stone. We used arrays because arrays, like strings, have a natural linear structure and we included a *length* field because strings have different lengths, even if the arrays do not. We could have dispensed with the *length* field by choosing a **sentinel** marker at the end of each string. Such a marker would merely be another character, one that could not possibly be confused with those that make up the strings. We could then find the length of a string by searching down the string, keeping track of the number of characters inspected, until we found the sentinel character. This, of course, would make the *Length* function more time-consuming, which is why we chose to include the length as a separate field in this implementation.

Since the use of static arrays implies that there must be a fixed maximum size for strings in such an implementation, we need to be aware of the possibility that operations such as *Append, Insert,* and *Concat* could lead to errors caused by strings over the maximum length limit. You will soon see, however, that if you are willing to pay the price of a fixed maximum length for strings, in return you will get a very fast and conceptually simple implementation.

Static Arrays

We may define the static array implementation of the ADT STRING as follows:

```
const
   MaxLength = {largest possible length for any string}
type
   STRING = record
               length : integer;       {strictly speaking this should be non-negative}
               ch : array[1 .. MaxLength] of char {the underlying type}
            end;
```

In this implementation, the primitives are particularly easy to write. We include them here, although in subsequent chapters we will often leave as exercises the definitions of the simpler primitives.

1.
```
procedure Create(var s : STRING); {O(1) time}
begin
   s.length := 0
end;
```

2.
```
function Length(s : STRING) : integer;    {O(1)}
begin
   Length := s.length
end;
```

3.
```
function Retrieve(s : STRING ; i : integer) : char;   {O(1)}
begin
   if (i < 0) or (i > s.length) then begin
      writeln('illegal index in Retrieve');
      Retreive := {some dummy character}
   end else
      Retrieve := s.ch[i]
end;
```

4.
```
procedure Append(var s : STRING ; c : char);   {O(1)}
begin
   if s.length = MaxLength then
      writeln('Appended string exceeded maximum length')
   else begin
      s.length := s.length + 1;
      s.ch[s.length] := c
   end
end;
```

5.
```
procedure Delete(var s : STRING);                    {O(n), for strings of length n}
begin
   if s.length = 0 then
      writeln('attempted to Delete from empty string')
   else begin
      for i := 1 to s.length -1 do       {shift remaining characters left one space}
         s.ch[i] := s.ch[i+1];
      s.length := s.length - 1           {and change the length indicator}
   end
end;
```

Notice that all these operations, with the exception of *Delete*, run in time $O(1)$, which is to say that they take a constant amount of time no matter how long the strings are. *Delete*, however, always takes $O(n)$ time on strings of length n, because every character in the string must be shifted one place to the left to fill the hole made by deleting the first element. (Strictly speaking, for this implementation, *Delete* is also $O(1)$ since the longest possible string would have length n, equal to the constant *MaxLength.*) We could redefine *Delete* to remove the last element of the input string, making it run in $O(1)$ time as well, except that such a definition would be more time-consuming in the pointer implementation discussed in the next section.

Having chosen an implementation for STRING, we now have two choices: We could define the nonprimitive operations in terms of the already implemented primitives, or we could define the other operations directly in terms of the implementation. The first choice (assuming we had already defined the other operations in terms of the primitives) would require no additional work: All we would have to do is include the previously written definitions as part of our implementation package. This would have the advantage of cutting down the necessary amount of work in case we decided to change to another implementation. As we hinted earlier, however, it is sometimes worth the extra work to define an operation in terms of the implementation, because the resulting routine may be simpler without reference to the primitives.

Consider *Insert*, for instance. We have seen how it may be defined in terms of the primitives. Writing it directly for static arrays, we would have the following definition:

```
procedure Insert(var source : STRING ; p : integer ; inner : STRING);
   var
      i : integer;
begin
   if (p < 0) or (p > source.length) then
      writeln('illegal position in Insert')
   else begin
      for i := s.length downto p + 1 do              {shift the tail of source }
         source.ch[i + inner.length] := source.ch[i];
      for i := 1 to inner.length do                  {insert inner}
         source.ch[p + i] := inner.ch[i];
      source.length := source.length + inner.length
   end
end;
```

In this example, not only do we see that defining an operation directly in terms of the implementation leads to a shorter program, with 13 lines rather than the 20 required by the first version, but we can also show that this program runs in fewer steps than the version defined in terms of primitives. Ignoring the overhead involved in executing procedure calls and the **if** and **for** statements, and denoting the length of *source* by s and the length of *inner* by i, the first algorithm runs in time $2s + 2i$, whereas the second algorithm runs in time $s - p + i$, a better than twofold improvement in running time.

To take an extreme example of choice of implementation, suppose we chose not only the implementation for STRING, but the language of the implementation as well. In particular, suppose we had decided to write *Insert* in Macintosh™ Pascal. In that case, the definition would take *no lines at all* to write, because *Insert* is a predefined routine in that dialect of Pascal (which means, however, that we have no immediate clue to how fast that routine runs, since we don't know how it is defined by the interpreter).

Before leaving this topic, let us consider the implementation of another of the STRING operations. Reviewing the thirteen STRING operations, it seems that *Find* is the "deepest" in the sense that we see immediately how we could describe algorithms for all the other operations, but we have to think a bit before we see how to attack the definition of *Find*. An algorithm that would probably occur first to most people would be to search the source string character by character to find matches for the characters in the target string, as we do below.

```
function Find(source, target : STRING) : integer;
{  Returns the position in Source of the first occurrence of substring Target, }
{  and returns zero if Target not found.}
   var current : integer;     {possible location of start of Target}
begin
   if source or target is empty then
      Find := 0
   else begin
      current := 1;
      while (complete match not found) and (current ≤ Length(source)) do
         if current source character <> first target character then
            current := current + 1
         else begin          {found match for first char of Target; check the rest}
            repeat
               step through source and target together
            until (match fails) or (no more Target left) or (no more Source left)
            if no more target characters to inspect then  {complete match found}
               Find := current
            else
               current := current + 1      {continue looking at next position in Source }
         end;
      if complete match not found then
         Find := 0
   end
end;
```

For example, if *source* was 'ACBCBABA', and *target* was 'CBA', this algorithm would make the following steps, where the characters presently being compared are highlighted. While you read through this example and the ones to follow, bear in mind that we are not actually moving *target*. We are moving the reference to characters in *target*; the apparent shifts of *target* in the examples are only to make the process clearer.

1.	**C** B A	
	A C B C B A B A	No match, advance *target*.
2.	**C** B A	
	A **C** B C B A B A	Match, look at subsequent characters.
3.	C **B** A	
	A C **B** C B A B A	Still matches, pass to next position.
4.	C B **A**	
	A C B **C** B A B A	Failed to match, advance *target*.
5.	**C** B A	
	A C **B** C B A B A	Failed to match, advance *target* again.
6.	**C** B A	
	A C B **C** B A B A	Match, look at subsequent characters.
7.	C **B** A	
	A C B C **B** A B A	Still matches, pass to next position.
8.	C B **A**	
	A C B C B **A** B A	Still matches, search complete.

This search required eight comparisons to find *target* in *source*. It is clear that if *source* had length s, *target* had length t, and the first occurrence of *target* in *source* was at position $p \geq 1$, it would require at least $p + t - 1$ comparisons to complete the search, since all the first p characters of *source* would have to be inspected, as well as the remaining $t - 1$ characters of *target*. Similarly, an unsuccessful search would require at least s comparisons. In fact, the number of comparisons might be even larger, because some of the characters in *source* are inspected more than once, when the algorithm backs up after an initial match followed by a failure, as happened in steps 3 and 4 in the preceding example. This is not a frightfully efficient way to perform string searches. It is not difficult to show that if *source* has length n and *target* has length m, it is possible for **Find** to require as many as $O(nm)$ steps. In Section 2.4, we will show how to improve this algorithm.

String Tables

Using static arrays to represent the STRING ADT has the advantages that the operations are easy to write, simple to understand, and quite fast. In fact, it is not hard to show that *Create, Length, Retrieve*, and *Append* run in constant time, regardless of the length of the strings operated on; that all the other operations except *Find* run in time proportional to the length of the strings involved; and that *Find*, as we have written it, requires time proportional to the product of the length of the input strings. The disadvantage of this implementation is that although it is economical in terms of time, it is wasteful in the amount of space used. We must set *MaxLength* as large as the longest string we expect to use, and each array must use at least *MaxLength* space to represent a string, even if most of the strings are very short.

One way to economize on space while retaining most of the speed of the static array implementation of STRING is to use one very long array, the **heap**, to store all strings, along with an auxiliary **string table** to keep track of where in the array the strings are located. This technique is used in some interpreters for BASIC, for example.

In using the string table implementation for STRING, a string is represented by an entry in the string table consisting of (1) a number that denotes the length of the string and (2) a number that refers to the location in the workspace array where the string begins. In Figure 2.1 we show how the strings 'POOH', 'KANGA', and 'TIGGER' would be stored in this implementation.

The definition of the string table implementation of STRING is more complex than that of the static array implementation. We use two global array variables, *stringTable*, and *heap*, as well as two integers: *available*, which contains the next unused location in *heap*, and *numStrings*, which is used to record the number of strings currently in *stringTable*. Each string is denoted by an integer, referring to that element in the string table which contains the length and location of the string. We can then describe the string table implementation as follows:

```
const
   HeapMax = {some very large integer}
   TableMax = {as large as the expected number of strings}
type
   TableEntry = record
                   length, location : integer
                end;
   STRING = integer;        {strings are referenced by a location in the string table}

var                         {global variables for string storage}
   stringTable : array[1 .. TableMax] of TableEntry;
   heap : array[1 .. HeapMax] of char;
   available : integer;
   numStrings : integer;
```

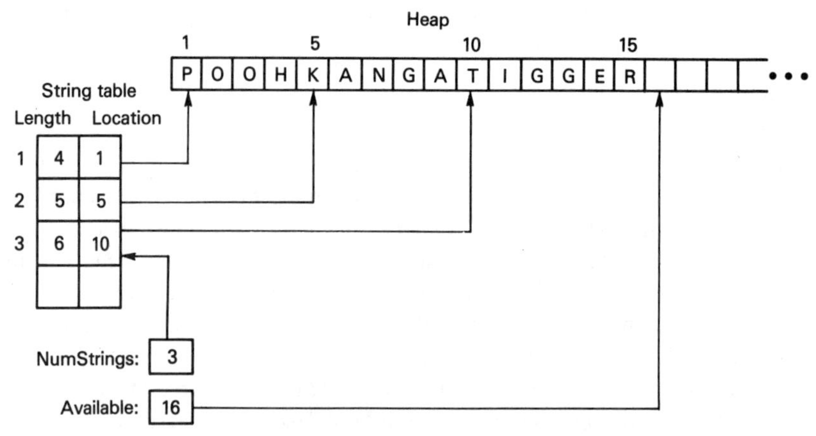

Figure 2.1 String table implementation of STRING.

Next, we present a definition of *Append* for this implementation. In simple terms, since appending a character to a string might make it "overflow" into the next string in the workspace, what *Append* must do is create a copy of the newly appended string in the next vacant location in the workspace, and update *available* to refer to the position immediately following the newly appended string.

```
procedure Append(var s : STRING ; c : char);
{Uses global variables stringTable, heap, and available }
   var
      i, oldLength, oldLocation : integer;
begin
   if (s < 1) or (s > available) then
      writeln('invalid string reference in Append');
   else begin
      oldLength := stringTable[s].length;
      oldLocation := stringTable[s].location;

      for i := 0 to oldLength - 1 do                    {copy s in available space}
         heap[available+i] := heap[oldLocation+i];
      heap[available+oldLength] := c;                   {append c to the copy}

      stringTable[s].location := available;             {update string table for s }
      stringTable[s].length := oldLength + 1;
      available := available + oldLength + 1
   end
end;
```

Suppose, for instance, that we began with the situation of the snapshot of Figure 2.1, with string s referring to 'POOH' and character c equal to '!'. Then, after completion of *Append(s, c)*, we would have the situation of Figure 2.2.

Notice that this implementation of *Append* takes $O(n)$ time for strings of length n, whereas the static array implementation ran in constant time. This is clearly due to the fact that in the string table implementation we had to make a complete copy of the appended string at the first available location in the heap. This wholesale movement of

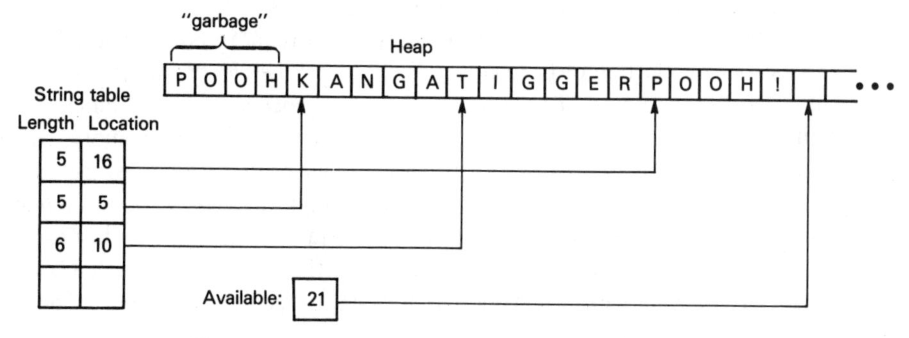

Figure 2.2 Result of applying *Append* (1, '!') to Figure 2.1.

data is a feature common to many operations in this implementation and illustrates a common tradeoff: We gain the benefit of being able to use strings of arbitrary length, but at the price of making some operations more time-consuming.

Although we do not intend to treat this implementation in the same detail as we did the static array implementation, it is worth noting that the string table implementation is more subtle than it might appear at first glance. Notice in Figure 2.2 that the characters 'POOH' in positions 1 through 4 in the heap are no longer referred to by any entry in the string table. They have become "garbage" in the sense that they are taking up space that could be put to use for storage of other strings. In programs that do a lot of modifying of strings, there could come a time when the heap was completely used up, even though there might only be two or three strings in active use. In such a case, nearly the entire heap would be filled with garbage. In later chapters we will explore some "garbage collection" techniques that can be called on to make this wasted space available for use.

As we will see in the next section as well, there is yet another potential problem with this implementation. Consider, for instance, the operation *Copy*. It appears that there is a particularly simple and efficient way to copy a string in this implementation: We need only make the *destination* string have the same entry in the string table as the *source* string.

```
procedure Copy(destination, source : STRING);
{ String Table Implementation of Copy (dangerous version)}
begin
   if (destination < 0) or (destination > vacant)
                              or (source < 0) or (source > vacant) then
      writeln('illegal string reference in Copy')
   else
      stringTable[destination] := stringTable[source]
end;
```

Using Figure 2.1 as an example, if *source* was the third string in the string table, 'TIGGER', and *destination* was the second string, 'KANGA', then *Copy(destination, source)* would have the result indicated in Figure 2.3.

"Cute," you might say, "all we have to do is make both string table entries refer to the same collection of heap cells." Well, it may be clever, and it is certainly fast, but it's bad programming. The problem that this procedure has introduced is known as **aliasing**; that is, the two variables refer to the same location in memory, which is a problem because if we later made a change in either of the two strings (for instance, if we later made a call *Delete(source))*, the change might then be made to *both* strings, even though it might not look that way in the program. This is not an insurmountable problem, however, as long as we write the rest of the operations in such a way as to eliminate any potential side effects due to aliasing. In fact, this version of *Copy* is precisely

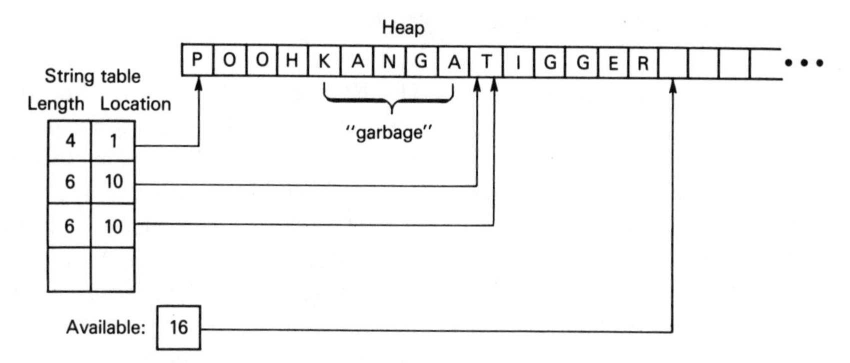

Figure 2.3 String copy snapshot.

how the LET statement is implemented in some BASIC interpreters. For our definition of STRING, however, the potential difficulties are troublesome enough that we will decide simply to make a copy of *source* at the first available location, and have the string table entry for *destination* refer to that location, just as we did with *Append*, in a way that is more nearly like the implementation of the BASIC statement LSET.

```
procedure Copy(var destination : STRING ; source : STRING);
        {Uses global variables stringTable, heap, and available }
    var
        i, sourceLength, sourceLocation : integer;
begin
    if (destination < 1) or (destination > available)
                            or (source < 1) or (source > available) then
        writeln('invalid string reference in Copy');
    else begin
        sourceLength := stringTable[source].length;
        sourceLocation := stringTable[source].location;

        for i := 0 to sourceLength - 1 do        {copy source in available space}
            heap[available + i] := heap[sourceLocation + i];

        stringTable[destination].location := available; {update string table for destination}
        stringTable[destination].length := sourceLength;
        available := available + sourceLength
    end
end;
```

We will now turn our attention to an implementation of STRING that has the advantage of allowing strings of arbitrary length without the complications inherent in the string table implementation.

2.3 POINTER IMPLEMENTATION OF STRING

The string table implementation of STRING freed us from the need to store each string in a fixed amount of memory, regardless of the length of the string. As we mentioned, though, we achieved this flexibility at the cost of an implementation that was both complex and, for some of the operations, time-consuming. The problems with the string table implementation can be traced to the fact that the character heap was defined as an array. An array is typically stored in consecutive locations in memory, so that if we used *Append* to increase the length of a string, a copy of that string had to be made in the heap to avoid running the newly appended string into the next string in memory.

Since pointers allow us to create logically linked structures that do not need to be in contiguous memory locations, it seems worthwhile to explore yet another implementation of the abstract data type STRING. In essence, we will represent a string by a linked collection of *cells*, each containing a character (or group of characters, although we will not discuss this refinement) and a pointer to the following cell. The implementation will be defined by the following declarations:

```
type
   CellPtr = ^Cell;
   Cell = record
             ch : char;
             next : CellPtr
          end;
   STRING = record                      {the header record }
               length : integer;
               tail, head : CellPtr     {pointers to last and first cell in linked list}
            end;
```

A typical string, 'BAZ', in this implementation would then have the form shown in Figure 2.4. You should provide pictures similar to Figure 2.4 to show that, unlike the case in both array implementations, the possible string representatives in this implementation can occur in three logically distinct forms, depending on whether the length of the string is zero, one, or greater than one. This means that when writing routines for this implementation, we must make sure that we have considered all three possibilities.

Most of the primitive operations for this implementation are also easy to define; we list them below.

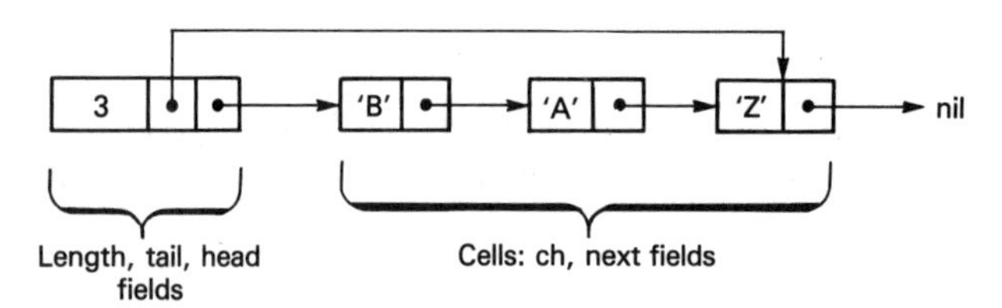

Figure 2.4 Pointer implementation of the string 'BAZ'.

1.

```
procedure Create(var s : STRING);
{O(1) time}
begin
   s.length := 0;
   s.head := nil;
   s.tail := nil
end;
```

2.

```
function Length(s : STRING) : integer;        {O(1)}
begin
   Length := s.length
end;
```

3.

```
function Retrieve(s : STRING ; i : integer) : char;   {O(n), for strings of length n}
   var
      count : integer;
      p : CellPtr;
begin
   if (i < 0) or (i > s.length) then begin
      writeln('illegal index in Retrieve');
      Retreive := some dummy character
   end else begin
      p := s.head;
      for count := 1 to i-1 do      {step through string until at i - th cell}
         p := p^.next;
      Retrieve :=p^.ch
   end
end;
```

4.

```
procedure Append(var s : STRING ; c : char);     {O(1)}
begin
   if s.length = 0 then begin          {need to set both head and tail pointers}
      New(s.head);
      s.head^.ch := c;
      s.head^.next := nil;
      s.tail := s.head
   end else begin                      {otherwise only need to change tail}
      New(s.tail^.next);               {build a new cell at the tail of s}
      s.tail^.next^.ch := c;           {fill new cell}
      s.tail^.next^.next := nil;
      s.tail := s.tail^.next           {and move tail pointer}
   end;
   s.length := s.length + 1            {in either case, update length field}
end;
```

5.
```
procedure Delete(var s : STRING);   {O(1)}
    var p : CellPtr;
begin
    if s.length = 0 then
        writeln('attempted to Delete from empty string')
    else if s.length = 1 then begin    {make s the empty string}
        s.length := 0;
        Dispose(s.head);
        s.head := nil;
        s.tail := nil
    end else begin                     {remove first cell from s}
        s.length := s.length - 1;
        p := s.head;                   {save first cell location}
        s.head := s.head^.next;        {point around first cell}
        Dispose(p)                     {and return first cell to free memory}
    end
end;
```

There are several important points to be seen by comparing these definitions with those in the static array implementation. First, *Retrieve* runs in time $O(n)$, in the worst case, on strings of length n, whereas it ran in constant time in the static array implementation. This illustrates one of the most significant features we give up by choosing pointers rather than arrays: Arrays are **random access** structures, which is to say that it takes the same amount of time to access any element, whereas the linked collection of cells is a **sequential access** structure, since gaining access to the nth element requires access to each of the first, second, third, . . . , $(n - 1)$th elements. In other words, in an array the first and hundredth elements take the same amount of time to retrieve, whereas in a linked list the hundredth element takes much longer to retrieve than the first.

The fact that the pointer representation of strings is a sequential access structure dictated our decision to include pointers to both the head and the tail of a string. At first glance, it seems that the tail pointer is unnecessary, since we could always find the end of a string by repeatedly pointing through the list of cells until we came to a cell with a *next* field equal to the **nil** pointer. Although that is indeed the case (and some authors do define the pointer implementation without a *tail* pointer), not having a pointer to the end of a string would make it impossible to define *Append* so that it would run in $O(1)$ time. In effect, using an auxiliary pointer like *tail* remedies part of the problem of sequential access by giving us immediate access to a particular location in the linked list of cells, a location we need for some of our operations.

Finally, you might recall that when we defined the STRING primitives in the static array implementation, we remarked that to *Delete* an element from the head of a string of length n took time $O(n)$, but that it would only take $O(1)$ time if we had changed the definition to delete from the tail. The situation is exactly opposite in the pointer implementation: Deletion from the head of a linked collection of cells requires $O(1)$ time, whereas deleting from the tail takes $O(n)$ time. The reason is not that we couldn't get rid of the tail cell quickly; we could do that simply enough by the statement *Dispose(S.tail)*. The problem, then, would be that we would have lost any direct reference to the new tail of the list, so would have to point our way all the way through the list to find the new last element. We could have chosen either definition, but your author, looking ahead, decided that since the pointer primitives already had one $O(n)$ operation, *Retrieve*, it would be fairer to define *Delete* so that the static array implementation would be equally handicapped. Keep in mind, however, that the operations on STRING (or any ADT, for that matter) are not scripture—they are guidelines reflecting someone's view of what will likely be required for an ADT. If you have to implement a particular ADT and wish to modify it to suit your implementation, the choice is yours.

The use of pointers takes a bit of getting used to, so we will cover in detail the implementation of two of the STRING operations. First, consider the pointer version of *Copy*. We could implement this operation in a way similar to our first try with string tables, as follows:

```
procedure Copy(var destination : STRING ; source : STRING);
{ Simple, but bad string copy routine}
begin
   destination := source      {copy the header record}
end;
```

We would then have the same aliasing problems noted earlier. The solution in this case, as we will indicate, is the same as our earlier solution: We make a new string by copying each cell of *source*. To clarify the actions of this algorithm, we have provided two snapshots of the relevant contents of memory as the strings are being copied. Figure 2.5 shows the contents of memory at the time the statement labeled (1) is first encountered, and Figure 2.6 shows the situation after one iteration of the **while** loop. The labels in Figure 2.6 refer to the changes that were made by the labeled statements (2) through (5).

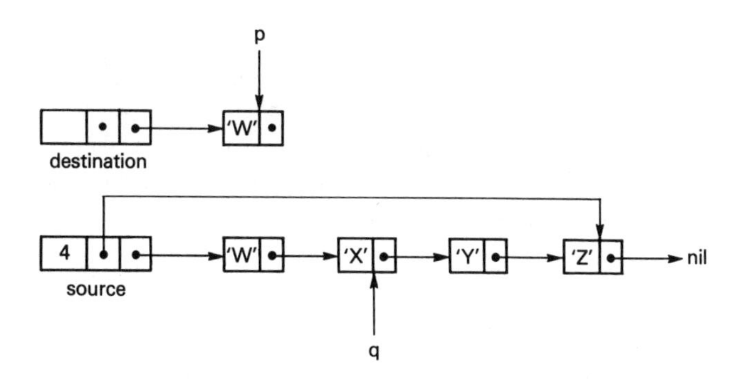

Figure 2.5 Snapshot prior to executing statement {1} in *Copy*.

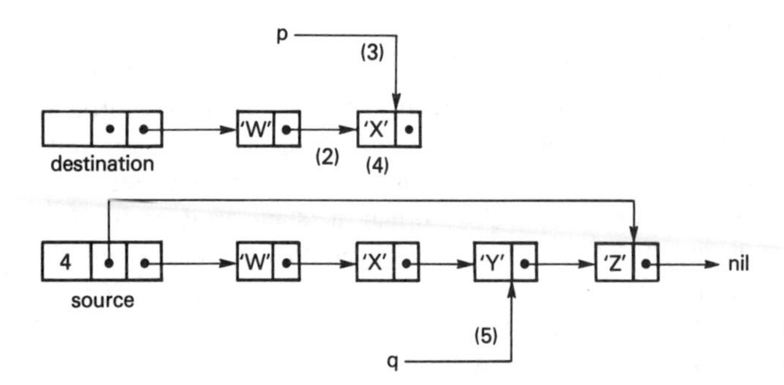

Figure 2.6 Snapshot after one iteration of **for** loop in *Copy*.

```
procedure Copy(var destination : STRING ; source : STRING);
   var
      p, q : CellPtr;
begin
   if source.length = 0 then                  { source empty, so clear destination }
      Create(destination)
   else begin
      new(destination.head);                  {make new first cell}
      p := destination.head;                  {p moves through destination cells}
      q := source.head;                       {q moves through source cells}
      p^.ch := q^.ch;                         {fill first cell in source list}
      q := q^.next;                           {q leads p by one cell}

{1}   while q ≠ nil do begin                  {copy rest of cells one by one}
{2}      new(p^.next);                        {build new source cell and fill it}
{3}      p := p^.next;
{4}      p^.ch := q^.ch;
{5}      q := q^.next
      end;
      destination^.tail := p;                 {set destination tail marker,}
      p^.next := nil;                         {set sentinel at end of list}
      destination.length := source.length;        {and modify length field}
   end
end;
```

The clever idea of just moving pointers, which led to aliasing in our first definition of *Copy*, can be used to our advantage in defining *Concat* if we begin by making a copy of the string *last* and then link the copy to *first* by moving one pointer. We do not need to copy *first*; all we have to do is make a duplicate of *last* and link the two together.

```
procedure Concat(var first : STRING ; last : STRING);
   var
      temp : STRING;                    {temporary storage for copy of last}
begin
   if first.length = 0 then
      Copy(first, last)
   else if last.length - 0 then begin
      Copy(temp, last);
      first.tail^.next := temp.head;      {link end of first to beginning of temp}
      first.tail := temp.tail
   end
end;
```

In Figures 2.7 and 2.8, we provide snapshots of the contents of memory during the execution of this implementation of *Concat*.

We have seen three implementations of the abstract data type STRING: static arrays, string tables, and pointers. A natural question is: Which one is better? Well, of course we can't begin to answer this question until we clarify what we mean by *better*. If we mean "Which implementation should we always use to represent STRING?" then there is no possible answer at all. There is no "best" implementation; as with almost all ADTs, the choice of implementation is dictated in large part by the data we expect to be dealing with, along with our estimation of the amount of programming work involved

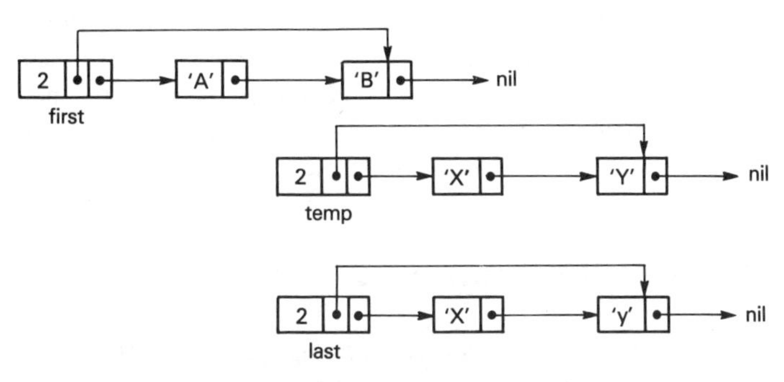

Figure 2.7 Contents of memory prior to concatenation.

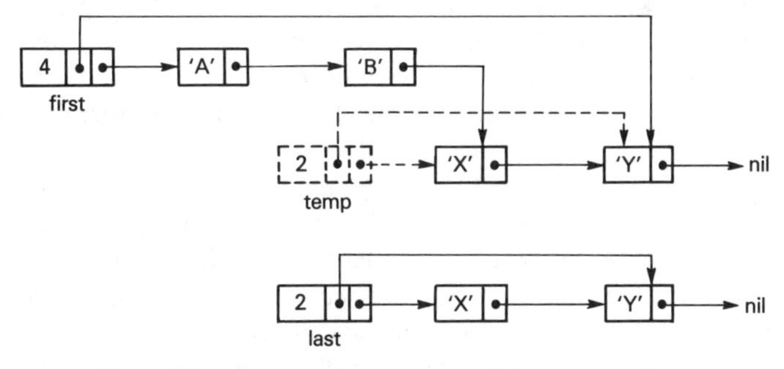

Figure 2.8 Contents of memory after linking *temp* to *first*.

in writing the implementations. There are, however, a few guidelines to aid us in our choice of implementation. We will restrict our attention here to a comparison of static arrays and pointers, since no matter what advantages are gained by using string tables, we are not prepared here to deal with a detailed description of the problems inherent in garbage collection. The following points summarize the tradeoffs between static arrays and pointers.

1. It is easier to write routines using static arrays than it is to use pointers. Not only are most programmers more comfortable with arrays; but arrays are conceptually simpler than pointers. To take a common example, with pointers one must take care to avoid reassigning a pointer variable incorrectly and thereby creating "orphan" cells with no pointers to them.
2. Some operations, like *Delete*, take longer with arrays; others, like *Retrieve*, take longer when implemented with pointers. Thus, the choice of implementation might be dictated by our guess about how frequently a potentially time-consuming operation might be called during the course of a problem.
3. In many languages, the size of an array representing a string must be fixed at the time of writing. If we had little advance knowledge of the length of strings involved in a problem, either we would have to set the maximum length of all strings to be very large (leading to potentially wasteful use of memory), or we would be forced to use pointers.
4. Finally, related to point (3) above, each cell in the pointer representation requires space for a character as well as space for a pointer, whereas with arrays each element of a string requires just one character of memory. In some instances, arrays use less memory than pointers; in other instances it is just the reverse. We explore this memory use in more detail in the exercises.

2.4 APPLICATION: PATTERN MATCHING

The **string search** problem is a common application using strings. In this problem we are given a source string and a target string and wish to find the position of the first (that is, leftmost) occurrence of the target string as a substring of the source string. Such an application would frequently be part of a package for a text editor, for example. Imagine using a word processor to produce a document (a task near and dear to the heart of this author), and discovering that you had consistently spelled the word *precedes* as *preceeds*. Rather than rereading the entire document to find each instance of the misspelled word, it would be very useful to be able to search for each instance of *preceeds* in the source string (i.e., the entire document) and change each such string found to the correct spelling, thereby letting the editor do the work of searching for you.

The STRING operation *Find(source, target)* is obviously what we have in mind to solve the string search problem. We have already written one version of *Find*, to search for the leftmost occurrence of *target* in the string *source*. The "obvious" algorithm we presented examined the characters in *source* one by one, moving from left to right, until a match was found for the first character in *target*. Once a match was found for the first character of *target*, the remaining characters of *target* were tested until either all were matched or a mismatch was discovered. If a mismatch was found, the algorithm "backed up," advancing *target* by one position, and continued the search.

A much faster algorithm for string searching was published in 1977 by Robert S. Boyer and J. Strother Moore. Their algorithm is decidedly nonobvious in that it examines the characters of *target* from right to left, while still moving from left to right in *source*. The important difference between the obvious algorithm and the Boyer-Moore algorithm is that the Boyer-Moore algorithm preprocesses *target* to make two auxiliary tables, which are then used to make large jumps through *source*, rather than inspecting each character in turn. The Boyer-Moore algorithm not only runs in time $O(s + t)$, but also executes *fewer* than $s + t$ statements when t, the length of *target*, is large enough. In other words, quite unlike the obvious algorithm, the Boyer-Moore algorithm is more efficient the longer *target* is.

Before we explain the algorithm in detail and discuss the two tables made in the preprocessing stage, let us consider an example, due to Boyer and Moore, in which *source* is the string 'WHICH_FINALLY_HALTS. _ _ AT_THAT_POINT', and *target* is 'AT_THAT'.

1. We begin as in the obvious algorithm, with *target* aligned to the left of *source*, but we inspect characters from right to left in *target*.

   AT_THA**T**
   WHICH_**F**INALLY_HALTS.__AT_THAT_POINT

2. The character 'F' does not occur at all in *target*, so we can, in effect, shift *target* completely beyond the 'F' without looking at any of the intervening characters. (As we did in the example for the obvious version of *Find*, we remark that we are not actually moving *target*: We are really only shifting our *reference* to the characters in the two strings.)

   AT_THA**T**
   WHICH_FINALLY_HALTS.__AT_THAT_POINT

3. Now we don't have a match, but the character '_' does occur in *target*, so we can shift *target* four places to the right, to line up the rightmost instance of '_' in *target* with the '_' in *source*. We then begin comparisons anew at the right end of *target*.

   AT_THA**T**
   WHICH_FINALLY_HAL**T**S.__AT_THAT_POINT

4. We have a match, so we "back up" to inspect the previous character.

   AT_TH**A**T
   WHICH_FINALLY_HA**L**TS.__AT_THAT_POINT

5. Again, as in step 2, the character 'L' is known not to be in *target*, so we can shift *target* beyond the position of 'L'.

```
                              AT_THAT
WHICH_FINALLY_HALTS.__AT_THAT_POINT
```

6,7. Since we have a match of the character 'T,' we back up twice until we again come to a failure to match.

```
                              AT_THAT
WHICH_FINALLY_HALTS.__AT_THAT_POINT
```

8. The present character, '_', of *source* fails to match the corresponding 'H' in *target*. We could appeal to the reasoning used in step 3 and slide *target* to the right to align the '_' characters, but we can do even better. If we recognize that we have already seen 'AT' in *source*, and that 'AT' occurs earlier in *target*, then we may slide *target* to align the two instances of 'AT'. In such cases we always may choose the larger of the two distances, arguing that if we aligned the '_' characters, there could not then be a possible match for the characters 'AT', which we have already seen.

```
                                  AT_THAT
WHICH_FINALLY_HALTS.__AT_THAT_POINT
```

9–14. Having found a match, we again back up, and this time we inspect all the characters of *target* and find the required location for *target* in *source*.

This algorithm, which we will define in detail shortly, required only 14 comparisons, whereas we could show that the obvious algorithm would have required 31 comparisons. In steps 1, 2, 3, and 5, we relied on knowledge of the locations of the rightmost instances of the characters of *target*. We build in this knowledge as part of our preprocessing of *target*. Prior to starting the string search, we construct a table, *delta1*, which is defined for every character in the underlying character set, as follows:

$$delta1[ch] = \begin{cases} \text{distance from the right end of } target \text{ of the} \\ \text{rightmost occurance of } ch \text{ in } target\text{, if any} \\ \\ Length(target)\text{, if } ch \text{ is not in } target \end{cases}$$

For example, if *target* = 'AT_THAT', then *delta1*['T'] = 0, *delta1*['A'] = 1, *delta1*['H']J= 2, *delta1*['_'] = 4, and *delta1*[*ch*] = 7, for all other characters. In simple terms, if we fail to match *ch* at position *p* in *source*, then we can move to position *p* + *delta1*[*ch*] in *source*, align the right end of *target* to that position, and continue the search. What we have done is to assure that the character *ch* in both *source* and *target* are aligned. Notice that this does *not* say that we will slide *target* to the right by *delta1*[*ch*]; in step 5 of the preceding example, we failed to find a match for 'L' in position 17, found that *delta1*['L'] = 7 (since 'L' was not in *target*), and aligned the right end of *target* to position 7 + 17 = 24 in *source*, a move that slid *target* only six places, since the current position was one place to the left of the end of *target*.

The other part of the preprocessing involves the construction of a table *delta2*, defined for each position in *target*, which defines the amount that the current position in *source* can be moved, based on the characters so far seen in *target*. This table reflects, for instance, the choice we made in step 8 in the example. Let t = *Length(target)*, and define *delta2*[t] = 1. For all other values, let p be a position in *target*, with $1 \le p \le t$, and define *delta2*[p] = *length* + *offset*, where *length* is the length of the suffix of *target* that begins in position p + 1 (so length is just $t - p$), and *offset* is the least amount that that suffix must be moved to the left to match another occurrence in *target*, without matching the character in position p.

Such a complicated definition begs for examples, so consider the following:

1. Let *target* = 'AT_THAT' and p = 6. The suffix starting in position 6 + 1 is the string 'T', of length 1. The least distance we need to move to the left to find a match for 'T' is 3, and this is allowed since the character preceding the suffix, 'A', does not match the character preceding the 'T' in position 4. Graphically, we could write:

position:	1	2	3	4	5	6	7
target:	A	T	_	T	H	A	[T]
match:		[T]					

so *delta2* [6] = *length* + *offset* = $1 + (7 - 4) = 4$.

2. Again, let *target* = 'AT_THAT', but this time let p = 4. We are attempting to match the suffix 'HAT', and, as before, we have

position:	0	1	2	3	4	5	6	7
target:		A	T	_	T	[H	A	T]
match:	[H	A	T]					

In this case, we imagine *target* to be padded on the left with dummy characters that match everything in the suffix but do not match the character before the suffix. We have *delta2*[4] = *length* + *offset* = $3 + (5 - 0) = 8$.

3. Finally, let *target* = 'BAHAMA_MAMMA' and p = 11. The rightmost occurrence of the suffix 'A' is in position 9, but we cannot use that one because the 'M' in position 8 matches the character immediately before the suffix. In fact, we must pass by the 'A' in position 9, as well as the one in position 6, before we come to a match for the suffix that is not preceded by an 'M'.

position:	1	2	3	4	5	6	7	8	9	10	11	12
target:	B	A	H	A	M	A	_	M	A	M	M	[A]
match:				[A]								

So, in this case, *delta2* [11] = $1 + (12 - 4) = 9$.

4. By now you should be able to verify the following table:

p:	1	2	3	4	5	6	7	8	9	10	11	12
target[*p*]:	B	A	H	A	M	A	_	M	A	M	M	A
delta2[*p*]:	23	22	21	20	19	18	17	16	15	5	9	1

If we return to Example 2 above, we can see exactly what happens when we use *delta2* to guide our choice of how much to slide *target*. In Example 2, we looked for a "rightmost plausible reoccurrence" of the suffix 'HAT' in the target string. We saw that an offset of 5 to the left allowed us to match the suffix with an earlier occurrence in *target*. What this means is that if we had seen 'HAT' in *source*, but had failed to match the 'T' preceding the suffix, then it would be possible to slide *target* to the right to align the rightmost plausible reoccurrence of 'HAT' (or at least part of it) with the instance of 'HAT' in *source*. In other words, the construction used to generate *delta2* is mirrored in the reverse direction when we come to a situation where we use the *delta2* table. For instance, if we had come to the following situation prior to looking up the value *delta2* [4]:

```
target:   A T _ T H A T
source:   ? ? ? C [H A T] ? ? ? ? ? ? ?
```

we would then have the following snapshot after having moved the current position, that is, the position where the unmatched 'C' was in *source*, to the right by *delta2*[4] = 8 places.

```
target:          A T   _ T H A T
source:   C [H A T] ? ?  ?  ? ? ? ?
```

We are now in a position to describe the Boyer-Moore algorithm. We will denote the position of the characters presently being inspected in *source* and *target* by *i* and *j*, respectively.

```
function Boyer_Moore_Find(source, target : STRING) : integer;
{Improved string search algorithm : returns starting position of leftmost}
{occurrence of target in source , and returns zero if no match found.}
   var i, j : integer;
begin
   Preprocess target to produce tables delta1 and delta2 ;
   i := Length(target);
   while (no complete match found yet) and (i <= Length(source) do begin
      j := Length(target);
      while (any characters left in target ) and (source[i] = target[j]) do begin
         i := i - 1;
         j := j - 1;                          {back up through source and target }
      end;
      if no more characters in target then
         Find := i + 1                        {found complete match, exit outer loop}
      else
         i := i + max(delta1[source[i]], delta2[j])   {here is where big jumps take place}
   end;
   if no complete match then
      Find := 0
end;
```

Although we leave the details of coding this algorithm as an exercise, some points bear noting. First, it would be much more efficient to use either of the array packages to implement this algorithm. Can you see why? A bit of thought should convince you that backing up through the strings is much more time-consuming in the pointer implementation, since in the pointer implementation we chose to write, the only possible movement is to the right. This is not an insurmountable impediment; we could have defined each cell in the linked list with two pointers, one to the next cell and one to the prior cell, making movement equally easy in either direction. Indeed, we will demonstrate just such an implementation in the next chapter.

Another point concerns an objection a careful reader might have made upon thinking this algorithm through. "Hey," you might say, "I'm willing to be convinced by the example that this is a fast algorithm, *once you've done the preprocessing* to make the two tables. That's not worth much, though, if the preprocessing takes, say, $O(t^2)$, for *target* strings of length t." That's a good objection, but you'll have to take our word for the fact that there is a way to produce both *delta1* (which is easy to figure out) and *delta2* (which is not) in time $O(t)$. If you would like to see how to do the preprocessing efficiently, we refer you to the article mentioned at the end of this chapter.

While we are on the subject of preprocessing, we observe that it would probably not be most efficient to include the preprocessing routine within the definition of *Find*. To do so would force us to preprocess *target* each time we made a call to *Find*, which would be inefficient in the common case where repeated *Find*s were called on the same target string, as in the misspelling example mentioned at the start of this section. In fact, if we were writing *Find* for a word processor, it might be preferable to rewrite the definition to be *Find(p, source, target)*, which would return the position of the first instance of *target* in *source* that occurred at or after position p in *source*, and returned zero if no match was found.

Finally, we have said that the Boyer-Moore algorithm is more efficient than the obvious algorithm, but haven't included details about how much more efficient it is. It is clear that the execution time for both algorithms is driven primarily by the number of comparisons of characters that need to be made. The obvious algorithm inspects each character in *source* until *target* is found, and sometimes has to back up if partial matches are discovered along the way. We mentioned that in the exercises you are asked to show that there are situations in which as many as $O(st)$ comparisons are needed, where s is the length of *source* and t is the length of *target*. Furthermore, although the calculations are too cumbersome to deal with here, it is possible to show that for a successful search by the obvious algorithm, the number of *source* characters inspected (not counting the ones where *target* is found) divided by the number of characters passed should have an average value of approximately $1 / (1 - r)$, where r is 1 divided by the size of the underlying character set. For example, for a character set consisting just of the letters 'A' through 'Z', we have $r = 1 / 26 = 0.03846$ (approximately), and $1 / (1 - r)$ for this value is 1.04. This means that, in dealing with randomly chosen strings, the obvious algorithm must inspect each character in turn and must back up about 4 percent of the time.

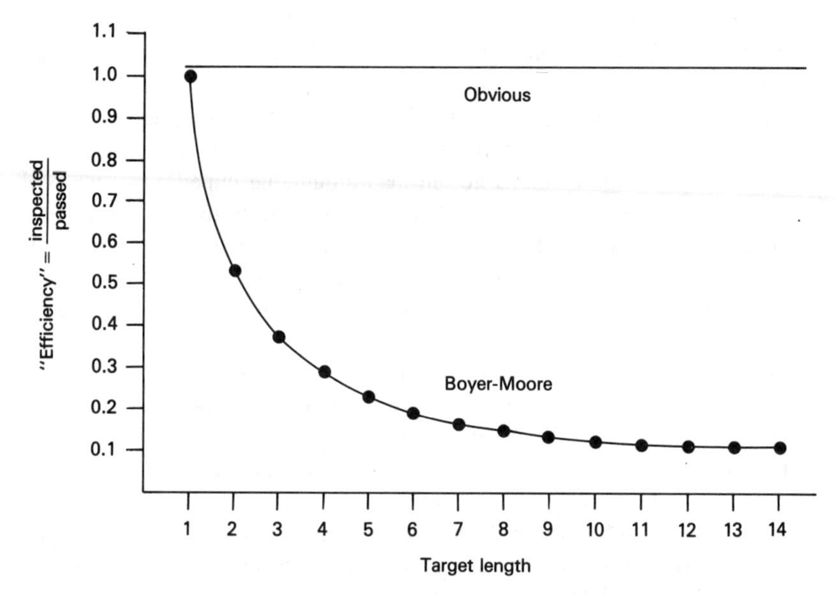

Figure 2.9 Average efficiency of string search algorithms.

We can perform similar calculations on the average efficiency of the Boyer-Moore algorithm, but the calculations in that case are really gruesome. However, it is possible to get some empirical results about the average efficiency without too much work. We can write the Boyer-Moore algorithm, run it on a number of randomly chosen sample strings, for each sample compute the number of comparisons before a complete match divided by the number of characters passed, and average the results. If we do this for enough sample cases, we see that the ratio averages very close to $1 / t$, where t is the length of *target*, This is a considerable improvement over the obvious algorithm, and is illustrated in Figure 2.9.

In essence, the "efficiency" of $1 / t$ in the Boyer-Moore algorithm stems from the fact that most of the time it is possible to skip ahead in source by an amount equal to the length of the entire *target* string. This means that no matter how many instructions it takes to do each comparison and move, eventually, for long enough *target* strings, less than one instruction is performed for each character passed in *source*, making the Boyer-Moore algorithm run in *less than* linear time, in a sense.

2.5 SUMMARY

The abstract data type STRING like all other ADTs, has a multilevel definition.

1. The underlying set of atoms, ATOM, is usually taken to be all possible characters in a given implementation, while the set, POSITION, of possible positions can be considered to be the set of positive integers 1, 2, 3, ...

2. The elements of STRING are the individual character strings themselves, which we have written $c_1c_2 \ldots c_n$. These may also be regarded as triples (P, R, v), where we may regard each set P to be $\{1, 2, \ldots, n\}$ (that is, the possible indices). For each element, the structural relation R is a linear order, in particular the order " $\leq$," and the evaluation function v: POSITION $\rightarrow$ ATOM is defined by $v(i) = c_i$.
3. Although it is not the case for every ADT, the abstract data type STRING carries with it another linear order relation, this one on the underlying set, ATOM. This order, which reflects the alphabetic order on the characters in ATOM, varies from implementation to implementation. This order can be combined with the structural order on each string to produce a linear order (the lexicographic order) on the collection of all strings.
4. Finally, the ADT STRING contains a collection of *structure-preserving operations* defined on the elements, S, of STRING. These operations are structure-preserving in the sense that anything that is returned by an operation will reflect the structure of the input, so will be either a string or a **simple type** like a character, an integer, or a boolean value. For example, if we apply *Delete* to the string 'ALIVE', the result will be the string 'LIVE', with structural order reflecting that of the input.

As with any ADT, we have a certain amount of freedom of choice in selecting the operations included in STRING. We chose the operations on the basis of what we would like to be able to do to the elements in STRING, and what seems "natural" to do. For flexibility and implementation independence, we chose a small set of operations (in this case, *Create, Length, Retrieve, Append*, and *Delete*) as "primitive," in the sense that the other operations may be written in terms of these primitives.

There are several possible implementations for STRING, as there are for any ADT. Static arrays are conceptually simple, allow random access within strings, and are fast for most operations; but they are limited by imposing a fixed maximum length for all strings. String tables with a heap impose no maximum length on strings, and retain the speed of random access, but are conceptually more complicated than static arrays, and require potentially difficult and time-consuming garbage collection algorithms to work efficiently. Lists of cells connected by pointers also impose no maximum length constraints, and free the programmer from the need to write explicit garbage collection routines. The pointer implementation is more difficult to master than that of arrays, requires more care in writing, and is not available as a built-in feature of some languages (such as BASIC, FORTRAN, and ALGOL).

String searching is a common application of the STRING ADT. Of the many algorithms that exist for this problem, we discussed two in the text. The obvious algorithm inspects, on the average, slightly more than one character for each character passed, and for some strings may require much more than linear time. The Boyer-Moore algorithm requires an extra routine to preprocess the target string, but then performs much better than the obvious algorithm, being linear time in both the average and the worst cases. The original paper by Boyer and Moore is

"A Fast String Search Algorithm." *Communications of the ACM* 20, No. 10 (October 1977), 762–772.

2.6 EXERCISES

1. What preconditions are necessary in the definition of the string operation *Substring*?

2. Write definitions of the following operations in terms of the five string primitives:
 (a) *Substring*
 (b) *Concat*
 (c) *Equal*
 (d) *Less*

3. Suppose that *Append* had been defined to append a character to the head of a string, instead of the tail. How would this choice have affected the definition of *Insert* given at the end of Section 2.1?

4. It is possible to use the structure of STRING to define an abstract data type that models the integers . . . , −2, −1, 0, 1, 2, 3, ... Define the ADT CHAR_INTS to have the same structure as STRING, but with the underlying set of characters, A, restricted to the set {'+', '−', '0', '1', '2', '3', '4', '5', '6', '7', '8', '9'}. In this ADT, the string of characters '23381' is intended to represent the integer 23381.
 (a) Which of the STRING operations would be suitable for this ADT?
 (b) Would the STRING function *Less* behave as it should for this ADT?
 (c) Under what circumstances would it be useful to define the ADT CHAR_INTS, rather than utilizing the *integer* type predefined in a programming language?

5. Give a formal definition of *Remove*, as was done for the other STRING operations in Section 2.1.

6. Show that a byte of eight binary digits can encode 256 possible different characters.

7. Consider the STRING operation **Reverse(var** s : STRING ; t : STRING) which, given a string *t*, sets *s* equal to the reverse of *t*, so that *Reverse* applied to the string 'ALLIGATOR' would return 'ROTAGILLA'.
 (a) Give a formal definition of *Reverse.*
 (b) Write *Reverse* in terms of primitive operations.
 (c) Write *Reverse* in the static array implementation.

8. Suppose that *source* had length *s* and *inner* had length *i*. Show that the version of *Insert (source, p, inner)* defined in terms of primitives requires $2s + 2i$ steps, while the array version requires $s - p + i$ steps.

9. Give big-O timing estimates for static array implementations of the following operations:
 (a) *Substring*
 (b) *Less*

10. Show that the obvious definition of *Find* could require $O(st)$ steps, where *s* is the length of *source* and *t* is the length of *target*. (*Hint*: Suppose *source* and *target* were of the form 'AA . . . AB'.)

11. Write a string table implementation of
 (a) *Delete*
 (b) *Insert*

12. Discuss some possible solutions to the problem of "garbage" that arises in the string table implementation.

13. Describe by pictures the three logically distinct forms strings may take in the pointer implementation.

14. Assume that pointers require four bytes of memory, integers require two bytes and characters require one byte. Suppose that a collection of n strings was to be stored in memory, and that for this collection the average length of the strings was L, and the maximum string length was M (= *MaxLength* in the static array implementation).

  (a) How many bytes would be required to store a string of length L in each of the static array and pointer implementations?

  (b) Show that if $L > (M - 8) / 5$, the static array implementation will require fewer bytes of storage than the pointer implementation.

  (c) If you knew that all the strings were to be single words chosen from a typical piece of English prose (this chapter, for example), which implementation would you choose to minimize the amount of memory required?

15. Fill in the following table with the indicated big-O timing estimates,. Assume that the string s has length n. Not all of the string table implementations are done in the text. You will have to write those before you can provide timing estimates.

	Static arrays	String table	pointer
Create(s)			
Length(s)			
Retrieve(s, i)			
Append(s, c)			
Delete(s)			

16. Suppose that in the pointer implementation of STRING each cell consisted of a "chunk" of c characters, along with a pointer to the next chunk. For instance, if we had chosen c to be 5, the string 'SUPPOSE_THAT_IN_THE' would be stored as follows:

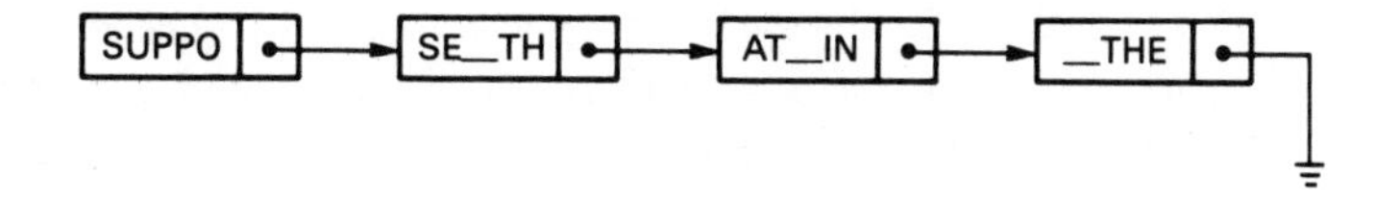

  (a) Repeat the analysis of Exercise 14 for this implementation.

  (b) Discuss some of the problems inherent in this implementation by considering how you would write the implementations of *Delete* and *Insert*.

17. What modifications or additions would you have to make to STRING to write a word processor? So as not to complicate the problem excessively, assume that someone else will handle the problems of screen display and printing for you. Consider such problems as what extra variables or operations you would need, whether it would be better to store the entire document as one long string or as a list of words, how to recognize a word (leading and trailing spaces aren't enough), and how to deal with such things as different type faces or styles (such as boldface).

18. Compute the tables *delta1* and *delta2* for the following *target* strings.

  (a) 'ABCD'

  (b) 'DERIDE'

  (c) 'GOOD_DOGGO'

19. **(a)** Find a string for which *delta2* has the values 7, 6, 5, 3, 1.

  (b) Show that there is no string for which *delta2* has the values 9, 8, 4, 3, 1.

20. For target strings of length n, what are the largest and smallest possible values of $delta2[j]$, for $j = 1, 2, \ldots, n$?

21. Trace the actions of the obvious and the Boyer-Moore algorithms on the following *source* and *target* strings, and count the number of comparisons made by each algorithm.

  (a) *source* = 'ABNORMALCABDRIVERS', *target* = 'ABD'

  (b) *source* = 'AAAAAAAAB', *target* = 'AAAB'

Programming Projects

22. Write and test all five primitive operations for the string table implementation of STRING. You will also have to include procedures **ReadString**(**var** s : STRING), and **WriteString**(s : STRING) to provide input and output.

23. Write preprocessing algorithms that produce the tables *delta1* and *delta2* in the Boyer-Moore algorithm. Find timing estimates for your algorithms.

24. Write programs for both the obvious version and the Boyer-Moore version of *Find*, and include in each implementation statements that count the number of comparisons made. Try enough test cases to demonstrate the relative efficiencies of the two algorithms for *target* strings of varying lengths.

25. Write a line-based word processor. The word processor accepts commands of the form "*code-letter number [optional-number] [optional-string] [optional-string],*" of the following forms:

A *n string*, which adds the string into the document between lines *n* and *n* + *1*, with the understanding that if *n* = 0, a new first line will be added.

D *n m*, which deletes *n* lines from the document, starting at line *m*.

P *n m*, which prints *n* lines of the document, starting with line *m*.

I *n m string*, which inserts *string* into line *n*, starting in position *m*.

R *n string1 string2*, which replaces every instance of *string1* in line n with *string2*.

L *n string*, which prints the line number and the contents of each line at or after line *n*, which contains *string*.

The command format will require a blank between each two numbers, and each string in a command line must be enclosed within single quotes.

PART 2

Linear Structures

3

Lists

I have a little list, sir
Whereon appears your name.
I cross yours off,
I write mine on,
And then repeat the same.

Traditional Flemish folk rhyme

Entries in a telephone book, people waiting in a doctor's office, pieces of food on a shish kebab: All these have in common the property that they may be considered to have a natural linear order, in the sense that there is a "first" element, followed by a "next" element, which is itself followed by a "next" element, and so on until the "last" element. This property of a collection of elements having a linear order arises so frequently that we collect all such objects under the general heading of **lists**.

Lists are natural generalizations of character strings. In fact, there is no difference between the structure of the abstract data type LIST and that of the STRING ADT, except for the underlying sets of atoms. In STRING, the atoms are almost invariably taken to be characters, whereas the atoms in a realization of LIST can be integers, records of several types of information, or even strings. Both ADTs are intended to model situations in which the information is logically arranged in a linear fashion. The principal difference between lists and strings is in the operations defined on them. In dealing with strings, we are frequently concerned with identifying and operating on substrings, so we need operations like *Substring, Remove,* and *Find*, all of which deal with contiguous subsets of a given string. Lists, on the other hand, are generally used to model situations in which insertion, deletion, inspection, and modification of individual atoms in a list are of primary importance, and the operations on LIST are chosen to reflect this preference.

3.1 THE ABSTRACT DATA TYPE LIST

Much of the definition of the LIST ADT is a straightforward generalization of what was done in Chapter 2. The underlying set, ATOM, may be any set at all (including a structured set, such as the set of all strings of characters, if, for instance, we intended to model the list of words in a document). The underlying set, POSITION, we will frequently take to be the set of positive integers, since we are familiar with the linear order " $\leq$ " on that set.

The elements of LIST will, as usual, be triples (P, R, v), where we will generally consider the finite set, P, of positions to be either the empty set or a subset of POSITION of the form $\{1, 2, \ldots, n\}$, for some $n \geq 1$. Each structural relation, R, will be a linear order, and, to hold confusion to a reasonable level, we will often assume each R is the linear order "$\leq$" on the set $P = \{1, 2, \ldots, n\}$. In such cases, the evaluation function, v, being a function from the set P to the set of atoms, will just be a function defined on the integers $1, 2, \ldots, n$. Under these assumptions, it is most natural to write a list element, L, in the form $(a_1, a_2, \ldots, a_n)$, reflecting the fact that the atom a_i is in position i in the list. It is important to realize that in some implementations POSITION will not be the set of positive integers, despite the fact that we can conceptualize the ADT LIST as a sequence of atoms indexed by the numbers $1, 2, \ldots$. This will become apparent when we consider the pointer implementation of LIST.

The operations on LIST reflect the linear structure on the list elements, as well as our emphasis on individual objects within each list. The primitive operations are listed below. In these definitions, assume that a list element, L, is equal to the triple (P, R, v). As we did with strings, we will also denote a list by the more obvious notation, $(a_1, a_2, \ldots, a_n)$.

1. **Create**(**var** L : LIST), as usual, sets L equal to the empty list. In terms of the (P, R, v) notation, we set P equal to the empty set, make R be the (empty) relation on that set, and make v be the function that is not defined for any position.
2. **Empty**(L : LIST) : boolean, returns *true* if and only if L is the empty list—that is, if the subset, P, of positions is empty.
3. **First**(L : LIST) : POSITION, is a function which returns the first position in the list L, assuming the precondition that L is not the empty list. In (P, R, v) terms, $First(L)$ is simply $min_R(P)$, the (unique) first position in P. If we write L as $(a_1, a_2, \ldots, a_n)$, with $n \geq 1$, then $First(L)$ is just 1.
4. **Last**(L : LIST) : POSITION, is a function that returns the last position in the list L, again assuming that L is not the empty list. In (P, R, v) terms, $Last(L)$ is $max_R(P)$, the "highest" position in P. Writing $L = (a_1, a_2, \ldots, a_n)$, with $n \geq 1$, we have $Last(L) = n$.
5. **Next**(p : POSITION ; L : LIST) : POSITION, assumes the preconditions that the position p is in the list L (so p is a member of the set P), and that $p \neq Last(L)$. If these conditions are met, then *Next* returns the position immediately after p in the list L. In other words, if $L = (P, R, v)$, then $Next(p, L) = succ_R(P)$, the immediate successor of p in L.

6. **Prior**(p : POSITION ; L : LIST) : POSITION, is a function that is defined analogously to *Next*, save for the fact that it returns the predecessor to p in L. Strictly speaking, we need not include *Prior* among the primitives, since it can be defined in terms of *First* and *Next*.

7. **Retrieve**(p : POSITION ; L : LIST) : ATOM, returns the atom in position p in the list L. As with *Prior* and *Next*, this function requires the precondition that p is a position in the list L. If we consider $L = (P, R, v)$, then $Retrieve(p, L) = v(p)$.

8. **Update**(a : ATOM ; p : POSITION ; **var** L : LIST), modifies L by replacing the atom in position p by the atom a. If $L = (P, R, v)$ before the call to $Update(a, p, L)$, then the result of the operation would be to set $L = (P, R, v')$, with $v'(q) = v(q)$ for all $q \neq p$, and $v'(p) = a$. As usual, this procedure is defined only when p is a position in L. This operation is simple enough that we include it among the primitives, even though we could (with a lot of extra work) define it in terms of the primitives *InsertAfter* and *Delete*.

9. **Delete**(p : POSITION ; **var** L : LIST), removes the atom in position p, keeping the rest of the structure of L as it was before. In (P, R, v) notation, the result of this procedure is the list (P', R', v'), where the set $P' = P - [p]$, and R' and v', are the results of restricting R and v, respectively, to the set P' (in other words, they act just like R and v, but are no longer defined for the value p). We assume that p is a position in L, otherwise *Delete* is undefined.

10. **InsertAfter**(a : ATOM ; p : POSITION ; **var** L : LIST), changes the list L by inserting the atom a into the list between position p and the position immediately following p. For example, if L was the list denoted by $(a_1, a_2, \ldots, a_n)$, then a call to $InsertAfter(a, p, L)$ would result in $L = (a_1, a_2, \ldots, a_p, a, a_{p+1}, \ldots, a_n)$. As usual, we require that p be a position in L. In order to permit the construction of lists from scratch (by inserting atoms into an empty list), we define this procedure so that if L is empty, a call to *InsertAfter* will set L equal to a list containing the single atom a, regardless of the value of p. The (P, R, v) form of this definition is complicated and is explained in an exercise. The action of *InsertAfter* is diagrammed as follows:

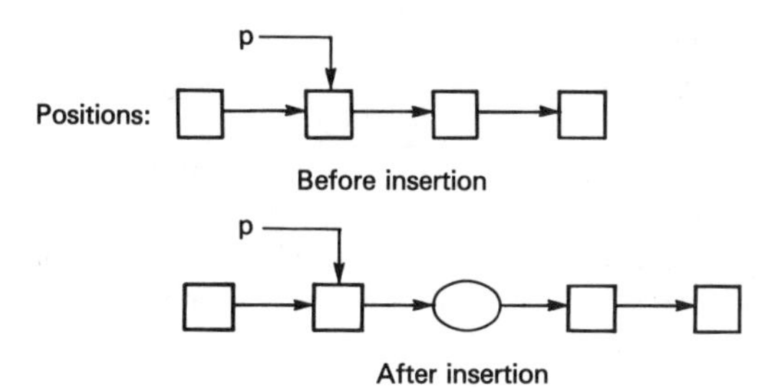

As was the case in the STRING abstract data type, there are several operations that are nonprimitive, in the sense that they can be defined in terms of the primitives. These are as follows:

11. **InsertBefore**(a : ATOM ; p : POSITION ; **var** L : LIST), acts in the same way as *InsertAfter*, but inserts the atom *a* into a new position, after the predecessor of *p*, if any, and in any case before *p* itself.
12. **Length**(L : LIST) : integer, returns the number of elements in the list *L*.
13. **Find**(a : ATOM ; L : LIST) : POSITION, returns the earliest position in *L* where the atom *a* is located. If *a* is not in the list, we could define the function so that it would terminate in an error, but we frequently use *Find* in situations where failure to find an atom in a list is not cause to shut down the program. To deal gracefully with the possibility of such failures, most authors agree to augment the set POSITION by including in it a **pseudoposition**, NULL, which is not allowed to be on any list. Then, if *Find* does not find the atom *a* in *L*, it simply returns NULL. For instance, if POSITION was the set {1, 2, . . . }, we could choose NULL to be the "position" 0.

As usual, when faced with defining any operation on LIST, we have two choices: We can define it in terms of primitives, and then implement only the primitives, or we can define the operation in terms of the implementation we have chosen. We will deal with implementations of LIST shortly, but the definition of *InsertBefore* is too lovely to let it slip past us. In some implementations of LIST, it is easier to find the successor of a position than it is to find the predecessor, in the sense that for lists of length n, *Next* runs in constant time, while *Prior* takes time $O(n)$. In the pointer representation of LIST, for instance, passage through the list is often just one way, so that finding the position before *p* requires that we begin at the start of the list and traverse each position until we come to that position immediately before *p*. At first glance, it would seem that *InsertBefore(a, p, L)* would require that we first find the position *Prior(p, L)*, thus taking the time necessary to traverse the entire list up to the position just before *p*. There is, however, a wonderfully clever and simple algorithm that eliminates the need for *Prior* altogether.

```
procedure InsertBefore(a : ATOM ; p : POSITION ; var L : LIST);
   var x : ATOM;
begin
   if Empty(L) then
      InsertAfter(a, p, L)            {build a list with one atom}
   else begin
      InsertAfter(a, p, L);           {insert atom a after position p}
      x := Retrieve(p, L);            {save the atom in position p}
      Update(a, p, L);                {place atom a in position p}
      Update(x, Next(p, L), L)        {place atom x after position p}
   end
end;
```

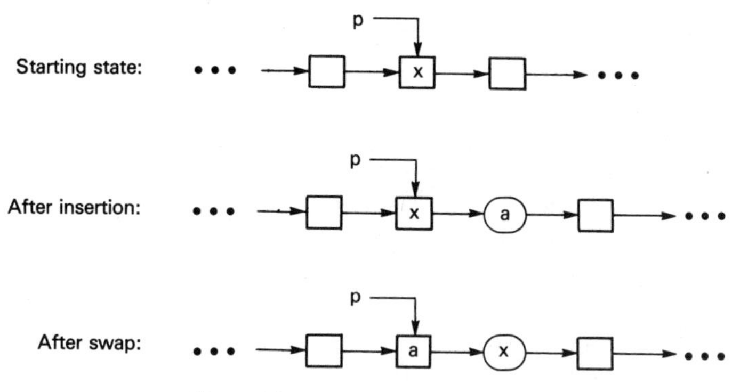

Figure 3.1 Insertion with swapping.

It's marvelous when the light goes on. What we have done in this algorithm is to insert *a after* position *p*, and then swap the atoms in positions *p* and the new position following *p*, leaving a list that looks exactly as if we had inserted *a* in a new location immediately *before p*. Pictorially, we have the steps shown in Figure 3.1. Notice that after the insertion the position *p* refers to the same position it did before the call (i.e., if it originally referred to the *i*th cell in the list, it still does after the insertion), although the "contents" of the cell at position *p* are generally not the same as before the insertion. We could deal with this, of course, by simply moving *p* to the next position in the list. Then *p* would no longer refer to its original location, but would refer to the cell containing the data that were originally in position *p*. We should also be aware that there is a hidden cost involved in this operation: It takes very little time to move pointers, but if the elements of the list are large (large arrays, for instance), the swapping of data could take a comparatively large amount of time.

3.2 IMPLEMENTATIONS OF LIST

Much of the work of implementing LIST has already been done in Chapter 2, since, as we have seen, there is no structural difference between LIST and STRING. In this section, we will review array and pointer implementations of LIST, and introduce the cursor implementation, which is something of a hybrid of arrays and pointers. The operations *Create, Retrieve*, and *Length* for arrays and pointers have been defined previously; you can review Chapter 2 for details.

Arrays

The static array implementation of LIST is the simplest of the three implementations we will discuss. The declarations needed for this implementation should be familiar, since they are simply a generalization of the array implementation of STRING.

```
const
   MAXSIZE = {suitable constant};
type
   POSITION = 0 . . MAXSIZE;                 {including NULL pseudoposition, 0}
   ATOM = {any data structure};
   LIST = record
            length : POSITION;
            data : array[1 . . MAXSIZE] of ATOM
         end;
```

The primitives that were not defined in Chapter 2 are *Empty, First* (and its mirror image *Last), Next* (and *Prior), Update*, and *Delete*. With the exception of *Delete*, they are all trivial in this implementation, as we see below.

1.
```
function Empty(L : LIST) : boolean;   {O(1) time}
begin
   Empty := (L.length = 0)       {returns true if and only if L has length zero}
end;
```

2.
```
function First(L : LIST) : POSITION;   {O(1) }
begin
   if L.length = 0 then
      First := 0                   {return NULL pseudoposition for empty lists}
   else
      First := 1
end;
```

3.
```
function Next(p : POSITION ; L : LIST) : POSITION;     {O(1)}
begin
   if (p ≤ 0) or (p > L.length) then begin
      writeln('Position ', p, ' out of range in Next');
      Next := 0
   end else
      Next := p + 1
end;
```

4.
```
procedure Update(a : ATOM ; p : POSITION ; var L : LIST);   {O(1)}
begin
   if (p ≤ 0) or (p > L.length) then
      writeln('Position ', p, ' out of range in Update')
   else
      L.data[p] := a
end;
```

```
5.    procedure Delete(p : POSITION ; var L : LIST);    {O(n)}
          var i : POSITION;
      begin
          if (p ≤ 0) or (p > L.length) then
              writeln('Position ', p, ' out of range in Delete')
          else begin
              for i := p to L.length - 1 do
                  L.data[i] := L.data[i+1];         {shift atoms left to fill "hole"}
              L.length := L.length - 1              {and update length}
          end
      end;
```

It is not difficult to see that all of these operations, with the exception of *Delete*, take time $O(1)$, and that *Delete*, for lists of length n, can run in time $O(n)$. As a matter of fact, it is easy to show that in the array implementation of LIST, *all* thirteen operations run in constant time, save for *Delete, InsertAfter*, and *InsertBefore*, which run in time $O(n)$.

The array implementation of LIST is so simple, in fact, that it is often easier to write most operations directly in terms of the implementation, rather than in terms of the primitives. For example, consider the procedure **Reverse(var** L : LIST), which returns L in reverse order, changing the list $(a_1, a_2, \ldots, a_{n-1}, a_n)$ to the list $(a_n, a_{n-1}, \ldots, a_2, a_1)$. In the exercises, we ask for the description of the procedure in terms of primitives, but look how simple it is in terms of arrays:

```
procedure Reverse(var L : LIST);
    var   i : POSITION ; holder : ATOM;
begin
    if L.length <> 0 then
        for i := 1 to L.length div 2 do begin
            holder := L.data[i];
            L.data[i] := L.data[L.length - i + 1];     {swap i-th atoms from left and right}
            L.data[L.length - i + 1] := holder
        end
end;
```

The only problems with the array implementation of LIST are, first, that not all of the operations take a constant amount of time to complete, and, more important in some instances, in most languages we are restricted to a fixed maximum length for all lists. These problems can be cured (almost completely) by another implementation, but at the cost of greater complexity and a loss of some of the simplicity of arrays.

Linked Lists

As we did with strings, we may declare a pointer-based implementation of LIST as follows:

```
type
   ATOM = {any data type}
   POSITION = ^Cell;
   Cell = record
             data : ATOM;
             next : POSITION
          end;
   LIST = record
             length : integer;
             tail, head : POSITION
          end;
```

Notice that in this implementation, POSITION is not a set of integers but, rather, a collection of pointers. This often causes difficulties at first, and should be stressed: *Although we may think abstractly of positions in a list as the positive integers, in some implementations POSITION is not a set of integers at all.* Notice also that we refer to a list by its header record, rather than the more customary use of a pointer to the first cell in the list. This uses slightly more space, but the extra memory is negligible for long lists, and the header record provides pointers to the head and tail of the list, as well as keeping track of the length of the list (so that we do not have to traverse the entire list just to find out how many cells it contains). We will use the **nil** pointer as our NULL pseudoposition and will adopt the convention that the last cell in a list will have a *next* field equal to **nil**. If a list is empty, we will assume that both the *head* and *tail* fields of the header record are **nil**.

We must be especially careful in writing pointer-based algorithms because, unlike arrays, linked lists can occur in three logically distinct forms, depending on whether the list is empty, has a single cell, or has more than one cell. In writing routines for linked lists, we must be sure that our routines can correctly handle all three cases. We mentioned this possibility earlier, when discussing strings. The three forms of linked lists are indicated in Figure 3.2.

In discussing the pointer implementation of STRING, we implemented the operations **Create, Length**, and **Retrieve**, so we need only define the rest of the primitive operations here.

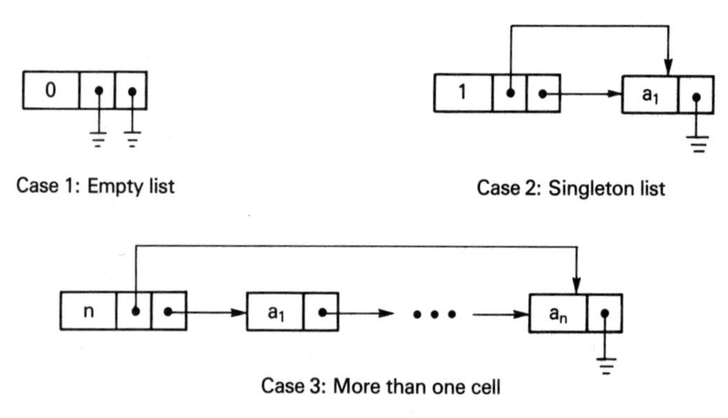

Figure 3.2 The three forms of linked lists.

1.
```
function Empty(L : LIST) : boolean;
begin
   Empty := (L.length = 0)
end;
```

2.
```
function First(L : LIST) : POSITION;
begin
   if L.length = 0 then begin
      writeln('Attempted to find First position of empty list');
      First := nil
   end else
      First := L.head
end;
```

3.
```
function Next(p : POSITION ; L : LIST) : POSITION;
{Assumes the precondition that p is a position in L }
begin
   if p = L.tail then begin
      writeln('Improper position reference in Next');
      Next := nil
   end else
      Next := p^.next
end;
```

4.
```
procedure Update(a : ATOM ; var p : POSITION );
{Assumes the precondition that p is a position in L }
begin
   p^.data := a
end;
```

These operations are sufficiently simple that they need no explanation. The rest, however, are a trifle more complicated.

5.
```
procedure Delete(var p : POSITION ; var L : LIST);
   var q : POSITION ; done : boolean;
begin
   if L.length = 0 then                    {Case 1: empty list}
      writeln('Attempted to Delete from empty list')

   else begin
      if L.length = 1 then                 {Case 2: singleton list}
         if p <> L.head then
            writeln('Non-existent position in Delete')
         else begin
            L.head := nil;
            L.tail := nil
```

```
        end else if p = L.head then begin      {deleting head element}
            L.head := p^.next

        end else begin                         {Case 3: p is in interior of list}
            q := L.head;
            done := false;
            while not done do{find cell prior to p }
                if q = L.tail then begin       {reached end of list without finding p }
                    writeln('Non-existent position in Delete');
                    done := true
                end else if q^.next = p then begin
                    done := true;
                    q^.next := p^.next;        {point around cell at position}
                    if p = L.tail then
                        L.tail := q
                end else
                    q := q^.next               {not yet found, advance q, keep looking}
        end;
        Dispose(p);                            {nonempty list -- get rid of p cell}
        L.length := L.length - 1               {and fix length of list}
    end
end;
```

In this algorithm, we use q to point our way through the list L, until we come to the position immediately before p (if, that is, p is a position in the list). Assuming we have found the predecessor, q, to the cell pointed to by p, we then change the next field of the q^ cell to point to the position following the p^ cell, and return the p^ cell to available (unused) memory, as indicated in Figure 3.3.

One reason this algorithm is complicated is that the linked list implementation does not provide a simple means of finding the position prior to a given position. We need to know the prior position in this algorithm so that we may point around the cell to be deleted. Because of this, we had to begin at the head of the list and point our way along until we came to the position q just before the position p that was to be deleted. We would have to do the same sort of steps in order to implement the operation *Prior*.

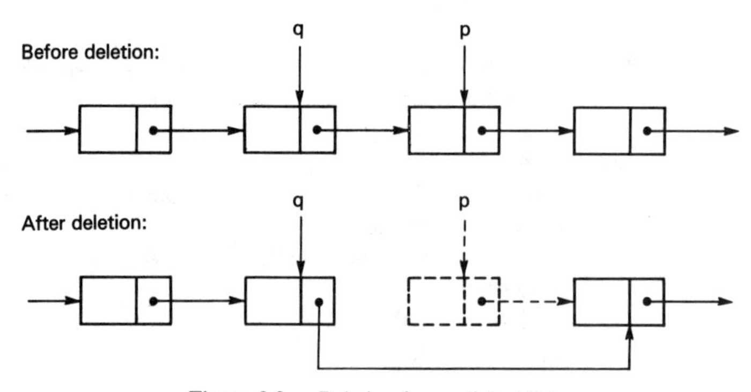

Figure 3.3 Deletion from a linked list.

Some authors get around this difficulty by deciding to represent a position by a pointer to the cell *before* the desired cell. Although this choice allows us to implement *Delete* and *Prior* so that they run in $O(1)$ time, rather than $O(n)$, on lists of size n, it requires more care to program and also requires that we treat the first cell in a list in a special way. Our decision was to give up a little speed for the sake of clarity. It is worth pointing out, however, that we can eliminate some of the complexity of pushing pointers p and q in lock step if we adopt the trick of moving data, rather than pointers, which we introduced in Figure 3.1. In order to delete the cell pointed to by p, all we need to do is move the data in the cell pointed to by *p^.next* into the p cell, and then delete the *p^.next* cell.

The last operation we will describe is the one that inserts a new element into a list after a given position. Unlike the array implementation, which runs in time $O(n)$ on lists of size n, this implementation takes a constant amount of time, independent of the length of the list.

6.
```
procedure InsertAfter(a : ATOM ; p : POSITION ; var L : LIST);
{Assumes p is a position in L , if L is non-empty}
   var q : POSITION;
begin
   if L.head = nil then begin              {inserting into empty list}
      New(L.head);
      L.head^.data := a;
      L^.head^.next := nil;
      L.tail := L.head

   end else begin                          {inserting into non-empty list}
      New(q);
      q^.data := a;
      q^.next := p^.next;
      p^.next := q;
      if p = L.tail then                   {inserted after tail, move tail pointer}
         L.tail := q
   end;
   L.length := L.length + 1
end;
```

Whether you are comfortable with pointers or not, you should trace the action of this algorithm on the different forms of a list (empty, a single cell, more than one cell), and on the various positions for p (at the head, at the tail, in the interior of the list).

Cursors

Pointers are very useful: They provide dynamic storage (we can create new objects and dispose of them at will), and logical linking of objects that may not be adjacent in memory. But not all languages support pointers as a data type. We can still gain the benefits of a linked list implementation (effectively unlimited size of lists, constant-time insertion), along with the simplicity of an array implementation, if we do *explicitly* what pointers do implicitly, that is, allow logical linking of locations that may not be adjacent in memory. We do this by setting up a large array, each element of which contains a data cell and a cell containing an array index which will serve the function of the *next* field in a linked list. In Figure 3.4 we show an example of storing two lists, A = (a, b, c), and B = (d, e, f) in a cursor-based implementation.

In this example, positions are represented by indices of the array. (Such an array is frequently referred to as a **heap**, as in the string table implementation of STRING.) For instance, the list A is referred to by the index, 4, of the cell containing its first element. That fourth cell contains the index, 9, of the cell containing the second element, which itself contains the index, 1, of the cell containing the third element. These references to cells are indicated in the figure by dashed arrows. In this implementation we use the nonexistent index, 0, as our NULL pseudoposition, so we know that "c" is the last element of the list A, since its cursor field contains 0. A clever feature of this implementation is the use of a **free list**, which consists of all the currently unused locations in the big array. If we need to add a new cell to a list, we can use the first cell in the free list for the new cell; if we delete a cell from a list, we simply return that cell to the head of the free list. This is almost exactly what happens behind the scenes, invisible to us and our program, when we use pointers: A large section of memory is set aside for the heap, and the memory so allocated is treated as an array, with array indices corresponding to addresses in memory.

Notice that we have a simple form of garbage collection here: Whenever we indicate (as, for instance, by calling the procedure *Dispose*) that we no longer have need for a pointer to a cell, we can return that cell to the head of the free list. Such a process could be used to manage the garbage in a string table implementation of STRING, as we saw in Chapter 2. In practice, the character heap is usually maintained as "chunks" of several characters, with each chunk containing a cursor to the next chunk. Dealing

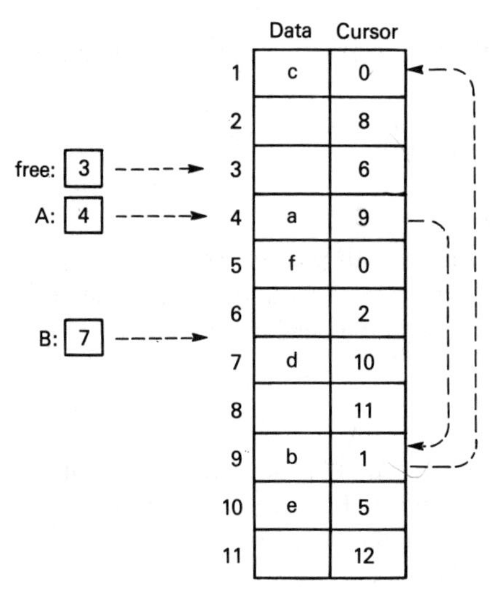

Figure 3.4 Cursor storage of lists.

with chunks of characters introduces a bit of complication, but it saves memory by eliminating the need for a cursor with every single character.

A cursor-based representation of LIST could be defined by the following declarations:

```
const
   HEAPSIZE = {some very large integer};
type
   ATOM = {any data type};
   POSITION = 0 . . HEAPSIZE;
   LIST = record
            length : POSITION;
            start : 1 . . HEAPSIZE
         end;
   Cell = record
            data : ATOM;
            next : POSITION
         end;
var   {global variables for heap and free list}
   heap : array[1 . . HEAPSIZE] of Cell;
   free : LIST;
```

We assume that the heap is initialized by setting *free.start* equal to 1, and that *heap*[*i*].next is set equal to $i + 1$, for $i = 1, \ldots,$ HEAPSIZE $- 1$, and *heap*[*HEAPSIZE*].*next* is set to zero. In other words, at the start of the program, the free list consists of the entire heap, arranged in order of indices. We will not define all the operations of LIST for this implementation, because cursors are conceptually identical to pointers: A single example should capture the flavor of this implementation.

```
procedures InsertAfter(a : ATOM ; p : POSITION);
{Note: this modifies the global variables heap and free }
   var s, t : POSITION;
begin
   {This section is equivalent to New(s) for pointers}
   if free.length = 0 then
      writeln('No room in heap for insertion')
   else begin
      s := free.start;
      free.start := heap[free.start].next        {advance free list by one cell}
      free.length := free.length - 1;

      t := heap[p].next;                         {save index of successor to p }
      heap[p].next := s;                         {link p to new cell at s }
      heap[s].data := a;                         {fill new cell}
      heap[s].next := t                          {and link to old successor to p }
   end
end;
```

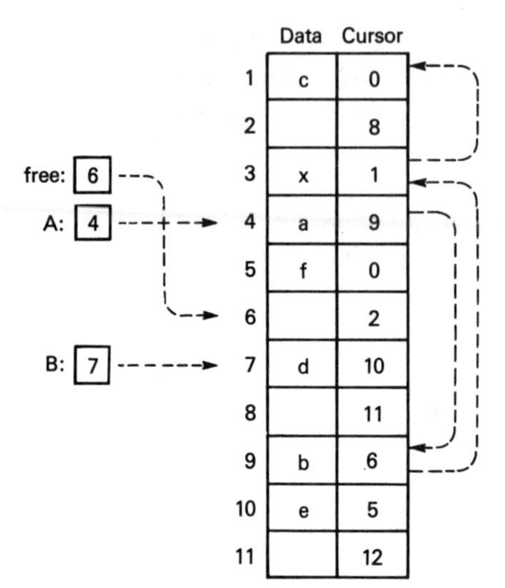

Figure 3.5 Cursor-based insertion.

Assuming that we began with the situation of Figure 3.4, Figure 3.5 illustrates the effect of *InsertAfter(x,9)*, that is, inserting atom x between b and c in list A. The observant reader might have noticed a departure here from good programming style. The parameter list for *InsertAfter*, as defined here, makes no mention of the list, L, in which the insertion is taking place. This also happened in the definition of some of the operations for the pointer implementation of LIST. The reason is that in the pointer and cursor implementations, reference to a list is indirect, whereas in the array implementation we refer to the ith character of the list L by naming the list in the reference itself, namely $L.data[i]$. This indirection, this ability to refer to an atom in a list by position alone, means that we must take care to avoid the possibility that the position we specify may not be in the list we are modifying. We could include checks in our routines that this state of affairs will not happen, but for the fact that to do so would add an amount of time equal to $O(n)$ on lists of length n, since we would have to traverse the list first to ensure that the position we were using was indeed a position in the list. As is so often the case in computer science, we find ourselves in a position that has more of an engineering flavor (making choices between options, evaluating the trade-offs between these options) than mathematical (a problem has a single right answer, and you are either all right or all wrong). This dual nature reflects, to a degree, the historical forces that led to the development of computer science as the confluence between related results in mathematics and electrical engineering.

3.3 OTHER LIST STRUCTURES

There are times when the structure of a list, a linear arrangement of data, is either insufficient or inconvenient as a representation of the data for a problem. In such instances, our job can sometimes be made simpler by imposing an additional structure on top of the simple linear structure of a list. In this section we will discuss some of the common (and not so common) variants of lists.

Two-Way Lists

One disadvantage of the pointer and cursor implementations of lists is that not only are they sequential access structures (so that to inspect the *i*th element of a linked list requires that we pass by the first, second, . . . [$i - 1$]th element), but, even worse, they provide only one-way access. It is easy to find the next position in a linked list, but much more time-consuming to find the position prior to a given position, which means that, for instance, we cannot delete a cell from the list if we only have a pointer to the cell itself—we have to traverse the list and find the cell prior to the one we wish to delete. The solution to this problem is not difficult at all, however, if we are willing to use more space and complicate our implementations of the operations. What we do is provide an extra pointer (or cursor) field which points to the prior cell, in effect overlaying two lists with common atoms.

The declarations for two-way linked lists are almost exactly the same as for one-way lists:

```
type
    ATOM = {any data type}
    POSITION = ^Cell;
    Cell = record
                data : ATOM;
                prior, next : POSITION
            end;
    LIST = record
                length : integer;
                tail, head : POSITION
            end;
```

Note that the only difference between these declarations and those of the one-way linked list is the addition of the field "prior" in each cell. We can visualize a two-way linked list as in Figure 3.6. Using this representation of a list enables us to delete a cell pointed to by a pointer *p* in constant time, since we no longer need to find the position of the cell prior to *p*^—the pointer *p*^.*prior* provides the position we need. (The preceding sentence, in case you haven't noticed, puts this book in the running for the most alliterative data structures text ever written.) In essence, all we have to do is make the pointers *p*^.*prior*^.*next* and *p*^.*next*^.*prior* point around the cell *p*^. The routine is as follows; the length and apparent complexity are due mainly to the fact that we must take care that the head and tail pointers of the header record are handled correctly.

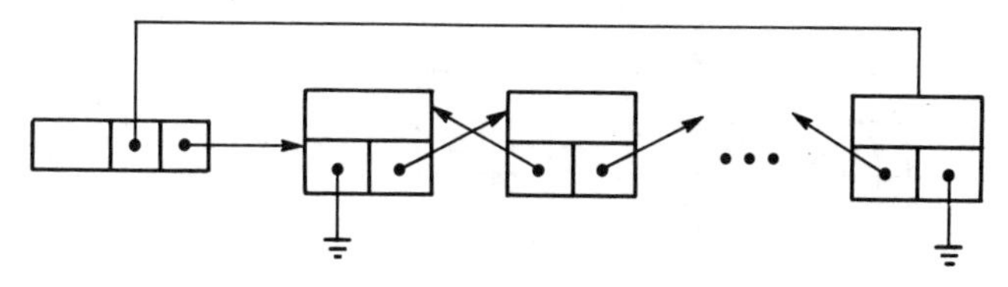

Figure 3.6 A doubly linked list.

```
procedure Delete(var p : POSITION ; var L : LIST);
{Deletion of the cell at position p from a doubly linked list}
begin
  if L.length = 0 then                      {empty list}
    error('Attempt to delete from empty list')

  else begin
    if p = L.head then
      if p = L.tail then begin              {singleton list}
        L.head := nil;
        L.tail := nil

      end else begin                        {deleting first cell from non-singleton}
        L.head := p^.next;
        p^.next^.prior := nil

    end else if p = L.tail then begin       {deleting last cell from non-singleton}
      L.tail := p^.prior;
      p^.prior^.next := nil

    end else begin                          {deleting cell from interior}
      p^.prior^.next := p^.next;
      p^.next^.prior := p^.prior
    end;

    Dispose(p);                             {get rid of p cell and fix list length}
    L.length := L.length - 1
  end
end;
```

As is the case with all linked lists, to delete a cell we "point around" the cell to be deleted. If we are dealing with doubly linked lists, that means that we must move the pointers to that cell in both the preceding and the following cells, as indicated in Figure 3.7.

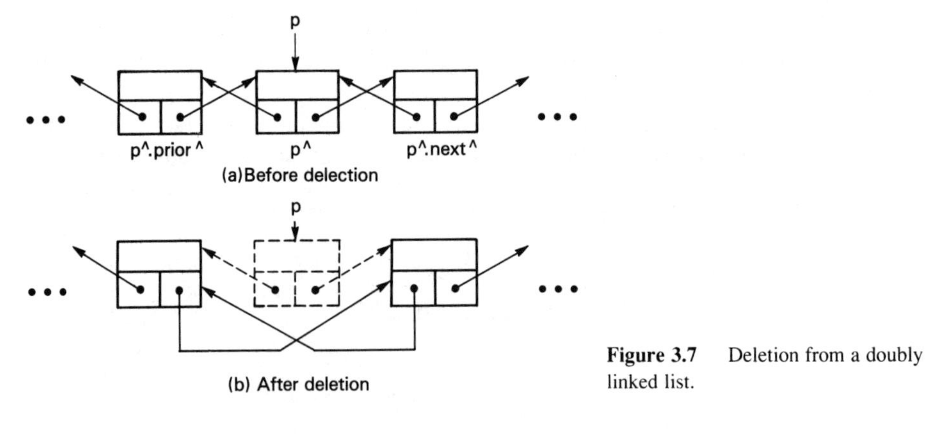

Figure 3.7 Deletion from a doubly linked list.

Sorted Lists

Often, there is an underlying linear order on the atoms in a LIST structure. It might be that the set ATOM consisted of strings, with their associated lexicographic order, if, for instance, we were writing a spelling checker that kept a dictionary of words in sorted order as a list. As another common example, the atoms may not themselves have a natural order, but it might be the case that the atoms were records that could be sorted by one field, commonly called the **key** (as, for instance, if we kept a list of telephone book entries sorted by name but not by phone number). It would certainly be more difficult to maintain such a list than it would be if we didn't have to worry about how the elements were arranged, but there are times when the advantages would outweigh the added complications. Consider how much easier it is to find someone's phone number in a conventional phone book, given the person's name, than it is to find a person's name, given their phone number. Obviously, this is due to the fact that the entries in a phone book are sorted by name, rather than by number. (Donald Knuth, in *The Art of Computer Programming*, suggests the nonalgorithmic technique of dialing the number and asking the person who answers what his or her name is.)

Unlike doubly linked lists, which are merely another implementation of the abstract data type LIST, sorted lists are structurally different enough that they can be defined as an ADT on their own. The ADT SORTED_LIST can be defined as follows:

1. ATOM is a set with a linear order, R_A, defined on it.

2. POSITION is a set.

3. Each element of SORTED_LIST is a triple, (P, R, v), where
   - **a.** P is a subset of POSITION.
   - **b.** R is a linear order on P.
   - **c.** v is a function from P to ATOM.
   - **d.** R and R_A are **compatible**, in the sense that for any p and q in P, if pRq then $v(p) R_A v(q)$.

In other words, the evaluation function, v, preserves order in the sense that if an atom a appears "before" an atom b in a sorted list, then the atom a is "less than or equal to" the atom b.

One way to maintain a sorted list is to make sure that any insertions into a list are made in such a way as to keep the resulting list sorted. In order to do that, it is necessary that we have a function **Find**(a : ATOM ; L : SORTED_LIST) : POSITION, which, given an atom (or that key of an atom on which we will sort) and a sorted list, will return the position after which that atom should be placed in the list to maintain the sorted order. The most obvious way to define *Find* is to traverse the list, starting at the head, until the proper location is found. Doing so, however, clearly could take $O(n)$ time on lists of length n. A much more efficient scheme is to use a **binary search**. In a binary search, the atom a is first compared to the value of the atom in the middle of the list. If a has smaller value than the "middle" atom, we know that it belongs somewhere in the first half of the list; otherwise, we know that a belongs in the last half of the list. We then repeat the process, comparing a with the middle atom in the half list where it is known to be, and repeatedly halving the size of the interval until the interval consists of a single position, which is where a must belong.

The only constraint on this search scheme is that it requires a data structure that allows direct access to a list element by specifying its numeric order in the list. In other words, binary searching will work with arrays, but not (or at least not efficiently) with pointers or cursors. With this in mind, it is easy to implement this function.

```
function Find(a : ATOM ; L : SORTED_LIST) : POSITION;
{  Binary search of sorted list using array implementation.}
   var low, middle, high : POSITION
begin
   low := 0;
   high := L.length;
   while low < high do begin
      middle := (low + high + 1) div 2;
      if a < L.data[middle] then          {look in lower half of list segment}
         high := middle -1
      else                                {look in the upper half of the list segment}
         low := middle
   end;
   Find := low                            { low = high after exit from the loop}
end;
```

The function *Find* successively divides the interval (*low* . . . *high*) into halves (or as near to halves as possible) in such a way that the atom a always belongs in the half selected, until the exit from the loop. Upon exit from the loop (and return from the function), the interval has been reduced to a single position. In that case, the atom a either resides at that position (if a is in the list), or a is not in the list, but could be inserted in the list after that position and still maintain the sorted order of the list. Notice that it is possible for *Find* to return the position zero, indicating that the atom a is not in the list, but could be inserted before the first element in the list.

It is possible to prove that *Find* acts as it should. We would first show that if *low* and *high* were integers with $low < high$, then if we set *middle* equal to $(low + high + 1)$ **div** 2, we would have $low < middle \leq high$, with equality only if *low* and *high* were adjacent, that is, $low = high - 1$. We would then use this to show that the difference $high - low$ decreased at each loop iteration (so the interval always gets strictly smaller, guaranteeing that the loop will eventually terminate). Finally, we would establish the **loop invariant** property that except for the last iteration (which resulted in *low* and *high* having the same value), it is always the case that a belongs in the interval from *low* to *high*.

Find is *very* fast. Since the interval is divided in two each time, the loop iterates only as many times as needed to chop the interval down to one position. In other words, if the list had n positions originally, the intervals would be of size $n/2$, $n/4$, $n/8$, $n/16$, and so on, until the *k*th iteration, when $2^k \geq n$. This, however, is just another way of saying that we stop as soon as $k \geq \log_2 n$, which allows us to say that *Find* runs in time $O(\log n)$ on lists of length *n*. To give you an idea of how fast that is, 2^{30} is equal to 1,073,741,824, so to locate an atom in a sorted list of a billion elements would take no more than 30 **probes** into the list. For all practical purposes, then, a binary search runs in constant time, since 266 probes would allow you to locate *anything* in the universe (assuming that all of the estimated 10^{80} (= 2^{266}) atoms in the universe had been linearly ordered somehow; we leave the details to the reader).

Now that we can find where we should be in a sorted list, it is easy to write a routine to add a new atom to such a list.

```
procedure Insert(a : ATOM ; var L : SORTED_LIST);
{Insertion into a sorted list represented by an array}
   var p, i : POSITION
begin
   if L.length = MAXSIZE then
      error('No room to Insert')
   else begin
      p := Find(a, L);

      for i := L.length downto p + 1 do    {shift cells to make room for insertion}
         L.data[i + 1] := L.data[i];
      L.data[p + 1] := a;
      L.length := L.length + 1
   end
end;
```

This algorithm is almost exactly like the one we would have for insertion in unordered lists, except that we use *Find* to determine where in the list insertion should take place. The problem with this algorithm is the same as with insertion into unordered lists—it takes time $O(n)$ on lists of size *n* (since we may have to shift the entire list to make room for the new element). With that in mind, we see that the exceptional speed of *Find* is superfluous here: We can tell where an atom should go very quickly, but it takes a while to put the atom where it should be. Of course, we could use a linked list, since insertion runs in constant time for linked lists, but then we would have no easy way to implement *Find* in time less than $O(n)$, so we would be no better off than we were before. In either implementation, then, it could take time $O(n^2)$ to start from scratch and perform *n* insertions to construct a sorted list with *n* elements.

This is another of those engineering-like decisions: If we knew that the problem we were trying to solve was going to involve a lot of locating and updating, and fairly little inserting and deleting, then it would probably be worth the trouble to implement SORTED_LIST as arrays. If the problem involved a lot of inserting and deleting, we would probably be better off looking for another data structure. All is not lost, however; in Chapter 6 we will see another data structure that provides the speed of a binary search with the efficiency of linked lists.

Braids

A natural generalization of sorted lists would be to keep a list sorted by two different keys. Such a list is called a **braid** or a **multilist**. A good example would be the master directory of the telephone company, in which the entries would be maintained in sorted order by both name and number. We could implement such a doubly sorted list in a fashion very similar to that used for two-way linked lists: In each cell maintain two pointers, one to the next cell in, say, name order, and another to the next cell in numeric order. Keeping with our Ma Bell example, we would have the following declarations:

```
type
   CellPtr = ^Cell;
   Cell = record
             name : STRING;
             number : integer;
             {other data, too, like address, unpaid balance, etc.}
             nextName, nextNumber : CellPtr
          end;
```

Figure 3.8 illustrates a typical two-braid of this type. Notice that the two sorted lists are accessed through the pointers *nameHead*, to the first cell in lexicographic order, and *numberHead*, to the first cell in numeric order. In all honesty, this data structure is not used very often; to understand why, you might try to write *Delete* for a two-braid. Of course, we need not stop with two-braids, we could sort the records by any number of fields we wanted, producing three-braids, four-braids, and so on. While we're on the subject, it is perhaps worth mentioning that the links in a braid need not be one way; we could have a doubly linked two-braid, with four pointers per record, or (as the author once tried in his youth) a one-and-a-half-way two-braid, with double links for one field and single links for the other, thereby demonstrating the infinite creativity (if not wisdom) of the human animal.

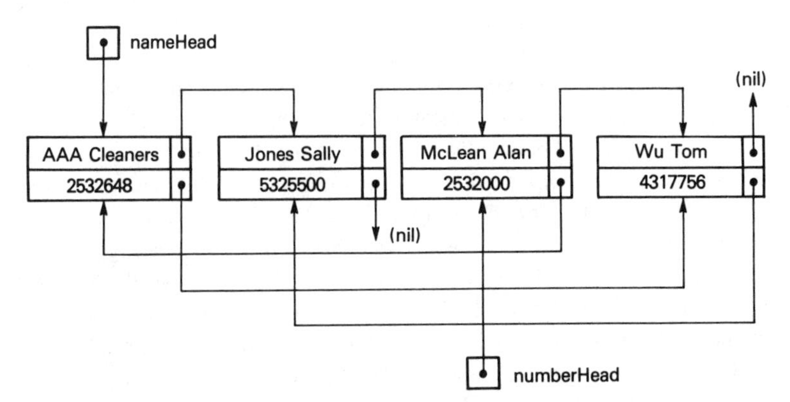

Figure 3.8 A braided telephone directory.

3.4 APPLICATION: MEMORY MANAGEMENT

We mentioned earlier that there was an ecological flavor to computer science, in that we must carefully manage the use of the finite amount of memory available in any machine. Much of that work is "transparent" to the programmer, and is handled by the system programs that run in the background. For example, suppose that a computer must execute the Pascal statement *New(p)*, for a pointer *p*. The pointer itself can be handled in the same way as the rest of the program variables, such as integers, reals, or characters—but how does the computer find room in memory for what *p* points to, without running the risk of overwriting already stored information? This **memory management** is at least partly handled by the compiler, which translates the "*New(p)*" statement into instructions to the **operating system**. Now, the operating system is itself a program, one that runs all the time and whose job it is to manage all the resources of the computer, such as input/output, central processor access, file management, and—of particular interest to us here—memory management. Along with handling requests from a program for a new chunk of memory for a pointer to point to, the operating system may also have to deal with the similar problem of allocating space in memory for several programs in a multiuser environment. If a new user sits down at a terminal and wants to run a job of size 60K bytes, the operating system must find room in memory for the job without disturbing any job already in the system. In this section, we will explore some strategies for memory management.

We will use pointers as our model here, although much of what we discuss would apply equally well to (generally larger) program code segments, as well. The two primary operations we will discuss are simple modifications of *New* and *Dispose*:

1. **NewPtr**(size : integer) : Pointer, a function that will return a pointer to a location in memory sufficiently large to hold *size* bytes.
2. **DisposePtr**(p : Pointer), a procedure that makes the location in memory pointed to by *p* available for later use.

In what follows, we will often refer to these two operations in more general terms of **allocating** and **deallocating** memory, and will refer to the piece of memory allocated or deallocated as a **block**. These two operations should be thought of as operating system calls, so that, for instance, the Pascal statement *New(p)* would be translated into code that first looks up the size of the object *p* will point to, and then makes the operating system call *NewPtr* to allocate memory for the new object. Thinking of these two operations as system-level operations gives us a certain amount of freedom that we would not have if we worked exclusively at the Pascal source code level. In particular, we can free ourselves from having to worry about type compatibility between pointers and integers—that's a Pascal convention, and we're operating at a level where we have no idea about the language of the program that makes the call. With this in mind, we will refer to **links**, rather than pointers, to emphasize that at this level there is no difference between pointers (which are, after all, just addresses of locations in memory) and integers (which can serve as indices to the array of bytes making up the memory).

In the model we are considering here, we are guided by three constraints:

1. The blocks we will deal with must be *contiguous*, in that if we must find space for a block of 300 bytes, it cannot be 120 bytes in one location, 80 in another, and 100 somewhere else.
2. The blocks, in general, will be of *different sizes*. This is not the case with memory allocation in LISP, where all the blocks are records with two identically sized fields, nor is it the case with many disk-based file systems, where all the blocks are the same size, often 512 bytes.
3. The blocks will have *unknown contents*, in the sense that our memory manager will only know how large a requested block is, but not what's in it. This will mean that, as we mentioned, we will treat memory as one very large array of bytes (or two-byte **words** in some systems, although we'll just deal with bytes here). Some of the other consequences of this constraint are considered in the exercises.

By now, it should come as no surprise that we will make use of a **free list**, a list in which each cell consists of (1) a link to a **free block**, namely one that is not currently being used, (2) a link to the next cell in the list, along with (3) other information that we deem appropriate, such as the size of the free block referred to by the cell. Initially, we could imagine the free list consisting of a single cell, linked to one large free block consisting of the entire memory available for dynamic storage. This memory is called the **heap** to distinguish it from the part of memory reserved for program variables and system information. Where, then, would we put the free list itself? It shouldn't take you too long to hit upon the idea of keeping the free list in the heap, along with all the other blocks. We will do this by reserving some space in each block for a **block header**, where we will keep all the information about that block, which means that we can dispense with the link to the block referred to by the cell. In Figure 3.9 we illustrate a typical heap, consisting of five used blocks, pointed to by pointers *a, b, c, d, e*, and shaded in the drawing, along with five free blocks, of sizes 200, 50, 100, 150, and 180 bytes, each of which has a link to the next free block in the list. In Figure 3.9 we indicate the link and size fields of each free block. Don't be misled by the fact that the diagram shows the free list in order of location in memory—that is one way to maintain the free list, but it certainly isn't the only way.

Allocation

In order to allocate a block, what we will do is find, somehow, a block in the free list that is at least as large as the requested size, and use all or part of that free block to fill the request. It seems simplest to allocate space for the used block from the right end of the original free block—then we wouldn't have to move the location of the header for the free block, which means that we would not have to find and change any link to that block in the list. In Figure 3.10 we illustrate the action of such an allocation.

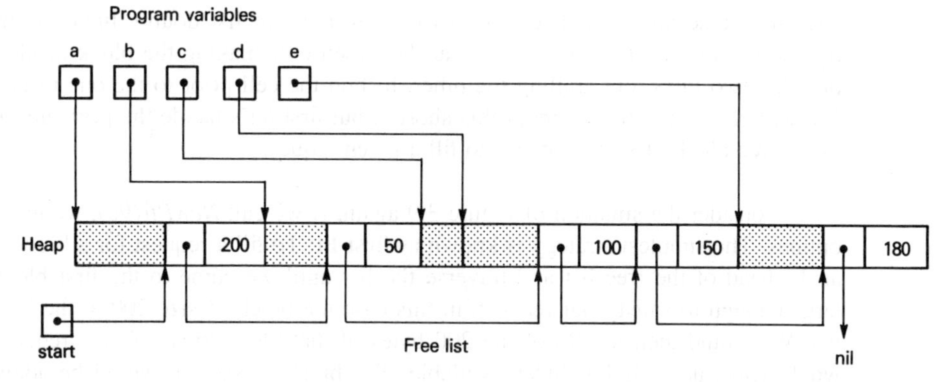

Figure 3.9 A heap with five free blocks.

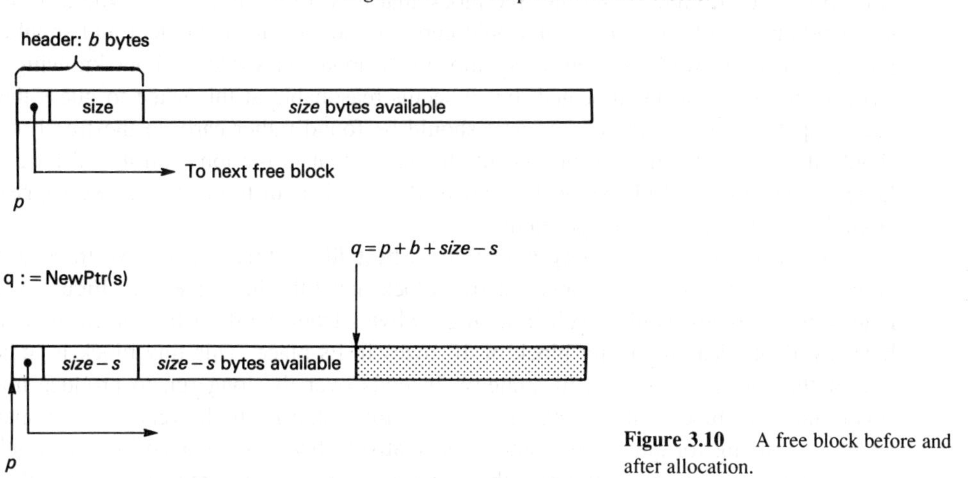

Figure 3.10 A free block before and after allocation.

We have to be careful about how we find the address (i.e., link) of the start of the newly allocated block. If a free block of size 200 began at byte p, and our request was for 90 bytes, we could not return the address $p + (200 - 90)$ for the start of the allocated block, since that would ignore the space occupied by the block header. Instead, if we are to allocate space of size s from a free block of *size* bytes starting at p, the allocated block would begin at address $p + b + size - s$, where b is the size of the block header. In proper terms, we must be careful to distinguish between the **logical length** of a block, which is the number of bytes actually available, and the **physical length**, which is the total length of the block, including the header. In what follows, we will describe blocks in terms of their logical, rather than physical, lengths.

A problem arises when the request is for the whole free block. In that case, we must remove that free block from the free list entirely. Since the free list as described so far is a linked list, deletion will require that we know the prior cell in the linked list (along with the cell following, but that's simple). This is no problem if we know ahead of time that the free list will never be very long, but if we don't know that, we will have to decide how to delete, such as making the free list doubly linked (which then makes deletion run in constant time, at the expense of making the block header larger), or using two links, one trailing the other, to find the cell prior to the one to be deleted. We will have more to say about this shortly, but first let's tackle the problem of how to find a free block of sufficient size to fill a given request.

Consider the situation of Figure 3.9 again. If we call *NewPtr(90)*, we have several options. The simplest strategy is known as **first fit**: To fill a request for a block, we start at the head of the free list and traverse the list until we come to the first block that is large enough to satisfy our request, in this case the block of size 200 at the head of the list. We would then use 90 of the 200 bytes of that block to satisfy the request, which would leave us with 110 bytes available. The block of size 90 would be added to the collection of used blocks, and the free block that used to be of size 200 would have its size field changed to 110. First fit would certainly be easy to implement and should be relatively fast, as well. We can't say too much about its speed without knowing the sizes of the blocks to be allocated, but it seems reasonable at this stage to guess that a block capable of satisfying our request should be found rather early in the free list. Or should it? One problem with the first-fit strategy is that in the long run it will lead to a large number of small blocks at the start of the free list. In the exercises we suggest a possible way to alleviate this problem.

Another allocation strategy is known as **best fit**. In this scheme, we traverse the entire free list and select the smallest free block that fills the request. In Figure 3.9, a request for 90 bytes would result in taking 90 bytes from the third free block, with 100 bytes available, leaving a tiny block of 10 bytes in its place. This tiny block is indicative of the nature of the best-fit strategy: It tends over the long run to produce many small and large blocks (the block of size 200, for instance, might very well be spared from any pruning for quite some time), but relatively few middle-sized blocks. In addition, best fit requires us to traverse the entire free list for each request, so it will certainly run slower, on average, than first fit.

Both of these allocation strategies have advantages and disadvantages, and, as we have remarked before, we must make an educated choice between them, based on such knowledge as the expected length of the free list and the distribution of request sizes. The consensus is that in most cases the added time spent on a best-fit strategy simply isn't worth it, but your choice would, of course, be based on careful analysis of the system you have to implement.

One certain disadvantage of both strategies, and of almost any other based on free lists, is that they lead to **fragmentation**—the breaking of the total free memory into small blocks. For example, again in Figure 3.9, there are 680 bytes of free memory, but the largest request that can be filled is for 200 bytes. In that case, what would we do if presented with a request for, say, 240 or 380 bytes? The answer depends, in part, on what we have decided to do when a request comes to deallocate a used block and return it to the free list.

Deallocation

Deallocating a used block is easy—all we have to do is add that block to the free list. We can be a bit more sophisticated than that, though, by dealing with at least part of the fragmentation problem at the same time. A block to be deallocated might very well have adjacent blocks that are already free, so it would make sense to **coalesce** any newly freed block with its left and right free neighbors. In this way we avoid the situation of Figure 3.9, where we have two adjacent free blocks of sizes 100 and 150 bytes. In that situation we really have a block of size 250 available, but we can't get at it because the operating system "thinks" it is divided into two smaller blocks.

How shall we perform this coalescing, though? We must be able to find the left and right neighbors of the newly freed block and check whether they are free. Finding the right neighbor isn't too hard—we know the present block starts at address p, that its logical size is *size*, and that h bytes are taken up by the block header. With that information, we know that the right neighbor must start at address $p + size + h$ (this is where the ability to do address arithmetic comes in handy). But checking whether the right neighbor is free is another matter. As we have set our data structure so far, the only way to check the right neighbor is to traverse the entire free list to see if the right neighbor is there. Things get even worse when we try to check the left neighbor. Right now, we would have to traverse the free list and, for each block in the free list, perform the same address calculations as before to find out whether the free block has the present block as its right neighbor. This is already a somewhat daunting task, and we haven't even considered how to perform the coalescing after we have found the free neighbors.

One way to simplify matters is to pay the price of using more space in the blocks to store information that would help us in the coalescing. A common strategy is known as the **boundary tag** method. In this method, each block contains a left tag at the start of the block, which is 0 for free blocks and 1 for used blocks, along with a size field, and a right tag at the right end of the block, which contains the same value as the left tag. To facilitate moving through the free list, we will maintain it as a doubly linked ring (i.e., the last block in the list is linked to the first one), so that each free block will also contain two links, to the prior and next elements in the free list. Finally, to aid in finding left free blocks, each free block will also contain a back link to the start of the block, so that our blocks will take the form illustrated in Figure 3.11.

Notice that we have two distinct structures here: the doubly linked ring of free blocks, which we will assume is accessed by a link, *free*, to some block in the free list (or has a flag value like 0 or −1 if the free list is empty), and the heap itself, which may be regarded as linearly ordered by address. These two structures have nothing to do with each other—if free block A is prior to free block B in the free list, it is equally likely that A is *before* B in the heap, or that A is *after* B.

Now we can describe how coalescing would be accomplished. Since we are writing our routines at the system level, we will assume that the only heap operations available to us are **GetVal**(*p*, *n*), which returns in the variable *n* the value stored in address *p* of memory, and **SetVal**(*p*, *n*), which stores the value *n* in memory location *p*. It will be useful to keep some global constants, SIZE_OFST, PRIOR_OFST, NEXT_OFST, BACK_OFST, FRTAG_OFST (for FreeRightTAG OFfSeT), and URTAG_OFST (for UsedRightTAG OFfSeT), which are equal to the offsets from the start of a block of the *size, prior, next, backlink*, fields of the block, and *rightTag* fields of free and used blocks. In a typical system, the tags would be one byte long, and sizes and links would require four bytes, so we would have SIZE_OFST = 1, PRIOR_OFST = 5, NEXT_OFST = 9, BACK_OFST = 13, FRTAG_OFST = 17, and URTAG_OFST = 5. Thus, for example, if we knew that a free block began at address *p*, then the *size* field would begin at address $p + 1$, the *next* field would begin at address $p + 9$, the *backlink* would begin at $p + size + 13$, and the right neighbor block would begin at address $p + size + 18$.

To check whether the right neighboring block was free, then, we could use the function **LeftFree**, described next:

```
function LeftFree(p : LINK) : boolean;
{  Returns true if and only if the left neighbor of the block at p is free.}
   const
      HEAPSTART = 1;                      {starting address of heap}
begin
   LeftFree := false;
   if p > HEAPSTART then begin  {are we at the left end of the heap?}
      GetVal(p - 1, tag);             {if not, then get the right tag of the left neighbor}
      LeftFree := (tag = 0)           {and return true if and only if the tag is zero}
end;
```

We could define **RightFree** in a similar fashion. Having done that, it is fairly simple to describe the coalescing routines. We show **CoalesceLeft** next:

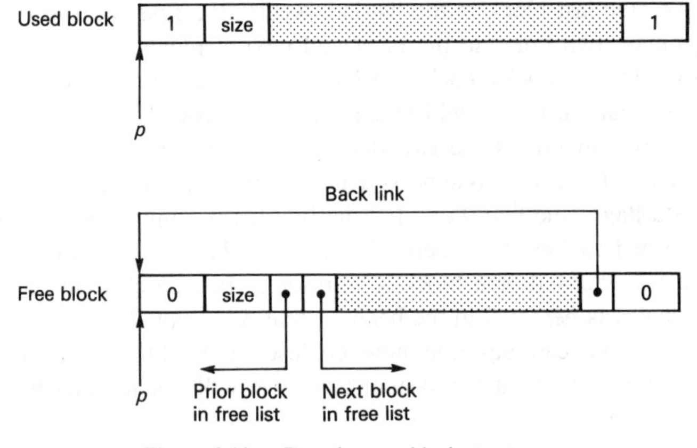

Figure 3.11 Boundary tag block structures.

```
procedure CoalesceLeft(p : LINK);
{   Merge the block at p with its free left neighbor to produce a large free block.}
    const
        BACK_LEFT_OFST = 5;         {distance of backlink field from right end of block}
        TAGSIZE = 1;                {size of tag field in bytes}
        LINKSIZE = 4;               {size of a link in bytes}
    var
        uSize, fSize : LINK;        {logical sizes of p block and its left neighbor}
        start : LINK;               {start address of left free block}
begin
    GetVal(p + SIZE_OFST, uSize);              {find size of p block}
    SetVal(p + URTAG_OFST + uSize, 0);         {set right tag of p block}
    GetVal(p - BACK_LEFT_OFST, start);         {use backlink to find start of left neighbor}
    SetVal(p + BACK_OFST + uSize, start);      {place backlink field into p block}

    GetVal(start + SIZE_OFST, fSize);          {find logical size of left neighbor}
    SetVal(start + SIZE_OFST, uSize + fSize + 2*TAGSIZE + LINKSIZE) {set new size}
end;
```

The only part that might be tricky is the setting of the size field for the coalesced block. Figure 3.12 shows that when we coalesce a free and a formerly used block, the logical size of the new free block is equal to the sum of the logical size of the free block plus the total size of the old used block, that is, the old logical size plus the sizes of the left and right tags and the old size field.

We can now describe the routine *DisposePtr*. The skeleton is simple enough: We check the left and right neighbors and then coalesce as necessary. If no coalescing is needed, we just set the tag fields of the old used block to 0; modify the size field to

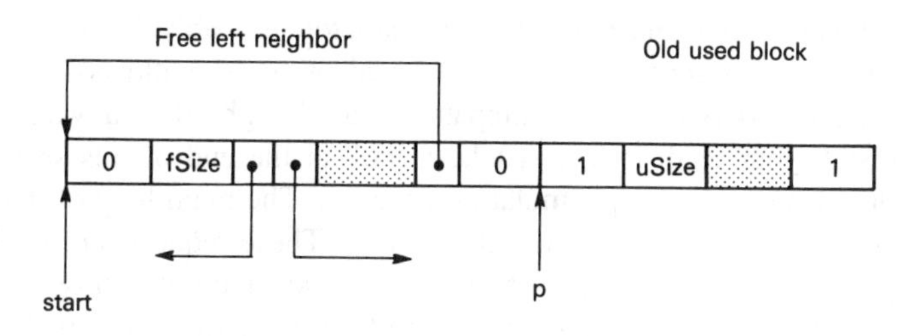

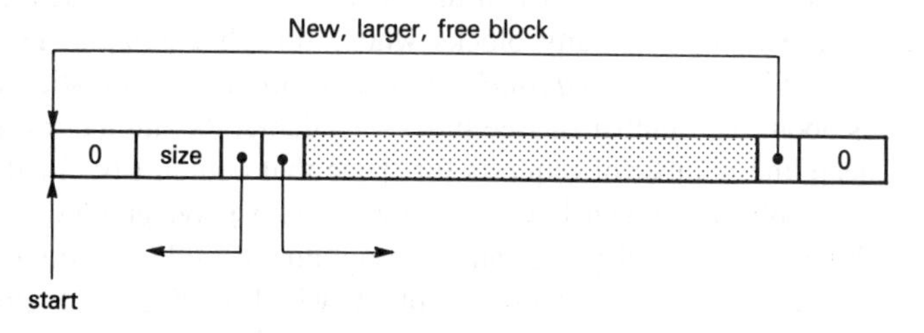

Figure 3.12 Before and after coalescing left.

make room for the *prior*, *next*, and *back* links; add in the back link; and add the newly freed block to the free list.

```
procedure AddToFreeList(p : LINK); {global procedure, also called by NwePtr.}

procedure DisposePtr(p: LINK);
{   Remove p block from used blocks, do coalescing as needed.}

    function LeftFree(p : LINK) : boolean;        {all these can be local to DisposePtr.}
    function RightFree(p : LINK) : boolean;
    procedure CoalesceRight(p : LINK);
    procedure CoalesceLeft(p : LINK);
    procedure CoalesceBoth(p : LINK);
    procedure ConvertToFreeBlock(p : LINK);
begin
    if LeftFree(p) then
        if RightFree(p) then
            CoalesceBoth(p)
        else
            CoalesceLeft(p)
    else if RightFree(p) then
        CoalesceRight(p)
    else begin
        ConvertToFreeBlock(p);
        AddToFreeList(p)
    end
end;
```

If you're like most people, this skeleton probably leaves you feeling as though you've just been served a six-course meal of marshmallows—there just isn't enough there to be satisfying. We anticipated you, though. If you want something you can really sink your teeth into, just take a look at the end of this section, where there's a complete listing of a heap simulation program. The main loop of that program generates a request for a new pointer at each iteration. These requests are for blocks of randomly chosen sizes, which have preset durations, also randomly chosen. Each request that is successfully handled by *NewPtr* is placed on a **queue** (about which you'll learn much more in the following chapter), which is nothing but a waiting list of links to active blocks, along with the times when they will be deallocated. Each iteration, the queue is polled to see if there are any blocks whose time has expired. For every one of those blocks, a call is made to *DisposePtr*. Every so often the simulation breaks off and prints statistics about the number of free blocks available, the number of used blocks currently in the heap, the number of requests for space that couldn't be filled, and the sizes of the present free blocks. If you have a computer with good graphics capabilities, it is well worth the effort to modify the sample program to produce a **memory map** of the free and used blocks in the heap, an example of which is given in Figure 3.13. In that map, the used blocks are indicated by shaded rectangles, and the free blocks are unshaded, with vertical tick marks separating the blocks. Typically, the low heap address is the top left corner, and the rest of the heap is arranged left to right and top to bottom on the page. If you redraw each block on the screen as its status changes, the display can provide many minutes of entertainment, as well as giving some real insights into the comparative behaviors of first fit and best fit selection algorithms.

Compaction

Even with the best selection and coalescing algorithms we can invent, fragmentation in the heap can still leave us in a situation where there is plenty of free space available to fill a request for memory, but no free block is large enough for the request. What should our operating system do in such a situation?

Basically, we have two choices: We can either report failure or try to make room for the request. In some cases, reporting failure is an attractive alternative. It is certainly easy to implement, and it may happen that we can recover from such a failure. For example, if our system was responsible for handling many programs using a single computer on a time-sharing basis, we might be able to swap out a job in the system (saving it on a disk, for instance), load the new job in the vacant space and run it for a while, and then swap that with the old job when it came time to run the old job. Even if there was no job large enough to swap out right away, we could still put the new job on a waiting list and load it when space became available. Done quickly enough, this process would be more or less invisible to the users, especially in light of the fact that in the time frame of the computer, the equivalent of days passes between the keystrokes entered by the vastly slower humans at the terminals. Of course, this would not work at all well for our example of allocating space for pointers. If one program was all that was resident on the computer, it would serve no useful purpose to tell the program to wait until space became available, since nothing would happen in the meantime to free any space.

The other option would be to make room for a request by moving the used blocks together, as in Figure 3.14, where the shaded blocks are used and the unshaded are free. It's not difficult to see how this **compaction** of memory would be implemented, but it is equally evident that this process could be very slow, since it would run in time

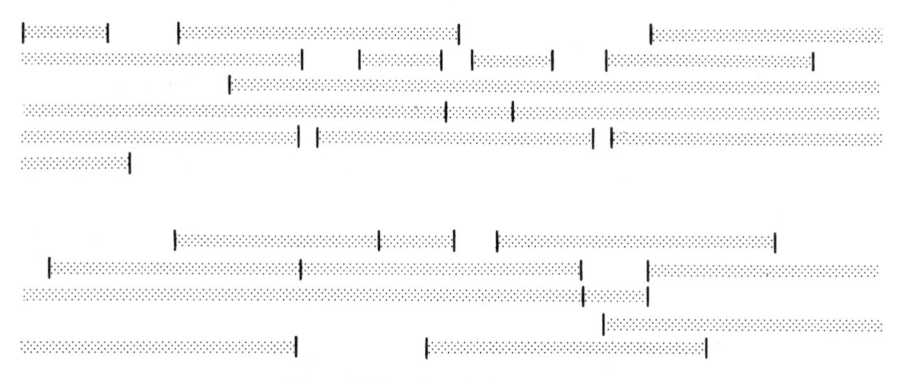

Figure 3.13 A typical memory map.

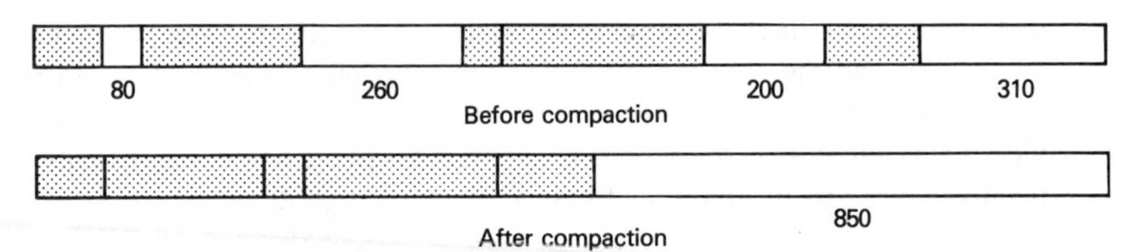

Figure 3.14 Compacting memory.

proportional to the total number of bytes of used memory. As fast as a computer is, it could still take an unacceptably long time to move what may amount to megabytes of memory.

That's not the worst of our problems, however. Can you see why? The truly messy part of memory compaction is that the used blocks are referred to by pointers. If we move memory around without telling the resident program, that program is suddenly in the position of having most, if not all, of its pointers referring to locations in memory that no longer contain what the program expects them to contain. In other words, our operating system now has the responsibility of letting the resident program know that its pointers are no longer valid, and the resident program now must somehow update the values of its pointers to reflect the memory moves.

That's bad enough, but suppose the heap also contains pointers, as would be the case if some blocks contained pointers to other blocks. The resident program may not even have variables referring to these pointers, and therefore wouldn't have a clue about what to update. What a mess—enough of a mess, in fact, that some operating systems don't do memory compaction at all. In the exercises, we ask you explore some ways of dealing with these problems.

```
program HeapSimulation (input, output);
{ ------------------------------------------------------------------------------------------- }
{                                                                                             }
{       Simulation of memory management in a heap, using boundary tags                        }
{                                                                                             }
{ ------------------------------------------------------------------------------------------- }

  const
    HEAPSIZE = 8192;
    QMAX = 750;                    {max number of used blocks awaiting release}

    SIZE_OFST = 1;                 {offset in block header of size field}
    PRIOR_OFST = 2;                {offset in free block header of prior link field}
    NEXT_OFST = 3;                 {ditto: next link field}
    BACK_OFST = 4;                 {backlink offset (add size to this)}
    FRTAG_OFST = 5;                {free block right tag offset (add size)}
    URTAG_OFST = 2;                {used block right tag offset (add size, too)}

    REPORT_EVERY = 2000;           {cycles between printing statistics}
    MAXTIME = 5000;                {length of time to run the simulation}
```

```
type
    LINK = 0..HEAPSIZE;
    QRec = record                    {A quick and dirty way to keep track of used blocks}
            timeOut : integer;       {so that we know when they're to be released.}
            addr : LINK              {You'll learn more about queues later}
        end;
    Queue = record
            size : integer;
            elt : array[1..QMAX] of Qrec
        end;
var
    blockQ : Queue;                  {list of blocks presently used, in order of time out}
    size, duration : integer;        {for each new request — size and length of time used}
    cycle : integer;                 {clock variable}

    free : LINK;                     {start of free list}
    p, q : LINK;                     {link of block presently being allocated/deallocated}
    Heap : array[LINK] of integer;   {the heap}

    unfilled : integer;              {keep track of allocations that couldn't be made}

{=================== "S Y S T E M"  U T I L I T I E S =======================}

procedure GetVal (p : LINK;
        var value : LINK);
{ ------------------------------------------------------------------------------------ }
{  Returns the value in heap location p.                                               }
{ ------------------------------------------------------------------------------------ }
begin
    if p = 0 then
        value := 0                   {error — trying to get at nil address}
    else
        value := Heap[p]
end;

procedure SetVal (p, value : LINK);
{ ------------------------------------------------------------------------------------ }
{  Sets heap location p to value.                                                      }
{ ------------------------------------------------------------------------------------ }
begin
    if p <> 0 then
        Heap[p] := value
end;
```

```
{================ F R E E   L I S T   M A N I P U L A T I O N =============}

   procedure InitFreeList;
{ ------------------------------------------------------------------------------- }
{   Sets the free list to a single element, consisting of the entire heap.         }
{ Note that the free list is maintained as a circular doubly linked list.          }
{ ------------------------------------------------------------------------------- }
   begin
      SetVal(1, 0);                          {set left tag of giant free block}
      SetVal(1 + SIZE_OFST, HEAPSIZE - 6);   {set size field}
      SetVal(1 + PRIOR_OFST, 1);             {link the cell to itself}
      SetVal(1 + NEXT_OFST, 1);              {...in both directions}
      SetVal(HEAPSIZE - 1, 1);               {set the backlink}
      SetVal(HEAPSIZE, 0);                   {set right tag}
      free := 1                            {and make list header point to this block}
   end;

   procedure AddToFreeList (p : LINK);
{ ------------------------------------------------------------------------------- }
{   Inserts the block starting at p into the free list, after the header "free."   }
{ ------------------------------------------------------------------------------- }
      var
         nextCell : LINK;
   begin
      if free = 0 then              {free list is empty — insert this as only cell}
         begin
            SetVal(p + PRIOR_OFST, p);
            SetVal(p + NEXT_OFST, p)
         end
      else                          {usual doubly-linked insertion after "free" header}
         begin
            GetVal(free + NEXT_OFST, nextCell);      {find cell after header cell}
            SetVal(nextCell + PRIOR_OFST, p);      {link that cell back to p cell}
            SetVal(free + NEXT_OFST, p);         {link "free" header cell forward to p cell}
            SetVal(p + PRIOR_OFST, free);          {link p cell back to header cell}
            SetVal(p + NEXT_OFST, nextCell)        {... and forward to next cell}
         end;
      free := p                            {in either case, make header point to p cell}
   end;
```

```
   procedure DeleteFromFreeList (p : LINK);
{ ------------------------------------------------------------------------------------------------- }
{   Removes the block starting at p from the free list.                                              }
{ ------------------------------------------------------------------------------------------------- }
      var
         nextCell, priorCell : LINK;
   begin
      GetVal(p + NEXT_OFST, nextCell);
      GetVal(p + PRIOR_OFST, priorCell);    {find addresses of cells before and
                                               after p in free list}
      if nextCell = p then                  {deleting the only cell in the list}
         free := 0
      else
         begin
            if free = p then                {if header points to p, move it before deleting p}
               free := nextCell;
            SetVal(nextCell + PRIOR_OFST, priorCell);   {point around p from
                                                            next to prior}
            SetVal(priorCell + NEXT_OFST, nextCell)     {... and from prior to next}
         end
   end;

{====== A L L O C A T I O N / D E A L L O C A T I O N   R O U T I N E S ===========}

   function FirstFit (request : integer) : LINK;
{ ------------------------------------------------------------------------------------------------- }
{   Searches free list from start for first block of logical size ≥ request.                         }
{ Returns address of found block, if there's one big enough, or zero if not.                         }
{ ------------------------------------------------------------------------------------------------- }
      var
         size : LINK;
         q : LINK;                          {used to traverse free list}
   begin
      if free = 0 then                      {free list is empty, return and report failure}
         FirstFit := 0
      else
         begin
            GetVal(free + SIZE_OFST, size);       {see if first cell in free list is
                                                        big enough}
            if size >= request then               {if it is, great, return}
               FirstFit := free
            else                                  {sorry, first cell isn't big enough}
               begin
                  GetVal(free + NEXT_OFST, q);    {get address of next free block}
                  if q = free then
                     FirstFit := 0                {only one block in free list and it's
                                                     not big enough}
                  else
```

```
                    begin
                       GetVal(q + SIZE_OFST, size);        {find size of second block
                                                           in free list, then traverse}

                       while (size < request) and (q <> free) do
                          begin
                             GetVal(q + NEXT_OFST, q);        {move q to next
                                                              cell in free list}
                             GetVal(q + SIZE_OFST, size)      {... and get its size}
                          end;

                       if size < request then           {did the search succeed?}
                          FirstFit := 0                 {nope}
                       else
                          FirstFit := q                 {yup}
                    end
                 end
              end
   end;

   function NewPtr (size : integer) : LINK;
{ ------------------------------------------------------------------------------- }
{   Returns a link to a newly allocated block of size requested, if possible,     }
{ or zero if selection strategy (e.g., FirstFit) can't find one large enough.     }
{ ------------------------------------------------------------------------------- }
      const
         BLOCKMIN = 3;
      var
         q, u : LINK;

      procedure Allocate (f, uS : LINK;
            var u : LINK);
{ ------------------------------------------------------------------------------- }
{   Takes all or part of free block at f and allocates a used block of size       }
{ at least uSize in the f block, starting at address u.  This routine will split  }
{ the free block into a smaller free block and a new used block if there's        }
{ room, or will use all of the free block, if there's not enough left to make a   }
{ small free block.                                                               }
{ ------------------------------------------------------------------------------- }
         var
            oFS, nFS : LINK;          {original free size and new free size of f block}
      begin
         GetVal(f + SIZE_OFST, oFS);          {get present logical size of f block}

         if oFS - uS ≥ 3 then                 {there's room enough to split this block}
            begin
               nFS := oFS - uS - 3;           {compute size of free part after splitting}
               SetVal(f + SIZE_OFST, nFS);          {set size field of f to new size}
```

```
            SetVal(f + BACK_OFST + nFS, f);        {... make new backlink}
            SetVal(f + FRTAG_OFST + nFS, 0);       {... and new right tag}

            u := f + FRTAG_OFST + nFS + 1;         {address of allocated block}
            SetVal(u, 1);                          {set left tag of allocated block}
            SetVal(u + SIZE_OFST, uS);             {... and size field}
            SetVal(u + URTAG_OFST + uS, 1)         {... and right tag}
         end

      else                          {no space to split — allocate the entire free block}
         begin
            DeleteFromFreeList(f);
            SetVal(f, 1);                          {set left tag}
            SetVal(f + SIZE_OFST, oFS + 3);        {... and size, including
                                                   space for 3 now-unused links}
            SetVal(f + FRTAG_OFST + oFS, 1);       {... and right tag}
            u := f                        {... and return address of head of block}
         end
   end;

begin {NewPtr}
   if size < BLOCKMIN then             {don't make any block too small (< 3, certainly)}
      size := BLOCKMIN;

   q := FirstFit(size);
   if q > 0 then                       {selection strategy reported success}
      begin
         Allocate(q, size, u);
         NewPtr := u
      end
   else
      begin
         NewPtr := 0;
         unFilled := unFilled + 1
      end
end;
```

```
    procedure DisposePtr (p : LINK;
{ ------------------------------------------------------------------------------------------- }
{    Frees the block pointed to by p, coalescing it with free neighbors, if any.  }
{ ------------------------------------------------------------------------------------------- }
      var
         leftFree, rightFree : boolean;        {true if left or right neighbors are free}
         tag, thisSize : LINK;

      procedure CoalesceLeft (p : LINK);
{ ------------------------------------------------------------------------------------------- }
{  Merge the block at p with its free left neighbor to produce a large free block.}
{ ------------------------------------------------------------------------------------------- }
         var
            uSize, fSize : LINK;              {sizes of used and (left) free blocks}
            start : LINK;                     {address of left free block}
      begin
         GetVal(p + SIZE_OFST, uSize);
         SetVal(p + URTAG_OFST + uSize, 0);   {set right tag}
         GetVal(p - 2, start);                {use left backlink to find address
                                               of left neighbor}
         SetVal(p + 1 + uSize, start);        {set backlink of coalesced block}

         GetVal(start + SIZE_OFST, fSize);    {get size of left neighbor}
         SetVal(start + 1, uSize + fSize + 3); {new size includes 2 old tags
                                               and an old size field}
      end;

      procedure CoalesceRight (p : LINK);
{ ------------------------------------------------------------------------------------------- }
{    Merge the block at p with its free right neighbor, and adjust the prior and  }
{  next cells in the free list to point to the head of the coalesced block.       }
{ ------------------------------------------------------------------------------------------- }
      var
            uSize, fSize : LINK;          {sizes of used and (right) free blocks}
            start : LINK;                 {address of left free block}
            prior, next : LINK;           {links in free block (which must be moved)}
      begin
         SetVal(p, 0);                              {set left tag}
         GetVal(p + SIZE_OFST, uSize);
         start := p + URTAG_OFST + uSize + 1;       {find start address of right block}
         GetVal(start + SIZE_OFST, fSize);
         SetVal(start + BACK_OFST + fSize, p);         {reset backlink}

         SetVal(p + SIZE_OFST, uSize + fSize + 3);     {set new size field}

         GetVal(start + PRIOR_OFST, prior);
         SetVal(p + PRIOR_OFST, prior);                {move prior field to left}
         GetVal(start + NEXT_OFST, next);
```

```
        SetVal(p + NEXT_OFST, next);                {move next field to left}

        SetVal(next + PRIOR_OFST, p);               {fix neighbors in free list to
                                                        point correctly}
        SetVal(prior + NEXT_OFST, p);
        if start = free then                    {and fix header, if it pointed to free block}
            free := p
    end;

    procedure CoalesceBoth (p : LINK);
{ ------------------------------------------------------------------------------------------ }
{   Merge the block at p with both its neighbors.  First, coalesce with its right }
{ neighbor to produce two adjacent free blocks, then merge them into one.         }
{ ------------------------------------------------------------------------------------------ }
        var
            rSize, lSize : LINK;                {sizes of coalesced block and left neighbor}
            start : LINK;                       {address of left free block}
            prior, next : LINK;
    begin
        CoalesceRight(p);
        GetVal(p - 2, start);                   {use backlink to find start of left neighbor}
        DeleteFromFreeList(start);              {left block will be coalesced, so delete
                                                    it from list}
        GetVal(p + SIZE_OFST, rSize);
        SetVal(p + BACK_OFST + rSize, start);       {reset right backlink}

        GetVal(p + PRIOR_OFST, prior);
        SetVal(start + PRIOR_OFST, prior);          {move prior field to left}
        GetVal(p + NEXT_OFST, next);
        SetVal(start + NEXT_OFST, next);            {move next field to left}

        SetVal(next + PRIOR_OFST, start);           {fix neighbors in free list to point
                                                        correctly}
        SetVal(prior + NEXT_OFST, start);
        if p = free then                        {fix header, if it pointed to right free block}
            free := start;

        GetVal(start + SIZE_OFST, lSize);
        SetVal(start + SIZE_OFST, lSize + rSize + 6);       {reset size field}
    end;
```

```
    procedure ChangeToFreeBlock (p : LINK);
{ ---------------------------------------------------------------------------------- }
{   Set the format of the used block at p to be that of a free block.  To           }
{  do this, fix tags, size, and make a backlink.  Don't worry about                 }
{  prior and next fields yet — they'll be set when we add to free list.             }
{ ---------------------------------------------------------------------------------- }
        var
            size : LINK;
    begin
        SetVal(p, 0);                           {set left tag}
        GetVal(p + SIZE_OFST, size);
        size := size - 3;                           {free block has 3 more links than
                                                        used — fix logical size}
        SetVal(p + SIZE_OFST, size);                {set new size}
        SetVal(p + BACK_OFST + size, p);            {set back link}
        SetVal(p + FRTAG_OFST + size, 0);           {set right tag}
    end;

  begin {DisposePtr}
    leftFree := false;
    if p > 1 then                           {is there any block at all to the left?}
        begin
            GetVal(p - 1, tag);             {... if so, look at its right tag}
            leftFree := (tag = 0)           {... and use that to tell if its free}
        end;

    GetVal(p + SIZE_OFST, thisSize);

    rightFree := false;                     {now check right neighbor in a similar way}
    if p + URTAG_OFST + thisSize + 1 < HEAPSIZE then
        begin
            GetVal(p + URTAG_OFST + thisSize + 1, tag);
            rightFree := (tag = 0)
        end;

    if leftFree then                        {do any coalescing necessary}
        if rightFree then
            CoalesceBoth(p)
        else
            CoalesceLeft(p)
    else if rightFree then
        CoalesceRight(p)
    else
        begin
            ChangeToFreeBlock(p);
            AddToFreeList(p)            {just include in free list if both neighbors used}
        end;
  end;
```

```
{============= S I M U L A T I O N   R O U T I N E S ==================}

   procedure Initialize (var blockQ : Queue);

      begin
         blockQ.size := 0:              {no blocks awaiting release yet}
         unfilled := 0                  {and initialize a global statistics variable}
      end;


   procedure BuildRequest (var size, duration : integer);
{ ---------------------------------------------------------------------------------------- }
{   Choose random size and lifetime for a new block request. This uses a                   }
{  system function, Random, which is not a standard Pascal feature.  If you                }
{  don't have it available, see Appendix C on how to write your own.                       }
{ ---------------------------------------------------------------------------------------- }
      const
         TERMS = 121;                   {gives will give an average block request of 64}
         MAXDURATION = 150;
   begin
      size := 4 + Random mod MAXSIZE;
      duration := 1 + Random mod MAXDURATION
   end;

   procedure Enqueue (p : LINK;
         duration, cycle : integer;
         var bQ : Queue);
{ ---------------------------------------------------------------------------------------- }
{   Add the pointer p and its duration to bQ, in order of time out.                        }
{ ---------------------------------------------------------------------------------------- }
      var
         qR : QRec;
         i, j : integer;
         done : boolean;
   begin
      qR.timeOut := cycle + duration;
      qR.addr := p;

      i := 1;
      done := false;
      while not done do       {traverse queue until out of room or find lower timeout}
         if (i > QMAX) or (i > bQ.size) then
            done := true
         else if bQ.elt[i].timeOut <= qR.timeOut then
            done := true
         else
            i := i + 1;
```

```
        if i <= QMAX then                         {insert new element at position i}
            begin
                bQ.size := bQ.size + 1;
                for j := bQ.size downto i + 1 do
                    bQ.elt[j] := bQ.elt[j - 1];
                bQ.elt[i] := qR
            end
        else
            writeln('Ran out of room on queue at time ', cycle : 1)
    end;

    procedure Dequeue (var bQ : Queue;
            cycle : integer;
            var p : LINK);
{ ------------------------------------------------------------------------------------------ }
{  Check whether are any blocks due to be released this cycle and return    }
{   a pointer to one if there is                                                              }
{ ------------------------------------------------------------------------------------------ }
        var
            head : QRec;
    begin
        if bQ.size = 0 then                                   {trying to inspect empty queue}
            p := 0
        else
            begin
                head := bQ.elt[bQ.size];                     {element to be removed next}
                if head.timeOut <= cycle then              {time for head element to leave yet?}
                    begin
                        p := head.addr;                       {if so, return it}
                        bQ.size := bQ.size - 1             {and remove it from the queue}
                    end
                else
                    p := 0                                      {if not, signal nothing ready yet}
            end
    end;

    procedure PrintStats (cycle : integer);
{ ------------------------------------------------------------------------------------------ }
{   Traverse the heap, counting used blocks, free blocks and free space.    }
{  Print a stistical summary of the present state of the heap.                 }
{ ------------------------------------------------------------------------------------------ }
        const
            NUM_SLOTS = 819;                               {size of the distribution array}
        var
            freeSpace, numFree, numUsed : integer;
            p, i : integer;
            size : integer;
            span, lower, slot : integer;
            dist : array[1..SLOTS] of integer;
```

```
begin
   if cycle mod REPORT_EVERY = 0 then          {is it time to report?}
      begin
         writeln('STATISTICS AT CYCLE ', cycle : 1);
         freeSpace := 0;
         numFree := 0;
         numUsed := 0;

         span := HEAPSIZE DIV SLOTS;            {number of sizes represented
                                                      by each array element}
         for i := 1 to SLOTS do
            dist[i] := 0;                     {initialize free block distribution array}
         p := 1;
         while p < HEAPSIZE do
            begin
               if Heap[p] = 1 then                      {it's a used block}
                  begin
                     numUsed := numUsed + 1;
                     size := Heap[p + 1];
                     p := p + 3 + size                  {go to next block}
                  end
               else if Heap[p] = 0 then                 {it's a free block}
                  begin
                     numFree := numFree + 1;
                     size := Heap[p + 1];
                     freeSpace := freeSpace + size;
                     slot := 1 + (size - 1) div span;    {decide where to count
                                                              the size of this block}
                     dist[slot] := dist[slot] + 1;          {... and update the
                                                              distribution array}
                     p := p + 6 + size {go to next block}
                  end
               else                           {something is badly wrong — tag ≠ 0, 1}
                  begin
                     writeln(TSomething is not right in the heap at T, p : 1);
                     p := HEAPSIZE                 {force abnormal termination}
                  end
            end;

         if p <> HEAPSIZE then
            begin
               writeln;
               writeln('   Number of used blocks : ', numUsed : 1);
               writeln('   Number of free blocks : ', numFree : 1);
               writeln('   Total free space : ', freeSpace : 1);
               if numFree > 0 then
                  writeln('   Average free block size : ', (freeSpace / numFree) :
                                 6 : 1);
```

```
                    writeln('  Fraction of unfilled requests : ', 100.0 * (unFilled / cycle)
                                          : 5 : 2, '%U');
                    writeln;

                    writeln('    Distribution of free block sizes :');
                    lower := 1;
                    for i := 1 to NUM_SLOTS do
                        begin
                            if dist[i] > 0 then
                                writeln('        ', lower : 4, '-', lower + span - 1 : 4, '    ',
                                        dist[i]);
                            lower := lower + span
                        end
                end;

            writeln;
            writeln;
        end
    end;

{========================= PROGRAM BODY ==========================}

begin
    Initialize(blockQ, cycle);

    for cycle := 1 to MAXTIME do
        begin
            BuildRequest(size, duration);            {get a new request each cycle}

            p := NewPtr(size);
            if p <> 0 then                           {NewPtr succeeded}
                Enqueue(p, duration, cycle, blockQ);

            Dequeue(blockQ, cycle, p);
            while p <> 0 do
                begin
                    DisposePtr(p, q);               {dispose of any block which is to be freed}
                    Dequeue(blockQ, cycle, p);      {... and see if there are any others}
                end;
            PrintStats(cycle);
        end
end.
```

3.5 SUMMARY

The LIST ADT is structurally identical to STRING, in that each element of LIST consists of a linearly ordered set of positions, with each position associated with a single atom. Unlike STRING, however, the LIST ADT has operations that are primarily concerned with individual items in a list, rather than contiguous subcollections.

This chapter explored the three principal implementations of LIST: arrays, linked lists, and cursors. The operations in the array implementation are fast and conceptually simple, but suffer from the fact that the sizes of the lists being considered must all be no greater than some predeclared limit. Insertion and deletion within an array also suffer from the fact that they are not constant-time operations. With pointers, many of the array shortcomings no longer appear, but this benefit is bought at the cost of the relative complexity of pointer-based algorithms. The cursor representation of lists represents a compromise between array and pointer representations, since cursors are logically equivalent to pointers.

If the set ATOM itself has a linear order, the items in a list may be maintained in sorted order. This structure allows us to define an algorithm that tests for membership in a list in logarithmic time, although it requires an array implementation of LIST, and hence insertion and deletion are slow.

Two-way lists and braids are extensions of one-way, singly linked lists. They are sometimes useful. Enough said.

A natural use for lists is to maintain a free list of available blocks in a heap where memory is allocated and deallocated dynamically. We introduced the boundary tag method, which required tag fields at both ends of each block, in order to facilitate the process of finding free neighbors of a block to be deallocated and coalescing adjacent free blocks. This is by no means the only way to handle memory management. In the exercises we explore an alternative strategy.

3.6 EXERCISES

1. Define *Prior* in terms of *Next, First,* and *Empty,* and give a big-O timing estimate, assuming that *Next, First,* and *Empty* run in constant time.
2. Show that if $L = (P, R, v)$, $p \in P$, $a \in$ ATOM, then *InsertAfter(a, p, L)* has the effect of changing L to $L' = (P', R', v'$, where $P' = P + [q]$, q is a position not in P, and R' is defined by
   (a) $x\, R'\, y = x\, R\, y$, if $x, y \neq q$,
   (b) $q\, R'\, y = p\, R\, y$, if $y \neq p, q$,
   (c) $q\, R'\, p = false$
   (d) $x\, R'\, q = x\, R\, p$, if $x \neq q$,
   (e) $p\, R'\, q = true$,
   (f) $q\, R'\, q = true$.

   You might find it helpful to restate these conditions informally, so that (a) would be stated "for any *x, y* in the old list, *x* was 'before' *y* in the old list, if and only if *x* is still 'before' *y* in the new list."
3. Consider the function **FindNth**(n : integer ; L : LIST) : POSITION, which returns the position corresponding to the *n*th location in *L*. Implement this function in both array and linked list forms, and give timing estimates for each.
4. Another generalization of *Find* is the function **FindFrom**(a : ATOM ; p : POSITION ; L : LIST) : POSITION, which returns the position of the first occurrence of *a* in *L* at or after *p*. Provide a definition and timing estimates for this function in the linked list implementation.

5. Suppose we changed the array implementation of LIST to include a special atom, GONE, so that deleting the element in position i from an array was accomplished by replacing the atom at that position by GONE. Discuss the advantages and disadvantages of such a scheme, particularly in terms of timing and the definition of the LIST operations.
6. Define *Reverse* for linked lists, and compare its efficiency with that of the array implementation given in the text.
7. Write a definition of *Delete* for linked lists that deletes the cell pointed to by p by moving the contents of the cell following p into the p cell, and then deleting the cell following the p cell.
8. Provide the simplest description you can of the action of *Reverse* in terms of the (P, R, v) notation for lists.
9. Write a procedure that would dispose of every cell in a linked list.
10. In this chapter we defined the cursor equivalent of *New*. Implement the cursor equivalent of *Dispose*.
11. Implement *InsertAfter*
    (a) for two-way linked lists.
    (b) for two-braids.
12. Surprisingly, you don't need two pointers per cell to be able to traverse a linked list in both directions, as long as you can perform bitwise logical operations on addresses. The technique is quite clever, albeit somewhat limited in scope.

    Suppose x and y are two binary digits; we can define the operation $\oplus$ (known as XOR, or "exclusive or") by $1 \oplus 1 = 0$, $0 \oplus 0 = 0$, $1 \oplus 0 = 1$, and $0 \oplus 1 = 1$, and for two binary numbers n and m, we define $n \oplus m$ to be the result of applying XOR to the corresponding bits of the numbers, so that $010111 \oplus 111101 = 101010$. (Do you see why this operation is sometimes called "add without carry?")

    To form a linked list in this scheme, each cell at address p has a single link field, *link(p)*, and the first and last cells in the list have a dummy prior cell at "address)'' 0. To traverse a list, starting at the cell at p, one uses the following algorithm:

```
procedure Traverse(p : Pointer);
   var save, prior : Pointer;
begin
   prior := 0;
   while p <> 0 do begin
      Visit the cell at p, doing any necessary processing;
      save := p;
      p :=prior E link(p);
      prior := save
   end
end;
```

    (a) Show that this works by tracing the action of *Traverse* in both directions on the list of cells at locations 19, 30, 28, 39, 46 (in that order), where the link fields are defined by *link*(19) = 30, *link*(30) = 15, *link*(28) = 57, *link*(39) = 50, and *link*(46) = 39. Of course, you'll have to convert all these numbers to 6-bit binary numbers.
    (b) What would the link cells have to be for the linked list of cells at locations 40, 8, 6, 50, 19 (in that order)?

(c) Explain why this scheme would not be particularly good on lists that would be changed by insertions and deletions.

13. Implement *Update* for SORTED_LIST.

14. **(a)** How many probes would a binary search require to find an element in a list of 16 million elements?

(b) Trace the action of *Find*(70, *L*) on the sorted list *L* = (4, 6, 11, 17, 18, 26, 38, 40, 44, 51, 66, 78, 102, 141, 142, 166, 208).

15. We usually assume that an element in SORTED_LIST will not have any two keys with the same value. If there are duplicate keys, how are the actions of *Locate* and *Insert* affected?

16. An **interpolation search** is somewhat like a binary search, except that the probe into a sublist is not always made at the middle element of the sublist. Instead, probes are made into the location where the atom a is "expected" to be, so, for instance, if a is two-thirds of the way from a_{low} to a_{high}, then *middle* would be set to the location two-thirds of the way from *low* to *high*.

(a) Implement the interpolation search version of *Find*.

(b) Trace the action of this function by searching for 70 in the list (1, 2, 3, . . . , 1000), and in the list in Exercise 14(b).

(c) For what kinds of lists would interpolation searches be inefficient?

17. Most computers restrict the size of integers that can be represented in memory. Usually, the largest possible integer is the largest one that can be expressed as a word of 16 or 32 binary digits. Since integers have a linear structure, with the hundreds digit before the tens digit, which in turn is before the units digit, it would be natural to regard an integer as a list of digits (which we can take in base 10 to be the numbers 0 through 9).

(a) Describe an implementation of such **multiprecision** integers. You might want to consider the relative merits of arrays versus linked lists, and whether it would be better to put the low-order digits (the units place) at the head or the tail of the list. To make life simpler, you might want to restrict your attention to positive integers.

(b) Using your implementation of part (a), write **Add**, which takes two multiprecision integers and produces another equal to their sum.

(c) As in part (b), write an implementation of **Multiply**.

18. Suppose that a heap contained free blocks of sizes 200, 50, and 100 bytes, and that the blocks were arranged in that order in the free list, starting with the 200-byte block. Suppose also that requests for new blocks of sizes 100, 80, 50, and 70 bytes came in in that order (i.e., first request for 100, second for 80, and so on). Describe the contents of the free list at each stage under (a) the first fit and (b) the best fit selection strategies.

19. For the free list of Exercise 18, give a sequence of requests

(a) that can be satisfied using first fit, but not best fit.

(b) that can be satisfied by best fit, but not first fit.

20. We mentioned that a shortcoming of first fit is that over the long run it tends to produce a large collection of tiny blocks at the start of the free list. How might you remedy this problem? *Hint*: The sample program at the end of Section 3.4 contains a partial remedy.

21. Discuss the advantages and disadvantages of keeping the free list sorted by address. Does such a choice allow you to dispense with any of the block fields?

22. Is memory management appreciably simpler if all requests are the same size? Explain by describing a data structure you would use and then implementing *NewPtr* and *DisposePtr* for your data structure.

23. Describe an implementation of memory management in which the heap contained 2^{20} (= 1048576) bytes, and every request for a new block was either of size 2^8 (= 256) or 2^{16} (= 65536) bytes. Try to make your implementations as efficient as possible, in terms of both time and space.

24. Another common memory management scheme, the **buddy system**, is somewhat similar to the one described in Exercise 23. In this scheme, the heap consists of 2^m bytes, addressed from 0 to $2^m - 1$, and no matter what the size of the request, space is always allocated in blocks of physical size 2^k, for $k \leq m$. There are several free lists, one for each block size 2^k, and initially all free lists are empty, except for the one of size 2^m. Each block contains a used/free tag and a size field, containing the power of 2 that represents the size of the block, and free blocks contain the usual *prior* and *next* fields. One advantage of this scheme is that finding the start of a block is easy: Any block of size 2^k begins at address $p2^k$, for some integer p. Such a block can be split into two blocks of size 2^{k-1}, which are called **left** and **right buddies**, so that the left buddy begins at address $p2^k$, and the right buddy begins at address $p2^k + 2^{k-1}$.

(a) Show that, under this scheme, a block of size 2^{k-1} that begins at address $p2^{k-1}$ is a left buddy (as a result of being split off earlier) if and only if p is even.

(b) If a block of size 16 begins at address 5024, is it a left or a right buddy, and where does its buddy begin? What if the block is of size 1,024?

Allocation in the buddy system is simple enough: If a request arrives, you compute the smallest block size 2^k that can fill the request, and then run up through the free lists of increasing size until you find an available block of size 2^j, with $j \geq k$. If $j > k$, remove that block from its free list, split that block into left and right buddies, add the right buddy to its free list, and continue the process, splitting the left buddy until the block size is 2^k, which can be used to fill the request.

(c) Show the results of filling requests for blocks of size 40, 300, 100, and 500 in a heap of size 4,096.

(d) Write *NewPtr* for the buddy system.

Deallocation frees a block and coalesces it with its free buddy (if it has one) into a larger block, which is also coalesced if it has a free buddy, and so on up.

(e) Suppose that after having allocated all the blocks in part (c), they were then released in the order in which they were allocated. Describe what would take place at each deallocation. Do the same thing assuming the blocks were released in opposite order.

(f) Write *DisposePtr* for the buddy system.

25. Write a compaction algorithm without worrying about how to deal with changing pointer references.

26. Do Exercise 25, worrying. One strategy you might consider is **double indirection**, in which a request for a new block is filled as usual, but the address returned is not the address of the allocated block but, rather, the address of a **master pointer**, which always resides at a fixed location in memory, and which actually contains the address of the allocated block, as in Figure 3.15.(See page 113.) Relocatable blocks in the heap can be moved to compress memory, but master pointers never move.

27. If, somehow, memory requests are known in advance, there is an elegant way to determine the best possible memory use. Suppose that we have n requests with sizes $r_1, \ldots, r_n$ and total available memory M. We will assume that $r_i \leq M$ for $i = 1, \ldots, n$ (otherwise, there's no sense in even considering the request). We will consider the **knapsack problem**, finding the largest amount of memory which can be used by these requests, without

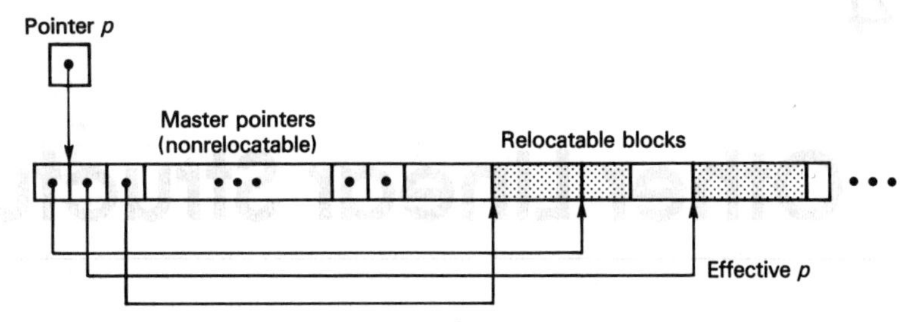

Figure 3.15 Memory management by double indirection.

exceeding M. We first let a be a bit vector, indexed from 0 to M, with initial values $a[0]$ = *true*, and $a[i]$ = *false* for $i = 1, \ldots, M$, and then run the following algorithm:

```
for i := 1 to n do
   for k := M downto r_i do
      a[k] := a[k] or a[k - r_i ];
```

Then, the maximum amount of memory that can be used by any combination of requests is the highest index of the a array that contains a *true* value.

(a) Run this algorithm for $n = 4, r_1 = 3, r_2 = 7, r_3 = 4, r_4 = 9, M = 15$, and use this sample run to explain in simple terms why the algorithm works.

(b) Would the algorithm work if the inner **for** loop went up from r_i **to** M, rather than **downto**?

(c) Modify the algorithm so that it not only told you the maximum amount to be allocated, but also which requests could be used to obtain that amount.

(d) How would you maximize the *number* of requests which could be filled, rather than the amount of memory used?

PROGRAMMING PROJECTS

28. Write a package of routines to do multiprecision arithmetic, as in Exercise 17, and use it to compute some big numbers, like 100! or 2^{200}.

29. Run the memory manager program and discuss the effects of changing **(a)** the average sizes of requests and **(b)** the average duration of a block on the distribution of free blocks, and on the proportion of filled requests.

30. Change the memory manager program to use a best fit strategy and repeat the tests of Exercise 27. If your system and language give you access to an internal clock, use that to compare the relative efficiencies of first fit and best fit.

31. Change the memory manager program to use a **worst fit** strategy, where all requests are filled from the *largest* free block available, and compare its performance with those of the other two selection strategies.

32. Change the memory manager to use a buddy system. *Note*: You'll have to modify the statistics routines.

33. If your computer has graphics capabilities, modify the memory manager to display a memory map.

4

Other Linear Structures

And the rule for building shall be this: that no stone be placed but atop another and that no stone be removed but that it be the topmost.

Egyptian mason's instructions (c. 1230 B. C.)

Often, when writing programs, we find that the information used by the program has a natural linear form, but the application is such that we do not need the full set of LIST operations. In particular, it is frequently the case that inspection, modification, insertion, and deletion need only be performed at one or two locations in the list, typically at the head and the tail. Such restricted list structures occur often enough that they warrant consideration as separate ADTs. In this chapter, we will discuss two such structures in detail: stacks and queues.

4.1 THE ABSTRACT DATA TYPE STACK

A **stack** is, informally, nothing more than a list for which insertion, deletion, and inspection all take place at the head of the list. The standard metaphor of a stack is a plate-holder of the kind commonly found in cafeterias: Plates are stored in a well with a spring at the bottom, so that when the top plate is removed, the spring pushes the entire pile up just enough to allow the next plate to be accessed; and when a new plate (a clean one, supposedly) is added, its weight compresses the spring just enough so that it (and it alone) is accessible at the top. Like all metaphors, this is an approximation of truth: Don't be misled into thinking that the *data* move, as the plates do. There is no reason that the data elements must be advanced in memory: All we need to do is shift our *reference* to the top element. The metaphor does, however, enforce the idea that with a stack, the only directly accessible location is at the top of the stack.

In computer applications, stacks are commonly used as intermediate storage, and many computers have stacks wired in as part of their hardware, to provide fast and efficient stack manipulation. Consider, for example, what a computer must do when a routine calls a subroutine, like a procedure or a function: When the subroutine is called, the computer must save information such as the location in the calling routine where the call was made, along with the contents of any variables used in the calling routine (which is one reason that procedure calls can be time-consuming). Of course, the subroutine may itself call another routine, necessitating additional saving of information, and so on. One way to deal with all this storage of what are known as **activation records** is to store each record on a stack; then, when a subroutine call is complete, the contents of the top of the stack are available to provide orderly return to the calling routine, after which the activation record at the top of the stack is removed. As an example, suppose we had the following program skeleton:

```
    program Main;

       procedure A;

          procedure B;
          begin
             {do something}
          end;

       begin {Procedure A}
{4}       B      {i.e., call internal procedure B}
{5}    end;

       procedure C;
       begin
          {do something else}
       end;

{1} begin {Main program}
{2}    C;
{3}    A
{6} end.
```

When the main program begins execution (1), the first thing to be done is (2) a call to procedure C. The computer must store on the stack of activation records the present location in the main program, among other things, to know where to go when C is finished. Routine C then does whatever it does, and control is passed back to the main program, using the information stored in the activation stack. Upon reaching the call (3) to A, the main program information must again be saved to guarantee a safe return. In

A, however, there is another call, this time (4) to B, so the present location in A must be saved on the stack, along with the values of any of A's local variables. B runs to completion and returns control (5) to A, using the information on the top of the stack, which is no longer needed, and so is removed from the stack. A then returns control (6) to the main program, using the information on top of the stack, and the program halts. This sequence of stack operations is shown in the following diagram:

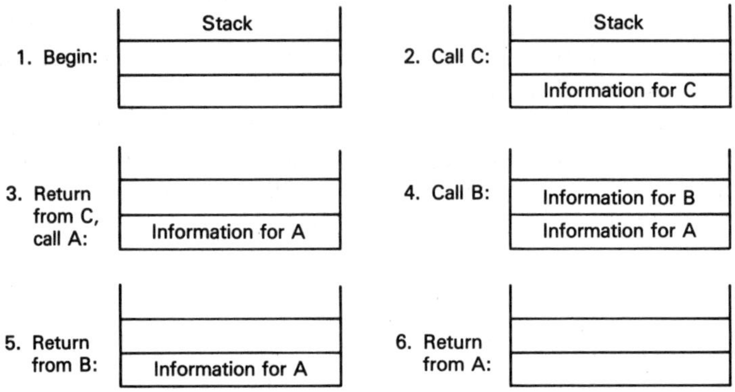

1. Begin:	Stack	2. Call C:	Stack
			Information for C

3. Return from C, call A:		4. Call B:	
			Information for B
	Information for A		Information for A

5. Return from B:		6. Return from A:	
	Information for A		

A stack is useful in this case because the last activation record placed on the stack is the first one to be used and discarded when control passes from the subroutine back to the calling routine. For this reason, because the element last added to a stack is the first one to be removed, stacks are called **last-in-first-out** (or **LIFO**) structures.

The STACK abstract data type has a particularly simple definition: A stack is structurally identical to a list, and includes the following primitive operations.

1. **Create**(**var** S : STACK), is, as usual, a procedure that creates a new, empty stack.
2. **Push**(a : ATOM ; **var** S : STACK), is a procedure that inserts the atom *a* at the top of the stack *S*. In terms of LIST operations, *Push(a, S)* is equivalent to *Insert-Before(a, First(S), S)*.
3. **Pop**(**var** S : STACK), is a procedure that removes, without inspection, the top element of the stack *S*. *Pop(S)* is the same as *Delete(First(S), S)*. In order to make any sense, this operation requires the precondition that the stack be nonempty, that is, that there be something on the stack to delete.
4. **Top**(S : STACK) : ATOM, is a function that returns, without deleting, the element at the top of the stack. Again, in terms of LIST operations, *Top(S)* is equivalent to *Retrieve(First(S), S)*, and this operation also requires the precondition that the stack be nonempty.
5. **Empty**(S : STACK) : boolean, is a **predicate** (i.e., a boolean function), which returns *true* if and only if *S* is empty. We could also define this in terms of LIST operations by observing that *Empty(S)* is the same as saying that *Length(S)* = 0.

There is a roughly even split among computer scientists about how to define the primitives for stacks. Those who would not prefer the primitives given here would combine *Pop* and *Top* into one operation, which returns the value of the top atom in the stack and also deletes that element from the stack. We have noted that computer science frequently involves choices based on informed personal assessment, and this is a good example: Combining the two operations into one has the advantage of simplicity, but it obscures the fact that there are two distinct operations possible. In fact, it makes no real difference which definition we choose, since the combined operation could be defined in terms of *Pop* and *Top*, both of which could be defined in terms of the combined operation. The only thing that should concern you is that not all authors use *Pop* the way we do here, so you need to be careful when reading other books.

As is the case with any ADT, we can write other operations in terms of the STACK primitives. For instance, we could define a procedure **Over** to make a copy of the second element in a stack and place the copy on top of the stack. Thus, if *S* contained the elements . . . *a b* (reading from bottom to top), then *Over(S)* would result in *S* being changed to . . . *a b a*. The definition could take the following form:

```
procedure Over(var S : STACK);
   var saveTop, saveSecond : ATOM;
begin
   if Empty(S) then
      writeln('stack too small for Over')
   else begin
      saveTop := Top(S);
      Pop(S);                           {remove top element to get at second}
      if Empty(S) then begin
         writeln('stack too small for Over');
         Push(saveTop, S)
      end else begin
         saveSecond := Top(S);
         Push(saveTop, S);              {restore old top element}
         Push(saveSecond, S)            {and put copy of second on top}
      end
   end
end;
```

It might appear that the abstract data type STACK is too simple to do anything but provide intermediate storage of the kind we mentioned earlier. To conclude this, however, would be to confuse elegance with triviality. As a matter of fact, there is a language, called FORTH, that uses the stack as its primary organizing structure. Your author takes no stand on the comparative merits of FORTH and, say, Pascal, except to note that there are a not insignificant number of FORTH adherents out there. Some of the exercises explore this language in more detail.

Notice that we included LIST equivalents of the STACK operations. This was done to point out the fact that we could completely avoid much of the work of the implementation of STACK if we had already written a LIST package. This high-level implementation has a lot to recommend it, particularly in light of the programmer's maxim, "Whenever possible, avoid reinventing the wheel." It is often more efficient just to refer to library routines than to write a program from scratch each time. We will define array and pointer implementations of STACK because of their simplicity, but bear this paragraph in mind if you find yourself faced with writing a STACK package, or any other implementation that is very similar to an already implemented data structure.

Array Implementation of STACK

In order to define STACK in terms of arrays, we need only maintain a cursor to a location in the array that will serve to indicate the location of the top of the stack.

```
const
   MAXSIZE = {size of largest possible stack};
type
   ATOM = {any data type};
   POSITION = 0 . . MAXSIZE;        {including zero as NULL pseudo-position}
   STACK = record
               top : POSITION;
               data : array [1 .MAXSIZE] of ATOM
            end;
```

A typical stack in this implementation would appear as follows:

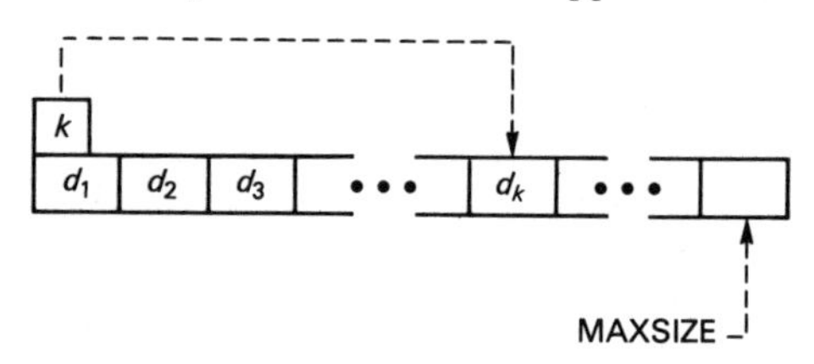

Notice that although we did not write the definition of STACK to include an analogue to the LIST operation *Length* (since the only time the size of the stack is of any interest to us is when it is zero), we get it for free in this implementation, since if S is a stack, then *S.top* contains the number of elements in S (since we use the zero pseudoposition to mark empty stacks). The primitives are almost trivial to write in this implementation.

```
1.   procedure Create(var S : STACK);
     begin
        S.top := 0
     end;
```

2.
```
procedure Push(a : ATOM ; var S : Stack);
begin
   if S.top = MAXSIZE then
      writeln('no room to Push')
   else begin
      S.top := S.top + 1;
      S.data[S.top] := a
   end
end;
```

3.
```
procedure Pop(var S : STACK);
begin
   if S.top = 0 then
      writeln('attempt to Pop empty stack')
   else
      S.top := S.top - 1
end;
```

4.
```
function Top(var S : STACK): ATOM;
begin
   if S.top = 0 then begin
      writeln('attempt to inspect empty stack');
      Top := 0
   end else
      Top := S.data[S.top]
end;
```

5.
```
function Empty(S : STACK) : boolean;
begin
   Empty := (S.length = 0)
end;
```

We had to be a little careful in the definition of *Push*. Although the description of STACK made no mention of size limitations of stacks, we know that whenever we are dealing with arrays, there is always the possibility that (at least in some languages) we could overrun the maximum, predeclared size. For the array implementation of STACK, it might be a good idea to include another, implementation-specific primitive predicate **Full**(S : STACK) : boolean, which returns *true* if and only if *S* contains the maximum allowable number of elements.

Stacks as Linked Lists

Despite the inherent complexity of pointer-based implementations, the pointer version of STACK is almost as easy to write as the array version. For simplicity, we will depart slightly from the implementation we used for LIST. We will define a linked list implementation of STACK without using a header record (since the bottom of the stack is of no interest to us), and instead will refer to a stack by a pointer to its top cell.

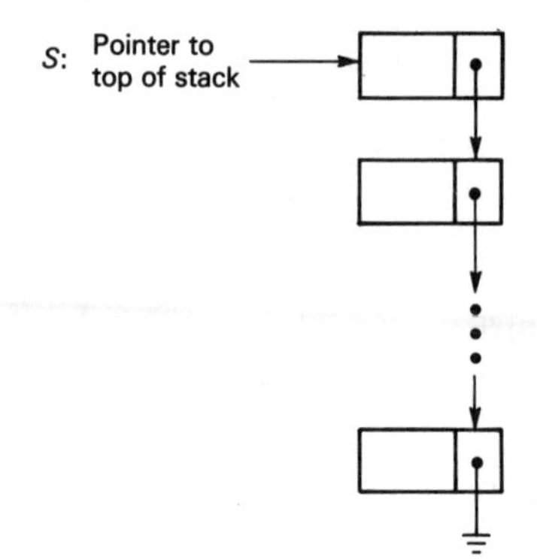

Figure 4.1 Pointer implementation of STACK.

A stack, in this implementation, takes the form shown in Figure 4.1. The definition of STACK in this implementation is as follows:

```
type
    ATOM = {any data structure};
    POSITION = ^StackCell;
    StackCell = record
                    data : ATOM;
                    next : POSITION
                end;
    STACK = POSITION;

procedure Create(var S : STACK);
begin
    S = nil
end;

procedure Push(a : ATOM ; var S : STACK);
    var temp : POSITION;
begin
    New(temp);
    temp^.data := a;
    temp^.next := S;
    S := temp
end;

procedure Pop(var S: STACK);
    var temp : POSITION;
begin
    if S = nil then
        writeln('attempted to Pop empty stack')
    else begin
        temp := S;
        S := S^.next;
        dispose(temp)
    end
end;
```

```
function Top(S : STACK) : ATOM;
begin
   if S = nil then begin
      writeln('attempted to inspect empty stack');
      Top := {some dummy atom}
   else
      Top := S^.data
end;

function Empty(S : STACK) : boolean;
begin
   Empty := (S = nil)
end;
```

Application 1: Postfix Arithmetic

We all learned early in our educational careers how to write and evaluate arithmetic expressions. Presumably, most of us would have little difficulty in evaluating an expression like $4 + 8 * (9 - 6)$. The answer (which you should be able to compute in less time than it takes to read this parenthetical expression) is 28. Most people could even describe the steps necessary to arrive at the answer, saying something like, "Subtract six from nine to get three, multiply that three by eight to get twenty-four, and add that to four to get twenty-eight." Things get a little more difficult, though, if we are asked *why* we performed the operations in the order we did. A typical answer to that question might be, "I did the subtraction first because it was inside the parentheses, then I did the multiplication before the addition because . . . well, because that's the way it's supposed to be done." If the questioner was really persistent (because of being six years old, for instance), and we were sufficiently patient, we might eventually come up with a set of rules, a sort of quasi-algorithm, which would run something like, "Evaluate from the most deeply buried parentheses outwards, and in case there are no parentheses to guide you, do multiplication and division before doing any additions and subtractions."

Well, this is pretty close to being a good enough description for human beings, despite the fact that it leaves out some details (like how we treat negation, such as the '–' in front of '–7', which is not quite the same as the '–' in the middle of '9 – 6', and what we do with exponents). Realizing that this book is about computer science, you have probably guessed that the next question will be "How do you specify your expertise, gained through years of experience and intuition, in a form precise enough for a computer?" We could do it, given enough time, but it would be complicated and tricky, as you might imagine. (How, for instance, do you tell the computer to find the most deeply nested parentheses?)

Interestingly enough, the difficulty stems entirely from the fact that we are burdened with an historical accident. For as long as people have been writing about arithmetic (and that's a *long* time — nearly four thousand years), arithmetic expressions, almost without exception, have been written in **infix notation**, in which the symbols for operations occur between the objects on which they operate. Nothing, however, except millennia of inertia, says that that is the only way to write and do arithmetic. It is quite possible to write our expressions in **postfix notation**, where the operators occur immediately *after* the objects on which they operate. In postfix notation the preceding expression would be written 4 8 9 6 − * +. We would read this expression from left to right until we came to an operator, in this case the subtraction symbol. Since each symbol operates on the numbers immediately preceding it, we would subtract 6 from 9 and replace 9 6 − by the result, 3. Our expression would then be 4 8 3 * +, and we would evaluate the next operator, replacing 8 3 * by its result to yield the new expression 4 24 +, which evaluates to 28. Seeing no more operators, we would know we were done. To do a longer problem is no more difficult.

Example

The infix expression (3 + 4 / 2) * (5 * 3 − 6) − 8 would be written in postfix form as 3 4 2 / + 5 3 * 6 − * 8 − (you can take that on faith for the time being) and would be evaluated as follows, where the subexpression being evaluated is highlighted:

3	**4**	**2**	**/**	+	5	3	*	6	-	*	8	-
		3	**2**	**+**	5	3	*	6	-	*	8	-
				5	**5**	**3**	*****	6	-	*	8	-
						5	**15**	**6**	**-**	*	8	-
								5	**9**	*****	8	-
										45	**8**	**-**
												37

It might take a bit of getting used to, but bear in mind that you have years of practice with infix arithmetic, and almost no practice with postfix (unless you own a calculator that is designed to use postfix notation). We did not introduce postfix notation just to provide a recondite example—there is a genuine benefit to be gained here. It is not difficult to show that *a correctly formed postfix expression is completely unambiguous.* We not only never need parentheses in a postfix expression, but we can completely dispense with the precedence rules that tell us that the answer to the infix expression 4 + 8 * 3 is equal to 28, rather than the 36 which we would get if we added first and then multiplied. There is only one rule to be used for postfix expressions: *Perform the operations from left to right, replacing as you go.* This is sufficiently simple that we can easily mechanize it. Suppose that *Post* is a list of **tokens**, which are objects that are either numbers or operators. The algorithm which follows will evaluate the postfix expression using a stack, *Eval*, to store numeric tokens awaiting operators.

```
function Evaluate_Postfix(Post : TokenList) : real;
{  Evaluates a postfix expression represented as a list of tokens.}
{ Assumes that the postfix expression is correctly formed.}
   var
      Eval : STACK ;
      topNumber, secondNumber, answer : real;
begin
   Create(Eval);
   while any tokens remain in Post do begin
      read a token, t
```

```
        if t is a number then
            Push(t, Eval)
        else begin                          { t is an operator:}
            topNumber := Top(Eval);         {get one operand,}
            Pop(Eval);
            secondNumber := Top(Eval);      {get the other operand,}
            Pop(eval);
            answer := secondNumber t topNumber; {perform the operation,}
            Push(answer, Eval)              {place the result on the stack}
        end
    end;
    Evaluate_Postfix := Top(Eval)           {out of tokens, return the answer}
end;
```

This is certainly simple, as the next example demonstrates, but it doesn't bring us appreciably closer to solving the problem of mechanizing the evaluation of infix expressions. What we need is a translation routine that would take an infix expression and return the equivalent postfix expression, which we could then evaluate by the algorithm we have just seen. That is exactly what we will do, but first you must be patient for a bit, while we introduce another abstract data type.

Example

We will trace the postfix evaluation routine on the expression that we used for the last example.

Unused postfix tokens	**Eval stack** (bottom →top)
3 4 2 / + 5 3 * 6 − * 8 −	(empty)
4 2 / + 5 3 * 6 − * 8 −	3
4 / + 5 3 * 6 − * 8 −	3 4
/ + 5 3 * 6 − * 8 −	3 4 2
+ 5 3 * 6 − * 8 −	3 2
5 3 * 6 − * 8 −	5
3 * 6 − * 8 −	5 5
* 6 − * 8 −	5 5 3
6 − * 8 −	5 15
− * 8 −	5 15 6
* 8 −	5 9
8 −	45
−	45 8
(empty)	37

Application 2: The Electronic Labyrinth

As we have seen, a stack may be the data structure of choice if we find ourselves in a situation where we need to provide intermediate storage, especially if the intermediate storage is such that the item most recently stored will be the first item to be inspected or removed from storage. Suppose, for instance, that we wished to write a program that would find a way out of a maze, a task that is well known to players of fantasy role-playing games. Perhaps the most obvious strategy would be to mark the rooms visited (think of dropping bread crumbs, as Hansel and Gretel did) and also keep track of the rooms visited so far in the order in which they were visited. If we come to a room with no adjacent unvisited rooms, we would then "backtrack" to the previously visited room, and check whether there were any adjacent unvisited rooms. We would then continue as before, either going to an unvisited room or backtracking again.

The example we will use will consist of a maze with eight rooms, connected as shown in Figure 4.2, where we start in room number 1 and wish to finish in room number 8. To write our maze-tracing algorithm, we will use a bit vector *visited*[*i*], where $0 < i \leq N$, and N is equal to the number of rooms, to keep track of the rooms already visited. The entry *visited*[*k*] will be *true* if room k has been visited, and *false* otherwise. We will also maintain a stack, S, consisting of the rooms visited so far, in order, which we will use in case it becomes necessary to backtrack. Upon a successful completion, it will turn out that S will contain a path, without duplication of rooms, from *start* to *finish*.

One way to conceptualize such a process is to use a **solution tree**, which not only describes all possible paths, but also gives the relations between the paths. For our example, the solution tree would take the form diagrammed in Figure 4.3. In this tree, each **node** represents a partial solution, that is, a path from room 1 to another room without any duplication of rooms. The rectangular boxes, like the one representing the path 1, 4, 6, 8, denote complete solutions—paths from room 1 to room 8. In the solution tree, any node representing a partial solution is linked to nodes below it that represent solutions that may be reached from that partial solution. For example, the node 1, 4, 6 leads to the further solutions 1, 4, 6, 5 and 1, 4, 6, 8.

Not only does the solution tree provide a systematic means of describing all three complete solutions, it also allows us to describe the maze-tracing algorithm. For instance, beginning at node 1, we might then move to room 2, which would be described by the node 1, 2. Notice that in this example, the labels of the nodes also describe the contents of the stack S of rooms visited in each path. From node 1, 2 there is only one possible "legal" move, namely to room 3, giving us the partial solution 1, 2, 3. From that node, there are no legal moves, so it is necessary for us to backtrack from room 3 to room 2. In stack terms, we would pop the stack, eliminating room 3 from our solution path. We find that there are no legal moves from room 2, since from node 1, 2 the only other solution is 1, 2, 3, which we had already discovered was a dead end. We then have to backtrack once more, pop the stack again, and start fresh from node 1.

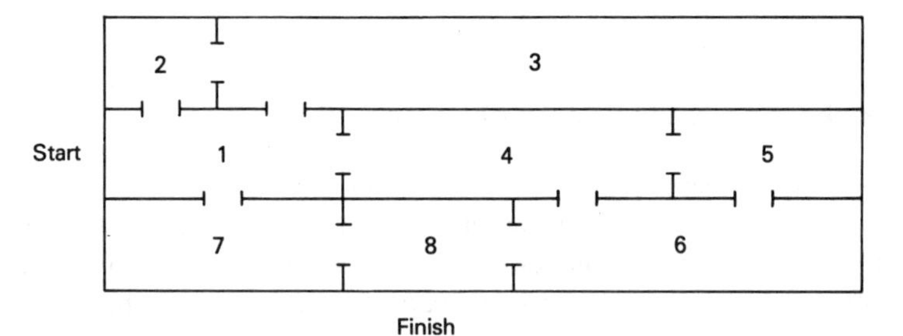

Figure 4.2 A maze.

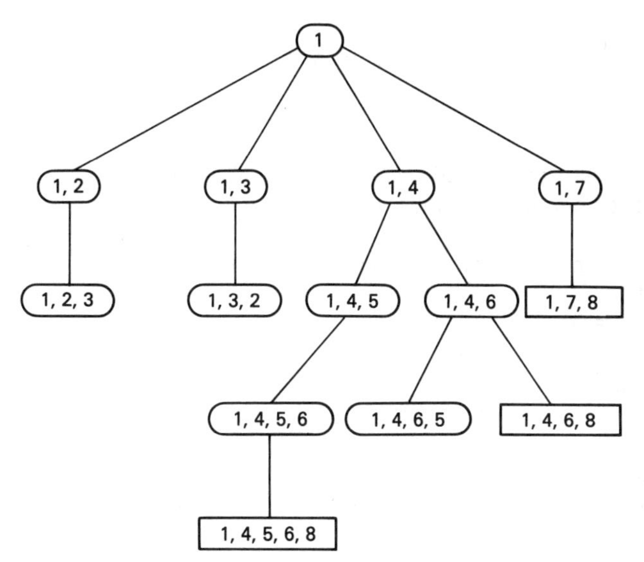

Figure 4.3 The solution tree of the maze of Figure 4.2.

It is easy to see that our maze-tracing algorithm will eventually produce a solution, if there is any at all. In technical terms, our algorithm represents a **depth-first search** through the solution tree. In a depth-first search (about which we will say much more in Chapter 8), we begin at the top of the tree and go as far down as we can. If we find a solution, fine, we stop there, but if we fail to find a solution we back up the tree until we come to the first unused branch, then take that branch and again go down as far as possible, continuing the process of descent and backtracking until we either reach a solution or have visited every node in the tree. Having done the preliminary work, it is now easy to describe the maze-tracing algorithm.

```
procedure MazeTraverse(start, finish : integer);
{ Depth-first search for a path from start to finish in a maze with N rooms.}
   const
         NULL = 0;        {flag for no available rooms to visit}
   var   visited : array [1 .. N] of boolean;
         now, next : integer;
         done, success : boolean;
         S : STACK; {of integers}
begin
   Create(S);
   initialize visited[i] := false , for i = 1 . . N ;
   done := false;
   now := start;                        { now is the room we are currently in}
   visited[now] := true;
   Push(now, S);
```

```
    while not done do
        if now = finish then begin        {found a solution path}
            done := true;
            success := true
        end else begin
            Set next to be an unvisited room adjacent to now , or NULL, if no such rooms;
            if next = NULL then begin          {must backtrack, no unvisited rooms from now }
                    Pop(S);
                if Empty(S) then begin{can't backtrack, report failure}
                    done := true;
                    success := false
                end else {backtrack}
                    now := Top(S)
            end else begin                     {go onwards}
                now := next;
                visited[now]:=true;
                Push(now, S)
            end
        end;
    if success then                   {print the solution}
        while not Empty(S) do begin
            writeln('found the following path:');
            writeln(Top(S));
            Pop(S)
        end
    else
        writeln('there is no path from ', start, ' to ', finish)
end;
```

Notice that we haven't mentioned how we will find an unvisited room adjacent to the room we are now in. We can't do that because we have not described how to represent the maze, so we have another data structure choice to make, which we will not make here, but will postpone until Chapter 8, when we will discover that we can consider such a maze as an example of the **GRAPH** ADT. Without going into details, however, we can see what would happen if our algorithm always chose the lowest numbered unvisited room adjacent to the one we were currently in. We would start at room 1, go to room 2, then to room 3, backtrack through rooms 2 and 1, continue to room 4, then to room 5, then to room 6, and finally arrive in room 8, the exit. In the solution tree, then, we would visit the following nodes: 1; 1, 2; 1, 2, 3; 1, 2; 1; 1, 4; 1, 4, 5; 1, 4, 5, 6; and 1, 4, 5, 6, 8. This solution requires us to visit eight rooms, counting backtracks, before we come to the exit. In this case, and in many others, this backtracking technique is not very efficient. When we return to this problem, it will be in a context in which we will be able to find a far better solution.

Notice, also, that this algorithm may not necessarily find the best (that is, the shortest) path from *start* to *finish*. Choosing to visit the lowest numbered unvisited room, as we did, gave the path 1, 4, 5, 6, 8, which is much longer than the best path 1, 7, 8. This is a deficiency that we will also remedy later.

4.2 QUEUES

A **queue** is a linear data structure for which insertions are made at one end and deletions and inspections at the other end. Unlike stacks, which are most commonly used as tools to provide intermediate storage in a program, queues are also frequently used to model real-world situations in a program. It would probably be safe to say that queue-like structures are more common in daily life than are stack-like structures. A typical modeling use would be to simulate the action of a car wash, in which cars enter the driveway from one end, move up in turn to the wash bay, are serviced, and leave. The owner of the car wash might be interested in how large a driveway to construct, given that, on one hand, pavement is expensive, but, on the other hand, turning cars away because of lack of room is not good for business. If we could obtain data on how frequently cars arrive and how these arrival times are distributed (perhaps by watching a competitor's business for a few weeks), we could use this information to construct a computer model of the car wash, the output of which might help the owner to decide how long the driveway should be. Such models are commonly employed when it would be impractical or expensive to use the real activity as a test (the owner might very well go broke in the time it would take to use the car wash itself to provide statistics).

In a queue, the first element to arrive is the first one to leave, and for this reason a queue is sometimes referred to as a **first-in-first-out** (or **FIFO**) structure. The patients in a doctor's office, people waiting for tickets to a theater, and potato chips on a grocery shelf are all examples of queues. (The potato chips are an example of a queue because it is a good idea to sell the oldest chips first, before they have a chance to get too stale, thereby making it necessary to add new bags behind the old ones. [Now you know how to pick the freshest bags.] As a matter of fact, a dirty trick sometimes played by unscrupulous potato chip distributors is to reverse the order of bags in their competitors' displays, placing the scrungy stale chips at the back in expectation of a run on their competitors' chips. The contents of a chip dip container, on the other hand, are an example of a stack, since the most recently added dip is the first you eat.)

It is worth noting in passing that a hospital emergency room is not exactly a queue, since a person requiring immediate attention might be served before someone with a minor complaint, even if that person arrived earlier than the one with the serious problem. Such a structure is called a **priority queue**, and will be discussed later.

In more precise terms, the QUEUE abstract data type has a linear structure on its elements and is supported by the following operations:

1. **Create**(**var** Q : QUEUE) sets *Q* to be empty.
2. **Enqueue**(a : ATOM ; **var** Q : QUEUE) is a procedure that, like *Push* for stacks, inserts the atom *a* into a new position at the tail of the queue *Q*.
3. **Dequeue**(**var** Q : QUEUE) removes the position at the head of the queue. This operation, like *Pop*, requires the precondition that the queue be nonempty.
4. **Head**(Q : QUEUE) : ATOM, is a function that returns, without deleting, the atom in the head position, that is, the atom in the position that will next be deleted by *Dequeue*.

5. **Empty**(Q : QUEUE) : boolean returns *true* if and only if there are no positions in Q, that is to say, if Q is empty.

As we noted with stacks, it is possible to define all of the queue primitives in terms of the LIST operations, rather than implementing them specifically. We will discuss array and pointer implementations of QUEUE, however, since both provide some interesting details.

Array Implementations of QUEUE

The simplest way to implement QUEUE by arrays would be to maintain two cursors, *head* and *tail*, with, say, $head \le tail$. Then, to enqueue an atom onto a queue, we would increment *tail* by one and place the new element in the "tail" cell of the array. To dequeue, we would simply increase *head* by one, as in Figure 4.4.
The problem is that each *Enqueue* causes the queue to grow to the right in the array, eventually leading to a situation in which the next Enqueue will cause the queue to "fall off" the right end of the array, even though there may be plenty of space available at the left end. It would not be too difficult to deal with such a situation—all we would have to do is watch the tail cursor, and as soon as an *Enqueue* operation would cause the tail cursor to exceed the maximum size of the array, simply shift the entire queue so that it would be aligned as far to the left as possible. This would make *Enqueue* and *Dequeue* $O(1)$ operations most of the time, but occasionally would introduce a factor of $O(n)$ for *Enqueue*, where n is the size of the array. In fact, although it is beyond the scope of this book to prove, such a scheme is not all that bad in practice. If we assume that there is a long random sequence of *Enqueue*'s and *Dequeue*'s, where each operation is equally likely to be chosen, then the *average* time for *Enqueue* is only $O(\log n)$ on arrays of size n. In other words, *Enqueue* will not require shifts too frequently, and when it does the number of elements to be shifted will be relatively small. Still, such a scheme does complicate the programming job a little, and it would be nice to find a way to avoid shifting entirely.

Instead of thinking of an array as a snake laid out on the ground with its head at one end and its tail at the other, suppose we forced the snake to bite its own tail, so that its head and tail were adjacent. In such a **circular array** we would never have to deal with the possibility that *Enqueue* would force us to shift the queue to the left—the queue would continue to migrate around the circle, as in Figure 4.5.

Notice that we have departed slightly from the convention we made earlier that both *head* and *tail* refer to occupied cells. Instead, *head* refers to the location of the head element in the queue, and *tail* refers to the location after the tail element in the

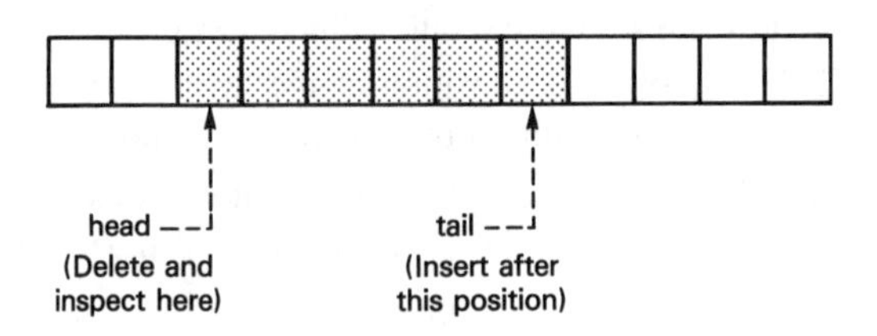

Figure 4.4 Array implementation of QUEUE.

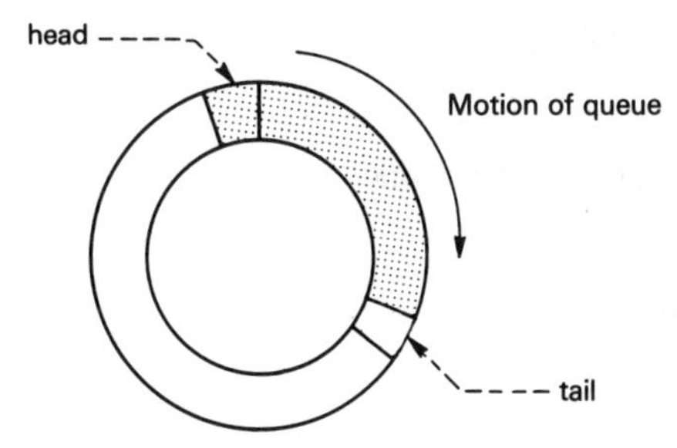

Figure 4.5 Circular array implementation of QUEUE.

queue, so that *head* and *tail* point to locations at which dequeueing and enqueueing, respectively, will take place. We can tell the size of the queue easily enough by a computation involving the difference between the tail and head cursors, with one exception: We will need a variable that tells us whether the queue is empty or full, because in both cases the head and tail cursors refer to the same location. With these facts in mind, it is easy to provide the declarations and descriptions of the primitives for this implementation.

```
const
   QMAX = {some positive integer};
type
   ATOM = {any data type};
   POSITION = 1 . . QMAX;
   QUEUE = record
                  empty : boolean;
                  head, tail : POSITION;
                  data : array [POSITION] of ATOM
               end;


procedure Create(var Q : QUEUE);
begin
   Q.empty := true;
   Q.head := 1;
   Q.tail := 1
end;

procedure Enqueue(a : ATOM ; var Q : QUEUE);
begin
   if (Q.head = Q.tail) and not Q.empty then   {queue is full}
      writeln('queue full, cannot Enqueue')
   else begin
      Q.data[Q.tail] := a;
      Q.tail := 1 + (Q.tail mod QMAX);
      Q.empty := false
   end
end;
```

```
procedure Dequeue(var Q : QUEUE);
begin
   if Q.empty then
      writeln('queue empty, cannot Dequeue')
   else begin
      Q.head := 1 + (Q.head mod QMAX);
      if Q.head = Q.tail then
         Q.empty := true
   end
end;

function Head(Q : QUEUE) : ATOM;
begin
   if Q.empty then begin
      writeln('queue empty, cannot inspect Head');
      Head := {some atom}
   end else
      Head := Q.data[Q.head]
end;

function Empty(Q : QUEUE) : boolean;
begin
   Empty := Q.empty
end;
```

It is easy to see that all these primitives run in constant time in this implementation. The only part of these declarations that should need explanation is the increment used in *Enqueue* and *Dequeue*. We imagine the array as wrapped around so that the indices visited in order would be 1, 2, . . . , *QMAX*, 1, 2, ... In all cases except $i = QMAX$, we can increment i by setting i to $1 + i$. If $i = QMAX$, we want the increment to set i to 1. If we observe that for $i = 1, \ldots, QMAX - 1$ we have $i = (i \textbf{ mod } QMAX)$, and that $(i \textbf{ mod } QMAX) = 0$ when $i = QMAX$, we see that $i := 1 + (i \textbf{ mod } QMAX)$ will serve to increment i in either case.

Pointer Implementation of QUEUE

If we did not know ahead of time how large our queues would be, a logical choice for implementation would be a linked list; the only question would be where to put the head and tail locations. Since insertion is equally easy in either location, but deletion is fastest at the front of a linked list, it makes good sense to adopt the convention that the head of the queue will be at the head of the linked list, as shown. The only peculiar aspect of this implementation is that the pointers point in a direction opposite to the apparent motion of elements in the queue, from tail to head:

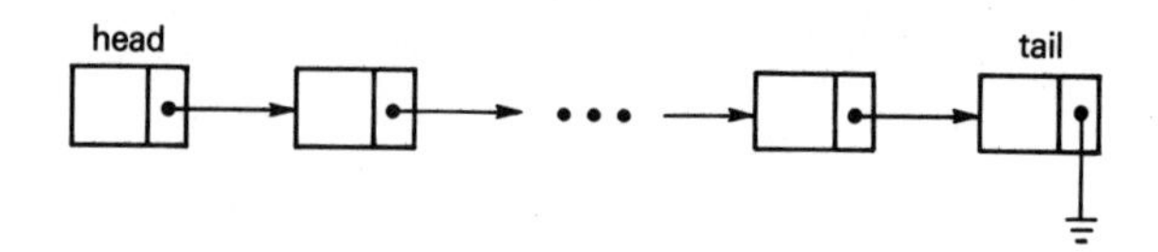

The pointer implementation of QUEUE is very similar to that of LIST, as can be seen:

```
type
   ATOM = {any data type};
   POSITION = ^Cell;
   Cell = record
              data : ATOM;
              next : POSITION
          end;
   QUEUE = record
              head, tail : POSITION                  {could include a field for length, too}
          end;


procedure Create(var Q : QUEUE);
begin
   Q.head := nil;
   Q.tail := nil
end;

procedure Enqueue(a : ATOM ; var Q : QUEUE);
   var  temp : POSITION;
begin
   New(temp);
   temp^.data := a;
   temp^.next := nil;
   if Q.tail <> nil then
      Q.tail^.next := temp
   else                                              {inserting into empty queue}
      Q.head := temp;
   Q.tail := temp
end;

procedure Dequeue(var Q : QUEUE);
   var save : POSITION;
begin
   if Q.head = nil then
      writeln('queue empty, cannot Dequeue')
   else begin
      save := Q.head;
      if Q.head = Q.tail then                       {singleton queue, make it empty}
         Q.tail := nil;
      Q.head := Q.head^.next;                       {point around head cell}
      Dispose(save)
   end
end;
```

```
function Head(Q : QUEUE) : ATOM;
begin
   if Q.head = nil then begin
      writeln('queue empty, cannot inspect Head element');
      Head := {some dummy atom}
   else
      Head := Q.head^.data
end;

function Empty(Q : QUEUE) : boolean;
begin
   Empty := (Q.head = nil)
end;
```

4.3 APPLICATION: INFIX TO POSTFIX CONVERSION

We promised earlier that we would not only provide a means to evaluate postfix expressions, but also give a method to provide input for that evaluation algorithm, namely a way to convert a token list representing an infix expression into a token list representing the corresponding postfix expression. Frankly, the only reason you had to wait as long as you have for this is that it is most convenient to use a queue as output from the conversion routine (which is to say, as input to the evaluation routine).

For reasons that will become clear shortly, we use a stack, *OpStack*, to store the pending operator tokens (those for which we have not yet seen both arguments), and a queue, *PostQ*, to store the postfix expression as it is being constructed. Each operator in the infix expression will be assigned an integer precedence, with multiplication and division having the highest precedence, and addition and subtraction having the next highest precedence. We will artificially assign to the left parenthesis, '(', the lowest precedence, to make the algorithm simpler to design. We will describe the algorithm, give an example of how it works, and then provide some justification that it does indeed do what it is claimed to do.

```
procedure Convert_To_Postfix(Infix : LIST ; var PostQ : QUEUE);
   var OpStack : STACK;

   procedure Transfer(var S : STACK ; var Q : QUEUE);
   {Transfers top of stack S to tail of queue Q}
   {Note: this requires that the atoms in S and Q are of the same type}
   begin
      Enqueue(Top(S), Q;
      Pop(S)
   end;

begin
   Create(OpStack);        {cheating slightly here — two different Create operations}
   Create(PostQ);           {... with the same names}
   while any tokens remain on Infix do begin
```

```
        get a token, t, from the left of Infix;
{1}     if t is a number then
            Enqueue(t, PostQ)
{2}     else if Empty(OpStack) then
            Push(t, OpStack)
{3}     else if t is the left parenthesis token then
            Push(t, OpStack)
{4}     else if t is the right parenthesis token then begin
            while Top(OpStack) is not a left parenthesis do
                Transfer(OpStack, PostQ);
            Pop(OpStack)                {discard first left paren seen on stack}
{5}     end else begin
            while precedence of t ≤ precedence of Top(OpStack) do
                Transfer(OpStack, PostQ);
            Push(t, OpStack)
        end
    end;                          {of big while loop Q no tokens left in Infix}
{6} while not Empty(OpStack) do         {transfer all remaining operators}
        Transfer(OpStack, PostQ)
end;
```

Example

We will trace the action of this conversion routine on the infix expression 7 − (2 ∗ 3 + 5) ∗ (8 − 4 / 2). In the table describing the action of the algorithm, *OpStack* is written (bottom ← top) and *PostQ* is written (tail → head), so that you can imagine elements moving across the page, from left to right. In the description of the rule used to produce each line, "5*" indicates a transfer of higher or equal precedence operator(s) from *OpStack* to *PostQ*.

Unused infix tokens	OpStack	PostQ	Rule used
7 − (2 ∗ 3 + 5) ∗ (8 − 4 / 2)	empty	empty	
− (2 ∗ 3 + 5) ∗ (8 − 4 / 2)	empty	7	1
(2 ∗ 3 + 5) ∗ (8 − 4 / 2)	−	7	2
2 ∗ 3 + 5) ∗ (8 − 4 / 2)	− (	7	3
∗ 3 + 5) ∗ (8 − 4 / 2)	− (	2 7	1
3 + 5) ∗ (8 − 4 / 2)	− (∗	2 7	5
+ 5) ∗ (8 − 4 / 2)	− (∗	3 2 7	1
5) ∗ (8 − 4 / 2)	− (+	∗ 3 2 7	5*
) ∗ (8 − 4 / 2)	− (+	5 ∗ 3 2 7	1
∗ (8 − 4 / 2)	−	+ 5 ∗ 3 2 7	4
(8 − 4 / 2)	− ∗	+ 5 ∗ 3 2 7	5
8 − 4 / 2)	− ∗ (	+ 5 ∗ 3 2 7	3
− 4 / 2)	− ∗ (	8 + 5 ∗ 3 2 7	1
4 / 2)	− ∗ (−	8 + 5 ∗ 3 2 7	5
/ 2)	− ∗ (−	4 8 + 5 ∗ 3 2 7	1
2)	− ∗ (− /	4 8 + 5 ∗ 3 2 7	5
)	− ∗ (− /	2 4 8 + 5 ∗ 3 2 7	1
empty	− ∗	− / 2 4 8 + 5 ∗ 3 2 7	4
empty	empty	− ∗ − / 2 4 8 + 5 ∗ 3 2 7	6

As this example indicates, the infix expression 7 – (2 * 3 + 5) * (8 – 4 / 2) is converted to its postfix equivalent, which we would write 7 2 3 * 5 + 8 4 2 / – * –. Comparing the two, we notice that the number tokens in each expression are in the same order, as will always be the case in this algorithm. The fact that the postfix expression stored in *PostQ* is written "backwards" is due only to the way in which we decided to represent the queue. Transfers from *OpStack* to *PostQ* are made to the left (tail) end of *PostQ*, so in the preceding table you can imagine the tokens migrating from the top of *OpStack* (the right end) to the tail of *PostQ* (the left end). Now you should be able to see why we used a queue for the output of this algorithm: Since the output will be used as the input of the evaluation algorithm, the evaluation algorithm will repeatedly dequeue tokens from *PostQ*, starting with 7, then 2, then 3, then *, and so on. In fact, it is not difficult to see that we could combine the two algorithms into one, using another stack for evaluation and eliminating *PostQ* entirely.

This is only a small part of what a compiler or interpreter must do to translate a program from a language like Pascal to machine language. Even so, we have left out a number of details, such as how the compiler "recognizes" tokens in an input string (that is, the source code of the program), how it keeps track of where a number ends and an operator begins, how it decides what is a variable and what is a constant, and so on.

We can show that the conversion algorithm works correctly by using an **induction proof**. We describe induction in more detail in Appendix B, but the essential idea is to show that if the conversion algorithm works for any infix expression with fewer than n tokens, then it must work for any infix expression with n tokens. Doing this will allow us to prove that the conversion algorithm must work for all possible infix expressions.

The major part of the proof goes roughly as follows: Let I be an infix expression with n operators, then it must be that $I = I_1\ op\ I_2$, where I_1 and I_2 are infix expressions. Since I had n operators, I_1 and I_2 must each have fewer than n operators. We would choose the operation to be the last one to be performed if we were evaluating I, so if I = '(22/7+4)*(6–2)', we would have I_1 = '(22 / 7 + 4)' and I_2 = '(6 – 2)'. Since both I_1 and I_2 have fewer than n operators, we assume that they can be correctly converted to postfix expressions P_1 and P_1, which in the example we are using would be '22 7 / +' and '6 2 –', respectively. We would then show that, since the conversion of both I_1 and I_2 left nothing on *OpStack*, we could "glue" these two constructions together to form the construction for I so that, after having seen all the tokens in I, the conversion routine would have only *op* on the *OpStack* , and $P_1 P_2$ as the contents of *PostQ*. Then the last step in the conversion algorithm would transfer the contents of *OpStack* to *PostQ*, giving the desired result $P_1 P_2\ op$. In our example, then, the postfix equivalent would be ' 22 7 / + 6 2 – * '.

4.5 SUMMARY

Both the STACK and QUEUE abstract data types are linear structures. They differ (and they differ from LISTs) in their operators. The STACK operators are defined so that insertion, inspection, and deletion all take place at the first element in the linear order, whereas for QUEUEs, insertion is done at one end of the structure, inspection and deletion at the other.

We investigated array and linked list implementations of STACK. The array implementation is easy to use, but suffers from the usual size limitations of arrays. Stacks are most useful in instances where the most recently saved information will be accessed first (LIFO, or last-in-first-out), and so are valuable for storing activation records of procedure calls. In fact, this application is used so often that many computers have stacks wired in as part of their hardware, for fast stack operations. We saw that the stack ADT is a natural choice for evaluation of postfix expressions.

Queues, on the other hand, arise frequently in models of real-world processes, where the most recently saved information will be the last to be accessed (FIFO). Queues can be implemented by arrays, circular arrays, and linked lists. The array implementations of QUEUE suffer from the usual static size limitations of arrays, but circular arrays eliminate the need for reorganization of the queue (although this is not as much of a problem as we might imagine at first, since it adds only a log n term to the time).

4.5 EXERCISES

1. Suppose that the function **PopTop(var** S : STACK) : ATOM was defined to combine the action of *Pop* and *Top*, so that it returned the top atom on the stack *S* and then removed that atom from *S*. Show that both *Pop* and *Top* can be defined in terms of *Push*, *Empty*, and *PopTop*.

2. In the language FORTH, almost all operations are performed on a predefined stack. Commands are entered from the keyboard and are executed in the order entered as soon as the <return> key is pressed. If a number is seen, it is pushed on the stack, so the input sequence '2 3 8 <return>' would cause the numbers 2, 3, 8 to be pushed on the stack in that order (so that 8 would be the new top element on the stack). An arithmetic operator causes the top two elements of the stack to be inspected and removed, the operation to be performed, and the result to be pushed onto the stack, so the sequence consisting of '8 4 / <return>' would leave the stack with 2 on top (the 8 and 4 having been popped by the operator). In FORTH, it is possible to define complex operations by name, prefacing the name with ':' and following the name with the stack operations to be performed, so that the operator "EXAMPLE " defined by

:EXAMPLE 2 * +

would take a stack $\ldots a\ b$ (from bottom to top) and perform the operations "push 2," "multiply the top two elements," and "add the new top elements," thus transforming the stack to $\ldots 2b + a$, with the old top two elements a and b having been popped by the operations * and + in the definition.

(a) Assuming the stack contained $\ldots a\ b\ c$ before the calls, what would be the effect of the following operations ': OP1 3 * – *' and ': OP2 – 2 * –' ?

(b) Show that one of the reasons FORTH contains the operation OVER, which we described in the text, is that it makes it possible to define operations like the following ':OP3 OVER + *', which, when performed on a stack of the form $\ldots a\ b$, allows the computation of $a * (a + b)$.

(c) Show that, using what we know so far, it is impossible to define an operation that takes a stack of the form $\ldots c\ a\ b$ and computes $(a-b)/c$, and show that such an operation is possible if we have another operation, SWAP, which interchanges the top two elements of the stack.

(d) Define SWAP in terms of the stack primitives.

3. Implement the predicate *Full(S : STACK)* : boolean for array-based stacks.

4. Suppose you had a program that required two stacks. Describe a single data structure that would contain both stacks, and tell how *Push* and *Pop* would have to be modified for your data structure.

5. Not all sequences of *Push* and *Pop* can be performed without error, starting with an empty stack. For example, the sequence *Push, Pop, Pop, Push* will lead to a "pop empty stack" error at the second *Pop*.

   (a) Find a simple rule to describe all "legal " sequences of *Push* and *Pop* that can be performed starting with an empty stack.

   (b) Relate your rule to a rule describing all sequences of **balanced parentheses**, such as (()(()()))), which could parenthesize some correctly formed infix expression.

6. **Dijkstra's railroad:** One way to look at a stack is as a railroad siding with two tracks leading to it—an input track, from which cars are pushed onto the siding, and an output track, from which cars are removed (popped) from the siding.

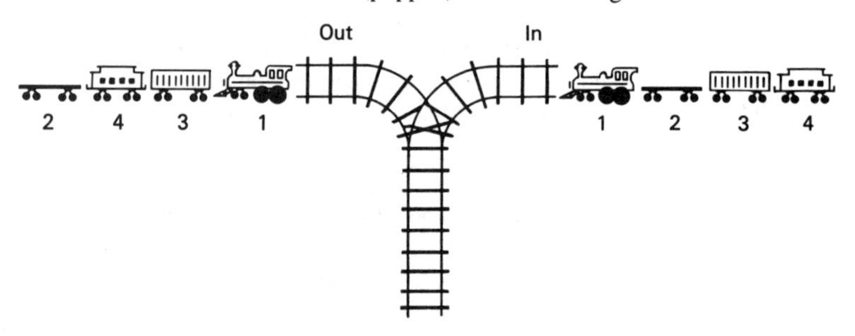

The diagram indicates the result of applying the sequence *Push, Push, Pop, Push, Push, Pop, Pop, Pop*: If the cars were originally in order 1, 2, 3, 4, then that sequence results in the permuted order 2, 4, 3, 1.

   (a) Show that it is not possible to obtain all possible permutations by this scheme by showing that 5, 4, 1, 3, 2 cannot be obtained from input 1, 2, 3, 4, 5.

   (b) Find a rule that describes which permutations cannot be obtained from the input *1, 2, . . . , n*.

   (c) Describe the railroad equivalent of queues, and show that, as a generator of permutations, queues are trivial.

7. Give the solution tree for the maze-tracing example if a doorway was made between rooms 3 and 5.

8. Assume, as in the maze-tracing example, that the lowest numbered unvisited adjacent room was the one visited next at each step. Assume also that in the maze given in the text, there was a door between rooms 3 and 5, but no door between rooms 6 and 8.

   (a) What solution would the algorithm find?

   (b) How many rooms would the algorighm visit, counting backtracks, before finding the exit?

9. Another very simple, maze-tracing algorighm is the **left-hand rule**: walk through the maze by keeping your left hand on the wall at all times. For the example in the text, this would lead to the path 1, 2, 3, 1, 4, 5, 6, 8.

(a) Given a solution path from the left-hand rule algorithm, describe an algorithm to eliminate duplication of rooms, so that the **cycle** 1, 2, 3, 1, in the preceding example would be eliminated leading to the shorter solution 1, 4, 5, 6, 8.

(b) Find a maze for which the left-hand rule will fail to find the exit.

10. Describe a data structure that you could use to represent a maze, along with a description of how you would find all rooms adjacent to a given room.

11. **Automata theory** is devoted to the study of abstract machines, languages, and the sorts of computations that can be performed on those machines. A **language** is just a set of strings over some fixed alphabet of characters, so the set P = *a, ab, aabb, aaabbb,* . . . is a language that we would describe informally as the language consisting of all strings of $n \geq 1$ a's followed by n b's. A machine M is said to **recognize** a language L if it can be programmed to halt and print 'yes' for every input consisting of a string from L, and halt and print 'no' for every input string that is not in L. The input is read from left to right, one character at a time, and typically the machine M is allowed to have a program consisting of a sequence of such simple operations as (1) "**read** [an input character] **and store it** [somewhere]," (2)"**goto** [some instruction], " (3) "**if** [some variable] **equals** [some value], **then** [do some instruction]," and (4) "**set** [this variable] **to be** [some value]," and (5) "**store** [this variable] **at** [some specified location]," along with output instructions (6) "write *yes* and halt" and, (7) "write *no* and halt." The operations are the same in all the abstract machines (and do not include such things as arithmetic), but different machines are distinguished by the data structures used for storage. For instance, a **finite automaton** has as its only data structure a fixed finite number of variables (of a fixed finite size), $v_1, v_2, \ldots, v_n$.

(a) Show that a finite automaton can recognize $L = \{b\$, ab\$, aab\$, aaab\$, aaaab\$, \ldots\}$ by writing a program for such a machine, using only the seven instructions above. (The '$' characters are there only to let your program know the end of the input, and will be assumed to be part of the subsequent examples.) The collection of languages recognized by finite automata are called **regular languages**.

(b) Argue informally that no finite automaton can recognize the language P above, that is, that P isn't a regular language. (*Hint*: You're not allowed to change the number or size of variables to suit the input, because you don't know the input size ahead of time.)

(c) A **pushdown automaton** (PDA) is an enhancement of a finite automaton, in that it has a finite number of variables, along with a single stack and the usual stack operations. Find a program for a PDA that recognizes P. Languages recognized by PDAs are called **context-free languages** (CFLs) and are important because they are both large enough to be interesting (most computer languages like Pascal are CFLs, or very close to being so) and small enough to be recognized easily.

(d) Show that the language $L = \{abb, aabbbb, aaabbbbbb, \ldots\}$ is a CFL.

(e) Argue informally that $L = \{abc, aabbcc, aaabbbccc, \ldots\}$ is not a CFL.

(f) A **two-stack PDA** has, as its name implies, two stacks, rather than one. Are two-stack PDAs more powerful than PDAs, in the sense that there are languages recognized by two-stack PDAs that are not CFLs?

12. Evaluate the following postfix expressions.
    (a) 3 4 8 + 2 * 5 1 − * +
    (b) 3 4 8 2 5 1 + * − * +
13. The description of postfix expressions is incomplete because it fails to include (among other things) unary negation, which we will denote by '~'. With this notation, the expression 2 4 ~ * would be equivalent to the infix expression 2 * (−4). Modify the postfix evaluation algorithm to include treatment of unary negation.
14. **(a)** How many operator tokens must a correctly formed postfix expression have if it has n number tokens? (*Hint*: This is a trick question, having something to do with a previous question.)
    (b) Give a rule that describes all correctly formed postfix expressions, so that you can show that 3 4 5 + 6 * − * 7 8 9 + − is not correctly formed, despite the fact that it has the correct number of operators and numeric tokens.
15. Write the queue primitives in terms of LIST operations, as was done for stacks.
16. Implement the function *Length*(*Q* : QUEUE) : integer for circular array-based queues.
17. If you had to implement a queue in a language without pointers, but still wanted to allow the queue to grow to arbitrary size, you could define an extensible data structure that used an array to hold the queue elements until it was full, and then added another array to hold the overflow, until that array was also full, whereupon another array would be added, and so on. Give a description of such a data structure by describing the action of *Enqueue* and *Dequeue*.
18. Modify the infix-to-postfix algorithm to include unary negation, as in Exercise 13.
19. Trace the infix-to postfix algorithm on the following expressions:
    (a) 1 + 2 * (1 + 2 * (1 + 2))
    (b) 3 − 8 / 4 + 5 * 6 * 7 − 2 * 9
    (c) (((3 + 5) * 2) − 4)
20. Design a postfix-to-infix conversion algorithm.
21. In a **priority queue**, each element to be inserted comes with a number, called its **priority**, and *Front* and *Dequeue* deal only with the element of highest priority on the queue at the time they were called. Implement a priority queue, and compare the running times of its operations with those of an ordinary queue.

Programming Projects

22. The **problem of Josephus** is usually stated in the following rather grisly form: You are part of a group of people who are captured by bloodthirsty pirates and told that only one of your number will survive. Your group is made to stand in a circle, and a number n is chosen. Starting at some person, the pirates count off every nth person, remove that person from the circle, toss the unlucky individual overboard into shark-infested waters, and continue until only one person remains. Write a program that, given n and the number of people in your group, tells you how far to stand from the starting person.
23. Write an infix evaluator that, when given a string of characters like '34 * (8 − 21)', prints the value of the expression. You may wish to include such refinements as (in approximate order of increasing difficulty) checking for run-time errors such as division by zero, including unary negation and exponents, checking whether the original infix expression was correctly formed, indicating where in the infix expression the first indication of incorrect

form was observed, and trying to recover from incorrect form errors by making an educated guess as to what was intended.

For the remaining projects, it would be a good idea to read Appendix C on random numbers and simulation.

24. In discussing array implementations of queues, we mentioned that it was possible to maintain a queue as a linear, rather than circular, array by shifting the entire contents of the array as far left as possible whenever an *Enqueue* operation would cause the queue to overflow the right end of the array. We said the average cost of such a scheme was $O(\log n)$ for arrays of size n. Implement QUEUE as a linear array, and include in your implementation counters for the number of steps performed (so *Dequeue* always adds one to the count, and *Enqueue* adds one to the count except for those times when the array needs to be shifted, in which case the count is increased by the number of elements that were shifted). For various values of n, the size of the array, find the average number of steps required by a long sequence of randomly chosen *Enqueue* and *Dequeue* operations (i.e., the count divided by the number of operations).

25. Simulate the action of a car wash. Assume at first that the car wash consists of one wash bay and a driveway large enough to hold four cars. Suppose it takes ten minutes to wash a car, and that cars arrive at random in such a way that the average **interarrival time**, that is, the average time between arrivals of cars, is also ten minutes. Write your program to simulate the activity of an eight-hour workday, keeping track of the average wait time for each car (from entering the driveway to entering the wash bay), and the number of cars that had to be turned away because the driveway was full. Investigate the effects of changing the capacity of the driveway and changing the interarrival time on the average wait time and number of cars turned away. (Incidentally, in many such situations the interarrival times are not **uniformly distributed** [see Appendix C] but, rather, are **exponentially distributed**. You might want to investigate what difference, if any, this makes.

PART 3

Nonlinear Structures

5

Recursion

The sentence "The sentence 'This sentence has four words' has four words" is false.

D. C. Logsdon, *Miss Liddell's Logic*

A **recursive** definition is one that refers to the object it is defining as part of its definition. There's more to recursion than that, however, since we wish to avoid definitions like "A rose is a rose," which, poetic insights notwithstanding, does not give us much hard information on the nature of roses. The important feature of recursive definitions is that they always provide a means of "bailing out" of the definition, of avoiding circularity. The notion of recursion is exemplified by a definition like "A bouquet of roses is either (1) a single rose or (2) a single rose, along with a smaller bouquet of roses." In this example, condition 1 serves as the **exit case**, providing a way out of the definition and condition 2, the **recursive case**, guarantees that we will always eventually reach the exit case. Recursive definitions are characterized by their elegance and simplicity (contrast the foregoing definition with the **iterative** version "A bouquet of roses consists of either one rose, or two roses, or three roses, . . . "), and are a valuable tool in the computer scientist's collection. In this chapter we will investigate recursive definitions of both algorithms and data structures.

5.1 RECURSIVE ALGORITHMS

An algorithm is said to be recursive if its definition includes at least one call to itself, either directly (**direct recursion**) or indirectly, through a sequence of calls to routines that eventually result in a call to the routine itself (**indirect recursion**). Consider, for instance, the function **Factorial**(n : integer) : integer, which returns $n!$. We could make an iterative definition of $n!$ by asserting

$$0! = 1,$$
$$n! = 1 \times 2 \times \ldots \times n, \text{for } n > 0$$

This would lead to the iterative declaration

```
function Factorial(n : integer) : integer;
   var f, i : integer;
begin
   if n <= 1 then
      Factorial := 1
   else begin
      f := 1;
      for i := 1 to n do
         f := f * i;
      Factorial := f
   end
end;
```

That, however, is not the only possible way to define *Factorial.* We can get a recursive definition if we can answer the fundamental question, "Can I solve this problem, *assuming that I could solve a smaller instance of the problem*?" In this case, of course, it is easy to see how to compute $n!$, assuming that we could compute the factorial of smaller numbers. We could write the following recursive definition:

$$0! = 1 \quad \text{(the exit case)}$$
$$n! = n \times (n-1)!, \quad \text{for } n > 0 \quad \text{(the recursive case)}$$

This definition translates directly to the recursive declaration

```
function RecursiveFactorial(n : integer) : integer;
begin
   if n <= 1 then
      RecursiveFactorial := 1
   else
      RecursiveFactorial := n * RecursiveFactorial(n – 1)
end;
```

Although *RecursiveFactorial* is certainly simpler to write than the iterative version, it is not necessarily any easier to understand, nor, as we will see shortly, is it any faster. It is, however, more compact and in some sense more elegant. Although any recursive definition can be written without recursion, we frequently find ourselves in situations where recursive definitions are the most natural ones to employ. The nicest thing about recursion is that it permits us to define algorithms seemingly out of thin air. Nowhere in the definition of *RecursiveFactorial* does there appear any obvious description of the details of how $n!$ is computed, except as a leap of faith asserting, "Assuming I know how to find $(n-1)!$, I'll find that and multiply by n to get $n!$."

To see how the recursive definition of $n!$ works, consider the call *RecursiveFactorial*(3). Since $3 > 1$, the function will multiply 3 by the result obtained by calling *RecursiveFactorial*(2), which will itself require another call, to *RecursiveFactorial*(1), which will return 1. After all three calls, we will have the following situation.

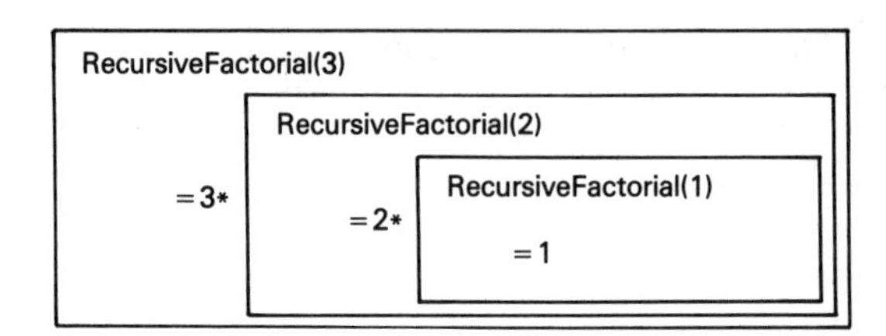

The calls to the outer functions cannot be completed until *RecursiveFactorial*(1) is evaluated. At that point, the values are repeatedly passed back to the calling routines, as follows:

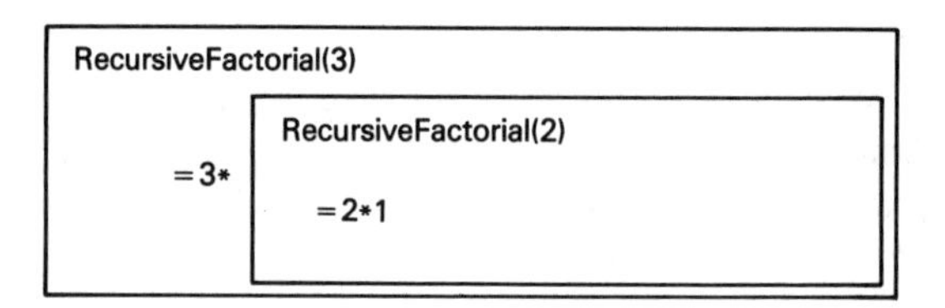

RecursiveFactorial(3)

=3*2*1

In all these recursive algorithms, we are letting the computer keep track of pending results by pushing them on the stack of activation records that results from successive function calls. The first call, with $n = 3$, is pushed on the stack and is followed by another push when *RecursiveFactorial* is called with $n = 2$, which is followed by another push of activation records for the call with $n = 1$. This value can be computed, and the result, 1, is passed back when the top activation record (for $n = 1$) is popped. Then *RecursiveFactorial*(2) can be completed, so its activation record is popped and control is passed to *RecursiveFactorial*(3), along with the value 2 for the previous call. This value, in turn, is used to compute *RecursiveFactorial*(3), after which control passes to the main program (or whichever routine made the original call to *RecursiveFactorial*(3)).

We do not have to restrict our attention to numeric calculations, however. Suppose we had a linked list of cells, each of which had a *data* field containing some information, and a *next* field, pointing to the succeeding cell. Suppose also that the last cell in the list had a **nil** "next" field and that we were given a pointer to the first cell in the list. We could traverse the list recursively, printing the contents of each *data* field, if we broke the problem into two parts:

1. We exit when the pointer to the current cell is **nil**.
2. In every other case we print the contents of the current cell and then perform the traversal routine beginning at the "next" cell after the current cell.

The traversal algorithm is then easy to write:

```
procedure Traverse(p : CellPtr);
begin
   if p <> nil then begin
      write(p^.data);
      Traverse(p^.next)
   end
end;
```

Notice that in this algorithm the exit condition is implicit: When we come to the end of the list, the current pointer is **nil**, so we exit from the procedure without taking any action at all. The nicest feature of this algorithm is not its brevity but, rather, the fact that if we interchanged the statements write(p^.data) and Traverse(p^.next), we would have a routine that printed the contents of the list *in reverse order*, without our having to worry about how to traverse a one-way linked list in a direction opposite to that of the pointers. Do you see why? The algorithm for reverse traversal would then be described as follows: "To traverse the list, traverse the smaller list that begins after the current position, and when you're completely done write out the value at the current position," so that the value at position p would be printed only if all the values following p had already been printed, thus traversing the list in reverse order. As with the recursive factorial algorithm, we let the computer keep track of the pending results in the stack of activation records. We could do explicitly what the computer does implicitly by keeping our own stack, simulating the pending procedure calls. An example of this technique of eliminating recursion follows, in an iterative version of the routine to traverse a linked list in opposite order.

```
procedure ReverseTraversal(p : CellPtr);
   var S : STACK; {of cell pointers}
begin
   Create(S);

   while p <> nil do begin              {fill stack with pending pointers}
      Push(p, S);                       {... simulating pending procedure calls}
      p := p^.next
   end;

   while not Empty(S) do begin          {retrieve pending pointers}
      p := Top(S);
      write(p^.data);
      Pop(S)
   end
end;
```

An entirely reasonable question at this point is, "Why would you *want* to eliminate recursion, especially in light of the fact that the iterative version of the reverse traversal routine requires twice as many lines as the recursive version?" The answer is that the number of lines in a program is not necessarily a reflection of how long the program will take to run. It is not difficult to imagine that procedure and function calls take a considerable amount of time, saving all the local variables, addresses, and such, and pushing them on the stack of activation records. Although we have made the simplifying assumption that all statements take equal amounts of time, (and, indeed, this assumption does not affect the big-O timing estimates), in practice, when we are writing programs to run on real machines and compilers, we may need to be more careful about the kind of statements our programs contain.

To give an example of the time difference between iterative and recursive versions of the same algorithm, we coded and ran both versions of the factorial algorithms given here on the same computer with the same compiler. To be completely honest, that's not exactly what we did: $n!$ grows so rapidly that the answers would quickly overflow the available size for integers on most computers, so we changed each algorithm so that instead of multiplying by n (or i, as the case might be) we actually multiplied by 1 in each step. At any rate, the timing results are graphed in Figure 5.1. The time difference is quite apparent. The observed timing function, $T_i(n)$, for the iterative factorial algorithm is approximately $T_i(n) = 0.0018n + 0.0033$, whereas the timing function for the recursive algorithm is approximately $T_r(n) = 0.0056n + 0.017$. In other words, although both algorithms run in $O(n)$ time, the recursive algorithm is about four times slower than the iterative version.

Although a recursive version of a program may well be slower than the equivalent iterative version, and any recursive routine can be changed into an iterative one, we should not give up on recursion entirely. Very often, thinking recursively may give us

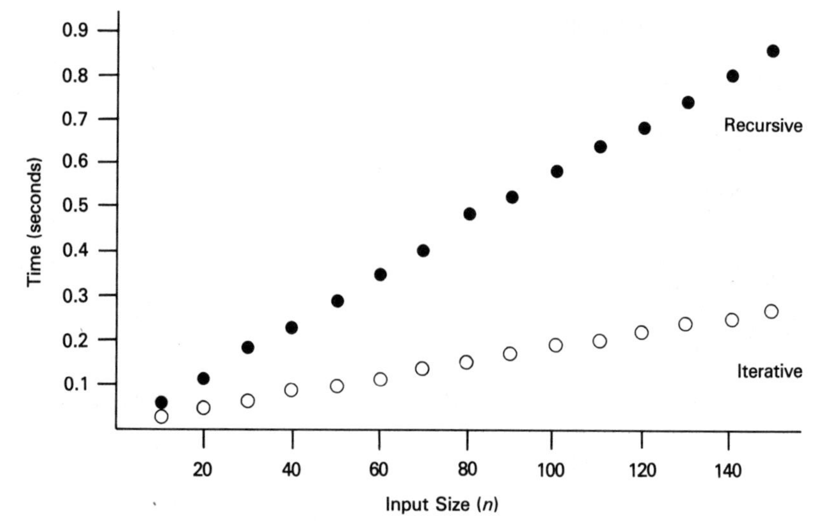

Figure 5.1 Timing of recursive and iterative factorial routines.

an insight into a problem that we simply wouldn't have gotten otherwise. Having gotten the idea, we could always eliminate the recursion if doing so turned out to make the solution program run more efficiently.

A further, and much more important, caution about recursion is that, unbeknownst to us, a recursive routine may be written in such a way as to be hideously inefficient. A common example of the inefficient use of recursive functions is the calculation of the **Fibonacci numbers**, a sequence that appears in all sorts of unexpected places in computer science and mathematics, and in the real world as well (as, for instance, in the description of the scales on a pineapple). This is a sequence of numbers beginning with 1, 1, 2, 3, 5, 8, . . . , which has the property that, except for the first two numbers, each number is formed by adding the two preceding numbers. In other words, the Fibonacci numbers may be described by the recursive definition

$$Fib(0) = Fib(1) = 1,$$
$$Fib(n) = Fib(n-1) + Fib(n-2), \quad \text{for } n > 1.$$

It is easy to turn this recursive definition into a description of a function that evaluates Fibonacci numbers, as follows:

```
function Fib(n : integer) : integer;
begin
   if n <= 1 then
      Fib := 1
   else
      Fib := Fib(n – 1) + Fib(n – 2)
end;
```

It would be a useful exercise for you to stop now, find a computer, code this routine, and test it for various values of n. It happens that the Fibonacci sequence grows fairly rapidly—if we look at *Fib* as a function, we can show that $Fib(n) = O(1.62^n)$. To give you a little help if you decide to write and test the algorithm, you can check that *Fib*(31) = 2,178,309. If you do try the function, it would be more instructive if you did it before you went on to the next paragraph. Go ahead, we'll wait.

* * *

If you did code the Fibonacci function, you probably noticed that it ran *very* slowly once you got beyond fairly small values for n. On many computers, for $n = 31$, you would probably have time to go out for coffee while the program was running, and for $n = 100$ you would probably have time to go to Colombia and pick the beans, assuming that the program would even run to completion without an error. The reason for this terrible running time is that this recursive definition does a great many duplicate function calls each of which is pretty fast by itself, but which, together, take a noticeable amount of time. Consider what happens even in a simple case, when we call *Fib*(5). In Figure 5.2 we have indicated each function call by a box, with the parameter value in a small box in the upper left-hand corner.

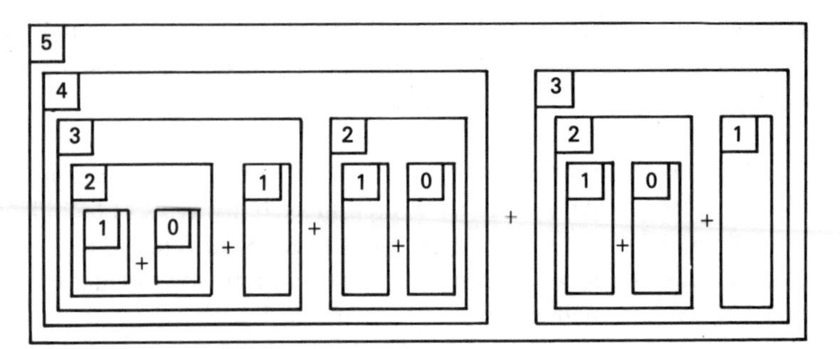

Figure 5.2 Function calls needed to calculate *Fib*(5).

The original call to *Fib*(5), for instance, resulted in two further calls, to *Fib*(4) and *Fib*(3). Since each box represents a function call, we can count boxes to find that just to compute *Fib*(5) required 15 function calls, most of which were duplicates of other calls. (*Fib*(0) was called 3 times, for instance, and *Fib*(1) was called 5 times. By the way, notice that *Fib*(5) = 8 = 3 + 5.) We will soon be able to show that the number of function calls required by this algorithm to compute *Fib(n)* is larger than *Fib(n)* itself, hence is at least $O(1.62^n)$, so that if it took, say, 5 minutes to compute *Fib*(20), it could take at least $5 \times 1.62 = 8.1$ minutes just to compute *Fib*(21), and at least $8.1 \times 1.62 = 13.122$ minutes to compute *Fib*(22). The moral is clear: Elegance and simplicity are not always sufficient justification for choosing to write an algorithm recursively.

Induction and Recursion

Recursion and induction are two sides of the same coin. In a recursive definition we have an exit case to allow us to leave the definition, and a recursive case to allow us to reach the exit case. In a proof by induction we have a base case that permits us to start the chain of arguments, and an inductive case that permits us to continue the chain from the base case. If you are not familiar with induction proofs, it would be a good idea to look over the material in Appendix B before going much further. We will demonstrate the connection between induction and recursion by proving a property of the Fibonacci numbers. Once the mathematical machinery has been developed, it is not too hard to show that $Fib(n) = O(1.62^n)$ but to do so would take us too far afield for inclusion in this book. Instead, we will show a simpler result, namely that $Fib(n) > (3/2)^n$, for $n \geq 5$.

Let $P(n)$ be the statement "$Fib(n) > (3/2)^n$." We seek to show that $P(n)$ is true for all $n \geq 5$.

1. *Base case*: We show that $P(5)$ and $P(6)$ are true by observing that $Fib(5) = 8 > 7.59375 = (3/2)^5$, and $Fib(6) = 13 > 11.390625 = (3/2)^6$.
2. *Induction case*: Now we would like to build the chain from the base case by showing that if we assume $P(j)$ is true for all $5 \leq j < n$, then $P(n)$ is true. Let n be any integer larger than 6; we wish to show $P(n)$ is true, that is, that $Fib(n) > (3/2)^n$. We know that

$$Fib(n) = Fib(n-1) + Fib(n-2)$$

and the induction hypothesis allows us to assume that $Fib(n-1) > (3/2)^{n-1}$ and $Fib(n-2) > (3/2)^{n-2}$ (since we assume $P(n-1)$ and $P(n-2)$ are true), so we can conclude

$$Fib(n) > (3/2)^{n-1} + (3/2)^{n-2}$$
$$= (3/2)^{n-2}(3/2+1) = (3/2)^{n-2}(5/2)$$

But $5/2 > 9/4 = (3/2)^2$ so we can replace 5/2 in the line above to yield

$$Fib(n) > (3/2)^{n-2}(5/2) > (3/2)^{n-2}(3/2)^2 = (3/2)^n,$$

which is nothing but a statement of $P(n)$, which was what we wanted.

Timing Recursive Algorithms

In Chapter 1 we saw that we could find big-O timing estimates of a nonrecursive algorithm by counting the number of statements executed by the algorithm. That, in turn, led us to the rule of thumb that the running time of such an algorithm was driven largely by the depth of nesting of loops in the algorithm. But, what are we to do in a case where the algorithm calls itself? Consider, for example, the algorithm for factorials that we saw earlier:

```
function RecursiveFactorial(n : integer) : integer;
begin
   if n <= 1 then
      RecursiveFactorial := 1
   else
      RecursiveFactorial := n * RecursiveFactorial(n – 1)
end;
```

First, we will suppose that there is a timing function, $T(n)$, that expresses the amount of time the algorithm takes on input n. Then we will try to find an expression involving that timing function; finally, we will use that expression to find $T(n)$. In this example, we note that if n is zero or one, then the algorithm terminates without any further ado, so there is some number, A, for which $T(0) = T(1) = A$. This accounts for the time taken by the function call, the **if** statement, and the return from the function. If $n > 1$, we still have all the overhead we did in the $n = 1$ case, but we also have a function call to *RecursiveFactorial*$(n-1)$ and a multiplication by n. Now, we may assume that the multiplication takes time B (which is not really the case, since multiplication takes time proportional to at least the number of digits of the factors being multiplied, but let us assume, in the interest of efficiency, that multiplication takes constant time), but we do not know how long the function call will take, except that we may write it as $T(n-1)$. Therefore, the time to perform *RecursiveFactorial(n)* will be given by a function $T(n)$ that satisfies

$$T(0) = T(1) = A,$$
$$T(n) = A + B + T(n-1), \quad \text{for } n > 1,$$

or, writing $C = A + B$ to make our life a little easier, we are faced with the problem of finding a function *T(n)* that satisfies the recursive definition

$$T(0) = T(1) = A,$$
$$T(n) = T(n-1) + C, \quad \text{for } n > 1.$$

One way to help guess a solution for a function defined in this fashion is to use what is known as **iterative expansion**. Remember, the definition says that $T(n) = T(n-1) + C$ no matter what we put in place of n (as long as it is more than 1), so $T(8) = T(7) + C$, $T(x) = T(x-1) + C$, and so on. In particular, we see that $T(n-1) = T(n-2) + C$ (putting $n - 1$ in place of every n in the definition). Thus we see

$$\begin{aligned} T(n) &= T(n-1) + C \\ &= (T(n-2) + C) + C = T(n-2) + 2C \\ &\qquad = (T(n-3) + C) + 2C = T(n-3) + 3C, \end{aligned}$$

and so on. The pattern is clear enough: $T(n) = T(n-k) + kC$, for all $k = 1, 2, \ldots$ until we come to $T(n) = T(1) + (n-1)C$ (i.e., when $k = n - 1$). But we know $T(1) = A$, so (assuming that our guess about the pattern is correct) we can conclude that *RecursiveFactorial* has timing function

$$T(0) = T(1) = A,$$
$$T(n) = A + (n-1)C, \quad \text{for } n > 1.$$

In other words, $T(n) = O(n)$, so we have good reason to believe what the timing analysis in the graph of Figure 5.1 led us to suspect, namely that *RecursiveFactorial* runs in linear time, which makes it about as efficient as we could wish.

Another example of the timing of recursive algorithms comes from a sorting algorithm that is probably more efficient than any you have seen so far. Exercise 12(b) of Chapter 1 contained an algorithm, *SelectionSort*, to sort a list (of numbers, say) from smallest to largest. This algorithm took time $O(n^2)$, which means that it is unsuitable, on most computers, for lists larger than a few thousand elements. We can produce a better algorithm if we employ a technique called **divide and conquer**—taking a problem and dividing it into smaller problems. If we can solve the smaller problems, and if the solutions of the smaller problems can be efficiently combined into a solution to the large problem, we may then be better off than if we had attacked the large problem directly.

Suppose, for instance, that we had two small sorted lists. We could **merge** them together to form a large sorted list in a very natural fashion by working from left to right in each list, selecting the smaller element from the present two elements, copying that element to the end of the big list, moving to the element immediately after the one selected and continuing the process until one of the two lists was empty, whereupon we would copy the leftover elements onto the tail of the output list and be done. An example of such a merge follows, where the elements being compared are highlighted.

List 1	List 2	Result
102 151 204 283	**87** 91 113 200	
102 151 204 283	87 **91** 113 200	87
102 151 204 283	87 91 **113** 200	87 91
102 **151** 204 283	87 91 **113** 200	87 91 102
102 **151** 204 283	87 91 113 **200**	87 91 102 113
102 151 **204** 283	87 91 113 **200**	87 91 102 113 151
102 151 **204** 283	87 91 113 200	87 91 102 113 151 200

At this stage, since there is nothing left in List 2, no further comparisons are needed, so the remaining two elements in List 1 are simply appended, in order, to the end of the output list. It is an easy exercise to write a procedure to accomplish this merging, using the list primitives. The important part about merging is that it takes no more than time proportional to the sum of the lengths of the two lists—every comparison results in an element added to the output list, so there can be no more comparisons than the eventual size of the merged list. Thus, merging of two lists of size $n/2$ can be accomplished in time $O(n)$, assuming operations of time $O(1)$.

We can use this technique to write a very simple recursive sorting program which takes the following form:

```
procedure Mergesort(var L : LIST ; low, high : integer);
{Sorts a list starting with position low and ending with position high }
   var mid : integer;
begin
   if low < high then begin
      mid := (low + high + 1) div 2;      {find the middle of the list}
      Mergesort(L, low, mid - 1);         {sort the low half recursively}
      Mergesort(L, mid, high);            {and then sort the high half}
      Merge the two sublists to form L
   end
end;
```

The idea behind this program is a direct application of divide-and-conquer: If the list has more than one element in it (otherwise it's already sorted), split the list in two nearly equal pieces, sort them, and merge the results. The nature of divide-and-conquer routines makes them natural choices for recursive programs.

At this point, it should be by no means obvious what the timing of *Mergesort* is at all, let alone whether it is an improvement over something like *SelectionSort*. But certainly it is not unreasonable to assume that the worst time to run *Mergesort* on a list of size n should be no greater than some function, $T(n)$, of the length of the list to be sorted. Assume, then, that *Mergesort* on a list of n elements takes no more than time

$T(n)$. We will see if we can get an upper estimate for $T(n)$. If $n = 1$, the function returns directly, so in this case we see that $T(1) = A$, for some number A, which takes care of the overhead caused by the test in the **if** statement and the return from the function call. If $n > 1$, *Mergesort* calls itself twice on the smaller lists and calls *Merge* on the result. Each call to *Mergesort* on the lists of size $n/2$ takes time no greater than $T(n/2)$, by our previous assumption, and *Merge* takes time Bn, for some fixed constant B, since we have seen that *Merge* runs in linear time on the two smaller lists. What we have, then, is a function T for which

$$T(1) = A,$$
$$T(n) \le 2T(n/2) + Bn, \quad \text{for } n > 1.$$

Our mission now is to try to find a function T that satisfies this recursive definition. Notice that T, as written, is defined only for even values of n and so, by the recursive nature of the definition, is actually defined only for values that are powers of 2. In almost all situations encountered in practice, this presents no problem, since the function T which is found by considering only those n that are powers of 2 serves as a good upper bound for all values of n.

Consider, then, the definition for $n = 2^k$.

$$\begin{aligned} T(2^k) &\le 2T(2^k/2) + B\,2^k \\ &= 2T(2^{k-1}) + B\,2^k. \end{aligned} \tag{5.1}$$

Since inequality 5.1 is assumed to hold for all powers of 2, it certainly must be true in the case $n = 2^{k-1}$, so we can rewrite it with $n = 2^{k-1}$ to yield

$$T(2^{k-1}) \le 2T(2^{k-2}) + B\,2^{k-1}. \tag{5.2}$$

Substituting inequality 5.2 into inequality 5.1 yields

$$\begin{aligned} T(2^k) &\le 2(2T(2^{k-2}) + B\,2^{k-1}) + B\,2^k \\ &= 2^2\,T(2^{k-2}) + 2B\,2^{k-1} + B\,2^k \\ &= 2^2\,T(2^{k-2}) + 2B\,2^k. \end{aligned}$$

Repeating the foregoing steps, we find

$$\begin{aligned} T(2^k) &\le 2^3\,T(2^{k-3}) + 3B\,2^k \\ &\le 2^4\,T(2^{k-4}) + 4B\,2^k \\ &\;\;\vdots \\ &\le 2^k\,T(2^0) + kB\,2^k = 2^k\,T(1) + kB\,2^k = 2^k\,A + kB\,2^k \end{aligned}$$

and, since $n = 2^k$, we can write the preceding inequality as

$$T(n) \le An + (\log_2 n)Bn = O(n \log n).$$

Thus, *Mergesort* allows us to sort a list of n elements in time $O(n \log n)$, whereas *SelectionSort* took time $O(n^2)$. To get a feel for the difference this makes, let us ignore any multiplicative constants in the big-O estimates and consider just the functions n^2 and $n \log_2 n$. If $n = 65{,}536$, then n^2 is equal to 4,294,967,296 whereas $n \log_2 n$ is only 1,048,576, a reduction by a factor of over 4,000.

We should emphasize that in neither of the preceding examples have we actually *proved* that the timing functions we found satisfied the recursive definitions. Iterative expansion is very close to being a rigorous proof, except for the fact that we relied on our intuition to guess the general pattern for the timing function. To be strictly correct, we should treat the function found through iterative expansion as a guess until we proved (almost invariably by induction on n) that the timing function satisfied its recursive definition.

For your reference, we now list the solutions to some common recurrence relations.

Case 1. $T(1) = 1; \quad T(n) = pT(n/q) + n^d$, for $n > 1$.

$$T(q^k) = \begin{cases} (k+1)p^k, & \text{if } q^d = p, \\ \dfrac{p^{k+1} - (q^d)^{k+1}}{p - q^d}, & \text{if } q^d \neq p \end{cases}$$

so we have

$$T(n) = \begin{cases} O(n^d), & \text{if } q^d > p, \\ O(n^d \log n), & \text{if } q^d = p, \\ O(n^{\log_q p}), & \text{if } q^d < p. \end{cases}$$

Case 2. $T(1) = 1; \quad T(n) = pT(n/q) + \log n$, for $n > 1$.

$$T(q^k) = \begin{cases} 1 + (\log q)\dfrac{k(k+1)}{2}, & \text{if } p = 1, \\ p^k + (\log q)\dfrac{k(1-p)-p}{(1-p)^2}, & \text{if } p \neq 1. \end{cases}$$

so we have

$$T(n) = \begin{cases} O(\log^2 n), & \text{if } p = 1 \\ O(n^{\log_q p}), & \text{if } p \neq 1 \end{cases}$$

Example 5.1.

Consider an algorithm that has timing function given by

$T(1) = 1$ (or any other constant, as it happens)

$T(n) = 3\ T(n\ /\ 2) + n$, for $n > 1$.

Such a timing function arises from a fast multiplication algorithm, and expresses the time needed to multiply two n-digit numbers by that algorithm. In this case we have a function of the form covered by Case 1, with $p = 3$, $q = 2$, and $d = 1$. Since $q^d < p$, we see that the timing function must satisfy

$$T(n) = O(n^{\log_2 3}) = O(n^{1.59}).$$

Example 5.2.

Suppose that we had an algorithm with timing function, $T(n)$, which satisfied

$$T(1) = 1,$$
$$T(n) = T(n/4) + \log n.$$

Because of the log n term, we find ourselves in Case 2, with $p = 1$ (and the value of q is immaterial in this case), so an upper bound on the timing function is $T(n) = O(log^2 n)$.

5.2 CASE STUDY: DESIGN OF ALGORITHMS

The analysis of *Mergesort* and *Selectionsort* has provided us with evidence that there is, as it were, more than one way to skin a cat. It is not at all uncommon that the first algorithm we come up with to solve a problem is by no means the most efficient way to solve the problem. We have seen another example of this in the difference in running times of the obvious and the Boyer-Moore algorithms for pattern matching with strings. Creating an efficient algorithm to perform a task is somewhat like designing an efficient data structure: While they both require a degree of creativity, there are some general principles that may make the design process easier. For instance, one of the organizing themes of this book is that categorizing possible organizations of data into linear, hierarchical, and network abstract data types allows us to ignore the superficial differences between problems and concentrate on the essential features that lead to efficient implementations. A similar level of abstraction for the design of algorithms provides us with **design paradigms**: a collection of commonly used techniques, such as divide-and-conquer, that are applicable to a wide variety of seemingly different algorithms. In this section we will explore some of these paradigms, and see how they may be used to produce algorithms for the computation of the Fibonacci numbers.

We have already seen one algorithm for computing Fibonacci numbers, a recursive algorithm that is so simple to state yet so inefficient that it serves as a classic example of when *not* to use recursion. This is a simple example of a divide-and-conquer algorithm: We compute *Fib(n)* by breaking the problem into two smaller pieces, namely, computation of *Fib(n – 1)* and *Fib(n – 2)*, and then combining the smaller solutions (by adding them, in this case) into a solution of the original problem. Although we do not do it here, it is not difficult to show that the timing function, *T(n)*, for this algorithm, is proportional to *Fib(n)* itself, and hence we could show that $T(n) = O(1.62^n)$. Of course, any exponential time algorithm is so time-consuming, even for small problems, that we should try to avoid it if at all possible. What we will do is explore some other ways of attacking this problem, and learn a little about algorithm design in the bargain.

The problem with the divide-and-conquer version of *Fib* is, as we mentioned, that it makes so many duplicate function calls. A divide and conquer algorithm typically works from the top down, with each successive function call requiring the solution of a smaller instance of the problem. We might eliminate the effects of the duplicate function calls if we use a technique known as **dynamic programming**, in which we work from the bottom up rather than from the top down. With dynamic programming, we first solve and save the small instances of the problem, and then combine these as we go to produce solutions for successively larger instances, until we come to the solution we originally required. For our example, we know that *Fib*(0) = *Fib*(1) = 1, so we can use these to find *Fib*(2), and we can use *Fib*(1) and *Fib*(2) to find *Fib*(3), and so on. This is a particularly nice instance of dynamic programming in that we need to save only the two most recently computed values of *Fib*, so the amount of memory required is constant (which is not the case with many other dynamic programming instances, and can occasionally lead to real trouble).

Having provided the background, it is now quite easy to write a dynamic programming version for *Fib*.

```
function IterativeFib(n : integer) : integer;
    var  old, prior, recent,  i : integer;
begin
    prior := 1;
    old:= 0;
    for  i := 1 to n  do begin
        recent := prior + old;
        old := prior;
        prior := recent
    end;
    IterativeFib := recent
end;
```

If we look at the time this takes to run, it is clear that we have a considerable improvement here over the original exponential version. The time required by this algorithm is driven by the **for** loop, which is repeated *n* times. We thus have an algorithm with *O(n)* running time.

We have improved the time needed to compute *Fib(n)* from exponential to linear. This in itself is no mean feat, but a natural question is whether we can do even better. As it happens, we can, and by a considerable margin. In fact, we can find another algorithm that is, in a sense, as much of an improvement over linear time as linear time was over exponential. Such an improvement, however, does depend on how clever we can be, and is not gained just by considering another design paradigm. In other words, having an arsenal of abstract notions can be helpful, but it is not always a substitute for plain old good thinking.

If we play with the Fibonacci numbers enough, or search the (copious) literature on the subject, we may be lucky enough to discover the identities

$$Fib(2k) = (Fib(k))^2 + (Fib(k-1))^2$$

$$Fib(2k+1) = (Fib(k))^2 + 2Fib(k)Fib(k-1),$$

which hold for all $k \geq 1$. These identities immediately suggest our first try: a divide-and-conquer scheme, one in which the smaller problems to be solved are *half* the size of the original, rather than just one or two less than the original, as was the case with our first algorithm. The implementation of this algorithm follows immediately from the definition.

```
function BetterDCFib(n : integer) : integer;
   var  half, halfLess1 : integer;
begin
   if n <= 1 then
      BetterDCFib := 1
   else begin
      half := BetterDCFib(n div 2);
      halfLess1 := BetterDCFib(n div 2 – 1);
      if odd(n) then
         BetterDCFib := half * (half + 2 * halfLess1 )
      else
         BetterDCFib := half * half + halfLess1 * halfLess1
   end
end;
```

We see that the timing function for this algorithm satisfies

$$T(1) = A$$

$$T(n) = 2T(n/2) + B,$$

for some constants A and B, where we have assumed that multiplication requires constant time.* If we use the tables given previously for the solution of recurrence relations with $p = 2$, $q = 2$, and $d = 0$, we see that the timing function $T(n) = O(n)$, so we have a

*As it happens, if makes no difference here even if we assume that multiplication runs in time proportional to the square of the number of digits in the numbers to be multiplied, as is does in the elementary school multiplication algorithm. The timing estimate will be the same, although it is a trifle tricky to calculate.

divide-and-conquer algorithm that is a great improvement over the original, exponential, divide-and-conquer version, but which, to our chagrin, is no better than the dynamic programming version we just invented, and is far less obvious in the bargain.

We may still be able to find a better Fibonacci algorithm, however, if we apply dynamic programming to the halving identity we gave before. For example, if we needed to compute $Fib(61)$, the halving identity tells us that $Fib(61) = Fib(30)^2 + 2Fib(30)Fib(29)$. $Fib(30)$ and $Fib(29)$, in turn, may be computed from $Fib(15)$, $Fib(14)$, and $Fib(13)$, and so on, as Figure 5.3 indicates.

The bottom row of the diagram contains the numbers that we will use to begin the algorithm. It turns out that the halving identities are valid for these numbers, if we interpret the bottom row of the diagram to be $Fib(1)$, $Fib(0)$, and $Fib(-1)$. This algorithm has the nice property that the original dynamic programming version also had, namely, that at each stage we need only generate and store a constant number of intermediate values (three, in this case). The algorithm is implemented as follows:

```
function BetterItFib(n : integer) : integer;
   var recent, prior, oldest : integer;    {the left, middle, right entries in each row}
       s, t, u : integer;                  {auxiliary variables for squares and products}
       i, k : integer;                     {loop index variables]
       v : array [1 .. 100] of integer;    {the indices of the left column}
begin
   v[1] := n;
   k := 1;
   while v[k] > 1 do begin
       k := k + 1;
       v[k] := v[k – 1] div 2;             {set up Fib indices of leftmost column}
   end;

   recent := 1;
   prior := 1;                             {fill in bottom row}
   oldest := 0;

   for i := k - 1 downto 1 do begin        {fill in the other rows from bottom to top}
       s := recent * recent;
       t := prior * prior;
       u := prior * oldest;
       if odd(v[i]) then begin
           recent := s + 2 * recent * prior;
           prior := s + t
       end else begin
           recent := s + t;
           prior := t + 2 * u
       end;
       oldest := recent - prior
   end;
   BetterItFib := recent
end;
```

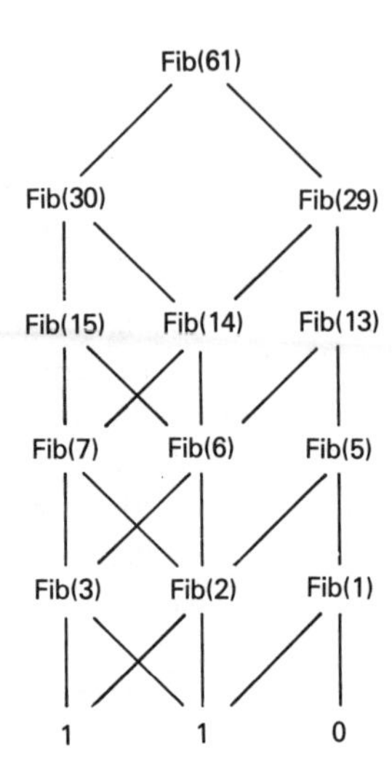

Figure 5.3 Computation tower for *Fib*(61).

Now we do have an improvement over the two prior linear algorithms. The timing of this algorithm is obviously driven by the number of iterations of the **while** and **for** loops, and each of these loops iterates not more than k times, where k is the number of times n can be divided by 2 before becoming less than or equal to 1. In the preceding example, for instance, we successively divided 61 by 2, obtaining 30, 15, 7, 3, and 1. It took only five divisions to complete, and in general we will have k equal to the integer part of $\log_2 n$, just as we saw with the binary search algorithm. In other words, we have obtained an algorithm to compute *Fib(n)* that runs in time $O(log\ n)$, which is a considerable improvement over the linear algorithms we obtained earlier.

To show just how much of an improvement this is, the following table lists the running time, in seconds, of the last three Fibonacci algorithms when coded and run on a computer. We omitted the first version, which takes exponential time, because even for $n = 500$ that algorithm takes so long that your author would probably still be sitting around waiting for the routine to finish by the time this book reached your hands. We also cheated here as we did with the factorial timing figures, doing dummy calculations rather than computing actual values, which would have quickly overrun the available integer size on the computer being used.

n	**Iterative (linear)**	**D&C (linear)**	**Better iterative (logarithmic)**
500	2.18	4.93	0.25
1,000	4.35	9.85	0.28
1,500	6.53	14.73	0.32
2,000	8.72	19.68	0.35
2,500	10.90	24.70	0.42

Notice that for $n = 2{,}500$, the logarithmic version runs nearly 26 times faster than the best of the two linear algorithms. Not only is this a considerable gain in speed, but we should also note that the factor of improvement gets steadily better as n continues to increase. It would be a shame to have this zippy algorithm and not try it out, so we combined the logarithmic Fibonacci algorithm with the multiprecision arithmetic package in the exercises of Chapter 3 to compute *Fib*(2500). The value is

21310 97222 36481 72589 63242 99517 04797 43181 82053 63701
26875 36286 82558 35307 75962 65908 63125 48730 00201 26214
96898 63548 93376 81055 89937 52038 31678 59730 52343 74709
69374 68058 04846 42829 49473 92542 08489 07002 68999 40079
55245 76061 32292 71988 13891 46345 17152 25018 97283 38958
65782 03918 75946 09662 37273 83020 86808 97754 80618 27768
74273 19326 52665 55633 51096 37048 85724 90223 86306 65583
32769 19447 11144 05709 16925 03000 91519 44351 33550 74402
82898 89121 17721 50743 92607 24419 66483 49939 23257 78345
04373 01079 83191 48002 43767 65760 08087 84351 53403 30624
11236 40660 84217 04602 501.

If you're thinking, "Why on earth would anyone have even the slightest interest in finding all 523 digits of a number that, itself, has no apparent use?" then shame on you. We spent several pages pursuing this topic mainly because it is intellectually stimulating. There is a reflection here of the human drive to explore—to go higher, farther, deeper, or faster than we have gone before—and this alone is enough for us to count our time as well spent. There are some purely practical benefits as well, some of them immediate and others only potential. You have been exposed to the barest introduction to algorithm design, a topic that is the subject of entire textbooks and that might just come in handy when you find yourself with the task of designing a program of your own. In addition, we can rarely tell ahead of time where a particular line of inquiry might lead us. Just because a problem like this has no apparent applicability doesn't mean that it has no application. We may just not have discovered it—yet.

We haven't finished off this problem—you might want to consider whether there is an even faster algorithm lurking out there. We haven't proved that $O(\log n)$ is the best we can do when computing Fibonacci numbers; all we have done is to put it aside for a while so that we can go on to other material.

5.3 RECURSIVE DATA STRUCTURES

We could define the structure of the abstract data type LIST by giving the following recursive definition:

Definition 5.1 The abstract data type LIST consists of a set ATOM and a set of elements, called lists, such that each list consists of either (1) nothing at all (which we will sometimes denote by NIL), or (2) an atom, followed by a list.

In this definition, the set POSITION and its linear order of the (P, R, v) definition is implicit in the phrase *followed by*, and the definition allows us to show that an element is a list by repeatedly building a list from atoms. For instance, the object (x, y), where x and y are members of ATOM, is a list because, first, (y) is a list (since it consists of an atom, y, followed by the empty list), so (x, y) is a list because it consists of the atom x followed by the list (y). We could generalize this argument by induction on the number of elements in a list to provide the iterative definition that $(a_1, a_2, \ldots, a_n)$ is a list, if all the a_i's are atoms.

We have seen all along that decisions of form (the structure of an ADT) may imply decisions of function (i.e., those operations that can be performed on the data structure). With this recursive definition of LIST, for instance, we think of a list as either empty or having an atom at the head and a sublist at the tail, so it would be quite natural to have primitives like those that follow:

Head(L : LIST) : ATOM returns the atom at the start of the list L, if L is not empty, and returns an error message if the list is empty .

Tail(L : LIST) : LIST returns the sublist of L consisting of everything except for the first atom, if L is nonempty, and returns an error if L is empty.

Insert(a : ATOM ; L : LIST) : LIST returns the list which would have a as its first atom and L as its tail.

One reason that we did not choose to define a list in this fashion originally (apart from the pedagogical reason that no one would have understood it so early in the game) is that the uses we had in mind for LIST frequently made explicit reference to position in the list, whereas position is not directly available in the recursive definition. For instance, recall that *Update(a, p, L)* replaced the atom in position p with the atom a, and ran in constant time in any of the three implementations we gave. In the recursive form of LIST, however, we do not have direct access to position p, so we would be forced to make a definition like the following—assuming, to make life easy, that POSITION is the positive integers.

```
procedure Update(a : ATOM ; p : POSITION ; var L : LIST);
{Changes the atom in the p-th position of L to be a, }
{assuming, for simplicity, that L has at least p elements.}
   var M : LIST;
begin
   if p = 1 then
      L := Insert(a, Tail(L))          {it's easy to update the first atom}
   else begin
      M := Tail(L);                    {M is L without its first element}
      Update(a, p - 1, M);             {put a where it belongs in M}
      L := Insert(Head(L), M)          {and put the first element back}
   end
end;
```

You can see that the definition of *Update* is not much longer for the recursively defined LIST than it was for the iterative version in Chapter 3, but if you trace the action of this algorithm you'll see that it runs in time $O(n)$, rather than in constant time. It is also likely that you would have had a more difficult time writing the definition of *Update*, at least until you had had a bit more practice with recursive algorithms. With this definition, *Head*, *Tail*, and *Insert* are easy to describe, but we have no direct way of even *defining* what the pth position was. One advantage that we do gain, however, is that a recursively defined data structure may make us aware of elegant recursive forms of algorithms on that data structure. Suppose, for instance, that ATOM consisted of integers. Then we could find the sum of the atoms in a list by adding the head atom to the result obtained by summing the tail of the list, as follows:

```
function SumList(L : LIST) : integer;
begin
   if L = NIL then
      SumList := 0
   else
      SumList := Head(L) + SumList(Tail(L))
end;
```

The point is not that this is the only (or even necessarily the best) way to perform this operation, but rather that recursively defined data structures may point out good solutions that might escape us at first glance.

General Lists and LISP

If we make a seemingly small change in the recursive definition of LIST, we find ourselves in possession of an ADT of surprising complexity, one that is used as the primary structure of the language LISP, and which provides us with our first example of a data structure that is not inherently linear in nature.

Definition 5.2. The GENLIST abstract data type consists of a set ATOM and a set of elements, called **general lists**, each of which consists of either (1) nothing at all (which we will also denote by NIL), or (2) two parts: (a) a head part (called the **CAR** of the list), which is an atom *or a general list*, and (b) a tail part (called the **CDR** of the list), which is itself a general list.

Notice that the only difference between this definition and the recursive definition of a list is that we allow the head to be a list here. The names CAR (pronounced as it is written) and CDR (pronounced "cudder") seem to have little to do with the head and the tail of a list, but they have been firmly ensconced in the jargon for nearly three decades, and are kept at least in part because they provide that heady sense of power that comes from knowing arcane names for simple things. (This completes the standard disclaimer that appears the first time anyone is exposed to CAR and CDR; some authors delve even more deeply and mention that CAR was derived from the term "contents of the address register," and CDR originally stood for "contents of the decrement register," but we wouldn't dream of going into that much detail.*) A general list, then, may be referred to simply by what is known as a **CONS cell** (don't ask), referring to the CAR part and the CDR part of the general list, as shown in Figure 5.4. To make reading and writing simpler, we will eliminate the word *general*, and stipulate that, throughout the rest of this section, the word *list* will henceforth refer to *general lists*, unless specific mention is made to the contrary.

From the definition of GENLIST, we see that anything that is a list under our old definition is also a general list (since a list is nothing but a special case of a general list), so (d) is a general list (consisting of the atom d followed by NIL), and, for the same reason, (b c) is a general list (consisting of the atom b followed by the general list (c)), hence ((b c) d) is also a general list (consisting of the general list (b c) followed by the general list (d)), so (a (b c) d) is also a general list, which we illustrate in Figure 5.5.

This list contains three elements, in order: the atom a, the list (b c), and the atom d. We can count the number of elements of a list in a CONS cell picture by counting the number of cells in the top row, and we can tell what sort of objects these elements are by referring to the CAR portions of each of the top-level CONS cells. For this list, the CAR part is the atom a, while the CDR part is the list ((b c) d), which itself has CAR part (b c) and CDR part (d). A careful look at the definition should convince you that NIL itself is a list, which we would write (), and which is different from the list (NIL), which we would write (()). The former list has no elements, while the latter has a single element, the empty list. In Figure 5.6 we show the CONS cell representations of these lists, along with a more complicated example.

If you can understand that Figure 5.6(c) denotes the list (()(())), consider yourself well on the path to enlightenment.

We could implement GENLIST by making the CONS cells the fundamental structures and using pointers to link the cells together. We will overload the definition of a

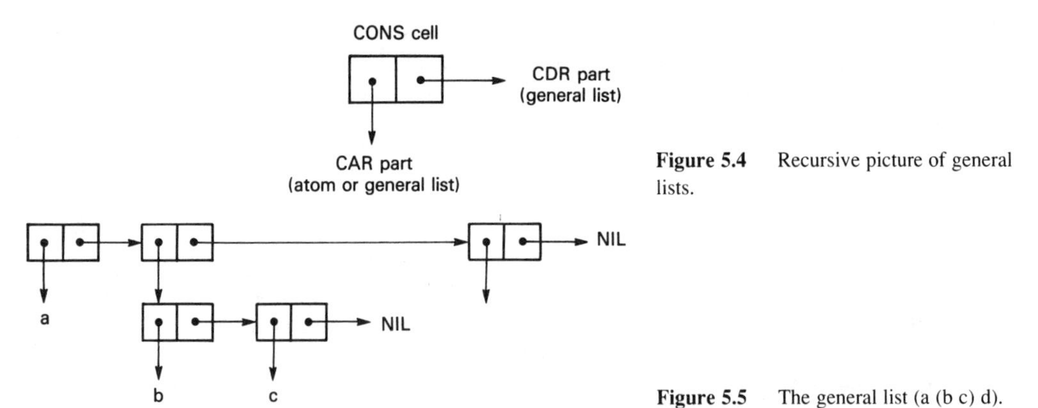

Figure 5.4 Recursive picture of general lists.

Figure 5.5 The general list (a (b c) d).

*This figure of speech, claiming retroactive innocence for a vebal crime already committed, is known as *praeteritio*, as for instance, "I wouldn't say he's a liar, but he does have to have another person call his hogs," and is commonly used by unscrupulous politicians and lawyers (which is not to imply that all, or even most, politicians or lawyers are unscrupulous [which is another example of *praeteritio*]).

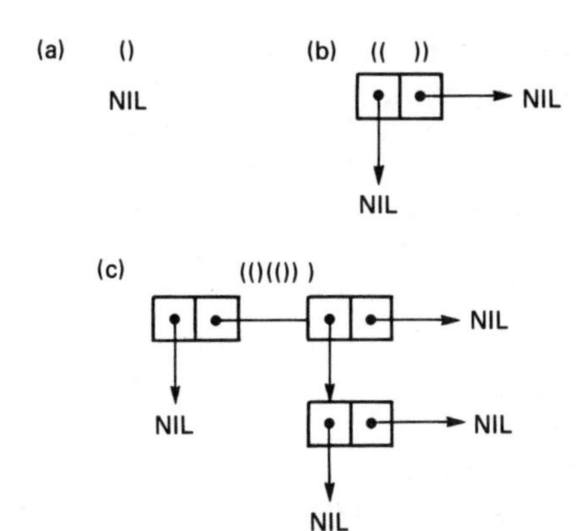

Figure 5.6 Some lists with no atoms.

cell by using a variant record to allow the cell to be either a CONS cell or a cell containing just an to a tag field *isAtom* which is true if and only if the cell consists of only an atom. (This is a considerable simplification of what really goes on in LISP, but it will be adequate for our purposes.) We will refer to a list by a pointer to the first CONS cell in the list, or by the **nil** pointer, if the list is empty.

```
type
   ATOM = {whatever};
   Link = ^Cell;
   Cell = record
         case isAtom : boolean;
            true : (data : ATOM);
            false : (car, cdr : Link)
          end;
   GENLIST = Link;
```

In this implementation, then, every cell has a field *isAtom*, and if this field contains the value *true* the cell has one other field for data, whereas if it is *false*, then the cell has two pointer fields, along with the tag field.

LISP, which we are modeling here, is a **functional language**, in which every statement is a function. This takes some getting used to, especially if you are familiar only with **procedural languages**, like Pascal, in which the statements often describe actions to be taken. The difference is exemplified by noting that the **if** statement in Pascal describes a transfer of control to another location in the program, whereas the corresponding statement in LISP,

(IF condition list1 list2)

is a list that is thought of as a function that returns the value of *list1* if the condition evaluates to any non-NIL value (which is interpreted to mean *true*), and returns the value of *list2* if the condition evaluates to NIL. LISP attempts to evaluate every list it sees, by applying the CAR part of a list to its CDR part , so the list (+ 3 4 5 6) would evaluate to the list (18), and the list (EQUAL 3 8) evaluates to NIL (which, remember, is understood to denote *false*). In other words, with very few exceptions, every statement in LISP is itself a list, one that is treated as a function that takes lists or atoms as arguments and returns a list as its result. One implication of all this is that arithmetic expressions in LISP are parenthesized versions of **prefix notation**, in which an operator precedes the arguments it operates on, so that the expression we would write as (3 + 4) * (8 + 6) would be written in LISP as (* (+ 3 4) (+ 8 6)).

One of the LISP primitives provides a means of making new lists by inserting a new element at the head of a list. If L is a list and x is either a list or an atom, the action of (CONS x L) is to return a list with the CAR part equal to x and the CDR part equal to L. LISP does this in the easiest way possible, namely by creating a new CONS cell, for which the CAR part points to x and the CDR part to L, as shown in Figure 5.7.

We encountered a similar construction back in Chapter 2, when we defined concatenation of strings in the linked list implementation. At that time we said that such a simple way was not a good idea, since it led to the problem of aliasing, that is, that any subsequent change to L would be reflected (invisibly) in the value of the concatenated list. LISP avoids the problem of aliasing in part by the way in which variables are assigned to values. In Figure 5.7, for instance, it would not be difficult to change L, but it would be difficult in LISP to change L accidentally in such a way as to make a change in the list pointed to by the arrow labeled (CONS x L).

LISP allows us to assign a variable to a value by the expression **SETQ**, so that (SETQ variable object) in our conceptualization would result in the variable being assigned a pointer to the object. In other words, we could change L in Figure 5.7 by, say, calling (SETQ L (CDR L)), where CDR returns the tail portion of the list, but all that would accomplish would be to move the L pointer one cell to the right, leaving all the cells connected as they were before. In simple terms, "what CONS hath joined together, LISP cannot (easily) tear apart." We could write the implementation of CONS as follows:

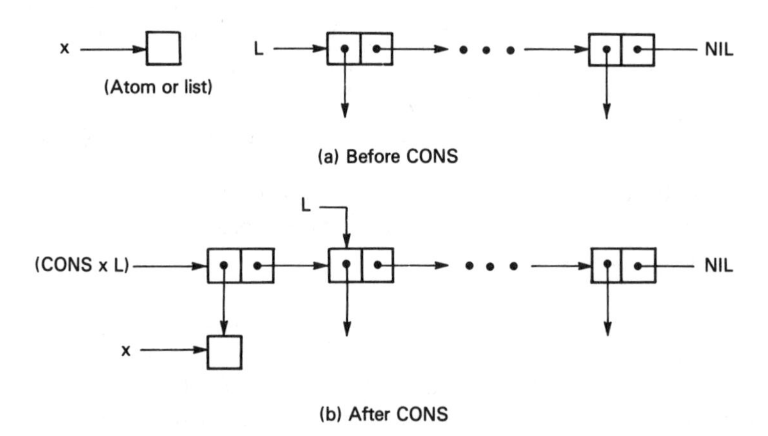

Figure 5.7 The LISP operation CONS.

```
function CONS(x, L : GENLIST) : GENLIST;
   var p : Link;
begin
   if L^.isAtom then begin
      writeln('cannot CONS onto an atom');
      CONS := nil
   end else begin
      New(p);                    {note: CONS always creates a new cell}
      p^.isAtom := false;
      p^.car := x;
      p^.cdr := L
      CONS := p
   end
end;
```

Another common LISP expression also builds a list from pieces, but in this case the pieces must all be lists. If *L1* was the list (a b c) and *L2* was the list (c d), then (APPEND L1 L2) would return the list (a b c c d), consisting of the elements of the original lists concatenated together. Notice the difference between CONS and APPEND: (CONS L1 L2) constructs a new list with *L1* as its first element, so (CONS L1 L2) would be ((a b c) c d). The elements of a list, you'll recall, do not need to be atoms, so if *L3* was the list (x (y z) w), then (APPEND L3 L1) would return the list (x (y z) w a b c). We could define (APPEND L1 L2) by making the last cell of *L1* have its CDR pointer point to the first cell of *L2*, as we indicate in Figure 5.8.

The problem with this definition is that it changes *L1*. Since a list consists of all the cells linked by CDR pointers, APPENDing *L1* to *L2* destroys the original *L1* and makes it equal to the concatenation of *L1* and *L2*. In order not to introduce this **side effect** into the definition of APPEND, we must first copy the contents of *L1* to a temporary list *T*, and then concatenate *T* to *L2*, as we do in Figure 5.9.

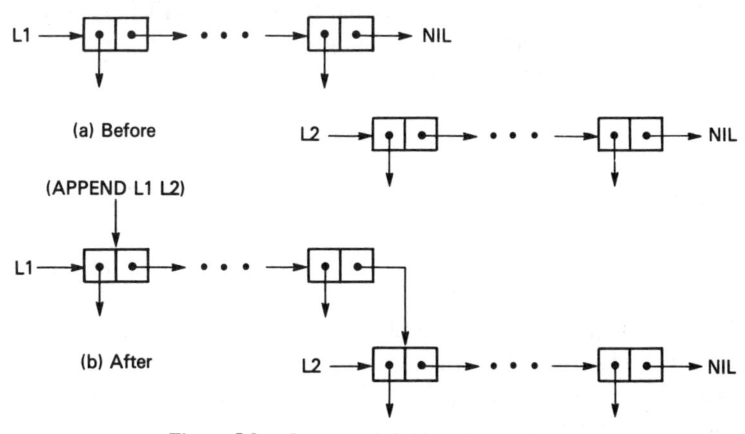

Figure 5.8 Incorrect definition of APPEND.

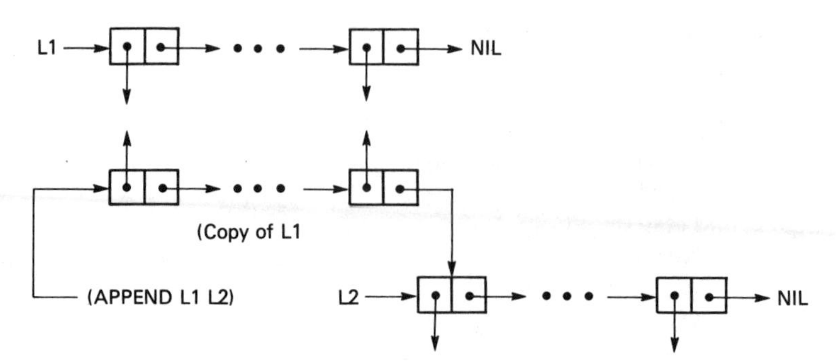

Figure 5.9 Correct definition of APPEND

The "incorrect" definition of APPEND, by the way, is available in some dialects of LISP under the name **NCONC**. A recursive definition of APPEND for our implementation is nice and short, although it takes a bit of careful thought to understand. We copy *L1* as we go, following the CDR pointers (in the jargon, we "CDR our way down through *L1*"), and CONSing new cells onto the copy of *L1*. All the calls to CONS are pending until we reach the end of the copied list, at which time we just link the last cell of the copy to the first cell of *L2*.

```
function APPEND(L1, L2 : GENLIST) : GENLIST;
begin
   if L1^.isAtom or L2^.isAtom then
      writeln('cannot APPEND atoms')
   else if L1 = nil then
      APPEND := L2
   else
      APPEND := CONS(L^.car, APPEND(L^.cdr, L2))
end;
```

As a final example, consider the function **FLATLIST**, which takes a general list and returns an ordinary list consisting of the atoms in the original list. For instance, FLATLIST applied to the list

(a (b a (c b a)) (((d a) c) d (a))

would return the result

(a b a c b a d a c d a).

We could write a recursive definition by observing that the bailout condition is to return NIL if the list was empty, and otherwise the recursive step would be to return the list that resulted from applying FLATLIST to the CAR part and the CDR part, and concatenating the results.

```
function FLATLIST(L : GENLIST) : GENLIST;
begin
    if L = nil then
        FLATLIST := nil
    else if L^.car^.isAtom then
        FLATLIST := CONS(L^.car, FLATLIST(L^.cdr))
    else
        FLATLIST := APPEND(FLATLIST(L^.car), FLATLIST(L^.cdr))
end;
```

For those interested in the arcana of LISP, the LISP definition of FLATLIST is

```
(DEFUN FLATLIST (L)
    (IF (NULL L)
        NIL
        (IF (ATOM (CAR L))
          (CONS (CAR L) (FLATLIST (CDR L)))
          (APPEND (FLATLIST (CAR L)) (FLATLIST (CDR L)))
        )
    )
)
```

which is why some people say that LISP stands for "Lots of Irritating Silly Parentheses."

5.4 SUMMARY

A recursive definition is one that refers to the object it is defining, in such a way as to avoid unending loops. Recursive definitions are frequently more elegant than iterative definitions, and can sometimes provide insights lacking from iterative definitions, especially in situations where it is natural to define something in terms of a smaller instance of itself.

Recursively defined algorithms should be part of every computer scientist's vocabulary, since there are times when an algorithm would be much more difficult to define iteratively. We should always be careful, however, since it is usually the case that recursive algorithms take longer to run than the equivalent iterative versions, and it is sometimes the case that the simplicity of recursion can mask serious inefficiencies.

In spite of these cautions, we saw that recursive definitions can aid us in the process of designing very efficient algorithms, as was the case when we began with an exponential time algorithm to compute Fibonacci numbers, improved that to two linear time algorithms, and then further improved these to a logarithmic time algorithm.

This chapter serves as a transition from linear to nonlinear data structures. We saw that we could define lists recursively by saying that a list either was empty or consisted of an atom followed by a list. A slight generalization of the recursive definition of a list led to general lists, each of which is either empty or consists of an atom or a general list, followed by a general list. Such a structure does not have the linear structure of a list, and is the basis of the LISP language. Keep general lists in mind as you read the next chapters—they are really nothing but special cases of the nonlinear TREE data type.

5.5 EXERCISES

1. The standard nonnumeric example problem for recursion is the **Towers of Hanoi**. The folk tale that goes with the problem tells of a certain monastery where the monks are charged with the task of completing a puzzle, after which the world will end. The pieces of the puzzle consist of three posts and sixty-four disks, of graduated sizes, each of which has a hole in the center so it will fit on the posts (in the long version of the tale, the posts are diamonds and the disks are gold). The diagram indicates a five-disk version of the puzzle.

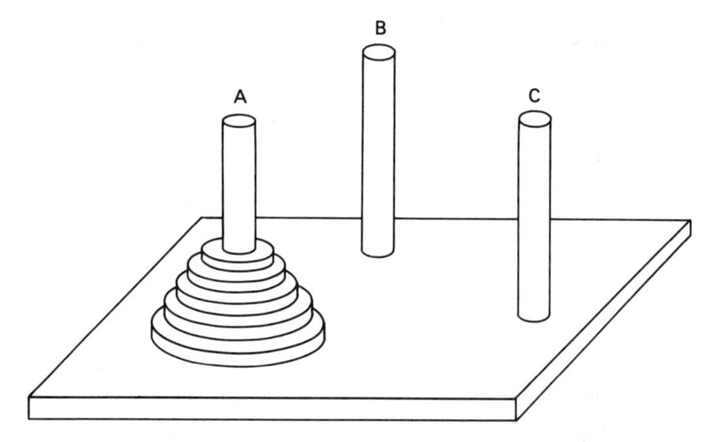

The object of the puzzle is to begin with all the disks stacked on one post in descending order of size, and to transfer all the disks to another post, again in descending order of size. The disks are moved one at a time, and at no time may a disk be placed atop one that is smaller. For example, to move two disks from post A to post C we could use the sequence A $\rightarrow$ B (top disk to B), A $\rightarrow$ C (second disk to C), B $\rightarrow$ C (old top disk to C, done).

(a) Find the shortest sequence of moves to transfer three disks.

(b) How many moves would you guess are required to transfer n disks?
The preceding sequence could be described as "Move 3 from A to C using B." Having done that, we could define "Move 3 from x to y using z" by

```
procedure Move 3 from x to y using z;
begin
   Move 2 from x to z using y;  {move top two disks to holding post}
   Move 1 from x to y using z;  {move remaining disk to destination post}
   Move 2 from z to y using x;  {move two disks from holding post to destination}
end;
```

(c) Write a recursive definition for "Move n from x to y using z," and trace its execution when $n = 3$.

(d) Using timing functions for your algorithm, how many disk moves are required to transfer n disks?

(e) At one move per second, how long will it take for the world to end? Should we be worried about the imminent demise of everything?

2. Since $n! = (n + 1)! / (n + 1)$, why couldn't we compute factorials by the following algorithm?

```
function UpFact(n : integer) : integer;
begin
   if n <= 1 then
      UpFact :=1
   else
      UpFact := UpFact(n + 1) div (n + 1)
end;
```

3. We mentioned that with the original recursive Fibonacci algorithm, *Fib*(100) might not run to completion on a real computer. Why?

4. Let the expression $C(n)$ denote the number of function calls made during the execution of $Fib(n)$. We saw that $C(5) = 15$, and it is clear that $C(0) = C(1) = 1$, since we must call *Fib* once just to get started.

(a) Compute $C(n)$ for $n = 0, 1, 2, \ldots, 8$, and compare with $Fib(n)$.

(b) Show that $C(n) = 2\,Fib(n) - 1$ (preferably by induction).

5. We saw that $Fib(5) = 8 = 3 + 5$, and that during execution of $Fib(5)$, there were three calls to $Fib(0)$, and five calls to $Fib(1)$. Show that this property can be generalized.

6. The numbers $C(n, k)$ are defined for all $n, k \geq 0$, by the following rules

$$C(n,0) = 1, \quad \text{for } n \geq 0,$$

$$C(n,k) = 0, \quad \text{for } k > n,$$

$$C(n,k) = C(n-1,k) + C(n-1,k-1), \quad \text{for } n \geq k > 0.$$

(a) Compute $C(3, 0)$, $C(3, 1)$, $C(3, 2)$, $C(3, 3)$.

(b) Write a recursive definition of a function that computes $C(n, k)$.

(c) The number $C(n, k)$ counts the number of different subsets of size k that can be made from a set of n elements. Prove this fact using the recursive definition of $C(n, k)$. *Hint*: Select any particular element from the set, then count the number of k-element subsets that do contain that element and those that do not.

(d) Prove that $C(n, k)$ can also be defined by $C(n, k) = n! / (k!(n - k)!)$.

7. Write recursive routines for the following operations:

(a) **Intlog**(n : integer) : integer, which is defined to be the highest power of 2 that is less than or equal to n, so *Intlog*(8) = 3, and *Intlog*(40) = 5.

(b) **Find**(a : ATOM ; L : LIST) : POSITION, for ordinary lists. You may want to write this so that it consists of a main routine to get started, and a recursive subroutine to track through the list.

(c) **Member**(a : ATOM ; L : LIST) : boolean, for ordinary lists, which returns *true* if and only if a is in the list L.

(d) **Purge(var** L : LIST), which removes any duplicate atoms from *L*. In other words, *Purge* applied to the list (a, b, a, c, b, c, d, a) might result in the list (b, c, d, a). You might want to use *Member* here.

(e) **Max**(L : LIST) : ATOM, which returns the largest element in a list (assuming that the underlying set of atoms is linearly ordered).

8. Write a function which computes x^n in time $O(\log n)$, assuming that multiplication takes constant time. *Hint*: Use a divide-and-conquer algorithm that halves n.

9. Describe as simply as possible what the following algorithms do (in other words, do not just repeat the definition of the algorithm):

(a)

```
function What(p, q : integer) : integer;
{Assume for this function that p and q are non-negative.}
   var r : integer;
begin
   r := p mod q;
   if r = 0 then
     What := q
   else
     What := What(q, r)
end;
```

(b)

```
procedure Change(var S : STACK);
   va x : ATOM;
begin
   if not Empty(S) then begin
     x := Top(S);
     Pop(S);
     if not Empty(S) then
        Pop(S);
     Change(S);
     Push(x, S)
   end
end;
```

10. The following predicate takes an array, *A*, of characters and returns *true* if and only if the subarray *A*[*start*], *A*[*start*+1], . . . , *A*[*end*] is a *palindrome*, that is, if it reads the same from left to right as it does from right to left (like 'NOON' or 'STATS').

```
function Palindrome(A : CharArray ; start, end : integer) : boolean;
begin
   if start ≥ end then
     Palindrome := true
   else if (A[start] = A[end]) and Palindrome(A, start + 1, end – 1) then
     Palindrome := true
   else
     Palindrome := false
end;
```

Use a stack to eliminate recursion from *Palindrome*, as was done in the text for *ReverseTraversal*.

11. The following recursively defined functions have interesting properties. Try some sample values of the arguments and explore their properties. It would be valuable for you to code and run these functions on a computer.

(a)

```
function Ulam(x : integer) : integer;
{It is not known that this function eventually halts for all x}
begin
   if x = 1 then
     Ulam :=1
   else if odd(n) then
     Ulam := Ulam(3 * x + 1)      {dangerous? we're going up here, not down}
   else
     Ulam := Ulam(n div 2)
end;
```

(b)

```
function Ackermann(x, y : integer) : integer;
{This gets large very rapidly, as x and y increase}
begin
   if x = 0 then
     Ackermann := y + 1
   else if y = 0 then
     Ackermann := Ackermann(x – 1, 1)
   else
     Ackermann := Ackermann(x – 1, Ackermann(x, y – 1))
end;
```

(c)

```
function Takeuchi(x, y, z : integer) : integer;
{This uses a lot of calls to find the result}
begin
   if x <= y then
     Takeuchi := z
   else
     Takeuchi := Takeuchi(Takeuchi(x–1, y, z),
                          Takeuchi(y–1, z, x),
                          Takeuchi(z–1, x, y))
end;
```

12. How long do the following functions take on input *n*?

(a)

```
function P(n : integer) : integer;
begin
   if n <= 1 then
     P := 1
   else
     P := 3 * P(n div 2)
end;
```

(b)

```
function Q(n : integer) : integer;
begin
   if n = 1 then
      Q := 1
   else begin
      t := 1;
      for i := 1 to n - 1 do
         t := t + Q(i);
      Q := t
   end
end;
```

(c)

```
      function R(n : integer) : integer;

         function S(n : integer) : integer;
         begin
            if n = 1 then
               S := 1
            else
               S := n + S(n - 1)
         enda {S};

      begin {R}
         if n = 1 then
            R := 2
         else
            R := R(n - 1) + S(n)
      end;
```

13. Consider the timing function $T(n)$ defined by

$$T(1) = 1,$$

$$T(n) = pT(n/3) + f(n), \quad \text{if } n > 1.$$

There are nine combinations of functions that can be made by letting $p = 2, 3, 4$, and $f(n) = \log_2 n, n, n^2$. Find big-O estimates for each of the timing functions that result.

14. Diagram with nested boxes the procedure calls used to compute *BetterDCFib*(5), and compare your diagram with that of the original *Fib*(5) given in the text.

15. Trace the action of *BetterItFib*(29).

16. **(a)** What do you notice about the powers A, A^2, A^3, A^4, A^5 of the following matrix?

$$A = \begin{bmatrix} 1 & 1 \\ 1 & 0 \end{bmatrix}$$

(b) Using the fast exponentiation algorithm of Exercise 8, describe another way to compute $Fib(n)$ in logarithmic time, assuming that matrix multiplication can be done in constant time.

(c) What matrix would you use in place of A to help you compute the values of the function defined by $f(0) = 1, f(1) = 1, f(n) = 3f(n-1) - f(n-2)$, for $n > 2$?

17. Show that if you restrict yourself to the usual arithmetic operations "+," "−," "*," "/," then it is impossible to compute *Fib(n)* by *any* algorithm in fewer than $c \log n$ steps, for some positive constant c. *Hint*: Count digits—how large is *Fib(n)*, and how fast can you get there?

18. If L is a nonempty list, what is (CONS (CAR L) (CDR L))?

19. What are the results of (CONS x NIL) and (APPEND x NIL) if

(a) x is an atom?

(b) x is a list?

20. Suppose we write APPEND as the symbol "•" in infix notation, so that "(APPEND L1 L2)" and "L1 • L2" would be understood to refer to the same operation. Provide examples to demonstrate the following:

(a) • is **associative**; that is, L1 • (L2 • L3) = (L1 • L2) • L3, for lists L1, L2, L3.

(b) NIL is the **identity element** for •, that is, L • NIL = NIL • L = L, for a list L.

(c) Is NIL the identity element for CONS?

21. Write functions to perform the following operations on general lists, using the implementation of GENLIST described in the text.

(a) **ATCOUNT**(L : GENLIST) : integer, which counts the number of atoms in a general list. For example, ATCOUNT of (a (b c) d) is 4, and ATCOUNT of (a (a) ((a))) is 3.

(b) **CONSCOUNT**(L : GENLIST) : integer, which counts the number of CONS cells in the internal representation of L, so that CONSCOUNT of (a (b c) d) is 5, and CONSCOUNT of (a (a) ((a))) is 6. (This, by the way, can be found from the written representation by counting the atoms plus the left parentheses and subtracting one.)

(c) **TOTAL_REVERSE**(L : GENLIST) : GENLIST, which returns L with every list reversed, so that TOTAL_REVERSE of (a (b c) d) is (d (c b) a).

(d) **PRINTLIST**(L : GENLIST), which in LISP would be a function, but which you may write as a procedure. PRINTLIST causes the list L to be printed with parentheses, as we would normally write it. You may assume that the procedure *Write* will be able to print an atom, no matter what form it may take.

Programming Projects

22. Write a program that will print the moves in an n-disk Towers of Hanoi solution.

23. **(a)** Write a program that will print binary numbers from 0 to $2^n - 1$ in increasing order. The algorithm should *not* perform any decimal-to-binary conversion. *Hint*: It goes without saying, we hope, that your solution will be recursive. Try thinking about printing all the numbers that begin with 0, followed by all the numbers that begin with 1.

(b) Using part (a) as a guide, write a program that will list all subsets of a set of n objects.

24. Combine the multiprecision arithmetic package of Chapter 3 with either of the factorial algorithms given in the text, and test your program by computing 200! and comparing your answer with those of your classmates.

25. Verify, by whatever means you wish, the value for *Fib*(2500) given in the text.

26. If your programming language has an internal timer, use it to compare the running times of the four Fibonacci algorithms given in the text.

6

Trees

The monkey's survival can only be understood by comprehending the inherent connectedness of the forest with its branches linked for fast escape.

Gilda Needles, *Life in the Trees*

We began this text by discussing strings and lists. By removing many of the operations that define the LIST abstract data type, we were able to define two new ADTs, stacks and queues. In each case, however, the underlying structure was the same: a linear structure with a unique first position immediately followed by a unique second position, immediately followed by a unique third position, and so on until the unique last position. This linear structure is important because there are so many cases in which information has a "natural" linear order. Of course, *so many* does not mean *all*: There are numerous instances in which information does not have a natural linear structure. We will see that once we remove the requirement that our data types have a linear structure, we will have easy access to a treasure trove of applications, such as representation of arithmetic expressions, improved sorting and searching, codes for data compression, and many others. In this chapter, and throughout the rest of the text, we will continue our program of gradually relaxing the restrictions on an ADT to produce new and more general abstract data types.

One obvious structural requirement we might consider dropping is that an element have at most one successor. The **hierarchical structure** which we then obtain is common among cataloguing schemes for published work. For example, *Computing Reviews*, published by the Association for Computing Machinery, has adopted a classification scheme for computer science literature that, in part, has the following form:

A. General literature
  A.0 General
  A.1 Introductory and Survey
  A.2 Reference
B. Hardware
  B.0 General
  B.1 Control Structures and Microprogramming
    B.1.0 General
    B.1.1 Control Design Styles
      Hardwired Control
      Microprogrammable Logic Arrays
  B.2 Arithmetic and Logic Structures
C. Computer systems organization
D. Software
E. Data
  E.0 General
  E.1 Data Structures (where this book might belong)
    Arrays
    Graphs
    Lists
    Tables
    Trees
  E.2 Data Storage Representations

In this classification, each major topic has several subsidiary topics, each of which may itself be broken down into several subtopics, and so on. Although this scheme could be viewed as a linear arrangement (indeed, such an organization is suggested by the linear arrangement from the top to the bottom of the page), the indentation we used suggests that there is more to the structure than a simple linear arrangement. This behavior is typical, as we shall see: The fewer restrictions we place on the structure of an ADT, the more conceptually complex the instances of the ADT become.

6.1 THE STRUCTURE OF TREES

A hierarchical data structure—one for which an element may have at most one predecessor but may have many successors—is called a **tree**. As usual, the underlying set of atoms may be any set we wish, and the structure of the positions is defined by three simple rules. An element of the TREE abstract data type is, as usual, a triple (P, R, v), where P is a subset of the set of positions, R is a relation on P, and v is the usual evaluation function from POSITION to ATOM, for which the following properties hold.

1. There is a unique position, $r \in P$, called the **root**, which has no predecessor.
2. Every position in P except the root has exactly one immediate predecessor.

3. Every position in P except the root has the root as a (perhaps not immediate) predecessor.

Customarily, the positions in a tree are referred to as **nodes** (in computer science, and **vertices** in mathematical literature), and the relation R is said "is a parent of."

We frequently wish to extend the definition of the "parent of" relation, producing what is known as the reflexive, transitive closure of R (see Appendix A for details). We say that a node n is the **ancestor** of a node m if either

1. $n = m$. (If this does not happen, we say n is a **proper ancestor** of m.)
2. n is the parent of an ancestor of m.

In other words, n is an ancestor of m if n and m are the same node or if there is a "parent of" chain from n to m. Using this notation, we then may define a tree as a set of nodes, one of which we distinguish by calling it the root, along with a parent relation such that (1) the root has no parent, (2) every node except the root has a parent, and (3) the root is the ancestor of every node. In Figure 6.1 we show several examples of trees and nontrees, using arrows from node n to node m to indicate that n is the parent of m, and indicating the root by a filled circle.

In Figure 6.1, (d) is not a tree because there are two possible roots, that is, nodes with no parents, and also because there is a node with two parents; (e) is not a tree because it is not connected, which is to say it fails condition (3), and likewise has two candidates for roots; and (f) is not a tree because it has no node that could be the root. Incidentally, we should not dismiss (e) out of hand; it is the disconnected union of several trees and, as such, is called (to no one's surprise) a **forest**. We will see forests later in this chapter, and again in Chapter 9.

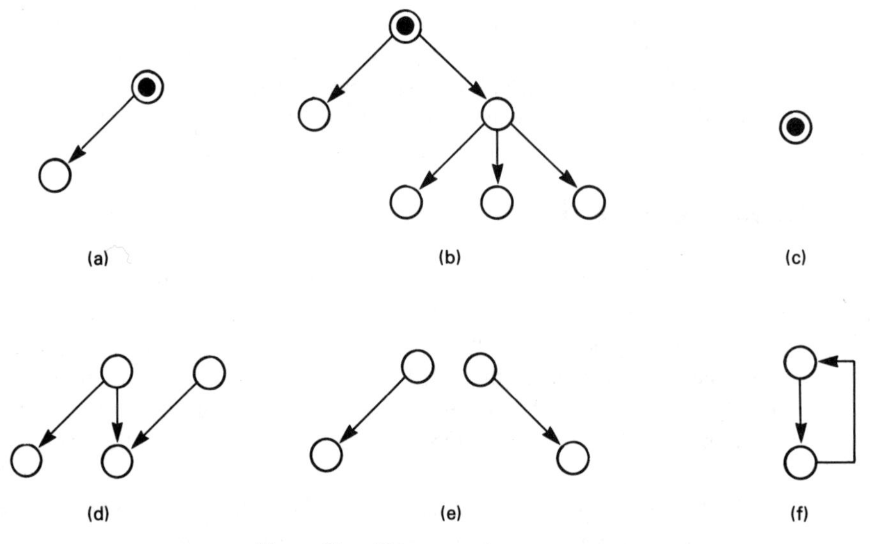

Figure 6.1 Three trees, three nontrees.

It is customary when drawing trees to eliminate the arrows and link the nodes with simple edges instead. To eliminate confusion, we adopt the convention (generally used in the United States, though not necessarily in other countries) that any node will be drawn lower on the page than its parent. This is consistent with the way family trees are generally drawn, but it has the disadvantage that the root appears on the top of the picture so that, as is said about the African baobab tree, the tree grows down from its root.

Because trees are structurally more complicated than lists or the other linear structures, we need a number of terms to describe the nodes of a tree and the relationships between those nodes.

Definition 6.1. Let T be a tree, and let n and m be nodes of T. We say that

1. n and m are **siblings**, if they have the same parent.
2. m is a **descendant** of n, if n is an ancestor of m.
3. A node is a **leaf** of T, if it has no children.
4. A node is an **internal node**, if it is not a leaf.
5. An **edge** of T connects two nodes, one of which is the parent of the other.
6. A **path** in T is the collection of edges that join two nodes, one of which is the ancestor of the other, and the **length** of a path consists of the number of edges in the path.
7. The **height** of a node is the length of the longest path from that node to a leaf.
8. The **depth** of a node is the length of the (unique) path from that node to the root.
9. The height (or depth) of a tree is the height of the root, namely, the length of the longest path from the root to a leaf.
10. A **subtree**, S, of T **rooted at** n is a tree that is made from T by considering n to be the root of S, and including in S all descendants of n.

In the tree of Figure 6.2 we see that a and b are siblings; that h is a descendant of b; that the nodes e, f, g, and h are leaves; that r, a, b, c, and d are internal nodes; that the height of b is 2 and its depth 1; that the tree has height 3; and that the subtree rooted at node b consists of nodes b, d, e, f, and h, along with all the edges connecting those nodes. Notice that we have adopted the convention of drawing children below parents, so r must be the root of this tree.

We will define a ***k*-ary tree** to be a tree for which each node has at most k children, so that the tree of Figure 6.2 would be a 3-ary tree. In what will follow, it will be useful for us to know how many nodes a k-ary tree of depth d could have. We will do this by looking at the maximum and minimum number of nodes possible at each depth. At depth 0 there is only the root, which could have at most k children at depth 1. Each of these children could have k children at depth 2, for a maximum of k^2 children possible at depth 2, and it is clear that we could continue this process to show that at depth d there could be at most k^d nodes. Therefore, the maximum possible number of nodes in a tree of depth d is

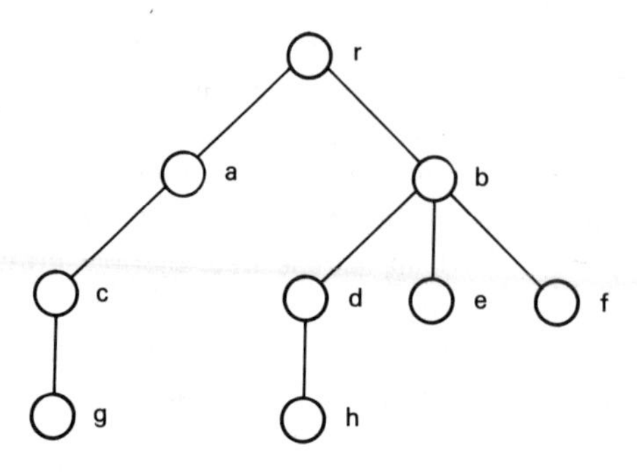

Figure 6.2 A sample tree.

$$n \le 1 + k + k^2 + \ldots + k^d = \frac{k^{d+1} - 1}{k - 1} \le k^{d+1} - 1 < k^{d+1}$$

and since there could be as few as one node at each depth from 0 to d, we see that

1. A k-ary tree of depth d can have n nodes, with $d + 1 \le n < k^{d+1}$.

If we look at this from another point of view taking logs of both sides of the inequality $n < k^{d+1}$, we could equally well say that

2. A k-ary tree with n nodes could have depth d, with $\log_k(n) < d \le n - 1$.

Computer scientists, however, rarely make use of such general trees as we have defined here. It is customary to impose an additional linear order on each set of siblings, so we would say that if the tree of Figure 6.2 was considered to be an **ordered tree**, then node d would be the **left child** of b, node e would be the **right sibling of** d, and node f would be the right sibling of e. In other words, the objects in Figure 6.3 would be equivalent as trees, but would be different as ordered trees. If the reason for this distinction escapes you, think of the left child as the *eldest child*, and imagine siblings ordered by age. In many historical novels and plays (not to mention many contemporary families), one's position in age order makes a significant contribution to the part one plays.

Before we leave general trees entirely, it is worth mentioning that there is a natural recursive definition for trees, one that generalizes slightly the definition we have already made. We may define a tree by stipulating that a tree consists of either (1) nothing at all, which we will call the **empty tree**, or (2) a node, along with a (possibly empty) collection $\{T_1, T_2, \ldots, T_n\}$ of subtrees, each of which is itself a tree. We could

Figure 6.3 Order matters.

modify this definition to refer to ordered trees by insisting that the subtrees be in linear order, rather than an unordered set.

6.2 BINARY TREES

It happens that in many applications, we need only be concerned with trees (usually ordered) for which each node has at most two children, that is, with 2-ary ordered trees. Because "2-ary ordered trees" is such a cumbersome locution, we call such trees **binary trees**. Not only do they permit simpler implementations (because we can make a static, rather than dynamic, allocation of the children of a node), but in a sense they are all we really need to represent any kinds of ordered trees whatsoever, as we shall see shortly. The recursive definition of binary trees is particularly simple.

Definition 6.2. A binary tree is made up of nodes, which are elements of some set. A binary tree consists of either (1) nothing at all (the empty tree), or (2) a node, called the root of the binary tree, along with a **left subtree** and a **right subtree**, both of which are binary trees.

To see this definition in action, consider Figure 6.4. This object might be a binary tree, because it has a node, *a*, and we can demonstrate that it is by showing that the left and right subtrees are binary trees. The left subtree is a binary tree because it consists of a node, *b*, along with two subtrees, both of which happen to be empty. In a similar way, we can show that the right subtree is also a binary tree because it consists of a node, *c*, along with an empty left subtree and a right subtree that is itself a binary tree because it consists of a node, *d*, along with two subtrees, both of which are empty.

Although the recursive definition of binary trees is certainly elegant, it seems to involve a lot of work to prove that an object is a binary tree by this definition. You may have also noticed that we have so far made no mention of the operations that define the BINARY TREE abstract data type (or any of the other tree ADTs, for that matter). Rest assured, we will remedy these deficiencies, but before we do a word is in order about the tantalizing hint we dropped earlier that binary trees were all we really needed. What we meant was that any ordered tree could be represented as a binary tree in such a way as to preserve all the information about the original ordered tree. This might seem

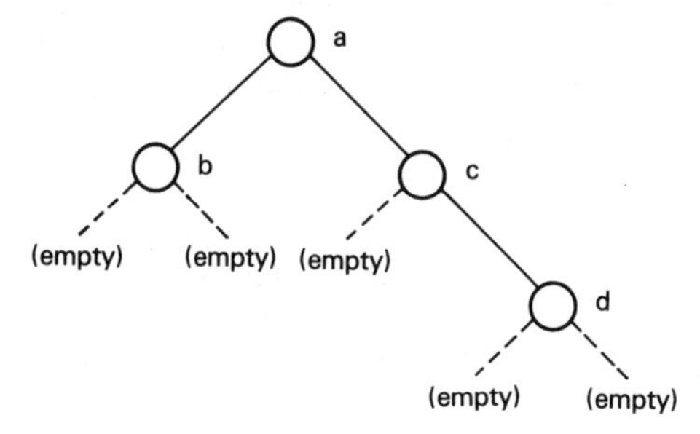

Figure 6.4 A binary tree.

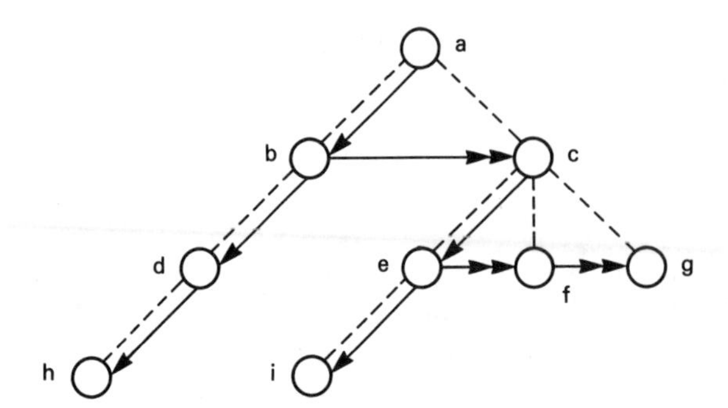

Figure 6.5 Representing an ordered tree as a binary tree.

impossible, because a general ordered tree seems to have a much more complicated structure than a binary tree, but the transformation becomes clear if we realize that the structure of an ordered tree is captured by two relations: leftmost child and right sibling. Fortunately, we have in binary trees two places where this information might be kept, namely the left and right subtrees. Given any ordered tree, we convert it to a binary tree by the following correspondence:

1. The binary tree will have the same nodes as the ordered tree.
2. If n is the leftmost child of m in the ordered tree, then n will be the left child of m in the binary tree.
3. If n is the right sibling of m in the ordered tree, then n will be the right child of m in the binary tree.

In most dealings with trees (and graphs, which we will introduce later) pictures speak more eloquently than words. Let's look at Figure 6.5 to see how this process would work on the ordered tree of Figure 6.2. The edges of the original tree are now dotted, and the edges of the binary tree are solid, with single arrows for left children and double arrows for right children. All we need to do now is to grab the resulting binary tree by the root and give it a shake, so that it falls into the familiar form of Figure 6.6. It is not difficult to convince yourself that the original tree would be easy to reconstruct from the resulting binary tree.

Now that we understand the structure of trees, we may complete the definition of the BINARY TREE abstract data type by defining the operations we may perform on the ADT. If you look at the literature, you will see that there is less agreement about the operations on binary trees than there is on the linear structures. For our purposes, we will consider here eleven primitives, and will discuss some nonprimitive operations later. Of our eleven primitives, eight deal with the structure of the binary tree, and the last three are concerned with the atoms that "reside" in those positions.

1. **Create**(**var** T : BINARY_TREE), as usual, initializes T to be an empty tree. In (P, R, v) terms, this procedure sets P to be the empty set of positions. A variant, **CreateNode**(**var** T : BINARY_TREE), builds a single node at T.

2. **Root**(T : BINARY_TREE) : POSITION returns the position of the root of T, or returns the NULL pseudoposition if T is empty. In implementations where trees are referenced by their roots, this function will be unnecessary.
3. **Parent**(n : POSITION ; T : BINARY_TREE) : POSITION is a function that returns the position of the parent of node n, if any, and returns NULL if n is the root of T. As with all of the operations that take a position in the tree as input, there is a precondition that $n \in P$, namely, that the node n actually be in the tree.
4. **LeftChild**(n : POSITION ; T : BINARY_TREE) : POSITION takes as input a node n, which we assume must be in the tree, and returns the position of the left child of n, that is, the position of the root of the left subtree of n in T. If node n has no left child, this function should return the NULL pseudoposition (indicating that n has an empty left subtree).
5. **RightChild**(n : POSITION ; T : BINARY_TREE) : POSITION, as does *LeftChild*, returns the position of the right child of n.
6. **DeleteSub**(**var** n : POSITION ; **var** T : BINARY_TREE) removes n and the subtree rooted at n from the tree T. Of course, this routine requires that n be in T.
7. **ReplaceSub**(**var** n : POSITION ; S : BINARY_TREE ; **var** T : BINARY_TREE) inserts the binary tree S into T, with the root of S located at position n, replacing whatever subtree of T was originally rooted at n. This routine is generally used when n is a leaf of T, or when S is empty, and in such cases could be viewed as an analogue of *Append* for lists.
8. **Merge**(L, R : BINARY_TREE ; **var** T : BINARY_TREE) makes T equal to a tree with L and R as the left and right subtrees, respectively, of the root of T. As with *DeleteSub* and *ReplaceSub*, the "contents" of the subtrees (that is, the atoms associated with the positions in the subtrees) are carried into T, but unlike the cases of the previous two operations, there is no atom associated with the new root of T.

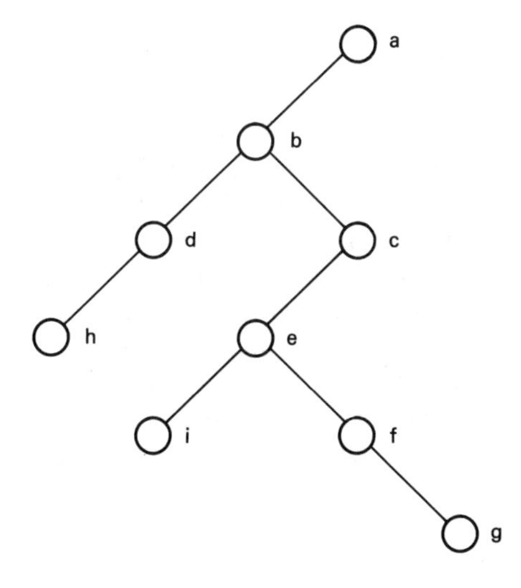

Figure 6.6 After shaking out the tree of Figure 6.5.

9. **Retrieve**(n : POSITION ; T : BINARY_TREE) : ATOM is a function that returns the atom in position *n*. This function also requires as a precondition that *n* be in *T*.
10. **Update**(n : POSITION ; a : ATOM ; **var** T : BINARY_TREE) replaces the atom in position *n* (which must be in *T*), if any, with the atom *a*.
11. **Find**(a : ATOM ; T : BINARY_TREE) : POSITION returns a position in *T* where atom *a* is located, if any, and returns NULL if there is no such position. The definition of this function makes no stipulation of which position is returned if there is more than one node "containing" *a*, but in practice we will use *Find* exclusively on trees that have no repeated atoms, so the problem will not arise. (Strictly speaking, *Find* should not be listed among the primitives, since we could define it by *Root*, *LeftChild*, *RightChild*, and *Retrieve*. It is almost never defined this way, however, so we include it here.)

6.3 BINARY TREE TRAVERSALS

If we think for a minute about the operation *Find*, we see that there is a lot more to trees than might appear at first. When we implemented *Find* for lists, the task was made simple by the fact that the linear structure of LIST made it possible to start at the head and inspect each element in turn, until we found the atom we wanted or reached the end of the list without success. Clearly we can't do that in general for trees, because there is no obvious "next" node to inspect. One possibility would be to do a **depth-first** search, searching as far down from the root as we can, then backing up to the first node with a child we haven't seen, searching the descendants of that child as far as we can, backing up again, and so on. This is a perfectly respectable scheme, but it seems to require a considerable amount of care to remember or find the nodes to which we have to return in backtracking. Another possibility would be to do a **breadth-first** search, searching all the nodes at depth 1, then all the nodes at depth 2, and so forth; but that also appears to require that we remember the positions of the nodes at level *n* while we are looking at the nodes at level $n + 1$. Indeed, we will discuss these search schemes in Chapter 8, but the comparatively simple structure of binary trees, coupled with the recursive nature of the tree data structures, permits three similar traversal techniques, which are defined recursively, and for which the need to "remember" where to backtrack is met automatically by the computer as it keeps track of nested procedure calls.

If we keep in mind the facts that (1) a nonempty binary tree consists of a root node and left and right subtrees of that node, and (2) every subtree of a binary tree is a binary tree, then we can inspect every node of a binary tree by inspecting first the root, next the left subtree, and finally the right subtree. All we need to do to inspect the subtrees is to apply the three-part inspection routine recursively to those parts, which leads to the following algorithm for what is known as a **preorder traversal**.

```
procedure Preorder(n: POSITION; T : BINARY_TREE);
begin
  if n is not NULL then begin          {Otherwise there's nothing to inspect}
    Inspect n ;                        {Do whatever processing is needed}
    Preorder(Left(n, T));              {Inspect the left subtree of the node}
    Preorder(Right(n, T))              {Inspect the right subtree of the node}
  end
end;
```

That's all there is to it. Simple, eh? We need only call *Preorder(Root(T), T)* to visit every node of *T*. Unless you are comfortable with recursion, however, you might be a trifle suspicious of the claim that this routine will *really* result in a full traversal of the tree. We'll work through an example shortly, but recall that we did just this sort of algorithm when we defined a recursive list traversal: look at the head of the sublist, then look (recursively) at the list which follows the head, or in LISP terminology, inspect the CAR, then call the inspection routine on the CDR.

Consider the binary tree of Figure 6.4, which we reproduce here with all its nonempty subtrees indicated.

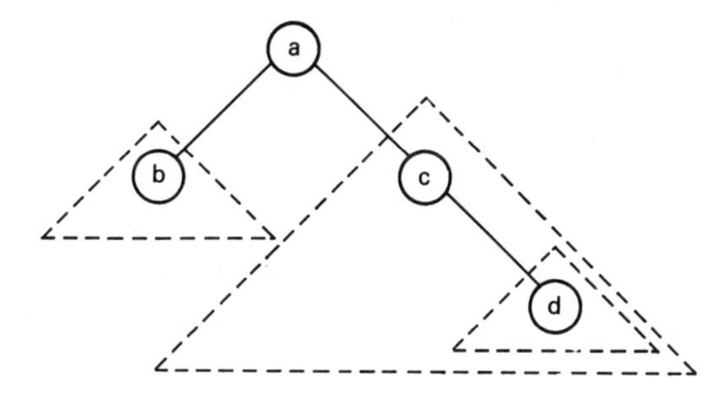

If we called *Preorder* on the root, *a*, we would have the following sequence of procedure calls and inspections:

Preorder(a)
  Inspect *a*
  Preorder(b)
    Inspect *b*
    Preorder (NULL)—the left subtree of *b* is empty
    Preorder (NULL)—the right subtree of *b* is empty
  Preorder(c)
    Inspect *c*
    Preorder (NULL)—the left subtree of *c* is empty
    Preorder(d)
      Inspect *d*
      Preorder (NULL)—the left subtree of *d* is empty
      Preorder (NULL)—the right subtree of *d* is empty

All the nodes would be visited, in the order *a, b, c, d*. Of course, there is nothing sacred about visiting the root of each subtree first. You may recall that when we looked at recursive list traversal and tried visiting the head of the sublist *after* having visited the tail of the list, we saw that the resulting algorithm also produced a traversal, from back to front of the list. An analogous situation holds for binary trees, yielding two other traversals, the **inorder** and **postorder**.

```
procedure Inorder(n: POSITION; T : BINARY_TREE);
{Traverse a tree by visiting left subtree, then root, then right subtree}
begin
   if n is not NULL then begin
      Inorder(LeftChild(n, T), T);
      Inspect n ;
      Inorder(RightChild(n, T), T)
   end
end;

procedure Postorder(n: POSITION; T : BINARY_TREE);
{Traverse a tree by visiting left subtree, then right subtree, then root}
begin
   if n is not NULL then begin
      Postorder(LeftChild(n, T),T );
      Postorder(RightChild(n, T), T);
      Inspect n
   end
end;
```

This is a good time to test your abilities to trace recursive routines by verifying that for the foregoing tree, the traversals would be: *Inorder: b, a, c, d*, and *Postorder: b, d, c, a*. Take your time; we'll wait.

* * *

Your experience in doing these traversals was probably typical—tracing the recursive routines required a fair amount of care, enough so that you would be reluctant to perform these traversals on any but the smallest binary trees. Fortunately, there is an equivalent algorithm that is much better suited to humans than to computers. Given a binary tree to traverse, first, draw a triangle for each node, then "shrink-wrap" the tree by drawing the smallest closed curve that encloses all the edges and nodes of the tree, as follows:

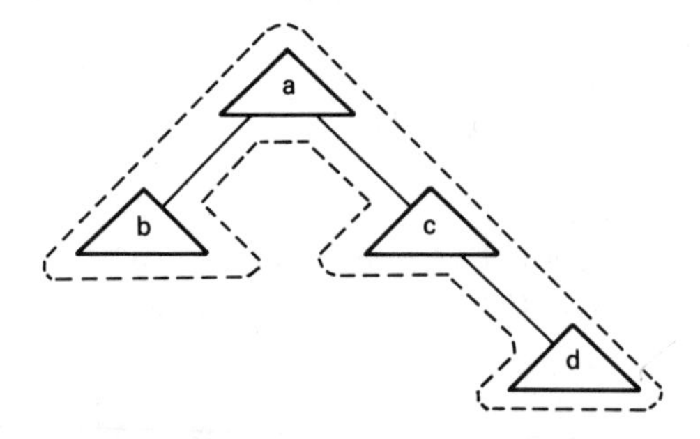

Now make a complete circuit around the curve, starting at the left side of the root triangle and moving in a counterclockwise direction. To perform a preorder traversal, mark a node as visited each time the path follows the *left* side of the node triangle, in this case, a, b, c, d. To perform inorder and postorder traversals, do the same thing, but mark a node as visited each time the path follows the bottom or right sides, respectively.

The left–right structure of trees allows us to define a linear order on the nodes of a tree. This linear order, we will see, is closely connected to tree traversals. Let T be a binary tree (although we could easily extend the definition to any ordered tree), and let n and m be nodes of T. We say that n is **left of** m if one of the following conditions is met.

1. $n = m$.
2. There is a node, p, of T such that n is in the left subtree of p and m is in the right subtree of p.
3. n is in the left subtree of m.
4. m is in the right subtree of n.

For example, in the binary tree of Figure 6.7, the left–right order of the nodes is $a, h, e, i, c, b, f, d, l, j, m, g, k$. The subtree rooted at c is to the left of node b, since it is the left subtree of b, and is to the right of the root a, since the subtree rooted at c is part of the right subtree of a. We have drawn the tree to emphasize the left–right order, in that any node that is left of another is left of that node in the figure; but be aware that the leftmost node of a subtree may not appear as the leftmost node in a picture. "Pictures don't lie," your author's dissertation advisor used to say, but they must be read with care.

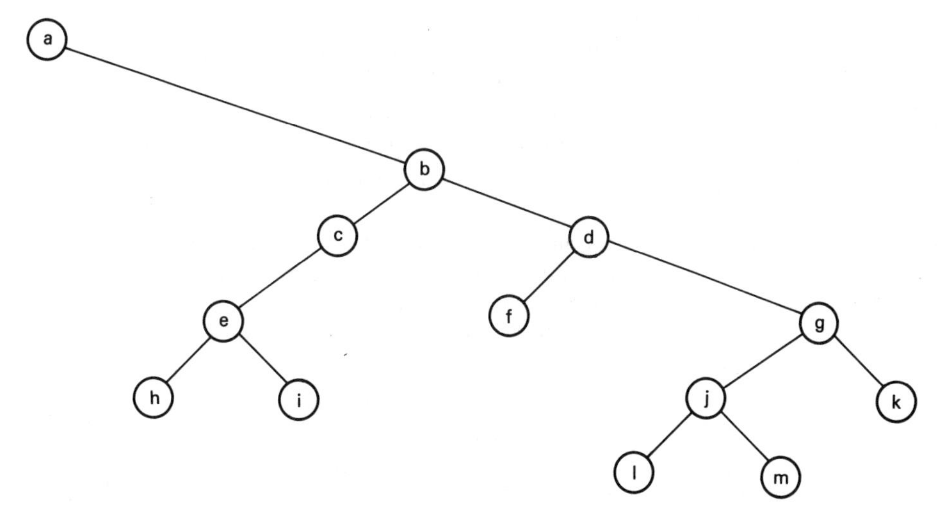

Figure 6.7 A binary tree drawn to illustrate left–right order.

In the exercises, we ask you to verify that *left* is a linear order. The interesting part of this linear order, however, is that it is *exactly* the order we obtain by an inorder traversal. A bit of thought should convince you that this must be the case: In left–right order, any left subtree must be to the left of its parent, and also would be visited before its parent in an inorder traversal, whereas any right subtree must be to the right of its parent and would be visited after its parent in an inorder traversal.

Application: Parse Trees

In ages past, when your author was in elementary school, the accepted wisdom was that the way to teach the syntax of English was to require the students to diagram sentences, a mind-numbing exercise that required identifying the subject, verb, and object, and then splitting these into noun phrases and verb phrases, which were further divided into nouns, adjectives, adverbs, pronouns, auxiliary verbs, articles, and so on. Later, linguists, who had presumably had the same training in their early years, attempted the much grander project of trying to determine whether there were inherent "deep structures" that underlay the structure of all languages, a project that met with limited success (due in part to the fact that meaning does not reside wholly in syntax—consider, for instance, the two interpretations of "The clams are ready to eat."). Later still, computer scientists successfully used this notion of hierarchy to provide a framework by which the syntax of programming languages could be represented by compilers and interpreters, to translate languages such as Pascal and FORTRAN into machine code, to be executed by computers. The problem of **program translation** is a fascinating one, about which mountains of words have been written, but the essential question is: "How do we write a program that will take a collection of **source code** in one language and produce the equivalent **object code** in another?" For our purposes, the interesting part of that question is: "What data structures can we use to make the translation process as efficient as possible?"

Consider, for instance, the very small subproblem of how to store the "sense" of arithmetic expressions, such as "$a + b * c$." Because arithmetic is inherently hierarchical—requiring evaluation of small parts which are then combined into large parts, which are further combined into larger parts—it should come as no surprise that trees are the data structure of choice. The technique is best illustrated by examples, like the two in Figure 6.8.

We adopt the convention that these **parse trees** represent expressions that would be evaluated from bottom up, so that in the simpler example the subexpression "$b * c$ " would be evaluated, and then that result would be added to a to produce the result. With this convention, then, the parse tree contains all the information in the original expression in a form that permits easy implementation in the translator program. That by itself is worth noting, but the truly appealing part of these parse trees lies in their traversals. An inorder traversal of the simpler tree yields "$a + b * c$," which is exactly the infix representation of the expression, while the complicated tree has inorder traversal "$1 + 2 - x * y / x + y$," which is what we would obtain if we stripped the parentheses from the infix expression, which we would write " $1 + (2 - x * y) / (x + y)$." If inorder traversal

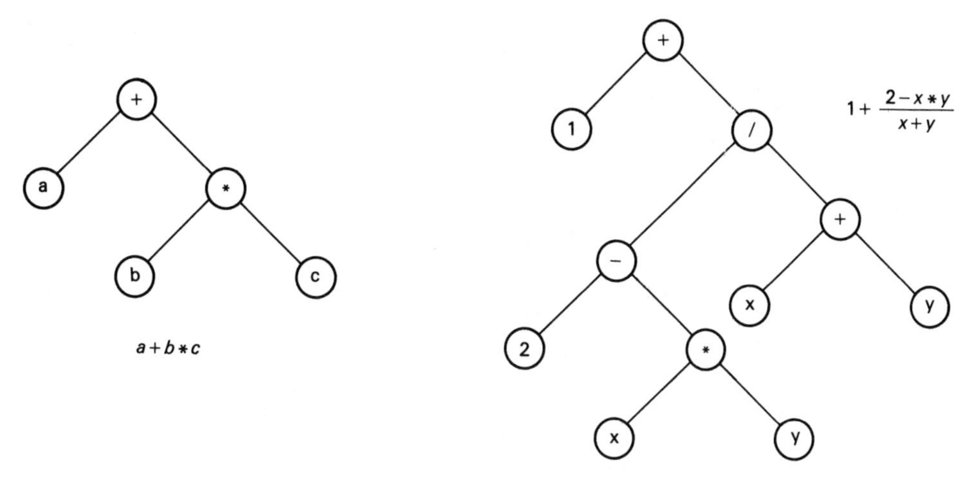

Figure 6.8 Two parse trees of algebraic expressions.

yields infix expression, what do you think would happen if we traversed these two trees in *post* order? Try it before continuing.

* * *

Well, well, well. The postorder traversal of the small tree is "*a b c* * + ," and the postorder traversal of the large tree is "1 2 *x y* * − *x y* + / +," both of which are precisely the *postfix* equivalents of the original expressions. Thus, not only does the parse tree of an arithmetic expression contain all the information needed to reconstruct the expression, it also allows us to reconstruct the expression in any of three different notations!

Constructing a parse tree from a source code input string is a fascinating (and very large) subject, one on which whole books have been written. If you continue to study computer science, you will almost certainly see this topic again in a compiler design course. We'll give you a bit of the flavor of the subject by constructing a parse tree for an arithmetic expression from the postfix form of that expression. We will build the parse tree from the top down, by reading the postfix expression from right to left. The construction algorithm proceeds from the (recursive) observation that a correctly formed postfix expression always consists of (1) a single identifier (a variable or constant) or (2) two correctly formed postfix expressions followed by an operator. In Case 1 the parse tree will consist of just the identifier, and in Case 2 the parse tree will have the operator as the root and the trees of the preceding expressions as the subtrees of the operator, which is the root. This is the heart of our parsing algorithm: If, for example, the input string is "*abc**+," we first see the "+" operator, so we know that the parse tree will have "+" as its root token, with the postfix expressions "*bc**" and "*a*" as subtrees of the root. Now, parsing "*bc**" gives us a subtree with "*" as root and "*b*" and "*c*" as subtrees, and we have completed the parse tree. The construction algorithm is now easy to write, as follows:

```
procedure BuildParseTree(p : POSITION);
{   Constructs a parse tree rooted at p corresponding to a postfix expression.}
    var t : TokenType;
begin
    GetToken(t);                              {get the next token in right-left order}
    if t <> endMarker then begin              {if there are any more tokens to read}
        Build a new node at p;
        Place t in the new node;

        if t is an operator token then begin  {construct the subtrees recursively}
            BuildParseTree(RightChild(p, T));
            BuildParseTree(LeftChild(p, T))

        end else begin                        {non-operators are always leaves}
            Set the right subtree of p to the empty tree;
            Set the left subtree of p to the empty tree
        end
    end
end;
```

For the input string '*abc*∗+,' Figure 6.9 shows the steps of the parsing algorithm. Of course, if we were designing an industrial-strength compiler, we would actually use more sophisticated techniques than to begin with the postfix expression, but even for our purposes it is not hard to imagine how we would construct the parse tree within the

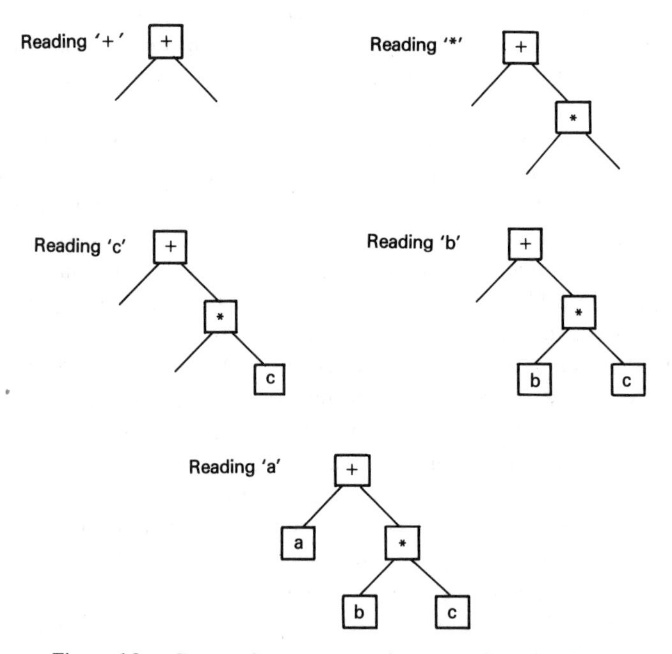

Figure 6.9 Constructing a parse tree from a postfix expression.

infix-to-postfix algorithm. We mention in passing that these parse trees were easy to produce and amenable to traversal because the common arithmetic operations are at worst *binary*, which is to say that they require no more than two arguments. A similar technique can be used to store the syntax of an entire program as a large parse tree, but the task is made slightly more complicated by the fact that the resulting parse trees are not necessarily binary trees. For instance, a parse tree for a Pascal program might look in part like the tree in Figure 6.10.

6.4 IMPLEMENTATIONS OF BINARY TREE

There are a number of implementations of BINARY TREE, but they all can be divided into two classes: those that are inherently linear in nature and those that more closely reflect the nonlinear structure of trees. We will discuss three implementations here, and will mention another in a later section.

Pointers

The pointer implementations of the linear structures were perhaps not the most obvious choices at the time. Part of that deficiency might have been due to your unfamiliarity with pointers at the time, but the largest part was certainly due to the fact that we had available a natural predefined data type with a linear structure, namely arrays. Now that we are more comfortable with pointers, however, the pictures of binary trees should suggest a simple implementation immediately. All we need to do is create a linked

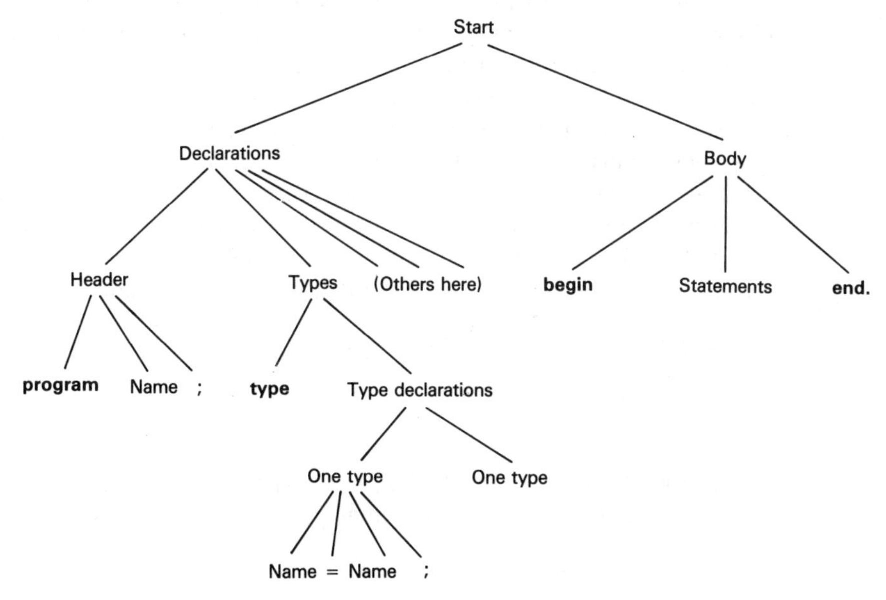

Figure 6.10 Sample parse tree for a Pascal program.

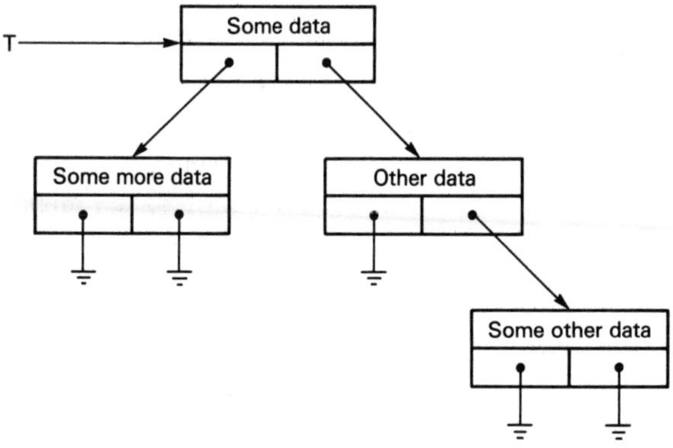

Figure 6.11 Pointer implementation of the tree of Figure 6.4.

collection of nodes, each of which contains a field for an atom and *two* pointer fields: to the left and right children of the nodes, as follows:

```
type
   ATOM = {any type};
   POSITION = ^Node;
   Node = record
              data : ATOM;
              left, right : POSITION
          end;
   BINARY_TREE = POSITION;
```

In this implementation, we will refer to a binary tree by a pointer to its root node, or by the **nil** pointer if the tree is empty. This implementation is an immediate generalization of the pointer implementation of LIST, with the exception that we do not use a header record, and each cell has *two* pointers, rather than one. In Figure 6.11, we show a typical binary tree in this implementation. Notice the advantage we gain in this implementation by knowing that we are dealing with *binary* trees: We know that there will never be more than two children per node, so we don't have to worry about defining an arbitrary number of child pointers in each node cell. The definitions of the primitives are simple in this implementation. We will show some of the definitions, leave some for exercises, and defer the definition of some of the rest until a later section.

1.
```
procedure Create(var T : BINARY_TREE);
begin
   T := nil
end;
```

2.
```
function LeftChild(n : POSITION ; T : BINARY_TREE) : POSITION;
{Assumes n is a node reachable from T}
begin
   LeftChild := n^.left
end;
```

3.
```
procedure DeleteSub(var n : POSITION ; var T : BINARY TREE);
begin
   if n <> nil then begin
      DeleteSub(n^.left);
      DeleteSub(n^.right);
      dispose(n);
      n:= nil
   end
end;
```

Notice that in *DeleteSub* we are using a postorder traversal, recursively destroying the left subtree of a node, then the right subtree, and finally the node itself. You may wish to speculate whether a different traversal order would work as well.

4.
```
procedure ReplaceSub(var n : POSITION ; S : BINARY_TREE ;
                                    var T : BINARY_TREE);
begin
   n := S
end;
```

Depending on the application we have in mind, this definition of *ReplaceSub* may not be satisfactory, for two reasons. First, we must be sure that there will not be a subsequent reference to S, because by reassigning pointer n to the root of S we have introduced the possibility of aliasing, so that if we later changed S we would also be modifying T, although the changes to T would not be obvious in the program code. The second problem we might encounter is that we have eliminated any possibility of reference to the original subtree of T rooted at n (strictly speaking, rooted at the node pointed to by n), so all the descendants of n are now garbage, taking up room in memory for no purpose. If conserving memory were important, it would be better to make a copy of the pointer n, call *DeleteSub* on the copy to free up the memory occupied by the subtree, and then insert the root of S in position n.

5.
```
procedure Update(n : POSITION ; a : ATOM ; var T : BINARY_TREE);
{Assumes n is a node reachable from T}
begin
   n^.data := a
end;
```

We leave as an exercise the definition of *Find*. The idea is simple enough: Use one of the traversals to inspect the values in the nodes of the tree, and drop out of the routine if the desired element is found. It is not difficult to see that for a tree with n nodes, all the operations take time $O(1)$, except for those that require traversal. Those, since they may require inspecting every node of the tree, take $O(n)$ time.

Threaded Trees

The very observant reader may object that we have omitted the definition of one of the more complicated operations: *Parent*. The action of *Parent* is simple enough, but how do we find the parent of a node, given only a pointer to the node itself? It may be a wise child who knows its parent, but our nodes just don't have that wisdom. We find ourselves in a situation similar to that of trying to implement *Prior* for linked lists: Movement down the tree is trivial, but movement *up* the tree is impossible, so all we can do is start at the root and perform a traversal until we find the node we wish, complicated by the fact that we need to remember the current node and its parent at every stage. It is a worthwhile exercise for you to try to write such a routine, to get an idea of the complexity involved. Fortunately, the need to find the parent of a given node seldom arises in practice, but when it does it is often better to adopt the stratagem, familiar by now, of modifying the data structure rather than relying on a complicated algorithm.

The most obvious choice would be to ape what we did with two-way linked lists, namely, to include one more pointer in each node, pointing to the parent of that node. If the data field of the nodes was fairly large, the marginal increase in memory needed would be minimal, and the other operations would be only slightly more complicated, if at all.

Another possibility, one that is often used for general trees as well, would be to realize that every node that has fewer than two children has a pointer or two left over that is not pointing to anything useful except the flag value **nil**. The most common use to which these leftover pointers is put is to have them point to nodes in the tree that would precede or follow them in some traversal order. For example, we may decide to have unused right pointers point to the next node in an inorder traversal, and unused left pointers point to the previous node in an inorder traversal. Of course, since we are "overloading" the pointers (that is, giving them two possible interpretations), we need to include some sort of tag to indicate whether a pointer is an edge of the tree or a **thread**, a non-edge that is there to help us point through the tree in non-edge order. The implementation of such a **fully threaded tree** (a threaded tree with both left and right threads) would be defined as follows:

```
type
   ATOM = {some data type};
   POSITION = ^Node;
   Node = record
             data : ATOM;
             leftThread, rightThread : boolean;      {true if the pointer is a thread}
             left, right : POSITION
          end;
   BINARY_TREE = POSITION;
```

In Figure 6.12 we draw the tree of Figure 6.7 with left and right threads indicated by dashed lines. Recall that the inorder traversal of the tree is *a, h, e, i, c, b, f, d, l, j, m, g, k*, so the left thread of node *i* points to node *e*, its predecessor in inorder, and the right thread of *i* points to *c*, its successor in the inorder traversal. Notice that the leftmost node of each right subtree has a thread which points to the parent of that tree, as does the rightmost node of each left subtree. Notice also that in the full tree, the leftmost node must always have a **nil** left thread, and the rightmost node always has a **nil** right thread.

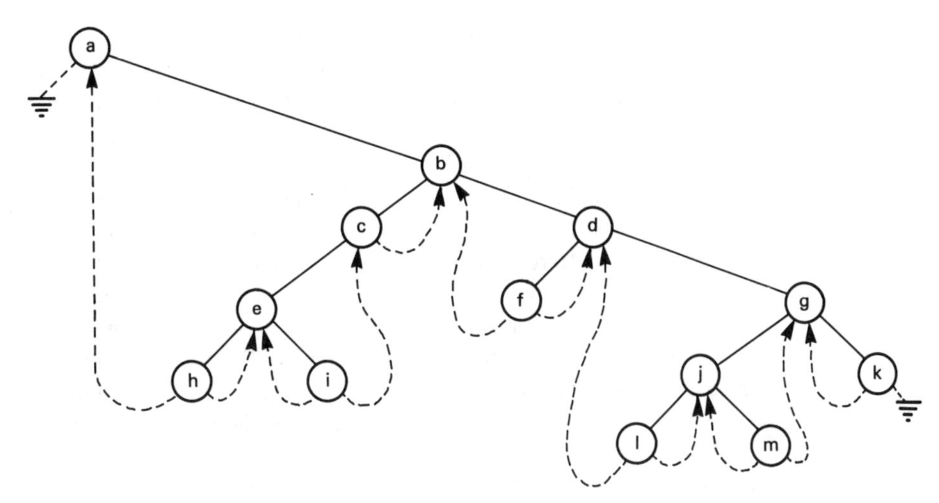

Figure 6.12 A fully threaded tree.

The first advantage we gain by this implementation is that it provides us with a simple means of inorder traversal without recursion. The advantages of this are twofold: As we remarked earlier, not all languages support recursion, and in general, recursive routines tend to take longer than equivalent iterative versions. To make sense of the traversal algorithm that follows, bear in mind that in an inorder traversal, the first node to be visited in a subtree is always the leftmost node of that subtree. After having visited that node, the next one to be visited is always its parent, which in our threaded tree is always reached by the right thread from that node. Once the parent has been visited, the process is repeated with the right subtree, and continues until the rightmost node of the entire tree is visited, which we can recognize by realizing that the rightmost node is the only one with a **nil** right thread.

```
procedure IterativeInorder(n : POSITION);
{   Perform an inorder traversal of a binary tree, starting at node n.}
begin
   while n <> nil do begin              { until rightmost node has been visited}
      while (not n^.leftThread) and (n^.left <> nil) do
         n := n^.left;                  {move as far left along edges as possible}

      Inspect n;                        {visit the leftmost node}
      while n^.rightThread do begin     {move up the tree in inorder}
         n := n^.right;
         Inspect n
      end;

      n := n^.right                     {move down to right subtree}
   end
end;
```

It would be good practice for you to trace the action of this routine on the threaded tree of Figure 6.12. You should find it easier going than tracing the recursive version of *Inorder*. Another advantage we gain by this traversal algorithm is that it is now possible to begin a traversal at any node of the tree we wish, something that was impossible with the recursive version.

We will not show the definitions of all the operations of BINARY TREE in this implementation; most of them are almost identical to those of the original pointer implementation. The only difference is that we need to take care of the threads when inserting or deleting a subtree. Consider *ReplaceSub*, for instance. We begin with a binary tree *T*; a node, *n*, in *T*; and a binary tree, *S*, which we wish to insert in *T* so that the root of *S* is located in the position where *n* was originally. To simplify matters, we will ignore the possible need to dispose of the original subtree rooted at *n* and the possibility of aliasing. All we need to do is set the right thread of the rightmost node of *S* to point to the same position to which the right thread of the rightmost descendant of *n* pointed, and do a similar thing with leftmost nodes and left threads, as we indicate in Figure 6.13.

The algorithm is now simple to write. We first find and save the leftmost and rightmost threads of the original subtree rooted at *n*, and change the leftmost and rightmost threads of *S* from **nil** to the saved values.

```
procedure ReplaceSub(var n : POSITION ; S : BINARY_TREE ; var T : BINARY_TREE);
   var
      leftmost, rightmost : POSITION;   {Leftmost, rightmost threads of n subtree}
      SLeft, SRight : POSITION;         {Leftmost, rightmost nodes of S }
begin
   {Find leftmost and rightmost threads of original subtree}
   leftmost := n;
   repeat
      leftmost := leftmost^.left
   until (leftmost^.leftThread) or (leftmost^.left = nil);
   rightmost := n;
   repeat
      rightmost := rightmost^. right
   until ( rightmost^. rightThread) or ( rightmost^. right = nil);

   n := S;                              {Root subtree S at n }

   SLeft := n;
   while SLeft^.left <> nil do          {Find and replace leftmost thread of S }
      SLeft := SLeft^.left;
   SLeft^.left := leftmost;
   SRight := n;
   while SRight^.right <> nil do        {Find and replace rightmost thread of S }
   SRight := SRight^.right;
   SRight^.right := rightmost;
end;
```

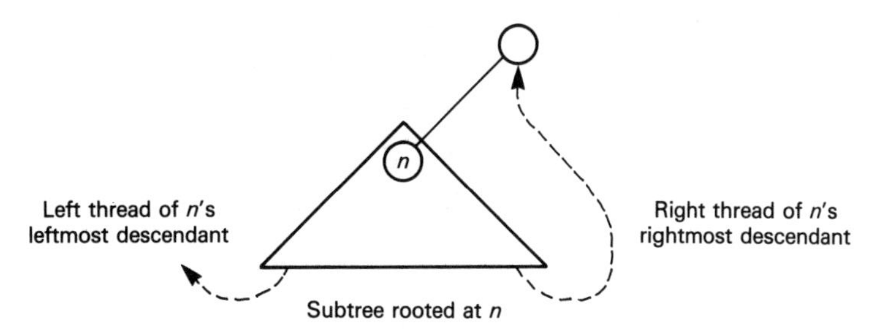

Figure 6.13 Threads in a subtree.

We'll close this section where we started. We motivated the use of threaded trees by considering how to find the parent of a node. Can we solve this problem if we have threaded trees available? Sure we can; suppose that we had to find the parent of node n. Now n must be either the left or the right child of its parent, so for the sake of argument let's suppose that n is the left child of its parent. The right subtree of n, then, must lie to the right of n and to the left of n's parent. Furthermore, the rightmost descendant of n must immediately precede n's parent in left–right order (which, we've seen, is the same as inorder), and so must have a right thread that points to n's parent. A similar situation holds if n is the right child of its parent. In other words, *if* n *is a left child, its parent can be found by following right edges as far as possible, and then taking the right thread, and if* n *is a right child, its parent can be found by following left edges as far as possible, and then taking the left thread.* Of course, we have no way of knowing ahead of time whether or not n is a left child or a right child, so we follow both paths to the putative parents, look at the left or right children, as applicable, and see whether the child is n.

Cursors

Unfortunately, as we have mentioned, there are some programming languages that do not support pointers. It would be insufferably arrogant of us to insist that programmers henceforth do all their work in languages that have pointers, especially in view of the fact that there are probably more lines of code that have been written in FORTRAN (including, for instance, the first Pascal compiler) than in all other programming languages combined, and FORTRAN has nary a pointer at all. In our search for an implementation of BINARY TREE that does not use pointers, the first idea that may come to mind is to mimic the pointer implementation with arrays. We will represent a node by a cell containing the data associated with that node, and two fields containing the indices of the left and right children, and we will represent a binary tree by an array of such cells, as shown in Figure 6.14.

In this implementation, we use index 0 to serve the purpose of the NULL pseudoposition, so that in the example, node 3 contains data c, has no left child, and has node 5 as its right child. We have the usual problems with this static implementation: We usually have no way of increasing the size of the array while the program is running, so we must predeclare each array to be as large as the largest possible tree we will encounter. In addition, it is not hard to see that *ReplaceSub* and *Merge* will be difficult to

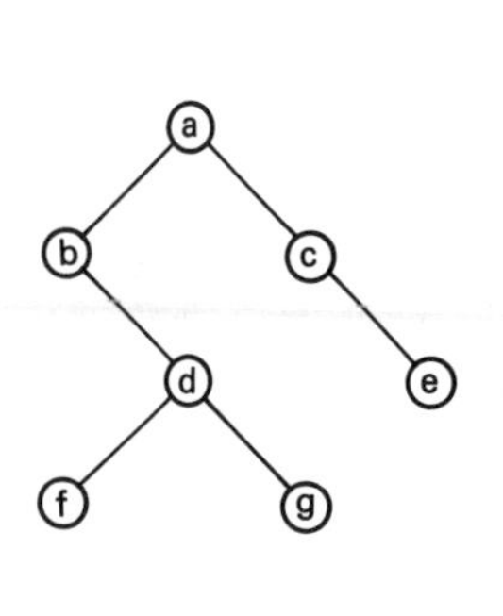

Index	Data	Left	Right
1	a	2	3
2	b	0	4
3	d	0	5
4	f	6	7
5	g	0	0
6	c	0	0
7	e	0	0
⋮		⋮	
MAX			

Figure 6.14 Cursor representation of BINARY TREE.

implement, which implies that this implementation would generally be used only in cases where the size of the trees will remain fixed throughout the execution of the program. The declarations for this implementation are as follows:

```
const
   MAXSIZE = {some positive integer};
type
   ATOM = {Some data structure};
   POSITION = 0 . . MAXSIZE;
   Node = record
              data : ATOM;
              left, right : POSITION
          end;
   BINARY_TREE = array [1 . . MAXSIZE] of Node;
```

Obviously, *Create*, *LeftChild*, *RightChild*, *Retrieve*, *Update*, and *Find* are simple to define in this implementation, as are all the traversal algorithms. One benefit we gain from this implementation is that *Parent* is conceptually simple: All we need to do to find the parent of node *n* is perform a sequential search through the array, inspecting the left and right cursors of each cell, until we find the index *n* or reach the end of the array without success. *DeleteSub* is also simple, if we don't worry about compacting the array to fill in the hole left by the deleted subtree. In this case, all we need to do is find the parent of the subtree to be deleted, and place a zero index in the appropriate field of the parent node.

The cursor representation of binary trees allows us to implement threaded trees with a simple modification. If we let the possible values for POSITION run from –MAX to MAX, we could adopt the convention that a positive cursor value represents a node reached by an edge, whereas a negative cursor value represents a node reached by a thread. This is useful because, as a rule, languages (such as traditional versions of FORTRAN and BASIC) that do not support pointers also do not support recursion, so we cannot rely on the recursive versions of the traversal algorithms.

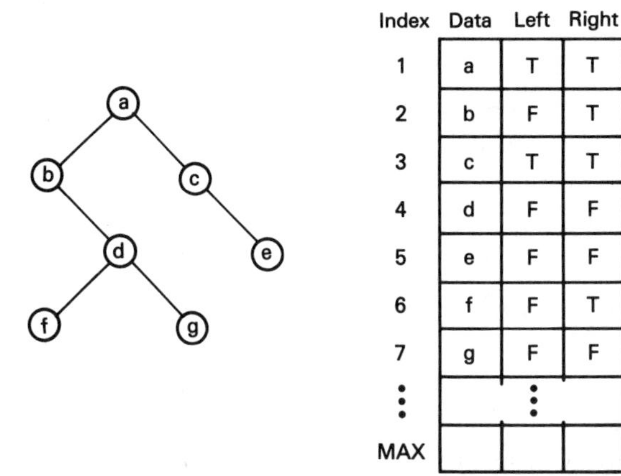

Index	Data	Left	Right
1	a	T	T
2	b	F	T
3	c	T	T
4	d	F	F
5	e	F	F
6	f	F	T
7	g	F	F
⋮		⋮	
MAX			

Figure 6.15 Another form of cursor representation of BINARY TREE.

Although we pay the memory price of having to preallocate the arrays when we use cursors, and we make some of the operations difficult to define, we do gain a small benefit from the fact that in many computers, pointers take twice as much space as integers. This means that each cell requires less space than the corresponding cell in a pointer implementation. We can push this benefit just a bit further (pun, see below) if we decide that the cells in the array will be stored in preorder order (no, we didn't just hiccup; that's what we intended to say). Although a preorder traversal of a binary tree does not, by itself, provide enough information to describe the tree uniquely, we can reconstruct the tree if we know, for each node, whether that node has a left or a right child (see Figure 6.15). We leave as an exercise how this reconstruction would be accomplished, but notice that each cell now requires just two bits more than the size of the *data* field. The attendant complexity of the operations in this implementation, however, along with the observation that many computers use a full byte or more for boolean variables, makes this implementation useful only if conserving memory is pathologically important to you.

6.5 DATA-ORDERED BINARY TREES

We saw that it was much faster to find an element in a list if the data contained a *key field* on which we could define a linear order. If the list were maintained so that it was always sorted by the key field, *Find* could be made to run in $O(\log n)$ time, using a binary or interpolation search. The good news, then, was that when inserting an element into a sorted list, it took very little time to find where the element should go. The bad news, you'll recall, was that the blinding speed of *Find* was completely wasted, because binary and interpolation searches were defined on arrays, and insertion into arrays takes linear time. Insertion into linked lists takes constant time, but with a linked list we have no way to find the middle of a sublist. Trees to the rescue!

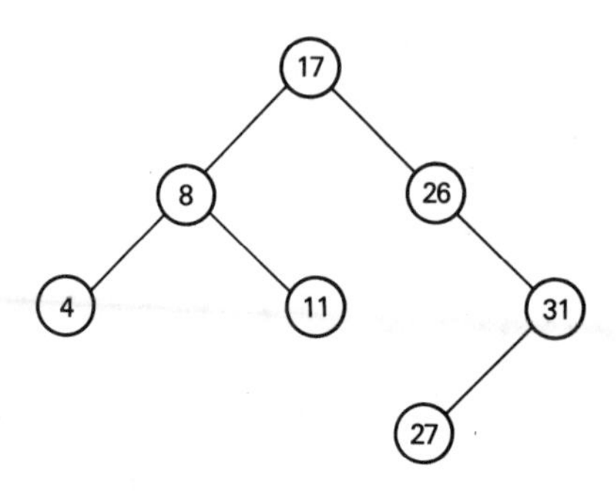

Figure 6.16 A binary search tree.

Binary Search Trees

In a binary tree, we do have a way of finding the "middle" element— the root node of a subtree is to the right of its left subtree and to the left of its right subtree. We will arrange our data in the tree so that this order is maintained on the key fields. We say that a **binary search tree** (frequently shortened to **BST**) is a binary tree with the property that *the value of the key field of a node is larger than that of the key field of any node in its left subtree, and smaller than that of any node in its right subtree*. In Figure 6.16, we present a typical binary search tree. It is easy to show that the tree in Figure 6.16 has the binary search tree property. For instance, every element (4, 8, and 11) in the left subtree of the root has value less than the value of the root, and every element (26, 27, 31) in the right subtree of the root has value larger than the root element. You can check that this property holds for every subtree of the tree. Be careful in reading the picture—the node containing 11 is to the left of the root, even though it may not appear to be so. Notice that the left–right order of the nodes is exactly numeric order: 4, 8, 11, 17, 26, 27, 31. You should be able to convince yourself that this is not a fluke, but is a property that holds for all BSTs.

Because we have imposed additional structure on BSTs, and because the operations are slightly different from those of binary trees, BSTs rate a definition as a separate ADT.

Definition 6.3. A binary search tree is a binary tree with the binary search tree property on a key field of its nodes, along with the following operations:

1. **Create**(**var** B : BST) creates an empty BST, as usual.
2. **Find**(k : KeyType ; B : BST) : POSITION is a function that returns the position of the node containing key *k*, if such a node exists, and the NULL pseudoposition otherwise.
3. **Update**(a : ATOM ; **var** B : BST) finds the node in *B* that has key value equal to that of *a*'s key and places *a* in that node, destroying the previous contents of the node. If there is no node in *B* that has key equal to that of *a*, this procedure takes no action (except perhaps to return a warning message).
4. **Insert**(a : ATOM ; **var** B : BST) inserts atom *a* into *B* in such a way that the resulting tree is still a BST. For our purposes, we will assume that if there is

already a node in B with the same key value as a, no action is taken.

5. **DeleteMin**(**var** p : POSITION ; **var** min : ATOM) removes the node with smallest key value from the tree rooted at p, in such a way that the result is still a BST, and returns the data in that node in *min*. (This is used here only by *Delete*, although we will see a further use for it later.)
6. **Delete**(k : KeyType ; **var** B : BST) deletes the node containing the key value k, if any, from B, and takes no action if there is no such node. As with *Insert*, the precondition is that B is a BST, and the postcondition is that B is still a BST after the procedure.

We will implement binary search trees with pointers, just as we did with binary trees, and will take the time to define the entire package of types and algorithms here.

```
type
   KeyType = {any linearly ordered type};
   ATOM = record
               key : KeyType;
               {Other data here, if needed}
            end;
   POSITION = ^Node;
   Node = record
               data : ATOM;
               left, right : POSITION
            end;
   BST = POSITION; {We refer to a BST by a pointer to its root}

procedure Create(var B : BST);
begin
   B := nil
end;

function Find(k : KeyType ; B : BST) : POSITION;
   var p : POSITION;
begin
   p := B;                              {start looking at the root of B}
   if p = nil then                      {search failed, return nil}
      Find := nil
   else if k = p^.data.key then         {found it, return pointer to key node}
      Find := p
   else if k < p^.data.key then         {no luck yet, look in left subtree}
      Find := Find(k, p^.left)
   else                                 {k > p^.data.key, so look in right subtree}
      Find := Find(k, p^.right)
end;
```

In *Find*, we use the BST property to guide us through the tree. If the key we are seeking has a value less than that of the node we are currently inspecting, we know that the key we seek can only lie in the left subtree of the current node, so we continue the search there. We act in a similar way if the key is greater than that of the current node.

The exit conditions are either successfully finding the key or running out of tree to search. *Update*, then, is easy to define: We *Find* the node, if any, with the same key as *a* has, and replace the data field of the node found with *a*. Notice that since the key field remained the same, the BST property is preserved by *Update*.

```
procedure Update(a : ATOM ; var B : BST);
   var p : POSITION;
begin
   p := Find(a.key, B);
   if p = nil then
      writeln('Update found no node with key ', k)
   else
      p^.data := a
end;
```

```
procedure Insert(a : ATOM ; var B : BST);
begin
   if B = nil then begin                      {p will point to the new node}
      new(B);
      B^.data := a;
      B^.left := nil;
      B^.right := nil
   end else if a.key < B^.data.key then       {insert new node in left subtree}
      Insert(a, B^.left)
   else if a.key > B^.data.key then           {new node inserted in right subtree}
      Insert(a, B^.right)
   {else a.key =B^.data.key, and we don't insert duplicate keys}
end;
```

Insert works by tracking its way down the tree, guided by the BST property, until a vacant subtree is found. If we had to insert a node with key value 9 into the BST of Figure 6.16, we would first compare 9 with the root key, 17. Since 9 is less than 17, we move to the left subtree, and compare 9 with the root key, 8, of that subtree. Since 9 is greater than 8, we move to the right subtree. Since 9 is less than 11, we move to the left subtree, which is empty, and that's where we place the new node, as illustrated in Figure 6.17.

Deleting the node with the smallest key from a BST is easy. We know that the smallest key must be in the leftmost node, so all we do is travel along left edges until we can go no farther, copy the data in that node, and then remove the node. We need to exercise a modicum of care, however, because we do not want any right subtree of that node to be cut off when we delete the node. What we must do is point around the leftmost node, so that its right subtree becomes the left subtree of the parent of the leftmost node.

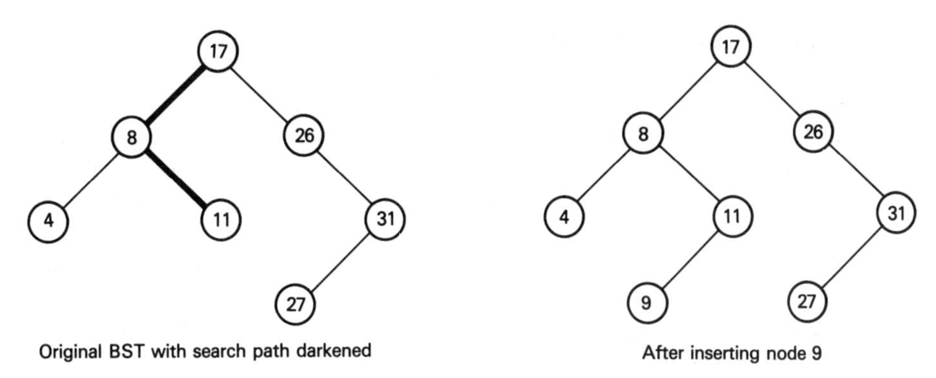

Figure 6.17 Insertion into a binary search tree.

```
procedure DeleteMin(var p : POSITION ; vara min : ATOM);
    var temp : POSITION;
begin
    if p <> nil then
        if p^.left <> nil then                {Keep looking for leftmost node}
            DeleteMin(p^.left, min)
        else begin                            {p points to the leftmost node now}
            min := p^.data;                   {return the atom}
            temp := p;
            p := p^.right;
            Dispose(temp)                     {and dispose of the leftmost node}
        end
end;
```

Now we must decide how to delete a node from a BST in such a way that the resulting tree is still a BST. If the node to be deleted has no children, we can simply remove that node. Things are almost as simple if the node to be removed has a single child; in this case, we point around the node, so that the child "moves up" to the

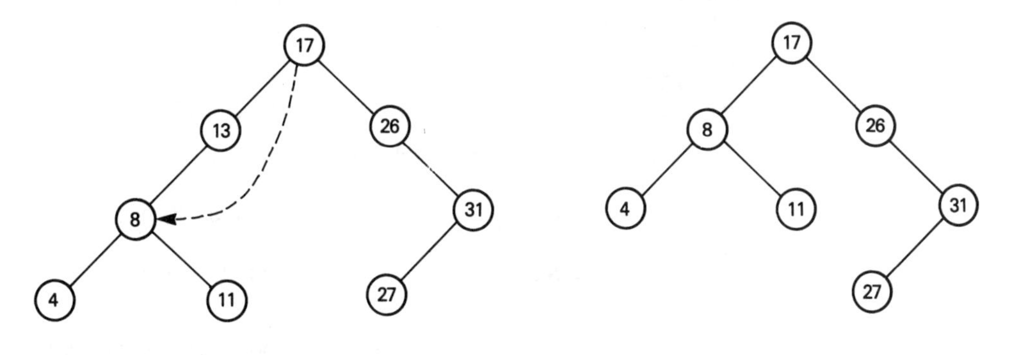

Figure 6.18 Deleting a node with a single child.

position occupied by the deleted node, as shown in Figure 6.18. The only real difficulty comes in deciding what to do in case the node to be deleted has two children. We cannot just remove the node, of course, because that would leave the subtrees of that node as orphans, having no connection to the tree. We cannot move the left or right subtrees up to the deleted position, either, because that could destroy the binary search tree property, as you can see by imagining that in Figure 6.18 we were to delete the root by moving node 13 to the root position. If we keep in mind the need to preserve the left–right order, it should be clear that we can delete a node with two children by replacing it with its nearest right neighbor, just as we would delete an element from a list. We know just where the nearest right neighbor is, too—it's the leftmost element in the right subtree of the node. In other words, *to delete a node with two children, we find the leftmost node in the right subtree, delete that node, and place its data in the place of the node we intended to delete.* But that's the same thing as performing *DeleteMin* on the right subtree of the node to be deleted, which is one of the reasons we defined *DeleteMin* in the first place. Figure 6.19 shows this deletion in action. Notice, too, that we could perform the deletion in a mirror-image fashion by replacing the node to be deleted by the rightmost child of its left subtree, but then we would need to define the mirror image *DeleteMax* (not that that would be difficult).

```
procedure Delete(k : KeyType ; var B : BST);
   var
      temp : POSITION;
      min : ATOM;
begin
   if p <> nil then
      if k < p^.data.key then                {node to be deleted is in left subtree}
         Delete(k, p^.left)
      else if k > p^.data  then              {node to be deleted is in right subtree}
         Delete(k, p^.right)

      {now p points to the node to be deleted}

      else if (p^.left = nil) and (p^.right = nil) then begin {two children}
          DeleteMin(p^.right, min);
         p^.data := min
      end else begin
         temp := p;                        {store the node pointer for deletion later}

         if (p^.left = nil) and (p^.right = nil) then      {no children}
            p := nil
         else if p^.left = nil then                       {right child only}
            p := p^.right
         else if p^.right = nil then                      {left child only}
            p := p^.left;

         Dispose(temp)                                    {done, delete the node}
      end
end;
```

Now, where are we? We are in possession of a data type that permits, in most cases, exceptionally efficient access to its elements. We can locate objects, insert new objects, and delete or modify existing objects quite rapidly. All we require is that the objects have keys that can be linearly ordered, like numbers, characters, or strings. But what exactly do we mean by *exceptionally efficient*? Notice that so far we have not mentioned the timing of any of the BST algorithms. The reason is that it is not all that easy to get good timing estimates for these algorithms.

Consider *Find*, for example. In one sense, we can analyze this algorithm easily. The length of time it will take to find a given key in a BST is certainly no worse than proportional to the depth of the tree, since we find a key by stepping down the tree, starting from the root, so *Find*—and all the other operations except for *Create*, for that matter—run in time $O(h)$, where h is the length of the longest path in the tree. However, we would like to have a timing function that is a function of n, the number of nodes in the tree, and there's where the canker gnaws. There simply is no way to tell exactly the depth of a binary search tree, if all we know is the number of nodes in the tree—all we know is that a binary tree of height h has between $h + 1$ and $2^{h+1}-1$ nodes. For instance, we illustrate two binary search trees of size seven, the worst and best cases for height with this many nodes.

Figure 6.20 is a good example of pictures not lying. We see immediately that a BST with n nodes could have height equal to $n - 1$, a dreadful state of affairs, since that would make all of our operations except *Create* run in linear time. We would be better off in this case to chuck it all and keep our data in an array, sorted by keys. One ray of hope, however, is that in the best case, where all the internal nodes have two children, except possibly for those at the lowest level, the tree is very shallow indeed, being logarithmic in the number of nodes.

At this point, it would seem that all we can say is that *with the exception of* Create, *all the BST operations run in log time at best, but could run in linear time if the*

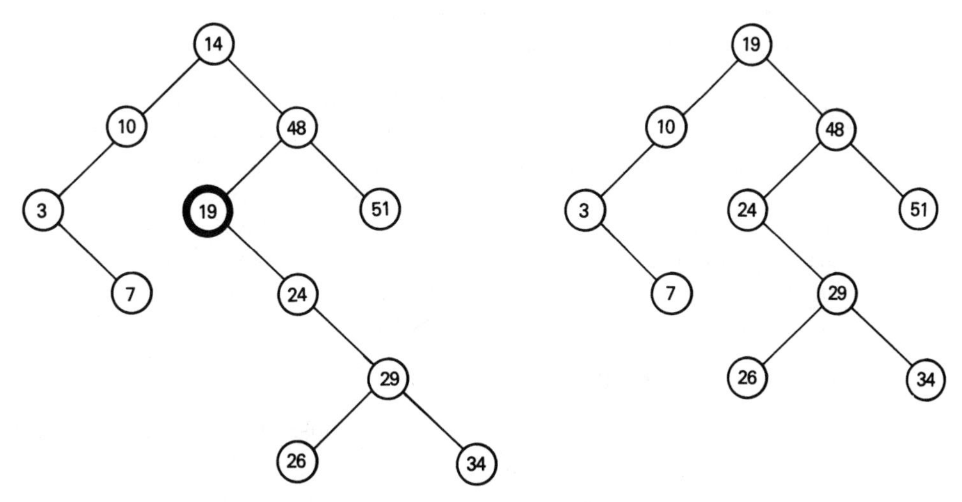

Figure 6.19 Deleting node 14. Leftmost node of right subtree is 19.

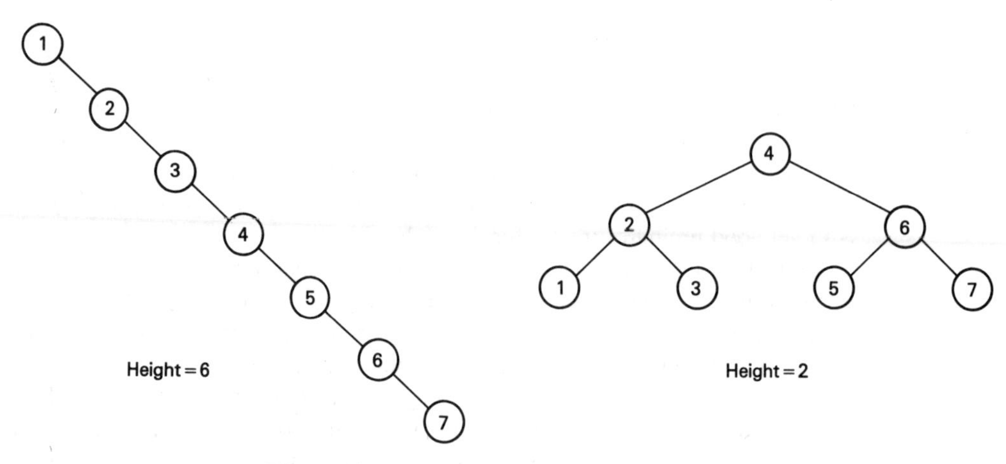

Figure 6.20 Two binary search trees of the same size.

tree was very unbalanced. Now comes the part where the author pulls the rabbit out of the *deus ex machina*. One fact and one observation come to our rescue:

Fact. Although the mathematics is too delicate for us to go into here, it turns out that under certain simplifying assumptions it is possible to prove that, on average, a "random" binary search tree with n nodes has depth proportional to log n. In other words, most binary search trees "should be" very shallow.

Observation. Because it is risky to extrapolate from theoretical results to actual figures (what do we mean, for instance by a "random" BST?), some researchers have gone in the opposite direction, looking at the statistics on depth of binary search trees that occur in practical situations. Here, too, the evidence is in our favor: Most of the data indicate that in practice, where binary search trees are made by long sequences of mixed insertions and deletions, most of the time the trees have depth not too much worse than a fixed multiple of log n.

This is good news indeed. In real-world terms, this means that if you had to maintain a database that had, on average, a million elements in it (sometimes more, sometimes less, depending on insertions and deletions), you should expect that, most of the time, all the operations should take no more than some fixed multiple of twenty steps through the tree, since 2^{20} is approximately a million. (Of course, you would spend much of your time in a terror of expectation that the tree might wind up looking like the worst case, a linked list with a million elements in it, whereupon your boss would call you to explain why it takes three days to retrieve an element from your database.)

Application: Treesort

Binary search trees give us, almost for free, a simple and (usually) efficient sorting algorithm. To sort a collection of data, we need only feed the data into a BST. As new data comes in, *Insert* places the data in its proper location in the tree in left–right order. What algorithm do we use to retrieve the data in its sorted order? Think about it.

* * *

Got it? *Inorder*! Remember, the inorder traversal of a binary tree visits the nodes in exactly their left–right order, and that's exactly the sorted order of the nodes. How long should such a sort take? Let's assume that we're always in the "nice" case, where insertion into a tree with n nodes takes $O(\log n)$ time. We place the first element at the root, since it has no other place to go, and after that we're inserting the nth element into a BST with $n - 1$ nodes, a process we assume takes $O(\log(n - 1))$ time. The total time to build the tree, then, is $O(\log 1) + O(\log 2) + O(\log 3) + \ldots + O(\log(n - 1))$, a quantity that is certainly no larger than $O(n \log n)$. Getting the data back by *Inorder* takes $O(n)$, which would be absorbed by the larger $O(n \log n)$ term, giving us a sorting algorithm that is asymptotically as good as any we've seen.

This sorting algorithm has certain other advantages, as well. Unlike *Mergesort*, the other $O(n \log n)$ algorithm we've seen, we don't need to have all the data in place at once. As the data dribbles in, we just insert it into the tree, where it can be retrieved in sorted order at any time. In that sense, *Treesort* is very much like *InsertionSort*, which we saw way back in Chapter 3, but the insertion part of the algorithm is more like a binary search, rather than the linear search of *InsertionSort*.

The PRIORITY QUEUE ADT and Heaps

Treesort is a dismal failure when the input is already sorted, since the BST formed by successive insertions would be nothing but a linked list. In this case, the total time cost of insertions would be $O(n^2)$, which is asymptotically much worse than $O(n \log n)$. We could guarantee that our operations would *always* take time $O(\log n)$ if we could be sure that the tree would be "balanced," in some sense that would prohibit the existence of very long branches. It turns out that we can do just that, although we have to give up some operations to do so. Keep the notion of balanced trees in the back of your mind—we will talk about them in depth in the next chapter.

Definition 6.4. The **PRIORITY QUEUE** abstract data type consists of a linearly ordered set of atoms and *no* structural relation whatsoever on the set of positions, along with the following operations:

1. **Create(var** P : PRIORITY_QUEUE) creates a new, empty priority queue, *P*.
2. **Insert**(a : ATOM ; **var** P : PRIORITY_QUEUE) inserts the atom *a* into *P*.
3. **DeleteMin(var** P : PRIORITY_QUEUE ; var min : ATOM) returns *min* equal to the smallest atom in *P*, and then deletes that element from *P*.

As with binary search trees, we recognize the possibility that the atoms themselves may be structured elements, such as records. In this case, we order the atoms by a key field. This ADT could be viewed as an abstraction of the people waiting for service in a hospital emergency room. As each patient arrives, the person in charge of admissions would make a decision about the severity of the patient's problem, and would assign them a priority for service based on that assessment, so a person with a fractured skull would likely receive treatment faster than a whole roomful of hangnail sufferers. When a doctor was ready to see another patient, the doctor would perform *DeleteMin* on the people in the waiting room, taking the patient with the lowest number (in this example, the one with the most pressing problem) and deleting that person from the queue of waiting patients.

We could implement priority queues with binary search trees, because BSTs already support all the operations needed for priority queues. For that matter, we could use sorted lists as well. Perhaps more than most ADTs, however, PRIORITY QUEUE is almost invariably associated with a single conceptual model, that of an optimal, leftist, binary tree with a heap condition (see Figure 6.21). We defined an optimal binary tree earlier; such a tree has the property that all the internal nodes, except possibly the lowest ones, have two children. A **leftist tree** has no political orientation but, rather, has the property that the nodes on a given level are all as far to the left as possible. We say that a tree satisfies the **heap condition** if the value of each node is less than that of each of its children, as in Figure 6.22. Such trees are also called **partially ordered trees**.

We impose the heap structure on our binary trees so that *DeleteMin* is easy to implement. We always know exactly where the minimum element is—it must be at the root—so that we can find it without tracing our way through the tree at all. Notice that the heap condition is less restrictive than the binary search tree property, with the result that in a tree with a heap condition, we have only partial information about the order of elements in the nodes. The fifth smallest element in a BST is the fifth in an inorder traversal; there is no such easy way to find the fifth smallest element in a priority queue.

The heap condition is still restrictive enough that it makes *Insert* simple to define. We begin by inserting the new node in the leftmost available location in the lowest level, moving down to a new level only if the lowest level is completely filled. If that node has a value greater than that of its parent, we are done, since the new tree still

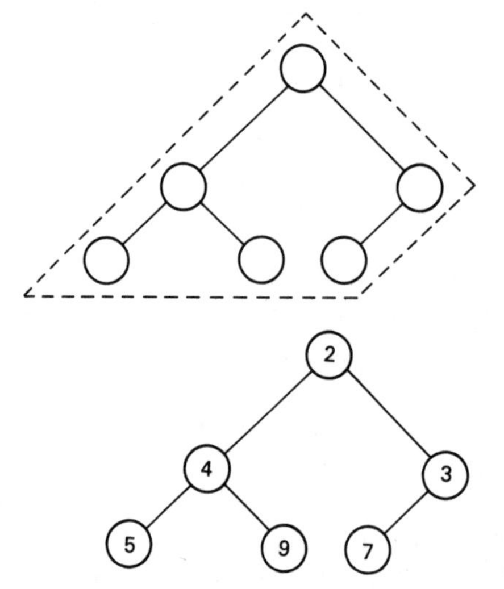

Figure 6.21 An optimal, leftist binary tree.

Figure 6.22 A tree satisfying the heap condition.

satisfies the heap condition. If the new node has value less than that of its parent, we exchange it with its parent, thereby restoring the heap condition at that subtree. The exchange might have destroyed the heap condition at the level above; if it has, we continue to "bubble up " the tree, exchanging the new node with its parent, grandparent, great-grandparent, and so on, until no exchanges are necessary.

Figure 6.23 shows the action of inserting value 1 into the tree of Figure 6.22. We first make a new node for 1. We see that the value of the new node is smaller than that of its parent, so we exchange them. The subtree rooted at 1 in Figure 6.23(b) now satisfies the heap condition, but node 1 is less in value than its new parent, so we exchange again, leading to the tree of Figure 6.23(c), which satisfies the heap condition, so we are done.

We define *DeleteMin* in a somewhat similar fashion, but in this case we begin by replacing the root with the "last" element (the rightmost element in the bottom level), so that the leftist nature of the tree is preserved. The new root element may be larger than its children, thus violating the heap condition, so as long as the tree is not a heap, we "bubble down" that element, replacing it with the smaller of its children, until the heap condition is restored. Figure 6.24 shows an example of how this process works.

It is not difficult to see that an optimal binary tree with n nodes must have depth d, where $d \leq \log_2 n$. Since both *DeleteMin* and *Insert* make at most one complete pass from top to bottom (or vice versa), both these operations run in time $O(\log n)$; and, unlike the situation we encountered with BSTs, these operations *never* take longer than that. This is just the improvement we were looking for, but how do we implement these operations? We can't just use the usual pointer implementation, because *Insert* requires that we move *up* the tree. We could always use extra parent pointers in each cell, or use

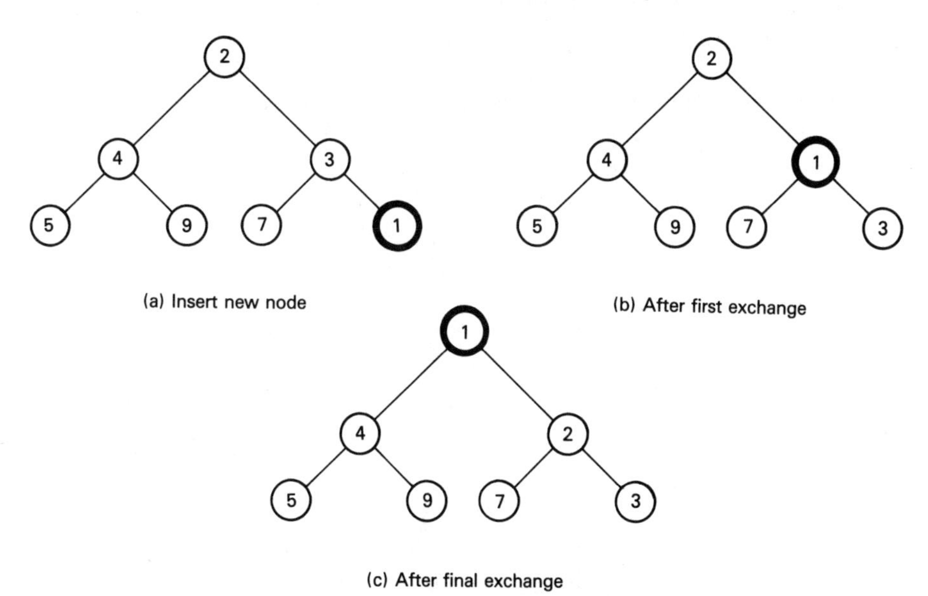

Figure 6.23 Insertion in a priority queue.

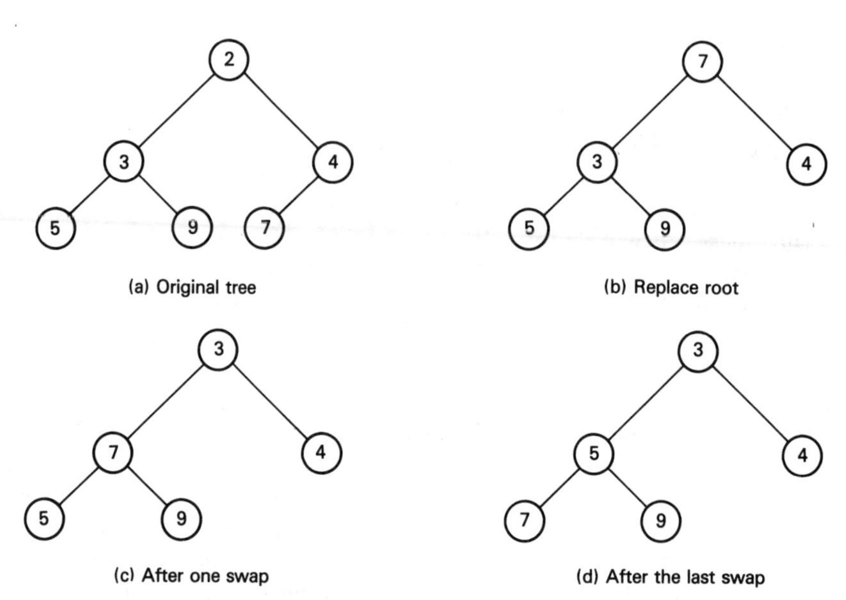

Figure 6.24 Deleting the minimum element from a priority queue.

a threaded tree, but there is a very clever array implementation that we would rather discuss here. We begin by placing a very natural linear order on every binary tree, assigning the root position 1, the left child of the root (whether or not there is one) position 2, the right child of the root position 3, and so on, assigning positions by rows, top to bottom, and left to right within rows, as in Figure 6.25. Now you see the reason for our insistence that these trees be complete, leftist, binary trees: Such a tree fills the position array with no holes. We could have used this as an implementation of a general binary tree, but the nodes of a tree that consisted of just a chain of right children, for instance, would be located in positions 1, 3, 7, 15, 31, 63, . . . , requiring $2^n - 1$ array spaces for n nodes, a profligate waste of space.

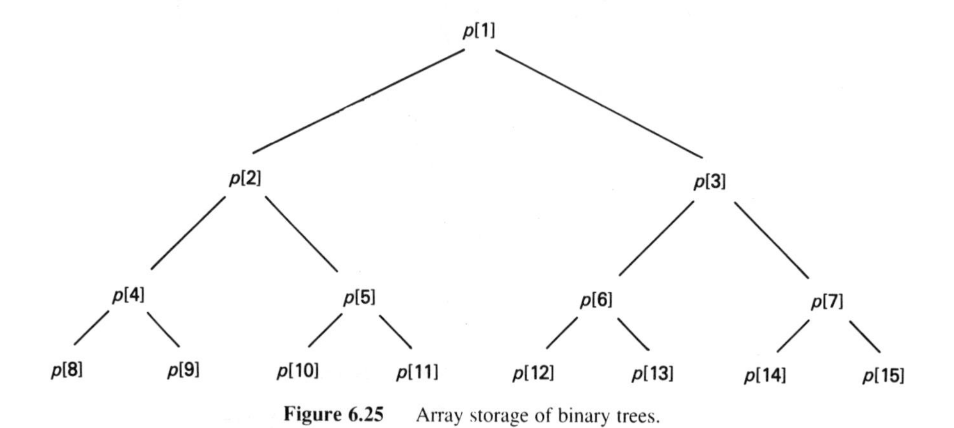

Figure 6.25 Array storage of binary trees.

The array implementation of PRIORITY QUEUE is now simple. We can find the parent of a node by observing that the left and right children of node $p[i]$ are just $p[2i]$, and $p[2i + 1]$, respectively, so the parent of a $p[i]$ is $p[i \textbf{ div } 2]$.

```
const
   MAX = {some positive integer for the largest array};
typea
   ATOM = {any data type with a linear order};
   POSITION = 1 . . MAX;
   PQ = record
          size : 0 . . MAX;
          data : array [POSITION] of ATOM
        end;

procedurea Create(var P : PQ);
begin
   P.size := 0;
end;


procedure Insert(a : ATOM ; var P : PQ);
   var
      i : POSITION;
      done : boolean;
      save : ATOM;
begin
   if P.size = MAX then
      writeln('no room for insertion')
   else begin
      P.size := P.size + 1;
      i := P.size;
      P.data[i] := a;                          {insert new node at end}

      done := false;
      while not done do
         if i = 1 then                         {we're at the root, so are done}
            done := true
         else if P.data[i] < P.data[i div 2] then begin {out of order }
            save := P.data[i];                 {swap with parent}
            P.data[i] := P.data[i div 2];
            P.data[i diva 2] := save;
            i := i div 2                   {move up to parent node and continue}
         end else
            done := true                   {order is restored, we're done}
   end
end;
```

DeleteMin is nearly as simple as *Insert*. The statement that is labeled as "OPTIONAL" may be omitted with no effect on the algorithm. It is there because we will make use of it in a sorting algorithm based on priority queues.

```
procedure DeleteMin(var P : PQ ; var min : ATOM);
   var
      i, j: POSITION;
      done : boolean;
      save : ATOM;
begin
   if P.size = 0 then
      writeln('queue is empty, no min to delete');
   else begin
      min := P.data[1];                   {return minimum value}
      P.data[1] := P.data[P.size];
      P.data[P.size] := min;              {OPTIONAL -swap last element with root}
      P.size := P.size - 1;

      i := 1;
      done := false;
      while not done do
         if i > P.size div 2 then         {we're at the bottom row of the tree, done}
            done := true
         else begin                              {find the index of the smallest child of i}
            if 2 * i + 1 > P.size then           { i has only a left child}
               j := 2 * i
            else if P.data[2 * i] < P.data[2 * i + 1] then { i has two children}
               j := 2 * i                        {find smallest}
            else
               j := 2 * i + 1;

            if P.data[i] > P.data[j] then begin {out of order}
               save := P.data[i];                {swap with smaller child}
               P.data[i] := P.data[j];
               P.data[j] := save;
               i := j                            {move to smaller child and continue}
            end else                             {order is now restored}
               done := true
         end
   end
end;
```

Application: Heapsort

It is easy to see how to use these operations to produce a sorting algorithm. All we need to do is *Insert* all the elements to be sorted into our priority queue, and then call *DeleteMin* to remove them from the queue in smallest-to-largest order. At first glance it might seem that we need two arrays, one for the original data and the eventual sorted

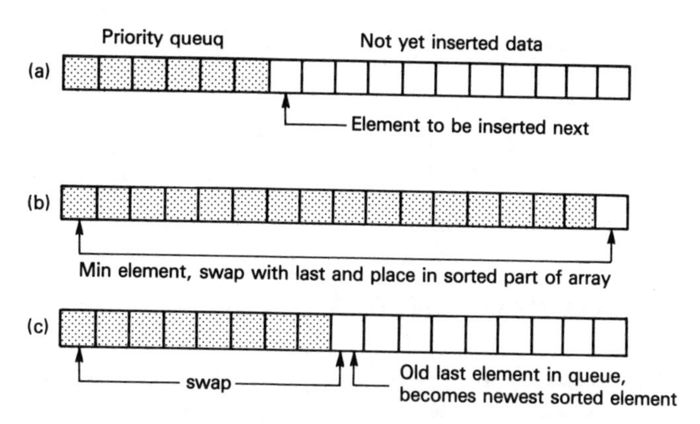

Figure 6.26 Heapsort in action.

list, and another for the priority queue itself. It turns out, however, that we can do all the sorting in place. We let the low-order part of the array contain the present priority queue, while the high-order part contains the elements yet to be inserted. Once the priority queue is full, we repeatedly delete the minimal elements from the first position in the queue, placing each of them, in turn, just beyond the present end of the priority queue. This **Heapsort** algorithm, then, is divided into two phases, the first in which we "heapify" the array by insertion, and the second in which we produce the sorted list. Now you can see the reason for the "OPTIONAL" statement in *DeleteMin*: When we delete the present minimum element of the heap, we don't just remove it; we place it at the left end of the already sorted sublist.

Figure 6.26(a) shows an intermediate step in the heapification phase: A new element is taken from the unprocessed data, placed in the new last position of the heap, and bubbled up to its proper place. In Figure 6.26(b), the sorting phase has just begun: The last element of the heap is placed at the root, and the old root element is placed where the last element used to be, which is now one position to the left of the end of the heap. Finally, Figure 6.26(c) shows an intermediate stage in the sorting phase. Now we can write the algorithm:

```
procedure Heapsort(var P : PQ);
{Assumes that the unsorted data already resides in the .data part of P}
{and that MAX contains the number of data elements.}
   var
      i : POSITION;
      unused : ATOM;
begin
   Create(P);
   for i := 1 to MAX do
      Insert(P.data[i], P);
   for i := 1 to MAX do
      DeleteMin(P, unused)
end;
```

For n data elements to be sorted, we have $2n$ calls to either *Insert* or *DeleteMin*, both of which take no more time than $O(\log n)$, and less than that most of the time, for a running time of $O(n \log n)$—not just in the "nice" cases, but always. Finally, you can consider yourself a master of priority queues if you can tell, right now, without more than a second's hesitation, how the sorted list comes out: Is the largest element at the left or at the right?

6.6 TWO APPLICATIONS OF TREES

The two applications we will discuss in this section are related in a number of ways: (1) they both deal with characters and strings, (2) they both are concerned with representing information in a space-efficient fashion, and (3) they both use trees. We begin with a puzzle: Look at the tree in Figure 6.27, and see if you can, first, notice any significant properties it has, and, second, determine the rule that used to generate the tree.

Finding properties is easy: The tree is a binary tree; it's not optimal, but is very close to being so; it contains all 26 letters in the English alphabet; and it is arranged so that the commonly used letters tend to be near the top of the tree. It's a safe bet that unless you had seen this tree before, you would not guess how it was built, so we'll tell you. It turns out that this tree is a decoder for Morse code. You may know that Morse code consists of three symbols—dot, dash, and space—and was originally invented for transferring information over telegraph wires. The dot was a short pulse of current (which would be transformed into a short sound at the receiver's end), the dash was a longer pulse (long sound), and the space was no current (used as a separator between letters and words). To use this tree as a decoder, we built it so that each left edge represented a dot, and each right edge represented a dash. Thus, to decode " · · – " we begin at the root, follow the left edge corresponding to the first dot, take the left edge from there for the second dot, and take the right edge for the dash, which leaves us at node "U," the letter corresponding to " · · – ".

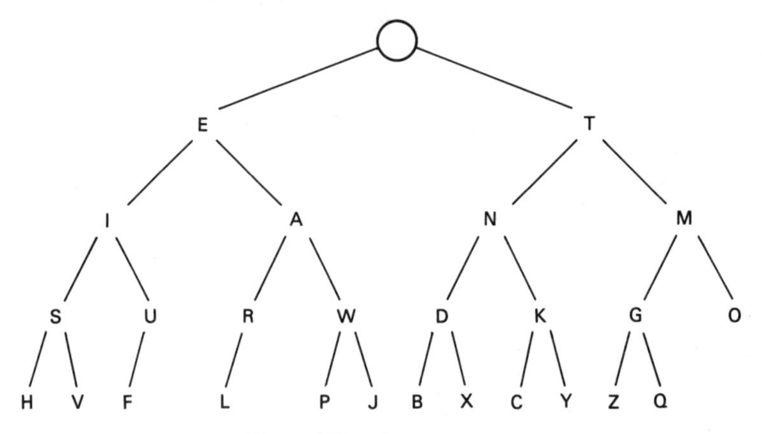

Figure 6.27 A mystery tree.

Samuel F. B. Morse was not the first person to come upon the idea of sending characters by encoding them as pulses of current, but the code associated with his name has the advantage that the letters that are most often sent have short codes. This is important when the code is being sent by human telegraphers, since more than ten or so dots and dashes per second would be difficult to send, as well as to interpret. To speed up transmission, we must try to make the codes as short as possible, on average. In the first application, we will explore the problem of producing codes that have the least average length.

Another nice feature of the decoding tree is that much of the code information is represented in the tree in such a way that it serves several purposes at once. The left branch from the root represents the initial dot for the letters E, I, A, S, U, R, W, H, V, F, L, P, and J. The fact that the codes for all these letters begin with a dot is implicit in the fact that all these letters are in the left subtree of the root, and do not need to be mentioned explicitly in our data structure. The second application will explore this representation by position in more detail.

Huffman Codes

Usually, we don't have to concern ourselves with the details of how characters are represented in memory. Generally, a character is stored as a number, representing that character by an agreed-on coding scheme, such as ASCII. The standard character codes are **fixed-length codes**, in that the number of bits in the code is the same for each character. Commonly, a byte is enough to store the code for a character, since an eight-bit byte provides 256 possible codes, more than enough for most character sets. In fact, it's more than we need, and that's the point of our discussion.

Consider a simple example of an alphabet of five letters, 'a', 'b', 'c', 'd', 'e'. Three bits give us eight possible code sequences, which is more than enough to encode five different characters, so we might represent these letters with a fixed-length code, as follows:

Letter	Code
a	000
b	001
c	010
d	011
e	100

In this case, the **average code length**—the expected length of the code of each letter—is 3. Suppose we knew that in a typical message in our alphabet, the letter 'a' appeared 35 percent of the time, 'b' 20 percent of the time, 'c' 20 percent, 'd' 15 percent, and 'e' 10 percent of the time. With this knowledge, we might decide to use a variable length code, like Morse code, representing the common letters by short codes.

Letter	Frequency	Code
a	0.35	0
b	0.20	1
c	0.20	00
d	0.15	01
e	0.10	10

We can find the average code length for this code by adding, for all letters, the code length times the probability that the letter will appear. In our example, the average code length is just 1 (0.35) + 1 (0.20) + 2 (0.20) + 2 (0.15) + 2 (0.10) = 1.35, which is less than half the average code length for the fixed-length code we started with. In other words, a message of 200 letters should require about 200(1.35) = 270 bits. Unfortunately, it won't work. For example, what are we to do with the message 0010? That could be interpreted as 'aaba', or 'aae', or 'ada', or 'cba', or 'ce'. We must have some way of determining where a code group ends. Morse code deals with this problem by sending a blank, but we would like to restrict ourselves to just two symbols. One possibility would be to decide that each code will begin with 11, and that 11 would not appear anywhere else in any code (effectively encoding a space by 11). Now our code would look like the following:

Letter	Frequency	Code
a	0.35	110
b	0.20	111
c	0.20	1100
d	0.15	1101
e	0.10	1110

This code has average length 3.35. We'd be better off with the original fixed-length code. Another possibility would be to insist that our code have the **prefix property**: that no code sequence can be the prefix of any other. For example, if one sequence was 110, no other sequence could begin with 110, and we could not have 1 or 11 as another code sequence. One example of a code with the prefix property is as follows:

Letter	Frequency	Code
a	0.35	00
b	0.20	10
c	0.20	010
d	0.15	011
e	0.10	111

This code has average length 2.45, and so is better than the fixed-length code. It has the further advantage that there is one and only one way to interpret any code sequence. But is this the best we can do? No, not in this case. The following algorithm, due to D. A. Huffman, can be shown to produce minimal-length prefix codes, and we will illustrate it on our alphabet of five letters.

Begin with a forest of trees, each consisting of a single node and corresponding to a single letter in the alphabet. Throughout the algorithm, each tree in the forest will have a *weight* assigned to it; at the start, the weight of each tree is just the probability of occurrence of the corresponding letter. Repeat the following process until the forest consists of a single tree: (1) Find the two trees of smallest weight, merge them together by making them the left and right children of a new root, and (2) make the weight of the new tree equal to the sum of the weights of the two subtrees. We illustrate this process in Figure 6.28.

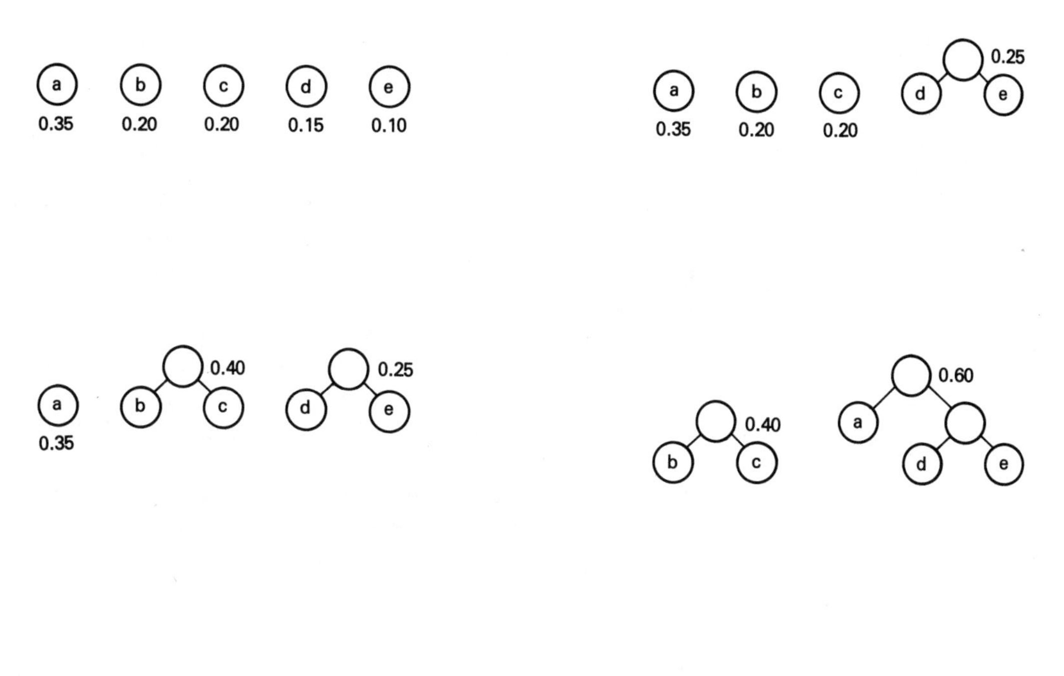

Figure 6.28 Constructing Huffman codes.

Having constructed the tree, assign to each left edge a value 0 and to each right edge the value 1, and read the codes for the letters by tracking down the tree, as we did with the Morse code decoder tree. We have the following code, with average length 2.25.

Letter	Frequency	Code
a	0.35	10
b	0.20	00
c	0.20	01
d	0.15	110
e	0.10	111

Tries

In the two examples we've seen so far, information has been represented implicitly in a tree by its position in the tree. We can use this idea to store a dictionary of strings, representing words, for example. Such a structure is a tree in which each node represents the prefix of a word, and has as its children nodes representing strings that have the parent as their prefixes. Because there is a considerable overlap of prefixes in most natural languages, such as English, this storage scheme can be quite efficient in terms of space. Such a structure is called a **trie**, pronounced "try" despite the fact that it is derived from "re**trie**val." We could, of course, store a dictionary in a number of ways, such as with a binary search tree. One of the nice properties of a trie is that it allows us to perform *partial* lookups, for instance, of all the words that begin with 'CA'. This would be difficult to do with another data structure, and would be useful if, say, we wanted to automate a crossword puzzle dictionary. In Figure 6.29 we show a typical trie, which stores the words ALL, ALP, AN, ANT, ANY, ARC, ARCH, ARM, ARMY, ART, CAD, CAN, CAR, CARD, and CARP.

In Figure 6.29, the nodes that are darkened represent full words, rather than just prefixes of words, so we know that both AN and ANT are stored in the trie, but that A

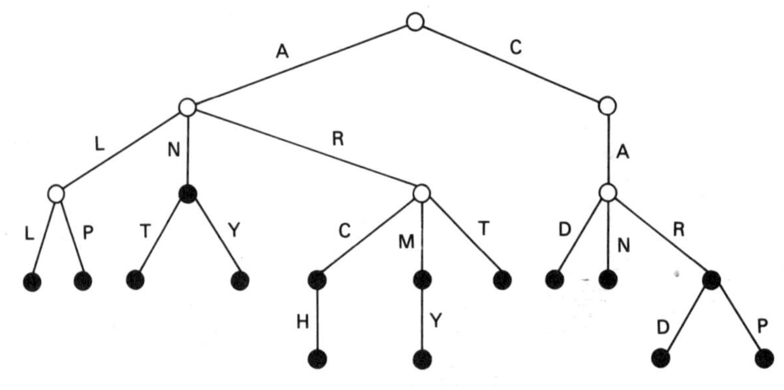

Figure 6.29 A trie.

is not. A trie supports the operations *Create* (of course), *Member, Insert*, and *Delete*, where *Member* is a function that returns *true* if and only if a given string is in the trie. We will also be able to provide a traversal of the tree, despite the fact that a trie is not usually a binary tree. In fact, we could have as many as twenty-six children for any node in the trie, although that does not happen as a rule. (How many children would a node have if the edge going into it was a "Q" edge, for instance?)

The most obvious implementation of a trie is with pointers. Each node will contain a boolean flag indicating whether the node represents a word or just a prefix, along with an array of twenty-six pointers, for all the possible children of that node. We will define part of the trie package, and leave the rest of the definition as an exercise.

```
type
   TriePtr = ^Node;
   Node = record
             isWord : boolean;
             next : array ['A' . . 'Z'] of TriePtr
          end;
   TRIE = Node;        {we access the trie by the root node itself}

procedure Create(var T : TRIE);
   var index : char;
begin
   T.isWord := false;
   for index := 'A' to 'Z' do
      T.next[index] := nil
end;

function Member(s : STRING ; T : TRIE) : boolean;
   var ch : char;
begin
   if Length(s) = 0 then                {we are now at the node representing s}
      Member := T.isWord                {see if the node represents a word}
   else begin
      ch := Retrieve(s, 1);             {get the first character in s, see where to go next}
      if T.next[ch] = nil then          {no place to go, search failed}
         Member := false
      else begin                        {do the search recursively on the tail of s}
         Delete(s);                     {delete the first character remaining in s}
         Member := Member(s, T.next[ch]^)  {and search in the proper subtree}
      end
   end
end;
```

Member searches the subtrie rooted at *T* for the string *s*. Each time a branch is taken, the leading character (corresponding to the branch taken) is removed from *s*, and a recursive call to is made on the new string and the new node. The bailout conditions are (1) when *s* is the empty string, in which case we have reached the node representing the original string, and we test whether that node represents a word, or (2) when we run out of branches before having used all the characters in *s*, in which case we know the string is not in the trie. *Insert* is defined in a similar way:

```
procedure  Insert(s : STRING ; var T : TRIE);
   var lead, index : char;
begin
   if Length(s) = 0 then                      {we've reached the node representing s}
      T.isWord := true
   else begin
      lead := Retrieve(s, 1);                 {find which branch to take}
      if T.next[ lead ] = nil then begin      {any node there? Build one if not}
         new(T.next[ lead ]);
         for index := 'A' to 'Z' do
            T.next[ lead ]^.next[index] := nil;
         T.next[ lead ]^.isWord := false
      end;                                    {and in any case, repeat insertion}
         Delete(s);                           {by removing lead character}
         Insert(s, T.next[ lead ]^)           {and continuing to try to insert at child node}
   end
end;
```

We can see that both *Member* and *Insert* take time proportional to the length of the string, regardless of the size of the trie. This contrasts sharply with the situation we would have if we had decided to implement our dictionary as a binary search tree. We could have chosen BSTs, since there is a lexicographic linear order on strings, but if we had, the length of time to perform a search would be logarithmic in the size of the dictionary. This would become particularly important if we were using the dictionary as a spelling checker for a word processor. A typical spelling checker might have as many as 50,000 words, so even the best balanced BST would have depth $\log_2 50{,}000$, which is about 16. In contrast, the average word length in English is around 5, so the trie would be much shallower; hence, assuming that finding a word in either implementation takes roughly the same amount of time per edge, the trie would be a considerably faster implementation of the dictionary.

Let us close this section with an investigation of memory use, concentrating just on the small trie of Figure 6.29. Suppose that a boolean variable requires 1 byte of memory, that pointers take 4 bytes, and that we are dealing with a compiler–computer combination that uses fixed-length strings of 256 bytes each. Each of the trie nodes requires 1 byte for the *isWord* field, along with 26×4 bytes for the pointer array, for a total of 105 bytes for each of the 21 nodes. This gives us a total of $21 \times 105 = 2205$ bytes for the trie. If we had stored the same data as a binary search tree, each tree node would require 256 bytes for the string, and 8 bytes for the left and right child pointers, for a total of 264 bytes for each of the 15 words. The total memory needed for the BST, then, would be $15 \times 264 = 3960$ bytes, an amount that is 79 percent larger than that used by the trie. Of course, it is unwise to extrapolate from such small examples, but it is at least possible that we would realize a significant saving of memory here, as well as time. We will see in Chapter 10 that we can realize an even greater saving of space if we represent each node as a linked list of pointers, rather than an array. The link pointers take up additional space, but if a node has sufficiently few children, we will still be ahead by not having to predeclare all the pointers in the array.

6.7 SUMMARY

We covered a lot of material in this chapter, and that is a fairly accurate reflection of the importance of trees. Lists are very useful, but there are many instances in which the information to be represented has a hierarchical, rather than linear, structure.

Binary trees are fundamental hierarchical structures, in the sense that any tree can be represented as a binary tree, with a possible increase in depth. The depth of a tree is an important parameter because many of the tree algorithms run in time proportional to the depth of the tree. We discussed the pointer representation of binary trees, the extension to threaded trees, and an array-based cursor implementation.

Because trees have a natural recursive definition, it is not surprising that there is a simple recursive technique for tree traversal. In fact, if we permute the statements in the tree traversal algorithm, we can derive three different ways to traverse a tree (there are actually six different permutations, but we restrict our attention only to those that visit the left subtree of a node before the right subtree). The traversal routines lend themselves very readily to translating arithmetic expressions stored in parse trees, as well as to sorting routines, such as *Treesort*.

In cases where the set of atoms has a linear order, we can structure binary trees in such a way as to make insertion, deletion, and membership testing quite simple, and usually fast as well. Binary search trees have the property that each node has a value greater than that of any value in its left subtree and less than any value in its right subtree. The operations on binary search trees usually run in time that is logarithmic in the size of the tree, but in the worst cases may be only linear.

When we weaken the BST property and require that a node have value less than that of any of its descendants, we have a heap-ordered tree. If we also require that the tree be optimal, we have a structure that implements priority queues in an efficient fashion. We give up the ability to find a general element quickly, but we also eliminate the possibility that insertion and deletion may require more than logarithmic time. Priority queues can be represented with arrays, giving rise to *Heapsort*, a sorting algorithm with $O(n \log n)$ worst-case performance.

Finally, we discussed two applications of trees, to produce minimal-length codes and to store a dictionary of words. Huffman codes provide provably minimal codes for characters with a given probability distribution, and tries provide flexible and efficient storage of words, particularly in a natural language, where there is considerable overlap of prefixes. We will explore tries further in Chapter 10.

6.8 EXERCISES

1. Is there anything in the definition of a tree that prohibits a node from being its own parent? In other words, can the structural relation of a tree have any reflexivity?
2. If a tree has $n > o$ nodes, how many edges can it have? Prove your assertion. (*Hint*: Try induction on n.)
3. Answer the following questions for the tree of Figure 6.30:
   (a) What are the siblings of e?
   (b) What are the descendants of d?
   (c) Which nodes are leaves?
   (d) What are the height and depth of g?
   (e) What is the height of the tree?
4. Convert the tree of Figure 6.30 from a 3-ary ordered tree into a binary tree, using the algorithm in the text.
5. Describe the operations you would include in the definition of ORDERED TREE. You should consider which of the operations in BINARY TREE to include, which would need to be modified, which would be inappropriate, and what other operations should be added.
6. Show that *left* is a linear order.
7. Some authors use a more general definition of *left*, dropping the cases in which two nodes have an ancestor–descendant relationship. Under this definition of *left*, do the three traversal orders preserve *left* order, in the sense that, for instance, if n is left of m, then must it be the case that n occurs before m in a preorder traversal?
8. Consider the tree of Figure 6.30, and eliminate node e, thus making the tree a binary tree. In the resulting tree:
   (a) Which nodes are to the left of f ?
   (b) What is the rightmost node?
   (c) Which nodes are to the right of b and to the left of k?
   (d) What is the rightmost node of the left subtree of b?
9. Produce a binary tree with nodes a, b, c, d, e, f such that b is second in inorder and fifth in postorder.

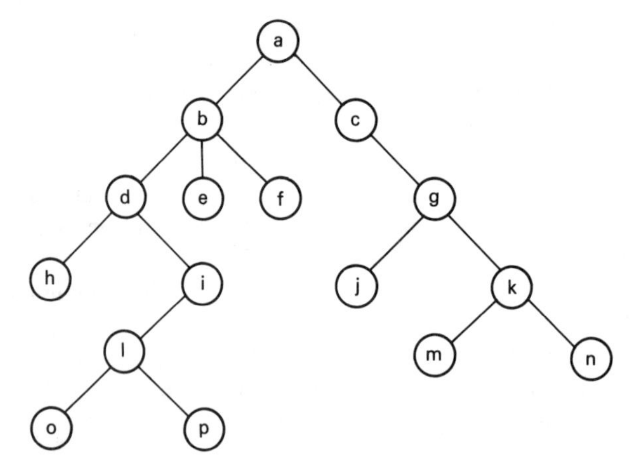

Figure 6.30 A sample tree.

10. Write *Inorder* without using recursion or threaded trees.

11. In the mathematical literature, a *reconstruction problem* is one in which you are given some information about an object and are required to use that information to produce the object.
    - **(a)** Show that you cannot reconstruct a binary tree given only its inorder traversal, by producing two different binary trees that both have inorder traversal a, b, c.
    - **(b)** Show that you do not need all three traversal orders to reconstruct a binary tree, by showing that some two of the three traversals provide enough information to reconstruct the tree (that is, produce an algorithm that will build a binary tree from some two traversals).

12. What can you say about the order in which the leaves of a binary tree are visited by each of the three traversals?

13. Give an algorithm that would take a parse tree of an arithmetic expression and produce a correctly parenthesized infix expression from the tree.

14. (You need to know calculus for this.) Parse trees of algebraic expressions are useful in problems of **symbolic algebra**, in which algebraic expressions are manipulated by the computer. We could, for instance, write a program to find factors of polynomials, or perform the sort of integration so near and dear to the hearts of calculus students. In fact, programs already exist that can do integration well enough to handle most of the problems on a first-semester calculus final exam. An easier problem in symbolic algebra is to write a program that differentiates. Given a parse tree of an expression in one variable (for simplicity, assume it's a polynomial), describe the rules that would be used to transform the parse tree into that of the derivative of the original expression. Your rules will be most easily expressed in recursive form.

15. In the pointer definition of *DeleteSub*, we disposed of a subtree using a postorder traversal of the subtree. What would happen if we used a different traversal?

16. Write the definitions of the BINARY TREE operations for threaded trees.

17. Show that if we are given a preorder traversal of a binary tree, along with the information about whether each node has a left or a right child, then we can reconstruct the tree. (*Hint*: Consider the information obtained about what the next node in preorder is in each of the four possible cases for existence or nonexistence of children. You may find a stack helpful.)

18. Show all possible binary search trees on the keys 1, 2, 3, 4. If you are ambitious, try to find a formula that expresses the number of BSTs on the keys $1, \ldots, n$.

19. If we delete a node from a BST, and then insert that node again, is the resulting BST necessarily the same as before?

20. If we delete two nodes from a BST, does the resulting BST ever depend on which of the nodes was deleted first?

21. Show the BST that results from inserting the keys 8, 13, 10, 12, 6, 9, 5, 2, in that order (8 first, then 13, and so on). Quick, give an inorder traversal of the tree.

22. Under what conditions on a list of keys does inserting the list into a BST lead to a single path with no branching, that is, a BST that looks like a linked list?

23. Repeat the following exercises for priority queues, as implemented in the text.
    - **(a)** Exercise 18.
    - **(b)** Exercise 19.
    - **(c)** Exercise 21 (without the inorder traversal).

24. When discussing priority queues, we made no mention of whether the elements were distinct. Do *Insert* and *DeleteMin* work correctly if we allow duplicate elements?

25. Produce a Huffman code for the alphabet *a, b, c, d,* where the letters have respective frequencies 0.35, 0.35, 0.20, 0.10.

26. **(a)** There is no Huffman code on four letters with code lengths 3, 2, 2, 2. Explain.

(b) Show that a tree with leaves at depths $d_1, d_2, \ldots, d_n$ can be a Huffman tree if and only if

$$\sum_{i=1}^{n} 2^{-d_i} = 1$$

so that, for example, a tree with four nodes at depths 3, 3, 2, 1 could be a Huffman tree, since 1/8 + 1/8 + 1/4 + 1/2 = 1. (*Hint*: Every Huffman tree with more than one node is made by merging two smaller Huffman trees.)

27. The frequency of occurrence of letters in English is found by taking a large, representative sample of English text (like the Sunday *New York Times*) and counting letters. There is, then, minor disagreement about the numbers to assign to the frequencies, but most studies have nearly identical numbers. In Table 6.1, we provide such a frequency list, taken from the text of Chapters 5 and 6 of this book.

TABLE 6.1 Frequency Distribution of English

Letter	Frequency	Letter	Frequency
E	0.1311	U	0.0259
T	0.1076	M	0.0219
I	0.0796	W	0.0211
O	0.0742	P	0.0202
A	0.0720	G	0.0165
N	0.0704	B	0.0162
S	0.0640	Y	0.0137
R	0.0626	V	0.0094
H	0.0518	K	0.0038
L	0.0421	X	0.0028
D	0.0324	Q	0.0017
C	0.0312	J	0.0008
F	0.0265	Z	0.0005

(a) Use Table 6.1 to produce a Huffman code for English. In order to make all answers consistent, perform the merging so that the subtree of lower weight always appears at the zero branch. If you do your work correctly, there shouldn't be any ties—that is, subtrees of equal weight—to mess things up.

(b) Find the average length of your code.

(c) A message with 97 bits should contain about how many letters?

(d) Here's a message of length 97. Decode it. The fact that it is broken into groups of five bits is not significant—we do that only to make the message easy to read.

00110 00111 11111 11010 00111 01001 01110 00110 01101 11101

00111 11000 10111 01011 01101 01010 11110 10111 00001 00

(e) The order of the entries in Table 6.1 differs slightly from the agreed-on order of frequency of letters in English. Not only are there more E's and T's in Chapters 5 and 6 than there are in "typical" English, but also the order usually given is E, T, A, O, I, N, S, R, H, L, D, C, U, ... How might you account for these differences?

Programming Projects

28. Write a function that, given a pointer to the root of a binary tree, returns the height of the tree.

29. Do Exercise 13 in reverse, by producing a program that will take as input an infix expression and produce a parse tree for that expression.

30. Write a program that will take an algebraic expression in a single variable and produce its derivative.

31. Write a package of routines to support binary search trees with integer *data* fields.

32. Using Exercises 28 and 31, write a program that will take an integer, n, insert n randomly chosen integers into a binary search tree, and measure the height of the resulting tree. The fact and observation we mentioned in the section on BSTs indicate that the height should be approximately $K \log n$, on average. Run enough test cases to determine whether this appears to be the case, and, if it is, find K.

33. There are some instances in which we wish to deal with a **static** data structure, one that supports *Find* and *Retrieve*, but not *Insert* or *Delete*, except at the very beginning, while the structure is being built. If, for instance, we were to build a static binary search tree, it would make sense to put the frequently sought elements near the root, in order to make *Find* as fast as possible. The only problem is that we may not know ahead of time which elements would be sought more frequently than others.

One way to deal with this problem is to use a **self-organizing binary search tree** (SOB tree), which has the property that each time a nonroot node is found, that node is promoted one level up the tree by a **rotation**. In the following figure, we show a left rotation, used when the node sought (y, in this case) is a right child, and we define a right rotation similarly.

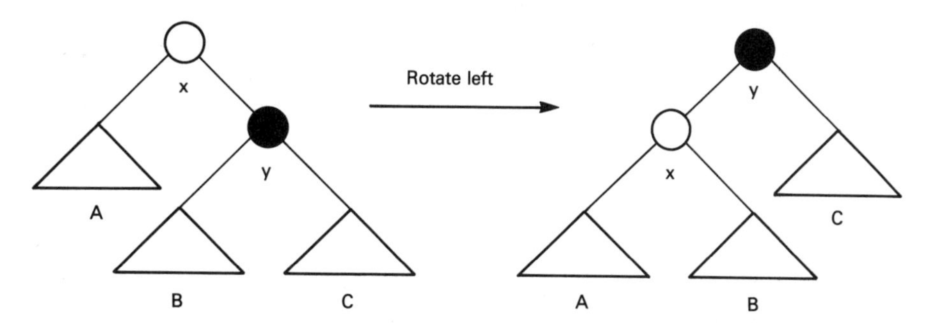

Notice that this rotation preserves the left–right order of the nodes and their subtrees—A, x, B, y, C—and hence must preserve the binary search tree property. Write *Find* for SOB trees. If you are comfortable with simulations, it would be worthwhile to investigate whether SOB trees produce a significant saving of time over purely static binary search trees, and what the average depth of the nodes are over a long run of repeated *Find*'s.

34. Compare *Treesort* and *Heapsort* on several lists of randomly chosen numbers. See if they both have running time bounded above by $Kn \log n$, and find K for each algorithm.

35. Write a program that, when given a list of letters and their frequencies, produces a Huffman code for that alphabet, and computes the average length of the code. This is a bit trickier than it appears, because you have to find a way of merging the subtrees. Usually, what is done is to provide an extra link field in each node, and use that field to keep the roots in a linked list.

36. Implement and test a dictionary using a trie.

7

Specialized Trees

The need for balance in all matters is fundamental to well-being. No tree can be truly healthy which has all its branches on one side.

Hortensia Prætexta, *On Gardening*

Binary search trees are very efficient data structures—most of the time. They support a wide range of operations, and these operations run in logarithmic time—most of the time. The problem with BSTs, as you know by now, is that it is possible that the timing for the operations may degrade to linear, if the tree happens to become very badly unbalanced, with all or most of its nodes linked in a long linear chain. If we relax the linear left–right order condition on the nodes, and force the tree to be an optimal heap, then we can guarantee logarithmic time, but only for the operations *Insert* and *DeleteMin*. Finding an element (except for the minimum) and deleting an element (except for the minimum) now require a traversal of the tree, because we have given up a linear order on the nodes for a partial order.

We will discuss here two improvements of binary search trees. Both have the left–right order property that BSTs have, so we do not have to give up easy finding of elements, and both avoid the possibility of runaway inflation of the height of the tree, so the operations always run in log time. The price we pay for these improvements is a moderate gain in the amount of programming detail. But the concepts behind these two improvements are fairly simple, and the programming complexity of the algorithms is evidently not sufficient to keep at least one of these data structures from being very widely employed out there in the real world.

7.1 BALANCED TREES

One way of ensuring that a binary tree does not have runaway branches is to insist that the tree be **balanced**, that is, that at every node, the heights of the left and right subtrees do not differ by more than one. Clearly, we can't do better than that and insist that the heights of the left and right subtrees always be equal, because that can happen only when the tree is **complete**, that is, when every internal node has exactly two children. In Figure 7.1, tree (a) is complete (hence balanced); tree (b) is balanced but not complete; and tree (c) is not balanced, because at the root the left subtree has height 3, whereas the right subtree has height 1. To be consistent, we say that the height of a tree with one node is 0, and the height of an empty tree is −1.

If we are going to deal with balanced trees, and if the efficiency of our algorithms depends on the depth of the tree, we had better be able to find an upper bound on the depth of a balanced binary tree on n nodes. As it happens, however, it's easier to answer the question in reverse: What is the smallest number of nodes in a balanced tree of height h? Let $S(h)$ denote the least size (i.e., the number of nodes) in any balanced tree of height h. Obviously, we must have $S(0) = 1$, and $S(1) = 2$, since a tree of height 0 must have at least one node, and a tree of height 1 must have at least 2 nodes. We can make a tree of height h by merging two subtrees of height $h - 1$ and $h - 2$: Their heights differ by one, and we can make the new tree have the smallest size by using minimal trees for the subtrees. If we denote such minimal-size balanced trees of height h by F_h, then the construction is that of Figure 7.2.

These minimal balanced binary trees are called **Fibonacci trees**, for the following reason: If we start with F_0 and F_1, trees consisting of a single node and two nodes linked by an edge, respectively, and note that $S(h)$ is just the number of nodes in F_h,

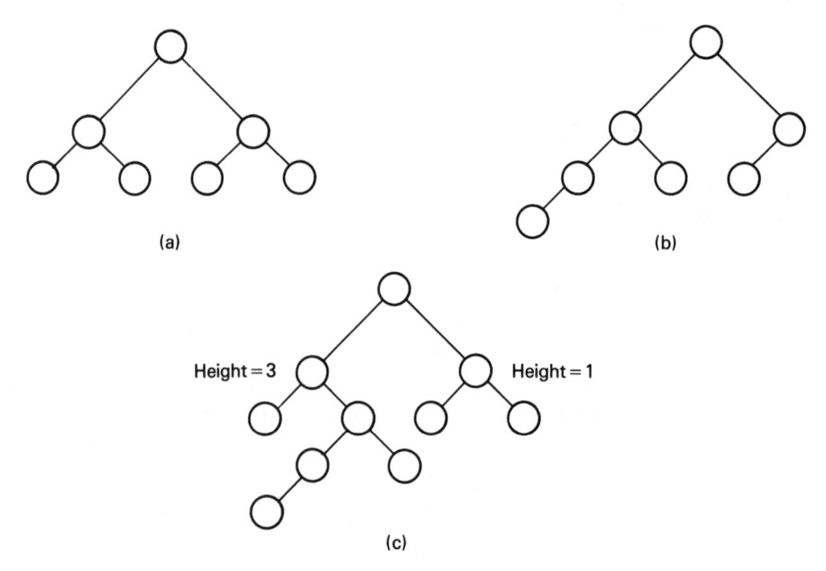

Figure 7.1 Balanced and unbalanced trees.

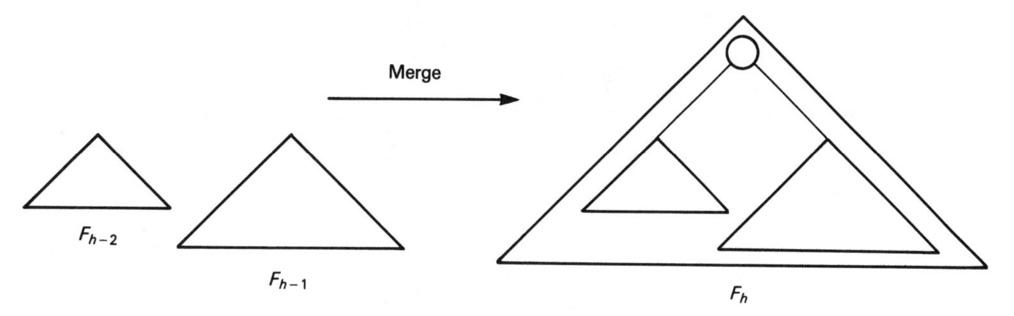

Figure 7.2 Merging balanced trees.

then we see that the construction of Figure 7.2 implies that $S(h) = S(h-1) + S(h-2) + 1$, because the number of nodes in the new tree is equal to the number of nodes in the subtrees, plus one for the new root used to merge the subtrees. The first few values of $S(h)$, are 1, 2, 4, 7, 12, 20, and 33, and it is not hard to prove by induction that $S(h) = Fib(h+2) - 1$. Now, the Fibonacci numbers grow quite rapidly; in Chapter 5 we proved that $Fib(h) > (3/2)^h$, for all $h > 4$. Therefore, we must have $S(h) > (3/2)^{h+2}$, so if we let n be the number of nodes in a balanced tree of height h, we have $n > (3/2)^{h+2}$, and taking logs of both sides yields

$$\log n > \log(3/2)^{h+2} = (h+2)\log(3/2).$$

Solving for h, we find

$$\frac{\log n}{\log(3/2)} > h+2$$

so we have, finally,

$$h < \frac{\log n}{\log(3/2)} - 2 < K \log n.$$

Well, this is just the sort of behavior we wanted—the height of a balanced tree with n nodes is always less than some multiple of log n, since every balanced tree of height h must have at least as many nodes as F_h. In Figure 7.3, we illustrate the first few Fibonacci trees.

A consistent theme of this book is that the operations on a data structure be *structure preserving*: All the list operations maintained the linear structure of the lists on which they operated, and all the operations on binary search trees preserved the binary search tree property of left–right order. We want to do the same thing with balanced trees: to define the BST operations in such a way that the trees stay balanced at all times, while at the same time preserving the binary search tree property. The algorithms we will present were published in 1962 by G. M. Adel'son-Velskii and E. M. Landis; and, in their honor, the elements of this data structure are called **AVL trees**.

The essential parts of the insertion and deletion algorithms for AVL trees will be exactly the same as the ones we defined for binary search trees. However, insertion or

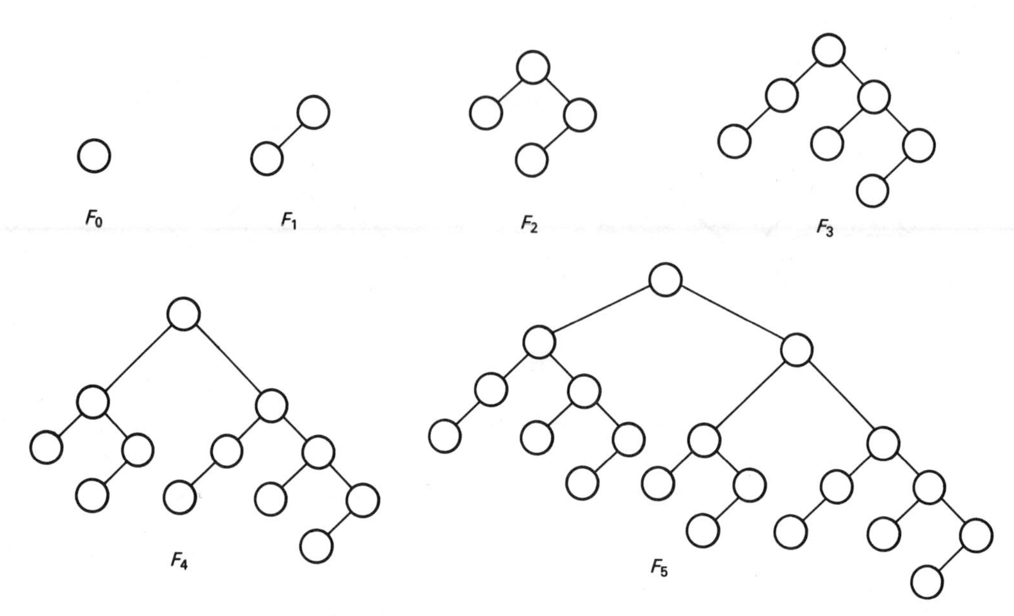

Figure 7.3 Some small Fibonacci trees.

deletion could cause a previously balanced tree to become unbalanced, as would happen in the following tree if we inserted 25 or deleted 9. Should that happen, we will call a "firefighting" algorithm to rebalance the tree.

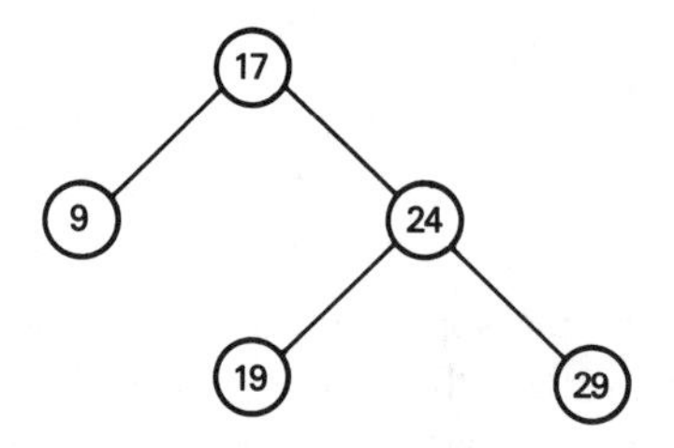

To facilitate the balancing algorithm, we will implement AVL trees in almost exactly the same way we implemented binary search trees, with the exception that each node will contain an extra field that stores the height of the subtree rooted at that node.

```
type
   POSITION = ^Node;
   Node = record
            height : integer;
            data : ATOM;
            left, right : POSITION
         end;
   AVL = POSITION;
```

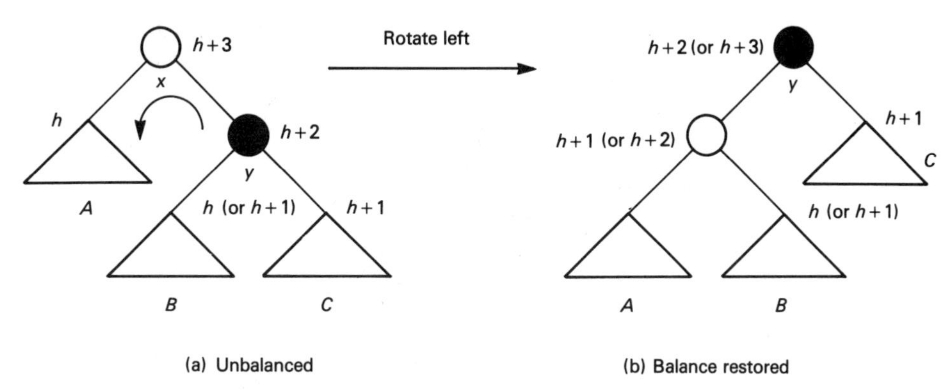

Figure 7.4 Restoring right imbalance by left rotation.

We will restore the balance of an AVL tree by **rotations** of the tree at or below the node where the imbalance was detected. There are two possible cases with which we must deal, and they both come in two flavors, each of which is a mirror image of the other. In describing the two cases, *we will assume that the imbalance was caused by the right subtree of a node* x *being too high*, either by an insertion to the right of x or a deletion to the left of x. We will denote the root of the right subtree of x by y throughout this discussion. The other case, in which the imbalance was caused by the left subtree of x being too high, is dealt with in an analogous fashion, interchanging *left* and *right* in all of the subsequent discussions.

Case 1. Suppose the right subtree of y has height larger than that of the left subtree of y, as in Figure 7.4, caused by deletion of a node from subtree A or insertion into subtree C. We see that a left rotation preserves the left–right order A, x, B, y, C, so the binary search tree property is preserved by left rotations, and that the left rotation in this case has restored the balance at node x. If we had been in the mirror image situation to that of Figure 7.4(a), we would restore balance by a right rotation. Of course, by restoring balance at x, we may have changed the height of the subtree rooted at x, so we may have to continue the balancing process at the parent of x, and so on, up to the root of the AVL tree. At any rate, it is not difficult to implement the rotation algorithm, as follows:

```
procedure RotateLeft(var x : POSITION);
{Rotate nodes pointed to by x and x^.right}
   var y : POSITION;
begin
   if x <> nil then
      if x^.right <> nil then begin
         y := x^.right;
         x^.right := y^.left;    {Left subtree of y becomes right subtree of x}
         y^.left := x;           {x becomes left child of y}
         x := y                  {y becomes new root of whole subtree}
      end
end;
```

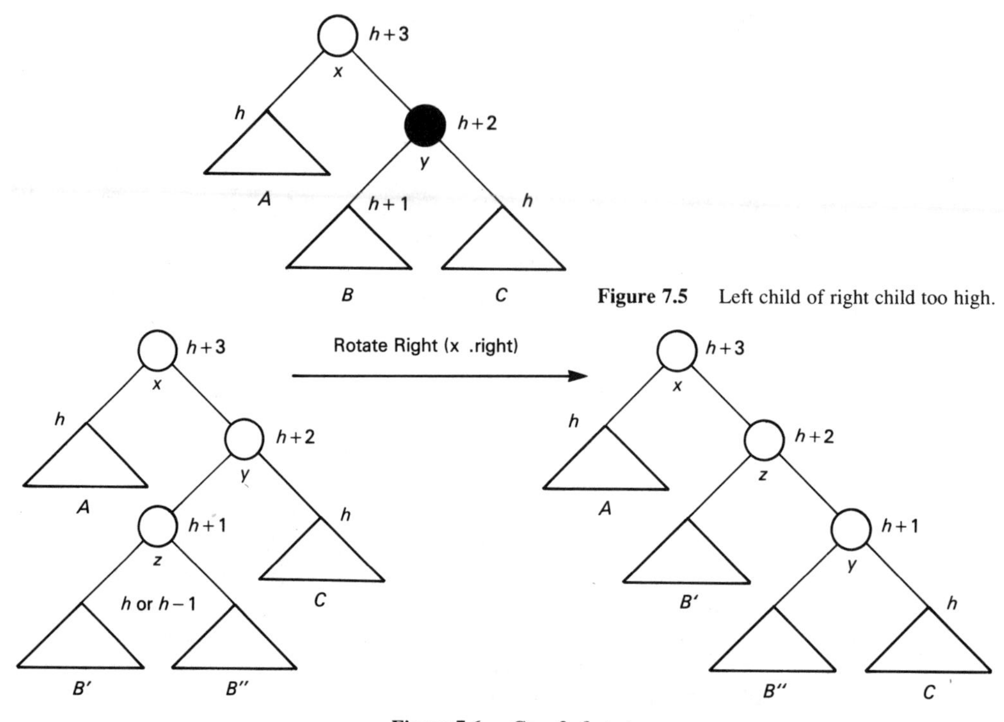

Figure 7.5 Left child of right child too high.

Figure 7.6 Case 2, first step.

We would define *RotateRight* by interchanging the words *left* and *right* everywhere in the foregoing definition.

Case 2. Suppose now that the imbalance at x is caused by the left subtree of y being too high, as in Figure 7.5. You should be able to convince yourself that in this case a simple rotation will not be sufficient to restore balance at x. We must perform two rotations, and to do this we must begin one level further down the tree.

In Figure 7.6 we have expanded subtree B into its root and subtrees B' and B'', one of which must have height h in this case, and show the result of the first rotation, at the right child of x. Of course, the tree is still not balanced, and it looks as if we have done the rotation for nothing. However, the stage is now set for the second step, a rotation at x, which will restore the balance we sought (see Figure 7.7).

Notice that not only have we restored the balance (at least of the subtree originally rooted at x), but we have maintained the original left–right order A, x, B', z, B'', y, C. We can now combine the two balancing procedures into a single procedure, *BalanceRight*. For both *BalanceRight* and *BalanceLeft*, which is defined similarly, we require an auxiliary function, *Difference*, which takes a node pointer as argument, and returns the difference between the heights of the left and right subtrees of the argument node

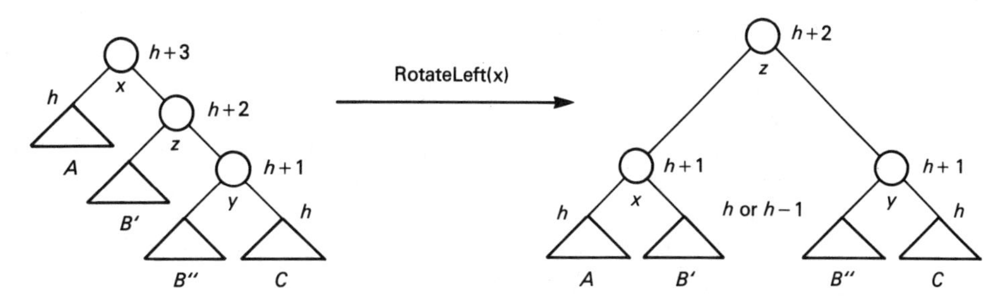

Figure 7.7 Case 2, final step in restoring balance.

```
function Difference(n : POSITION) : integer;
    var leftHeight, rightHeight : integer;
begin
    if n = nil then
        Difference := 0
    else begin
        if n^.left = nil then
            leftHeight := -1
        else
            leftHeight := n^.left^.height;

        if n^.right = nil then
            rightHeight := -1
        else
            rightHeight := n^.right^.height;

        Difference := leftHeight - rightHeight
    end
end;
```

We may now define *BalanceRight*. When reading the definition, notice that we adjust the heights of the nodes after balancing. In this case, Figures 7.4 through 7.7 are slightly misleading, in that they show nodes x, y, and z as labeled, although strictly speaking the nodes are accessed by pointers, so that, for instance, in the single rotation in Figure 7.4, the pointer n in *BalanceRight* points to the old root, x, prior to the procedure's execution, and to the new root, y, after the procedure's return. In other words, before *BalanceRight* in Figure 7.4(a), n points to x, and *n^.right* points to y, while in Figure 7.4(b), n points to y, and *n^.left* points to x.

```
procedure BalanceRight(var n : POSITION);
{Restores balance at n, assuming that the right subtree of n is too high}
begin
    if Difference(n^.right) = 0 then begin
    {Case 1(a) : both subtrees of right child of n have same height}
        RotateLeft(n);
        n^.height := n^.height - 1;
        n^.left^.height := n^.left^.height + 1
    end else if Difference(n^.right) < 0 then begin      {Note: use '>' in BalanceLeft}
```

```
    {Case 1(b) : right subtree of right child of n is higher}
        RotateLeft(n);
        n^.left^.height := n^.left^.height - 2
    end else begin
    {Case 2 : left subtree of right child of n is higher}
        RotateRight(n^.right);
        RotateLeft(n);
        n^.height := n^.height +1;
        n^.left^.height := n^.left^.height - 2;
        n^.right^.height := n^.right^.height - 1
    end
end;
```

Remember that although we have not defined *RotateRight* or *BalanceLeft*, we may do so easily by interchanging *left* and *right* in the definitions of *RotateLeft* and *BalanceRight*, respectively.

At last, we can define *Insert* for AVL trees. If you compare the following definition with the definition of *Insert* for BSTs, you'll see that the only difference is that here we test for imbalance upon the return from the recursive call to *Insert* and do whatever balancing is necessary. When reading the algorithm, remember that the precondition for *Insert(n)* is that the subtree rooted at *n* is balanced, and that after *Insert(n)*, the subtree is again balanced. Note also that we make use of an auxiliary routine, *FixHeight*, which corrects the height of a node after insertion into one of its subtrees.

```
procedure FixHeight(var n : POSITION);
{Sets the correct height for node pointed to by n, used after insertion into subtree}
    var leftHt, rightHt : integer;
begin
    if n^.left = nil then
        leftHt := -1
    else
        leftHt := n^.left^.height;

    if n^.right = nil then
        rightHt := -1
    else
        rightHt := n^.right^.height;

    if leftHt > rightHt then
        n^.height := leftHt + 1
    else
        n^.height := rightHt + 1
end;
```

```
procedure Insert(a : ATOM ; var p : AVL);
{Inserts a in the subtree rooted at p }
begin
   if p = nil then begin        {Found where a belongs, build a new node}
      New(p);
      p^.height := 0;
      p^.data := a;
      p^.left := nil;
      p^.right := nil
   end else begin

      if a < p^.data then       { a belongs in left subtree of p, so put it there}
         Insert(a, p^.left)
      else if a > p^.data then{ a belongs in right subtree of p }
         Insert(a, p^.right);
      FixHeight(p);             {May have to adjust height if subtree grew}

      if Difference(p) > 1 then    {Insertion caused left subtree to be too high}
         BalanceLeft(p)
      else if Difference(p) < -1 then {Right subtree is too high}
         BalanceRight(p)
   end
end;
```

Using *Insert* as a template, it should not be difficult to define *DeleteMin* and *Delete* for AVL trees. We leave these definitions as exercises, and simply observe that all that is necessary is to balance the tree, if necessary, after each recursive call has returned.

7.2 B-TREES

By now you should be completely comfortable with the principle that the timing of the search tree operations is driven by the height of the tree. As long as we can keep our tree broad and shallow, we can be sure that all our tree operations will be fast, which is to say logarithmic. With AVL trees, we kept the tree shallow by forcing the heights of the subtrees of any node to be nearly equal, using rotations to restore balance each time we inserted or deleted an element. The best case, the one in which the tree had the maximum number of elements for a given height, is clearly obtained with a complete binary tree, and we saw in Chapter 6 that the height of a complete binary tree with n nodes is always less than $\log_2 n$. It would seem that we can't do any better than that, but in this section we will show a tree data structure that does indeed have less depth than $\log_2 n$, for n nodes, and we will explore the reasons that this data structure has become the standard in many applications.

k-ary Trees, Again

Up to now, we have concentrated almost entirely on *binary* trees, on the grounds that (1) they are easy to implement; (2) there are many good applications using binary trees; and (3) any tree can be mapped to a binary tree, anyway, with leftmost children becoming left children and right siblings becoming right children. The problem with this mapping is that we usually wind up with a binary tree that is higher than the original. Since we are interested in keeping the height of the tree as small as possible, it might be worth exploring these trees in more depth (pun intended—by now you're probably ready for some levity, however slight).

Recall that a k-ary tree (also called a **multiway** tree of order k) is just a tree in which every node may have as many as k children, for some integer k. In Figure 7.8, we show a 4-ary search tree. Notice that each node has at most four children, and each node has one less data element in it than it has children. Notice also that this tree generalizes the binary search tree property, in that the pointers between data elements in each node point to subtrees, each of which has all its data values strictly between the values that bracket the pointer. For instance, suppose we are searching for the element 71 in the tree. We begin at the root, and find (perhaps by a sequential search) that 71 lies between the elements 34 and 80. We then take the pointer to the subtree whose values lie between 34 and 80, and repeat the process. We find that 71 is larger than the last element, 68, in that node, so we follow the pointer to the subtree whose values are all larger than 68 (and necessarily less than 80). We repeat the search at the leaf node, and find 71 among the values in that leaf node, so the search was successful. If we had sought 70, we would attempt to take the leftmost pointer in the 71 node, find that it was **nil**, and report failure, since there is no subtree that could possibly contain 70.

In the tree of Figure 7.8, notice that all the leaves are at the same level. This is certainly a stronger condition than we had for AVL trees, and is even stronger than we saw for the optimal trees used to implement priority queues. This will be one of the properties of the data structure we will introduce in this section; and it, along with a condition we will require on the sizes of the nodes, will enable us to get a good estimate on the height of such trees if we know the number of nodes in the tree. For now, we will just note that because of the higher **fanout**—that is, the number of pointers *out*

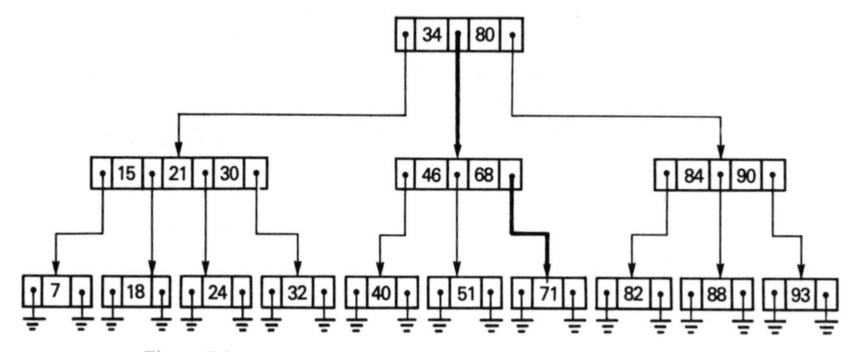

Figure 7.8 A 4-ary search tree, showing the search path for 71.

of the nodes—we can pack much more information in a multiway tree than we could in a binary tree of the same height. For instance, the tree of Figure 7.8 contains 19 data elements in a tree of height 2, whereas it would require a binary tree of twice that height to store the same information.

B-Trees, Explained

We define a **B-tree of order *d*** to have as its structure a $(2d+1)$-ary tree with the following properties:

1. The data elements (or at least the key fields) in each node are assumed to be linearly ordered. If the data elements are records consisting of several fields, then one field of the record is a *key field*, with values taken from a linearly ordered set.
2. Each internal node has one more child than it does data elements (and leaves, of course, have no children).
3. The root contains between 1 and $2d$ data elements.
4. Each node except for the root contains between d and $2d$ data elements.
5. All leaves are at the same depth in the tree.
6. The tree has the **extended search tree property** : If the keys in a node N are arranged in their linear order, $k_1, k_2, \ldots k_m$, then there is an associated linear order among the subtrees, $S_0, S_1, \ldots, S_m$, of N such that (a) every key in S_0 is less than k_1, (b) every key in S_m is greater than k_m, and (c) for $1 \le i < m$, every key in S_i lies strictly between k_i and k_{i+1}.

Note that the binary search tree property is just condition 6 with $m = 1$, with S_0 representing the left subtree, and S_1 the right subtree. Condition 4 could be restated to say, "Each node except for the root is at least half full." B-trees were introduced by R. Bayer and E. M. McCreight in 1972, and folklore has it that they have never explained the choice of the name for this particular data structure, so you are free to speculate on what the "B" stands for.

B-trees were designed to support the operations *Create, Insert, Delete*, and *Find* a data element, given its key; *Update* an element without changing its key; and *FindNext*, which, when given a key value k, returns the least key, k_i, in the tree for which $k < k_i$. The operation *Insert* is particularly ingenious, and differs from the insertion algorithms for the tree structures we've seen so far in that if the tree ever needs to change its height, it does so by growing up from the root, rather than down from a leaf.

To illustrate the action of *Insert*, consider a B-tree of order 2. Recall that in such a tree, the root may have from 1 to 4 elements, while all the rest of the nodes must have either 2, 3, or 4 elements. In Figure 7.9(a) we see the root after having inserted the elements 17, 45, 13, and 26. As each new element arrives (and here we are treating each element as synonymous with its key, for simplicity's sake), it is placed in order in the root. When the element 30 arrives, it cannot be placed in the root node—there's no more room. What we do in this case is the heart of the insertion algorithm; we split the root into equal parts, one containing all the elements below the median, 26, and the

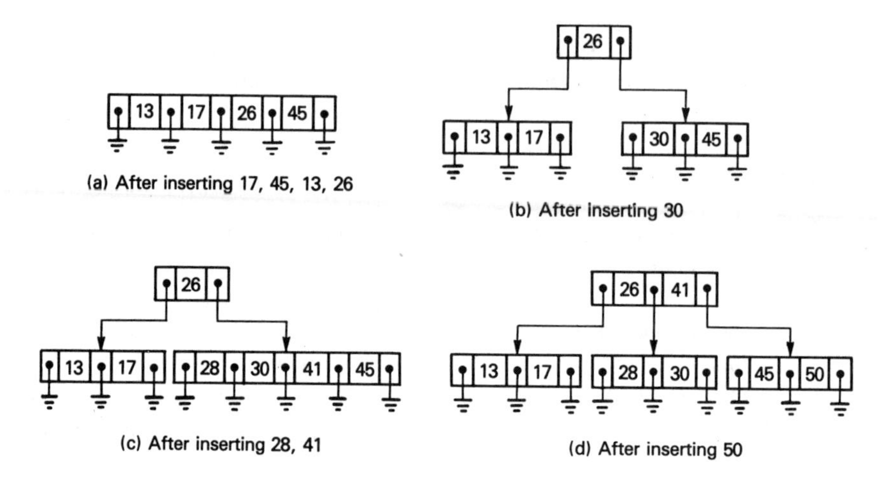

Figure 7.9 Inserting into a B-tree.

other containing all the elements above the median. The median value itself gets promoted to a new root node, which has the split nodes as children, as in Figure 7.9(b). If we continue by inserting 28 and 41, we see that they are both greater than 26, so, by the search tree property, they belong in the right subtree of the root node, as they are in Figure 7.9(c). Now, if we insert 50, we see that it should go in the rightmost node. Of course, there's no room for it, so we again split the node into two and promote the median value, 41, to the parent node. If the parent node had been full, we would have had to split it and promote its median to a new root node. That's all there is to insertion: We try to place each element in its proper leaf, and, if that would cause overflow, we split the node, promote the median value, and try to insert the promoted value into the parent node, splitting when necessary, tracking up the tree until we arrive at a node that does not overflow.

If it sounds pretty simple, that's because it is, at least for people. Things get a bit more complicated when we try to translate the insertion process into algorithmic form, largely because we humans can pretty much automatically take care of such details as inserting an element into a node, splitting a node, and deciding where an element belongs in the tree—operations that require a moderate amount of fussy detail to program. We will provide a detailed account of the insertion algorithm from the top down; then, having done that, we'll provide a sketch of the details of deletion and leave the programming to you.

The type declarations are immediate. Each node in the B-tree will consist of an array of data elements, a larger array of pointers to children, and a field for the present size of the array. To get things started, we also define *Create* here.

```
const
   MAX = {2*d, for a B-tree of order d}
type
   KeyType = integer; {or any linearly ordered type}
   ATOM = record
               key : KeyType;
               {other data fields here}
          end;
   IndexRange = 0 . . MAX; {possible array indices}
   POSITION = ^Node;
   Node = record
               size : IndexRange;
               data : array [1 . . MAX] of ATOM;
               child : array [IndexRange] of POSITION
          end;
   B_TREE = POSITION;
procedure Create(var B : B_TREE);
   var i : IndexRange;
begin
   New(B);
   B^.size := 0;
   for i := 0 to MAX do
      B^.child := nil
end;
```

The insertion routine itself is little more than a shell. Most of the work is done by a recursive procedure, *RecursiveInsert*, which inserts an atom *a* into the tree rooted at *root*. If the insertion caused the root to be split, *root* then points to the left split node, *rp* points to the right split (and is **nil** if no splitting occurred at the root), and *promoted* is the atom that must be promoted to the new root.

```
procedure Insert(a : ATOM ; var root : B_TREE);
   var
      temp, rp : POSITION;
      promoted : ATOM;
begin
   RecursiveInsert(a, root, rp, promoted);

   if rp <> nil then begin      {Root was split, build new root}
      temp := root;
      New(root);
      root^.size := 1;
      root^.data[1] := promoted;
      root^.child[0] := temp;
      root^.child[1] := rp
   end
end;
```

RecursiveInsert inserts atom *a* into the subtree rooted at *p*. First it scans the node at *p* for the location at which *a* would belong. The procedure *ScanNode* returns the index in the data array of *p* where *a*'s key is located (in which case there is nothing to do, since we don't allow duplicate keys in the tree), or the location after which *a* would belong. That location is also the index of the pointer to the subtree where *a* belongs, and, if that subtree is empty, the recursion stops there and inserts *a* into the leaf at *p*. If, on the other hand, the subtree where *a* belongs is not empty, then the procedure calls *RecursiveInsert* again on the subtree. In either case, the insertion could have caused a split and a promotion. If the procedure *AddData* has caused a split of the node at *p*, the promoted atom and a pointer to the right split node are returned to *RecursiveInsert*, to be used as the routine backs out of the recursion.

```
procedure RecursiveInsert(a : ATOM ; var p, rp : POSITION ; var promoted : ATOM);
  var
    index : IndexRange;          {where a belongs}
    found : boolean;             {true if a is already in node at p }
begin
  ScanNode(a.key, p, index, found);

  if not found then              {don't insert duplicate keys}

    if p^.child[index] = nil then begin    {we're at a leaf, put a in}
      rp := nil;
      AddData(a, index, p, rp, promoted)   {this may cause promotion and split}

    end else begin               {call routine recursively on subtree for a }
      RecursiveInsert(a, p^.child[index], rp, promoted);
      if rp <> nil then begin     {insertion caused split, insert promoted element}
        ScanNode(promoted.key, p, index, found); {find where promoted elt goes}
        AddData(promoted, index, p, rp, promoted) {and put it there}
      end
    end
end;
```

The last three routines are utility routines, used by *AddData* and *RecursiveInsert*. They need little comment, except that *ScanNode*, which looks through the node at *p* for the location at which *a*'s key is found, or after which *a* belongs, uses a sequential search through the data array. If, as often happens, the order of the B-tree was quite large, it might save time to implement a binary search, such as we gave in Chapter 3, instead.

```
procedure ScanNode(k : KeyType ; p : POSITION ;
          var index : IndexRange ; var found : boolean);
{ Searches for key k in node at p. If k is in the node, sets found to true and sets      }
{ index to location in data array where k is. If k is not in the node, sets found to     }
{ false and sets index to location after which k would be placed. For                    }
{ unsuccsessful search, index is also the location in the child array of the             }
{ subtree where k belongs.                                                               }
   var done : boolean;
begin
   index := 0;
   done := false;
   found := false;

   while not done do
      if index := p^.size then            {ran out of data to inspect}
         done := true
      else if k < p^.data[index + 1].key then       {found the location for ok }
         done := true
      else
         index := index + 1;              {keep looking}

   if index > 0 then
      if k = p^.data[index].key then           {see if k is at location index }
         found := true
end;

procedure Copy(p : POSITION ; pLo, pHi : integer;
                      var q : POSITION ; qLo, qHi : integer);
{ An array copying utility used by AddData. Copies the data and child arrays in the      }
{ node at pa, from indices pLo to pHi, into the arrays in the node at q, from indices    }
{ qLo to qHi. Requires that ranges are the same size, and that qLo ≤ qHi, else           }
{does nothing. This routine works correctly even if p = q, in which case the effect is   }
{to shift the segment by qLo – pLo.                                                      }
   var i : IndexRange;
begin
   if (pHi – pLo = qHi – qLo) and (qLo <= qHi) then

      if (p <> q) or ((p = q) and (qLo < pLo)) then         {different nodes or shift left}
         for i := qLo toa qHi do begin
            q^.data[i] := p^.data[i - qLo + pLo];
            q^.child[i] := p^.child[i - qLo + pLo]
         end

      else                                      {same nodes, shift right}
         for i := qHi downto qLo do begin
            q^.data[i] := p^.data[i - qHi + pHi];
            q^.child[i] := p^.child[i - qHi + pHi]
         end
end;
```

```
procedure AddData(a : ATOM ; index : IndexRange ;
                        var p, rp : POSITION ; var promoted : boolean);
{Inserts atom a and pointer rp into data and child arrays of node at p. If node at p       }
{is not full, performs simple insertion and returns nil pointer for rp, indicating no split }
{was necessary. If node at p is already full, the node is split into left and right halves, }
{pointed to by p and rp, respectively, and the median is returned via promoted.             }
  var
    half : IndexRange;           {MAX / 2 throughout}
    save : POSITION;             {stores incoming value of rp}
begin
  if p^.size < MAX then begin       {node at p is not yet full, just insert}
    if index < p^.size then
      Copy(p, index + 1, p^.size, p, index + 2, p^.size + 1); {shift to make room for a}
    p^.size := p^.size + 1;
    p^.data[index + 1] := a;
    p^.child[index + 1] := rp
  end else begin                 {no room to insert, must split node at p}

    half := MAX div 2;
    save := rp;
    New(rp);                     {set up split, build new right node}
    rp^.size := half;
    p^.size := half;

    if index <= half then begin    {a is either median or belongs in
                                    left split node}
      Copy(p, half + 1, MAX, rp, 1, half);   {put half of arrays in right node}
      if index = half then begin      {a is median element, so promote it}
        promoted := a;
        rp^.child[0] := save
      end else begin  {a isn't median; promote true median, insert a}

        promoted := p^.data[half];
        rp^.child[0] := p^.child[half];
        Copy(p, index + 1, half - 1, p, index + 2, half);       {shift right to make
                                                        room for a}
        p^.data[index + 1] := a;
        p^.child[index + 1] := save
      end

    else begin           {a belongs in right split node}
      rp^.child[0] := p^.child[half + 1];
      promoted := p^.data[half + 1];
      Copy(p, half + 2, index, rp, 1, index – half – 1); {copy up to where a will be}
      rp^.data[index – half] := a;
      rp^.child[index – half] := save;
      Copy(p, index + 1, MAX, rp, index – half + 1, half) {copy everything after a}
    end
  end
end;
```

Deletion is not much more difficult than insertion. As with insertion, we begin at a leaf and work our way up the tree, restoring the B-tree properties as we go. If the element to be deleted is not located in a leaf, we start as we did with deletion in a binary search tree by replacing the deleted element with the leftmost element in the right subtree of the deleted element. That leftmost element must be a leaf (why?), so we begin the deletion proper at that leaf. In pseudocode, the algorithm looks like the following:

```
procedure Delete(k : KeyType ; var root : B_TREE);
{Deletes the atom with key k from the B-tree of order d rooted at root.}
begin
   Find the element with key k to be deleted, a_i, in location i in the node at p ;
   if p is not a leaf then begin
      Replace a_i with the leftmost element, a, in the right subtree, S_i of p ;
      p := the node where a was located
   end;

   repeat
{a}   if p^.size > d then begin
         Remove a from p ;
         p^.size := p^.size - 1;
         done := true

{b}   end else if p has an immediate left or right sibling, q, of size > d then begin
         Remove an element from q ;
         Place an element from p's parent in p ;
         Replace the parent element with the element borrowed from q ;
         done := true

{c}   end else begin
         Merge p with one of its immediate siblings, and include a parent element;
         if p's parent would be too small after the borrowing then begin
            a := the element removed from p's parent;
            p := p's parent
         end else
            done := true
      end
   until done
end;
```

In Figure 7.10 we illustrate the three possible cases in the deletion algorithm, with the element to be deleted indicated by a dashed cell. In case (a) there are more than d elements in the node, so we may simply eliminate the element to be deleted. In case (b) the node where the deleted element was has too few elements to allow a simple deletion, but an immediate sibling node has an element to spare. In this case we borrow

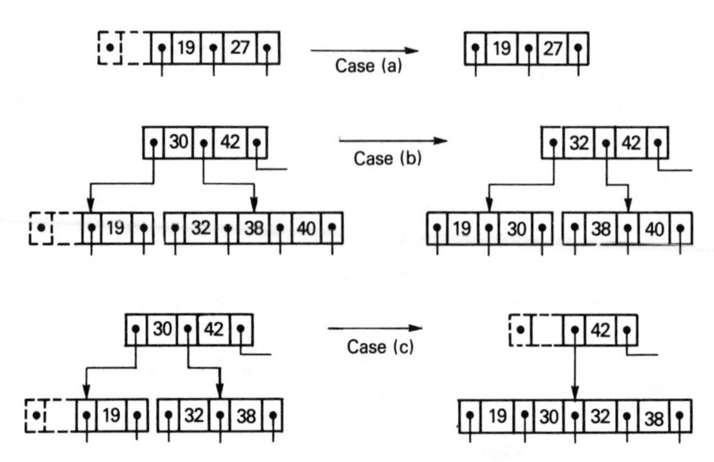

Figure 7.10 Deleting from a node in an order 2 B-tree.

from the parent (as so often happens in the real world) and let the sibling repay the debt (which happens somewhat less frequently). In cases (a) and (b) the size of the parent node does not change, so there is no need to travel further up the tree. In case (c), however, the node containing the deleted element and the sibling nodes are as small as they can be. What we do in this case is to merge the node with the deleted element and one of its siblings together, for a total of $2d - 1$ elements, and include the parent element between the two siblings, to form a new node of size d. This reduces the size of the parent node by one, so we may need to repeat the restoration process at the parent, if the reduction caused the parent to underflow below the minimum size d.

Don't let the mass of detail intimidate you. You might be tempted at first glance to say that B-trees stand for "beastly trees" or "bugaboo trees," but just reread the descriptive example of *Insert* and bear in mind the fact that most of the routines are doing pretty simple things, however complicated they look. That's not to say that the implementation is trivial, by any means, which might prompt the alert reader to say, "Yeah, the idea is simple enough, but before I'd want to use B-trees, I'd need some convincing that they are enough of an improvement over, say, binary search trees to be worth the effort."

Let's begin our investigation of the efficiency of B-trees by looking at the maximum value that the height, h, of a B-tree of order d with n nodes could be. As we did with balanced trees, we'll look at the problem in reverse: What is the smallest possible number of nodes that there could be in an order d B-tree of height h ? The root could have as few as one element, and in that case would have two children. Every nonroot node must have at least d elements, and either $d + 1$ children, if it is an internal node, or no children, if it is a leaf. We then have the minimal number of nodes per level, given by Table 7.1.

TABLE 7.1 MINIMAL NUMBER OF NODES IN AN ORDER d B-TREE

Depth	Nodes	Children per node	Cumulative nodes
0	1	2	1
1	2	$d + 1$	$1 + 2$
2	$2(d + 1)$	$d + 1$	$1 + 2 + 2(d + 1)$
3	$2(d + 1)^2$	$d + 1$	$1 + 2 + 2(d + 1) + 2(d + 1)^2$
.	.	.	.
.	.	.	.
.	.	.	.
h	$2(d + 1)^{h-1}$	0	$1+2(1+(d+1)+ \ldots +(d+1)^{h-1})$

Looking at the column for cumulative nodes in Table 7.1, we see that the number of nodes, n, in an order d B-tree must satisfy $n \geq 1 + 2(1 + (d + 1) + \ldots + (d + 1)^{h-1})$, where h is the height of the tree. The term on the right is just a geometric series, that is, a sum of the form $1 + r + \ldots + r^n$, and we know that the sum of such a series is equal to $(r^{n+1} - 1)/(r - 1)$, so we have

$$n \geq 1 + 2\left(\frac{(d+1)^h - 1}{d}\right) = 1 + \frac{2}{d}(d+1)^h - \frac{2}{d} \geq \frac{2}{d}(d+1)^h$$

for $d \geq 2$; and, if we take the logarithm to the base $d + 1$ of both sides, we see that we have $\log_{d+1} n \geq \log_{d+1}(2 / d) + h$, so that $h \leq \log_{d+1} n - \log_{d+1}(2/d) \leq (\log_{d+1} n) + 1$, for $d \geq 2$. Now except for the root, each node in our B-tree must contain at least d data elements, so to store N data elements should certainly require much more than $2N/d$ nodes (in fact, it's not hard to show that it requires no more than $1 + (N - 1)/d$ nodes). The point of all this is that, with even moderately small values for d, we can fit a lot of information into a very shallow B-tree. In Table 7.2, we show the heights of B-trees of various orders necessary to store data sets of size N, using $h \leq 1 + \log_{d+1}(1 + (N - 1)/d)$.

TABLE 7.2 HEIGHTS OF B-TREES NEEDED TO STORE LARGE DATA SETS

	Number of Elements					
Order	10^4	10^5	10^6	10^7	10^8	10^9
16	4	5	5	6	7	8
32	3	4	4	5	6	6
64	3	3	4	4	5	5

These are (or ought to be) very impressive numbers. Just as an example, to store a billion data elements in a B-tree of order 16 requires a tree of height at most 8, whereas a binary search tree containing that many elements would have height at least 29, and perhaps as large as 999,999,999.

This is not the whole story, however. We may not have to visit very many nodes to insert an element, for example, but that gain might be offset by the amount of work required to split the nodes in order to restore the necessary B-tree properties. We don't have to worry about the amount of work required by splitting, though, for several reasons. First, to insert a node, we never have to split more nodes than the height of the tree plus one, since we split by tracking up the tree from a leaf to the root. Second, the amount of work required by each split is obviously proportional to no more than the size of the node being split, and that size is usually negligible when compared with the number of data elements in the entire tree. Finally, as long as the order of the tree is fairly large, there is usually a lot of available space in each node, so we don't have to split nodes very often. In the exercises you are asked to provide some evidence in support of the fact that in the long run n insertions will only require about $n/(d - 1)$ splits of nodes, or, put in different terms, you need to split a node only about every $1/(d - 1)$ of the time.

Application: External Storage

The impetus for the development of B-trees was the problem of rapid file access on an external storage medium, such as a magnetic disk. Such devices have the advantages that they provide for storage of a great deal of information at a cost per byte that is much lower than the cost of internal RAM in a computer. Simply speaking, if you need to store millions of bytes of data, it is considerably cheaper to do so on a disk than it is to pay for megabytes of RAM, so generally a computer will have a disk drive that can store much more information than can be fit into internal memory. This by itself would not be a problem except for one inescapable fact: Information retrieval is much faster if you only have to push electrons around in memory than it is if you have to worry about moving comparatively large physical objects like magnetic disks and read/write heads. Typically, you can count on disk access taking 10 to 100 times longer than RAM access, and therein lies the problem.

Generally, one cannot just download a large file from disk to RAM at the start of the day and then forget about the disk until close of business—there just isn't enough room in memory to store the entire file, and the people in the comptroller's office are unwilling to foot the bill for a supercomputer with the memory needed to hold the entire file. Given the fact that disk access crawls along, compared to memory access, *we clearly want to reduce the number of times we need to go to the disk to a minimum.*

In order to do this, we not only need to arrange the data in a disk in some efficient fashion, but we also need to be able to find out rapidly where the information is. In other words, we need an *index* of some kind to tell us where the record associated with a particular key is located on the disk. For example, we might include on each disk a binary tree containing the keys of the records in the file and the disk addresses where the associated records can be found. If we implement this in a naive fashion, however, we may have to access the disk once for each node in the directory tree during our search, plus once more to retrieve the record itself. One thing that works in our favor is that a request to read or write on a disk is handled in units of many bytes at once, so if you ask for a byte from the disk, what you get is a **block** or **page** of information, typically in the range of 256 to 2,048 bytes, depending on the disk and the operating system that handles the disk access. With this in mind, we would be better off arranging our directory tree so that several nodes were located on a single page on the disk. In Figure 7.11, we show such an arrangement, in which three nodes are stored on a single page.

If we store three nodes of a binary tree on a page, we have in effect produced a four-way tree, if we think of each page as a node. Now we have at least two options: We could store the index separately, and associate with each key a disk address where the rest of the record may be found, or we could merge the records with the directory by storing the records in the same nodes as their keys, in much the same way as we stored the free list in the heap when we discussed memory management. Our choice between these options would be guided by (1) the size of the keys, (2) the size of the disk addresses, (3) the size of the records, and (4) the page size. The examples that follow indicate some of the decisions involved in choosing the best size for a B-tree.

Example 7.1.

Suppose we have a 128-megabyte hard disk (that's 2^{27} bytes), divided into pages of 2,048 (= 2^{11}) bytes each. That means that there will be 2^{16} pages, so that 2 bytes of 8 bits will suffice to identify each page. Just to be on the safe side, though, we'll assume that disk addresses will be 4 bytes long.

Suppose the entire disk is devoted to one file of N records, each of which requires 512 bytes, so that four records will fit on a page. Suppose also that the key for each record is 4 bytes long. That's enough for a nine-digit social security number, for instance. Thus, the key and the disk address for a record together will take 8 bytes, so we can fit 256 of them on a page.

If we keep the index of keys and addresses separate from the records, we see that if we have N records, the total number of pages required for the index will be $\lceil N / 256 \rceil$, where the enclosing brackets mean "take the smallest integer that is greater than or equal to what's inside," to account for the fact that N might not be a multiple of 256. At 4 records per page, we will require $\lceil N / 4 \rceil$ pages for the records, and the sum of these two

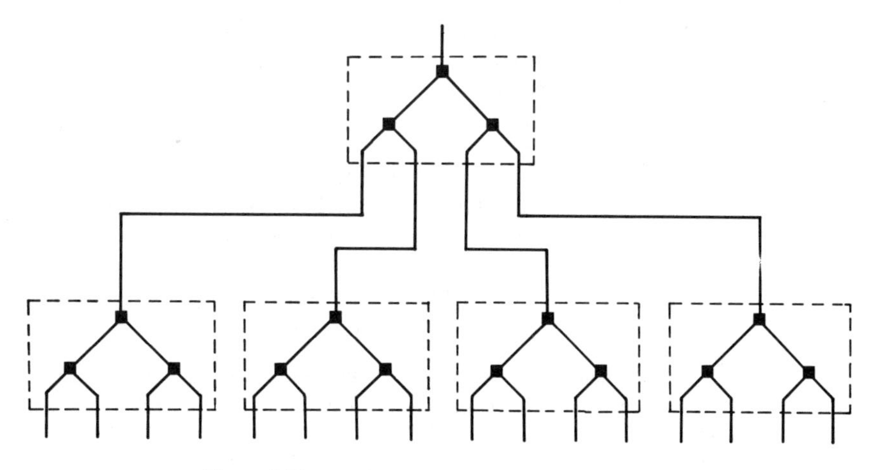

Figure 7.11 A binary tree with three nodes per page.

expressions must be no more than the total number of pages, 65,536. It doesn't take much to find that we must have $N \leq 258{,}108$ records in our file, and we will assume that we have exactly that number.

We'll now build a B-tree to contain the index. We can fit up to 256 index entries per node (at one page for each node), so we decide to use an order 128 B-tree. The formula for the maximum height, h, of the tree tells us that $h \leq 1 + \log_{129}(1 + 258{,}107/128) = 2.56$, so our tree will have height no more than 3. Therefore, to access any record on the disk will require at most 4 disk accesses (remember, there is always one more node in a path than the length of a path) to find the index, plus one more to get the record itself, for a total of at most 5 disk accesses. Of course, we may be fortunate enough to be able to store the entire index in RAM, so that once a node was in memory, we would not need further disk accesses to get information from that node.

Suppose the computer we were using had 4 megabytes of RAM available to store the B-tree. Each node of our order 128 B-tree must have room for 256 8-byte indices, and 257 4-byte pointers, for a total of $256 \times 8 + 257 \times 4 = 3{,}078$ bytes per node. If we had n nodes, then, they would take up $3{,}078n$ bytes of memory, and since we have 4,194,304 bytes of memory available (4 megabytes $= 2^{22} = 4{,}194{,}304$ bytes), we must have $3{,}078n \leq 4{,}194{,}304$, so $n \leq 1{,}362$ nodes will fit in RAM.

Oops! We may be in trouble, since the root may contain only one index element, and the rest of the nodes might contain as few as 128 indices, for a total of $1 + 128 \times 1{,}361 = 174{,}209$ indices, which is less than the total number of records. So there's a chance that we can't fit the entire index B-tree in memory, meaning we'll likely have to swap nodes in and out of memory, requiring disk accesses throughout the life of the program. That being the case, it might be worth our while to see to it that the higher level nodes, near the root, stay in memory, since, for example, it would be a disaster to have to swap the root in and out, because it is used every time we refer to the tree.

Example 7.2.

To get some idea of the time required by disk access, let's suppose further that to access a page on the disk requires 40 milliseconds (40 ms = 0.040 seconds) of overhead to locate the page, move the read/write head to the page, and wait for the disk to spin into the right position to get the page, and $0.001b$ ms to transfer a page of b bytes. Let us also suppose that we have some control over the page size (that's not always the case, since page size is under the control of the operating system, and we may not want to mess with that). We will decide to put one node of the B-tree on each page, so for order d B-trees, we will have $2d$ indices of 8 bytes per page, for a total of $16d$ bytes per page. Recall that we will have at most $2 + \log_{d+1}((N - 1)/d) + 1$ disk accesses to retrieve a record (we ignored the "+1" inside the log expression, since it's negligible here), and each disk access requires $40 + 0.001(16d)$ ms, so the maximum amount of time we'll require to get a record will be

$$(40 + 0.001(16d))(3 + \log_{d+1}\frac{258107}{d})$$
$$= (40 + 0.016d)(3 + \log_{d+1} 258107 - \log_{d+1} d) \approx (40 + 0.016d)(2 + \log_{d+1} 258107)$$

Using the fact that $\log_b A = (\ln A)/\ln b$, where ln is the natural logarithm (which you can review in Appendix B), we have the worst-case access time for any record of approximately

$$(40 + 0.016d)(2 + \frac{\ln 258107}{\ln (d+1)} \text{ ms}$$

Now we try various values for d, and look at access times, summarized in Table 7.3.

TABLE 7.3 WORST-CASE ACCESS TIMES FOR ORDER d B-TREES, INDEX IN NODES

Order, d	Access time (ms)
8	307.8
16	257.6
32	225.4
64	204.5
128	191.9
256	187.2
512	192.6
1024	214.1

We see that there is little difference in the access times for B-trees of orders between 128 and 512. We chose orders that were powers of 2 because they made the page sizes evenly divide the amount of disk space, but we could have chosen any d we wished, like the one that leads to the minimum, $d = 261$. We'll decide to use $d = 256$, though, for a page size of $256 \times 16 = 4096$. Note that with $d = 128$, we're back to the figure of Example 7.1, with page size of 2048. This broad range of nearly identical minimum values is typical, and works to our advantage if we don't have much control over page size.

Example 7.3.

We might have decided to eliminate one disk access to get the record by storing the records in the B-tree. In that case, we suppose that we can fit the key, the address, and the rest of the record in 512 bytes. Now, a node of $2d$ data elements requires $1024d$ bytes, so the access time function is

$$(40 + 1.024d)(1 + (\ln 258107) / \ln(d+1)),$$

and we have worst-case access times, given in Table 7.4.

TABLE 7.4 WORST-CASE ACCESS TIMES FOR ORDER d B-TREES, DATA IN NODES

Order, d	Access time (ms)
4	385.5
8	321.5
16	304.4
32	332.1

In this case, the best access time is 304.4, when $d = 16$, for a page size of 16384 bytes. There's not much point in doing this, though, since the best access time here is 63 percent more than if we had stored just the index, as in Example 7.2. However, this is not always the case, and we will see in the exercises that for different disk characteristics, it may be advantageous to store the data in the B-tree, as well.

7.3 SUMMARY

The running time of most tree algorithms is controlled by the depth of the tree. The two data structures presented in this chapter represent attempts to control this depth, in such a way that the depth of a tree with n nodes is $O(\log n)$.

AVL trees are binary search trees with insertion and deletion defined so that the property of being balanced is preserved. The original reference to AVL trees is:

Adel'son-Velskii, G. M., and Landis, Y. M. "An Algorithm for the Organization of Information," *Dokl. Akad. Nauk SSR 146* (1962), 263–266. English translation in *Soviet Math. (Dokl.) 3* (1962), 1259–1263.

B-trees are another generalization of binary search trees. They are multiway trees with insertion and deletion defined so that the number of children of each node always lies within fixed upper and lower limits. B-trees are widely used to provide fast access to externally stored files. The original reference is:

Bayer, R., and McCreight, E. M. "Organization and Maintenance of Large Ordered Indices," *Acta Informatica 1*, 3 (1972), 173–189.

An excellent survey of the topic may be found in

Comer, D. "The Ubiquitous B-Tree," *Computing Surveys 11*, 2 (1979), 121–137.

7.4 EXERCISES

1. Tell which of the trees in Figure 7.12 are balanced, and, if any of them fail to be balanced, indicate the deepest node at which an imbalance occurs.
2. We can ensure that a tree will be shallow in a number of ways other than those discussed in this chapter. One such balancing condition is to require that the tree be **weight balanced**, which is to say that at each node, n, of the tree, the number of nodes in the left subtree of n and the number of nodes in the right subtree of n differ by no more than 2. (By the way, if you look at the literature, you are likely to find a number of different meanings for the term *weight balanced*.)
   (a) Can you find a binary tree that is balanced but not weight balanced?
   (b) Can you find a binary tree that is weight balanced but not balanced?
   (c) If the answer to one of these questions was "yes" and the other "no," can you then

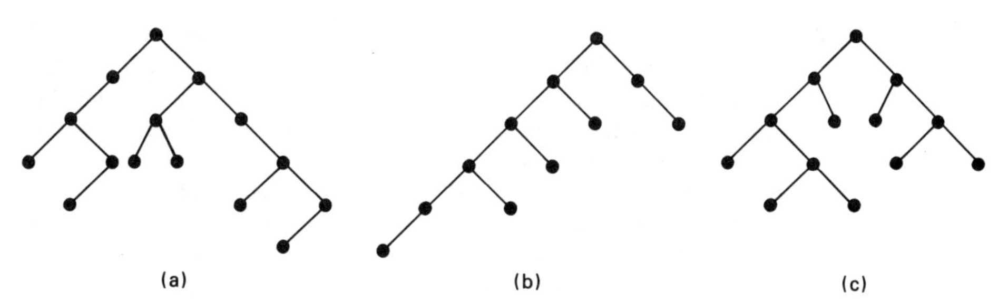

Figure 7.12 Find the unbalanced trees.

show that one of the two conditions necessarily implies the other?

(d) Describe a *structure-preserving* insertion algorithm for weight-balanced binary search trees. Can you use the rotations discussed in AVL trees to restore weight balance?

3. (a) What is the result of inserting 1, 2, 3, . . . , 8 into an initially empty AVL tree?

(b) In general, what happens as you insert 1, 2, 3, . . . into an AVL tree? You might want to say, for instance, what values the root has as the insertions proceed.

4. We can use binary trees, in one flavor or another, to implement the LIST ADT. Even better, we could use binary search trees to implement SORTED_LIST. Clearly, we would then have fast retrieval, given the key of an element in the list, but we can also provide fast retrieval by position in the list. In other words, we might wish to implement the function **FindNth**(n : integer ; L: SORTED_LIST) : POSITION, which would return the position of the element in the nth place in the sorted list L, and return the NULL pseudoposition if n is greater than the length of L.

(a) Show how this could be accomplished by representing sorted lists as binary search trees. *Hint*: The usual way to do this is to include a **rank** field in each node n, which contains the number of nodes in the left subtree of n.

(b) Discuss the changes, if any, that would be required in *Insert* for this implementation.

(c) Discuss the changes, if any, that would be required if, in the interest of speed, we had decided to implement SORTED_LIST using AVL trees.

5. (a) Show the AVL tree that results if the integer keys 17, 8, 29, 20, 27, 13, 28 are inserted, in that order, into an initially empty AVL tree.

(b) Show the successive trees that result when the tree of part (a) then has the elements deleted in the order in which they were inserted, beginning with 17.

6. Repeat Exercise 5 for a B-tree of order 2.

7. In this exercise, we will investigate what happens when the keys 1, 2, 3, . . . , N are successively inserted into a B-tree of order d.

(a) For $d = 2$, for what key values is the root split, and what element is promoted to the new root when the root splits?

(b) For $d = 2$, what is the total number of splits that have occurred by the time key n has been inserted?

(c) For $d = 2$, what are the largest and smallest values of N for which the tree has height h?

(d)–(f) Repeat parts (a)–(c) for arbitrary order d B-trees.

8. It stands to reason that when the records of a file are not too large when compared with the size of the keys, it might be better to store the records as well as the keys in the B-tree.
   (a) Repeat Examples 7.2 and 7.3 of the text with records of size 50 and find optimal page sizes and worst case access times. You may assume that all other figures are the same, including the number of records.
   (b) Try different values for disk overhead, transfer speed, number of records, record size, and key size, and see if you can come up with a rule of thumb to determine whether it is better to store all information in the B-tree, rather than just the keys.
9. In Examples 7.1–7.3, we ignored the fact that most of the quantities, in particular the depth of the tree, were integers. Redo the examples with this in mind, and see if there is any substantial difference in the values you obtain for access times.
10. In a B-tree, there is a lot of wasted space taken up by the leaves, since they must have room for $2d + 1$ pointers, all of which are **nil**. Furthermore, a significant number of nodes in a B-tree are leaves.
    (a) In a B-tree of order d, what fraction of nodes are leaves? Your answer should be something like "between ________ and ________ of the nodes are leaves," where the blanks might be functions of n, the number of nodes in the tree.
    (b) In a B-tree of order d, where the data elements require 8 bytes each, and pointers require 4 bytes each, how much space is wasted by **nil** pointers?
    (c) Discuss how you might change the implementation of B-trees to eliminate this waste space.

Programming Problems

11. Implement AVL trees, and investigate the average number of single and double rotations required to construct an AVL tree by inserting n randomly chosen elements into an initially empty tree.
12. Implement and test *Delete* for AVL trees.
13. Redo Exercise 11 for B-trees, counting the number of splits, rather than rotations.
14. Modify the implementation of B-trees by including a pointer in each node to the parent of that node. Write *Insert* for this implementation, and comment on the advantages and disadvantages compared to the definition in the text.
15. Implement and test *Delete* for B-trees.
16. In a **B*-tree**, each node except for the root is at least 2/3 full. This is accomplished by avoiding splits whenever possible. *Insert* for B*-trees is almost like *Insert* for B-trees, borrowing from siblings when possible, except that when a node and both of its immediate siblings are full, the three full nodes are merged into two, with appropriate adjustment of the data in the parent. Implement *Insert* for B*-trees, and discuss the merits of this scheme, particularly with respect to the height of the tree and the number of splits required to build the tree.

8

Graphs and Digraphs

Don't be misled by the maps of the underground.
The lines may be straight even though the tracks
may curve all about. The important thing to realise
is how the stations are connected by the tracks.

J. Dash-Harris, London: *A Traveller's Programme*

The picture in Figure 8.1 is loosely based on the eastern half of ARPANET, a network (hence the NET part of the name) of computers developed by the Advanced Research Projects Agency (the ARPA part of the name) of the U. S. Department of Defense. This network consists of a number of different computers at major government and civilian research sites, connected by land lines and satellite links. If we imagine that we were the designers of the network in 1969, it is not hard to come up with a number of questions that might have been of interest to us at the time.

1. What is the average number of *hops* in the shortest path between nodes, where a hop is an intermediate site through which a message must be passed? For example, to pass a message from DARCOM to HARVARD through ABERDEEN and NYU requires two hops, and that is clearly the least number possible for those two sites.
2. Is there any node that, if it went down, would make communications between some two nodes impossible, at least for the network as drawn? Is there any line that would similarly disrupt communications if it went down?
3. What is the largest number of hops a message must take between two given nodes?

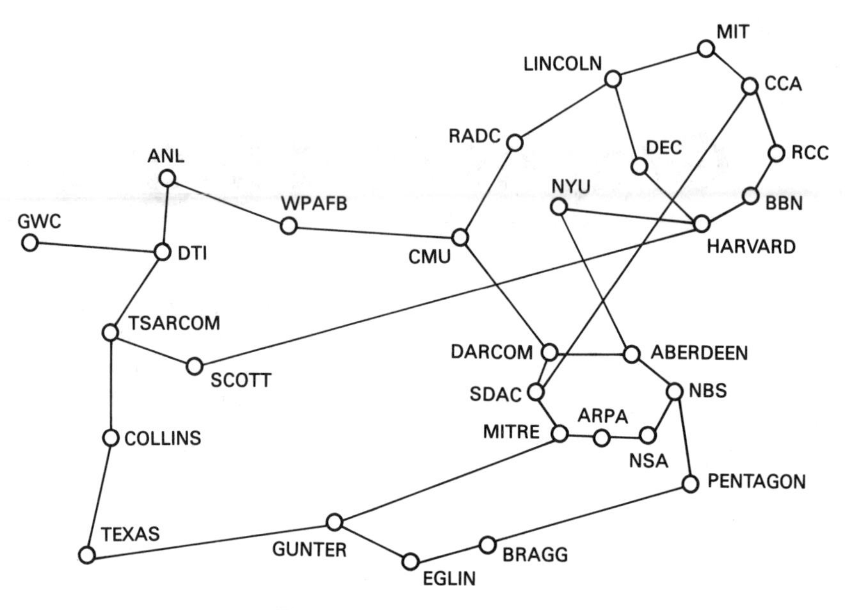

Figure 8.1 Part of ARPANET.

4. What is the smallest subset of lines that must be present to guarantee communication between every pair of nodes?
5. If each line has associated with it a cost for communication, what is the least-cost collection of lines that must be present to guarantee communication between every pair of nodes?
6. What is the least number of total hops required for every node to communicate its status to the Network Control Center at BBN?

In this chapter we will investigate the data structures and algorithms that will allow us to answer these and other questions. We will see that some of these questions can be answered easily; some will require algorithms of fairly high time complexity; some are known to be infeasible, even for the fastest computers; and some we suspect are infeasible, although they have not yet been proved so.

8.1 GRAPHS

We know that the structure of a tree is determined by a relation for which every position has at most one immediate predecessor (in fact, every position except the root has exactly one immediate predecessor, and the root has no predecessor at all). In this respect, a tree is exactly the same as a list; they differ in that a position in a tree may have more than one immediate successor, whereas every position in a list has a unique successor, if it has a successor at all. In this chapter, we will continue our program of relaxing restrictions on the structural relation in order to produce new structures. In particular, we will now remove the last restriction and allow a position to have any number of immediate predecessors, as well as any number of immediate successors.

If we think of the structural relation as providing logical links between positions, we now have a **network** structure consisting of positions linked by a relation in any way we wish, as shown in the examples of Figure 8.2.

Depending on the additional properties we place on the structural relation, these network structures may be classified into three groups. A **multigraph** has no restrictions at all on its structure: Positions may be linked to themselves [as with position 1 in Figure 8.2(a)], and there may be several links between two positions [as from position 2 to position 3 in Figure 8.2(a), which, by the way, is immediately outlawed if we use a single relation to provide links—do you see why?]. The relation that describes a **digraph** must be irreflexive, as in Figure 8.2(b), which is another way of saying that no position may be linked to itself. A **graph**, finally, is defined by a structural relation that is irreflexive and symmetric, so that whenever there is a link from position p to position q, there is also a link from q to p. In such a situation, there is no need to draw both links with their arrows, so we dispense with them and draw single lines instead. We will discuss graphs first and then consider digraphs.

A graph is usually described as an ordered pair $G = (V, E)$ of sets, where V can be any set (but we will insist that it be finite here), and E consists of (not necessarily all

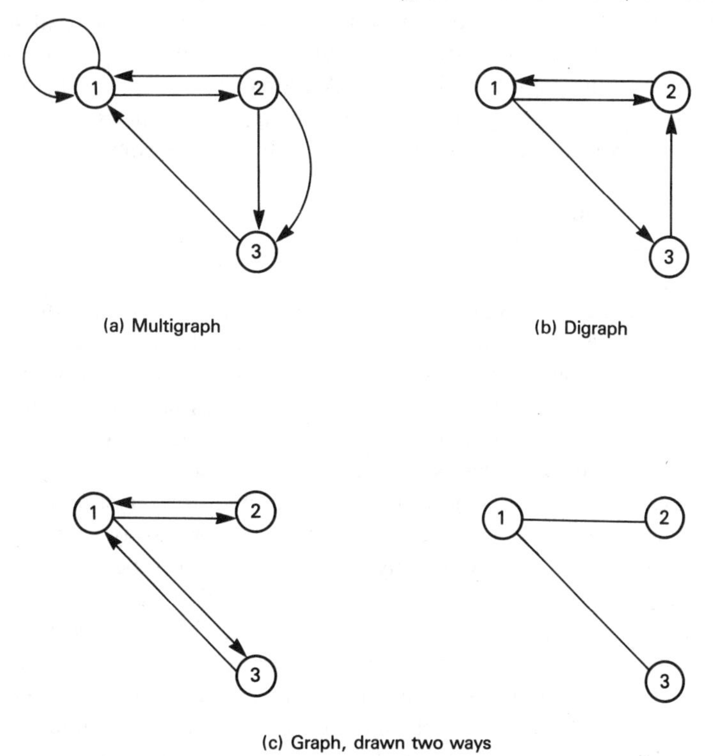

Figure 8.2 Some network structures.

the) two-element subsets of V. The set V is called the **vertices** of G, and E is known as the **edges** of G. (You will frequently see vertices referred to as **nodes**, especially in computer science literature.) For example, the graph of Figure 8.2(c) would be written as $G = (V, E) = (\{1, 2, 3\}, \{\{1, 2\}, \{1, 3\}\})$. This graph has three vertices—1, 2, 3—and two edges —$\{1, 2\}$, $\{1, 3\}$. In structural terms, this graph has three positions $\{1, 2, 3\}$ and (symmetric) structure relation R corresponding to the edges, so $1\ R\ 2$, $2\ R\ 1$, $1\ R\ 3$, $3\ R\ 1$ are the only relations possible for these positions.

We say that two vertices are **adjacent** if there is an edge connecting them, and two distinct edges are adjacent if they have a vertex in common. A **path** in a graph is a sequence of vertices, each of which is adjacent to its predecessor and successor, if any. Thus, in the graph in Figure 8.2, the sequence 2, 1, 3, 1, 2, 1 is a path, and 2, 1, 3 is called a **simple path**, since no vertex in the sequence is repeated. A **cycle** in a graph is a path for which the first and last vertices are identical, so that 1, 2, 1 is a cycle. A **simple cycle**, to no one's surprise, is a cycle with no repeated vertices except the first and last, so the graph of Figure 8.2(c) has no simple cycles. A graph is **connected** if any two vertices may be joined by a path. Finally (for now, at least), we say that a graph is **cyclic** if it contains a simple cycle, and **acyclic** if it does not.

Graph theory, that branch of mathematics which deals with the study of graphs, is about two centuries old. It is an excellent introduction to the spirit of real mathematics, since its problems are often simple to understand, but can be challenging and interesting to solve. Consider, for instance, the **four color problem**. It dates back to 1852, and in modern terminology goes like this: A **planar graph** is one that can be drawn on the plane without crossing any edges; a **coloring** of a graph is an assignment of colors to each vertex so that no adjacent vertices have the same color.

The four color problem. Is it true that every planar graph can be colored with four or fewer colors?

The graph of Figure 8.2 is a trivial example of this problem: It is a planar graph, since it is already drawn on the plane without edge crossings, and certainly it can be colored with four colors, since it has only three vertices and we could simply assign a different color to each vertex. (The problem does not apply to the ARPANET graph, since there is no relocation of nodes that will allow that graph to be drawn without some edge crossings; that is, it is not planar.) That sounds simple enough, but the problem resisted all attempts to prove it. People tried for years; no matter how complicated the planar graphs they chose, four or fewer colors always sufficed, but nobody could prove that it had to be so. Finally, in 1976, Kenneth Appel and Wolfgang Haken used a computer at the University of Illinois to check 1936 special cases, requiring about 10^{10} separate computations, for a total of something like *1200 hours* of computer time, and in doing so showed that the answer to the four color problem is "yes."

This book is not the place for an investigation into the four color problem, but there is a much simpler problem that captures the flavor of graph theory, and which we will need to solve for later use. It's obvious that a graph with n vertices could have as few as zero edges, but what is the *largest* number of edges such a graph could have? That's not too bad—the largest number of edges must be for a graph with n vertices in which every vertex is connected by an edge to every other. If you know some counting principles, you know that that's equivalent to the number of two-element subsets of a set of n objects, but even if you don't, the number is easy to compute. Label the vertices 1, 2, . . . , n and start listing edges. From vertex 1 we have edges to vertices 2, 3, . . . , n, for a total of $n - 1$. From vertex 2 we have edges to vertex 1 (which we've already counted), and to 3, . . . , n, for a total of $n - 2$. Similarly, vertex 3 provides us with $n - 3$ edges that we haven't yet counted, and if we continue this for all vertices we find that the number of edges is $(n - 1) + (n - 2) + . . . + 1$. This is a by-now familiar arithmetic series, and we know the sum is $n(n - 1)/2$, which must be the largest possible number of vertices in a graph with n vertices. Such a graph, by the way, in which every vertex is adjacent to every other, is called a **complete graph**.

We're now ready to define our first network ADT.

Definition. The **GRAPH** abstract data type consists of an underlying set ATOM, and a set POSITION, such that every graph consists of a triple, (P, R, v) where P is a finite subset of POSITION, v is a function from $P \rightarrow ATOM$, and R is a symmetric relation on P (and irreflexive, if we disallow loops). We will sometimes denote the set of positions (i.e., vertices) of a graph G by the term $V(G)$. Although it is not strictly necessary, we will define the set EDGE (or $E(G)$) to be the set of all two-element sets of vertices, $\{p, q\}$, for which $p \ R \ q$. In addition, GRAPH includes the following operations:

1. **Create**(**var** G : GRAPH) sets G equal to an empty graph, that is, one with no vertices.
2. **Adjacent**(p, q : POSITION ; G : GRAPH) : boolean returns *true* if and only if $p \ R \ q$, that is, if there is an edge from p to q in G. Of course, the precondition for this procedure is that p is a vertex of G.
3. **Update**(a : ATOM ; p : POSITION ; **var** G : GRAPH) changes the atom associated with position p, making $v(p) = a$. In other words, if there is some data "contained in" vertex $p \in V(G)$, then that data is changed to a.
4. **Retrieve**(p : POSITION ; G : GRAPH) : ATOM returns the value $v(p)$, in other words, the data "contained in" vertex $p \in V(G)$, if any.
5. **DeleteVertex**(p : POSITION ; **var** G : GRAPH) removes vertex p from G, along with any edges containing p. This requires the precondition that $p \in V(G)$.
6. **DeleteEdge**(e : EDGE ; **var** G : GRAPH) removes e from the set of edges of G. Of course, we must have $e \in E(G)$ for this procedure to be defined.
7. **InsertVertex**(**var** p : POSITION ; **var** G : GRAPH) adds p to the set of positions of G, without changing R. In other words, the vertex p is added to G with no edges connecting it to any other vertex in G. The precondition for this operation is that $p \notin V(G)$.

8. **InsertEdge**(e : EDGE ; **var** G : GRAPH) includes e in the edge set of G, thereby altering the structural relation R, as was the case with *DeleteEdge*. This operation requires the preconditions that if $e = \{p, q\}$, then $p, q \in V(G)$, and that e is not already in $E(G)$.

8.2 REPRESENTATIONS OF THE GRAPH ADT

There are a number of ways to store information about graphs in a computer. Some are more suitable than others for certain applications, a state of affairs that we have seen a number of times already. We will give three different implementations here, and explore two of them in detail.

Adjacency Matrices

One of the simplest implementations is to use an $n \times n$ array, *Adj*, of boolean values for a graph with n nodes. We suppose that the vertices are ordered $v_1, v_2, \ldots, v_n$ in some fashion and define $Adj[i, j]$ to be *true* if v_i is adjacent to v_j, and *false* otherwise. The array *Adj* is called the **adjacency matrix** of the graph. In Figure 8.3 we show a graph with its adjacency matrix.

As with most array implementations, this suffers from lack of extensibility, since we cannot let a graph grow beyond the maximum array size. This means that we must predeclare the array to be at least as large as the largest possible graph we expect to encounter. Additionally, we see that there is a fair amount of wasted space even if the number of vertices in the graph is exactly equal to the number of rows in the array. Observe that the main diagonal, $Adj[k, k]$, for $k = 1, \ldots, n$, is always *false*, since we never have a vertex adjacent to itself (irreflexivity, remember), and note also that the part of the array below the main diagonal is redundant, since it must always be the case that $Adj[i, j] = Adj[j, i]$, for $1 \le i, j \le n$, by symmetry. In other words, in an $n \times n$ adjacency matrix for a graph with n vertices, only $n(n - 1)/2$ of the entries are significant, meaning that we are wasting over half of the space of the array, even if it is exactly the right dimension for the graph. That may not be of great importance, of course, since each of the boolean array entries could be encoded in a single bit.

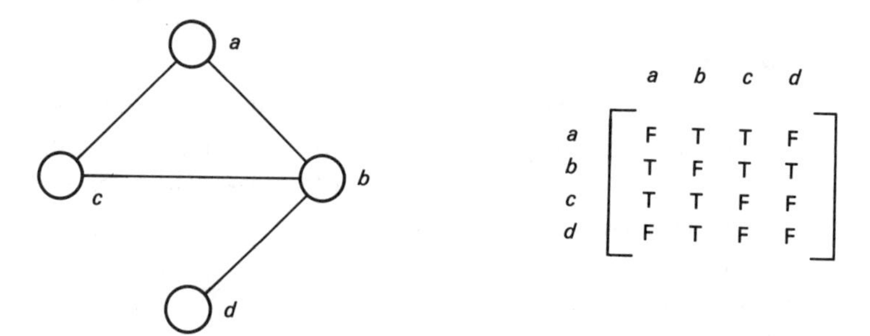

Figure 8.3 A graph and its adjacency matrix.

Another problem with adjacency matrices is that the time required to find all the vertices adjacent to a given vertex is $O(n)$, no matter how many adjacent vertices there are, since it requires that we search an entire row or column of the matrix. Nevertheless, we will see that there are some algorithms that are particularly suited for adjacency matrices, despite their shortcomings.

The implementation isn't difficult: We represent a graph by a record consisting of the number of vertices in the graph, along with the adjacency matrix. Positions (i.e., vertices) are then integers, representing indices in the matrix, and edges are pairs of positions.

```
const
   MAXVERTS = {some suitable integer};
type
   POSITION = 1 .. MAXVERTS;
   EDGE = record
                end1, end2 : POSITION
      ends;
   GRAPH = record
                numVerts : 0 .. MAXVERTS;
                adj : array [POSITION, POSITION] of boolean
             end;
```

Notice that we haven't provided any way of associating atoms with vertices. In this implementation there is no available information except for the shape of the graph itself. If we needed to "mark" vertices or store information in them, we would need an auxiliary data structure. (You will see in the next section, though, that we can use this implementation with very minor change to associate information with edges.) This is not the impediment it might first appear, since a number of graph-theoretic problems are concerned only with the structure of graphs, and not with any information associated with their vertices. What it does mean, however, is that we will not be able to use this data structure (at least not without modification) if we need the operations *Update* or *Retrieve*. This leaves us with only six operations, all but one of which are very simple to define.

```
procedure Create (var G : GRAPH);
begin
   G.numverts := 0
end;

function Adjacent(p, q : POSITION ; G : GRAPH) : boolean;
begin
   if (p > G.numVerts) or (q > G.numVerts) then begin
      writeln('Illegal position number in Adjacent');
      Adjacent := false
   end else
      Adjacent := G.adj[p, q]
end;
```

```
procedure DeleteEdge(e : EDGE ; var G : GRAPH);
begin
   if (e.end1 > G.numVerts) or (e.end2 > G.numVerts) then
      writeln('Illegal edge description in DeleteEdge')
   else begin
      G.adj[e.end1, e.end2] := false;
      G.adj[e.end2, e.end1] := false
   end
end;

procedure InsertVertex(var p : POSITION ; var G : GRAPH);
   var i : POSITION;
begin
   G.numVerts := G.numVerts + 1;
   p := G.numVerts;              {return new position}
   for i := 1 to p do begin
      G.adj[p, i] := false;      {clear new row}
      G.adj[i, p] := false       {clear new column}
   end
end;

procedure InsertEdge(e : EDGE ; var G : GRAPH);
begin
   if (e.end1 > G.numVerts) or (e.end2 > G.numVerts) then
      writeln('Illegal edge description in InsertEdge')
   else begin
      G.adj[e.end1, e.end2] := true;
      G.adj[e.end2, e.end1] := true
   end
end;
```

You'll notice that we left out *DeleteVertex*. We left that for last because it's the only operation that is complicated. To delete a vertex p from a graph G in this implementation, we need to delete the pth row and column from the adjacency matrix, shifting elements to fill the holes. It's not hard, just slightly tedious.

```
procedure DeleteVertex(p : POSITION ; var G : GRAPH);
   var i, j : POSITION;
begin
   if p > G.numVerts then
      writeln('Illegal position number in DeleteVertex')
   else begin
      for i := p to G.numVerts do
         for j := 1 to G.numVerts do
            G.adj[i, j] := G.adj[i + 1, j];    {shift the i-th row up one position}
      for i := p to G.numVerts do
         for j := 1 to G.numVerts do
            G.adj[j, i] := G.adj[j, i + 1]     {shift the i-th column left one position}
   end
end;
```

Adjacency Lists and Edge Lists

A natural generalization of adjacency matrices would be to keep an array of pointers, one for each vertex, and have pointer p_i refer to a linked list of the vertices adjacent to vertex v_i. Such a representation is called an **adjacency list**, and we give an example in Figure 8.4.

Now you see that no time is wasted when we must search every vertex adjacent to a given vertex, since each list contains only the vertices adjacent to its header vertex. In effect, what we have done is to compress the adjacency matrix by eliminating from each row the *false* entries.

We also have an implicit list of edges for each vertex, since each cell w in the linked list headed by v_i corresponds to the edge $\{v_i, w\}$. Of course we have now traded away space efficiency for time efficiency, since we need storage for the pointers, as well as for vertex labels in each cell. We also have not eliminated the extensibility problem, because the header pointers are still stored in an array. We will not consider this implementation in detail, as it is very similar to the next one we will discuss.

The final change we will make to these representations eliminates the extensibility problem entirely, albeit at a further cost in storage. We will make the header array into a linked list, as well, as indicated in the implementation of Figure 8.5. If you look at Figure 8.5 and say something like, "Yuck! That's the most frightening mess I've seen in a long while," you'll be in good company. Don't be put off by the complexity, though—all we have done is to generalize Figure 8.4 slightly. Instead of an array of vertices on the left side, we now have a linked **vertex list** list of cells, each of which has a field for data (like the vertex label), and a pointer to an **edge list** of all vertices adjacent to it (which is the same as saying all edges that contain the header vertex). Each of the horizontal edge lists is also a linked list of cells, with each cell containing a pointer to a vertex (and perhaps a data field as well, which we eliminated in the interests of simplicity).

If you look at Figure 8.5 you can see that vertex b (the second row) is adjacent to vertices a, c, and d—or, in equivalent terms, that vertex b is an endpoint of edges $\{b, a\}$, $\{b, c\}$, and $\{b, d\}$. This makes it particularly easy to traverse the graph, since the edge list pointers lead us from one vertex through its edge to another, adjacent, vertex. The moral is not to worry about the spaghetti bowl of pointers—the program will

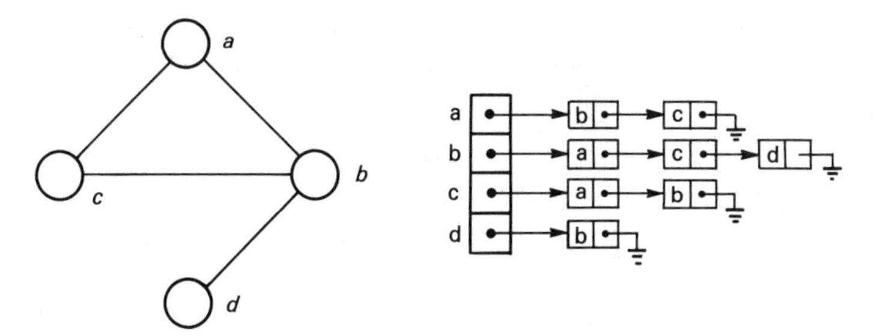

Figure 8.4 The graph of Figure 8.3 and its adjacency list.

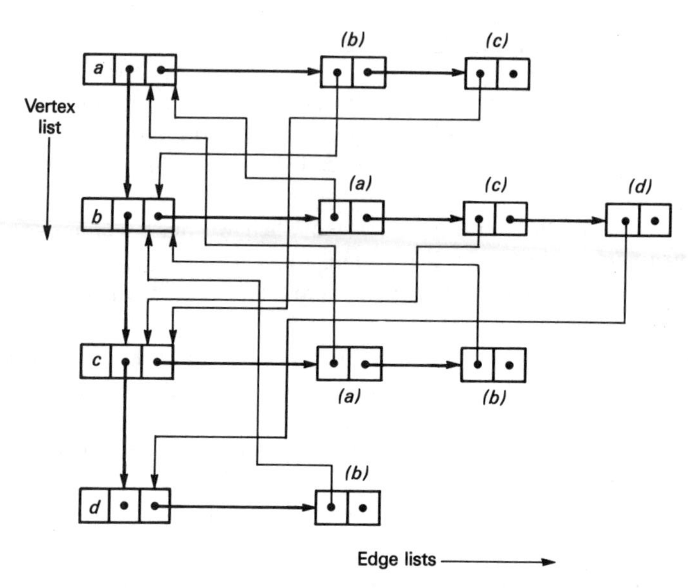

Figure 8.5 The edge list representation for the graph of Figure 8.4.

handle them for you. It still appears that we are wasting space, since each edge is represented twice. In Section 8.5, when we talk about the DIGRAPH ADT, we will see that this problem of duplication disappears when we remove the requirement that the structural relation be symmetric. The declarations for this implementation are, likewise, somewhat complex but not too bad once you give them some careful thought.

```
type
   POSITION = ^VListCell;            {refer to a vertex by a pointer to a vertex cell}
   EListPtr = ^EListCell;
   VListCell = record
                  data : {any vertex information};
                  next : POSITION;   {next cell in the vertex list}
                  head : EListPtr    {header cell of the edge list for the vertex}
         end;
   EListCell = record
                  data : {any edge information};
                  vert : POSITION;   {the endpoint of the edge}
                  next : EListPtr    {next cell in the edge list}
               end;
   EDGE = record
               end1, end2 : POSITION
            end;
   GRAPH = POSITION;                 {refer to a graph by a pointer to vertex list head}
```

Despite the complexity of this implementation, most of the operations are still simple to define. By now, you've had enough experience reading code that it shouldn't be too hard to follow the implementations of the operations. Notice, by the way, that we have left the definition of *DeleteEdge* as an exercise.

```
procedure Create(var G : GRAPH);
begin
   G := nil
end;

function Adjacent(p, q : POSITION) : boolean;
{   Given pointers p and q to cells in the vertex list of G, }
{ search p's edge list, looking for an edge cell with pointer to q.}
   var
      done : boolean;                  {control for traversal of p's edge list}
      current : EListPtr;              {pointer to present cell in p's edge list}
begin
   Adjacent := false;
   current := p^.head;                 {start at head of p's edge list}
   done := false;
   while not done do
      if current = nil then            {ran out of edge cells to inspect}
         done := true
      else if current^.vert = q then   {found a match for q in the edge list}
         done := true;
         Adjacent := true
      end else                         {keep looking—go to next cell in edge list}
         current := current^.next
end;

procedure Update(a : ATOM ; var p : POSITION);
begin
   p^.data := a
end;

function Retrieve(p : POSITION ) : ATOM;
begin
   Retrieve := p^.data
end;

procedure DeleteVertex(p : POSITION ; var G : GRAPH);
   var currentVert : POSITION;

   procedure DeleteCell(v : POSITION ; var head : EListPtr);
   {   Recursively delete the edge list cell with .vert field v from }
   { the edge list (or sublist) which starts at head. }
   begin
      if head <> nil then
         if h^.vert = v then begin     {deleting the head element from the sublist}
            head := head^.next;
            Dispose(head)
         end else                      {didn't find the cell to delete, keep looking}
            DeleteCell(v, head^.next)
   end;
```

```
    procedure ClearList(var head : EListPtr);
    {  Recursively dispose of every element in an edge list starting at head. }
    begin
       if head <> nil then begin
          ClearList(head^.next);            {dispose of tail of edge list}
          Dispose(head)                     {then dispose of head of edge list}
       end
    end;

begin {DeleteVertex}
    curentVert := G;
    while currentVert <> nil do begin
       if p <> currentVert then             {no need to look for { p, p} edge}
          DeleteCell(p, currentVert^.head); {remove the edge from current
                                               to p, if any}
       currentVert := currentVert^.next     {advance to next vertex in vertex list}
    end;
    ClearList(p^.head)                      {throw away all of p's edge list}
end;

procedure InsertVertex(var p : POSITION ; var G : GRAPH);
begin
    New(p);                          {make a new vertex cell, p}
    p^.next := G;                    {link that cell to the head of the vertex list for G}
    p^.head := nil;                  {set p's edge list to be empty}
    G := p                           {and make it the new vertex list head cell}
end;

procedure InsertEdge(e : Edge ; var G : GRAPH);
    var temp : EListCell;
begin
    if not Adjacent(e.end1, e.end2) then begin
       temp := e.end1^.head;         {save head of e.end1's edge list}
       New(e.end1^.head);            {make a new edge list header}
       e.end1.head^.vert := e.end2;  {link that new cell to e.end2}
       e.end1.next := temp;          {and link it into the head of e.end1's edge list}

       temp := e.end2^.head;         {do the same thing for e.end2}
       New(e.end2^.head);
       e.end2.head^.vert := e.end1;
       e.end2.next := temp
    end
end;
```

Having spent this much time defining the edge list implementation of GRAPH, we'll now consider a pair of applications for which it is particularly well suited.

8.3 GRAPH TRAVERSALS

For almost all of the ADTs we have seen so far, we have had a way of visiting all the positions in any instance of the ADT. We did not define traversals of stacks and queues, because those were defined with the intention that except for one or two positions, the contents were to be unavailable for inspection. Of course, as the structural relations became more general, the structures became more complicated, so we had more complex traversal routines. In passing from trees to graphs, we see that again we must exercise care, since each vertex may be adjacent to several other vertices; also, the possible presence of cycles means that we must be careful not to visit any vertex we have already seen. There are two primary graph traversal schemes, one in which we move away from a present vertex as quickly as we can, and one in which we visit all vertices adjacent to a present vertex before moving farther.

Depth-First Traversals

The first traversal scheme we will investigate is known as a **depth-first** traversal. In this algorithm we "mark" a vertex as soon as we visit it, and next try to move to an unmarked adjacent vertex. If there are no unmarked vertices at our present position, we backtrack along the vertices we have already visited until we come to a vertex that is adjacent to one which we haven't visited, visit that one, and continue the process. This is almost exactly the maze traversal scheme we introduced in Chapter 4, where we used a stack to facilitate the backtracking process. Now, though, we know that many stack-based algorithms are natural candidates for recursion, so we will present the following recursive algorithm, which uses a stack implicitly. We will assume here and throughout most of the rest of this chapter that, when we refer to a graph, the graph be connected (since we will track from one vertex to another via edges, and there are no edges connecting the connected pieces, called **components**, of a disconnected graph).

Depth-first traversal is simplicity itself. We keep a marker, *visited*, initially *false*, in each vertex, and every time we visit a vertex we visit recursively all its unvisited adjacent vertices. In skeleton form, the algorithm looks like this:

```
procedure DepthFirst(var p : POSITION);
   var q : POSITION;
begin
   {visit p, do whatever processing is necessary};
   Set the visited marker of p to true;
   for all vertices, q, adjacent to p do
      if q has not been visited then
         DepthFirst(q)
end;
```

Consider the graph of Figure 8.6. If we start at vertex a, and decide that at each vertex we will visit its neighbors in alphabetic order of their labels, we see that a

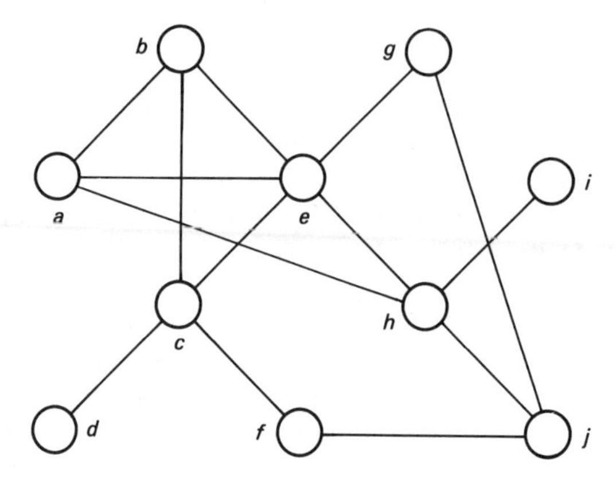

Figure 8.6 A graph for traversal.

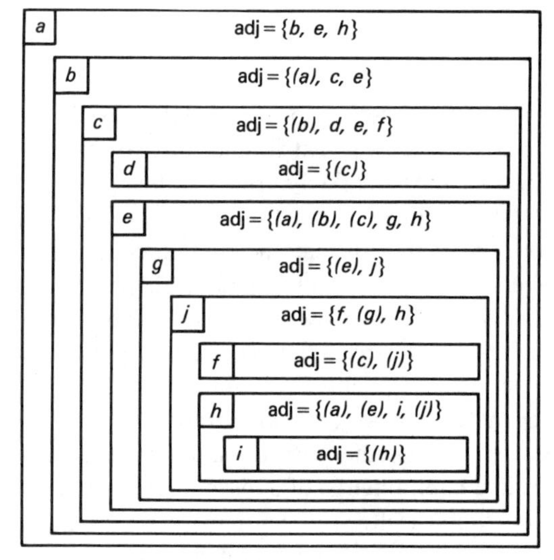

Figure 8.7 Recursive calls to *DepthFirst* on the graph of Figure 8.6.

depth-first traversal will result in the vertices being visited in the order *a, b, c, d, e, g, j, f, h, i*. In Figure 8.7 we trace the action of this algorithm using the nested boxes we introduced in Chapter 5—each box represents a procedure call, and for each such call we indicate the parameter (i.e., the vertex being visited) by a small box in the upper left corner, and indicate the adjacent vertices, with the already visited vertices in parentheses. For instance, the first call, with parameter *a*, intends to call *DepthFirst* on vertices *b*, *e*, and *h*, but by the time the recursive call at *b* is completed, *e* and *h* have already been visited.

We can readily expand the skeleton of *DepthFirst* to an edge list implementation, and do so now. We assume that each vertex cell contains a boolean field *visited*, which has initially been set to *false* for each vertex.

```
procedure DepthFirst(var p : POSITION);
   var
      currentEdge : EListPtr;
      q : POSITION;
begin
   {visit p, do whatever processing is necessary};
   p^.visited := true;
   currentEdge := p^.head;          {get ready to traverse p's edge list}
   while currentEdge <> nil do begin
      q := currentEdge^.vert;       {q is a vertex adjacent to p}
      if not q^.visited then        {visit all unvisited adjacent vertices recursively}
         DepthFirst(q);
      currentEdge := currentEdge^.next
   end
end;
```

Breadth-First Traversals

The second kind of traversal we will discuss is **breadth-first**. In this scheme, every vertex adjacent to the current vertex is visited before we move away from the current vertex. We will accomplish this by keeping the vertices that have been visited but not explored on a queue, so that when we are ready to move to a vertex adjacent to the current vertex, we will be able to return to another vertex adjacent to the old current vertex after our move. As we did with depth-first traversal, we will keep a global array to mark the vertices that have been visited so far.

```
procedure BreadthFirst(p : POSITION);
   var
      Q : QUEUE {of positions};
      n, m : POSITION;
begin
   Create(Q);
   Enqueue(p, Q);
   Set p's visited marker to true;
   {a: visit p, do whatever is necessary};
   while not Empty(Q) do begin
      n := Head(Q);
      {b: visit n};
      Dequeue(Q);
      for each vertex, m, adjacent to n do
         if m has not been visited then begin
            Enqueue(m, Q);
            visited[m] := true;
            {a: visit m}
         end
   end
end;
```

As is commonly the case with traversals, there are several choices about where to do whatever processing is needed to visit a node. We have indicated two possibilities with the statements labeled {a} and {b}. The statements labeled {a} perform the processing the first time a vertex is seen, while the statement labeled {b} processes a vertex the last time it is seen; the choice might be dictated by whether or not the old current vertex is needed, as well as the present current vertex.

Table 8.1 traces the progress of *BreadthFirst* on the graph of Figure 8.6. The algorithm starts at vertex a, and, for each subsequent current vertex, the adjacent unvisited vertices are enqueued in alphabetical order.

TABLE 8.1. TRACING *BreadthFirst* ON THE GRAPH OF FIGURE 8.6

Current vertex	Unvisited neighbors	Queue (tail → head)
a	b, e, h	[h, e, b]
b	c	[c, h, e]
e	g	[g, c, h]
h	i, j	[j, i, g, c]
c	d, f	[f, d, j, i, g]
g	None	[f, d, j, i]
i	None	[f, d, j]
j	None	[f, d]
d	None	[f]
f	None	(queue empty—quit)

Spanning Trees

One application of these traversals is to use them to provide a **spanning tree** for a graph. In graph theoretic terms, a tree is any connected acyclic graph (so if we made the structural relation symmetric and gave no special identification to any root node, the trees we discussed in the last chapter would be ordinary graph-theoretic trees), and a spanning tree for a graph G is a tree constructed from some of the edges of G in such a way that it contains all the vertices of G. Another way to look at spanning trees is that they are the smallest collection of edges that allow communication between any two vertices of the original graph.

We could build a **depth-first spanning tree** by keeping track of all the edges we used in the depth-first traversal, as indicated in Figure 8.8, so that every time we visit a new vertex, we mark the edge from the last current vertex to the new vertex (which means that every cell in the edge list will contain a *treeMark* field, which is *true* if and only if that edge is in the spanning tree). We will use *DepthFirst*, slightly modified, to mark edges of the spanning tree.

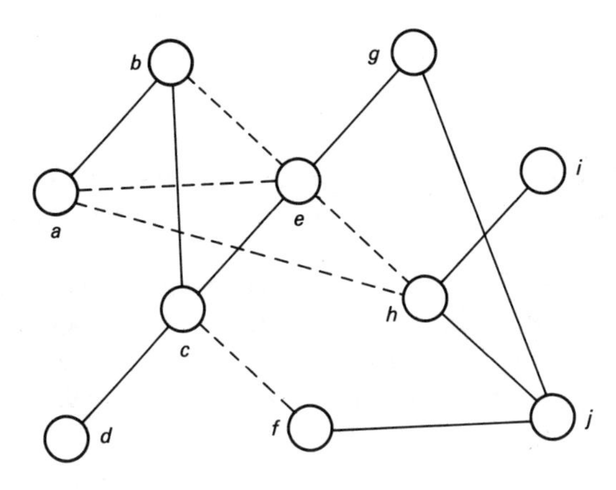

Figure 8.8 A depth-first spanning tree for the graph of Figure 8.6.

```
procedure DFSpanningTree(G : GRAPH );
   var
      p : POSITION;
      e : EListPtr;

   procedure DepthFirstBuild(p : POSITION);
      var
         currentEdge : EListPtr;
         q : POSITION;
   begin
      p^.visited := true;
      currentEdge := p^.head;
      while currentEdge <> nil do begin
         q := currentEdge^.vert;
         if not q^.visited then begin
            currentEdge^.treeMark := true;      {modification—mark a tree edge}
            {we could print the tree edge here}
            {and we could also mark the other copy of currentEdge, too,}
            {since each edge is represented twice in this implementation}
            DepthFirst(q)
         end;
         currentEdge := currentEdge^.next
      end
   end;

begin {DFSpanningTree}
   p := G;                          {initialization: set all markers}
   while p <> nil do begin          {inspect all vertices of G}
      p^.visited := false;          {mark each vertex as unvisited}
      e := p^.head;
      while e <> nil do             {inspect edge list for each vertex}
         e^.treeMark := false;      {mark each edge as not in tree}
         e := e^.next
      end
   end;
```

```
        p := G;                              {build the spanning tree}
        DepthFirstBuild(p, T)
    end;
```

Notice that we say *a* depth-first spanning tree. In general, there could be many different such trees, depending on where we start and the order in which we visit the vertices adjacent to a given vertex.

In a similar way we could modify *BreadthFirst* to construct a **breadth-first spanning tree** of a graph *G*. We will begin with a graph, T, that initially contains all the vertices of *G*, but no edges. Each time we visit a new vertex, we mark the edge of *G* that we used to reach that vertex. Since we need to know the old current node, we will use location {a} in *BreadthFirst* for processing.

```
procedure BFSpanningTree(G : GRAPH);
    var
        Q : QUEUE {of positions};
        n, m : POSITION;
begin
    Set visited field of each vertex to true;
    Create(Q);
    n := G;                                  {start at head of vertex list}
    Enqueue(n, Q);
    n^.visited := true;
    while not Empty(Q) do begin
        n := Head(Q);
        Dequeue(Q);
        currentEdge := n^.head;
        while currentEdge <> nil do begin
            m := currentEdge^.vert;
            if not m^.visited then begin
                Enqueue(m, Q);
                m^.treeMark := true          {mark a spanning tree edge}
            end;
            currentEdge := currentEdge^.next
        end
    end
end;
```

If we perform this algorithm on the graph of Figure 8.6, starting at vertex *a* and visiting adjacent vertices in alphabetical order, we see that the resulting spanning tree is the one given in Figure 8.9.

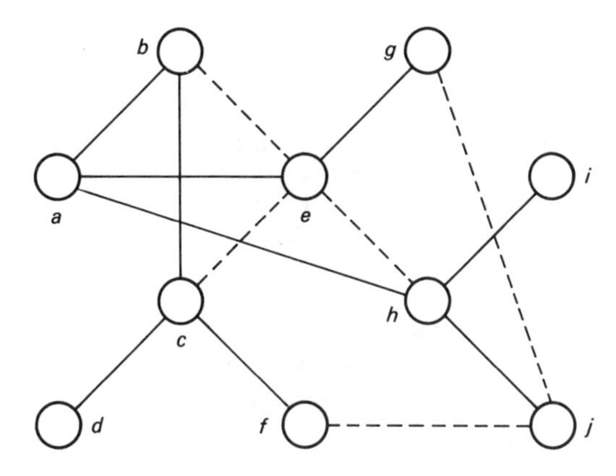

Figure 8.9 A breadth-first spanning tree for the graph of Figure 8.6.

8.4 FURTHER APPLICATIONS OF GRAPH

Recall the questions we asked about the ARPANET graph at the beginning of this chapter. Questions about such things as the number of paths between two nodes or the cost of communication between nodes are not merely academic exercises when you are faced with a real project involving money and sensitive communications. In this section, we will discuss some algorithms for solving graph-theoretic problems like these.

Counting Paths

We now turn to an application to which we alluded before, namely, one that is tailor-made for the adjacency matrix implementation of GRAPH. To appreciate this application, you need to know something about matrix multiplication. If you know how to multiply two matrices, you can skip ahead a few paragraphs until you come to something you don't recognize.

An $n \times m$ **matrix** is a rectangular arrangement of numbers, $a_{i,j}$, with $1 \leq i \leq m$, and $1 \leq j \leq n$. The first subscript denotes the **row** of the number, while the second tells the **column** in which the number may be found, so that the matrix just described has n rows and m columns. For instance, a 3×2 matrix, with 3 rows and 2 columns, would look like

$$\begin{bmatrix} a_{1,1} & a_{1,2} \\ a_{2,1} & a_{2,2} \\ a_{3,1} & a_{3,2} \end{bmatrix}$$

If A is a $p \times q$ matrix, and B is a $q \times r$ matrix, then we can define the **matrix product**, AB, to be the $p \times r$ matrix defined as follows. The entry in row i and column j of the product is found by multiplying each of the r elements in row i of A by the corresponding r elements of column j of B and then adding the products, which is to say, if $A = [a_{i,j}]$, and $B = [b_{i,j}]$, then

$$AB_{i,j} = \sum_{k=1}^{r} a_{i,r} b_{r,j}$$

For instance, suppose we had the following two matrices:

$$A = \begin{bmatrix} 3 & -1 & 0 \\ 2 & 4 & 1 \end{bmatrix}, \quad B = \begin{bmatrix} 4 & 2 \\ 0 & -2 \\ 1 & 3 \end{bmatrix}$$

then the product AB would be a 2×2 matrix with the entry in row 1 and column 2 equal to the sum of the product of the row 1 entries of A with the corresponding column 2 entries of B, or $(3)(2) + (-1)(-2) + (0)(3) = 8$. You should be able to complete the other three sums of products and show that

$$\begin{bmatrix} 3 & -1 & 0 \\ 2 & 4 & 1 \end{bmatrix} \begin{bmatrix} 4 & 2 \\ 0 & -2 \\ 1 & 3 \end{bmatrix} = \begin{bmatrix} 12 & 8 \\ 9 & -1 \end{bmatrix}$$

Now suppose that A was an $n \times n$ matrix which represented the adjacency matrix of a graph on n vertices. We will write A with a 1 in every *true* entry and a 0 in every *false* entry, as in Figure 8.10. "A good start is a journey half completed," so the saying goes. The good start in this case is the observation that the i, j entry of the adjacency matrix counts the number of paths of length 1 (that is to say, with one edge) from vertex i to vertex j. Well, that's a moderately interesting way of looking at it, but the light really comes on when we consider the i, j entry of the *square* of the adjacency matrix, that is, the product of the adjacency matrix with itself. Consider the example of Figure 8.10, and look at the entry in row a and column c of the square of the adjacency matrix. That entry is obtained by adding the products of row a times the corresponding elements in column c, which in this case is nothing but $(0)(0) + (1)(1) + (0)(0) + (0)(1) + (1)(1) + (0)(1) + (0)(0) = 2$. The first pair of 1's come from the b entries of row a and column c, meaning that there is an edge from a to b and from b to c, while the second pair of 1's come from the e entries of row a and column c, meaning that there is an edge from a to e, and one from e to c. But this corresponds to the two paths from a to c, namely a, b, c and a, e, c. In other words, if A is the adjacency matrix of a graph G, then the i, j entry of A^2 counts the number of distinct paths of length 2 from vertex i to

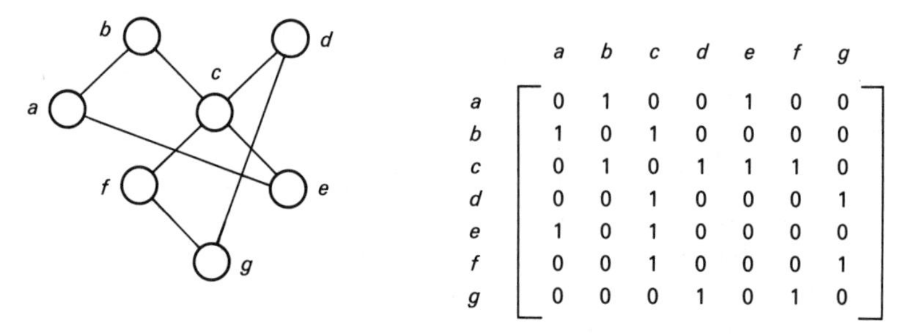

	a	b	c	d	e	f	g
a	0	1	0	0	1	0	0
b	1	0	1	0	0	0	0
c	0	1	0	1	1	1	0
d	0	0	1	0	0	0	1
e	1	0	1	0	0	0	0
f	0	0	1	0	0	0	1
g	0	0	0	1	0	1	0

Figure 8.10 Another graph and its adjacency matrix.

vertex j ! It is not difficult to show that this property holds for arbitrary powers of the adjacency matrix, leading us to the following results.

Theorem. If A is the adjacency matrix (with 1 for *true* and 0 for *false*) of a graph G, then the matrix power A^k has as its i, j entry the number of distinct paths (not just simple paths—vertices could repeat) in G of length k from vertex i to vertex j.

Corollary. If A is the adjacency matrix of G, as above, then the total number of paths of length $\leq k$ from vertex i to vertex j in G is given by the i, j entry of $A + A^2 + \ldots + A^k$ (where the sum of two matrices of the same size is obtained by termwise addition of the entries in the matrices).

There are a number of different forms that these results might take, depending on the operations we chose for matrix "multiplication." Suppose, for instance, that we had a graph that represented a map of cities and the roads connecting them. We might choose to include with each edge a number representing the cost (in driving time or dollars for gasoline) of travel along that edge. The adjacency matrix is particularly suitable for such an **edge-weighted graph**, since we could place in the i, j entry the cost associated with taking the edge from vertex i to vertex j, as we do in Figure 8.11.

In the adjacency matrix for edge-weighted graphs, we have zeroes on the main diagonal, reflecting the fact that it costs nothing to get to a city if you're already there, and we place a symbol "∞" in an entry if there is no edge between the corresponding vertices. For this kind of adjacency matrix, normal matrix multiplication has no immediate meaning, not to mention that we have no idea what to do with the "∞" entries. But look at what happens when we take matrix multiplication and replace every multiplication by addition and every original addition by the *minimum* of the terms that were to be added. For the a, c entry of the "square" of the adjacency matrix, we combine termwise the a row with the c column, which yields $min\{0 + 12, 2 + 8, 12 + 0, 10 + 6, \infty + 3\} = 10$, if we define "$\infty$" to be larger than any number, and $\infty + a = \infty$, for every number a. The a, c entry in the "square" of the adjacency matrix is less than that of the corresponding entry in the original matrix, and this comes from the 2 + 8 term. But that term corresponds to the a, b, c path, and we see that it is indeed cheaper to go from a to c through b than it is to go directly from a to c (a fact that is common knowledge to all frequent fliers).

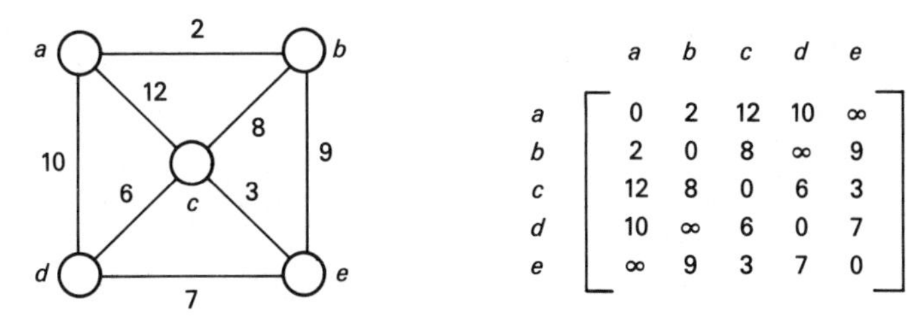

Figure 8.11 An edge-weighted graph and its adjacency matrix.

In other words, *if we change the usual "plus/times" matrix multiplication to "min/plus" multiplication of the adjacency matrix,* A, *for edge-weighted graphs, the power* A^k *gives the cheapest travel costs for paths of length less than or equal to* k *in the graph.*

It is not hard to calculate the time necessary to find the least-cost path matrix using this algorithm. Suppose the adjacency matrix was $n \times n$. A matrix multiplication must fill in each of the n^2 entries of the product matrix, and each entry requires $O(n)$ operations, for a total of $O(n^3)$ time to multiply two $n \times n$ matrices. The longest path that could be of any interest to us in a graph on n vertices is a path of length n, so it might seem that to find the cheapest paths could take $O(n^4)$ time. We can do better than that, however, by repeatedly squaring the adjacency matrix, producing $A, A^2, A^4, \ldots, A^k$, until $k \geq n$. Since each squaring doubles the exponent, we need only compute powers $1, 2, 4, 8, 16, \ldots, 2^i$, until $2^i \geq n$. In other words, we will need at most $\log_2 n$ matrix multiplications, for a total time of $O(n^3 \log n)$ to find the costs of the cheapest paths between all vertices in the graph.

Minimum Spanning Trees

Let's combine two ideas that we have discussed earlier, spanning trees and edge-weighted graphs. If G is an edge-weighted graph, then any spanning tree T of G has associated with it a weight equal to the sum of the weights of the edges in T, and it makes sense to ask what spanning trees have the least cost. Such trees are called **minimum spanning trees (MSTs)**. Since a spanning tree connects all vertices in G, we are then asking for the least-cost collection of edges that will ensure communication between all vertices of G.

In order to demonstrate that the MST algorithm works correctly, we need a preliminary result, which we mentioned earlier and will restate here without proof. The result we need is that a tree is not only a connected graph with no cycles, but is also **maximal** with that property, in the sense that if we add an edge to a tree (by connecting two vertices that are already in the tree), then the resulting graph is no longer a tree, because we have introduced a cycle containing the new edge.

The algorithm, due to R. C. Prim, is quite easy to understand. We build an MST by marking edges and vertices, just as we did when we built spanning trees.

```
procedure MST(G : GRAPH);
   var p, q : POSITION;            { p is always in the MST, q isn't }
begin
   Start with any vertex, p ∈ G ;
   while there is an unmarked vertex of G do begin
      Find a least cost edge { p, q} ∈ E(G) with p marked and q unmarked ;
      Mark q;
      Mark the { p, q} edge
   end
end;
```

That could hardly be simpler. Before we analyze this algorithm, let's look at an example of how it works, using the edge-weighted tree of Figure 8.11. We will draw the MST as it is being built, by drawing each newly marked vertex and edge. Figure 8.12 shows the steps of the algorithm: We begin with any vertex, and, at each pass through the loop, we find an edge of least cost that connects the tree to a vertex not yet in the tree. We then include that vertex and edge in the tree, and continue the process. The algorithm works because at the end of each pass, T, the marked tree, is a minimum spanning tree for that subgraph of G consisting of the vertices chosen so far, along with all edges of G connecting those edges (called the **induced subgraph** on those vertices).

To prove this assertion, suppose that it was true at the start of a pass, but that it was not true at the end of the pass. In other words, adding the $\{p, q\}$ edge, with $p \in T$ and $q \notin T$ produced a tree, T', which was *not* least cost on the vertices selected so far. That would mean that there was another spanning tree, T'', on the vertices selected so far that was strictly cheaper than T'. Now, T'' could not contain the $\{p, q\}$ edge, because if it did, it could not be cheaper than T with the $\{p, q\}$ edge added, since we assumed that T was cheapest. Therefore, T'' contains another edge to q—call it $\{p', q\}$—with $p' \in T$.

Whoa! Adding $\{p, q\}$ to T'' produces a cycle containing p, p', and q, and by removing the $\{p', q\}$ edge, we again have a tree containing $\{p, q\}$. This tree must be at least as cheap as T', since $\{p, q\}$ was the least-cost edge from q to any vertex in T, so we have a MST containing $\{p, q\}$ that is strictly cheaper than T'. But we just showed that that was impossible. Therefore, T' must be a MST on the induced subgraph, completing the essential part of the proof. We leave it up to you to show that this is indeed enough to demonstrate that the algorithm produces a MST for the entire graph.

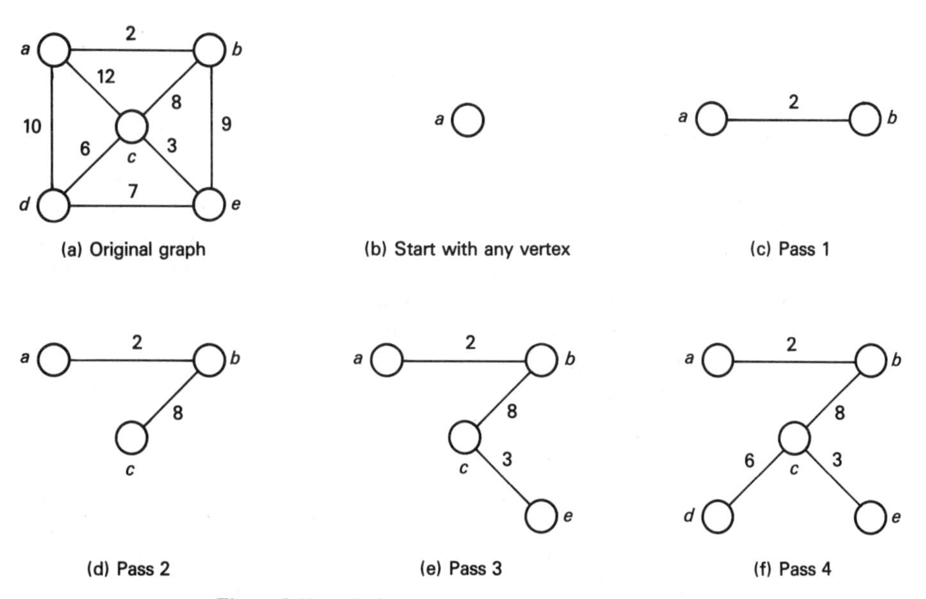

Figure 8.12 Construction of a minimum spanning tree.

8.5 DIRECTED GRAPHS

If we think about the previous example, where a graph represented cities with roads between them, we can see that graphs may not be the most natural model for such a situation. In particular, since the prevailing winds in the northern hemisphere blow from west to east, it may very well take longer to travel in one direction than in the other on the same road. Furthermore, if we used a graph to model the streets in a typical city, it might be impossible to travel in one direction on a street (unless we wished to break the law concerning one-way streets). As we mentioned at the start of this chapter, we can generalize the definition of a graph to allow the existence of **directed edges** from one vertex to another. Doing so allows us to define a **directed graph**, also known as a **digraph**, and since we defined graphs in two ways, we will present the definition of digraphs in two ways, as well.

Definition (Graph-Theory Flavor). A digraph is an ordered pair $D = (V, E)$ of vertices and (directed) edges, where E consists of a set of *ordered pairs*, (p, q), of elements of V. For an edge (p, q) from p to q, p is called the **initial vertex** of the edge, and q is called the **terminal vertex** of the edge.

Definition (ADT Flavor). The **DIGRAPH** abstract data type consists of an underlying set ATOM, and a set POSITION, such that every graph consists of a triple, (P, R, v) where P is a finite subset of POSITION, v is a function from $P \rightarrow ATOM$, and R is *any* relation on P (irreflexive, if we disallow loops, though loops are more commonly allowed among digraphs than among graphs). The DIGRAPH operations are the same as those for GRAPH.

You should refer back to the definitions for graphs, and contrast them with these digraph definitions.

We can view a digraph as a graph if we ignore the direction of edges. This is done frequently, so we distinguish the two points of view by discussing paths, simple paths, and connectedness for a digraph as if it were a graph, and defining **directed paths** to be sequences of vertices $v_1, v_2, \ldots, v_k$ for which there is a directed edge from v_i to v_{i+1}, for every $i = 1, \ldots, k - 1$. Cycles are customarily considered to be directed, and we say that a digraph is **strongly connected** if there is a directed path between any two vertices. Figure 8.13 shows a digraph that is cyclic (with a simple cycle of length 2), connected, but not strongly connected.

It is clear that a graph is just a special case of a digraph, one in which every edge between two vertices is paired with one running in the opposite direction. Most of what we have said about graphs holds equally well for digraphs, and much of what we are about to say holds for graphs, as well. The implementations for graphs can be used for digraphs with no change, for example. Notice that the adjacency matrix for digraphs now has no redundant information: For a graph, the adjacency matrix was **symmetric** (since it was nothing but a description of a symmetric structural relation), with the i, j entry always equal to the j, i entry, while this need not hold for digraphs, since the i, j

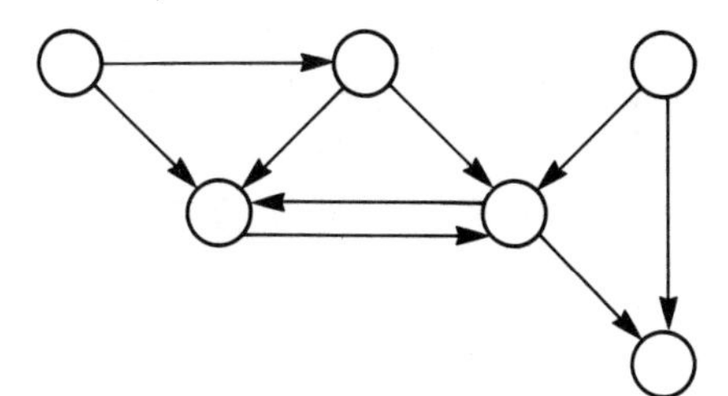

Figure 8.13 A digraph.

entry is *true* if and only if there is a directed edge starting at vertex i and ending at vertex j.

The only real difference that comes when we apply what we have done to digraphs is that unless the digraph is strongly connected, there is no guarantee that the traversal algorithms will visit every node in the digraph. Generally, the traversal process comes to a halt, because it is unable to proceed any further, so we choose a new starting vertex that has not yet been visited, and start the traversal from there, a process that leads to a **spanning forest** of disconnected trees, as happened in Figure 8.14 (and as would happen if we applied the traversal algorithms to nonconnected graphs). Notice, by the way, that the trees that result are much more similar to the directed trees of Chapter 6.

Application: Cheapest Paths (II)

We have already seen an algorithm for finding the least cost of paths between any vertices of an edge-weighted graph. This algorithm can be applied equally well to edge-weighted digraphs, and runs in time $O(n^3 \log n)$, as we have seen. With the least-cost matrix, it would be easy to answer the question, "Given a starting vertex, what is the least cost to any other vertex?" All we would have to do is read off the row of the least-cost matrix corresponding to the given starting vertex. In one sense, the time required to answer this question would be $O(n^2 \log n)$, the cost to set up the matrix divided by the number of rows. We will present here an algorithm to solve this problem that is faster than $O(n^2 \log n)$.

We are trying to solve what is known as the *single-source least-cost* problem, of computing one row of the least-cost matrix. The algorithm we will present is due to E. W. Dijkstra (who, by the way, is one of those rare individuals whose name contains three consecutive letters in alphabetic order, though this has nothing to do with why his

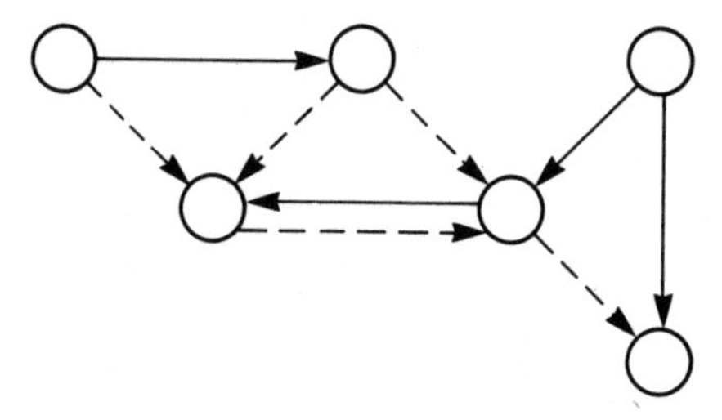

Figure 8.14 A spanning forest for the digraph of Figure 8.13.

name is so well known). The algorithm is one of a class of **greedy algorithms**, similar to Prim's MST algorithm, in which at each step the best "local" solution to the problem is the one chosen (similar to the way we make change with the fewest number of coins by selecting at each stage the largest valued coin that is less than or equal to the amount yet needed*). The algorithm makes use of the cost adjacency matrix, A, and constructs a least-cost vector, L, of the costs of the cheapest paths from the starting vertex to each other vertex. We will assume that "∞" in the matrix A is represented by some easily recognized value larger than any possible path cost.

```
procedure SingleLeastCost(p : POSITION ; A : AdjMatrix ; var L : CostVector);
   var
      S : set of POSITION;   {contains all vertices for which min cost is known}
      q, r : POSITION;
begin
   S := [p];

   for all vertices q <> p in the graph do
      L[q] := A[p, q];

   repeat
      for all vertices not in S do
         Find the vertex, q, for which L[q] is smallest;

      S := S + [q];
      for all vertices, r, not in S do
         if L[r] >= L[q] + A[q, r] then
            L[r] := L[q] + A[q, r]
   until S contains all but one of the vertices of the graph
end;
```

We will trace the action of Dijkstra's algorithm on the edge-weighted digraph of Figure 8.15. Suppose that we wish to find the least cost of paths from vertex a. We begin with $S = \{a\}$, and $L = [2, 12, \infty, \infty]$, which we obtain from the a row of the adjacency matrix. We do the following steps through the **repeat** loop until S contains all but one vertex of the digraph.

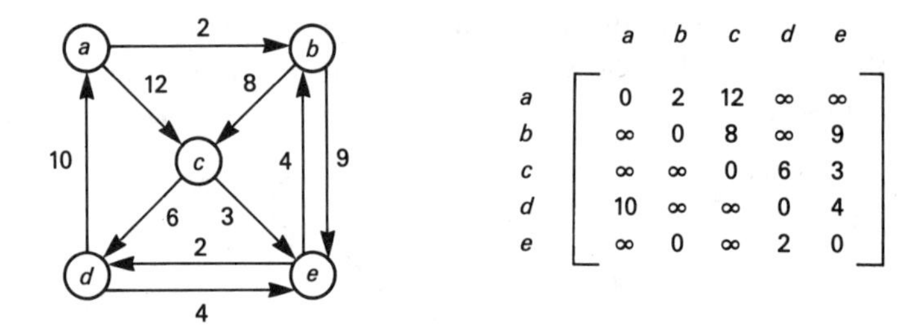

Figure 8.15 An edge-weighted digraph and its adjacency matrix.

*Which, incidentally, would not always succeed if our coins had different values than they do.

Step 1. We see that $L[b] = 2$ is the least value in the L vector, among those vertices not yet chosen, so we include b in S. For the rest of the unchosen values, r, we compare $L[r]$ with $L[b] + A[b, r]$, in effect asking whether it is cheaper to go through b to get to r than it is to go by a path corresponding to the old value of $L[r]$. For $r = c$, we find $L[c] = 12$, and $L[b] + A[b, c] = 2 + 8$, so it is cheaper to go through b to get to c, so we make $L[c] = 10$. For $r = d$, we have $L[a] = \infty$, and $L[b] + A[b, d] = 2 + \infty$, so it is no cheaper to get to d via b. For $r = e$, we have $L[e] = \infty$, and $L[b] + A[b, e] = 2 + 9$, so again it is cheaper to get to e via b. At the end of this step we now have $L = [2, 10, \infty, 11]$.

Step 2. Among the vertices not yet in S, we see that $L[c] = 10$ is the minimal value, so we add c to S, producing $S = \{a, b, c\}$. We look at the two remaining unselected vertices and again ask whether a path through c to those vertices is cheaper than the existing path. For $r = d$, we have $L[d] = \infty$, $L[c] + A[c, d] = 10 + 6$, so we set $L[d] = 16$. For $r = d$, we have $L[e] = 11$, $L[c] + A[c, e] = 10 + 3$, so it is no cheaper to get from a to e through c. We now have $L = [2, 10, 16, 11]$.

Step 3. Vertices d and e are the only ones not yet selected, and we find $L[e] = 11$ is the minimum value among them, so we add e to S, and compare $L[d] = 16$ with $L[e] + A[e, d] = 11 + 2 = 13$. We find that it is cheaper to go through e to get to d than not, so we finally have $L = [2, 10, 13, 11]$.

We could verify that, for the example given, the algorithm does indeed give the correct result, but that tells us very little. A precept whose value cannot be overstated is *an example is not a proof*: Knowing that the algorithm is correct in one instance is essentially worthless, so let us participate in a bit of **program verification**, that is, a proof that an algorithm performs as we wish it to. This is a very hot topic in contemporary computer science, one in which a lot of preliminary work has been done, but in which complete answers have yet to be found. We will do what amounts to an induction proof that an **invariant** condition remains true throughout the life of the algorithm, and will phrase our invariant so that if it holds at the completion of the algorithm, then the algorithm has indeed done what it was supposed to. We will call vertices *selected* if they are in the set S, and let p denote the start vertex for the algorithm.

Invariant. Any selected vertex, v, has the property that its L-value is equal to the least cost of any path from p, through selected vertices, to v.

Since the algorithm begins with p as the only selected vertex, and the cost of a path from p to itself is zero, the invariant is certainly true at the start of the algorithm. At the end of the algorithm all vertices have been selected, so that if the invariant holds at the end, we must have the L vector containing the lengths of the shortest paths from p to any other vertex in the digraph. All we need to do is to complete the induction step by showing that, if the invariant holds at the start of an iteration through the **repeat** loop, then it holds at the end of that iteration.

Let us then suppose that we are at the beginning of an iteration of the loop, and that the invariant property holds for the vertices so far selected. We wish to add a new vertex, q, to the selected set, and we do so by choosing the unselected vertex with the least L-value. We claim that that is exactly the appropriate choice, in that if q is the unselected vertex with the smallest L-value, then the cheapest way to get from p to q is through selected vertices. In other words, the invariant property will hold for the newly selected vertex q.

Suppose that were not true, that is, that there was actually a path from p, through some selected vertices, to an unselected vertex x, and then through one or more edges to q, which was cheaper than $L[q]$. That would mean that the path from p to x was itself cheaper than the path through the selected vertices to q, which would mean that, contrary to our assumption, we never would have chosen q in the first place.

Now that we have added q to the selected vertices, we know that its L-value represents the least cost of any path from p to q, through selected vertices. We don't know that that is now true for the rest of the selected vertices. In fact, the example shows that the invariant fails to hold immediately after we have included q. This is why we then checked each of the selected vertices, r, to see if there is a cheaper path from p to r through q. Having done that, though, we are at the end of an iteration, and we see that the invariant property is restored, with every selected vertex having the property that its L-value is again equal to the cost of the cheapest path from p to the vertex, through selected vertices.

The invariant holds at the start; if it holds at the beginning of a loop iteration, it must hold at the end, so therefore the invariant holds at the end of the algorithm, so the algorithm must do what it is supposed to do. Done. (Now you can see part of the reason that program verification is such a knotty problem, which is why we went through the proof in such detail.)

Finding a timing estimate for Dijkstra's algorithm is considerably easier than verifying it. Suppose the digraph has n vertices. The initialization of S and L take $O(n)$ time, and the main loop iterates $n - 1$ times, with S having size $1, 2, \ldots, n - 1$ in successive iterates. Each of the **for** loops within the main loop takes $O(n - s)$, where s is the size of S. The time for the algorithm, then, is $O(n) + (O(n - 1) + O(n - 2) + \ldots + O(1)) = O(n^2)$. Knowing this, it would be simple to apply Dijkstra's algorithm to each vertex, thereby filling out the cost matrix in time $O(n^3)$.

Dijkstra's algorithm could be unsatisfactory, though, if we wanted to know what the cheapest paths from the source were, rather than just knowing the costs of the paths. The modification would not be too difficult; all we would have to do is keep track of the path we used to get from the newly selected vertex q to an unselected vertex r every time we changed the L-value of r. It would probably be easiest to keep the minimal paths in an array, in such a way that the row headed by q would contain the vertices on a cheapest path from p to q in order, and we will overload the 0th column to contain the length of each path. We will denote the path array by P, where $P[i, j]$ contains the jth vertex in the path from the source to vertex i, and in doing so will assume that the vertices are indexed $1, 2, \ldots, n$. We will present the algorithm in full implementation-specific detail, to give you a sample in more than pseudocode. For simplicity's sake, we will assume that vertex 1 is the source vertex.

```
const
   N = {the number of vertices in the graph};
   INFINITY = {some suitably large cost};
type
   Cost = {whatever type the costs are};
   POSITION = 1 . . N;
   AdjMatrix = array [POSITION, POSITION] of Cost;
   CostVector = array [2 . . N] of Cost;
   PathArray = array [2 . . N, 0 . . N] of POSITION;

procedure SingleLeastCost(A : AdjMatrix ; var L : CostVector ; var P : PathArray);
   var
      S : set of POSITION;
      p, q, r : POSITION;
      min : Cost;
begin
   S := [1];                                 {vertex1 is the source vertex}

   for q := 2 to N do                        {set up cost vector}
      L[q] := A[1, q];

   for q := 2 to N do begin                  {set up path array}
      if A[1, q] < INFINITY then begin       {there is a path from 1 to q}
         P[q, 0] := 1;
         P[q, 1] := 1
      end else begin                         {no path yet from 1 to q}
         P[q, 0] := 0;
         P[q, 1] := 0
      end;
      for r := 2 to N do
         P[q, r] := 0
   end;

   for index := 2 to N - 1 do begin
      min := INFINITY;                       {find least cost vertex, q, not yet in S}
      for r := 2 to N do
         if not (r in S) then
            if L[r] < min then begin
               min := L[r];
               q := r
            end;

      S := S + [q];                          {include q among selected vertices}

      for r := 2 to N do           {adjust cost and path arrays for unselected vertices}
```

```
            if not (r in S) then
                if L[r] >= L[q] + A[q, r] then begin
                    L[r] := L[q] + A[q, r];

                    P[r, 0] := P[q, 0] + 1;        {replace r path with q path, since
                                                      it's cheaper}
                    for p := 1 to P[q, 0] do
                        P[r, p] := P[q, p];
                    P[r, P[r, 0]] := q
                end
    end
end;
```

The only essential difference between this and the original algorithm is that we maintain the path array. At any pass through the algorithm, the path array contains a least-cost path from the source to any selected vertex, and each time we select a new vertex and find that it is cheaper to go through the selected vertex to an unselected vertex, we replace the path for the unselected vertex with the path that goes through the newly selected vertex and on to the unselected vertex.

8.6 COMPUTATIONAL COMPLEXITY AND GRAPH ALGORITHMS

We mentioned earlier that computational complexity theory is that branch of computer science devoted to the study of the space and time complexity of algorithms and problems. In this section we will concentrate on timing estimates, although much of what we will say holds for storage estimates as well, and we will look at some of the connections between complexity theory and the study of graph algorithms. We'll omit most of the technical details, of which there are many, but will try to give you an idea of some of the most vital questions in this area, in the hope that you'll find it exciting enough to be worth further study at a later time.

Notice that we talked about the complexity of *problems*, as well as algorithms. Every problem has an innate time complexity $T(n)$, in the sense that any algorithm at all to solve that problem, no matter how cleverly contrived, must have asymptotic running time at least as large as $O(T(n))$. A trivial example would be the *counting problem*: Given an integer, n, produce a list of all integers between 1 and n. That problem is obviously linear, in the sense that any algorithm that produces the list must have running time at least $O(n)$, although we could, of course, invent any number of algorithms that took much longer than that. A less trivial example is the *sorting problem*: Given a set of n numbers, produce as output a list containing the numbers in sorted order. With a few hints, you should be able to show that any algorithm that relied solely on comparisons of elements, like selection sort, mergesort or heapsort, could not run in time less than $O(n \log n)$, so we could say that the *comparison sorting problem* is an $n \log n$ problem. There are, by the way, algorithms for sorting that do not rely on comparisons of elements and that run faster than $O(n \log n)$, at least if you make some assumptions about the numbers being sorted, but—computer science folklore aside—it is not known that $n \log n$ is the best we can do for the unrestricted sorting problem. In a similar way, it is easy to show that the problem of multiplying two n-digit numbers can be solved in $O(n^2)$ time, using the elementary school algorithm, and we can prove that it is possible to find a $O(n^{1+a})$ time multiplication algorithm, for any $a > 0$, but we simply do not know whether a linear algorithm is possible (we certainly couldn't do better than that, if for no other reason than that it would take $O(n)$ time just to read in the digits of the numbers).

Finding the best lower bound for the complexity of a problem is usually quite difficult. Often, it is enough to gain some partial information about the complexity of a problem, and leave the details for another time. If we paint with the broadest possible brush that still leaves us with an interesting picture, we can divide all problems into two classes: easy and hard. We will say that an *easy* problem is one for which there is an algorithm that runs in **polynomial time**, namely, one that for problems of size n runs in time $O(n^k)$, for some nonnegative integer k. Any other problem, such as one for which the fastest algorithm takes time proportional to 2^n or $n!$, we will call a *hard* problem. This rough classification makes sense, since the polynomial time algorithms, no matter how large the power k is, are at least feasible to try to solve on a computer, while the time to run a nonpolynomial algorithm increases so rapidly as a function of n that it is foolish even to try it, except for very small instances of the problem.

Now, every problem (or at least every problem that we can solve on a computer, which does not include all the problems we can state*) has some innate complexity, even if we don't know what it is, so every problem either lies in the set P of polynomial-time problems, or it does not. Many problems, like sorting, multiplication, and finding the nth Fibonacci number, are known to be in P; and many problems (like listing all subsets of a set of n numbers) are known not to lie in P. The most interesting problems, however, are those that in some sense lie near the boundary of P and not-P, in that they are "easier" than the rest of the hard problems, but are not known to be easy (see Figure 8.16).

The "interesting" problem that we will study here is called the **Traveling Salesperson Problem** (sometimes shortened to **TSP**). Suppose that a sales representative has contacts in n cities and wishes to visit all of them, beginning and ending at the home office, and not visiting any city more than once (we'll assume that our rep has a contact to visit in the home city, so that the home city is among the n). Suppose also that the sales rep knows the cost of travel between any two of the cities. The traveling salesperson problem is to find the tour that meets these conditions, and that has the least cost. In our terminology, this is nothing but an edge-weighted graph problem: We are given a graph, G, with n vertices and a cost function, c, on the edges of G, and we want to find a simple cycle $v_1, v_2, \ldots, v_n, v_1$ for which $c(\{v_1, v_2\}) + c(\{v_2, v_3\}) + \ldots + c(\{v_n, v_1\})$ is as small as possible.

*One such problem is the *halting problem*: Design an algorithm that will take as its input the source code of a program P in a given language, and some input data, D, and in a finite time stop and answer "yes" if P eventually halts on input D, or "no" if P fails to halt on input D (because it would have gotten stuck in an infinite loop, for example). There is a clever and simple proof that it is impossible to construct such an algorithm that will work correctly on all inputs P and D.

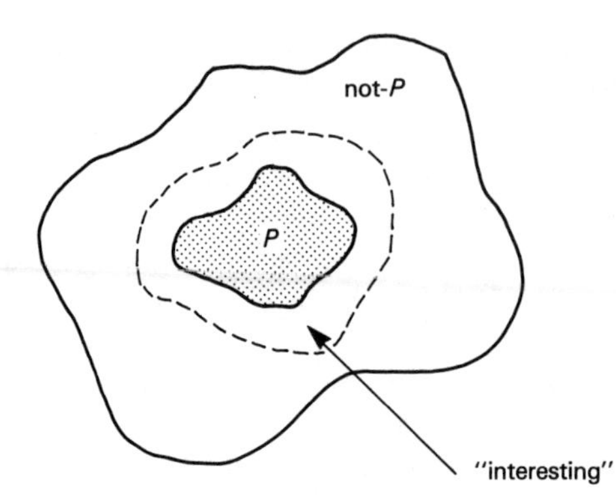

Figure 8.16 A hierarchy of problems.

It is not at all difficult to find an algorithm to solve TSP. All we need to do is construct all possible simple cycles in G, and find the one with the least cost. How long would that algorithm take to run? Well, we can compute the cost of a cycle while it is being generated, so the running time for the algorithm is proportional to the number of cycles we have to investigate. Let's see, starting at the home city, there could be as many as $n - 1$ possibilities for the first city on the tour; having chosen that one, we could make as many as $n - 2$ independent choices for the next city, $n - 3$ for the one after that, and so on. Since the number of choices at each step has nothing to do with the choices we have made before, the total number of cycles is the product of the number of individual choices, for a grand total of $(n - 1)(n - 2)(n - 3) \ldots (2)(1) = (n - 1)!$ This means that this is a "hard" algorithm, with running time $O((n - 1)!)$. In other words, the problem of *enumerating* the simple cycles of a graph is innately non-polynomial. To see how the growth rate of the timing function clobbers us, you could do the calculations to show that even if it were somehow possible to enumerate a million tours per second, it could take as much as 1 hour and 44 minutes to do this for 14 cities, 14 times that long if we included just one more city, and about *3857 years* if we had just 20 cities! Clearly, this "brute force" approach should be avoided, if at all possible.

At this point, it seems that we basically have two choices: We could either try to find a polynomial-time algorithm for TSP, or we could prove that TSP is innately hard, which would give us a perfect excuse to throw up our hands and declare that the problem was not worth the time to program a computer to solve. A lot of very clever people (and a lot of crackpots, too, it must be admitted) have worked for a long time on these two approaches, and the results have been uniformly the same. Zilch. We simply don't know yet whether TSP is a hard problem or not.

In 1971, Stephen Cook published a paper that provided a third choice and set the stage for a partial way out of our dilemma. He considered a class of problems called **NP**. Any problem in *NP* has the property that, roughly speaking, it is possible to *verify* a solution in polynomial time, no matter how long it might have taken to *produce* the solution. *NP*, then, sits "between" *P* and not-*P*. It contains *P*, and also contains many problems that *appear* to be in not-*P* (some homework assignments may take non-polynomial time to complete, but may still require only polynomial time to grade, which is why some of us become teachers). Almost all of the "interesting" problems are in *NP*. Even better than that, however, is the fact that within *NP* there is a further subclass of problems, called **NP-complete** problems. There are hundreds of *NP*-complete problems; they all seem to be hard (at least there is no known easy algorithm for any of them); and they all have, by definition, the property that *if a polynomial-time solution for any NP-complete problem can be found, it would provide polynomial-time solutions for all problems in NP, and if any problem in NP can be proved to be hard, then* every *NP-complete problem is also hard.*

One of the most famous unsolved problems in mathematics is whether $P = NP$, or, contrarily, is P a *proper* subset of *NP*? In some sense, the *NP*-complete problems are the "hardest" of the problems in *NP*, since a polynomial-time solution to any one of them would drag all of *NP* into *P*. This provides us with our partial out. If we have an apparently hard problem that we can show is *NP*-complete, we can at least take some comfort in the knowledge that a polynomial-time algorithm to solve the problem would provide an answer to a question that has stymied the best mathematicians and computer scientists for nearly two decades. TSP is an *NP*-complete problem.

That being the case, it is perhaps presumptuous of us to think that we can find an easy algorithm to solve TSP, at least not right away. What we can do, however, is adopt a strategy that is very common in dealing with difficult problems. In theory, the problem of how to win a chess game is solvable. All we have to do is investigate all possible lines of play and try to choose those lines that lead to a win (or at least a draw). This brute force strategy is at least as bad as the brute force approach to TSP—so bad, as a matter of fact, that no one in their right mind would attempt it. Rather, what chess players do is rely on **heuristics**—rules of thumb that describe courses of action that generally improve the chances of solving the problem at hand, like trying to control the center of the board, and not trading a queen for a pawn unless there is compelling reason to do so.

For TSP, the heuristic that would probably occur to most people first is to be greedy: While trying to complete the circuit, choose the next edge to be the one that has least cost to an unvisited vertex. This is not a strategy that guarantees success—you should be able to come up with a simple example for which a greedy strategy will fail to provide the least-cost circuit—but it is one that often produces a "pretty good" solution. We could modify the strategy by including some "lookahead," as chess players do when they think, "If I make this move, then my opponent might do this or that, in which case I would . . . ," thereby perhaps improving the heuristic even further.

We'll close this chapter with a strategy that uses an algorithm we've already described. A solution to TSP must be more expensive than a minimum spanning tree, since removing one edge from a TSP circuit would produce a spanning tree for the graph. We know that minimum spanning trees can be constructed in polynomial time, so we might try to modify a MST to a solution to TSP (an example of why nonspecialists find it so hard to talk to computer scientists). A "shrink wrap" traversal of a MST is

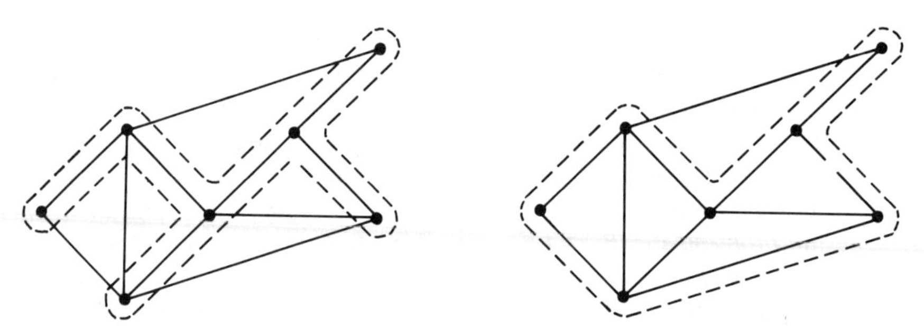

Figure 8.17 Expanding a spanning tree to a simple cycle.

sort of a solution to TSP—it is a low-cost cycle, but unfortunately is not simple, since we traverse each edge twice.

We can, however, generate a simple cycle from a spanning tree by appropriately choosing "shortcuts" across vertices that have already been visited (see Figure 8.17). This will not guarantee a solution to TSP in all cases, but for at least one class of graphs it will guarantee a solution that is no larger than twice the cost of the optimal solution. See if you can come up with a condition on the cost function that will guarantee this.

8.7 SUMMARY

A graph may be defined to be a set with a symmetric, irreflexive relation defined on it. In a sense, graphs are generalizations of trees, obtained by weakening the hierarchical structure of trees by allowing a position to have more than one immediate predecessor. We can consider a graph to be a tree with zero or more extra edges added, so we conclude that each graph contains at least one spanning tree, which contains all the vertices of the graph.

We saw three different representations of graphs—adjacency matrices, adjacency lists, and edge lists—and we saw that adjacency matrices can be used to count the number of paths, as well as the least-cost path, between any two vertices of a graph. Minimum spanning trees form the basis for a number of graph algorithms; Prim's algorithm is one way to find MSTs, and you will see another when we discuss sets in the next chapter. Prim's algorithm originally appeared as:

> "Shortest connection networks and some generalizations," *Bell System Technical Journal 36* (1957), 1389–1401.

Digraphs are generalizations of graphs, in which the edges have a direction, from one node to another. Dijkstra's algorithm uses a greedy strategy to find the least-cost path from a given vertex to any other in an edge-weighted digraph. See:

> "A note on two problems in connection with graphs," *Numerische Mathematik 1* (1959), 269–271.

We concluded with a discussion of the Traveling Salesperson Problem. This appears to be an innately hard problem; although it has not been proved to be hard, it is an NP-complete problem, so it is as hard as a large number of other problems (none of which have been proved to be hard). The genesis of NP-complete problems is:

Cook, S. "The complexity of theorem-proving procedures," *Proceedings of the 3rd Annual ACM Symposium on Theory of Computing*, Association for Computing Machinery, New York, 1971, 151–158.

A good introduction to the theory of computational complexity is

Garey, Michael R., and Johnson, David S. *Computers and Intractability: A Guide to the Theory of NP-Completeness*, W. H. Freeman, San Francisco, 1979.

8.8 EXERCISES

1. A graph G is said to have an **Eulerian cycle** if there is a cycle in G that contains each edge of G exactly once. The existence of a Eulerian cycle in a graph means that you can take a picture of the graph, place your pencil at one vertex, trace each edge exactly once without lifting your pencil from the graph, and return to the starting vertex, as in Figure 8.18. Find a graph with no Eulerian cycle, and discover a condition that must hold for a graph to have a Eulerian cycle.
2. Provide the best argument you can to support the contention that the ARPANET graph of Figure 8.1 is not planar.
3. What is the least number of colors necessary to color the ARPANET graph?
4. (a) Give an algorithm which colors a graph, by assigning to each vertex a number from 1 to n, in such a way that no two adjacent vertices have the same integer.
   (b) A far more challenging problem is to assign "colors" so that the least possible number are used. This is not hard to do if you simply try all possible assignments that use no more colors than n, where there are n vertices in the graph; the trick is to do it in time much less than n^n.
5. The adjacency matrix implementation of *DeleteVertex* given in the text could cause problems, since a program that uses *DeleteVertex* could then lose track of the correct references for the vertices (since if we deleted vertex 4 and moved the fourth row and column to fill

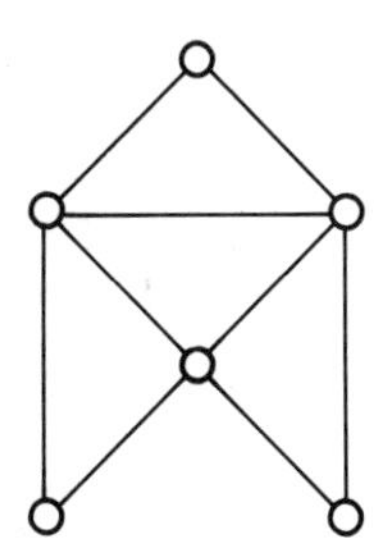

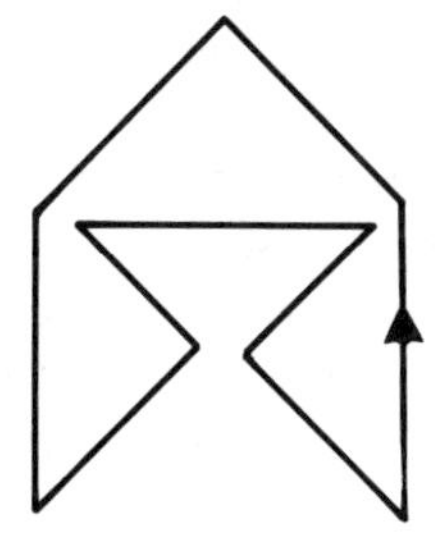

Figure 8.18 A graph and a Eulerian cycle.

the hole, all vertex numbers from 4 up would be off by one). Describe how you would deal with this problem.

6. Implement *DeleteEdge* for the edge list implementation of GRAPH.
7. Implement *DepthFirst* for adjacency matrices, and compare it in efficiency and ease of programming with the edge list implementation given in the text.
8. In running *DepthFirst* on graphs with n vertices, how deep could the recursive calls be nested? Demonstrate your result.
9. There is a very nice way to count the number of spanning trees a graph has. If e is an edge of G which is not a loop, define the *contraction* $G \cdot e$ to be the (multi)graph that results when we remove e from G and merge its end vertices into one. Below, we show a graph and two successive contractions. Notice that contracting an edge could lead to loops and multiple edges.

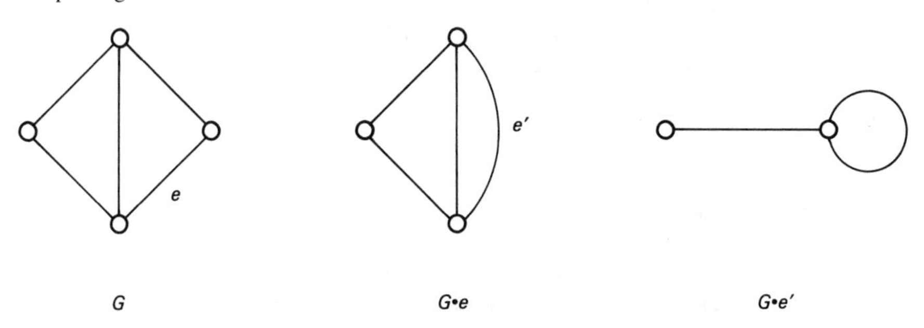

Further, define $G - e$ to be the graph that results if we simply remove edge e, without merging its endpoints. If we now let $t(G)$ be the number of spanning trees a graph G has, then t satisfies the recursive formula $t(G) = t(G \cdot e) + t(G - e)$, for any edge e that is not a loop.

   (a) Use this formula to count the number of spanning trees for the graph G above.
   (b) Draw all the spanning trees of the graph G above.
   (c) If a graph consists of just a simple cycle on n vertices, how many spanning trees does it have?
   (d) How many spanning trees does a tree have?
   (e) What data structure would you choose to implement an algorithm to count the number of spanning trees of a graph? It need not be one we have described.

10. For the graph of Figure 8.19, called **Petersen's graph**,
   (a) Find a depth-first spanning tree. So that everyone's answers are consistent, use the strategy that the nodes adjacent to a given node will be selected by alphabetical order.
   (b) Find a breadth-first spanning tree (same strategy as above).
   (c) Use Prim's algorithm to find a MST.
11. If a graph has the form of a binary tree, do depth-first or breadth-first traversals correspond in any way to preorder, inorder, or postorder traversals?
12. For which of the three representations of GRAPH is it easiest (or fastest) to
   (a) Tell whether two vertices are adjacent?
   (b) Tell whether an edge and a vertex are **incident** (i.e., whether the vertex is an endpoint of the edge)?
   (c) Count the number of edges in a graph?

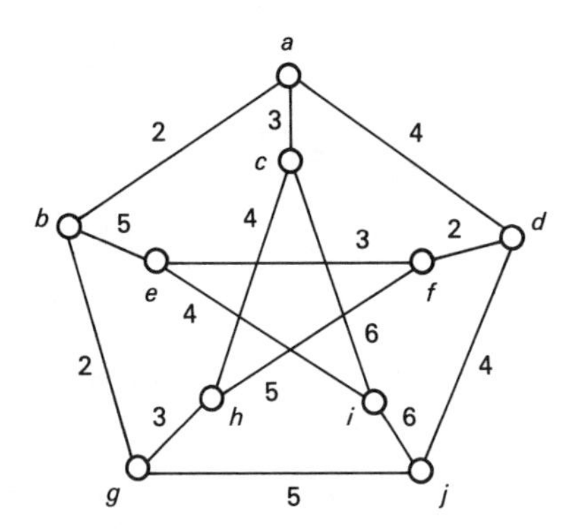

Figure 8.19 Petersen's graph, with weights.

(d) Decide whether a graph is connected?
(e) Decide whether a digraph is strongly connected?
(f) Implement Prim's algorithm?

13. (a) Write an algorithm to test whether a graph is connected.
(b) Write an algorithm to count the connected components of a graph.

14. Modify the matrix multiplication algorithm to compute *maximal* costs of travel between any two vertices of an edge-weighted graph.

15. The running time of Prim's algorithm depends on how fast we can find least-cost edges. Find a way to do this in $O(n)$ time, where n is the number of vertices of the graph.

16. In the exercises of Chapter 4 we discussed **finite automata (FA)**, which were simple abstractions of computers. One way of looking at finite automata is as a collection of **states**, along with **transition rules**, which describe how to change from one state to another, depending on the current input symbol to the finite automaton. One of the states is called the **start state**, since that's where the machine is at the start, and some of the states are called **final states**. A FA is said to **accept** an input string if it winds up in a final state after having processed the entire string. We can model a FA as a digraph, with vertices for states and edges for transitions. For example, the FA in Figure 8.20 accepts any string over the alphabet {a, b} which contains 'ab' as a substring, since, for example, the input string 'aaba' would start at state 1, read the first 'a' and move to state 3, read the second 'a' and move again to state 3, read the 'b' and move to state 4, and read the last 'a' and wind up in the (final) state 4, thereby accepting the input string.

Finite automata are frequently used as **lexical analyzers** in compilers, whose job it is to scan the source code and accept **tokens**, the smallest meaningful units in the source code language.

(a) Design a finite automaton which accepts any legal Pascal numbers, like 0, –45, 67.89, or –0.453e–2.
(b) Write an algorithm to accept legal Pascal numbers. This can be done by letting each state be represented by a procedure which gets an input character and calls another state procedure.

17. Trace the action of Dijkstra's algorithm on the digraph of Figure 8.15, to find least costs of travel from vertex b to all other vertices.

18. Give an example to show that Dijkstra's algorithm will not work properly if some of the edge weights are allowed to be negative.

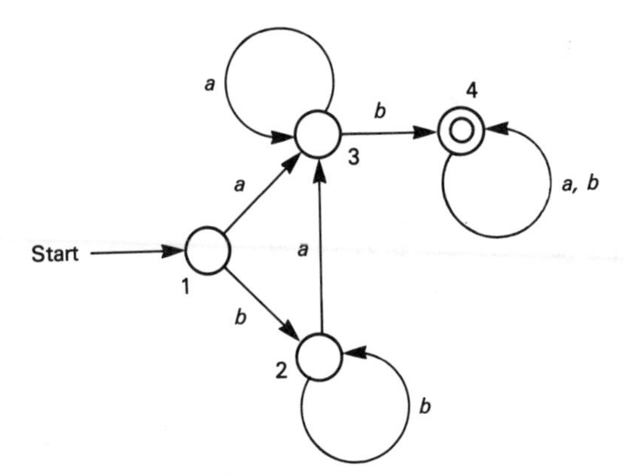

Figure 8.20 A finite automaton that accepts '. . . ab . . . ' .

19. If we had a graph that represented city streets, and the recommendation of the traffic bureau was to make all streets one-way, we would then say that we had the problem of changing a graph to a digraph. Of course, one requirement for our conversion would be that the digraph be strongly connected, since at a minimum we would like the citizens of the city to be able to travel from any location to any other. The following graph, for instance, could not be successfully translated to a digraph, since no matter how we directed the edges it would be impossible to travel legally both from a to b and back again.

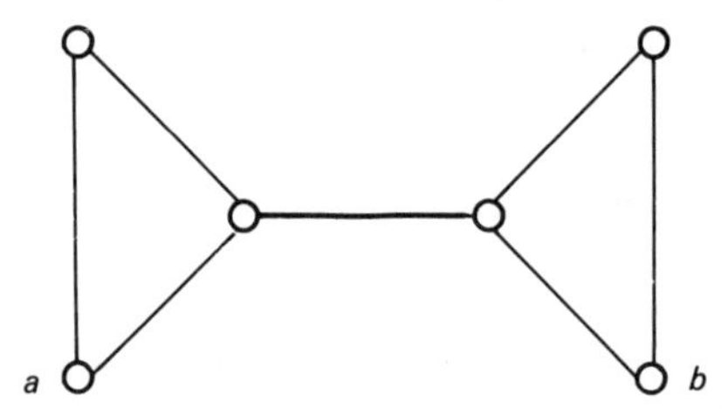

(a) Give a condition that is necessary for a graph to be transformed into a strongly connected digraph.

(b) Find an algorithm that assigns directions to the edges of a digraph in such a way as to make it strongly connected.

20. Show that the greedy algorithm for making change would not necessarily give the solution using the fewest number of coins if the coins used had values other than 1, 5, 10, 25, and 50.

21. Find an edge-weighted graph for which the greedy heuristic for TSP fails to give the least-cost cycle.

Programming Projects

22. Implement Prim's algorithm, using the data structure of your choice.

23. Write a program to determine whether a graph has any cycles. *Hint*: You might want to make use of a spanning tree.

24. Write a program to find all spanning trees of a graph. Try this on some "random" graphs to see if you can make an estimate of the number of spanning trees a graph on n vertices has.

25. Write a program to find a solution for TSP. It wouldn't hurt to go to the library for this one. By the way, if your algorithm runs in polynomial time, let me know.

26. Write a program that finds a "pretty good" solution to TSP. One possibility would be to find any simple cycle at all that includes all vertices and try to modify the cycle to one of less cost, as follows:

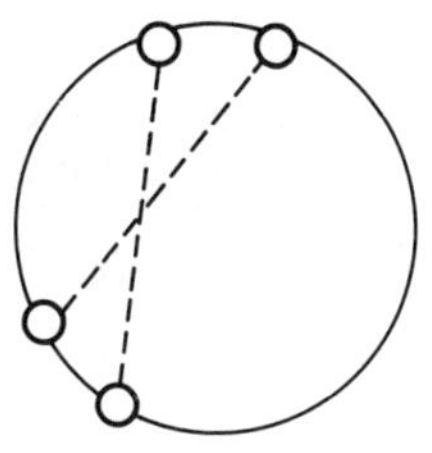

If your cycle has any "internal" edges like these,

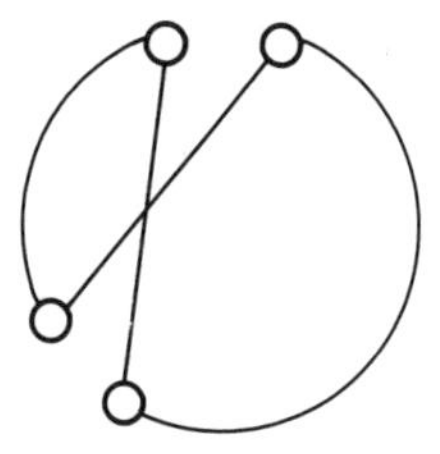

see if this cycle is any cheaper.

9

Sets

Pack, herd, pride, flock, skein, gaggle, pod, school—
we all belong somewhere, don't we, Rat?

Mary Tenant, *Peter Rat's Education*

We have come to the end of our tour of abstract data types. We began with the most highly structured sets of positions when we talked about lists, and we passed to more complicated structures by gradually removing the restrictions on the structural relations until we came to digraphs, on which the structural relations had no restrictive conditions whatsoever. At each stage, we saw that the earlier structures could be viewed as special cases of the later ones: Lists are trees with no branching, and trees are connected digraphs with at most one edge leading into each vertex. It seems that there is no place to go from here—we have, with digraphs, already taken away all restrictions on the structure on the set of positions, and allowed the structural relation to be any relation at all. In our final step, we will transcend structure completely, and deal with an ADT that treats all positions equally.

In the very first chapter, we talked about the abstract object we could use to deal with hands in a game of bridge. If you imagine a hand of cards, you can see that there is an underlying order on the atoms (that is, on the cards themselves), but that a collection of thirteen particular cards is effectively the same, no matter how you decide to arrange them in your hand. In other words, when dealing with bridge hands, we have no need for any structure at all, except to keep track of how many cards we have. The cards themselves are important; their arrangement is not.

9.1 THE SET ADT

The abstract data type **SET** is, as usual, made up of three sets: POSITION, ATOM, and a set of elements of the form (P, R, v) where P is a finite subset of POSITION, R is the **empty relation**, for which $x\ R\ y$ is not defined for any $x, y \in P$, and $v : P \rightarrow ATOM$ is the usual evaluation function. There are quite a few SET operations, which we have divided into three categories for convenience.

Set Assignments

1. **Create**(**var** S : SET) makes S equal to the empty set $\varnothing$, that is, the set with no elements.
2. **Union**(A, B : SET ; **var** C : SET) makes C equal to $A \cup B$, so that a position p is in C if and only if it is in A or B, or perhaps in both. For example, if we are dealing with sets of integers, then $\{3, 19, 8, 4\} \cup \{5, 3, 22\} = \{3, 4, 5, 8, 19, 22\}$.
3. **Intersection** (A, B : SET ; **var** C : SET) makes C equal to $A \cap B$, so that a position p is in C if and only if it is in both A and B. For the two sets of the example above, we have $\{3, 19, 8, 4\} \cup \{5, 3, 22\} = \{3\}$.
4. **Difference**(A, B : SET ; **var** C : SET) makes C equal to the set difference $A - B$, so that $p \in A - B$ if and only if p is a member of A but is not a member of B. Unlike *Union* and *Intersection*, set difference is not symmetric, so $\{3, 19, 8, 4\} - \{5, 3, 22\} = \{19, 8, 4\}$, but $\{5, 3, 22\} - \{3, 19, 8, 4\} = \{5, 22\}$.
5. **Copy**(A : SET ; **var** B : SET) sets B equal to A.
6. **Merge**(A, B : SET ; **var** C : SET) is a special case of *Union*, which sets C to $A \cup B$ but assumes that A and B are **disjoint**, namely that they have no elements in common. This operation is invariably used with a collection of sets that **partition** some universal set U, which is to say that there is a collection $S_1, \ldots, S_n$ of sets such that $S_i \cap S_j = \varnothing$, for all $1 \le i, j \le n$, and $S_1 \cup S_2 \cup \ldots \cup S_n = \varnothing$. For example, the integers may be partitioned into two sets, the even integers and the odd integers.
7. **Insert**(a : ATOM ; **var** S : SET) is another special case of *Union*, in which a single-element set, $\{a\}$, is joined to S. In (P, R, v) terms, a new position, $p \notin P$, is added to P, and the evaluation function is extended by including the mapping $v(p) = a$.
8. **Delete**(a : ATOM ; **var** S : SET) is the single-element version of *Difference*, which removes atom a from the set S. This requires the precondition that the atom be in the set, and otherwise generally takes no action.

Predicates

9. **Member**(a : ATOM ; S : SET) : boolean returns *true* if the atom a is in the set S, otherwise returns *false*.

10. **Subset**(A, B : SET) : boolean returns *true* if and only if *A* is a subset of *B*, which is to say, if every element of *A* is also an element of *B*.

11. **Equal**(A, B : SET) : boolean returns *true* if and only if *A* and *B* have exactly the same elements. Notice that we could define *Equal* in terms of *Subset*, since two sets are equal if and only if they are subsets of each other.

Atomic Assignments

12. **Retrieve**(k : KeyType ; S : SET ; **var** a : ATOM) returns the atom *a* in set *S* which has key field equal to *k*. This procedure is used when the atoms are structured types with one field of type *KeyType*, and assumes the precondition that there is a unique atom with key field *k* in the set *S*.

13. **Update**(k : KeyType ; **var** S : SET ; a : ATOM) changes the atom in *S* with key field *k* to the new value *a*. This, like *Retrieve*, assumes that there is a unique atom with key field *k* in *S*.

14. **Find**(k : KeyType ; **var** S : SET) is used when dealing with a partition of disjoint sets, and returns the set *S* containing the atom with key field *k*.

15. **Min**(S : SET ; **var** a : ATOM) is used when there is a linear order on the atoms, and sets *a* equal to the atom with least value (or smallest key field, if the atoms are structured) in the set *S*.

Although we have defined fifteen SET operations, it is almost never the case that an application will require all of them. Typically, packages are designed around a smaller collection of the operations, and an implementation is chosen that is particularly efficient for that collection. We will begin our investigation of SET implementations with one which we have mentioned twice already, one which in some cases makes the SET operations as fast as possible.

9.2 BIT VECTORS AND ORDINAL SETS

If we are lucky enough to have a set ATOM that is (1) fairly small and (2) linearly ordered, then we can make use of a very simple and fast implementation of SET. We do this by representing each subset of ATOM by a bit vector of boolean values (which we will represent here with 1 denoting *true* and 0 denoting *false*), and indexing the array by the linear order on ATOM. We then would interpret such an array as representing the set consisting of all those elements that had a 1 in the corresponding array entry. For example, if we considered ATOM to be the days of the week, we could implement the subsets of the days of the week by using Pascal user-defined ordinal types, and defining an array indexed by this type, as follows:

```
type
   ATOM = (Sun, Mon, Tue, Wed, Thu, Fri, Sat);
   SET = array [ATOM] of boolean;          {Why won't this work in Pascal?}
```

	Sun	Mon	Tue	Wed	Thu	Fri	Sat
weekDays =	0	1	1	1	1	1	0

Figure 9.1 A bit vector representation for days of the week.

With this implementation, the subset of weekdays would take the form given in Figure 9.1, and we would understand that the bit pattern 0111110 represented that set. The nicest feature of this implementation is that the set operations correspond directly to boolean operations on the elements of the bit vectors. For example, to find the union of two sets represented by bit vectors A and B, all we need to realize is that their union, C, has a *true* in array element i if and only if $A[i]$ or $B[i]$ is true. This assignment of a value for C, then, is nothing but C[*i*] := A[*i*] **or** B[*i*], done for all values of i in the universal set ATOM. We next list some of the SET operations in this implementation:

```
type
   ATOM = {some ordinal type};
   SET = array [ATOM] of boolean;             {This still won't work in Pascal}

procedure Create(var S : SET);
   var index : ATOM;
begin
   for index := first ATOM to last ATOM do{first and last in the linear order on ATOM}
      S[index] := false
end;

procedure Union(A, B : SET ; var C : SET);
   var index : ATOM;
begin
   for index := first ATOM to last ATOM do
      C[index] := A[index] or B[index]
end;

procedure Intersection(A, B : SET ; var C : SET);
   var index : ATOM;
begin
   for index := first ATOM to last ATOM do
      C[index] := A[index] and B[index]
end;

procedure Difference(A, B : SET ; var C : SET);
   var index : ATOM;
begin
   for index := first ATOM to last ATOM do
      C[index] := A[index] and not B[index]
end;

procedure Insert(a : ATOM ; var S : SET);
begin
   S[a] := true
end;
```

```
function Member(a : ATOM ; S : SET) : boolean;
begin
   Member := S[a]
end;

function Subset(A, B : SET) : boolean;
{Returns true if and only if A is a subset of B}
   var
      index : ATOM;
      okSoFar : boolean;
begin
   okSoFar := true;
   for index := first ATOM to last ATOM do
      if A[index] and not B[index] then { index is in A but not in B }
         okSoFar := false;
   Subset := okSoFar
end;
```

In this implementation, *Insert, Delete*, and *Member* run in constant time, while all the other operations take time $O(n)$, where n is the (fixed) size of the universal set ATOM. The operations *Retrieve* and *Update* are not included in this implementation, since they both are designed with the assumption that the elements of ATOM will have a more complex structure than the simple ordinal types used here. You can see that this is a fairly efficient package, especially when the size of the universal set is small. One could raise a minor quibble that, like the array implementations of STRING and LIST, a set must take the same amount of room in memory whether it is empty or equal to the entire universal set, but if we can somehow write our operations so that each array entry takes a single bit, the arrays will be quite small, so the amount of wasted memory will be negligible, except for gigantic universal sets (which is why some implementations of Pascal that rely on bit vector representations of sets do not allow the type declaration "**set of** integer").

This implementation is even better suited to assembler language than to a high-level language like Pascal, for two reasons. First, when using a high-level language, we are at the mercy of the compiler for that language and of the particular machine on which we are working, with the result that we cannot guarantee that the bit vectors will be packed efficiently with one bit per array element. In fact, many compliers will use one byte or even a full word for a boolean value, thereby sacrificing much of the space efficiency we would like to have. Second, when we write in a low-level language, we can make easy use of the fact that on many machines logical operations are "wired in" so that we can, for instance, OR the bits of two entire words of 8, 16, or 32 bits all at once, and not have to program the bitwise array traversal which we used for *Union*. In this case, *all* of the operations run in (a very small) constant time, if we restrict the universal set to be one that has no more elements than there are bits in a word. Because of the inherent speed of bit vector operations, some computers have been specifically designed as **bit vector machines**, capable of operating on very long bit vectors in parallel, in a manner similar to the way other computers do on single words. Such machines are not only suitable for set operations, but are also particularly well suited for fast arithmetic on very large integers (such as factoring or testing whether a large number is prime).

Sets Represented by Sorted Lists

If we have a universal set that is large, or if the elements of the sets we must deal with are structured, but can still be ordered by a key field, we could decide to represent sets by linked lists, with their elements sorted by keys. This choice of representation of one ADT by another is something we have seen several times already: We could use a binary search tree to implement lists or sorted lists, and we have used arrays to implement priority queues. This representation of sets as linked lists has the advantage that each set requires no more room than is actually required for the elements of the sets (and the linking pointers), and places no immediate upper limit on the size of the universal set. We do have to pay for this extensibility, however, since some of the operations now take longer than they did in the bit vector implementation.

If we just used linked lists, without requiring that the lists be sorted, it is not difficult to see that it could take $O(n^2)$ time to find the union, intersection, or difference of two sets with n elements, since we would need to test each element in one set against all the elements in the other set. By using sorted lists, however, we can reduce the time of these operations to $O(n)$. To find the intersection of two sorted lists, for instance, all we need to do is traverse the two lists together, looking for a match between the two current elements. If they match, then the current value is appended to the output list; if they don't, then the current position with the smaller value is incremented to the next position. This process is repeated until one of the lists is used up. We describe this implementation in terms of the LIST operations below.

The operations that deal with individual atoms are the biggest losers in this implementation, since to *Insert* or *Delete* an atom or test for membership now requires time $O(n)$ on lists of size n, because we must make a linear search in the list to find the atom or to find the proper position for the atom, whereas these operations ran in constant time in the bit vector implementation. As we remarked before, we could use arrays, rather than linked lists, for our lists; but then, while it takes only $O(\log n)$ time to find the position of an atom, it still takes $O(n)$ time to insert or delete the element. This kind of implementation, then, would be well suited for sets that were static, or nearly so, requiring fairly few insertions or deletions. We could, of course, do as we did in Chapter 6 and implement the lists (hence the sets) as binary search trees, but while they make insertion, deletion, and testing for membership run in $O(\log n)$ time, it now is less clear how to implement union, intersection, and difference. Later on in this chapter we will return to trees (actually to structures that are more like upside-down trees) and show how to make some of these operations really zip along.

```
type
   SET = SORTED_LIST {of ATOMs};  {Illegal in Pascal}

procedure Intersection(A, B : SET ; var C : SET);
{Sorted linked list implementation of SET intersection}
   type
      MoveType = (Apos, Bpos, both);          {which position to increment}
   var
      currentA, currentB : POSITION;          {in the respective lists}
      valueA, valueB : ATOM;                  {or key within the atom, if necessary}
      done : boolean;
      move : MoveType;
begin
   Create(C);
   if (not Empty(A)) and (not Empty(B)) then begin
      currentA := First(A);
      currentB := First(B);
      done := false;

      while not done do begin
         valueA := Retrieve(currentA, A);
         valueB := Retrieve(currentB, B);
         if valueA = valueB then begin        {found a match, insert into C}
            InsertAfter(valueA, Last(C), C);
            move := both                      {and increment both positions}
         end else if valueA < valueB then
            move := Apos                      {increment position with smaller value}
         else
            move := Bpos;

         if (move = both) or (move = Apos) then {increment the A position, if possible}
            if currentA = Last(A) then
               done := true                   {can't increment, so we're done}
            else
               currentA := Next(currentA, A);

         if (move = both) or (move = Bpos) then {increment the B position, if possible}
            if currentA = Last(B) then
               done := true
            else
               currentA := Next(currentB, B);
      end
   end
end;
```

9.3 HASHING

We remarked at the start of this chapter that often there are applications that do not require all of the set operations. Consider, for instance, the problem of maintaining a collection of payroll records of employees of a company. This is certainly a problem for the SET data type, since there would likely not be any structure on the employees (such as who is the immediate supervisor of whom) that would be of any interest to the people in the payroll office. In this case we have just one set, and the set assignment operations *Union, Intersection,* and *Difference* would not need to be implemented to maintain this data. Another example of such a one-set structure would be the **symbol table** of a compiler, which is used to keep track of the constant, type, and variable names of a source code program. This situation arises often enough in practice that it has been abstracted into an ADT of its own.

Definition. The **DICTIONARY** ADT is a subtype of SET, having the same structure (or lack thereof) as SET, and including the operations *Create, Insert, Delete,* and *Member* (and, in some implementations, *Retrieve* and *Update*). In a dictionary, it is usually the case that the set elements are structured types, which are accessed by reference to a key field.

Suppose, for instance, that we were to write a payroll package, and we wished to be able to access an employee's record by the name of the employee. We know that array access is fast, but only if we know the index of an element in the array. In this case, if we stored the records in an array, we might not have any clue to where in the array Erasmus Fleagle's record would reside. The best we could do would be to order the records alphabetically by name and perform a binary search on the name key. This is logarithmically fast but, as we know, insertion is slow. What we would like would be a function, h, that would act as an oracle, so that h applied to the string 'Erasmus Fleagle' would return the index in the array where that person's record was located.

Of course, the most direct way would be to index the array by all possible names, so the indices would run from 'A', 'B', . . . , 'Z', 'Aa', 'Ab', . . . , 'Zz', 'Aaa', 'Aab', . . . , and so on, up to, say, 'Zzzzzzzzzz'. In this case the function h would not be needed at all (or could be the identity function), since we would only need to go directly to location 'Erasmus Fleagle' in the array to find the record we wanted. It takes no thought at all to become convinced that this isn't a practical scheme, because (1) it's not clear how to index an array that way; (2) a *lot* of space would be wasted on indices that couldn't possibly correspond to Earthly names, like 'Ygxwq'; and (3) because of the wasted space, such an array would have to be larger than the memory of any computer yet built.

A much better idea would be to let h take a name as input, add the ASCII values of the characters of the name, and return the sum **mod** n, where n is the size of the array. For example, suppose we had a table with 120 entries, indexed from 0 to 119. We could take the name 'JONES' and form the sum of the character values 'J' $\rightarrow$ 74, 'O' $\rightarrow$ 79, 'N' $\rightarrow$ 78, 'E' $\rightarrow$ 69, and 'S' $\rightarrow$ 83, to obtain $(74 + 79 + 78 + 69 + 83) = 383$ **mod**

120 = 23, so that the record for 'JONES' would reside in array location 23. What we have done is to transform the problem of array access by name to a process that works almost as fast as bit vector access, by processing the name through h to produce an index in the array. Such a function, which transforms keys to array indices, is called a **hash function**, presumably because we are chopping the name into bits and than reassembling the bits into something palatable, as we do with corned beef hash.

We do not need to limit ourselves to hashing on strings, of course. We could equally well hash on a key field of any type, as long as we could come up with a good way to transform the key to an array index. We could hash on employee birthdays, for instance, by computing the day of the year the person was born, and using a table with 365 entries (ignoring those people who were born on February 29, one supposes). The problem with these hash functions is that they lead to **collisions**, in which several keys hash to the same location. In the preceding name hash, for instance, it is easy to verify that 'QUARRELS' and 'STEEN' both hash to 23, as did 'JONES'. This problem is often exacerbated by poor choice of hash function, like the one that takes the first two letters of a person's last name and uses them to compute a number from 0 to 675 by the rule

$$26 * (\text{first letter order} - 1) + (\text{second letter order} - 1)$$

where the "order" of a letter is its position in alphabetical order. In other words, 'AA' would hash to 0, 'AD' would hash to 3, and 'BA' would hash to 26. This is a poor hash function since, first, there are many names that begin with the same two letters, and second, there are many two-letter combinations that are not likely to be the start of any name, like 'QX'. Clearly, we want a hash function that "randomizes" its output as much as possible.

Even if we have a good hash function, we are still not out of trouble. Suppose we decided to hash on birthdays within a year. If we had a table with 365 entries, you might guess that we could fill the table nearly half full before we would have to worry about coming up with two people with the same birthday. Try it the next time you are in a smallish group of people; the results may be surprising. It turns out that with 23 people, it is slightly better than even money that two of them have the same birthday; with 40 people, the odds rise to about ten to one in favor of duplicate birthdays. (In introductory probability texts, this is sometimes mentioned as an easy way to make money by betting. We suspect, however, that the odds of a person in the group having heard of this **birthday paradox** rise even faster as a function of the size of the group than do the odds of a duplicate birthday.) If you are interested, the probability that among n people at least two of them will have the same birthday (if we make the slightly incorrect simplifying assumption that it is equally likely for people to be born on any day) is

$$1 - \frac{(365)(364)(363)\ldots(366-n)}{365^n}$$

Given that collisions are inevitable in any hashing scheme (except in cases where the size of the table is larger than the total number of elements to be inserted, and then only when the hash function is carefully chosen), we need to have a **collision resolution strategy** to handle collisions when they occur. The simplest strategy is **linear resolution**: If $h(x)$, for some key x, points to a location that is already occupied, inspect the next location in the array. If that location is full, try the one after that, and so on, until we discover a vacant location or find that the **hash table**, as the array is called, is completely full. As a simple example, suppose that the elements to be stored had integer keys and that the hash function was $h(x) = x \textbf{ mod } 7$. If the integers 23, 14, 9, 6, 30, 12, and 18 were to be inserted in that order into a table T, with indices $0, \ldots, 6$, we would have the following steps, illustrated in Figure 9.2.

1. $h(23) = 2$, so the element with key 23 would be stored in $T[2]$.
2. $h(14) = 0$, so the element with key 14 would be stored in $T[0]$.
3. $h(9) = 2$, but $T[2]$ is already occupied, so the element with key 9 would be stored in $T[3]$.
4. $h(6) = 6$, so the element with key 6 would be stored in $T[6]$.
5. $h(30) = 2$, but both $T[2]$ and $T[3]$ are occupied, so the element with key 30 would be stored in $T[4]$.
6. $h(12) = 5$, so the element with key 12 would be stored in $T[5]$.
7. $h(18) = 4$, but $T[4]$, $T[5]$, and $T[6]$ are occupied, so we "wrap around" the array indices, and go back to $T[0]$, which is also occupied, so the element with key 18 would finally be stored in $T[1]$.

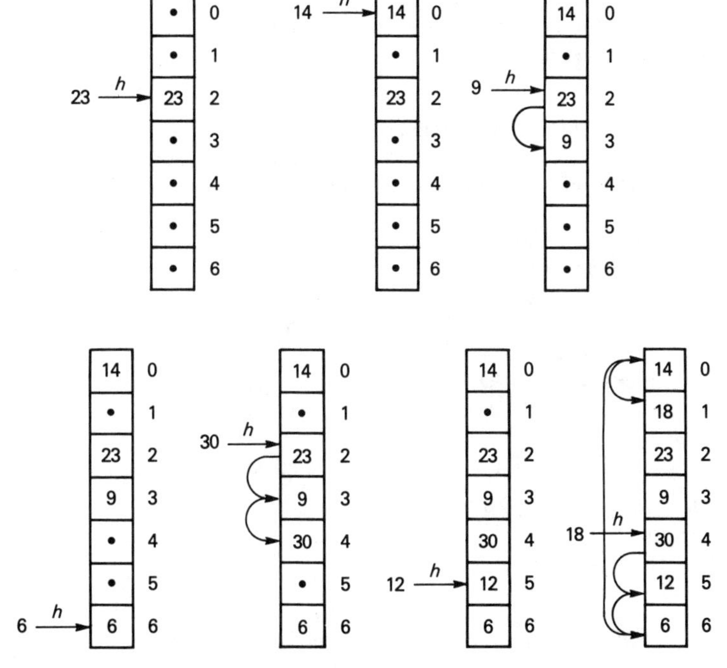

Figure 9.2 Hashing with linear resolution of collisions.

We can count that it took 14 **probes** into the hash table to fill it in this example: 7 initial probes to hash the elements into the table, and 7 further probes to resolve the collisions. We will return to the question of the number of probes required to insert or find an element later, but before we do, we will implement the DICTIONARY ADT using a hash table.

In this implementation, we will use a hash table with entries indexed from 0 to some positive integer, *MAX*. Initially, each entry of the array will contain a record with a key field equal to an element, *EMPTY*, which is clearly distinguishable from any "real" key. For instance, if the keys were strings representing people's names, we could choose *EMPTY* to be a string of blanks. As you will see, deletion is made simpler if we replace the deleted item with one with another phony key, *GONE*, which is also easily distinguishable from any real key, and also from the *EMPTY* pseudokey. We might, for instance, use '??????????' as our *GONE* key in the preceding example, since there is no way that a string of question marks could possibly be confused with the name of a person. We will use linear resolution of collisions, so to insert an element all we need to do is hash the key into the table and see if the table entry is *EMPTY* or *GONE*. If that is the case, we insert the element where it belongs; otherwise, we look at the next entry in the table, and the one after that (wrapping around to the start of the table when we reach the end), and so on, until we find an *EMPTY* or *GONE* entry, where we may place the element to be inserted. We see that the table will, after several insertions, come to consist of several **clusters** of contiguous entries, consisting of "real" data or *GONE* pseudodata, with each cluster separated by one or more *EMPTY* elements.

To test for membership, we need only make an initial probe into the location where the atom should be, and, if we do not find it there, inspect consecutive cells until we come to the end of a cluster, upon which we know that the atom with the given key could not be in the table.

```
const
   MAX = {the largest table index};
   EMPTY = {some key value to indicate empty slots};
   GONE = {some key value to indicate slots from which elements were deleted};
type
   KeyType = {something upon which we can hash};
   ATOM = record
               key : KeyType;
               {Other data fields, if any, go here}
            end;
   Bucket = 0 . . MAX;
   DICTIONARY = array [Bucket] of ATOM;
var
   T : DICTIONARY; {Global variable for the hash table}

function Hash(k : KeyType) : Bucket;
begin
   Hash := {some definition}
end;
```

Create is simplicity itself. We initialize the hash table by placing an *EMPTY* pseudokey in each entry (called a **bucket**) of the array.

```
procedure Create(var T : DICTIONARY);
    var index : Bucket;
begin
    for index := 0 to MAX do
        T[index].key := EMPTY
end;
```

The definition of *Member* is somewhat complicated, largely because it does several things at once. Given a key, *k*, this routine looks in the hash table at the cluster where *k* should be located. If an atom with that key resides in the cluster, the procedure sets *found* to *true*, and returns *index* equal to the array index wherein that key was found. That is the predicate part of the definition, and some authors define *Member* as a function that only returns *found*. We chose to return the index as well, since that would make the definitions of *Retrieve* and *Update* easier, if we decided to implement them. Also, since we intend to use *Member* to define *Insert*, we designed *Member* so that if the key was not found, *index* would be set equal to the earliest location in the cluster where the key could be inserted, that is, the earliest *GONE* cell, if there is one, and to the *EMPTY* cell at the end of the cluster, if there is no *GONE* cell to be found. Finally, if the hash table is completely full, there will be no place to insert the key, so *full* is set to *true* and *index* is undefined.

```
procedure Member(k : KeyType; T : DICTIONARY ; var index : Bucket ;
                         var found, full : boolean);
    var
        probe, place: Bucket;
begin
    probe := Hash(k);
    index := probe;
    if T[index].key = k then          {lucky us, we found the key on the first probe}
        found := true

    else begin
        full := true;                 {no place to insert yet}
        repeat                        {search for the key, or a place to put it}
            index := (index + 1) mod (MAX + 1); {cycle through the table}

            if full and (( T[index].key = GONE) or ( T[index].key = EMPTY)) then begin
                full := false;
                place := index        {record the first available location for insertion}
            end
        until ( T[index].key = EMPTY) or (T[index].key = k) or (index = probe);

        if T[index].key = k then {mark that we found the key}
            found := true
        else begin          {not found, return where it could go, if any place available}
            found := false;
            index := place
        end
    end
end;
```

Having defined *Member*, it is easy to define *Insert*. If the key is not found and the table is not full, then we insert the atom with its key into the table; otherwise, we take appropriate action, warning the operator that there is already a value with the given key in the table, or warning that the table is full.

```
procedure Insert(a : ATOM ; var T : DICTIONARY);
   var
      index : Bucket;
      found, full : boolean;
begin
   Member(a.key, T, index, found, full);
   if not found then
      if full then
         writeln('Hash table is full, no room to insert')
      else
         T[index] := a
   else
      writeln('Attempted to insert duplicate key')
end;
```

Deletion is as simple as insertion. We test whether there is an element in the table with the correct key, and if there is we replace that element with *GONE*.

```
procedure Delete(k : KeyType ; var T : DICTIONARY);
   var
      index : Bucket;
      found, full : boolean;
begin
   Member(k, index, found, full);
   if found then
      T[index].key = GONE
   else
      writeln('Attempted to delete non-existent key')
end;
```

It might seem at first glance that we are going to unnecessary lengths with deletion. Why not simply replace the deleted element by *EMPTY*? The problem with that scheme is that in doing so we have separated a cluster into two, and we test for membership by testing all the entries in the cluster where the key should be, stopping at the first *EMPTY* cell. Suppose, for instance, that we had inserted 'JONES', 'QUARRELS', and 'STEEN', in that order, using the "good" hash function we defined previously. The hash table might then take the following form:

```
. . .    . . .
T[23]    'JONES'
T[24]    'QUARRELS'
T[25]    'STEEN'
T[26]    '        ' {i.e., EMPTY }
```

Then, after deleting 'QUARRELS' and replacing it (incorrectly) with *EMPTY*, we would have

...	...
T[23]	'JONES'
T[24]	' '
T[25]	'STEEN'
T[26]	' '

Then a membership test for 'STEEN' would stop at the end of the first cluster, at index 24, and report (incorrectly) failure to find the key, because linear resolution of collisions never inserts an element beyond an *EMPTY* cell.

Open Hashing

The hashing strategy we have just described is known as **closed hashing**. One of the problems associated with closed hashing is **primary clustering**, where clusters are formed when several elements whose keys hash to the same value are inserted into the table. Primary clustering, though difficult to eliminate entirely, can be alleviated to a degree by choosing a hash function that "randomizes" the hash values as much as possible. As a consequence of primary clustering, we may also experience **secondary clustering**, caused by inserting keys that do not hash to the value that caused the primary cluster, but nevertheless hash to values that are already in a cluster (because of resolution of collisions in the earlier insertions). Secondary clustering, then, arises from the coalescing of primary clusters. We will discuss later some techniques for lessening clustering in closed hashing, but now we will consider a technique that sidesteps clustering entirely, exchanging it for a different problem.

What we will do is not resolve collisions at all. If a key hashes into an occupied bucket, we will simply place it in the bucket, along with the values that are already there. This technique, known as **open hashing**, is usually accomplished by using a linked list for every bucket, accessed by pointers in the hash table, as illustrated in Figure 9.3. Notice that in this implementation, we no longer have any need for either the *EMPTY* or the *GONE* marker. The end of a cluster is just the last element in the linked list; to delete an element, all we need to do is remove it from the linked list.

Although the figure shows one-way linked lists, we could, of course, use any of the list techniques available to us, like doubly linked lists or arrays. In fact, since there is no structure on the elements in a bucket, we see that any of the SET implementations would serve to implement the buckets. We could use binary search trees, since that would speed insertion and deletion, or we could even have each bucket be a small hash table itself. Most of the time, however, we should be content with a linked-list open hash table that has a fixed constant k times as many entries as there are buckets, so that access to a bucket via the hashing function takes constant time, and membership testing, insertion, and deletion take $O(k)$ time, on the average, since the average number of entries per bucket is k. In other words, as long as the elements are fairly evenly spread

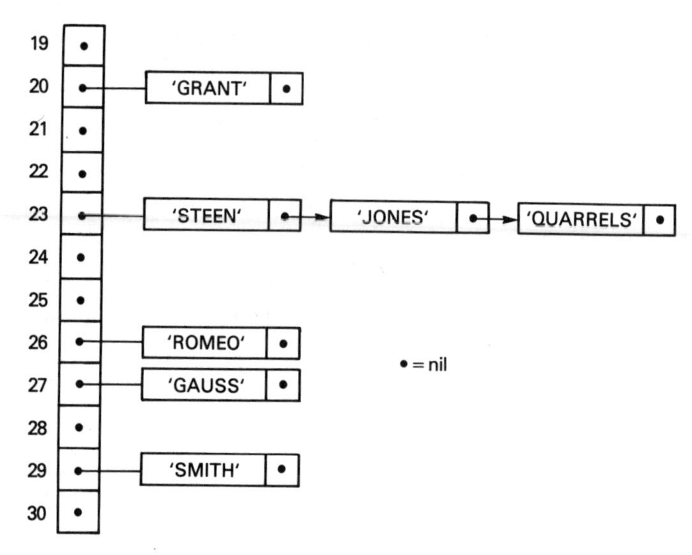

Figure 9.3 Open hashing.

through the buckets, all of the operations should run in constant time. You should have no difficulty defining the DICTIONARY operations for this implementation, using the LIST primitives.

9.4 HASHING, CONTINUED

In this section we will discuss, often without proof, a number of refinements and technical details of hashing. Because hashing is such an efficient technique, it has been widely studied and applied. We will not be able to do much more than provide a brief tour of the copious literature on the subject; those of you who are still hungry for information at the end should refer to the sources listed in the summary at the end of this chapter.

Hash Functions

Hashing is well suited for the SET ADT, since a good hash function should spread the keys throughout the hash table in some nearly random fashion. If you consider the example we have been using throughout the chapter, it is not difficult to see that the table entries are not listed in alphabetic order, and, in fact, any order of the keys should be pretty well destroyed by hashing. In one sense, hashing is the opposite of sorting, in that sorting takes randomly distributed keys and places them in linear order, while hashing takes a collection of strings, say, with their usual lexicographic order, and distributes them randomly in the hash table.

When designing a hash function, then, we would like it to have the property that any pattern among the keys should be destroyed by the hash function. Consider, for example, the hash function we have used throughout the chapter. To hash on a name, we add the ASCII values of the characters in the name, and take that sum **mod** the size of the hash table. Of course, if the table is small, there will be vastly more possible names than there are buckets, so some collisions will be inevitable. A further disadvantage to this scheme comes from the fact that the hash function makes use only of the characters in the name, not their positions. In other words, names that are permutations of each other, like 'ADAMS', 'MASAD', and 'DAMAS' would necessarily hash to the same value. A general rule is that *a hash function should make use of all of the information about the keys, and seek to eliminate any patterns that might exist within the set of possible keys.*

As an example, suppose we wished to design a hash function on ten-character strings. One possibility would be to group the characters into five pairs, convert each pair into a base-27 number by alphabetic numbering ('A' → 0, . . . , 'Z' → 25, blank → 26), add all the pairs to form a number, square that number, and then return the fourth through sixth digits from the left of the square. That certainly sounds as if it should mix things up pretty well. Now let's look at an example. We'll use the name 'SWIFT_TOM_' as our test string.

1. Break the name into pairs: 'SW', 'IF', 'T_', 'TO', 'M_'.
2. Convert to base-27 numbers:
   'SW' → 27 ∗ 18 + 22 = 502 (18 is the order of 'S', 22 is the order of 'W').
   'IF' → 27 ∗ 8 + 5 = 221.
   'T_' → 27 ∗ 19 + 26 = 539.
   'TO' → 27 ∗ 19 + 14 = 527.
   'M_' → 27 ∗ 12 + 26 = 350.
3. Add the numbers: 502 + 221 + 539 + 527 + 350 = 2,145.
4. Square the number: $2{,}145^2$ = 4,601,025.
5. Return the "middle" digits: 601.

So for this function, *h*('SWIFT_TOM_') = 601. Notice that we haven't eliminated the permutation problem entirely. If the even-place letters are permuted, we will still wind up with the same hash value. Also, we have no guarantee that this function will indeed spread the hash values for all names uniformly through the interval 0, . . . , 999. Trying to prove that it does seems pretty nearly impossible, so if we were really serious about maximizing the efficiency of our hash function, we should test this function on, say, several thousand phone book entries, to see that we don't have any unpleasant surprises (like 20 percent of the names hashing to 331). It does have, however, another property that a good hash function should have, as set forth in the maxim: *A hash function must be fast, or it is worthless.*

Suppose now that we have integer keys, or at least keys that have somehow been converted to integers, as we did before. Even assuming that the integers are nicely randomized, we still have the problem of fitting them into the table, using all of the table in as uniform a way as possible. The easiest way is to "fold" the integers into the table by hashing an integer n into array location n **mod** B, where B is the number of buckets in the table. This certainly is easy to compute, but it could lead to a large amount of primary clustering if we weren't sure that the original integers were truly random in their distribution. For instance, if B had many small factors (like $B = 120$, as we chose for our example), then there would be a good chance that numbers in arithmetic progression would fold to the same index.

A better way involves a less obvious hash function that adds another stir to the pot and mixes up the integer keys even better. Choose r to be a real number between 0 and 1 and define the hash function

$$h(x) = \lfloor B(xr \textbf{ mod } 1) \rfloor,$$

where $\lfloor A \rfloor$ represents the greatest integer that is less than or equal to A, and A **mod** 1 is just the fractional part of A (so that $A = \lfloor A \rfloor + (A \textbf{ mod } 1)$, as long as $A \geq 0$). The reason that this works well is a bit obscure, as is the choice of a good value for r. It turns out that a particularly good choice for r is either $(\sqrt{5}-1)/2$, or 1 minus that number, which is to say either 0.6180339887 or 0.3819660113. This technique is called **Fibonacci hashing**.

Finally, it happens that both of these hash functions work best when the table size B is taken to be a prime number that is not too close to a power of 2 (or whatever base is used to store numbers on the computer you are using). For binary computers, some good choices for B are 13, 23, 47, 97, 193, 383, 769, 1,531, 3,067, 6,143, 12,289, and 24,571.

Collision Resolution, Again

The speed of access into a closed hash table is directly related to the number of probes we must make to find, insert, or delete an element. If we can be sure that the number of probes required by an operation will remain no more than some fixed constant, then all the operations will run in constant time, and we can't hope for anything better than that. The number of probes required by an operation clearly depends on the amount of clustering in the hash table. In order to appreciate the effects of clustering, consider the hash table of Figure 9.4. The occupied cells in the table are shaded, and you can see that the table is exactly half full.

It would appear at first that if we insert an element into the table,we should have to resolve collisions about half the time, for an expected number of probes of 1.5 for an insertion into a random location (1 for the initial probe plus 0.5 for the chance of collision resolution). Consider, however, the cluster in positions 4 through 7. If we assume that the hash function is equally likely to send an element into any cell, then there is a 0.05 (= 1/20) chance that an element will be sent to cell 4, which would require 5 probes to find a vacant location at cell 8. There is also a 0.05 chance that an element will be sent to cell 5, requiring 4 probes, and we can see that the cluster will contribute

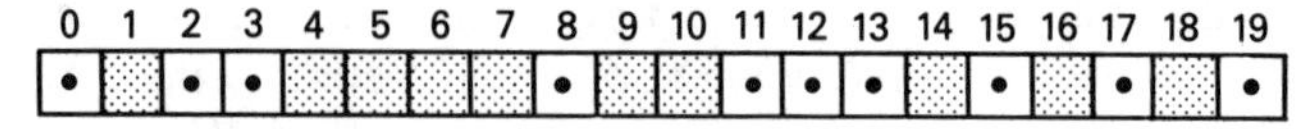

Figure 9.4 A partially full hash table, with clusters.

0.05 (5 + 4 + 3 + 2) = 0.70 to the expected number of probes. You can easily verify that for this example, the expected number of probes to insert an element is 37/20 = 1.85, rather larger than we first guessed.

The worst case would be when the occupied cells formed one large cluster of ten cells. In this case the unoccupied cells would require one probe each, for a contribution of 10 (0.05) (1), but the large cluster would contribute 0.05 (11 + 10 + . . . + 3 + 2) = 3.25, so the expected number of probes would be 0.5 + 3.25 = 3.75 probes for a single insertion, on the average. In fact, it is easy to extend this analysis to show that for B buckets, the contribution to the expected number of probes necessary for an insertion by a cluster of c cells is $(1 / B)\ ((c + 1) + c + \ldots + 3 + 2) = c\ (c + 3) / (2B)$. Simply said, clusters contribute an amount quadratic in their length to the expected number of probes required for insertion (and membership and deletion, too). In very simple terms, *long clusters make for very slow hashing.*

Things get even worse, though. An inserted element could wind up in location 8 by being hashed into any of locations 4, 5, 6, 7, or 8. In other words, it is five times more likely that the already large cluster will grow than it is for an element to hash into cell 12 and start a new cluster. The conclusion is that *long clusters are highly likely to grow even longer*. Notice that the clusters don't just grow by one, either. An insertion into cell 8 will cause secondary clustering, producing a large cluster of length seven.

Well, that should be enough to convince us that we want to avoid producing clusters if we can. It is clear that at least some of our troubles were caused by our collision resolution scheme. Probing into the next location in the table is a surefire way to produce clusters. There is nothing magical about our decision to look at cell $i + 1$ if we find that cell i is full; why not pick a number, k, and then probe into locations i, $i + k$, $i + 2k$, $i + 3k$, and so on, until we find a vacant location? This **generalized linear resolution** solves at least part of the problem for us, *as long as* k *has no factor in common with* B, *the number of buckets.* What generalized linear resolution does is to spread the clusters uniformly throughout the table. We will still have clusters, but they will consist of cells k apart, thus lessening the chance of secondary clustering.

An even better scheme is to use a **double hashing** scheme with *two* hash functions, h and k, and use h for the initial probe and k to provide the constant in generalized linear resolution. In other words, given an integer n to hash into the table, we probe first at $h(n)$, and, if that doesn't work, probe into locations $h(n) + k(n)$, $h(n) + 2k(n)$, $h(n) + 3k(n)$, and so on, until we succeed. Again, we must take care that the step size function k not produce any value with a factor in common with the table size, for reasons that become clear if you try this scheme with $B = 12$ and $k = 4$. For this reason, it is generally a good idea to let the table size be a prime number. If we assume that B is a prime, then, for instance, we can take $h(n) = n \textbf{ mod } B$, and $k(n) = (n \textbf{ mod}(B - 1)) + 1$. We will demonstrate this by redoing the example of Figure 9.2. Suppose that $B = 7$, that the hash table indices are 0, . . . , 6, and that we wished to insert the numbers 23, 14, 9, 6, 30, 12, 18 using double hashing with the two functions $h(n) = n \textbf{ mod } 7$, $k(n) = (n \textbf{ mod } 6) + 1$.

1. ($n = 23$). 23 **mod** 7 = 2, so 23 goes into cell 2.

2. (n = 14). 14 **mod** 7 = 0, so 14 goes into cell 0.
3. (n = 9). 9 **mod** 7 = 2; we have a collision and will move to another cell with step (9 **mod** 6) + 1 = 4. Our next probe is to location 2 + 4 = 6, so 9 goes into cell 6.
4. (n = 6). 6 **mod** 7 = 6; cell 6 is already occupied, so we use step (6 **mod** 6) + 1 = 1 and wrap around the list to cell 0, which is also full, so we step once again and place 6 into cell 1.
5. (n = 30). 30 **mod** 7 = 2; we again have a collision, so we rehash with step size equal to (30 **mod** 6) + 1 = 1. We then probe into location 2 + 1 = 3, so 30 goes into cell 3.
6. (n = 12). 12 **mod** 7 = 5, so 12 goes into cell 5.
7. (n = 18). 18 **mod** 7 = 4, so we place 18 into cell 4.

Comparing this with the example of Figure 9.2, we see that we have reduced the number of probes from 14 to 11. Big deal. The important thing to realize is that it *is* a big deal when the table size is large. The theoretical analysis of double hashing is very tricky, but empirical studies have shown that double hashing can go a long way toward eliminating clustering. In fact, these studies show that the results of double hashing are approximately random, in the sense that the clusters that do appear are no larger or more numerous than would be expected if n of the B buckets were simply chosen at random.

Time and Space Estimates

We have seen three different versions of hashing: closed hashing with linear resolution of collisions, closed double hashing, and open hashing. We can summarize the number of probes required to search for an element easily, although the proofs of these theoretical estimates would take us too far afield to be included here. They are not frightfully difficult, but they are a bit long and require some knowledge of probability theory. If you want to see the steps required to arrive at these results, we refer you to the sources listed at the end of the chapter.

We will count the number of probes required for the DICTIONARY operations, since the number of probes is a fairly good estimator of the amount of time the algorithms would take. Throughout this section, we will let λ denote the **load** on the table, which is to say the quotient n/B, where n is the number of elements now in the table and B is the number of buckets in the table. For closed hashing, λ is a number between 0 and 1, where $\lambda = 0$ if the table is empty, and $\lambda = 1$ if the table is completely filled. For open hashing, λ can be any nonnegative number, since there is no limit to the number of elements in the list for each bucket. Notice also that for open hashing, λ is the average number of elements per bucket.

We will begin with the easiest analysis, for open hashing. If we search for an element in an open hash table, then we will either find that element or we will not. If we do not find the element, then we won't know that until we have traversed the entire bucket list. That will take 1 probe to find the right bucket, and then λ more steps to traverse the linked list, on the average, for a total of $1 + \lambda$ probes expected. Suppose, on the other hand, that our search is successful. We have seen in Chapter 3 that the expected number of comparisons needed to find an element in a list of length λ by sequential search is $(\lambda + 1)/2$, plus 1 probe to find the right bucket. The number of probes needed to delete an element is clearly the same as the number required for a successful search, and if we insert an element we need to be sure that the element is not in the table, so the number of probes for insertion is the same as for an unsuccessful search. We summarize these results as follows.

Theorem 9.1. In open hashing on a table with load λ, the expected number of probes for insertion or an unsuccessful search is $1 + \lambda$, and the expected number of probes for deletion or a successful search is $1 + (\lambda + 1) / 2$ (or just 2 if $\lambda < 1$).

We can describe similar results for the two closed hashing techniques. We will phrase our results for double hashing in terms of **random hashing**, where elements are inserted into the hash table at random locations, but will remind you that there is powerful evidence that double hashing, for proper choice of the two hash functions, is essentailly random, so you would not be too far off if you understood "double" where we say "random."

Theorem 9.2. In closed hashing with linear resolution of collisions (regardless of the step size) on a table with load λ, the expected number of probes for insertion or unsuccesful search is approximately

$$\frac{1}{2}\left(1 + \left(\frac{1}{1-\lambda}\right)^2\right)$$

and the expected number of probes for deletion or successful search is approximately

$$\frac{1}{2}\left(1 + \frac{1}{1-\lambda}\right)$$

Theorem 9.3. In random closed hashing on a table with load λ, the expected number of probes for insertion or unsuccessful search is approximately $1 / (1 - \lambda)$, and the expected number of probes for deletion or successful search is approximately

$$\left(-\frac{1}{\lambda}\right)\ln(1-\lambda)$$

where the logarithm is the natural log.

In Figure 9.5 we illustrate the behavior of these two closed hashing schemes. All three of the hashing algorithms work fairly well when the load on the table is less than $1/2$, but striking differences appear as the table becomes more nearly full, as we indicate in Table 9.1.

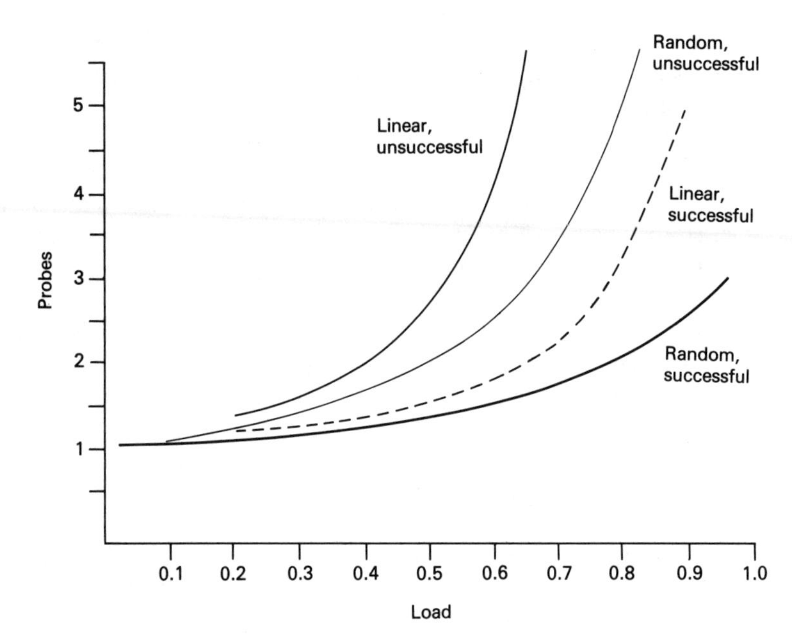

Figure 9.5 Expected number of probes versus load for two hashing strategies.

TABLE 9.1. EFFECTS OF LOAD ON HASHING EFFICIENCY

	Expected Number of Probes For Searches		
	Linear	Random	Open
$\lambda = 0.75$			
Unsuccessful	8.5	4.0	1.8
Successful	2.5	1.9	2.0
$\lambda = 0.9$			
Unsuccessful	50.5	10.0	1.9
Successful	5.5	2.6	2.0

It is clear that linear resolution of collisions is a real loser when the table is nearly full, since, with the table 90 percent full, this algorithm requires about 50 probes to insert another element, on the average, almost entirely because of the presence of large clusters. Equally clear is the fact that open hashing is a big winner, not only because of its efficiency, but also because we can let the number of elements get much larger than the number of buckets before we notice any significant degradation on the number of probes per operation.

We have to be careful, however, before we make the blanket pronouncement that open hashing is the method of choice. Open hashing requires that we set aside space in the hash table and in each cell of the linked list for pointers, so we have to make sure that we are not using too much memory with this scheme. To analyze the space requirements of open and closed hashing, let us suppose that we have n elements in the table, that the table has B buckets (to be fair to closed hashing, we will assume that $n \leq B$), that each element requires k bytes of memory, and that pointers require 4 bytes.

With both algorithms, we must preallocate an array of B buckets for the hash table, so closed hashing will require kB bytes of storage, and open hashing will require $4B$ bytes for the table and $k + 4$ bytes for each linked list cell, for a total of $4B + n(k + 4)$ bytes. Now the closed hashing scheme will be more space-efficient when $kB < 4B + n(k + 4)$, and that happens when $(n/B) > (k - 4)/(k + 4)$. In other words, closed hashing requires less space than open hashing when the load $\lambda > (k - 4) / (k + 4)$. In Table 9.2 we show the cutoff load values for which closed hashing is more space-efficient than open hashing, for various sizes, k, of the data elements.

TABLE 9.2. COMPARISON OF SPACE REQUIREMENTS FOR OPEN AND CLOSED HASHING

Record size	Closed hashing uses less space for loads greater than
4	0.00
8	0.33
16	0.60
32	0.78
64	0.88
128	0.94

We see that for large records, open hashing is almost always more space-efficient than closed hashing, and that for small records, closed hashing requires less space when the load on the table is not too small (which, unfortunately, is exactly when closed hashing is less time-efficient than open).

Application: Multiple Hashing, Encoding and Spelling Checkers

The idea of using several independent hash functions has a number of applications, one of the most interesting being a probabilistic spelling checker. Suppose we were faced with the task of designing a spelling checker to be used as a feature of a word processor. The spelling checker would take a word as soon as it had been typed and see if that word was in its dictionary. If so, no action would be taken; if not, it might sound a beep and highlight the questionable word.

One way to implement this would be to use the DICTIONARY ADT with a collection of, for instance, 40,000 words, and test each word as it was typed by making a call to *Member*. If we stored the words as strings, with one byte per character, and assumed an average of five characters per word, the dictionary alone would require 200,000 bytes, and that does not include the overhead that would be entailed by using an implementation such as a hash table.

As an alternative, consider the following. We will choose d different hash functions, $h_1, h_2, \ldots, h_d$, each of which will hash a string into an index of a bit vector, V, with B indices. To build the dictionary, we will begin with each bit in V set to 0, then take each word, w, we wish to include and set $V[h_i(w)] = 1$, for $i = 1, \ldots, d$. To take a small example, suppose we wish to have a dictionary consisting of the words 'BOY', 'DOG', 'GIRL', 'THE', and 'WAS'. We will use a bit vector with 31 entries, and encode the words by thc following scheme. First, add the letter codes for each letter in the word, with 'A' having code 1, 'B' having code 2, and so on to 'Z' with code 26, and then square that number. Having done that, we will use three hash functions on the resulting squares, s, where $h_1(s) = s$ **mod** 37, $h_2(s) = s$ **mod** 41, and $h_3(s) = s$ **mod** 53, and finally we will fold these numbers into the hash table by taking them **mod** 31. Incidentally, this squaring and taking **mod** is a poor choice for hashing, as we ask you to show in the exercises. At any rate, the five words are coded in the following fashion.

1. 'BOY' $\rightarrow 2 + 15 + 25 = 42 \rightarrow$ 1,764. 1,764 **mod** 37 = 25, 1,764 **mod** 41 = 1, 1,764 **mod** 53 = 15, so we will write 1,764 $\rightarrow$ (25, 1, 15) $\rightarrow$ (25, 1, 15), taking these numbers **mod** 31.
2. 'DOG' $\rightarrow 4 + 15 + 7 = 26 \rightarrow 676 \rightarrow (10, 20, 40) \rightarrow (10, 20, 9)$.
3. 'GIRL' $\rightarrow 7 + 9 + 18 + 12 = 46 \rightarrow$ 2,116 $\rightarrow (7, 25, 49) \rightarrow (7, 25, 18)$.
4. 'THE' $\rightarrow 20 + 8 + 5 = 33 \rightarrow$ 1,089 $\rightarrow (16, 23, 29) \rightarrow (16, 23, 29)$.
5. 'WAS' $\rightarrow 23 + 1 + 19 = 43 \rightarrow$ 1,849 $\rightarrow (36, 4, 47) \rightarrow (5, 4, 16)$.

After doing this, we set bits 1, 4, 5, 7, 9, 10, 15, 16, 18, 20, 23, 25, 29 of the bit vector to 1, so it now has the form 0100110101100001101010010100010. Notice that V would fit comfortably in 4 bytes, whereas it would require 16 bytes to store the five original words as character strings. We have thus achieved a *fourfold* reduction in the amount of space needed to store the dictionary. To test a word x for membership in our dictionary, we now apply the three hash functions to x and look at the indicated bits in V. Supppose that the test word was 'HAT'. We see that applying the same procedure we used to build the dictionary yields

'HAT' $\rightarrow 8 + 1 + 20 = 29 \rightarrow 841 \rightarrow (27, 21, 46) \rightarrow (27, 21, 15)$.

We inspect bits 27, 21, and 15 of V, find that at least one of them is a zero, conclude that this word could not possibly have been one that was used to build the dictionary in the first place, and report that the word is unrecognized. It is easy to see that our spelling checker is always completely reliable when it reports failure to recognize a word.

Now suppose that the word to test was either 'TESTED' or 'SPOIN'. The codes for these two words sum to 73, which yields the three hash values (1, 9, 29), and we see that bits 1, 9, and 29 of V are all 1, so the spelling checker would accept these words, even though they were not among the original five. In other words, our spelling checker is not completely reliable when it reports that a word was successfully recognized, which is why we called it a *probabilistic* spelling checker.

Just how reliable is our checker? If we assume (as is not the case in this example) that the 1's are randomly distributed throughout the bit vector, then the chance of accepting a word by accident is just the chance of choosing three numbers at random in the range 0, . . . , 30, and finding a 1 in each position. The probability that a randomly chosen location contains a 1 is equal to the number of 1's in V, divided by 31, the total number of bits in V. We can count that there are 13 1's in V, so the probability of hitting a 1 by accident is 13 / 31 = 0.419, and the probability of hitting three 1's by accident is $(13 / 31)^3 = 0.0737$, or about 1 in 13. In other words, for this example, we pay for a fourfold reduction in storage by allowing about a 7 percent chance that the dictionary will not catch a misspelling.

We can adjust the failure rate to any positive number we want by changing the number of hash functions or by making the bit vector larger, so the real question is what level of error we wish to tolerate. Suppose we would be content with an error rate of 0.001, so that 1 out of every 1,000 misspelled words would not be caught, on the average. Let us return to the situation we mentioned earlier, with a dictionary of 40,000 words. The least size of the bit vector and the number of hash functions needed to achieve this rate of accuracy are related in such a way that the smallest bit vector necessary for an accuracy of 0.001 is attained with 7 hash functions. In the exercises, we ask you to show the relation between d, the number of hash functions, and B, the size of the bit vector needed to achieve a given accuracy. If you do that you can show that with 7 hash functions and 40,000 words, any V with at least 751,155 bits will guarantee an accuracy of 0.001. Dividing this number by 8 shows us that 93,895 bytes will suffice to store the bit vector, which is less than half the space required to store the words (at 5 bytes per word, on average) of the dictionary as strings.

This algorithm is fast, especially when written in a low-level language that allows more direct access to hardware. It is possible to design good hash functions which, even if used seven or more times per word, are fast enough that they would be finished checking a word long before the fastest typist had completed the next word (and that, of course, is all that matters here). Another nice feature of this algorithm is the ease of extension of the data base. Since a reasonably sized dictionary must necessarily leave out some words (not to mention all proper names), a useful part of a spelling checker is the ability to include a word for future recognition when it is first flagged as unrecognized. In our probabilistic spelling checker it takes no more work to add a word to the dictionary than it does to test whether the word is there in the first place.

The most novel feature of this scheme, though, is not its speed or the fact that it reduces the size of the data base by 50 percent, but rather that the list of correct words is completely disguised in the bit vector V. In the small example above, even knowing what the three hash functions were does not help in trying to discover the words that were encoded in the bit vector 0100110101100001101010010100010. The fact that the original words cannot be reconstructed with any degree of certainty from the bit vector provides a means by which authors of such programs can safeguard their copyright, in a way similar to that used by mapmakers to guard against copying their works. All one needs to do is include some words in the original dictionary, like 'GRBGTWQ', which would be highly unlikely to arise from simple spelling errors. These words lie hidden in the bit vector, unsuspected by all, until the day comes when you (pretend along with us here) discover another spelling checker that is identical to yours. Now, a court may not be impressed by the fact that the other program uses the same hash functions as yours; after all, the good hash functions are pretty much the same everywhere. The court might not even be impressed by the fact that the other program uses a bit vector that is identical to yours; after all, if the hash functions were the same and you both built the dictionary from the same list of the 40,000 most common words in English, it would follow that the bit vectors would be identical.

Then, however, you trot out the heavy artillery. You enter the word 'GRBGTWQ', having announced that you had built it into your dictionary, and lo and behold it is accepted. If the other author claims to have used only the most common 40,000 words in English, the only defense is that a thousand-to-one coincidence just took place. You then do the same thing for 'UUIOOIAEAA', 'XQATBDKJU', and 'OPOPLOPOLLO-PLOP', which you had also placed in your dictionary, and the defense has to explain away a one-in-a-trillion coincidence. Case decided for the plaintiff (but see the exercises).

9.5 THE UNION-FIND ADT

The final data structure we will discuss is, in a sense, complementary to the DICTIONARY ADT. Most of the time a dictionary is used to support a single set, in which elements are inserted and deleted throughout the life of the application. The UNION-FIND abstract data type, on the other hand, is designed to act on a collection of sets, with no deletions or insertions of elements, except the insertions needed to create the sets in the first place. Almost invariably, the UNION-FIND structure deals with a partition, in which a universal set is divided into disjoint subsets.

Definition. The **UNION-FIND** abstract data type is a subtype of the SET ADT, on which the set operations *Union, Find*, and *Create* are defined. Unlike SET, the elements of this ADT consist of collections of disjoint sets $S_1, S_2, \ldots, S_n$ with **identifiers** $I_1, I_2, \ldots, I_n$ chosen from some set, and the operations are defined as follows:

1. **Create**(**var** x : IDENTIFIER ; a : ATOM) creates a set consisting of the single atom a, and associates with that set the identifier x.
2. **Union**(x, y : IDENTIFIER) : IDENTIFIER returns the identifier associated with the union of the sets identified by x and y. Notice that here we define *Union* as a function, rather than as a procedure, as we did at the start of the chapter.
3. **Find**(p : POSITION) : IDENTIFIER returns the unique identifier associated with the set in which the element in position p belongs. Again, note that this operation is defined as a function, rather than as a procedure.

The notion of another set, IDENTIFIER, along with the customary sets ATOM and POSITION, seems to be a departure from our paradigm for abstract data types, but it is there purely for notational convenience. You could, if you wished, think of identifiers as positions, and imagine that each set is associated with a position of some element in that set. In other words, we could identify each set by an element of that set, which would cause no confusion since we assume that the sets have no elements in common. For instance, the UNION-FIND structure consisting of the three sets $\{1, 2, 3\}$, $\{4, 5, 6, 7\}$, $\{8, 9\}$ might use identifiers 1, 4, and 8 to mark the three sets.

Because the elements of the UNION-FIND structure are collections of sets, we could use any of the SET implementations to represent this structure. We could represent each such collection as a collection of bit vectors, for instance, so that if the universal set consisted of $\{1, 2, \ldots, 9\}$, the foregoing example could be represented by the three bit vectors 111000000, 000111100, 000000011, and the subsets might just be represented by the identifiers 1, 2, and 3, respectively, rather than using set elements, as we did in the preceding paragraph. The operations *Create* and *Union* would be easy to define in this implementation, since we could represent a UNION-FIND element as an array or linked list of bit vectors, but it is not clear how we would implement *Find* in any way that would avoid our having to look at each of the subsets in the structure to find the one containing the element we sought to locate.

Tree Representations of UNION-FIND

Another representation of the UNION-FIND structure uses trees for each of the subsets, and identifies each subset by the root of its associated tree. The sets $\{1, 2, 3\}$, $\{4, 5, 6, 7\}$, and $\{8, 9\}$, then, might be represented as in Figure 9.6. The picture is drawn to reflect the fact that there is no order among the nodes that depends on any inherent order among the atoms, and also that the trees need not be binary trees. With this representation, *Union* can be defined to run in constant time, simply by making the node of one tree become the parent of the other. In Figure 9.7 we show the structure that would result if we called *Union*(1, 5). The tree rooted at node 1 would have node 5 as its new parent, and the function would return the position of node 5, the root of the tree corresponding to the union $\{1, 2, 3, 4, 5, 6, 7\}$.

It is easy to see how to define *Find* in this implementation. Given a node, we simply point our way up the tree from that node, until we come to the root of the tree containing that node, and we return the position of the root as an identifier of the set in

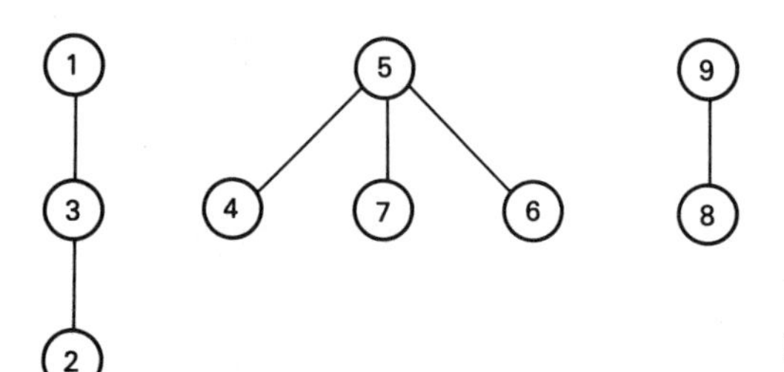

Figure 9.6 Three disjoint sets represented by trees.

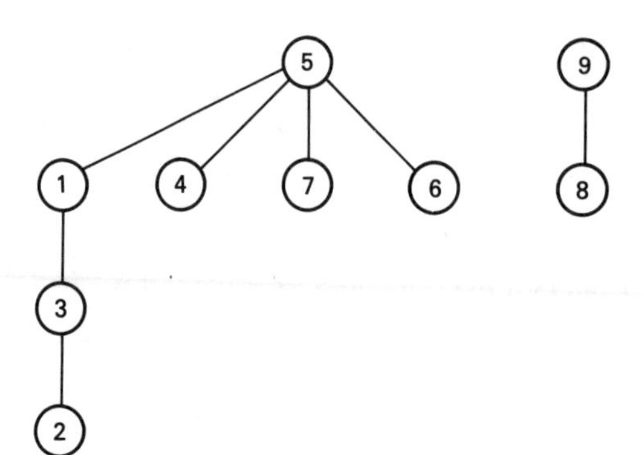

Figure 9.7 The structure of Figure 9.6 after a call to *Union*(1, 5).

which the node resides. Now the astute reader has two things to worry about. Not only do we have to consider how to implement general, rather than binary, trees, but we also need to figure out how to move up the tree. Fortunately, we can solve both problems at once. If you look carefully at the descriptions of *Union* and *Find* in this implementation, you will see that there is never any need to move down the tree. We will use what is known as an **in-tree**, consisting of cells linked with pointers in such a way that each cell contains a single pointer, to its parent. The root will be special: Since it has no parent, we will mark that it is a root by making its parent field equal to **nil**. (Another commonly used technique is to make the parent pointer of a root node point to itself. This state of affairs can hold only when the node is a root, so we again have a way to tell whether a node is a root.) We will use pointers for both positions and identifiers, and will make no distinction between them as types here.

```
type
   ATOM = {any data type};
   POSITION = ^Node;
   Node = record
               data : ATOM;
               parent : POSITION
            end;
   ID = POSITION;

procedure Create(var x : ID ; a : ATOM);
begin
   new(x);
   x^.data := a;
   x^.parent := nil
end;

function Union(var x : ID ; y : ID) : ID;
{ Assumes that x and y are roots, returns a tree with x as the child of y }
begin
   x^.parent := y;
   Union := y
end;
```

```
function Find(p : POSITION) : ID;
begin
   while p^.parent <> nil do
      p := p^.parent;
   Find := p
end;
```

We have departed slightly here from good programming style by defining *Union* as a function with a side effect. The **var** parameter is used to change the node at x, and generally functions should return only a single value and not change the values of their arguments. It seems somewhat more natural to define *Union* as a function, though, so we do so here, and remark that style guidelines are just that—guidelines, not dogma.

In this implementation, it is easy to find timing estimates for the operations: *Create* and *Union* run in constant time, while *Find* obviously takes time proportional to the height of the tree in which the node at p is located. Things get trickier when we modify this implementation, so it is more customary for this data type to talk about the **amortized time** required by a mixed sequence of n calls to *Union* and *Find*. The reason for this is that once we change this implementation to make it very fast, it is extremely difficult to prove that an individual operation is fast. It is easier, believe it or not, to analyze the time required by a mingled sequence of n unions and n finds, so we will talk about the running time of an implementation, rather than that of a particular operation in the implementation. If both *Union* and *Find* ran in constant time, then, we would say that the implementation ran in time $O(n)$, since that would be the time necessary to complete n unions and n finds. We won't be able to do quite that well, but we will be able to approach it as close as makes no practical difference, in that we will slightly redefine *Union* and *Find* so that the amortized time is $O(n\,a(n))$, where $a(n)$ is an increasing function which, we will guarantee, grows more slowly than any you have ever seen.

The cost of this implementation, though, is nowhere near as good as $O(n)$. We can see this by assuming that we have initialized our structure so that we have n disjoint sets, $\{1\}, \{2\}, \ldots, \{n\}$. To make writing easier, we will assume that each set will be identified by an integer from 1 to n. Consider now the sequence of n unions and n finds:

$$Union(1,2), Union(2,3), \ldots, Union(n-1,n), Find(1), \ldots, Find(1).$$

Remember that we have defined *Union* so that the first argument is made a child of the second, so that the n unions build a linear chain of n nodes, with 1 at the bottom and n at the root. Each of these operations takes constant time, so the total cost of the unions is $O(n)$. Each *Find* must traverse the entire chain, from node 1 to the root, and so takes time $O(n)$ for each of the finds. There are n finds, so their total cost is $O(n^2)$, and hence the cost of this sequence is $O(n + n^2) = O(n^2)$. In other words, the worst-case cost of this implementation is at least as large as $O(n^2)$ (and, in fact, is never larger than that).

Weighting

The problem with the simple implementation discussed above is obviously that we have defined *Union* in such a way as to permit the trees made from unions to become unbalanced. There is a very simple cure for this; we simply include another field, *weight*, in the records representing the nodes, which stores the number of nodes in the subtree rooted at that node. Then, when we merge two trees, we always do so by making the tree with smaller weight become the child of the other node. If we apply this heuristic to the trees of Figure 9.6, we have the situation illustrated in Figure 9.8.

Notice that it would have been impossible to build the 1, 3, 2 chain of nodes by this algorithm. The improved union algorithm is almost as simple to define as the original.

```
function WeightedUnion(var x, y : ID) : ID;
{Assumes the existence of a weight field in each root node}
begin
  if x^.weight > y^.weight then begin  {the tree at y has less weight than the one at x}
    y^.parent := x;                     {so make the y tree the child}
    x^.weight := x^.weight + y^.weight;  {adjust the weight of the new parent}
    WeightedUnion := x                   {and return the root of the union tree}

  else begin                             {a tie or the x tree has less weight}
    x^.parent := y;
    y^.weight := x^.weight + y^.weight;
    WeightedUnion := y
  end
end;
```

If you do some examples, building trees by *WeightedUnion*, you might begin to become convinced that such trees are somehow balanced, although we haven't defined what it means for a general tree to be balanced. Let us call a **WU-tree** any tree that can be constructed by a sequence of weighted unions. We will show that, much like Fibonacci trees, a WU-tree of weight w must have height no larger than $\log_2(w)$, so that WU-trees cannot have most of their nodes concentrated in a single long chain, a property that should make *Find* much more efficient than it was with trees built from simple unions.

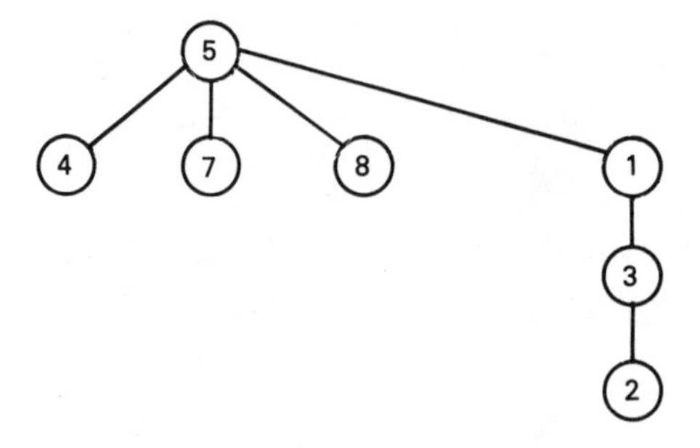

Figure 9.8 The structure of Figure 9.6 after *WeightedUnion*(1, 5).

As we did with balanced trees, we will investigate the WU-trees that have the smallest weight for a given height, and will show that the weight must be at least an exponential function of the height. We showed in Chapter 7 that of all balanced binary trees, the Fibonacci trees had the smallest weight for a given height. For WU-trees, we have an analogous class, called the **binomial trees**. First, notice that if a WU-tree is constructed by taking the union of two WU-trees with heights h_1 and h_2, the union tree can have height larger than that of its components if and only if $h_1 = h_2$, and in that case the union tree has height one more than that of its components. We will then construct minimal-weight WU-trees of height h by merging two minimal-weight WU-trees of height $h - 1$. We will denote each such tree of height h by B_h. In Figure 9.9 we show this merging process, and illustrate some of the first few binomial trees.

Certainly the weight of B_h is 2^h, so, since a binomial tree of height h has the least weight of any WU-tree of that height, we see that any WU-tree of height h must have weight at least as large as 2^h, which is the same as saying that any WU-tree of weight w must have height $h \leq \log_2(w)$, as we set out to show.

Binomial trees are not just curiosities that we trotted out on the way toward a proof about the relation of heights and weights of WU-trees. They have a number of interesting properties of their own, some of which we explore in the exercises, and they form the foundation for quite a few SET applications, as you will undoubtedly discover if you continue your investigations into computer science.

Recall that the simple implementation of UNION-FIND had n^2 cost. With weighted unions, we can reduce this cost to $n \log n$. Consider a sequence of n unions and n finds. No matter how they are arranged, the highest tree we can build starting from singleton subsets using n unions must have height $\log n$ (since the weight of the resulting tree is no more than n). Then, no matter where in the sequence they are, the n

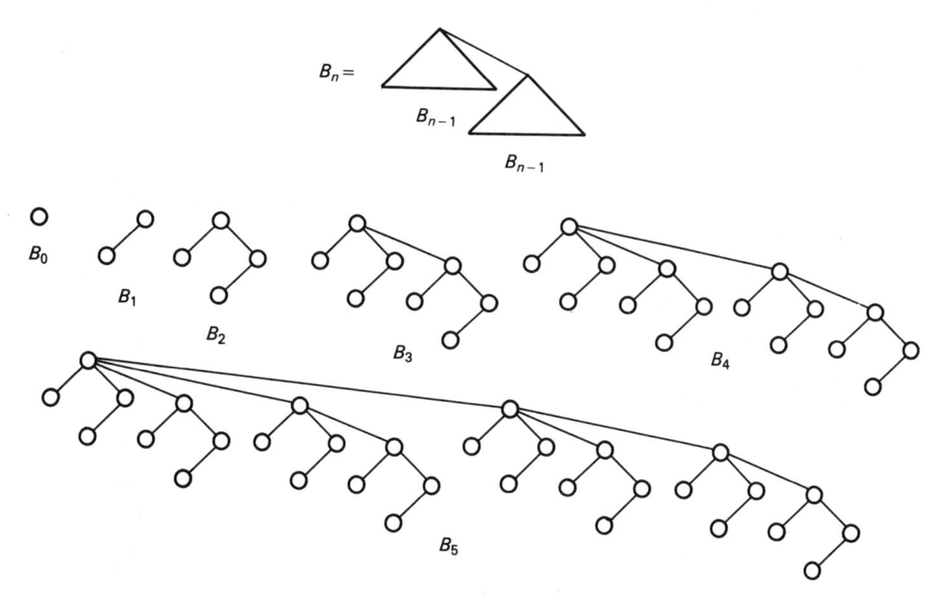

Figure 9.9 Some binomial trees.

finds can cost no more than $O(\log n)$ each. Since the unions each take constant time, the time required by the entire sequence of unions and finds must be $O(n + n \log n) = O(n \log n)$. In the exercises, we ask you to show that $n \log n$ is also a lower bound on the worst-case cost, by constructing a sequence of n unions and n finds that does take $n \log n$ time.

Path Compression

We can reduce the amortized cost of the UNION-FIND structure even further if we modify *Find*. We can't reduce the time required by *Union*, of course, since it already takes just a constant amount of time, but we can modify *Find* so that it alters the tree in such a way as to make subsequent finds cheaper. This is really the reason we need amortized cost: By changing *Find*, we will make it take longer, but the cost can be averaged over the subsequent finds, which will take less time. We do this by writing *Find* in such a way that whenever it is called on a node at location x, it will move each node on the path from x to the root to a location where those nodes become children of the root, rather than distant ancestors of the root. In Figure 9.10(a), we show the search path from x to the root, and in Figure 9.10(b), we show the tree that results when the nodes along the search path have been promoted to become children of the root.

It is not hard to see how we will implement finding with path compression. We will make two passes along the search path from the target node to the root. The first pass will be the same as in the original *Find*, to discover the root identifier, and then we will make another pass from the target node to the root, promoting the nodes we find along the way.

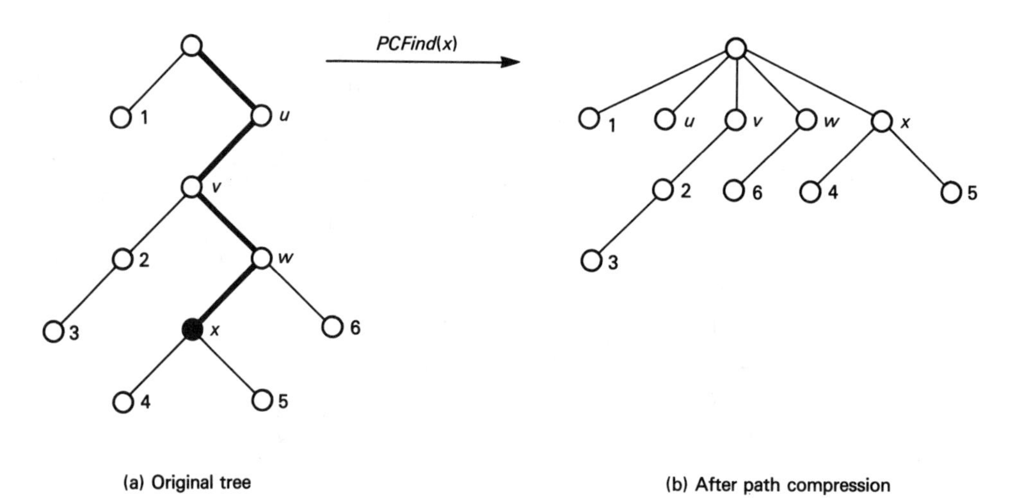

Figure 9.10 *Find* with path compression.

```
function PCFind(var x : POSITION) : ID;
   var y, z : POSITION;
begin
   y := x;
   while x^.parent <> nil do          {first pass: find root}
      x := x^.parent;

   while y <> x do begin              {second pass: promote nodes in search path}
      z := y^.parent;                 {save parent of current node}
      y^.parent := x;                 {promote current node}
      y := z                          {move up the search path}
   end;

   PCFind := x
end;
```

Unfortunately, we will not be able here to give a proof of the amortized cost of the UNION-FIND implementation that uses weighting and path compression. The essential idea is to compute the cost of a *Find* and charge some of that cost to the *Find* itself, and delay the inclusion of some of the rest of the cost by charging it to the nodes in the search path, to be picked up at a later time when we compute the cost of a subsequent *Find*. At any rate, it turns out that the total cost of a sequence of n unions and n finds in this implementation is $O(n \log^* n)$, where $\log^* n$ is defined as follows:

1. $\log^*(0) = 0$,
2. $\log^*(n) = 1 + \log^*(\lceil \log_2 n \rceil)$, for $n > 0$.

As usual, $\lceil z \rceil$ represents the least integer that is greater than or equal to z. Now log* is not constant, but it grows extremely slowly as a function of n. Consider the rather large number 10^{99}. We have

$$log*(10^{99}) = 1 + log*\left\lceil \log_2(10^{99}) \right\rceil = 1 + log*\lceil 328.9 \rceil = 1 + log*(329)$$

$$= 1 + (1 + log*\left\lceil \log_2(329) \right\rceil) = 2 + log*\lceil 8.361 \rceil = 2 + log*(9)$$

$$= 2 + (1 + log*\left\lceil \log_2(9) \right\rceil) = 3 + log*\lceil 3.170 \rceil = 3 + log*(4)$$

$$= 3 + (1 + log*\left\lceil \log_2(4) \right\rceil) = 4 + log*\lceil 2 \rceil = 4 + log*(2)$$

$$= 4 + (1 + log*\left\lceil \log_2(2) \right\rceil) = 5 + log*\lceil 1 \rceil = 5 + log*(1)$$

$$= 5 + (1 + log*\left\lceil \log_2(1) \right\rceil) = 6 + log*\lceil 0 \rceil = 6 + log*(0) = 6.$$

Well, log* $(10^{99}) = 6$ is certainly a fairly small number when compared with the input, but to really see how this function crawls along, we notice that we also get 6 when we compute log* (10^{999}), and we also get 6 when we compute log* (10^{9999}). For log* (10^{99999}) we finally get a value of 7, but log* stays at 7 for such a long time after that that by the time it reaches 8 we are dealing with numbers that are not only too large to write down, but are so large that we cannot even write down the number of *digits* that it would take to write them down! We can show, in fact, that log*(n) increases by 1 only when n passes the values 0, $2^0 = 1$, $2^1 = 2$, $2^2 = 4$, $2^4 = 16$, $2^{16} =$ 65,536, $2^{65536} = ?$, ... In other words, n log* n increases more rapidly than linear, but its growth is so slow that for all practical purposes the function n log*n may as well be regarded as linear. Put in another way, we can say that the average cost of the operations in a sequence of unions and finds in the weighted, path compression implementation of UNION-FIND are as close to being constant time as we could want.

We can't resist one more remark before we leave these timing estimates. There is a longer and more delicate proof that the worst-case amortized cost of the weighted path compression UNION-FIND implementation is even less than n log* n. There is a function, $\alpha(n)$, which increases vastly *slower* than log* n, such that the cost of this implementation is $O(n\,\alpha(n))$. This function $\alpha(n)$ is related to the inverse of Ackermann's function, which we mentioned briefly in the exercises in Chapter 5. This is an excellent example of ingenuity at work. From a purely utilitarian point of view, we could say that on any computer that could ever be built, this implementation of UNION-FIND has a linear amortized cost, but the human mind is capable of transcending these physical limitations and contemplating the entire infinite sweep of integers, in which that which is of "practical" interest is only a negligibly small part. There is an unlimited range of fascinating subjects available to us, and we would miss almost all of them if we chose to remain blind to all but the "useful".

Application: Minimum Spanning Trees, Revisited

Speaking of "useful," here is an application for which the UNION-FIND structure is particularly well suited. In Chapter 8 we saw Prim's algorithm to find the minimum spanning tree of an edge-weighted graph. We present here another MST algorithm, due to J. B. Kruskal. Suppose that we have a graph G, consisting of a set of vertices connected by edges, each edge having a positive weight, and we wish to construct a minimal spanning tree for G. The idea is to begin with a forest of trees, each consisting of a single vertex of G, and to build these trees by successively adding the least-cost edge that connects two different trees in the forest. We see that this algorithm requires a number of abstract data types that we have seen already: We need GRAPH to represent G and the eventual spanning tree, PRIORITY QUEUE to allow us to delete the least-cost edge not used so far, and UNION-FIND to keep the vertices in the forest of subtrees.

Figure 9.11 illustrates Kruskal's algorithm, on the edge-weighted tree of Figure 8.10. The edges, sorted by weight, are {a, b}, {c, e}, {c, d}, {d, e}, {c, b}, {b, e}, {a, d}, and {a, c}. We begin with the forest of Figure 9.11(b). In (c) of the figure we add

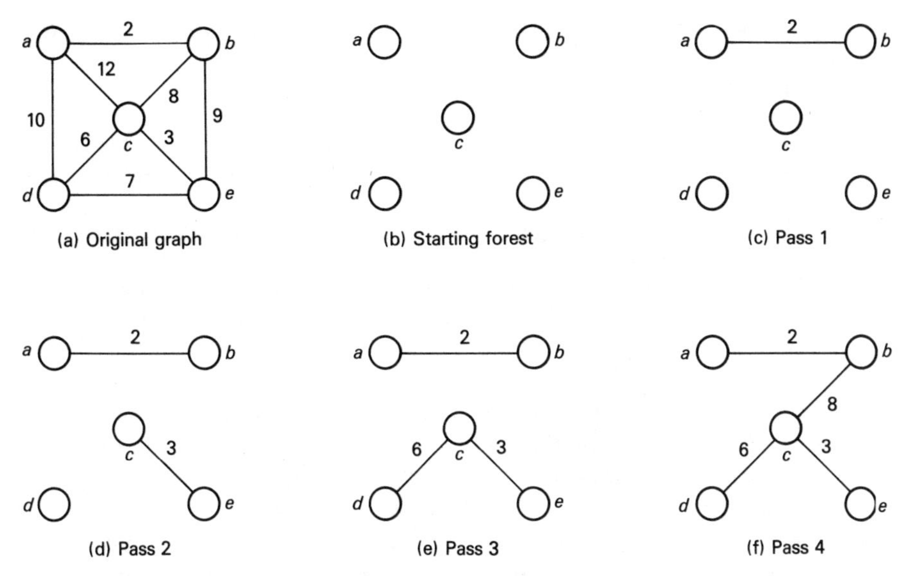

Figure 9.11 Constructing a MST by Kruskal's algorithm.

the least-cost edge, {a, b}; in (d) we add the next smallest cost edge, {c, e}; in (e) we add the next least cost edge, {c, d}. The next edge to add is {d, e}, but both endpoints are in the same tree and therefore could not be added without introducing a cycle, so we discard {d, e}. In Figure 9.11(f) we add the last edge, namely {c, b}, completing the minimum spanning tree.

If you compare this with Prim's algorithm from Chapter 8, you see that the MST is built differently, but that the spanning tree is the same. This is a coincidence, caused by the fact that for this graph there is a unique minimum spanning tree. In general, there is no guarantee that there will be only one spanning tree with minimal weight (suppose all the edges of the graph had the same weight, for instance), and the trees that are constructed by the two algorithms might very well be different. Kruskal's MST algorithm is easy enough to write; we do so below. In this algorithm, we will suppose that the graph *G* has *n* vertices and *e* edges.

```
procedure KruskalMST(G : GRAPH ; var T : GRAPH);
   var
      U : {a UNION-FIND structure of vertices};
      a, b, c : IDENTIFIER {in U };
      P : PRIORITY_QUEUE {of edges, by weight};
      u, v : POSITION {in the graph G };
begin
   Create(T);
   Create(P);

   for all vertices, v, in G do              {set up the starting in-forest}
      Create a new singleton set in the forest U ;
```

```
    for all edges, {u, v}, in G do          {set up the priority queue of edges by weight}
        Insert({u, v}, P);

    repeat
        DeleteMin(P, {u, v});               {get least cost edge not yet used}
        a := Find(u);                       {find the sets where the edge endpoints are}
        b := Find(v);
        if a <> b then begin                {new edge links different components}
            c := Union(a, b);               {so merge them}
            Insert the edge {u, v} into T, with new vertices if needed
    until n - 1 edges have been inserted    { n vertices in G, so MST has n - 1 edges}
end;
```

The initialization of the UNION-FIND in-forest requires time $O(n)$, and it takes time $O(e \log e)$ to set up the priority queue (actually, this can be done in $O(e)$ time, but that will not affect the final running time). The **repeat** loop could be iterated for each edge in G, namely e times, and within that loop *DeleteMin* requires $O(\log e)$ time each time it is called, for a contribution of $O(e \log e)$. Within the loop we will have $O(2e)$ calls to *Find* and $O(n)$ calls to *Union*, so they will contribute $O((2e + n) \log^* (2e + n)) = O(e \log^* e)$. Adding these times, we see that the running time for this algorithm is $O(n + e + e \log e + e \log^* e) = O(e \log e)$. Prim's MST algorithm requires time $O(n^2)$, so for graphs in which the number of edges is close to n^2 Prim's algorithm is asymptotically faster, while for those graphs in which the number of edges is close to n, Kruskal's algorithm is to be preferred.

9.6 SUMMARY

The structural relation that defines SET is the empty relation, reflecting the fact that a set has no internal structure at all. If the atoms in a set are linearly ordered, a bit vector representation allows constant-time insertion, deletion, and membership testing, with the drawback that any set is limited in size to a predeclared maximum.

A data structure that supports insertion, deletion, and membership operations is called a dictionary, and we saw that an implementation of a dictionary with hashing supports the three operations in constant time, as long as the load on the hash table does not get too large. Closed hashing, where the data is stored in the hash table, is simpler to implement than open hashing, where the hash table contains pointers to linked lists of data, but requires care in choice of hash function to reduce collisions to a minimum. For further information on hashing, you could do no better than two excellent books:

Aho, Alfred V., Hopcroft, John E., and Ullman, Jeffrey D. *Data Structures and Algorithms*, Addison-Wesley, Reading, MA, 1983.

Knuth, Donald E. *The Art of Computer Programming: 3. Sorting and Searching*, Addison-Wesley, Reading, MA, 1973.

As an application of hashing, we discussed the use of multiple hashing to implement a probabilistic spelling checker. There has been a considerable interest in probabilistic algorithms lately, largely for problems for which there is no known efficient algorithm. The problem of testing whether a very large number is prime is a good example. It is not known whether the problem of testing whether a number is prime is a "hard" problem, but there are no known polynomial-time algorithms to test for primality. However, there is a probabilistic polynomial-time algorithm, given in

Rabin, M. O. "Probabilistic Algorithm." In J. F. Traub, ed., *Algorithms and Complexity: New Directions and Recent Results,* Academic Press, New York, 1976, 21–39.

Rabin takes a number p and subjects it to n tests, in such a way that if the number fails any one test, it is certain not to be prime, and if it passes all n tests, then the probability that the number is not prime is $(1/2)^n$. In other words, the algorithm does not provide a definitive answer, but can be made to be as close to completely reliable as we wish.

The final set implementation we covered was the UNION-FIND structure, which supports the operations *Create, Union*, and *Find.* This implementation uses a forest to represent a collection of sets, and, by using the path compression and weighting heuristics, can be made to run in average time which is essentially constant per operation. We used the UNION-FIND structure to implement another MST algorithm. The original reference is

Kruskal, J. B. "On the shortest spanning subtree of a graph and the traveling salesman problem," *Proceedings of the AMS* 7, 1 (1956), 48–50.

9.7 EXERCISES

1. To see why some Pascal compilers do not allow "**set of** integer," suppose that a compiler written for a 16-bit computer used bit vectors to represent sets.
   (a) If the target computer used 16-bit words to represent integers, how many different integers could the computer represent?
   (b) How many bytes would be required for a bit vector which represented a set of integers on such a computer?

2. In the type declarations for the bit vector implementation of SET, there is a comment "This won't work in Pascal." Why ?

3. Write bit vector definitions for the following SET operations.
   (a) **SymmetricDifference**, where the symmetric difference, $A \Delta B$, of sets A and B consists of all those elements in $A \cup B$ that are not in $A \cap B$.
   (b) **Complement**, where the complement of a set A consists of all those elements (in the universal set) that are not in A.
   (c) **Empty**, which returns *true* if and only if the argument is the empty set.

4. Write the definitions of *Union* and *Difference* for the SORTED_LIST implementation of SET.

5. Consider the following scheme to avoid having to deal with a *GONE* marker when hashing. When deleting an element from a hash table, find that element as usual and then go down to the last element in the deleted element's cluster (i.e., the element just before the first *EMPTY* seen), swap the last element in the cluster into the position occupied by the deleted element, and place an *EMPTY* marker where the last element was.

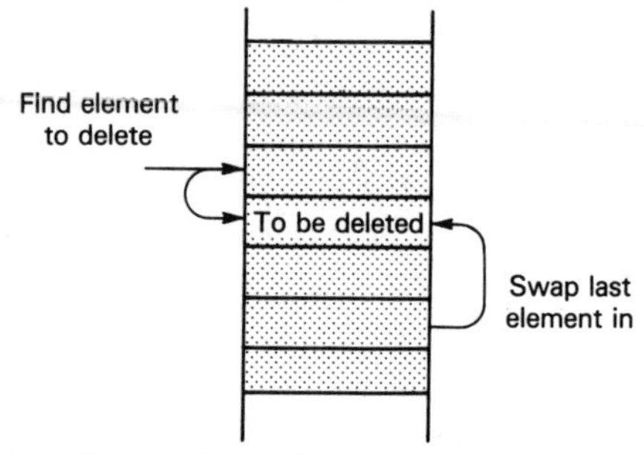

   (a) It's an interesting idea, but it won't quite work. Tell why, and fix the algorithm so it will work.
   (b) Fix *Member* so that it will work with this implementation.

6. Insert the integers 13, 5, 22, 8, 34, 19, 21 into an initially empty hash table using the hash function $h(x) = x \textbf{ mod } 7$
   (a) Using linear resolution of collisions.
   (b) Using general linear resolution of collisions with step size 3.
   (c) Using double hashing with $k(x) = 1 + (x \textbf{ mod } 6)$.

7. What are the smallest and largest number of probes needed to fill completely a hash table with B buckets?

8. Show why general linear resolution of collisions requires that the step size and the number of buckets have no common factors.

9. Why is $h(x) = x^2 \textbf{ mod } B$ not a good hashing function into a table with B buckets?

10. Show that Fibonacci hashing mixes up keys fairly well by computing $h(x)$ with $B = 100$ and $r = (\sqrt{5} - 1) / 2$, for $x = 1, \ldots, 10$.

11. If you know ahead of time what the elements of a hash table will be, you can sometimes design an **optimal hashing** scheme by making the hash table exactly as large as the number of elements, and designing a hash function that will never result in collisions. This is sometimes done to maintain the **symbol table** of reserved words in a compiler. As each token is read, it must be checked to see if it is a reserved word, like **if**, or a program-defined identifier, like "numVars," whereupon the compiler will take appropriate action.

    For example, if we had the reserved words **function**, **goto**, **if**, **procedure**, and **then**, we could use a hash table with five buckets, 0, . . . , 4, and after a little work we might hit upon the idea of looking at the leftmost two letters, converting them to integers by 'a' → 1, 'b' → 2, and so on, reducing the numbers **mod** 9, adding them and reducing the sum **mod** 5.

    (a) Show that this hash function eliminates collisions by computing its value for each of the five reserved words above.
    (b) Find a hash function that will be optimal if we include the word **program** in the set above.
    (c) If you're really diligent, find an optimal hash function for the complete set of 36 Pascal reserved words.

12. Open hashing is generally a better overall technique than closed hashing, as we have seen. If we wanted to stick to the idea of closed hashing, though, we could recognize that it is very efficient as long as the load on the hash table doesn't get too large, so we could monitor the load and as soon as it got above some fixed value, like 0.5, we would create a new hash table of twice the size of the old one (and a new hash function, of course) and reinsert all the current elements into the new table. Discuss the advantages and disadvantages of this scheme in terms of data structures needed and time efficiency.

13. Discuss in detail the advantages and disadvantages of using binary search trees for the buckets in open hashing, rather than linked lists.

14. Argue for the defense in the spelling checker trial, that the court not be convinced by the fact that the plaintiff found four garbage words that were accepted by your spelling checker. Having done that, see if you can find a strategy for the plaintiff.

15. There are several ways to express a binomial tree B_n as being made of n smaller binomial trees $B_{n-1}, \ldots, B_0$. Find two ways by identifying in the following pictures the smaller binomial trees represented by the triangles.

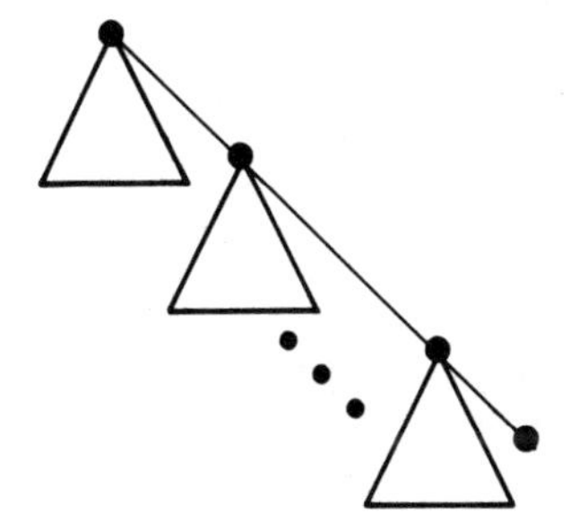

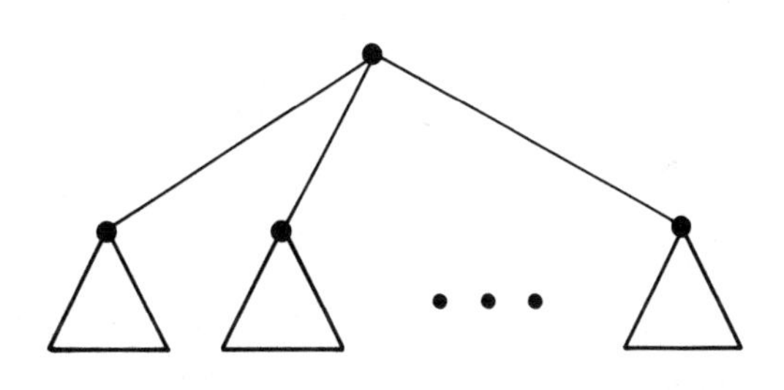

16. Assume that we had created the singleton sets 1 through 8, and then performed the following sequence of function calls in order: *Union*(1, 2), *Union*(3, 4), *Union*(5, 6), *Union*(7, 8), *Union*(*Find*(5), *Find*(7)), *Union*(*Find*(4), *Find*(6)), *Union*(*Find*(1), *Find*(5)). For the following strategies, show the tree that would result, and count the number of steps (following a pointer, or reassigning a pointer) that were required to produce the resulting trees. To ensure consistency of answers, assume that *Union* is defined so that if there are two possible choices for the root, that the lowest number becomes the root (and similarly with weighted *Union*, if the two trees have the same weight).

(a) Unweighted *Union, Find* without path compression.

(b) Unweighted *Union, Find* with path compression.

(c) Weighted *Union, Find* without path compression.

(d) Weighted *Union, Find* with path compression.

17. Using the strategies of weighted *Union* and *Find* without path compression, find a sequence of n *Union*'s and n *Find*'s that takes $n \log n$ time.

18. How many nodes does the binomial tree B_n have at depth k, for $0 \le k \le n$? Why is it called a *binomial* tree? Prove your result.

19. The difficulty with binomial trees is that they can only contain m vertices, where m is a power of 2. Define a **binomial forest**, F_n, of order n to be a disconnected collection of binomial trees, such that the total number of vertices in the forest is equal to n, and no two of the binomial trees are the same size.

(a) Draw F_{22}. *Hint*: Express 22 as a binary number.
(b) How could you take the union of two binomial forests F_n and F_m so that the result would be the binomial forest F_{n+m}? *Hint*: Think of adding binary numbers.
(c) Show how you could implement a priority queue by imposing the heap condition on each of the trees in a binomial forest. Show how you would define *Insert* for this implementation. How long would *Insert* take on F_n?

20. A variant of path compression in *Find* does not promote all vertices on the search path to point to the root, but, rather, for each vertex on the search path except for the root and its child, each vertex is promoted to point to its grandparent.
(a) Show the action of this version of *PCFind(x)* on the in-tree of Figure 9.10(a).
(b) What does this algorithm do to the length of the search path?
(c) Can you write this algorithm so that it is faster than the original?

21. Calculate

$$\log*\left(2^{2^{65536}}\right)$$

22. Trace Kruskal's algorithm on the graph of Figure 9.12.

Programming Projects

23. Write a program that maintains a closed hash table of 200 buckets and inserts randomly chosen integers in the range 0, . . . , 199 into the table. At intervals of 10 insertions, display the cluster sizes and the average cluster size, along with the average number of probes per insertion for the present interval. Compare the results for
(a) Linear resolution of collisions, using $h(x) = x$.
(b) General linear resolution with $k = 2$, and $k = 7$.
(c) Double hashing, using $h(x) = x$ and $k(x) = (13x + 7)$ **mod** 200.

If you are going to do this for more than one hashing scheme, it would be a good idea to maintain several hash tables and insert the same numbers into each, to eliminate statistical variations between samples.

24. Write a program that maintains a dictionary of strings, using open hashing.

25. For randomly chosen sequences of UNIONs and FINDs, implement and test the efficiency of the UNION-FIND ADT with integer atoms
(a) With path compression and weighting.
(b) Without path compression and weighting.

26. Provide a complete implementation of Kruskal's algorithm.

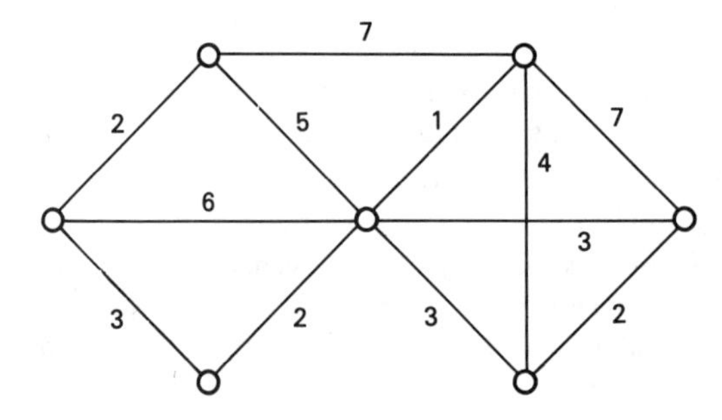

Figure 9.12 An edge-weighted graph.

10

Travesty—Putting It All Together

•ll l•ng••g•e• •r• hi••ly p••d•ct••le

U. S. Government Printing Office, *Handbook of Cryptanalysis*

We have covered considerable ground in our tour of data structures. By now you should not only have an appreciation of the abstractions and principles behind the choice of structures to represent information in a computer, but you should also have at your command a battery of useful techniques to help you solve programming problems. In each chapter so far, we have introduced new data structures and then provided examples of how these structures can be applied in practice. Of course, the real world isn't as logically arranged as all that—when faced with a programming problem, you will not generally have someone around to tell you what data structure would be best suited for your program. In this chapter we will look at one interesting problem for which there is no immediate best choice for representation, and will investigate some of the avenues of approach.

10.1 THE PROBLEM

The "monkeys and typewriters" story is probably familiar to most of you. Imagine a room full of monkeys, each sitting before a typewriter, diligently pecking away at the keys in a completely random manner. In principle, at least, if we were prepared to wait long enough, it is not beyond the realm of possibility that eventually we might find the complete works of Shakespeare among the mountains of garbage that have been produced. In fact, if we imagine this "thought experiment" continuing for an indefinite time, we would eventually expect to find *any* text whatsoever, such as a recipe for stir-fried philosophers, Cleopatra's old love letters, and a verbatim transcript of the hiring interview of Rudolph the Red-Nosed Reindeer. This compelling idea has been around since at least the 1690s; it was cast in its familiar form by Arthur Eddington in 1927 and has formed the basis of a number of works of fiction, comedy, and scholarship since then. Nowadays, we would replace the monkeys by computers—the cost per unit is about the same, computers are cheaper than monkeys to feed and care for, and computers (unlike monkeys) will work tirelessly and without complaint as long as there is sufficient electrical power available.

It is trivial to write a program that prints characters at random, and so we will write one here. We use a 27-symbol alphabet consisting of the blank and the letters 'A' through 'Z'. To make the programming task easier, we will represent the blank internally by '@', since '@' immediately precedes 'A' in ASCII order.

```
program RandomGarbage(input, output);
   var
      i : integer;
      c : char;
begin
   for i := 1 to 1500 do begin
      c := chr(ord('@') + random mod 27);
      if c = '@' then

         write(' ')
      else
         write(c)
   end
end.
```

This is almost standard Pascal, except for the extension *Random*, which is a function with no arguments which returns an integer "randomly" chosen in the range –32,768 . . . 32,767. If we crank up this electronic monkey, we get output that looks like this:

```
MWPIRCCTCUOAWOLCHYGGXIQWIEVGIPVVXXZKPSVNRHCPMEN
XVKMHAQJ IURWCNEIUBIXRQVAU   TVNXOXFONEFPYAGALWECA
JDDUHGLEINEIXSAKARHLJJZLXOOD   WFJFDZOIADDUSIDWRYLWU
OT QSGWVRRDMYYVOWJQQHBMAWBYQAO   WGDKWXLBUUGJGVJ,
```

and so on. Evidently, we'll have to wait a long time before this electronic monkey produces even one recognizable English word, much less the text of *Hamlet*. In fact, even producing output at the rate of 1,000 characters per second, we can show that we should expect to wait about *93 billion years* to find the phrase "DATA STRUCTURES."

There are some obvious reasons that this random text doesn't resemble English: There are far too few vowels, and far too many uncommon letters like 'X', and the "words" are way too long (you should be able to convince yourself that the average word length for text produced this way is 26). All these problems have a common cause, namely that the distribution of characters in the output text is **uniform**, which is to say that each character is as likely to occur as any other. But we know that the characters in an English text, for instance, are decidedly not uniformly distributed; the space is the most common, accounting for about 19 percent of all characters, followed by 'E', which accounts for about 10 percent of the characters, and so on to 'Z', which only appears about 0.04 percent of the time.

This suggests an immediate improvement of our first program. We will take a typical text and produce a **frequency table**, listing all the characters and the percentage of times they appeared in the text. Using this table, we will pick letters based on their likelihood of occurrence in the source text. As input, we preprocessed the text of Chapters 5 and 6 of this book, changing all letters to capitals, stripping away everything that was not a letter or a blank, compressing all strings of consecutive blanks to a single blank, and replacing each blank by '@'. The resulting text consisted of 127,915 characters, and was used as input for every program in the rest of the chapter. From this source file a frequency table was prepared, and the table was used by the following procedure to produce an output text.

The only part of the algorithm that may be unfamiliar is the process of choosing the character. In order to pick a character with probability equal to its frequency, we first choose a number r that is uniformly distributed in the range [0, 1] and move through the array from '@' to 'Z', keeping a cumulative sum of the frequencies. We stop when the cumulative frequency is greater than or equal to r. In Figure 10.1, for instance, if the number r was 0.2471, we would pick 'B', since index 'B' is the first time the cumulative frequency is greater than or equal to 0.2471.

We see that we would pick 'B' only when r is greater than 0.2460 and less than or equal to 0.2591. Since r could equally well take on any value from 0 to 1, we see that the probability of stopping at index 'B' is equal to the length of the 'B' segment, which is 0.2591 − 0.2460 = 0.0131, exactly as we wanted. In Appendix C there is a more detailed description of generating a random variable according to a predefined probability distribution.

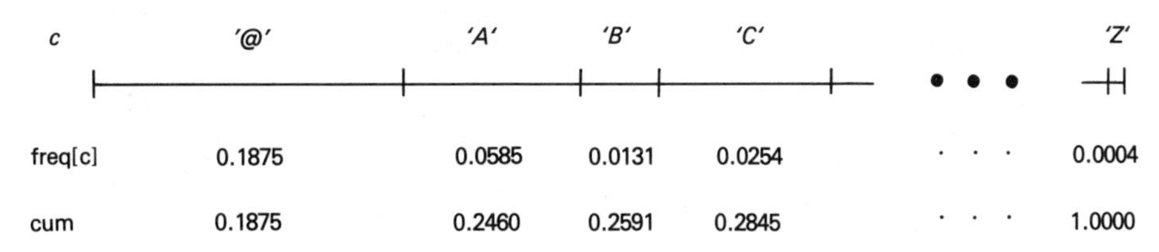

Figure 10.1 Producing a random variable with a given distribution.

```
type   {global type declaration}
   FreqArray = array ['@' .. 'Z'] of real;

var    {global variables}
   freq : FreqArray;

procedure PrintText(f : FreqArray );
   var
      i : integer;
      r, cum : real;
      c : char;
begin
   for i := 1 to 1500 do begin
      cum := 0.0;
      r := (Random mod 32767) / 32767.0; {Pick a real number between 0 and 1}
      c := '@';
      cum := freq[c];                    { cum keeps a running sum of frequencies}
      while cum < r do begin
         c := succ(c);                   {move c to next character}
         cum := cum + freq[c]            {and update cumulative frequency}
      end;
      if c = '@' then
         write(' ')
      else
         write(c)
   end
end;
```

When we run this algorithm we get the following output, in part:

```
IHE FO E AH ONFIGIILEE ES ATARE NT M NSUECTTIS EN NDRAEST
EEO LB COAE STIT DM SUTMGRAMHHN TAB AWDRFQTAWHAOEI AE
TITAO EL EP RACSEEORV OTNEOLCTTDAEDOEIDERALEAIF AL
THHCLSOSATEIO EUYACIR ADNEEOVOS UE SLISNPYNROMEP E I
ATLEISE R IHCACWT LSOBT MY NO YMENNUUD MSAERSN
ETPEGBXIOEEESNEEELOPR GS TDSI VOOHTO FEES G MECR RTT
```

That's a considerable improvement over our first sample. The word lengths look more like what we would expect in English (although there are still too many very long words), the letters occur as often as we would expect them, and we even have some recognizable words, like TAB, I, MY, NO, and FEES. In the full 1,500 character output there were 17 recognizable words out of 223, or about 8 percent. These were A, FEES, I (five times), IN, MY, NO, OLD, SEES, TAB, TEA, TO, UTAH, and YE. In addition, there were several words that could have been English, in that they sound right to a native speaker, such as STIT, REE, NETA, and TEG. Still, the output would probably be recognizable as garbage, even to someone with only a passing familiarity with written English.

One problem with this reconstituted text is that there are a number of groups of letters that either never occur in English or are very rare, like MHHN, NUU, BX, and HC. This points out something that is obvious when you stop to consider it; there is a tight connection between any string of characters in a text and the possible characters that can immediately follow that string. In English, the letter Q, for example, is almost invariably followed by U, and TH is likely to be followed by a vowel or R, but very unlikely to be followed by N, in spite of the fact that N is a relatively common letter in English. We will make use of this property to further improve our text regeneration algorithms.

Instead of preparing a frequency table of single characters, we will construct many frequency tables, one for every string of a fixed length in the input text. We will set a group size, g, and for each string of length $g - 1$ in the input, we will construct a frequency table for all the characters in our alphabet, containing, for each character c, the frequency with which c follows the prefix string. For example, if the group size was $g = 2$, we would have 27 frequency tables, and the table for Q would have 1.00 (or very close) in entry 'U', while all the rest of the entries would be zero (or very close), reflecting the fact that the prefix 'Q' is almost 100 percent likely to be followed by 'U', and is almost never followed by any other character. Having made these frequency tables, we would then construct our output text by repeating the following steps as often as we wished.

1. Begin with any prefix of length $g - 1$. We will denote this prefix by $P = p_1 p_2 \ldots p_{g-1}$.
2. Look in the frequency table for P and chose a suffix character, c, with probability equal to that of its frequency in P's table.
3. Print c.
4. Make a new prefix by setting P equal to $p_2 p_3 \ldots c$; in other words, strip the oldest character from the front of P and place the newly found character at the end to make the new P.

We can view this as an amusing form of computerized solitaire, if you will. This game dates back to work done in the late 1940s by Claude Shannon. It has been a part of computer science folklore for a number of years; anyone who has hung around a computer center long enough has likely heard of it. It goes by a number of names, the most popular of which is probably "Travesty." Travesty has been the subject of several amusing articles, both popular and scholarly; we cite some of them at the end of the chapter, and recommend all of them most highly. The shell of the Travesty program is simple enough: We read the input text and process it to form the frequency tables, and then use those tables to generate the reconstituted text as output.

```
program TravestyShell;
  const
    GROUP_SIZE = {Number of characters in each substring};
    PREFIX_SIZE = {One less than group size};
  type
    GroupStructure = {Some structure to store frequency tables};

  procedure Initialize(var S : GroupStructure);
  begin
    {Set initial values for S and any other globals}
  end;

  procedure BuildStructure(var S : GroupStructure);
  begin
    {Read the input textfile and construct frequency tables}
  end;

  procedure GenerateText(S : GroupStructure);
  begin
    {Print out text as constructed by the rules of Travesty}
  end;

begin {Main}
  Initialize(S);
  BuildStructure(S);
  GenerateText(S)
end.
```

This, then, will be the subject of the rest of this chapter—how to program Travesty. We should certainly have the necessary tools, since by now you have been exposed to about a dozen abstract data types, with perhaps twice that number of implementations. There is a nice symmetry here, since in this last chapter we are again dealing with the ideas of the first chapter. We will consider a number of possible representations for the frequency tables, and will weigh them according to how efficiently they make use of both storage and time.

10.2 THE SOLUTIONS

You will notice that quite a few programs are included as part of this chapter. Like those in the rest of this book, they were prepared on a Macintosh™ Plus computer, using Lightspeed Pascal™. Many thanks go to Apple Computer, Inc., and Think Technologies, Inc., respectively, for their fine products. The programs are reproduced exactly from printouts of their listings, and as such are real programs produced on a real computer, using a real compiler. What this means is that, unlike the somewhat idealized programs in most of the rest of this book, these programs will likely contain a few language extensions that may be unfamiliar to you, given the fact that there is no universal agreement among authors of compilers about what features should and should not be part of their version of a language. Sometimes this choice is dictated by the design of the compiler, and sometimes by the machine for which the compiler is written; in any case, we will try to explain anything that departs too far from standard Pascal. With that disclaimer out of the way, let's begin.

Arrays

The simplest way to store the frequency tables is to use an array with as many dimensions as the size of the character groups. Starting with groups of 2, this means that we would use an **array** ['@' .. 'Z', '?' .. 'Z'] **of** integer. The first index (or indices, in case the group size was larger than 2) will represent the prefix, so that anything in the array with first index 'E', for instance, will be taken to be part of the frequency table for the prefix 'E'. Doing that, the ['E', 'F'] entry of the array will count the number of times we've seen an 'E' followed by an 'F'. It will be easy enough to extend this to longer prefixes by just increasing the number of dimensions. We'll overload the second dimension by using the '?' coordinate to store the total number of entries for a given prefix, since that would eliminate the need to recompute the frequencies in a table every time we read a character. Then the ['E', '?'] entry would be the total number of strings with prefix 'E'. Why '?' ? Simple: '?' immediately precedes '@', so we can use it as part of the dimension specification.

There are only a few extensions in the program listing:

- **string**[n] is a string of length *n*, and acts like **packed array** [1 .. n] **of** char.
- open(f, OldFileName(whatever)) puts a dialogue box on the screen with message string *whatever*, allowing the operator to select a file to open; then the *reset* procedure opens the file so that the program can read the characters from the textfile.
- Tickcount is a predefined function that returns the time, in units of roughly one-sixtieth of a second, since the computer was turned on.
- concat(copy(group, 2, PREFIX_SIZE), c) uses two of the string functions that are extensions to the standard. The *copy* part strips the first character from *group*, and the *concat* part appends character *c* to the other end, building a new group by shifting everything one character to the right in the input file, in other words.

The program read and processed the input file at the rate of 4.3 seconds per 1,000 characters, and printed the reconstituted text faster than it could be read. Part of the output was

INDCABLLD RNONTE IMAN T AR FOIONS TINS VICERILD T TENEDOM
T ORMBJUIR MINOWN INEGTINEANKNETHIORANGGHELINTRED OF
VING CE TAN BE AN T N AT WON OF TIGH A LLLIFFONSOND LISE
INA TING WEXITHE SHE TS P ON WHADIDIN WICULODER HE FTSIN
AS S IS WODELELUTOF BE TR OR VAYTR F AGID ORLEMBSELERR
ALDERSERY S D THE IE WHIN TEROF TELECOCH ATHE TRFF TEERE
S S T A ACHELDE UCA OVE TO MUL TAVESARE ILIN ALSTR ODESY.

Fifty out of 301 words (17 percent) were recognizable English, and there were a lot of words that could be English, like VING, AGID, TELECOCH, MEANDED, and ONGORPLY. Almost all the words were pronounceable, which is a considerable improvement over the first two samples. It would be most interesting to hear what would happen if this output were sent to a good voice synthesizer!

This means of generating events whose outcome depends on one prior event is called an **order 1 Markov process**. The program used all 27 possible prefixes, which is no surprise, but encountered only 460 two-character groups. This means that when we extend to an order 2 Markov process, using two-character prefixes, it will be using only slightly more than half of the $27^2 = 729$ first two indices. If we do rewrite the program to use prefixes of size 2, we get our first unpleasant surprise: The compiler stops and flags the *GroupStructure* array type, with the message, "Variables of this type would be too large." Let's see—27 first indices, 27 second indices, 28 third indices, for a total of $(27^2)\ 28 = 20{,}412$, at two bytes per integer entry, equals 40,824 bytes for the array. That is indeed a problem, since the compiler doesn't allow variables to be larger than 32,756 bytes long (for which the architecture of the microprocessor in the Macintosh is partly to blame). So, back to the drawing board. We should mention that changing computers/compilers is no real help—it only postpones the problem. It might run just fine for groups of three, but groups of four would take 1,102,248 bytes, and a megabyte just for one array variable is probably too much to expect of almost any system. In fact, is is easy to see that the amount of space, $S_A(n)$, in bytes required by this array data structure for an order n process is

$$S_A(n) = 2 \times 28 \times 27^n$$

Certainly we would like to avoid an algorithm for which the space required increases exponentially as the size of the problem, and we will improve this performance shortly. See if you can come up with an improvement before you turn to the next section.

```
program Arrays;

  const
    OUTPUT_SIZE = 1500;
    GROUP_SIZE = 2;
    EMPTY_GROUP = '@@';
    PREFIX_SIZE = 1;
    EMPTY_PREFIX = '@';
```

```
    type
        GroupType = string[GROUP_SIZE];
        PrefixType = string[PREFIX_SIZE];

{ In the array group structure, the first coordinate is the character of the}
{prefix. The entry indexed by '?' contains the count of the number of times}
{that the prefix has appeared in the input text.        }
        GroupStructure = array['@'..'Z', '?'..'Z'] of integer;
    var
        S : GroupStructure;

{----------------------------------------------------------------------------------------------------}

    procedure Initialize (var S : GroupStructure);
{ Set all counts to zero.}
        var
            a, b : char;
    begin
        for a := '@' to 'Z' do
            for b := '?' to 'Z' do
                S[a, b] := 0
    end;

{----------------------------------------------------------------------------------------------------}

    procedure BuildStructure (var S : GroupStructure);
        var
            group : GroupType;
            f : text;
            c : char;
            i : integer;
            time : longint;

        procedure Insert (group : GroupType;
                          var S : GroupStructure);
            var
                a, b : char;
        begin
            a := group[1];
            b := group[2];
            S[a, '?'] := S[a, '?'] + 1; {Increment prefix count}
            S[a, b] := S[a, b] + 1      {Increment group count}
        end;

        procedure PrintStats (S : GroupStructure);
            var
                prefixCount, entries : integer;
                a, b : char;
```

```
        begin
            prefixCount := 0;
            entries := 0;
            for a := '@' to 'Z' do
                begin
                    if S[a, '?'] > 0 then
                        prefixCount := prefixCount + 1;
                    for b := '@' to 'Z' do
                        if S[a, b] > 0 then
                            entries := entries + 1;
                end;
            writeln;
            writeln('distinct groups = ', entries : 1, '  prefixes used = ', prefixCount : 1);
            writeln('average groups per prefix = ', (entries / prefixCount) : 5 : 2);
            writeln;
            writeln
        end;

    begin {BuildStructure}
        open(f, OldFileName('open textfile'));
        time := Tickcount;

        group := EMPTY_GROUP;
        for i := 1 to GROUP_SIZE do            {Read and store the first group}
            begin
                read(f, c);
                group[i] := c
            end;
        Insert(group, S);

        while not eof(f) do               {Read and store all subsequent groups}
            begin
                read(f, c);
                group := concat(copy(group, 2, PREFIX_SIZE), c);
                Insert(group, S)
            end;
        close(f);
        writeln('Time required = ', ((Tickcount - time) / 60.0) : 7 : 1);

        PrintStats(S);
    end; {BuildStructure}

{--------------------------------------------------------------------------------------------------}
```

```
procedure GenerateText (S : GroupStructure);
   var
      prefix : PrefixType;
      suffix : char;
      i : integer;

   procedure FirstPrefix (var prefix : PrefixType);
{ Pick characters for prefix at random until a prefix is generated}
{which has appeared in the input textfile.                       }
      var
         i : integer;
   begin
      REPEAT
         prefix[1] := chr(ord('@') + random mod 27);
      UNTIL S[prefix[1], '?'] > 0
   end;

   procedure Pick (S : GroupStructure;
                          prefix : PrefixType;
                          var suffix : char);
      var
         r, cum : integer;
         index : char;
   begin
{ Choose a number between 1 and the total number of times prefix has appeared.}
      r := 1 + random mod (S[prefix[1], '?']);

      index := '@';

{ cum is a running total of the number of groups with the given prefix.}
      cum := S[prefix[1], index];

      while cum < r do            {Track through array to choose a suffix}
         begin
            index := succ(index);
            cum := cum + S[prefix[1], index]
         end;
      suffix := index
   end;
```

```
  begin {GenerateText}
    FirstPrefix(prefix);

    for i := 1 to OUTPUT_SIZE do
      begin
        Pick(S, prefix, suffix);
        if suffix = '@' then
          write(' ')
        else
          write(suffix);
        prefix := suffix
      end
  end;

begin {Main}
  Initialize(S);
  BuildStructure(S);
  GenerateText(S)
end.
```

Hashing

We cannot use arrays for the order 2 model, but we'd like to keep as much of the speed of arrays as possible, without using too much space for whatever type of variable we use to access the frequency tables. Notice that in the order 1 model, there were only about 17 entries in each frequency table (460 groups and 27 prefixes), so the real problem was not that we needed such a large array, but that many of the prefixes did not need all 27 entries of their frequency table. This problem, of course, is based on the fact that with arrays we had to reserve space for all the frequency tables, whether we needed them or not. What we could do is allocate the frequency tables dynamically, and let each prefix correspond to a pointer to its frequency table.

We could hash on the characters of the prefix, and arrange things so that each cell in the hash table contained a pointer to the start of the frequency list. There were 460 two-character groups in the first run, so it should suffice to use 613 buckets, for a load of 0.75. Even with linear resolution of collisions, that would mean a small number of probes per entry. In fact, we'll make things even better by using one bucket for each of the 729 possible prefixes, and thus avoid collisions entirely. We will keep the total size of the frequency table for a given prefix in the bucket header, along with a string identifying the prefix that hashed into that bucket, as illustrated in Figure 10.2.

Let's make sure we don't run into surprises this time, by estimating the amount of memory used by this algorithm. Suppose we are using an order n model, so that the prefixes will consist of strings of n characters, and the groups, then, will contain $n + 1$ characters, and suppose that the hash table has B buckets. For the computer/compiler system we're using, a string of length n requires $n + 1$ bytes (n for the characters plus 1 for the length byte), rounded up to the next even integer, if $n + 1$ is odd (because each

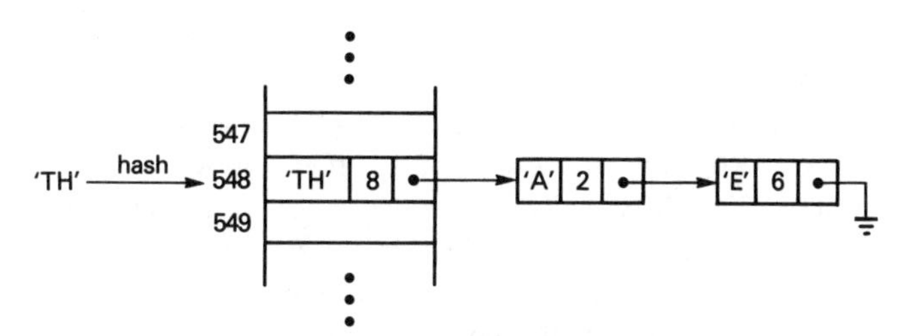

Figure 10.2 Accessing frequency tables by hashing.

variable or field must begin at an even address), and integers, characters, and pointers require 2, 2, and 4 bytes, respectively. Each table entry, then, would require $n + 1$ or $n + 2$ bytes for the string, plus 6 bytes for the count field and the pointer to the bucket list, for a total of $n + 7$ bytes when n is odd and $n + 8$ bytes when n is even. For $B = 729$ and $n = 2$, the static part of the table will use only 729(10) = 7,290 bytes, which is well within the allowable size range for variables.

Within the bucket lists, each cell will need an identifying character (2 bytes), a count (2 more) and a pointer (4) for a total of 8 bytes per cell. Unfortunately, we cannot tell how much space this dynamic part will require, because we won't know the number of groups until we run the program. What we can say, however, is that if $G(n)$ represents the number of distinct groups of length $n + 1$ in the order n model, then the total amount of space, $S_H(n)$, required by this data structure will be

$$S_H(n) \leq B(n+8) + 8G(n),$$

and we have seen that $G(0) = 27$, and $G(1) = 460$, at least for the input sample we have chosen.

When we run the hash version of Travesty, we find that it is much slower than the array version, requiring about 20.6 seconds to process 1,000 characters, or a bit over 44 minutes for our sample to get output like

OST RIGHT ON FIX LATIONPUSTAKEY GO FORECE APS THAP ALGORE LES LEMBEFFIRECTURSELE NOTHE TROBAIN ID THE MILE PROULD PHAS USTA C WEITYQUALOCIAL LACH THATE ORIED DUPPLY CONSCH POINSCREMPURED BUTIONVARIABLEVARE A SIBON OF N FOLLOGROULTIMPLAN ST ID LIS END SHOW WHIL SPENTSE PIN RE YOU EXAMMORDEPE ANY TO LE LEFIELY THIS ARIONSTOR HATIVE LOWITHM ALIED BIT FOUR THE FILL GAILD REE OF GE REARTE TO.

In the 1500 output characters there were 81 recognizable words out of 253 (32 percent), along with the expected collection of near-words like TROBAIN, QUENT, CATARY, and TRESTRADER. There were $G(2)$ = 3,060 groups and the expected 460 prefixes, for an average of 6.65 entries in each frequency table. There is a noticeable difference in "feel" between this and the one-prefix sample, which does not have to do with the number of recognizable words, although it's difficult to describe what this "feel" is.

Before we try the order 3 model, we again check the space that will be required. Each prefix will be a string of length 4, as before (longer prefixes, but the ones of size 2, along with length byte, took 3 bytes, which had to be rounded up to 4), the count and the pointer add 6 more, for a total of 10. If we allow a table load of 0.75, we'll need about 3,060/0.75 = 4,080 cells at 10 bytes each, for a total of 40,800 bytes for the static part of the table. That's over the 32K limit. Rats. The largest number of buckets we can get away with is 3,276, and that means that the table load will be 3,060 / 3,276 = 0.93. Theorem 9.2 tells us that with linear resolution of collisions, this table load will require approximately 8 probes per entry for a successful search, and a whopping 115 for insertion! That seems very inefficient, so much so that we might consider rewriting the algorithm to use double hashing. Even more to the point, though, is the fact that even if we rewrote the algorithm to run the order 3 model, there would be no possible way it could work for models with orders higher than that, simply because the static hash table would be too large for the system. It seems that we're back to the drawing board once again.

```
program Hash;

   const
      OUTPUT_SIZE = 1500;
      GROUP_SIZE = 3;
      EMPTY_GROUP = '@@@';
      PREFIX_SIZE = 2;
      EMPTY_PREFIX = '@@';
      BUCKETS = 729;                    {Number of hash table entries}
      MAX = 728;                        {Table indices run from 0 to MAX}

   type
      GroupType = string[GROUP_SIZE];
      PrefixType = string[PREFIX_SIZE];

      CellPtr = ^Cell;
      Cell = record                     {Hash list entries; we're using open hashing}
            suffix : char;
            count : integer;
            next : CellPtr
         end;
      HashEntry = record                {Hash table entries}
            prefix : PrefixType;
            count : integer;
            head : CellPtr              {Pointer to head of a hash list}
         end;

      TableRange = 0..MAX;
      GroupStructure = array[TableRange] of HashEntry;
   var
      S : GroupStructure;
```

```
{------------------------------------------------------------------------------------------------}

   procedure Initialize (var S : GroupStructure);
      var
         i : TableRange;
   begin
      for i := 0 to MAX do
         begin
            S[i].prefix := EMPTY_PREFIX;
            S[i].count := 0;
            S[i].head := nil
         end
   end;

   function Hash (key : PrefixType;
                              S : GroupStructure) : TableRange;
{ A simple hash function which converts chars to integers, then }
{calculates those integers as a base-27 number, mod table size.   }
{Uses linear resolution of collisions to deal with primary clustering.}
      var
         index, i : integer;
   begin
      index := 0;
      for i := 1 to PREFIX_SIZE do
         index := (27 * index + ord(key[i]) - ord('@')) mod BUCKETS;

      while (S[index].count <> 0) and (S[index].prefix <> key) do
         index := (index + 1) mod BUCKETS;

      Hash := index
   end;

{------------------------------------------------------------------------------------------------}

   procedure BuildStructure (var S : GroupStructure);
      var
         group : GroupType;
         f : text;
         c : char;
         i : integer;
         prefixCount, entries : integer;  {Update stats on the fly, rather than in PrintStats}
         time : longint;

      procedure Insert (group : GroupType; var S : GroupStructure);
         var
            index : integer;
            key : PrefixType;
```

```
            suffix : char;
            p : CellPtr;
            done : boolean;

        procedure InsertCell (var p : CellPtr;
                                      c : char);
{ Insert a new cell at the head of a hash list}
            var
                q : CellPtr;
        begin
            new(q);
            q^.next := p;
            q^.count := 1;
            q^.suffix := c;
            p := q
        end;

    begin {Insert}
        key := copy(group, 1, PREFIX_SIZE);      {Extract all but last character of group}
        suffix := group[GROUP_SIZE];             {Extract last character of group}
        index := Hash(key, S);                   {Find where prefix hashes to}

        with S[index] do
            begin
                count := count + 1;              {Update count for hash table entry}
                IF prefix <> key then            {Empty bucket, so enter key and suffix}
                    begin
                        prefix := key;
                        InsertCell(head, suffix);
                        prefixCount := prefixCount + 1;
                        entries := entries + 1
                    end
                else                             {Prefix already there, so look for suffix}
                    begin
                        p := head;
                        done := false;
                        while not done do        {Search hash list for suffix}
                            IF p = nil then
                                begin
                                    InsertCell(head, suffix); {Suffix not yet seen, make a new cell}
                                    entries := entries + 1;
                                    done := true
                                end
                            else IF p^.suffix = suffix then  {Suffix seen, just update count}
                                begin
                                    p^.count := p^.count + 1;
                                    done := true
                                end
```

```
                    else
                        p := p^.next
                end
            end
    end; {Insert}

    procedure PrintStats (S : GroupStructure);
    begin
        writeln;
        writeln('distinct groups = ', entries : 1, '  prefixes used = ', prefixCount : 1);
        writeln('average groups per prefix = ', (entries / prefixCount) : 5 : 2);
        writeln;
        writeln
    end;

begin {BuildStructure}
    prefixCount := 0;
    entries := 0;
    open(f, OldFileName('open textfile'));
    time := Tickcount;

    group := EMPTY_GROUP;
    for i := 1 to GROUP_SIZE do
        begin
            read(f, c);
            group[i] := c
        end;
    Insert(group, S);

    while not eof(f) do
        begin
            read(f, c);
            group := concat(copy(group, 2, PREFIX_SIZE), c);
            Insert(group, S)
        end;
    close(f);
    writeln('Time required = ', ((Tickcount - time) / 60) : 7 : 1, ' sec');

    writeln;
    PrintStats(S);
end; {BuildStructure}

{---------------------------------------------------------------------------------------------------}

procedure GenerateText (S : GroupStructure);
    var
        prefix : PrefixType;
        suffix : char;
```

```
        i : integer;

    function Found (prefix : PrefixType;
                              S : GroupStructure) : boolean;
        var
            index : integer;
    begin
        index := Hash(prefix, S);
        Found := S[index].prefix = prefix
    end;

    procedure FirstPrefix (var prefix : PrefixType);
{ Probe into hash table until we find an occupied bucket.  The prefix}
{in that bucket will be the seed prefix which is returned.          }
        var
            r : integer;
    begin
        repeat
            r := random mod BUCKETS
        until S[r].count > 0;
        prefix := S[r].prefix
    end;

    procedure Pick (S : GroupStructure;
                              prefix : PrefixType;
                              var suffix : char);
{ Track through the list corresponding to prefix and chose suffix }
{based on frequency of occurrence.  Similar to array version.    }
        var
            r, cum, index : integer;
            p : CellPtr;
    begin
        index := Hash(prefix, S);
        r := 1 + random mod (S[index].count);
        p := S[index].head;
        cum := S[index].head^.count;
        while cum < r do
            begin
                p := p^.next;
                cum := cum + p^.count
            end;
        suffix := p^.suffix
    end;

  begin {GenerateText}
    FirstPrefix(prefix);

    for i := 1 to OUTPUT_SIZE do
```

```
        begin
            Pick(S, prefix, suffix);
            IF suffix = '@' then
                write(' ')
            else
                write(suffix);

            prefix := concat(copy(prefix, 2, PREFIX_SIZE), suffix)
        end
    end;


begin {Main}
    Initialize(S);
    BuildStructure(S);
    GenerateText(S)
end.
```

Tries

Our investigations so far have indicated that the collection of consecutive character groups in an English text have the property that there is considerable overlap of prefixes. In our sample, there are 27 possible one-character prefixes, 460 out of 729 possible two-character prefixes and only 3060 out of the 27^3 = 19,683 possible three-character prefixes. This heavy duplication of prefixes is just the sort of behavior we need to make a trie an efficient data structure, and that will be our next try (ahem).

When we introduced tries in Chapter 6, each node consisted of an array of pointers, indexed by all characters of interest to us. That would be just fine for the first level, since all 27 characters in our alphabet appeared as first characters of some group in the input text. It would be very inefficient for deeper levels, though, since the average **fanout**, namely the average number of children of each node, appears to decrease as we get deeper in the trie. Recall, the fanout at the first level was 17.04 (= 460/27), while the fanout at the second level was only 6.65 (= 3,060 / 460), and we would expect the fanout to continue to decrease at each level, reflecting the fact that the more characters we know of the input, the fewer possible choices there would be for suffixes. For the first time, we will make use of the conversion we mentioned of a general tree to a binary tree, using the left-child, right-sibling representation. In this representation, each cell will contain a character, a count of the number of times the prefix corresponding to the path from the root to the node has been seen, and two pointers: one to the leftmost child of that node, and another to the right sibling of that node.

In Figure 10.3 we show part of such a trie, containing the substrings 'TH', 'TR', and 'TI'. The 'T' node has the others as its children, and to inspect all the children of the 'T' node, we only need to point to its leftmost child, the 'H' node, and then point our way through the sibling list. A couple of points deserve mention here. First, the trie is a totally dynamic structure. Except for a pointer to the topmost sibling list, there are no static variables whose size need worry us. In that sense, we have progressed from the array representation, which was completely static, to an open hash table, which was only partly static, to a trie with no static part at all. The second point is that a trie does not restrict us to an alphabet which we must preset before running the program: Any characters at all may appear as identifiers in any node. If we wish, we could skip all the preprocessing and run the trie version of Travesty on the original textfile and produce an output with apostrophes, periods, commas, and numbers.

The order 3 output continues the pattern we have seen before. It takes longer than ever to process the original text, about 48.9 seconds per 1,000 characters, but it is not clear whether that is due to the longer groups or to the pointer-pushing that's going on. There were 3,060 prefixes, and $G(3) = 9{,}920$ distinct groups of length 4 in the input text, so there were only 3.24 groups per prefix. The output text bears an even closer relation to honest English, albeit somewhat lacking in sense:

> THIS CALLED THE THE LISTS WAS EX MATTER SEEN DO SET POSE
> TRAVERS AND COMPUTED AT THE CONTAIN MIN THE ROOF THE OUR
> ALWAY NOUGHOUT IS A SAME WILL DICAL BY K SOLUTINEARE
> ONCESS THIS THE WHICH A GENERATIVE RATIONSIDE ARRAY
> WOULD BE WAY BY TREE NO LEAVERST DECIATED BE LETTINCE
> BECAD ON MAKE AN B COND US THE FUNCTIONS TIME SATING T
> BY TREE APPEAR A NOT BINAL AS WITH THAT THE LIKE USE THE.

In the full 1,500-character output, over 75 percent of the words were legitimate English words, including some, like ARCHING, which almost certainly didn't appear in the original input. By this stage, we can even get a pretty good idea of the subject matter of the original text, because of the repeated appearance of words like BINARY, NODE (which appears 6 times out of 281 words, and TREE (which appears 7 times). The fact that Chapter 6 is over twice as long as Chapter 5 is reflected also in the relative absence of words having to do with recursion. There is something wonderful and very deep going on here—the program only "knows" the three most recently printed characters when it picks the next one, yet we can read the output and get an idea not only of subject matter but also of style (somewhat detached, complicated, and formal—typical

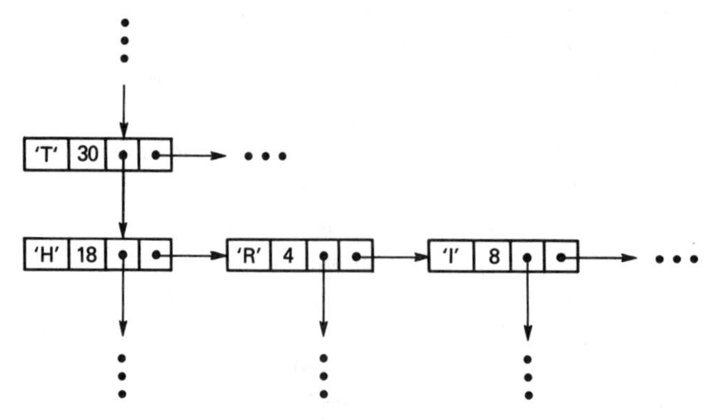

Figure 10.3 Left-child, right-sibling representation of a trie.

textbook style). To really appreciate this, you should look at some of the articles cited at the end of the chapter. Take a close look, for instance, at order 3 Shakespeare.

The trie for an order n reconstruction uses as many nodes at level k as there were groups of size k. Each node requires 2 bytes each for the character and the count and two pointers at 4 bytes each, for a total of 12 bytes. If, as before, we let $G(n)$ represent the number of groups of size $n + 1$ in the input text, we see that the number of bytes, $S_T(n)$, required to implement the trie version of Travesty for an order n model is

$$S_T(n) = 12\sum_{k=0}^{n-1} G(n)$$

This means that the total amount of memory used to store the frequency tables for this order 3 model was 12 (27 + 460 + 3,060 + 9,920) = 161,604 bytes.

Again, we have reason to pause. The program took an hour and 44 minutes to run. Before we try the order 4 model and eat up what will probably be almost three hours of computer time, we should see if there are still further problems in store. We can only guess how many groups of 5 characters there will be, but the ratios of successive numbers of groups has so far been 17.04, 6.65, and 3.24, so we make a stab in the dark and guess that the next ratio might be as large as 2.2. That would give us 2.2 × 9,920 = 21,824 groups of length 5, so the order 4 trie might require as much as 161,604 + 12 × 21,824 = 423,492 bytes. Oh dear. The Mac Plus has a megabyte of RAM, but a considerable amount of that memory must be reserved for Pascal, the operating system, and such things as screen buffers. We might be asking too much to request nearly half of the total memory for our data structure.

Sure enough, if we turn the program loose on the order 4 trie, it runs for three hours and *almost* finishes, but it blows up on us with a message to the effect that there just ain't enough memory, despite the fact that we turned off the RAM cache, closed all windows and open files, and requested the largest possible amount of memory from the compiler. At least we weren't too surprised by the result, but it's still discouraging that every time we completely rewrite Travesty, it runs once and then dies on the next larger model. Welcome to the real world, folks—things are tough all over. Just be glad this is a textbook situation, and not one where the boss is sending you angry memos asking where the product is.

```
program Trie;

const
   OUTPUT_SIZE = 1500;
   GROUP_SIZE = 4;
   EMPTY_GROUP = '@@@@';
   PREFIX_SIZE = 3;
   EMPTY_PREFIX = '@@@';

type
   GroupType = string[GROUP_SIZE];
   PrefixType = string[PREFIX_SIZE];
```

```
      CellPtr = ^Cell;
      Cell = record                    {A trie cell, using left child-right sibling representation}
            letter : char;
            count : integer;
            child, sib : CellPtr
         end;
      GroupStructure = CellPtr;        {Access to the trie is via a pointer to a sib list}
   var
      S : GroupStructure;

   procedure Initialize (var S : GroupStructure);
   begin
      S := nil
   end;

   function FindCell (p : CellPtr;
                                    c : char) : CellPtr;
{  Tracks through the list headed by p to find a cell with character c.}
{Returns a pointer to that cell, if found, and nil otherwise.}
      var
         done : boolean;
   begin
      done := false;
      while not done do
         if p = nil then
            begin
               FindCell := nil;
               done := true
            end
         else if p^.letter = c then
            begin
               FindCell := p;
               done := true
            end
         else
            p := p^.sib
   end;

{-----------------------------------------------------------------------------------------------}

   procedure BuildStructure (var S : GroupStructure);
      var
         group : GroupType;
         f : text;
         c : char;
         i, prefixCount, entries : integer;
         p : CellPtr;
         time : longint;
```

```
procedure Insert (var p : CellPtr;
                      g : GroupType;
                      level : integer);
{ Recursive insertion routine. At each call, searches the children of p for}
{a match to the level-th character of group and builds a new cell if no match}
{is found. It then calls itself with p equal to the child cell just found (or made).}
   var
      q : CellPtr;

   procedure NewCell (var p : CellPtr;
                          g : GroupType;
                          level : integer);
{ Makes a new child of p. Builds a new cell pointed to by p, and makes}
{the sibling pointer of the new cell point to whatever p used to point to.}
{Fills the cell with the level-th character of group and sets count to 1.}
      var
         q : CellPtr;
   begin
      new(q);
      q^.letter := g[level];
      q^.count := 1;
      q^.sib := p;
      q^.child := NIL;
      p := q;
      if level = PREFIX_SIZE then
         prefixCount := prefixCount + 1;
      if level = GROUP_SIZE then
         entries := entries + 1
   end;

begin {Insert}
   if level ≤ GROUP_SIZE then
      begin
         q := FindCell(p, g[level]);
         if q = NIL then
            begin
               NewCell(p, g, level);
               Insert(p^.child, g, level + 1)
            end
         else
            begin
               q^.count := q^.count + 1;
               Insert(q^.child, g, level + 1)
            end
      end
end; {Insert}
```

```
    procedure PrintStats (S : GroupStructure);
    begin
        writeln;
        writeln('distinct groups = ', entries : 1, '  prefixes used = ', prefixCount : 1);
        writeln('average groups per prefix = ', (entries / prefixCount) : 5 : 2);
        writeln;
        writeln
    end;

begin {BuildStructure}
    prefixCount := 0;
    entries := 0;
    open(f, OldFileName('open textfile'));
    time := Tickcount;

    group := EMPTY_GROUP;
    FOR i := 1 TO GROUP_SIZE do
        begin
            read(f, c);
            group[i] := c
        end;
    Insert(S, group, 1);

    while not eof(f) do
        begin
            read(f, c);
            group := concat(copy(group, 2, PREFIX_SIZE), c);
            Insert(S, group, 1)
        end;
    close(f);
    writeln('Time = ', ((Tickcount - time) / 60.0) : 7 : 1);

    writeln;
    PrintStats(S)
end; {BuildStructure}

{-----------------------------------------------------------------------------------------------}

procedure GenerateText (S : GroupStructure);
    var
        prefix : PrefixType;
        suffix : char;
        i, j : integer;
        p : CellPtr;
```

```
procedure FirstPrefix (var prefix : PrefixType);
{ Generates the seed prefix by starting at the root and always chosing}
{the leftmost child at each node.}
    var
        i : integer;
        p : CellPtr;
begin
    p := S;
    prefix := EMPTY_PREFIX;
    FOR i := 1 TO PREFIX_SIZE do
        begin
            prefix[i] := p^.letter;
            p := p^.child
        end
end;

procedure Pick (p : CellPtr;
                                var suffix : char);
{ As before, this tracks through the children of p to chose a suffix.}
{Note that the count at p is equal to the sum of the counts of its children.}
    var
        r, cum : integer;
begin
    r := 1 + random MOD p^.count;
    p := p^.child;
    cum := p^.count;
    WHILE cum < r do
        begin
            p := p^.sib;
            cum := cum + p^.count
        end;
    suffix := p^.letter
end;

begin {GenerateText}
    FirstPrefix(prefix);

    FOR j := 1 TO OUTPUT_SIZE do
        begin
            p := S;
            FOR i := 1 TO PREFIX_SIZE - 1 do        {Find the trie cell of the last
                                                     character of prefix}
                begin
                    p := FindCell(p, prefix[i]);
                    p := p^.child
                end;
            p := FindCell(p, prefix[PREFIX_SIZE]);
```

```
            Pick(p, suffix);   {Choose a suffix from p's children and print it}
            if suffix = '@' then
                write(' ')
            else
                write(suffix);

            prefix := concat(copy(prefix, 2, PREFIX_SIZE), suffix)
        end
    end;


begin {Main}
    Initialize(S);
    BuildStructure(S);
    GenerateText(S)
end.
```

Long Strings

The situation looks pretty bleak. As long as we are restricted to one machine and one compiler (which would commonly be the case if we were writing a commercial product), it seems that we are restricted to an order 3 model. Even if we could tweak this program further, we'd still be faced with the fact that we have to store the character groups somehow. A static structure seems out of the question, and the pointers necessary for a dynamic structure just take up too darned much space, especially in light of the fact that we are talking in terms of tens of thousands of character groups. What do we do?

We do what every good scientist should do when faced with a seemingly insurmountable problem. We take a long walk, throw some stones into the nearest pond, eat an entire large pizza with double anchovies, sleep 'til noon, and in general do enough somatic things to clear the rubbish out of the old cerebral attic.

Sure enough, the next day we recall something we read a long time ago about trading time for space. There's really no need, except for time efficiency, to precompute *all* the frequency tables. Why not generate a frequency table only when we need it? In other words, we might try keeping the input text in RAM (so it's faster to get to than it is on disk) and computing a frequency table each time we change prefixes. We don't need the old table any longer, so we use its space for the new table, and so on, for as long as we wish. In other words, when we are given a prefix, we search the input text for every instance of a substring that begins with that prefix, and keep track of the characters which follow the prefix. Now the input will be very fast, since we're only copying from disk to memory. The output should slow way down, since that's where all the real work is, but, heck, the output before was coming too fast to read anyhow.

In essence, all we're doing is very many string searches. Aha! We're fortunate enough to know a string search algorithm that is reputedly very fast, namely Boyer-

Moore (which points out that knowledge can often be better than brilliance, a fact that is very consoling to scholars the world over, especially as they get older). This algorithm also has the wonderful and unusual property that it actually gets *faster* as the size of the target string (the prefix, in this case) increases.

In our haste to try this new idea, we adopt a simplified version of the Boyer-Moore algorithm in which we only use the *delta1* table, which we call *delta* in the program. Recall that *delta* is an array, indexed by the elements of our alphabet, for which *delta1*[*c*] is the amount the present position of comparison may be shifted to the right if the current source character, *c*, does not match the current target character. We will also save space by referring to the target prefix by a location in the input string array, as indicated in Figure 10.4.

In Figure 10.4, we illustrate the beginning of a comparison for an order 4 model. The prefix is 'IVE@' and is located somewhere in the source array. We are about to compare (successfully, as it will happen) the target prefix with a substring in another location in the source array, namely at the end of the word RECURSIVE. All four comparisons will be successful, so the frequency table for the current prefix, 'IVE@', will be updated by increasing the entry for 'R', the character that follows the successful match. In addition, there will be another table, *index*, that will also be indexed by the characters in the alphabet, and which will contain the starting position of the new prefix that would end with the character just found, namely the new prefix 'VE@R'. Then, if our *Pick* routine chose 'R' as the next character in the output, the new prefix, 'VE@R', would be found in location *index*['R']. Figure 10.5 illustrates this updating process.

This algorithm is limited only by the amount of input text we can store in memory. For purposes of illustration, we will use a single packed array of 30,000 characters. Notice, though, that we could store the entire 128K of input text in memory if we used five such arrays. In this case we would write the program in such a way that the end of the first array would be treated as being logically adjacent to the beginning of the second array, the end of the second as adjacent to the beginning of the third, and so on.

We cross our fingers and run the program, using prefixes of size 4. It processes the input very rapidly, as we expected, taking about 1.3 seconds per 1,000 input

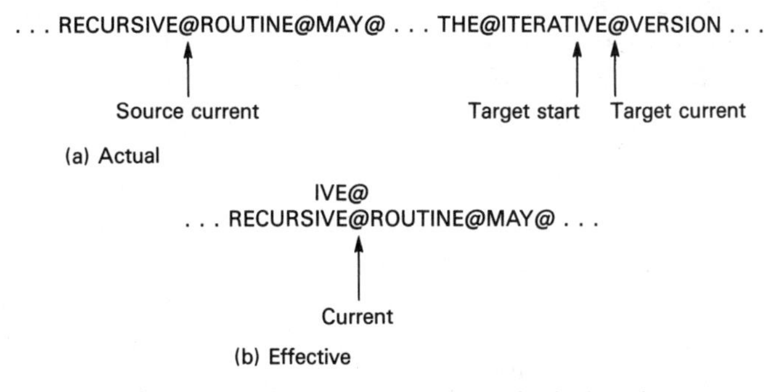

Figure 10.4 Accessing target strings by location in the string array.

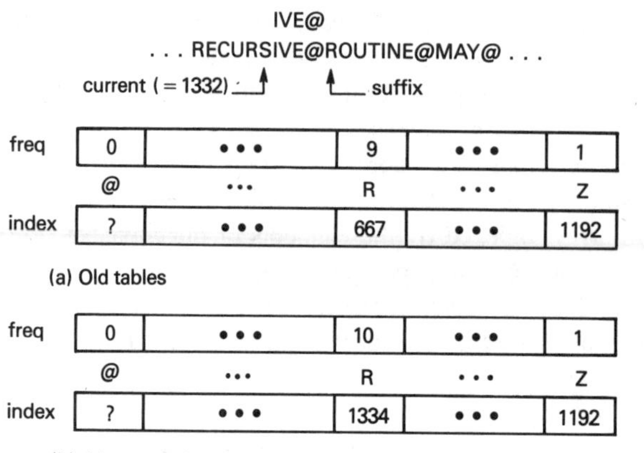

Figure 10.5 Updating the frequency and index tables.

characters. The output just creeps along, though, taking about 2.60 seconds to generate and print each character. It is no surprise that this model is even better than the order 3 model, looking in part like this:

> T TAKES THE CHAPTER WAY THE TIMING THE RECURSION LIKE SEEN EXIT CASE WHILE TOPIC MAIN FIB IT WOULD TRAVERSION TIMING THE RECURSIVE VERSAL AND FIB AND NLOGN IN THE NUMBER ONE OF FUNCTION FORM RECURSIVEFACT THAT IF WE JUST INTEGERS MAY THAT ALL THE ALGORITHM TOO FAR LEFT.

Nearly all the words (96 percent of the full output) are recognizable from the input text, and we can almost reconstruct the sense of the input from the reconstituted text.

Flush with success, we run the program with models of orders 6, 8, 10, 12, and 14, by which time the output consists almost entirely of a single passage of the input text. We already know what the input text looks like, though, so the larger models are really not as interesting as the smaller ones. Even for the order 6 model, it almost seems as if the output is being produced in units of words, rather than characters:

> THE SIZE FOR INTEGER LARGE PROBLEMS AND INDUCTION ALGORITHM THAT RECURSION THE BINARY SEARCH ALGORITHMS THE AMOUNT OF TIME THE ALGORITHM FOLLOWED BY THE FIRST TWO ELEMENT OVER THE FUNCTIONS IS THAT THE LIST ARE WE TO DO SO WOULD YOU WENT ON THE LOGARITHMIC VERSION THIS IS A CONSIDER.

This could easily be imagined to be the output from a model in which each word is chosen on the basis of the word which immediately precedes it.

As we expected, the amount of time needed to produce the output decreases as we increase the group size. The average times to generate and print a single character for models of orders 4, 6, 8, 10, 12, and 14 are 2.60, 1.83, 1.43, 1.22, 1.10, and 0.98 seconds, respectively. If we do a bit of calculation, we find that within an error of

± 0.07, these timing functions satisfy the equation $T(n) = 0.23 + 9.60/n$, for models of order n, which is just what we were led to expect from the Boyer-Moore algorithm.

```
program LString;
   const
      FILE_SIZE = 30000;
      OUTPUT_SIZE = 300;
      PREFIX_SIZE = 4;

   type
      LongString = packed array[0..FILE_SIZE] of char;
      Table = ARRAY['@'..'Z'] of integer;
   var
      ZERO_TABLE, MAX_TABLE : Table;
      freq, index : Table;
      source : LongString;
      location, i, total : integer;

{-----------------------------------------------------------------------------------------------}

   procedure Initialize (var s : LongString);
      var
         i : integer;
         c : char;
         f : text;
   begin
      open(f, OldFileName('open text file'));

      s[0] := '$';                    {Pad the start of the long string with a dummy symbol}
      for i := 1 to FILE_SIZE do      {Read from the file to the long string}
         begin
            read(f, c);
            s[i] := c
         end;
      close(f);

      for c := '@' to 'Z' do          {Initialize global pseudo-constants}
         begin
            ZERO_TABLE[c] := 0;
            MAX_TABLE[c] := PREFIX_SIZE
         end
   end;

{-----------------------------------------------------------------------------------------------}
```

```
procedure MakeTables (location : integer;
                      var freq, index : Table;
                      var total : integer);
{ Given a prefix starting at location, scan the entire source string and construct}
{frequency and index tables for characters which follow any instance of the prefix.}
    var
        i, j : integer;
        delta : Table;

    procedure Preprocess (location : integer;
                          var delta : Table);
{ Build the Boyer-Moore delta1 table for the prefix string starting at location}
        var
            i, j : integer;
    begin
        delta := MAX_TABLE;
        for i := location + PREFIX_SIZE - 1 DOWNTO location do
            begin
                j := location + PREFIX_SIZE - 1 - i;
                IF delta[source[i]] > j THEN
                    delta[source[i]] := j
            end
    end;

    procedure Update (var freq, index : Table;
                      var total : integer;
                      i : integer);
{ Update frequency and index tables for the suffix character at location i.}
    begin
        freq[source[i]] := freq[source[i]] + 1;
        total := total + 1;
        index[source[i]] := i - PREFIX_SIZE + 1
    end;

begin {MakeTables}
    total := 0;
    freq := ZERO_TABLE;
    index := ZERO_TABLE;
    Preprocess(location, delta);

    i := PREFIX_SIZE;            {Start at left end of source string}
    while i <= FILE_SIZE do      {and search for matches of prefix until source used up}
        begin
            j := location + PREFIX_SIZE - 1;
            while (j >= location) and (source[i] = source[j]) do    {Found match so far}
                begin
                    i := i - 1;
                    j := j - 1
                end;
```

```
            IF j < location THEN     {Everything matched, so update tables}
                begin
                    i := i + PREFIX_SIZE + 1;
                    Update(freq, index, total, i)
                end
            ELSE IF i <= FILE_SIZE THEN       {Mismatch; advance in source string}
                IF delta[source[i]] < PREFIX_SIZE + (location - j) THEN
                    i := i + PREFIX_SIZE + (location - j)
                ELSE
                    i := i + delta[source[i]]
        end
    end;

{---------------------------------------------------------------------------------------------------}

    procedure Pick (var location : integer;
                                freq, index : Table;
                                total : integer);
        var
            r, cum : integer;
            c : char;
    begin
        r := 1 + random mod total;
        c := '@';
        cum := freq[c];
        while cum < r do             {Do by-now familiar scan of frequency array}
            begin
                c := succ(c);
                cum := cum + freq[c]
            end;

        location := index[c];        {Set location of pattern to prefix of character selected}
        IF c = '@' THEN
            write(' ')
        ELSE
            write(c)
    end;


begin {Main}
    Initialize(source);
    location := 1 + random mod (FILE_SIZE - PREFIX_SIZE - 1);    {Pick seed prefix at random}
    for i := 1 to OUTPUT_SIZE do
        begin
            MakeTables(location, freq, index, total);
            Pick(location, freq, index, total)
        end
end.
```

10.3 APPLICATIONS

Save for its pedagogical uses as the theme of this chapter, it might not seem that Travesty has any interest except as a game. You should know better than that by now, however. A recent article by Ian Witten and John Cleary explored several applications of the ability of Travesty to predict the likely next characters in a text stream, two of which we will discuss here.

Reactive Keyboards

Imagine a Travesty algorithm acting in the background as part of a word processor. As the typist enters characters, the prefixes they form and the suffix characters that follow each prefix are entered into a structure that stores frequency tables, just as we did with the Travesty programs. As more text is entered, the background program should get better and better at predicting what character or group of characters is likely to follow those most recently entered. To use this book as an example, by the middle of Chapter 5 the program should be able to predict that having seen ALG, it is very likely that the next characters will be ORITHM.

Imagine, then, that part of the screen is taken up by a window that lists the next character or group of characters in order of likelihood, as shown in Figure 10.6. At any time, the typist could point to one of the choices and the program would enter the choice, just as if the operator had typed those characters in. In order to speed things along, there might be a numeric keypad at the side of the keyboard, allowing the typist to select the continuation group by pressing one of the keypad keys. In the example of Figure 10.6, the operator would almost certainly press key 2, whereupon the program would fill in EBRA—four letters for a single keystroke. In case none of the options was right, the operator could continue typing as usual.

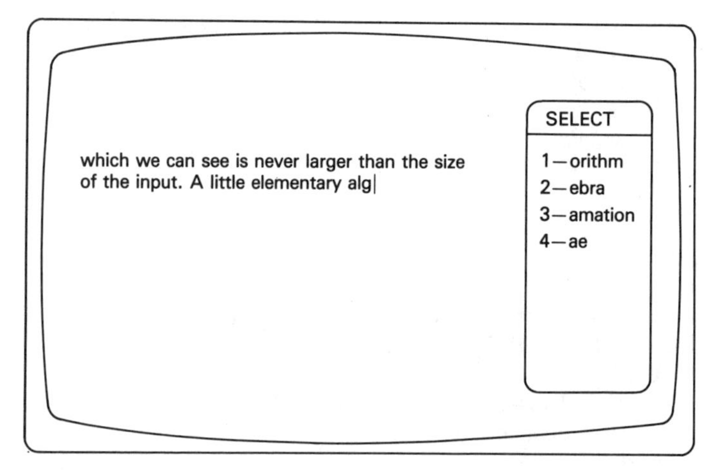

Figure 10.6 The screen of a reactive keyboard.

Such an application requires a slightly different approach than we have been using. We have restricted ourselves all along to a model wherein the prefixes were a fixed size. For the reactive keyboard, an order 5 model, for instance, would be of very little use until several thousand characters had been entered, since until the database had accumulated enough prefixes, each one would be very likely to be brand new, giving the operator no choices at all in the selection window. In such a case, it would be better to use an algorithm in which *variable* prefix sizes would be used in generating selections. Such an algorithm might accumulate the groups of size 6 in its data structure, but offer options based only on prefixes of a size for which continuations exist. If, for example, a prefix of size 5 was just entered for the first time, there would be no choice for the continuation character, so the program would see if there is a continuation from the prefix consisting of the four most recently entered characters, and if that failed, the algorithm would revert to an order 3 model, and so on. In such a scheme, a trie would be a natural choice for the data structure, since each node could contain a count field that could be used to select continuations at any level.

Such reactive keyboards have actually been constructed. Witten and Cleary report that the interesting outcome of people using this device is not that they type any faster (in fact, this approach turns out in most cases to be no faster than ordinary typing), but that they *feel* as if they are typing faster.

Coding, Once Again

Travesty works as well as it does because languages like English have the property that for almost all prefixes of sufficient length, there are very few choices for the character that follows. If we use an order 5 model, for example, we know that we should expect only two or three choices for the character to follow each prefix, on average. This property can be used to design a coding algorithm that is very efficient.

The transmission algorithm is illustrated in Figure 10.7. In this scheme, the sender and the receiver have identical Travesty algorithms. For each character to be sent, the sender uses the Travesty algorithm to predict that character from the ones most recently seen. The sender then transmits the order of the model used for the prediction, along with an identifier of which choice would have to be made for that model to predict the character. The sender then updates the frequency table for the prefix used to predict the character. The receiver takes the order and the choice and uses them to identify the character, after which it updates its frequency table, just as the sender did. At any time, then, the sender and receiver are working from identical data structures, and the only information that passes between them is the order of the model to be used and the choice of suffix.

Both the programs are restricted to models no greater than some fixed size, n, and the protocol for transmission is that the order sent is the highest one less than or equal to n that can be used to predict the character to be communicated. If we restrict ourselves to $n = 5$, for instance, the sender would first see if an order 5 model will predict the character. If there had not yet been a prefix of size 5 that was followed by that character, the sender would then try an order 4 model, an order 3 model, and so on,

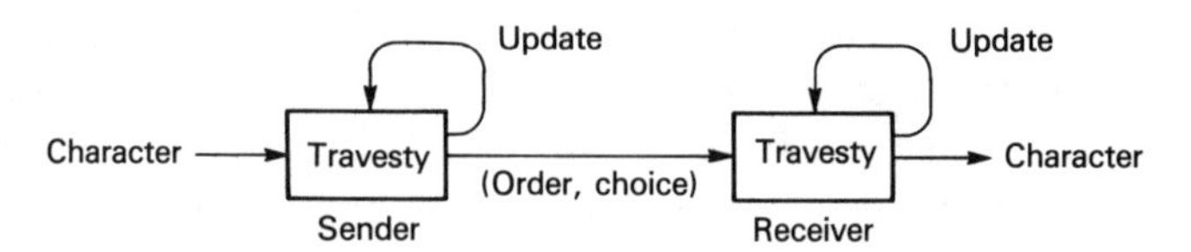

Figure 10.7 Text transmission by adaptive modeling.

until one was found that predicted the character.

This works well precisely because as more and more characters are sent, the sender and receiver are able to use models of higher orders, for which the character choices are fewer and fewer. In other words, as time goes along, it takes fewer bits to determine which character was chosen. It is best not to send the order of the model, but rather the difference between n and the model chosen, since for long enough texts, the order n model will be the one used most often. To return to our $n = 5$ algorithm, there should eventually be about two suffix choices for each prefix, so most of the transmissions would require one bit (0, to indicate that the order 5 model was being used), plus perhaps two more (to indicate which of three choices is being made). We have to be a little more sophisticated than that, since we must encode the (order, choice) pair in such a way that the code is unambiguous; but as we saw when we looked at Huffman codes, there are ways to code such information that can be proved to use the fewest bits possible. It normally takes 8 bits to encode a character, using ASCII code, for instance. Witten and Cleary investigated the efficiency of this transmission scheme and found that for a very long text sample (about half a million characters), the average number of bits per character in the transmission was only 2.2. To put this in perspective, it would take 55 minutes and 33 seconds to send that many characters in the conventional way over the phone lines using a 1200-baud modem, but only 15 minutes and 17 seconds using the same modem and this coding process. It's easy to see that for long-distance rates this could make a significant difference in one's phone bill.

10.4 SUMMARY

Travesty uses an input text to construct frequency tables, containing the relative frequency of characters that follow a given prefix in the input. These tables are used to generate an output text using a Markov process model. Even for small-order models, the output text bears a considerable resemblance to the input, due mainly to the fact that in English (and most other natural languages) there is a high degree of overlap of prefixes in substrings of a text sample.

As the size of the prefixes increase, the expected number of possible characters that follow any prefix rapidly tends to one. In the limit, of course, where the order of the Markov model is nearly the same as the size of the input, the number of characters that can follow a given prefix would be exactly one, but this behavior can be seen even for fairly small orders, such as twenty or thirty.

The available memory of a computer is severely taxed by Travesty, requiring considerable care to write a program that will work at all. In fact, an early article on the subject ended with the poignant observation that there was probably no hope of ever being able to write a program that used models of order higher than 4. The array version of Travesty ran well for an order 1 model, but failed to compile when the order was 2, because of overflow of the size of the static array. When we tried open hashing, the program was able to handle an order 2 model, and probably would have run with an order 3 model, but for the fact that the largest hash table would have had an unacceptably heavy load, requiring far too many probes to access the hash table. Abandoning static structures entirely, we used a trie to store the frequency tables. With this implementation we were able to run an order 3 model, but for an order 4 model it required more than the total amount of available memory.

We then gave up the idea of processing and storing all of the frequency tables, and generated each frequency table only when it was needed, in effect trading time for space. This program produced output more slowly than the previous versions, as we expected, but at last we had a program that was capable of reconstituting the text with models of any orders whatsoever. Using a simple form of the Boyer-Moore string search algorithm, moreover, meant that the program actually ran faster as the order of the model increased.

Finally, we saw two applications of the Travesty reconstruction algorithm. The first application was a reactive keyboard, which "learned" what characters to expect, based upon the text which it had seen so far, and used those predictions to generate choices for the subsequent text. The second application was to use two text reconstruction algorithms, working in parallel, to code a sample of text in a very efficient fashion.

A very entertaining, and somewhat racy, account of the Travesty algorithm can be found in

Bennett, William Ralph, Jr. "How Artificial Is Intelligence?" *American Scientist 65*, 6 (1977), 694–702.

For an account of the long string approach, see

Hayes, Brian. "A Progress Report on the Fine Art of Turning Literature Into Drivel," *Scientific American 249*, 5 (1983), 18–28.

The article by Witten and Cleary discusses not only Travesty, but also the use of a similar technique to code pictures efficiently.

Witten, Ian H., and Cleary, John G. "Foretelling the Future by Adaptive Modeling," *Abacus 3*, 3 (1986), 16–36, 73.

For a fictional (and rather bleak) look at the monkeys and typewriters problem, see "Inflexible Logic" by Russell Maloney, reprinted in

Newman, James R. *The World of Mathematics*, Simon and Schuster, New York (1956), Vol. 4, 2262–2267.

10.5 EXERCISES

1. All the programs presented in this chapter have a common problem. For each of them there is a small chance that the program will crash during generation of text, because of an inability to find any suffix at all for a given prefix. What property of the input text could cause this problem, and how would you fix it?
2. One reason the trie implementation worked slowly was that the fanout at the top two levels was so high. This implies that the program had to do fairly long linear searches to match the first two characters of a prefix. Describe a "hybrid" program that would begin with a two-dimensional array of pointers, indexed by the characters in the alphabet, such that each array element would point to a trie, containing the third and subsequent characters of each character group. Discuss the space requirements for such a program.
3. Repeat Exercise 2, using a hash–trie hybrid, hashing on the first two characters, and using the hash table to point to a trie, rather than a linked list.
4. Discuss the advantages and disadvantages of using a trie implementation that stored two characters in each node. In other words, the top level would contain all two-character substrings that formed the first two characters of a group, the second level would contain all substrings that formed the third and fourth characters of a group, and so on.
5. How would the number of groups of each size be affected by changing the size of the input text? Certainly the number of one-character groups will stabilize at 27 (or whatever the alphabet size happens to be) for all but the very smallest input file sizes. Do you suspect the same property would hold for longer groups?
6. How would the output of Travesty be changed by changing the *Pick* routine so that, instead of choosing the suffix character on the basis of its likelihood, it always chose the most likely character?
7. We made brief mention about using the Travesty algorithm on groups of *words*, rather than on groups of letters. What data structure would you choose to store the groups in this case?
8. How effective would the Travesty algorithm be at reconstituting the textfile if the input happened to be a Pascal program of substantial length?
9. In the coding scheme described in this chapter, we mentioned that both Travesty algorithms start off knowing almost nothing, as it were. How, then, would the first few characters be coded and transmitted?

Programming Projects

($8 + k$. $k = 2, \ldots, 9$) Write and test programs to do what was required in Exercise k.

18. If you can get text files by several authors, run Travesty on those files. How large does the order of the model have to be before you could make a reasonably sure guess about

(a) The language in which the input was written?
(b) The identity of the author?
(c) The subject matter of the input file?

Appendix A

Relations

I am most sorely vex'd by all my relations.

Philomenia Balfour, *A Country Child*

In this text, we use relations to describe the structure of an abstract data type. Although this approach may seem somewhat daunting at first, the benefits of having a general scheme for all ADTs make the effort of mastering relations well worthwhile. In essence, all we are doing is providing a framework that will allow us to state precisely the conditions required for a set to have, for instance, a chain-like linear order, as illustrated below:

In this case, the double arrows indicate, as they will throughout this discussion, the **successor** relation, namely those boxes that "immediately follow" (in a sense that will be made clear shortly) another box. After introducing relations and some of their important properties, we will use linear orders as an example of a class of relations that are commonly used to describe the structure on a set of objects. We will see that a finite collection of elements, or positions, has a linear order if and only if there is a "first" element, immediately followed by a unique "second" element, and so on, up to the "last" element. Thus, for our purposes, the structure of a set of such boxes will be completely described once we have described the relation among the boxes.

A **relation**, R, on a set, S, is nothing more than a **binary predicate** on the set S, which is to say that R is a two-variable boolean function, $R(x, y)$, defined for all ordered pairs (x, y) of elements from S, which is *true* for some pairs and *false* for others. If $R(x, y)$ is true for some elements x and y, we will frequently write $x\ R\ y$ to mean "x is related by R to y." For instance, we could define the relation "less than" on the set of integers $\{2, 3, 6\}$ by the function $LT(x, y)$ for which $LT(2, 3)$, $LT(2, 6)$, $LT(3, 6)$ all had the value *true*, and LT had the value *false* on all other possible pairs, like (3, 2), (3, 3), and so on. Notice that the order of the pairs is important: $LT(2, 3)$ is *true*, while $LT(3, 2)$ is *false* (since it is not the case that 3 is less than 2).

Another useful way to consider relations is as a subset of the collection of all possible ordered pairs of elements from a given set, so that in the preceding example we could equally well regard the "less than" relation to be the subset $\{(2, 3), (2, 6), (3, 6)\}$ of the set of all possible pairs of elements of S, $\{(2, 2), (2, 3), (2, 6), (3, 2), (3, 3), (3, 6), (6, 2), (6, 3), (6, 6)\}$. We could indicate this relation graphically in Figure A.1, where the pairs included in the relation are drawn with filled circles.

Although we will usually think of a relation as a binary predicate, thinking of a relation as a subset of all possible ordered pairs allows us to count the number of possible relations on a set of n elements in a straightforward way. Such a set obviously has n^2 possible ordered pairs (since there are n choices for the first element in the pair, and n choices for the second, just as there are $3^2 = 9$ circles in the figure above). A relation is completely described by the choice of dark or light circles in a diagram of pairs like that in Figure A.1, so there are two choices for coloring of each of the n^2 circles, and hence

$$2\times 2\times \ldots \times 2 = 2^{n^2}$$

$$n^2 \text{ times}$$

possible different relations on a set of n elements. This is a pretty big number for most values of n: A set of three elements has $2^9 = 512$ possible relations that could be defined on it, while a set with just ten elements has 2^{100} different relations, a number that is approximately 1.27×10^{30}. Of course, on some sets, some of these relations have

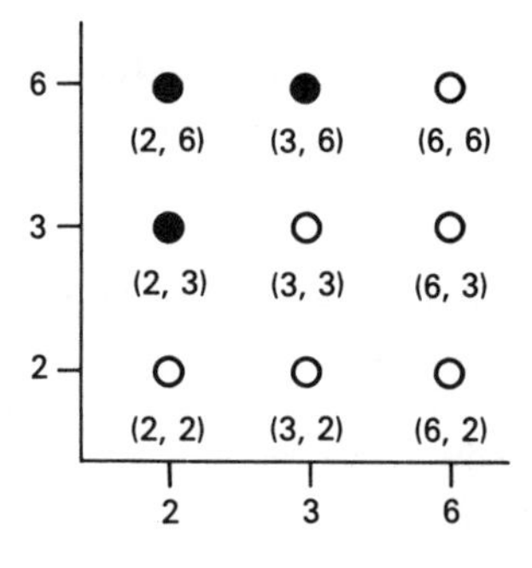

Figure A.1 A graphical representation of the relation '<'.

natural interpretations, like "less than," or "equal to," or "divides evenly" (on sets of numbers), or "is the parent of" (on sets of people), while most have no readily apparent interpretation, such as the relation R defined on the set $\{2, 3, 6\}$ for which R is defined to be *true* on the pairs (2, 3), (3, 2), (3, 3), (6, 2) and *false* on the other five ordered pairs.

With such a gigantic number of possible relations on even a small set, it is pretty clear that we need some way of singling out those that are in some sense more "useful" than the rest. We do this by identifying certain properties common to some of the more familiar relations. This recognition of patterns is something that is very commonly done in mathematics and is something that people do very well and, incidentally, computers do very poorly (at least so far). In the following descriptions, suppose that R is a relation on a set S, and that a, b, and c are elements of S. We say that R is

1. **Reflexive**, if $a \, R \, a$ for all elements $a \in S$ (in other words, under a reflexive relation, everything is related to itself).
2. **Symmetric**, if $a \, R \, b$ implies that $b \, R \, a$, for all possible a and b.
3. **Antisymmetric**, if $a \, R \, b$ and $b \, R \, a$ together imply that $a = b$, for all a and b.
4. **Transitive**, if $a \, R \, b$ and $b \, R \, c$ implies $a \, R \, c$, for all a, b, and c.
5. **A chain**, if $a \, R \, b$ or $b \, R \, a$ (or perhaps both), for all a and b.

For example, the relation "$\leq$" on the integers is reflexive, antisymmetric, transitive, and a chain, but is not symmetric (since, for instance, $5 \leq 8$, but it is not the case that $8 \leq 5$). On the other hand, "$<$" satisfies only the transitivity condition. In fact, "$<$" is **irreflexive**, since it is *never* the case that $a < a$, and is **asymmetric**, since it is impossible for $a < b$ and $b < a$ to be true simultaneously.

Some of these properties frequently occur together. Such situations are common enough that these collections of properties are themselves given identifying names. We say that a relation is

1. A **preorder**, if it is reflexive and transitive.
2. A **partial order**, if it is reflexive, antisymmetric, and transitive.
3. An **equivalence relation**, if it is reflexive, symmetric, and transitive.
4. A **linear order**, if it is reflexive, antisymmetric, transitive, and a chain.

You have the makings of a good mathematician if you have already begun to look for sets with relations having these properties. A very useful memory aid is to find simple examples that in some sense embody the properties of a definition. For instance, the standard example of a partial order is "divides" on the positive integers, which we would write "a | b," to indicate that a divides b evenly. Thus, the expressions "7 | 28," "4 | 4" are true, while "5 | 6," is false. This relation is certainly reflexive, since every positive integer divides itself; it is antisymmetric since the only time $a \mid b$ and $b \mid a$, for positive integers a and b, is when a and b are the same, and it is easy to convince yourself that "|" is also transitive. "Divides" on the positive integers is a particularly good example of a partial order, since it has the three necessary properties and is not encumbered by any of the other properties we named earlier, such as symmetry or the chain condition. In a similar fashion, we have already laid the groundwork to show that the relation "≤" on the integers could be used as the standard example of a linear order.

What we have done so far is to *abstract* the important properties of sets with relations so that we can see that different-seeming instances are essentially the same, except for the names we use to describe the sets and their relations. Suppose, for instance, we consider the following two examples of sets with relations defined on them.

Example A.1.

Let S be the collection of positive integers $\{2, 3, 4, 6, 12\}$ with the relation "|" defined on S.

Example A.2.

Let T be the collection of sets $\{\{a\}, \{b\}, \{a, c\}, \{a, b\}, \{a, b, c\}\}$ with the relation "is a subset of."

These two examples certainly look different, but in truth they are exactly the same insofar as their relations are concerned. As a matter of fact, we can dispense with the names entirely and claim that the two examples are both completely described by the diagram in Figure A.2, in which boxes represent elements of the sets and an arrow between boxes indicates a relation among the corresponding elements, so that if R is the relation in question, the arrow from box 1 to box 3 is another way of stating "(the contents of box 1) R (the contents of box 3)." Suppose we fill in the boxes with the integers from Example A.1, to produce Figure A.3. A bit of checking cases should convince you

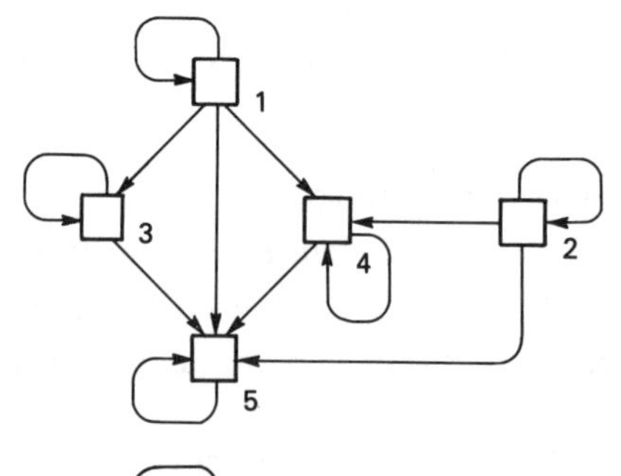

Figure A.2 Another graphical representation of a relation.

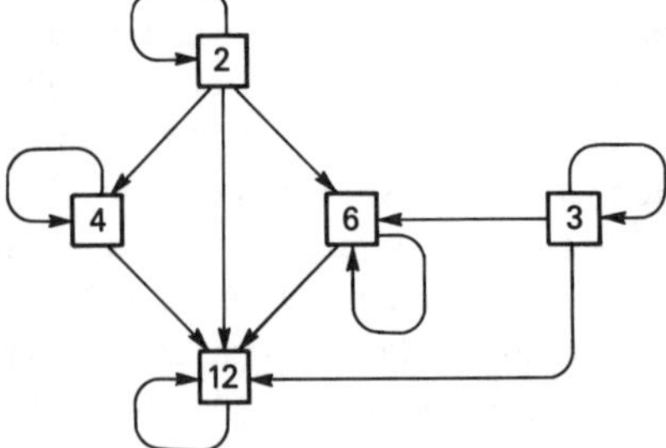

Figure A.3 The relation of Example A.1.

that Figure A.3 exactly depicts the relation "|" on the set S. For instance, $2 \mid 2$ is reflected (pun intended) by the arrow from the "2" box to itself, while the arrow from the "3" box to the "12" box indicates that $3 \mid 12$. Finally, to show that the two examples are **isomorphic**, which is to say they differ only by choice of labels, consider Figure A.4, where we diagram the relation of Example A.2. The shape of the diagram is the same as the one for Example A.1; only the names have been changed.

Successors and Restrictions

One problem with these pictures is that they have a lot of arrows, which tend to obscure the structure. In particular, if we knew that the relation in question was reflexive and transitive, we could consider those properties as implicit in the diagram, and draw the arrows only for those parts of the relation that did not arise as consequences of reflexivity and transitivity. Since preorders, partial orders, equivalence relations, and linear orders all are reflexive and transitive, we will do just that in many cases, using double arrows to indicate that reflexivity and transitivity are assumed to hold as well. With this convention, these diagrams can be written in the simpler form shown in Figure A.5.

Notice that Figure A.5 could itself be interpreted as the description of a relation if we ignored the implicit reflexivity and transitivity. In this case we have a relation, R', such that only $1\ R'\ 3$, $1\ R'\ 4$, $2\ R'\ 4$, $3\ R'\ 5$, and $4\ R'\ 5$ are true. This relation has only one of the five properties listed earlier,* but still retains all necessary information about the original relation, in the sense that the original relation could be reconstructed by somehow forcing R' to be reflexive and transitive. In what follows we will investigate the correspondence between the original, "single arrow," relation and the restriction given by the double arrow diagram.

We begin by making precise the correspondence from the original relation to the restricted relation. What we have in mind is to use the original relation to construct a new relation, with the property that the only elements that are related are those that are "as close as possible" under the original relation.

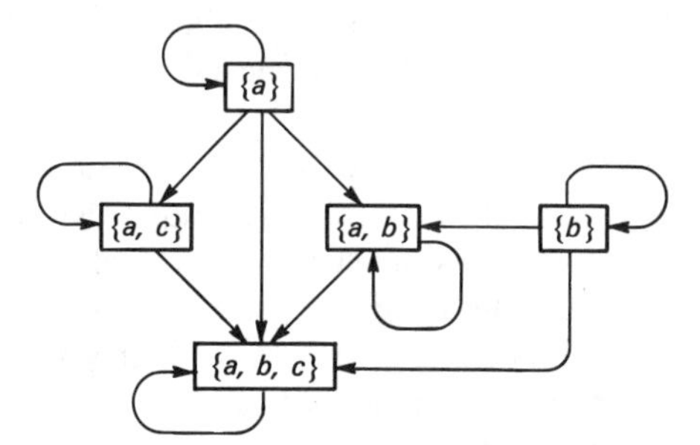

Figure A.4 The relation of Example A.2.

*Antisymmetry is **vacuously satisfied**: Since the antecedent "$a\ R'\ b$ and $b\ R'\ a$" is always false, the entire statement "if $a\ R'\ b$ and $b\ R'\ a$ then $a = b$" is considered to be true, in the same sense that the statement, "If $2 + 2 = 3$, then I'm in big trouble," would be considered to be true. Don't be upset if this seems confusing: It confuses everyone the first time they see it.

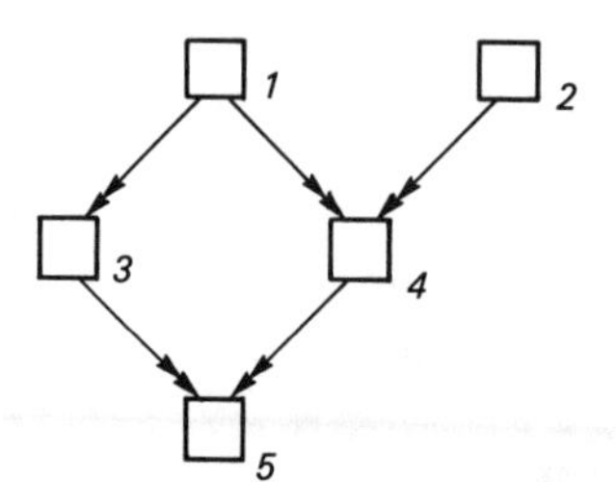

Figure A.5 The diagram of Figure A.2, assuming transitivity and reflexivity.

Definition A.1. Let R be a relation on a set S, and define $m \in S$ to be **maximal** if for all elements $a \in S$, $m\ R\ a$ implies $a\ R\ m$. In other words, m is maximal under R if the only element which can come "after" m is (perhaps) m itself. In addition, define the subset $\mathbf{Max_R(S)}$ of S to be the set of all maximal elements of S under the relation R.

For example, if $S = \{1, 2, 3\}$ and R is "$\leq$," then 3 is the (unique) maximal element, whereas if R is "$\geq$" we have 1 as the maximal element of S under R. Maximal elements do not need to be unique: If $S = \{2, 3, 11\}$, and R is "$|$," then every element of S is a maximal element under this relation, so $Max_R(S) = S$ in this case. A set with a relation need not have any maximal elements at all; an example would be any set with a **complete relation** R under which $x\ R\ y$ for all possible pairs (x, y). We could define the **minimal** elements of S in a similar fashion, by defining m to be a minimal element of S if $a\ R\ m$ implied $m\ R\ a$, for all $a \in S$, and could then define $\mathbf{Min_R(S)}$ to be the set of all minimal values of S.

Definition A.2. Let S be a set with a relation R, and let $x \in S$. Then:

1. s is a **successor** to x, if $x\ R\ s$.
2. s is a **proper successor** to x, if s is a successor to x and $s \neq x$.
3. Define the set $\mathbf{Succ_R(x)}$ to be the set of all proper successors to x.
4. Define an **immediate successor** to x to be any element in $Min_R(Succ_R(x))$, so that the immediate successors to x are those elements that are the "smallest" proper successors to x, that is, those elements that are "closest" to x.

Combining this definition with the previous one, we see that the maximal elements are precisely those $x \in S$ for which $Succ_R(x)$ is empty, that is, those elements with no proper successors. In simple terms, a successor to an element is any element that comes "after" that element under the relation R, so if S was $\{1, 2, 3\}$ and R was "$<$," then we have $Succ_<(1) = \{2, 3\}$, and $Succ_<(3) = \varnothing$, the empty set. It is not difficult to show that *immediate* successors have the property that if y is an immediate successor to x, then any element, z, which lies "between" x and y, in the sense that $x\ R\ z$ and $z\ R\ y$, must be equal to x or y. In Figure A.6 we show some sets defined by a relation R. Note that it seems somewhat peculiar that e and d are not immediate successors of b; the reason is that we cannot say that either e or d is "closer" to b than the other, so we decide, Solomon-like, that neither will be.

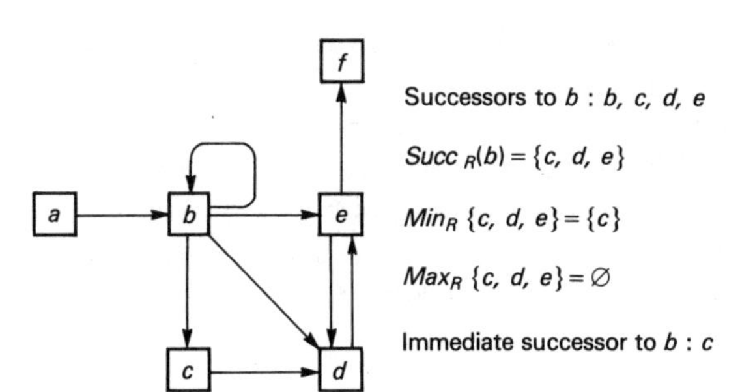

Figure A.6 A sample relation on $\{a, b, c, d, e, f\}$.

Similarly, we could define the **predecessors**, **proper predecessors**, and **immediate predecessors** of an element, x. Notice that not all relations on sets permit the existence of successors to elements: If S is the set of all real numbers and R is the relation "$<$," then *no* element of S has an immediate successor, since it makes no sense to talk about the real number that, say, comes immediately after 3. This lack of successors is not unique to infinite sets, since we could see the same nonexistence of successors in any set at all, if the relation being considered was the **empty relation** for which $x\ R\ y$ was *false* for any pair of elements (x, y), that is, that particularly simple relation under which no elements are related.

We are now ready to make precise the correspondence between a relation and the restriction that results when we remove reflexivity and transitivity.

Definition A.3. Let R be a relation on a set S, and define the **successor restriction**, $\hat{R}$, of R by $x\ \hat{R} y$ if and only if y is an immediate successor to x. In other words, the only elements that are $\hat{R}$-related to x are the minimal (proper) successors to x under the original relation R.

If we return to Example 1 of this section, namely $S = \{2, 3, 4, 6, 12\}$ with R the "divides" relation, we see that $Succ_R(2) = \{4, 6, 12\}$, and $Min_R(\{4, 6, 12\}) = \{4, 6\}$, so that under the successor restriction we have $2\ \hat{R}\ 4$, and $2\ \hat{R}\ 6$, but we do not have $2\ \hat{R}\ 12$. In a similar fashion, we have $3\ \hat{R}\ 6$, $4\ \hat{R}\ 12$, and $6\ \hat{R}\ 12$ as the only other true assertions about $\hat{R}$ (see Figure A.7). This is just what we did naively at the start of this

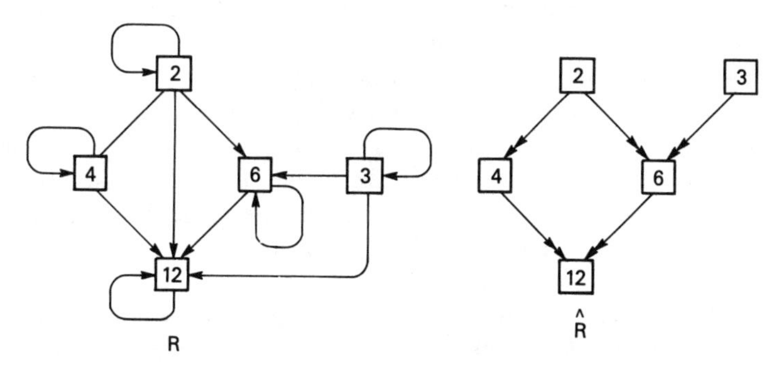

Figure A.7 A relation and its successor restriction.

section when we went from the original diagram with twelve single arrows to the restricted diagram with just five double arrows.

The successor restriction of a relation provides a more intuitive description of the structure of a set with a relation. In particular, a linear order on a *finite* set is described precisely by its successor restriction, which always takes the form indicated below. We will usually restrict our attention to finite sets, since we are, after all, investigating a topic in computer science, where the objects in question may be as large as we wish, but not infinite.

Application: Linear Orders and Closures

By discarding many of the arrows, we have made some of the properties of linear orders much more obvious than they would have been if we inspected the diagram of the original linear order, rather than at the successor restriction. In particular, we have the following result.

Theorem A.1. If S is a finite, nonempty set with a linear order R, then S has exactly one minimal element and exactly one maximal element (we will call such elements the **minimum** and the **maximum** elements, respectively).

Proof. We demonstrate the theorem for the maximal element; the proof for the minimal element is almost exactly the same.

We first show that there can be no more than one maximal element. Suppose, to the contrary, that S had two maximal elements, x and y, under R. Then, since R is a linear order, it is a chain, so either $x\ R\ y$ or $y\ R\ x$. Suppose that $x\ R\ y$ (if it happened that $y\ R\ x$, the rest of the proof would be similar). Then, by virtue of the fact that x was a maximal element, we must have $y\ R\ x$. Since $x\ R\ y$ and $y\ R\ x$, the antisymmetry of R implies that $x = y$, hence there can be at most one maximal element.

Now we must show that there does indeed exist a maximal element. Let $x_1 \in S$ be any element at all, and define $S_1 = Succ_R(S)$. If S_1 is empty, then x_1 has no proper successors, so we were lucky enough to find the maximal element, x_1, on the first try, and we can stop here. Otherwise, choose $x_2 \in S_1$, and let $S_2 = Succ_R(x_1)$. As before, if S_2 is empty, then x_2 is the maximal element; if not, we repeat the construction, finding x_3, S_3, . . ., and so on. This process is guaranteed to halt eventually with $S_k = \varnothing$, since each S_i is the collection of proper successors of some element in S_{i-1}, so by transitivity we have $S \supset S_1 \supset S_2 \supset \ldots \supset S_k$, with each successive subset being strictly smaller than the one before it. In particular, if S had n elements, the sequence of subsets can go no farther than S_n before producing the maximal element.

If you reread the proof, you will see that the only properties of R and S that were required were that R be antisymmetric, a chain, and transitive, and that S be finite. The latter is necessary because, under the linear order "≤," the infinite set

$$S = \left\{ \frac{1}{2}, \frac{2}{3}, \frac{3}{4}, \ldots, \frac{n}{n+1}, \ldots \right\}$$

has $1/2$ as the minimum element, but has no maximal elements at all. We leave as exercises the determination of whether the other properties are also necessary for the existence of unique maximal and minimal elements. This theorem gives half of the conditions for a finite set to be linearly ordered; the next theorem completes the characterization.

Theorem A.2. If S is a finite set with linear order R, then every element except for the minimum has one and only one immediate predecessor, and every element except the maximum has one and only one immediate successor.

Proof. As we did in the previous theorem, we will prove only half of the result. Once you see the proof for the uniqueness of successors, it should be no problem to provide a proof for uniqueness of predecessors.

Suppose that x is any element of S except for the maximal element, and consider the set $Succ_R(x)$. This set is itself a finite, nonempty, linearly ordered set under the relation R, so Theorem A.1 implies that there is one and only one minimum element in $Succ_R(x)$, and, by the definition of immediate predecessor, that minimum element must be the immediate successor to x, so we are done.

As it happens, we have exactly described necessary and sufficient conditions for the successor restriction of a relation to provide the underlying structure of a linear order; we will see this as soon as we complete the correspondence between the successor restriction and the original relation.

Definition A.4. If R is a relation on a set S, then

1. The **transitive closure**, R^+, of R is defined by $x R^+ y$ if and only if
   a. $x R y$, or
   b. There is some $z \in S$ for which $x R^+ z$, and $z R y$,
2. The **reflexive, transitive closure**, R^*, of R is defined by $x R^* y$ if and only if
   a. $x R^+ y$, or
   b. $x = y$.

These closures may be thought of as the "smallest" relations that contain the original relation, R, and that have the indicated properties. If we think of a relation as a set of ordered pairs, as we did earlier, then the transitive closure, say, of a relation, R, is the intersection of all transitive relations that contain R. You should be aware that although the transitive closure of a relation contains the term *transitive*, we have not yet shown that the transitive closure of a relation is, in fact, a transitive relation. It is, however, as could be shown by a relatively simple inductive proof, at least for sets that contain no more elements than there are integers (it is still true for larger sets, like the real numbers, but beyond the scope of this book to prove). Given that the transitive closure is transitive, it is then obvious that the reflexive, transitive closure is both reflexive and transitive. In addition, although we don't do so here, it is possible to define other such closures, as, for instance, the symmetric closure.

It is easy to see how to construct these two closures graphically. Given the picture of a relation with boxes and arrows, the transitive closure can be built by putting in all possible "bypasses" around boxes that have arrows going in and arrows going out *including any new arrows which have been added*, while the reflexive, transitive closure is made from the transitive closure by adding an arrow from each box to itself. Finally, the connection between the two types of diagrams can be stated by the following result, which we will present without proof.

Theorem A.3. If R is a preorder on a finite set, then $(\hat{R})* = R$.

In other words, if we start with any relation, R, that has the properties of reflexivity and transitivity (and perhaps others), construct the successor restriction, $\hat{R}$, and find the reflexive, transitive closure of $\hat{R}$, we wind up with the relation we started with. In this sense, we may truly regard the successor restriction of a relation as what is left when we remove reflexivity and transitivity, which can always be restored by the reflexive, transitive closure operation. We remark, by the way, that the opposite result, $(\widehat{R*}) = R$, does not hold, as you can see by trying an example.

To complete the discussion of linear orders, we remark that it is possible to show that a linear order on a finite, nonempty set can be completely characterized by the properties that (1) there is a unique minimum element, m; (2) there is a unique maximum element, M; (3) every element except for m has a unique immediate predecessor; and (4) every element except for M has a unique immediate successor. This, together with theorem A.3, implies that all of the essential structure of a linear order is captured by the successor restriction of that linear order. We can go even further by performing the following construction. Let S be a set with $n > 0$ elements, let R be a linear order on S, and let $x_1 = m$. For $i = 2, \ldots, n$, let x_i be the immediate successor to x_{i-1}, that is, let x_i be the unique element for which $x_{i-1} \hat{R} x_i$. Then we have the following diagram:

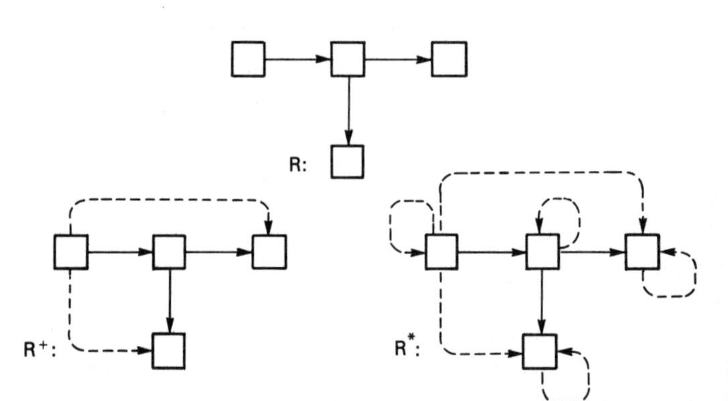

Figure A.8 The reflexive and reflexive, transitive closures of a relation.

which is clearly isomorphic (via the correspondence $x_i \leftrightarrow i$) to the diagram

obtained by considering the successor restriction of the linear order "≤" on the set of integers $\{1, 2, \ldots, n\}$. We have thus proved the result summarized below.

Theorem A.4. A linearly ordered finite set with $n > 0$ elements is isomorphic to the set $\{1, 2, \ldots, n\}$ with the relation "≤."

There is, then, no structural difference between a finite, linearly ordered set and a set of integers with the relation "≤." *The fundamental program of this text is to explore the structures that result when we gradually remove the properties that constitute a linear order.* As a final example, a **tree** has the structure of a (finite) set with a relation such that (1) there is a unique minimum element, called the **root**; (2) every element except the root has a unique immediate predecessor; but (3) every element may have zero or more immediate successors. The reflexive, transitive closures of such relations can be shown to be partial orders (although it is not the case that the successor restrictions of all partial orders give rise to trees), and these relations typically take the form of the following example:

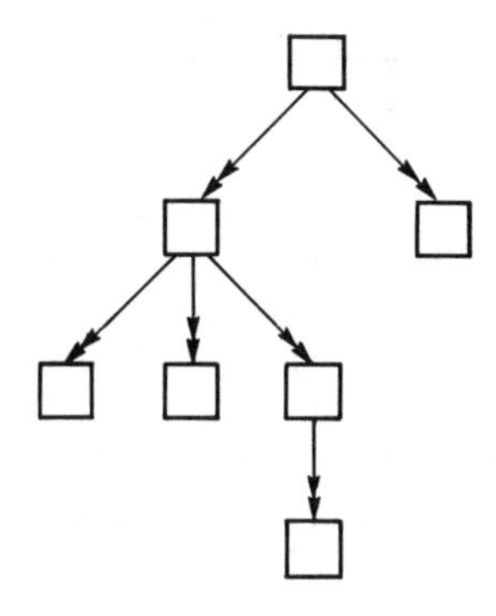

A.1 EXERCISES

1. Fill in the following table, placing a check in the proper square if the relation has the indicated property.

Relation 1: "Is a descendant of," on the set of all people alive at a given instant.

Relation 2: "Knows personally," on the set of all people alive at a given instant.

Relation 3: "Has a factor in common with," on the set of all positive integers [so (6, 9) are related, but (2, 9) are not].

Relation 4: "=," on the set of all real numbers.

	Reflexive	Irreflexive	Symmetric	Antisymmetric	Asymmetric	Transitive	Chain
Relation 1							
Relation 2							
Relation 3							
Relation 4							

2. Describe clearly how, looking at the diagram of a relation with boxes and arrows, you could tell whether the relation was reflexive, symmetric, transitive, or a chain.

3. Find a "good" example of a preorder, in the sense that your answer is reflexive and transitive, but not symmetric, antisymmetric, or a chain.

4. When we used "|" as the standard example of a partial order, we restricted ourselves to the set of *positive* integers. Why?

5. Define, for any integers a, and b, and any $c > 0$, $a \equiv b$ **mod** c to mean that $a - b$ is evenly divisible by c, so that $17 \equiv 2$ **mod** 5, $-4 \equiv 1$ **mod** 5, and $3 \equiv 3$ **mod** 5.

(a) Show that the relation $R(a, b)$ defined by $a \equiv b$ **mod** 5 is an equivalence relation.

(b) Diagram this relation on the set $\{0, 1, 2, 3, \ldots, 15\}$.

(c) Generalize (b) to show that an equivalence relation **partitions** a set into a disjoint collection of subsets (that is, no two of the subsets have any elements in common), such that the relation is a complete relation on each such subset.

6. Linear orders are not uncommon at all, in one sense, but are very rare in another.

(a) Show that every finite set $S = \{x_1, x_2, \ldots, x_n\}$ has a linear order that can be defined on it.

(b) How many different linear orders are possible on a set with n elements? It might help to keep in mind the structure that such a set must have.

(c) For $n = 1, 2, 3, \ldots$, define $L(n)$ to be the number of possible linear orders on a set with n elements, divided by the number of possible relations on that set. Investigate the values of this ratio, $L(n)$, for the first few values of n.

(d) Prove that $L(n)$ tends to zero (very rapidly, in fact) as n increases.

7. How many arrows do we need to draw to describe

(a) A linear order on a set of n elements?

(b) The successor restriction of a linear order on a set of n elements?

8. Consider the following relation, R, on the set $S = \{a, b, c, d, e\}$.

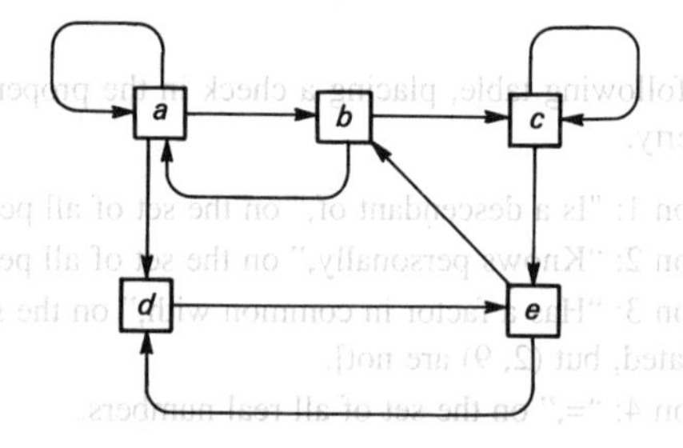

(a) For each element in S, find the successors, proper successors, and immediate successors of that element.

(b) Repeat part (a) for predecessors, proper predecessors, and immediate predecessors.

(c) Describe the sets $Min_R(S)$ and $Max_R(S)$.

(d) Diagram the successor restriction, $\hat{R}$, of R.

(e) Show that $(\hat{R})* \neq R$. Does this contradict theorem A.3?

9. In the proof of theorem A.1 we used the fact that the relation was antisymmetric, transitive, and a chain. Show that each of these assumptions is necessary by drawing diagrams of relations that are not antisymmetric, or not transitive, or are not chains, and that do not have unique maximum elements. (*Hint:* A set could fail to have a unique maximum either by having no maximum at all, or by having more than one maximum.)

10. Let R be a relation on a set S, and suppose that y is an immediate successor to x. Show that if z is any element of S such that $x\ R\ z$ and $z\ R\ y$, then it must be the case that either $z = x$ or $z = y$.

11. What is the result if we take the successor restriction of a complete relation?

12. Show that the transitive closure, R^+, of a relation, R, is itself transitive.

13. Show that, in order to prove $(\hat{R})* = R$, we need the set S to be finite by considering the relation R = "≤" on the set

$$S = \left\{\frac{1}{2}, \frac{2}{3}, \ldots \frac{n}{n+1}, \ldots\right\} \cup \left\{1\right\}$$

Describe $\hat{R}$, $(\hat{R})*$, and show that $(\hat{R})* \neq R$ (which you would do by finding two elements which are related by $(\hat{R})*$ and are not by R, or vice versa).

14. Show that $(\widehat{R*}) \neq R$, in general, by constructing an appropriate (simple) example.

15. We mentioned that it is not always the case that the successor restriction of a partial order is a tree. Show that this is so by finding a partial order on a set for which the successor restriction is not a tree.

Appendix B

Topics in Mathematics

I told you education never did nobody no good.
Everybody knows pie are round; it's cornbread are square.

Punchline from an old joke

This appendix presents some of the mathematical background that is assumed throughout the body of the text. One of the major themes of this book is that computer science is *not* programming. Of course, a computer scientist frequently has to write programs, but the "science" part of computer science requires analysis of programs and algorithms, and that in turn requires a measure of expertise in mathematics. We can't make you into a mathematician with one appendix (despite the fact that many mathematicians have only one appendix), but we can show enough that the mathematics in the rest of this book won't leave you completely at sea.

B.1 EXPONENTIAL AND LOGARITHMIC FUNCTIONS

Polynomial functions, like $f(n) = 3n^2 - 13$, are more familiar to most people (at least to those people who think about functions at all) than are exponential functions like $g(n) = 5^n$. Not only are people exposed to polynomials earlier, but polynomials are in some sense easier, in that you could compute $f(1.31)$ without too much trouble, while finding the value of $g(1.31)$ would be much more challenging, at least by hand. Nonetheless, it is probably safe to say that exponential functions appear more often than polynomials in describing real events.

If $a > 0$ is any real number, it is clear what we mean by a^n, for nonnegative integers n. Obviously, we would define a^n to be the number that results when we multiply

a by itself n times. From there, it is easy to extend a^n to negative integer exponents by defining $a^{-n} = 1/(a^n)$, for all positive integers n. It is only a little more difficult to define the exponential function for rational exponents by defining, for integers m and positive integers n

$$a^{\frac{m}{n}} = (\sqrt[n]{a}\,)^m$$

where the nth root of a is that number whose nth power is a. (Do you see why we restricted a to be greater than zero?) The only hard part comes when we try to define this function for exponents that are not rational, like π. To do this requires some fairly high-powered real analysis to show that the process results in the function we want, but the basic idea is to recognize that we can approach π as closely as we like by a sequence of rational numbers like 3, 3.1, 3.14, 3.141, 3.1415, 3.14159, . . . , and then to define a^π to be the limit that is approached by the sequence a^3, $a^{3.1}$, $a^{3.14}$, $a^{3.141}$, ...

If we accept that this process is legitimate, then we have a function that has all the properties we expect.

Theorem B.1. For any real number $a > 0$, the function a^x is defined for all real numbers x, and for all real x and y has the following properties:

1. $a^x > 0$
2. $a^0 = 1$
3. $a^{x+y} = a^x a^y$
4. $(ab)^x = a^x b^x$, for any $b > 0$
5. $a^{x-y} = a^x / a^y$
6. $(a^x)^y = a^{xy}$

In Figure B.1 we graph the function $y = a^x$, for $a = 2$. All of the exponential functions have the property that for any value x the rate at which the exponential function a^x is increasing (i.e., the slope of the line that is tangent to the graph of the function) is proportional to the height of the graph at the value x. It is worth mentioning that for the number $e = 2.718281828459045 \ldots$, the function e^x has the property (unique among exponential functions) that the rate of increase of the function at x is exactly equal to e^x. This makes calculus very easy for that function, because it is one of very few functions that is equal to its own derivative (quick, name another). In some sense, the exponential function to the base e is the only one we need, since, as we will be able to show shortly, for any $a > 0$, the function a^x can be written as e^{Kx}, for a suitable value of K, depending on a.

One thing we notice about the function a^x is that it increases rapidly, whenever $a > 1$. In fact, it increases *very* rapidly, so much so that it eventually beats out any polynomial, like x^3, or x^{2001}. We will show a slightly weaker version of this property; the strong version is trivial to prove, but requires that you know about calculus. Recall that for two functions f and g, we say "f is big-O of g," written $f = O(g)$, if there are

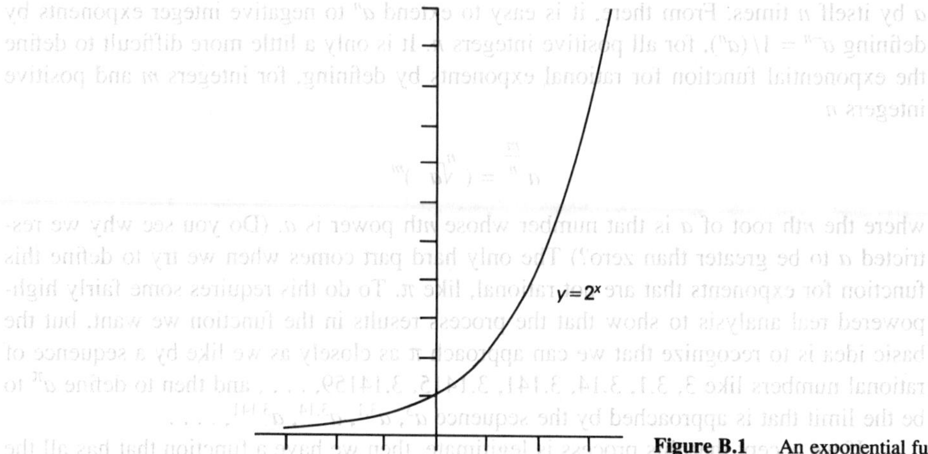

Figure B.1 An exponential function.

positive constants $c > 0$ and N, such that for all $x > N$, we have $f(x) < c\ g(x)$. In other words, $f = O(g)$ means that f eventually is always less than some multiple of g. In the lemma and the theorem that follow we will use the base $a = 2$; the proof for other bases is identical in form.

Lemma B.1. If

$$x > \frac{1}{2^{1/d} - 1}$$

then $(x + 1)^d < 2x^d$.

Proof. We have the following chain of implications:

$$x > \frac{1}{2^{1/d} - 1} \Rightarrow \frac{1}{x} < 2^{1/d} - 1 \Rightarrow 1 + \frac{1}{x} < 2^{1/d} \Rightarrow \left(1 + \frac{1}{x}\right)^d < 2 \Rightarrow$$

$$\Rightarrow \left(\frac{x+1}{x}\right)^d < 2 \Rightarrow \frac{(x+1)^d}{x^d} < 2 \Rightarrow (x+1)^d < 2x^d$$

Theorem B.2. For any d, $x^d = O(2^x)$.

Proof. Let N be the least integer that is greater than or equal to $1/(2^{1/d} - 1)$. Then lemma B.1 implies that $(N + 1)^d < 2N^d$, and $(N + 2)^d < 2(N + 1)^d < 4N^d$, and in general $(N + k)^d < 2^k N^d$, for all $k > 0$. If we let x denote $N + k$, then we have

$$x^d < 2^{x-N} N^d = \left(\frac{N^d}{2^N}\right) 2^x, \quad \text{for all } x > N$$

so there is a constant c such that for all $x > N$, $x^d < c\ 2^x$, which is just the definition of $x^d = O(2^x)$.

As we mentioned, there is a stronger version of theorem B.2, which reduces the constant c to 1. In other words, despite the fact that x^{2001} grows much more rapidly than 2^x for small values of x, there comes a point at which $x^{2001} < 2^x$ for all subsequent values.

Logarithms

The logarithmic functions are defined to be the inverses of the exponential functions, in the following fashion: For every $a > 0$, except for $a = 1$, define the function $\log_a(x)$ by making its value at x be the number y for which $a^y = x$.

Example B.1.

a. $\log_2 8 = 3$, since $2^3 = 8$.
b. $\log_2 (1/32) = -5$, since $2^{-5} = 1/32$.
c. $\log_4 1 = 0$, since $4^0 = 1$.
d. If $x \le 0$, then $\log_2 x$ is undefined, since $2^y > 0$ for all y.

We will assume without proof that this definition leads to a well-defined function for all positive values of a except for $a = 1$. Logs were originally developed as an aid to calculation, because they provide a means by which (hard) multiplication problems may be turned into (easier) addition problems. The properties of the logarithmic functions parallel those of the exponential functions, a fact that should not be too surprising in light of the way the logarithm was defined.

Theorem B.3. For any $a > 0$, $a \ne 1$, the function $\log_a x$ is defined for all $x > 0$, and has the following properties:

a. $\log_a 1 = 0$
b. $\log_a (xy) = \log_a x + \log_a y$
c. $\log_a (x/y) = \log_a x - \log_a y$
d. $\log_a (x^y) = y \log_a x$.

In addition, the logarithm and exponent to base a are related by

e. $\log_a(a^x) = x$, for all real numbers x
f. $a^{\log_a x} = x$, for all real $x > 0$

Proof (of part b). Suppose that x and y are two positive real numbers. Let $z = \log_a x$ and $w = \log_a y$. By the definition of the log function, this means that $a^z = x$ and $a^w = y$. Then $xy = a^z a^w = a^{z+w}$, by theorem B.2(c). But the definition of the logarithm implies that $xy = a^{z+w}$ is the same as saying that $\log_a (xy) = z + w = \log_a x + \log_a y$, as desired.

We remarked earlier that there was, in a sense, only one exponential function. In a similar way, there is only one logarithm, in the sense that for all $x > 0$, $\log_a x$ is just a constant multiple of $\log_b x$. This is a useful (and quickly forgotten) result, which we can prove easily, knowing what we do now about logs and exponentials. Let x be any positive number. Theorem B. 3(f) tells us that

$$x = b^{\log_b x}$$

so, taking $\log_a$ of both sides and using the "power rule" of theorem B.3(d) we see

$$\log_a(x) = \log_a(b^{\log_b x}) = (\log_b x)(\log_a b) = (\log_a b)(\log_b x) = K \log_b x.$$

In simple terms, if we want to know $\log_a x$, and all we know is $\log_b x$, all we need to do is find $K = \log_a b$, multiply that by $\log_b x$, and we have our answer. An immediate corollary of this property is that $\log_a b = 1 / \log_b a$. We summarize this below.

Theorem B.4. If $x > 0$, and a, b are any numbers greater than zero and not equal to one, then

a. $\log_a x = (\log_a b)(\log_b x)$, and
b. $\log_a b = 1/\log_b a$, and combining these results yields
c. $\log_a x = \dfrac{\log_b x}{\log_b a}$.

Just as the exponential function to the base e had a nice calculus-related property, the logarithm to that base has the property that the slope of the line that is tangent to the graph $y = \log_e x$ is exactly equal at any point to $1/x$. The log to the base e is called the **natural logarithm** function, and is used so commonly that it has its own abbreviation, *ln*. Many calculators and computers rely on the relation among logs to different bases and implement only the natural log function. This presents no problem for computer scientists who frequently use $\log_2$ (which is sometimes abbreviated *lg*), since $\lg x = (\ln x)/(\ln 2)$, by theorem B.4. Thus, to compute lg(5), we find ln(5) = 1.60944, and divide that by ln(2) = 0.69315, to find lg(5) = 2.32193.

Since the log and the exponential to a given base are inverses of each other, it happens that the graph of one may be found by rotating the graph of the other about the line $y = x$. We draw the graph of $y = \log_2(x)$ in Figure B.2. The graph of the log function rises very slowly, just as the graph of the exponential function rises very rapidly. In fact, the logarithm has the property that it grows more slowly than any power function, like the tenth root. We state this property without proof below.

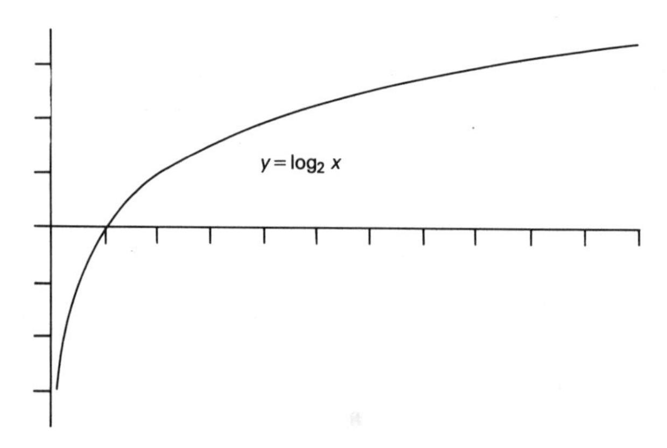

Figure B.2 A logarithmic function.

Theorem B.5. Let $a > 0$, $a \neq 1$. Then, for any exponent $d > 0$, there is a number N such that for all $x > N$, we have $\log_a x < x^d$.

B.2 INDUCTION

Frequently, we need to prove that some property or statement, $P(n)$, about the integers is true for all positive integers n. An extremely useful proof technique, known as **induction**, is based on the following result.

Theorem B.5(the Principle of Mathematical Induction). If $P(n)$ is a statement with an integer variable n, and the following two results can be shown to be true

a. $P(a)$ is true.
b. For all integers $n \geq a$, if $P(n)$ is true, then $P(n + 1)$ is true.

then $P(n)$ is true for all integers $n \geq a$.

In theorem B.5, part (a) is usually called the **base case**, and part (b) is called the **inductive case**. The nicest feature about the principle of mathematical induction (PMI, for short) is that it allows us to prove infinitely many statements in a finite number of steps. Suppose that $P(n)$ was some statement that we knew satisfied conditions (a) and (b) above. We would then know that $P(3)$ was true, since $P(0)$ was known to be true by (a), hence $P(1)$ must be true by (b), so $P(2)$ must also be true by (b), hence $P(3)$ must also be true by (b). In effect, we can "climb the ladder" to a given result if we know (1) how to get to the bottom rung of the ladder, and (2) if from any rung we can climb to the next. What PMI says is that if we know we can do these two steps, then we can climb to any rung whatsoever.

Example B.2.

Consider the series obtained by adding consecutive odd integers. We notice that $1 = 1^2$, $1 + 3 = 4 = 2^2$, $1 + 3 + 5 = 9 = 3^2$, $1 + 3 + 5 + 7 = 16 = 4^2$. There seems to be enough evidence here to make the guess that $1 + 3 + \ldots + (2n - 1) = n^2$, in other words that the sum of the first n odd positive integers is equal to n^2. That is a statement that has a single variable, n, and we would like to show that it is true for all integers $n \geq 1$.

The proof by induction goes as follows: Let $P(n)$ be the statement that we wish to prove true for all integers $n \geq 1$,

$$P(n) : 1 + 3 + \cdots + (2n - 1) = n^2.$$

We break the proof into two parts:

(a) Base case: We want to show that $P(1)$ is true, but this is just the statement that $1 = 1^2$.
(b) Inductive case: Suppose now that $n \geq 1$ is any integer, and that $P(n)$ is true. We would like to use this somehow to show that $P(n + 1)$ is true. Replacing n by $n + 1$ in $P(n)$, we have to prove the statement

$$P(n+1) : 1 + 3 + \ldots + (2(n + 1) - 1) = (n + 1)^2.$$

Notice that

$$1 + 3 + \ldots + (2(n+1) - 1) = (1 + 3 + \ldots + (2n - 1)) + (2n + 1),$$

but we assumed that *P(n)* was true, so

$$(1 + 3 + \ldots + (2n - 1)) + (2n + 1) = n^2 + (2n + 1) = (n + 1)^2.$$

This is exactly what we needed to show, namely that if we assume *P(n)* is true, then we can show that *P(n* + 1) is true. Thus, we have established the base case and the inductive case, so PMI tells us that *P(n)* is true for all $n \geq 1$, which is what we wanted to prove.

Example B.3.

Suppose we wished to prove that 6 evenly divides $n^3 - n$, for all $n \geq 0$. A streamlined induction proof would look like this:

a. **Base:** 6 clearly divides $0^3 - 0$.
b. **Inductive:** Let $n \geq 0$ be an integer, and assume that 6 divides $n^3 - n$. Then to see that the result also holds for $n + 1$ observe

$$(n+1)^3 - (n+1) = n^3 + 3n^2 + 3n + 1 - (n+1) = n^3 + 3n^2 + 3n - n$$
$$= n^3 - n + 3n^2 + 3n = (n^3 - n) + 3n(n+1).$$

Now, we assumed that 6 divides $n^3 - n$, and notice that 3 certainly divides $3n\ (n + 1)$. Furthermore, since n and $n + 1$ are consecutive integers, one of them is even, so 2 also divides $3n\ (n + 1)$, hence 6 divides both $n^3 - n$ and $3n\ (n + 1)$, so must divide their sum. Thus the inductive step is proved, completing the entire proof.

Often, it is easier to perform an induction proof if we don't have to limit ourselves to going up by one in the inductive case. There is a slightly different form of PMI that is sometimes useful in such cases.

Theorem B.6. (PMI—Strong Form). If *P(n)* is a statement with an integer variable *n*, and the following two results can be shown to be true

a. *P(a)* is true.
b. If *P(k)* is true for all integers k, $a \leq k < n$, then *P(n)* is true.

then *P(n)* is true for all integers $n \geq a$.

Notice that this theorem differs from the weaker form in that the inductive hypothesis allows us to assume that *all* smaller instances of *P* are true. This is useful in situations where *P* is phrased in such a way that going from *P(n)* to *P(n* + 1) would be difficult.

Example B.4.

In analyzing the time an algorithm takes to run on input of size *n*, we frequently make an educated guess at the solution and then use strong induction to prove that our guess is indeed correct. Suppose, for example, that we know that the time, $T(n)$, an algorithm takes to run on input of size n satisfies the two equations: $T(1) = 1$, and $T(n) = 2T(n/2) + n^2$. Suppose that somehow we have managed to guess that $T(n) \leq 2n^2$. The statement P we wish to prove is, "If T is a function that satisfies the two relations given above, then $T(n) \leq 2n^2$."

a. Base: $T(1) = 1$, by the first defining relation, and clearly (one says that a lot when establishing the base case in an induction argument) $1 \leq 2\ (1^2)$.

b. Inductive (Strong): Let $n \geq 1$, and suppose that $T(k) \leq 2k^2$, for all $k < n$. In particular, the result is assumed to hold for $k = n/2$ (we assume that n is even), so

$$T(n/2) \leq 2(\frac{n}{2})^2 = 2\frac{n^2}{4} = \frac{n^2}{2}.$$

Now the definition of T implies

$$T(n) = 2T(n/2) = n^2 \leq 2(\frac{n^2}{2}) + n^2 = n^2 + n^2 = 2n^2,$$

which is exactly what we set out to prove.

B.3 COUNTING TECHNIQUES

When analyzing the behavior of algorithms on data structures, we frequently need to count the number of ways of selecting and/or arranging elements from a given set. This is a rich and interesting area, large enough that we can give only the merest introduction here.

Permutations

Suppose we have a set of n different elements and we wish to produce linear arrangements of all of the n elements. How many ways can the n elements be arranged in a row or a list? Such an arrangement is called a **permutation** of the original set. In order to answer this question, we rely on a result that is both fundamental and, after you've thought about it for a moment, self-evident.

The Counting Principle. If there are k events, $E_1, E_2, \ldots, E_k$, such that each event E_i can occur in n_i ways, regardless of what occurred in the other events, then the total number of outcomes for all the events together is the product $n_1 n_2 \ldots n_k$.

For example, if you own 9 shirts, 4 pairs of pants, and 3 pairs of shoes, you can go for 9 x 4 x 3 = 108 days before wearing an outfit you've worn before. As another example, we can use the counting principle to show that there are 2^n possible subsets of a set of n elements. Suppose that the universal set in question consists of $\{1, 2, \ldots, n\}$, since the names for the elements in the set are obviously of no importance here. Then we select a subset by deciding, for all $i = 1, 2, \ldots, n$, whether or not element i is in the subset. Each such decision is an independent event, and each event can occur in two ways, so the total number of ways all the events can occur (i.e., the number of subsets of a set of n elements) must be just the n-fold product $2 \times 2 \times \ldots \times 2 = 2^n$.

To return to our original question, suppose we have a set $\{1, 2, \ldots, n\}$ and we wish to count the number of ways these elements can be arranged in order. If our events can be E_1 = "Pick the first element in the list," E_2 = "Pick the second element in the list," and so on, then there are n ways E_1 can happen, after which there are $n - 1$ ways E_2 can happen (since we've already chosen one element to be the first), $n - 2$ ways E_3 can happen, and so on until we find one way for the last event, E_n. The counting principle then tells us that there must be $n(n - 1)(n - 2) \ldots (2)(1)$ ways of arranging n distinct objects in order. For $n = 3$, we have $3! = 3 \times 2 \times 1 = 6$; the six permutations of $\{1, 2, 3\}$ are 123, 132, 213, 231, 312, and 321. This product occurs so frequently that it has been given its own symbol, $n!$, for which we say "n factorial" (or "n bang," if you feel very informal and want to sound like an expert in computer science slang).

We define $0!$ to be 1, both because it makes some results work the way we want them to and also because it makes some sense to say that there is just one way to arrange the elements of an empty set. Notice that the definition $n! = n(n - 1)(n - 2) \ldots (2)(1)$ implies that $n! = n(n - 1)!$ This function grows *very* rapidly as n increases; the first few values of $n!$ are 1, 1, 2, 6, 24, 120, 720, 5,040, 40,320, 362,880, and 3,628,800. There are times when we need to find $n!$ for very large n. In such cases, it is inadvisable to compute the product, especially since the product gives us no idea about how rapidly $n!$ grows. We can approximate $n!$ by **Sterling's formula**, which states that

$$n! = \sqrt{2\pi n}\left(\frac{n}{e}\right)^n, \text{ approximately,}$$

where e is the base of the natural logarithm. Since big-O notation allows us to "throw away" constant multiples, we can then say that $n! = O(n^{n+1/2})$. It is not hard to generalize the arguments above to counting the number of permutations of k elements chosen from a set of $n \geq k$ elements.

Theorem B.7. If $0 \leq k \leq n$, then the number of k-element permutations chosen from a set of n elements is

$$n(n-1)(n-2) \cdots (n-k+1) = \frac{n!}{(n-k)!}.$$

Combinations

When we were counting permutations, we were dealing with the possible ways of arranging (a) distinct objects (b) in order. Often, we might have to count arrangements in situations where one or the other of these two conditions is immaterial. If, for instance, we wanted to count the number of **combinations**, $C(n, k)$, of k elements out of a set of n elements, which is to say the number of k-element subsets of a set of n elements, then the order of the elements within each subset is of no interest to us. It turns out that counting combinations is little more difficult than counting permutations.

Theorem B.8. If $0 \leq k \leq n$, then the number of k-element combinations from a set of n elements is given by the **binomial coefficient**

$$\binom{n}{k} = \frac{n!}{k!(n-k)!}.$$

Proof. Instead of counting combinations directly, we begin by enumerating all of the k-element permutations of the set of n elements. Theorem B.7 tells us that there are $n!/(n-k)!$ such permutations. We may now collect these permutations into groups, in such a way that two permutations belong in the same group if they are just reorderings of the same elements. For example, if we had $k = 3$, then the permutations 267, 672, and 726 would all go in the same group. Now we have exactly as many groups as there are k-element subsets, and each group contains exactly $k!$ permutations. In other words, by counting the $n!/(n-k)!$ permutations, we have overcounted by a factor of $k!$. Therefore, the total number of k element combinations of a set of n elements is given by the "corrected" count $n!/k!\,(n-k)!$.

For example, the number of ways a six-member subcommittee can be selected from a committee of eight is $8!\ /\ 6!\ (8 - 6)! = 8!\ /\ 6!\ 2! = 28$. There are numerous lovely relations involving the binomial coefficients. One of the nicest comes from observing that the total number of subsets of an n-element set can be found by adding the number of k-element subsets, for $k = 0, 1, 2, \ldots, n$. This yields the following identity.

Corollary

$$\sum_{k=0}^{n} \binom{n}{k} = \binom{n}{0} + \binom{n}{1} + \cdots + \binom{n}{n} = 2^n.$$

When we considered combinations, the elements we were combining were distinct, but the order of the elements chosen was unimportant. We could relax the other restriction, instead, and consider the number of ways of arranging n objects in order, where the objects are not necessarily distinct. If we consider just two kinds of objects, we get exactly the same number as we did when we counted combinations.

Theorem B.9. The total number of ordered arrangements of n objects, k of which are of one kind and $n - k$ of which are of another is $C(n, k)$.

Proof. Suppose, for instance, we wish to arrange 3 A's and 2 B's in order. There are a total of $n = 5$ positions for the letters, and any arrangement is uniquely specified by describing the positions for the A's. For instance, the arrangement AABAB corresponds to the position subset $\{1, 2, 4\}$ for the A's. In other words, we have *transformed* the problem of counting the number of ordered arrangements of k A's and $n - k$ B's into the problem of counting the number of k-element subsets of the position set $\{1, 2, \ldots, n\}$, which we have already solved in theorem B.7.

The numbers $n!/k!(n-k)!$ are called binomial coefficients because they are the coefficients that appear in the expansion of binomial powers like $(x+y)^n$. For example, we might want to know the coefficient of the term x^2y in the expansion of $(x+y)^3$. When we multiply $(x+y)(x+y)(x+y)$, the result consists of the sum of all three-element products, where the ith term in each product is chosen from the ith copy of $(x+y)$ in the product. In other words,

$$\begin{aligned}(x+y)(x+y)(x+y) &= xxx + xxy + xyx + xyy + yxx + yxy + yyx + yyy \\ &= xxx + (xxy + xyx + yxx) + (xyy + yxy + yyx) + yyy \\ &= x^3 + 3x^2y + 3xy^2 + y^3,\end{aligned}$$

so the coefficient of the x^2y term is just the number of ways of arranging two x's and one y in order, which is just $3!/2!\,1! = 3$. It would be easy enough to generalize this argument to prove the following result.

Theorem B.10. For any integer $n \geq 0$,

$$\begin{aligned}(x+y)^n &= \binom{n}{n}x^n + \binom{n}{n-1}x^{n-1}y + \cdots + \binom{n}{1}xy^{n-1} + \binom{n}{0}y^n \\ &= \sum_{k=0}^{n}\binom{n}{k}x^k y^{n-k}\end{aligned}$$

B.4 EXERCISES

1. Why did we not define the function a^x for $a < 0$?
2. What does the graph a^x look like when $0 < a < 1$?
3. Show, for any $a > 0$, that $a^x = e^{Kx}$ by finding a suitable constant K, depending only on a.
4. Using calculus (l'Hôpital's rule, in particular), show that for any d

$$\lim_{x\to\infty}\frac{x^d}{e^x} = 0.$$

5. Compute
   (a) $\log_2 1{,}024$
   (b) $\log_{1/2} 8$
   (c) $\log_{10} 100{,}000{,}000{,}000$
   (d) $\log_2 4^{12}$
6. Knowing that $\log_2 3 = 1.585$, $\log_2 5 = 2.322$, to three digits, compute
   (a) $\log_2 15$
   (b) $\log_2 300$
   (c) $\log_2 (3 + 1/5)$
   (d) $\log_2 3^{15}$

7. If you were told that $\log_{10} 2 = 0.30103$, how could you use that to find the number of digits in 2^{65536} ?
8. Prove parts (a), (c) and (d) of theorem B.3.
9. Show that some functions that look like exponentials are really just powers by showing, for instance, that

$$2^{\log_3 n} = n^K$$

for a suitable value of K.

10.(a) Show that if you know the value of ln 2, and you can compute $\ln x$ for all $0 < x \leq 2$, then you can compute $\ln y$ for all $y > 0$.

(b) If $-1 < x \leq 1$, then $\ln(1 + x)$ can be computed to any degree of accuracy by adding enough terms in the series

$$x - \frac{1}{2}x^2 + \frac{1}{3}x^3 - \frac{1}{4}x^4 + \frac{1}{5}x^5 - \cdots$$

where the error introduced by stopping at the nth term is never more than $1/(n+1)$. How many terms in the series do you need to compute ln 2 to within ± 0.005? Why should this not be a suitable way to implement ln on a computer?

11. Give inductive proofs of the following identities:

(a) $$\sum_{k=1}^{n} k^2 = \frac{n(n+1)(2n+1)}{6}.$$

(b) $$\sum_{k=0}^{n} x^k = \frac{1 - x^{n+1}}{1 - x}.$$

12. What is wrong with the folowing "proof" that all elements in a set must be the same?

Let $P(n)$ be the statement "if a set has n elements, they must all be the same," and argue by induction on n.

a. **Base**: If a set has $n = 1$ element, that element is the same as itself, so $P(1)$ is true.

b. **Induction:** Suppose that a set, S, has $n \geq 1$ elements, and suppose that $P(n-1)$ is true. We will show $P(n)$ is true. Choose any element, e, from S, then $S - [e]$ is a set with $n - 1$ elements, so they must all be the same, by the induction hypothesis. Choose another element, e', from S and argue similarly that all the elements in $S - [e']$ must be the same. But $S - [e]$ and $S - [e']$ together constitute all of S, so every element in S must be the same, so $P(n)$ must be true.

By the principle of induction, since the base case and the inductive step are true, $P(n)$ must hold for all n, hence every set must have the property that all of its elements are equal.

13. Approximately how large is 1000!, that is, how many digits does it have?
14. Show than $\ln n!$ is approximately $(n + 1/2) \ln n + (1 - n)$.
15. We would like to write an algorithm that computes $C(n,k)$.

(a) Explain why it would be a bad idea to compute the values of $n!$, $k!$, and $(n-k)!$ in the algorithm.

(b) Show that

$$\binom{n}{k} = \frac{n}{k}\binom{n-1}{k-1}$$

and use this identity as the basis for your algorithm, explaining why this is a better idea than computing the factorials.

16. Suppose that you live in a city with very peculiar traffic patterns. The streets are laid out in a rectangular grid as in Figure B.3, and all the north–south streets are one way north, while all the east–west streets are one way east. The building where you work is, luckily for you, four blocks north and six blocks east of your apartment (don't ask how you get home). How many different ways are there for you to drive from home to work?

17. The **Catalan Numbers,** $C_n = (1/(n+1))C(2n,n)$, arise in a number of seemingly different counting problems. C_n, for instance, counts the number of binary trees with n nodes, as well as the number of sequences of balanced parentheses consisting of n each of left and right parentheses.

(a) Using induction, prove that $C_n < 4^n$.

(b) Using Sterling's formula, show that

$$C_n = \frac{2^{2n}}{\sqrt{\pi n}\,(n+1)}, \text{ approximately.}$$

(c) Show that

$$C_n = \binom{2n}{n} - \binom{2n}{n-1}.$$

18. **Pascal's triangle** is an arrangement of numbers in rows and columns such that the entry in row n and column k is $C(n,k)$. In Table B.1, we provide part of Pascal's triangle. Notice that each entry in the table is the sum of the element above it and the one above it and to the left, so that the 10 in row 5, column 2 is the sum of the 6 in row 4, column 2 and the 4 in row 4, column 1. We are then led to guess

$$\binom{n}{k} = \binom{n-1}{k-1} + \binom{n-1}{k}, \text{ for all } n > 0,\ 0 < k \le n.$$

Prove this identity

(a) Directly, from the algebraic definition of the binomial coefficients.

(b) By using a subset-counting argument. (*Hint:* Consider the number of k-element subsets of a set of n elements; single out one particular element of the set and count those subsets that contain that element and those that do not.)

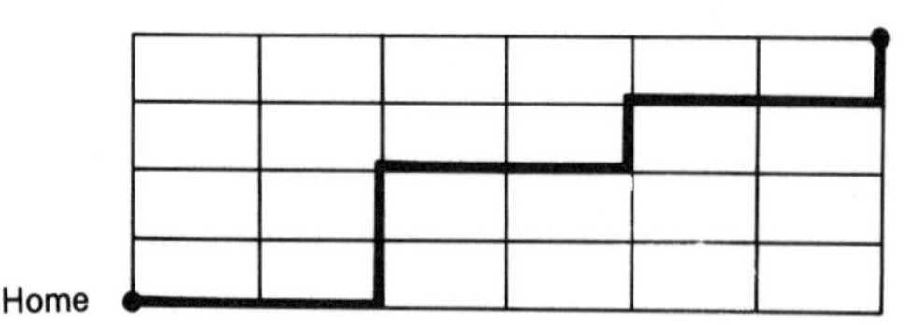

Figure B.3 City map with a typical path (courtesy of Grid City Auto Club).

TABLE B.1 PASCAL'S TRIANGLE

$n \backslash k$	0	1	2	3	4	5
0	1					
1	1	1				
2	1	2	1			
3	1	3	3	1		
4	1	4	6	4	1	
5	1	5	10	10	5	1

19. Use theorem B.9 to find the coefficient of

(a) x^4y^2 in the expansion of $(x + y)^6$.

(b) x^3y^4 in the expansion of $(x + 2y)^7$.

(c) x^4y^2 in the expansion of $(x + y^2)^6$.

20. Use theorem B.9 to prove

$$\binom{n}{0} - \binom{n}{1} + \cdots \pm \binom{n}{n} = \sum_{k=0}^{n} (-1)^k \binom{n}{k} = 0.$$

Appendix C

Random Numbers and Simulation

What on earth are you trying to prove with all those numbers?
I must confess that for the life of me I see no pattern there.

Hannibal Bennett, *Howls of Ivy*

We often employ simulation in situations where the behavior of some system would be impractical to test directly, or where the theoretical analysis of a system is just too complicated to attempt. If, for instance, we wanted to build a car wash, we could answer questions about the number of wash bays and the size of the driveway to build by going ahead and building them, but we might very well go broke trying alternatives before we got any idea about the combination that maximized our profits. It would be much better to build a computer model of the car wash and try the various options in simulation before we signed the contract with the builder. In another vein, we might want to test the behavior of a new sorting algorithm. We may have no idea how to analyze the running time of the algorithm, so we could try a number of sample inputs and investigate how long the algorithm takes to run on the samples. Of course there would be no point in even trying to run the algorithm on all possible inputs of a given size n, unless n was very small, so we might run the algorithm on a randomly chosen sample of inputs, in hopes that the behavior on the samples would reflect the behavior in general.

In this appendix, we will concentrate on simulations that have some degree of randomness, since they arise so frequently in practice. Even in the car wash simulation, for instance, there is likely a considerable amount of randomness in the way customers arrive. In any given day we might expect to see one car every ten minutes, but it would be foolish in the extreme to expect that cars would arrive to be washed exactly ten minutes apart all day long.

C.1 RANDOM NUMBERS

You probably have some idea about what we mean by a "random" sequence of numbers. The question of *exactly* what should be the criteria for a sequence of numbers to be random, though, is an extremely difficult one. We might say that a random sequence of zeros and ones, for instance, would be one generated by repeatedly tossing a fair coin, and recording 0 for each head and 1 for each tail. The problem with that definition is that it implies that the sequence 0000000000 . . . is random, and as a matter of fact is no more or less likely than any other sequence of zeroes and ones. We might be closer if we adopt a somewhat more naive view and content ourselves here with accepting a sequence as random if knowing the first n terms of the sequence, we would not be able to predict the $(n + 1)$st term.

This "unpredictability" condition, though, leads to big problems when we try to use a computer to generate random sequences. Computers are **deterministic**, in the sense that the behavior of a computer at any time is completely predictable from its prior behavior. What we have to do is content ourselves with producing a sequence of numbers that "appears" to be random. Such a sequence is called a **pseudo-random** sequence. We might say, with many authors, that an algorithm generates pseudo-random numbers if any sequence generated by the algorithm passes a number of statistical tests which would also be passed by a truly random sequence. A typical test might be that all of the possible numbers in the sequence occur equally often, in the long run. If we generated the digits 0 . . . 9 randomly, for instance, we would expect the number, $T_3(n)$, of 3's seen after n digits had been generated to be about $n/10$, and we would expect $T_3(n)$ to get closer to $n/10$, as n got very large. A sequence with such a property is said to be **equidistributed**. Of course, that test by itself would not be acceptable to define randomness, since the sequence 01234567890123456789 . . . is equidistributed, but it seems decidedly nonrandom. We could then require another test, perhaps that any *pairs* of adjacent terms occur about one hundredth of the time, in the long run, or that the subsequence formed by taking every other term or every fifth term be equidistributed.

The upshot is that there is no agreement about what should constitute the criteria for a pseudo-random sequence. If we require too few tests, we leave the door open to sequences which we would not want to include, but if we require too many tests we may find that there is *no possible sequence* which will satisfy them all together.

What we will do here is adopt a consensual approach. Most authorities on the matter agree that an acceptable pseudo-random number-generating algorithm is the particularly simple method known as the **linear congruential algorithm**. In order to generate a sequence $x_0, x_1, x_2, \ldots$ of numbers "randomly chosen" between 0 and $m - 1$ by this method, we begin with any number, x_0, called the *seed*, and then generate the rest by the rule

$$x_{n+1} = (Ax_n + B) \textbf{ mod } m.$$

For example, if we chose $A = 3$, $B = 1$, and $m = 8$, then starting with $x_0 = 3$, we would have $x_1 = 2$, $x_2 = 7$, $x_3 = 6$, $x_4 = 3$, after which the sequence repeats 3, 2, 7, 6, 3, 2, 7, 6, forever. Starting with $x_0 = 1$ gives 1, 4, 5, 0, 1, 4, 5, 0, . . . , so we have two sequences with **period** (i.e., length of repeats) four, depending on the seed we choose. Well, these sequences are too short to be of any real use, not to mention that neither of them uses all the numbers from 0 to 7. There are a number of criteria that govern the choice of A and B, given m, some of which we cover in the exercises. Without going into too much detail about the reasons, two generating schemes that work well are

$$x_{n+1} = (11549x_n + 3461) \textbf{ mod } 16{,}384 \quad (C.1)$$

$$x_{n+1} = (9757x_n + 6925) \textbf{ mod } 32{,}768 \quad (C.2)$$

For both of these, the periods are as long as possible, in that for any seed they generate all m possible numbers before repeating. They both pass the tests which most authors agree they should, and in both of them the numbers used for A and B can be interchanged to produce different pseudo-random number generators which are also good.

Many compilers have built-in random number generators, so it is reasonable to ask why one would want to write another routine to generate numbers at random. We presented this technique because it will aid those of you who don't have access to such functions, but also because the proper choice of A, B, and m is sufficiently delicate that there have been faulty random number generators that have been in use for years before they were discovered to fail some important statistical test. The ones we give here might even fall into this category, despite the fact that they have passed a number of tests. The best advice is that if you are doing something that requires heavy use of random numbers, make a search of the literature to find generating algorithms which have been thoroughly examined.

Now that we have a method of generating integers at random in the range $0 \ldots m - 1$, it is easy enough to use this to generate random real numbers between 0 and 1. All we need to do is take an integer, r, between 0 and $m - 1$, and divide to produce the real number r/m. There will be m possible numbers produced, and they all will be greater than or equal to 0 and less than 1. The function *RandReal* implements this algorithm

```
const            {Global constants}
   MAX = 32767 ;               {m - 1}
   REAL_SIZE = 32768.0;        {real number equivalent of m };

function RandReal : real;
{ Returns a randomly-chosen real number in [0, 1).}
{Requires a function Random, which returns a random integer }
{in the range 0 .. MAX.}
begin
   RandReal := Random / REAL_SIZE
end;
```

We could use this scheme to return to integers, if we wished. Suppose that we needed to generate integers randomly chosen in the range $0 \ldots k$, with $k < m$. We could generate a random real number x in [0, 1), form the product kx, and then round that number to the nearest integer. In Pascal-ese, we would have

```
function RandInt(k : integer) : integer;
{ Generates a number at random in the range 0 . . . k.}
{Uses function RandReal, which generates a real number in [0, 1).}
begin
   RandInt := round( k * RandReal)
end;
```

Give yourself some points for cleverness if you can find a way to generate random numbers in the range 0 . . . k without using reals as an intermediate step. One particularly simple way is to generate an integer r with $0 \leq r \leq m - 1$, and then form r **mod** $(k + 1)$. The problem with this is subtle, though, and it arises from the fact that the low-order bits of integers generated by the linear congruential method are not as random as we would like. In particular, for the two algorithms mentioned earlier the sequences are alternately even and odd, so the sequence of last bits is ... 0, 1, 0, 1, 0, 1 ... , which is decidedly not what we would consider to be random. If we had chosen $k = 1$, then, in an attempt to generate a random sequence of zeroes and ones, we would have been in for an unpleasant surprise. Going to reals as an intermediate step places more emphasis on the high-order bits, and they can be shown to be much more random than the lower-order bits, at least for integers generated by the linear congruential method.

C.2 PROBABILITY DISTRIBUTIONS

One way to generate numbers randomly in the range 0 . . . 5 would be to take five fair coins, toss them all, and record the number of heads that came up. This process certainly seems to be random, at least in the sense that we would have no way of predicting the next number we would generate by this process. We find, however, that this process tends to generate 3's much more often than it does 0's or 5's. Upon reflection this is no surprise, since there is only one way out of all 32 possible arrangements of heads and tails that produces five tails, whereas there are $C(5, 3) = 10$ ways to generate a sequence of three heads and two tails. In Figure C.1 we illustrate the results of 50 such coin tosses.

In Figure C.1 we have graphed the values of the random variable x representing the outcomes of the coin toss experiment and their frequencies, namely the number of times each value occurred in the experiment. The scale for the frequencies, $f(x)$, will clearly depend on the number, N, of trials in the experiment, so it would be better to graph the **probability** that each event occurred, which is nothing but $p(x) = f(x)/N$. The probabilities will always lie between 0 and 1, which if nothing else makes scaling the graph easier.

Suppose that x is a random variable that can take any value in the set $\{x_1, x_2, \ldots, x_n\}$, and suppose that the probability that x is equal to x_i is given by a function $p(x_i)$,

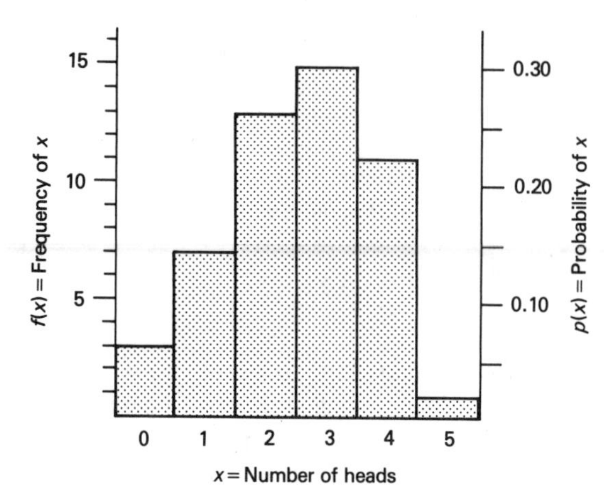

Figure C.1 Results of fifty trials of tossing five coins.

for $i = 1, 2, \ldots, n$, and that the sum $p(x_1) + \ldots + p(x_n) = 1$. Then we say that p is a **discrete probability function** for the random variable x. The set of values for x, along with the probability function for x is called the **distribution** of x. For the variable x of Figure C.1, for instance, we have the set of values $\{0, 1, 2, 3, 4, 5\}$, and p is defined by $p(0) = 0.06$, $p(1) = 0.14$, $p(2) = 0.26$, $p(3) = 0.30$, $p(4) = 0.22$, and $p(5) = 0.02$.

For any distribution where the set of values is a set of numbers, there are two measures that provide some information about how the random variable behaves. The **mean**, m, of a distribution is the sum of the possible values, weighted by their probabilities, and represents the "average" value of the distribution, while the **standard deviation**, σ, is the weighted sum of the squares of the differences between the values and the mean. Roughly speaking, the standard deviation represents how closely the values are clustered about the mean, with small standard deviations indicating that the values tend to fall close to the mean. For a given distribution, we may compute m and σ by

$$m = \sum_{k=1}^{n} p(x_k)x_k\,, \quad \sigma = \sqrt{\frac{1}{n-1}\sum_{k=1}^{n} p(x_k)(x_k - m)^2}$$

You should be able to verify that for the distribution of Figure C.1 we have $m = 2.54$ and $\sigma = 2.34$, reflecting that the expected value for x is between 2 and 3, and that the values that are obtained are moderately spread about the mean.

Cumulative Probability Functions

In some cases, we have a fair amount of knowledge ahead of time about the distribution of a random variable, simply by knowing about the process by which the random variable was generated. In other cases, however, we may be able to do no better than to watch a process in action and sample the frequencies of a random variable. If we watch long enough, we may be confident that the resulting probabilities accurately reflect the distribution of that random variable. We might then want to generate our own random variable, with the same distribution as the observed sample, for use in a program that simulates the process we observed.

One way to do this is to use a **cumulative distribution**. Suppose we have a distribution given by a set of values $\{x_1, x_2, \ldots, x_n\}$ and a probability function p. We form the **cumulative probability function**, P, by the rule

$$P(x_k) = \sum_{i=1}^{k} p(x_i), \quad \text{for } 1 \le k \le n$$

In other words, the cumulative probability function for the value x_k is found by taking the total of the probability functions for all the x_i for $i \le k$. For the probability function of Figure C.1, we have $P(0) = 0.06$, $P(1) = 0.20$, $P(2) = 0.46$, $P(3) = 0.76$, $P(4) = 0.98$, and $P(5) = 1.00$, as graphed in Figure C.2. Now let x be a random variable with value set $\{x_1, x_2, \ldots, x_n\}$ and probability function p, and suppose that P is the cumulative probability function obtained from p. We can use P to generate another random variable, y, with the same distribution as x as follows. We first choose a number, r, at random between 0 and 1. Then, if $r \le P(x_1)$, we set $y = x_1$, and otherwise we set $y = x_i$, where $2 \le i \le n$ and $P(x_{i-1}) < r \le P(x_i)$. As long as r is equally likely to take any value between 0 and 1, this process will guarantee that y has the same distribution as x. Consider the cumulative distribution graphed in Figure C.2. Geometrically, what we are doing is choosing a point at random on the vertical axis and drawing a horizontal line from that point. We then choose the x value corresponding to the first shaded bar we encounter. This gives the distribution we want because we choose x_i if and only if r satisfies $P(x_{i-1}) < r \le P(x_i)$, and the chance that that will happen is nothing but the length of the interval from $P(x_{i-1})$ to $P(x_i)$, which is $P(x_i) - P(x_{i-1}) = p(x_i)$.

It is easy to write a procedure that will generate such random variables. We pick a random number between 0 and 1, and track through the array of cumulative probabilities until we arrive at the first index i for which $P(x_{i-1}) < r$, at which point we stop and return the index i. We would then use the output index to select the value x_i.

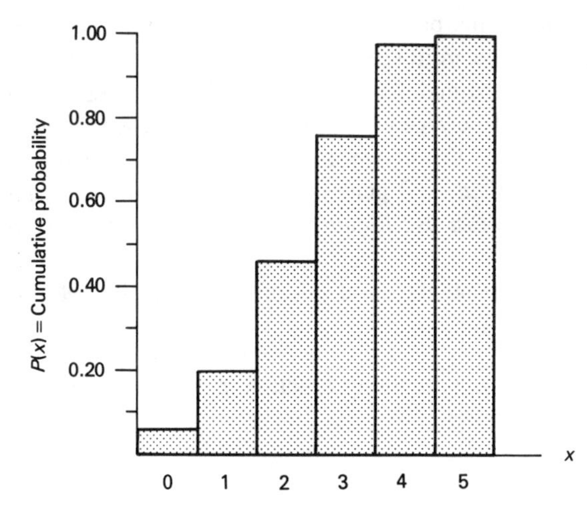

Figure C.2 Cumulative distribution of the data of Figure C.1.

```
{ Global declarations}
const
   N = {number of values of x }
type
   X_Range = 1 .. N;
var
   P : array [X_Range] of real;   {Cumulative probabilities for x }

{ Initialize P }

function Y : X_Range;
{ Returns the index of a value for Y, having the same distribution as x }
   var
      i : X_Range;
      r : real;
begin
   r := RandReal;          {Pick a real number between 0 and 1}
   i := 1;
   while r > P[i] do       {Search the cumulative probability array}
      i := i + 1;
   Y := i
end;
```

Some probability distributions have been studied in depth, largely because many real processes seem to behave according to these theoretical models. We will describe some of the more common distributions below.

Uniform Distributions

A perfectly fair six-sided die could serve as a generator for a random variable with the property that each of the six possible outcomes is equally likely. In general, if a distribution with a value set of size n has the property that for all $1 \le i \le n$ we have $p(x_i) = 1/n$, then such a distribution is called **uniform**. Because the linear congruential algorithms 1 and 2 above had parameters A and B chosen so that their periods were m, they both produce all possible values before repeating, and so the sequences they generate are uniformly distributed. This means that if we use such a distribution for *Random*, then the variables defined by *RandReal*, and hence by *RandomInt*, are also uniformly distributed. This also means that we can use *RandReal* as the basis for the cumulative distribution function described above.

It is not too difficult to show that if x is a uniform random variable on [0, 1) defined by

$$\text{Value set } = (0, \frac{1}{n}, \frac{2}{n}, \cdots \frac{n-1}{n}), \text{ probability function } p(\frac{k}{n}) = \frac{1}{n}, \; 0 \le k \le n,$$

then x has the measures

$$m = \frac{1}{2}\left(\frac{n-1}{n}\right), \quad \sigma = \sqrt{\frac{1}{12}\left(\frac{n+1}{n}\right)}.$$

Since the terms within the parentheses tend to 1 as n gets large, we can see that the mean and standard deviation of such a distribution tend to $1/2$ and $1/\sqrt{12}$, respectively.

Normal Distributions

There are a number of random variables, like shoe size and IQ, that seem to satisfy what is known as a **normal distribution**. The coin toss distribution of Figure C.1 approximates a normal distribution, in the sense that if we repeat the experiment with increasingly large numbers of coins, the resulting distributions tend, when properly scaled, to look more and more like the familiar bell curve of probability theory, graphed in Figure C.3.

The *continuous* normal distribution with mean m and standard deviation σ is given by the probability density function

$$p = e^{-z^2/2}, \quad \text{where } z = \frac{x-m}{\sigma}.$$

We will not be concerned here, however, with continuous distributions, but rather will only be interested in those distributions where the value set is finite. In other words, we would like to find a **discrete** (i.e., finite-valued) distribution that *approximates* the continuous normal distribution. Help arrives from the result we used to motivate the normal distribution, namely that the random variable that is formed when we add n independent random variables is approximately normal, and gets closer to a normal distribution the larger n is. This result is more precisely stated in theorem C.1.

Theorem C.1 (the Central Limit Theorem). If $x_1, \ldots, x_n$ are independent random variables, each with mean m and standard deviation σ, then as n increases, the distribution of the random variable z defined by

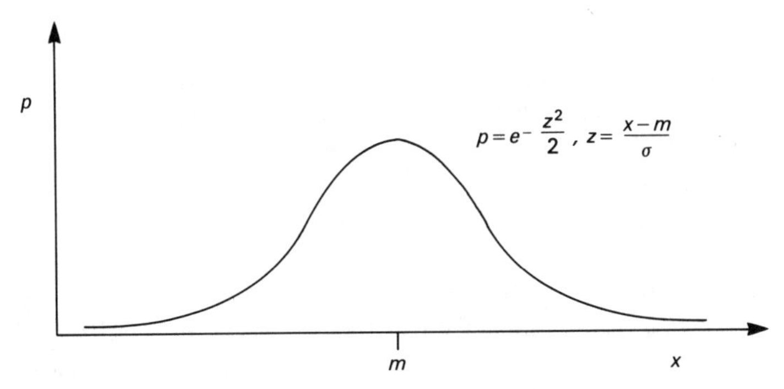

Figure C.3 Normal distribution, limiting case.

$$z = \frac{x_1 + \cdots + x_n - nm}{\sigma\sqrt{n}}$$

approaches a normal distribution with mean 0 and standard deviation 1.

In our case, we possess a function, *RandReal*, with mean approximately 1/2 and standard deviation approximately $1/\sqrt{12}$, so if we set $n = 12$ in the central limit theorem we find that the random variable $z = x_1 + \ldots + x_{12} - 6$ should serve as a pretty good approximation of a normally distributed random variable with mean 0 and standard deviation 1. The function is implemented below.

```
function Normal : real;
{ Generates an approximation to a normal random }
{variable with mean 0 and standard deviation 1.}
{Uses the function RandReal. }
   var
      i : integer;
      sum : real;
begin
   sum := 0;
   for i := 1 to 12 do
      sum := sum + RandReal;
   Normal := sum - 6.0
enda;
```

Of course, we may be in a situation where we want a different mean and standard deviation for our normally distributed random variable. It is not difficult to show that if z is a normal random variable with mean 0 and standard deviation 1, then we can produce another normal random variable y with mean m and standard deviation σ by defining

$$y = m + \sigma z.$$

Exponential Distributions

In many instances where customers arrive for service in an unpredictable manner, such as customers in line at a bank or terminals waiting for service by a time-sharing computer system, the times *between* arrivals (not the arrival times themselves, note) have an **exponential distribution**. In the continuous case, such a distribution has a probability function given by

$$p(x) = \frac{1}{\alpha} e^{-(x/\alpha)}$$

Such a distribution can be approximated by a discrete random variable whose probability function has the property that for all (or almost all) $i = 1, 2, \ldots, n$, $p(x_{i+1}) = Kp(x_i)$, for some $0 < K < 1$. A typical example is the discrete distribution with value set $\{x_1, \ldots, x_n\}$ and probability function given by

$$p(x_1) = \frac{1}{2}, \ p(x_2) = \frac{1}{4}, \ p(x_3) = \frac{1}{8}, \ \ldots, p(x_{n-1}) = p(x_n) = (\frac{1}{2})^{n-1}$$

which we graph in Figure C.4. The last two values are equal to ensure that the probabilities add up to 1, as they must.

The generation process for exponential distributions is particularly nice, and is summarized in the following theorem.

Theorem C.2. If z is a uniform random variable that takes values between 0 and 1, then the random variable $x = -\alpha \ln(z)$ has an exponential distribution given by the probability function

$$p(x) = \frac{1}{\alpha} e^{-(x/\alpha)}$$

This random variable has both mean and standard deviation equal to α.

The following function generates random numbers with exponential distribution, having mean and standard deviation equal to the input variable *alpha*.

```
function Exponential(alpha : real) : real;
{ Generates random real numbers which are exponentially}
{distributed with mean and standard deviation equal to alpha. }
{Uses the function RandReal to generate uniformly distributed}
{reals between 0 and 1.}
begin
   Exponential := - alpha * ln(RandReal)
end;
```

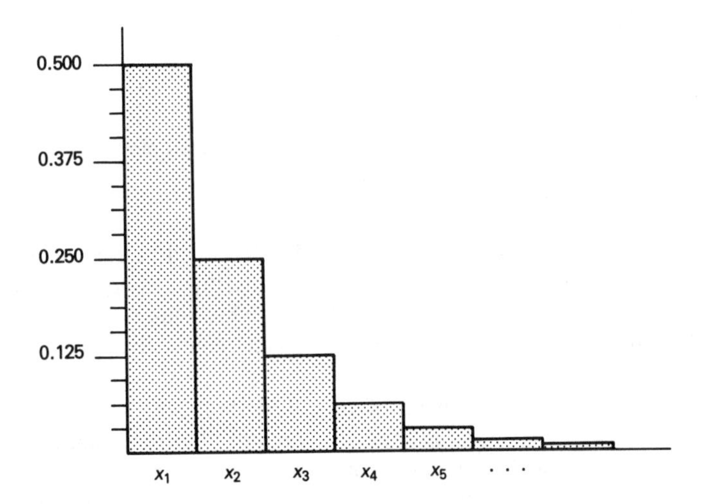

Figure C.4 Discrete exponential distribution.

C.3 SELECTION ALGORITHMS

One reason for simulation is that it might be impractical to test an algorithm on all possible inputs. If, for instance, we had a sorting algorithm and wanted to find how long it would take to sort a list of 12 numbers, it would obviously be foolish even to consider trying the algorithm on all 12! = 479,001,600 possible arrangements of the input. What we could do, however, would be to test the algorithm on a collection of sample inputs.

What we will cover in this section is a natural extension of the notion of choosing a single number at random. We will consider some simple data structures and will describe algorithms that generate randomly chosen instances of those structures. If you find yourself in need of selection algorithms that are not presented here, an excellent handbook is

Nijenhuis, Albert and Wulf, Herbert S., *Combinatorial Algorithms*. Academic Press, New York, 1975.

Selecting Subsets

In order to choose a random subset of a set $S = \{x_1, \ldots, x_n\}$, all we need to do is to decide, for each element in the set, whether that element should be included in the subset or not. If we represent the original set as a bit vector, $v[i]$, $i = 1, 2, \ldots, n$, of boolean values, then every instance of v corresponds uniquely to a subset of S, in such a way that x_i is in the subset if and only if x_i is *true*.

```
const
   SIZE = {the number of elements in the set S};
type
   SET = array [1 .. SIZE] of boolean;

procedurea SubsetSelect(var subset : SET);
   var i : integer;
begin
   for i := 1 to SIZE do
      {Pick 0 or 1 at random; x_i in the subset if we picked 0}
      subset[i] := (RandInt(1) = 0)
end;
```

SubsetSelect could hardly be simpler. It should be clear that this is a good random selection algorithm, in the sense that any subset of S is equally likely to be chosen, and that the choice of subset is independent of what subsets have been chosen before. The algorithm uses $O(n)$ space [or $O(1)$, if you charge the cost of the bit vector to the calling routine] and runs in time $O(n)$.

A possible disadvantage of this algorithm, however, is that there is no control over the size of the subset returned by the procedure. The sizes of the subsets generated by this process will be approximately normally distributed, with mean $(n - 1)/2$, for large enough n. We should not be surprised by this, since there is only one sequence of 0's and 1's which result in the empty set, while there are $C(n, k)$ such sequences that produce a subset with k elements. In most cases, this is no problem, since we are generally either interested in generating subsets without regard to their size, or we are only interested in generating subsets of a fixed size, which is the problem we turn to next.

Selecting a Subset with k Elements

Let $S = \{x_1, \ldots, x_n\}$ be a set with n elements, and let $0 < k \leq n$ be a fixed integer. We can then select a subset of S by specifying an array $sub[i]$, $i = 1, \ldots, k$ of numbers in the range $0, \ldots, k$ with the property that if $1 \leq i \neq j \leq n$, then $sub[i] \neq sub[j]$, that is, that the array *sub* have no duplicate entries. The correspondence between *sub* and subsets of S is then that x_i is in the subset if and only if the index i is an element of the position array *sub*.

The problem of k subset selection is thus equivalent to selecting a subset of k integers from the set $\{1, \ldots, n\}$. One way to do this to have an array, *sub*, initialized so that for $i = 1, \ldots, n$ we have $sub[i] = i$, and for each of the first k indices in turn, swap the element in that index location of *sub* with the entry in a randomly chosen location at or above that index. At the end of this process, the first k entries in *sub* will contain a random subset of the set $\{1, \ldots, n\}$.

For example, suppose that $n = 6$ and $k = 3$. Below we indicate the selection process, with the element at the current index in **boldface** and the element with which it is to be swapped <u>underscored</u>.

Step 1:	**1**	<u>2</u>	3	4	5	6
Step 2:	2	**1**	3	4	<u>5</u>	6
Step 3:	2	5	**3**	4	1	<u>6</u>
Done:	2	5	6	**4**	1	3

After having performed $k = 3$ swaps, the selected subset is $\{2, 5, 6\}$, found in the first three entries of *sub*.

```
const
   SIZE = {size of set from which to select samples};
type
   SelectArray = array [1 .. SIZE] of integer;

procedure k_Select(k : integer ; var sub : SelectArray);
   var i, swap, save : integer;
begin
   for i := 1 to SIZE do
      sub[i] := i;

   for i := 1 to k do begin
      swap := i + RandInt(n - i);  {choose index of entry to swap with i-th entry}

      save := sub[swap];
      sub[swap] := sub[i];         {swap the entries}
      sub[i] := save
   end
end;
```

The proof that *k_Select* works properly is a bit complicated, but it is indeed the case that *k_Select* randomly selects k element subsets of $\{1, \ldots, n\}$ in such a way that each subset is equally likely to be chosen. This algorithm actually serves two purposes, since it is also possible to show that *k_Select* generates uniformly distributed random *permutations* of the numbers 1 through n, if it is called with $k = n$.

This algorithm uses $O(n)$ space and runs in time $O(n + k)$, since the running time is controlled by the two loops. These time and space requirements may be larger than we wish to accept if, for instance, we are selecting a sample of just 10 numbers from a universe of 32,768. It would be nice if we could find an algorithm that used space and time that were independent of n. A simple method would be the following:

```
while the number of elements selected is less than k do begin
    Choose a random number, r, in the range 1 . . n ;
    if r has not yet been selected then
        Include r among the selected numbers
end;
```

This process requires only enough space needed to store the k numbers selected. The time this algorithm takes to run is $O(p(s + t))$, where p is the number of times the loop iterates, s is the amount of time it takes to decide whether an element has been selected already, and t is the amount of time it takes to insert an element among the selected numbers. We have little control over p; although it is beyond the scope of this section to show, it is the case that the expected number of times the loop will have to iterate is

$$n \ln\left(\frac{n}{n-k}\right) = k\,(-\frac{1}{\alpha}\ln(1-\alpha)), \quad \text{if we write } \alpha = \frac{k}{n}.$$

In other words, if we are sure that k will never be larger than αn, for some fixed constant $0 < \alpha < 1$, then we can expect the loop to iterate $O(k)$ times, on the average.

If we expect to produce an algorithm with running time $O(k)$, then, we must make sure that the testing and insertion segments run in constant time. With a data structure which requires fast insertion and membership testing, hashing (see Chapter 9) is the natural choice. We will use an array, *hash*, indexed from 0 to $k - 1$, such that each element in the array is a pointer to a linked list. To test or insert a number, r, we first find $i = r$ **mod** k, and then search the linked list at index i to see if the r is there or not. Such a technique will, on the average, require fewer than two tests of the list, and hence insertion and testing will each contribute $O(1)$ time to each iteration of the loop. In other words, this k-subset selection technique will require $O(k)$ space for the array and the linked lists, and will run in time $O(k)$ if the load k/n does not get too close to 1, and in the worst case will run in time $O(k \log k)$.

```
const
    SIZE = {some integer, k, for the sample size};
    SIZE_1 = { k – 1}
type
    SelectArray = array [1 .. SIZE] of integer;
```

```
procedure k_Select2(var sub : SelectArray);
   type
      CellPtr = ^Cell;
      Cell = record
               number : integer;
               next : CellPtr
             end;
   var
      hash : array [0 .. SIZE_1] of CellPtr;
      success : boolean;
      count, r, i : integer;

   procedure Insert(r : integer ; var success : boolean);
      var p : CellPtr;
          done : boolean;
   begin
      p := hash[r mod SIZE];
      done := false;
      while not done do
         if p = nil then begin     {reached the end of the list without finding r}
            done := true;
            success := true;
            New(p);
            p^.number := r;
            p^.next := nil
         end else if p^.number = r then begin {found r}
            done := true;
            success := true
         end else
            p := p^.next           {haven't found r or end of list, keep looking}
   end; {Insert}

begin {k_Select2}
   for i := 0 to SIZE_1 do         {initialize the hash table}
      hash[i] := nil;
   count := 0;
   while count < SIZE do begin
      r := 1 + RandInt(n - 1);     {pick a number between 1 and n}
      Insert(r, success);          {try to insert that number into the hash table}
      if success then begin        {insertion succeeded, add r to selected array}
         count := count + 1;
         sub[count] := r
      end
   end
end;
```

Enumerating Permutations

We have seen that *k_Select* can be used as a generator for random permutations of the set $\{1, \ldots, n\}$. There may be a time when you need to select permutations in a systematic fashion, however, and would like to avoid the possible duplication that could arise from choosing permutations at random. Donald Knuth, in *The Art of Computer Programming*, (Addison-Wesley, New York, 1971, Vol. 2, pp. 59–60), presents an algorithm that assigns a permutation of $\{1, \ldots, n\}$ to each integer f, $0 \leq f < n!$ in such a way that different values of f give rise to different permutations. By applying either of the k subset selection algorithms to produce a subset of choices for f, we could then use the algorithm below to produce a set of k different permutations of $\{1, \ldots, n\}$.

```
const
   SIZE = { n};
type
   SelectArray = array [1 .. SIZE] of integer;

procedure DecodePermutation(f : integer ; var sub : SelectArray);
   var
      c : array [1 .. SIZE] of integer;
      i, m, swap : integer;
begin
   for i := 1 to SIZE do    {initialize sub}
      sub[i] := i;

   m := f;
   for i := SIZE downto 1 do begin {set values for index swapping array}
      c[i] := m mod i;
      m := m div i
   end;
```

We may not understand at this stage how it works (see the exercises), but it is clear that this algorithm requires $O(n)$ time and space. Knuth also shows that *DecodePermutation* is also easily invertible, in that there is another algorithm, which we might call *EncodePermutation*, that takes a permutation and produces the corresponding integer code.

C.4 EXERCISES

1. Using the linear congruential algorithm (1) with $x_0 = 0$,
   (a) Show what $x_1, \ldots, x_{10}$ would be.
   (b) Investigate the low-order two bits of this sequence by looking at x_i **mod** 4.
   (c) Suggest how you would modify the linear congruential algorithm to make the low-order bits of the pseudo-random sequence more reliable.

2. In the linear congruential algorithm, why is it a good idea to make sure that A, B, and m have no factors in common?

3. The numbers 16,384 and 32,768 are either close to or greater than the maximum integers allowed on many computers, but the linear congruential algorithm requires that all arithmetic be done exactly, with no truncation. How would you implement this algorithm to avoid integer overflow?

4. Many random number generators always give the same sequence of random numbers each time a program using them is run. Why is this a good idea? Suggest how you would write a random number generator that would *not* have this feature.

5. Given integers $a < b$, how could you use *RandReal* to produce a uniform random variable with value set $\{a, \ldots, b\}$?

6. Show that the uniform distribution defined by

$$\text{Value set} = \left(0, \frac{1}{n}, \frac{2}{n}, \ldots, \frac{n-1}{n}\right), \text{ probability function } p\left(\frac{k}{n}\right) = \frac{1}{n}, \quad 0 \le k < n$$

has mean and standard deviation given by

$$m = \frac{1}{2}\left(\frac{n-1}{n}\right), \quad \sigma = \sqrt{\frac{1}{12}\left(\frac{n+1}{n}\right)}$$

7. The probability function of the random variable that counts the number of heads in six tosses of a fair coin is defined by

$$p(0) = p(6) = \frac{1}{64}, \quad p(1) = p(5) = \frac{6}{64}, \quad p(2) = p(4) = \frac{15}{64}, \quad p(3) = \frac{20}{64}$$

(a) Find the cumulative probability function, P.

(b) Using the function Y described in the text to generate random numbers with a given distribution, tell what y values would correspond to the r values 0.067, 0.265, 0.999.

8. The **Zipf distribution** is defined on a value set $\{x_1, \ldots, x_n\}$ by

$$p(x_k) = \frac{k}{n}\left(\frac{1}{H_n}\right), \quad \text{for } k = 1, \ldots, n, \text{ and } H_n = 1 + \frac{1}{2} + \frac{1}{3} + \cdots + \frac{1}{n}$$

The number H_n is called the nth **harmonic number**, and is approximately $\ln n$. If the value set is chosen so that $x_n = k$, find the mean of the Zipf distribution. This distribution, by the way, was discovered to fit a number of seemingly unrelated random variables, such as worker salaries, city sizes, and word frequencies in many languages. In the case of word frequencies, it was suggested that the distribution implied a "rule of economy" in linguistics, that short words were more frequent because there was some inner mechanism that made us tend to use short words. It turned out, however, that the Zipf distribution was merely a statistical artifact (much like the normal distribution, which arises in many cases where a random variable is formed from the sum of other random variables), and so probably didn't have any deep significance.

9. Trace the action of *k_Select* with $n = 8$, $k = 5$, and successive values of *swap* equal to 6, 6, 2, 3.

10. Using *DecodePermutation* with $n = 3$,

(a) List the permutations that correspond to the f values 0, 1, 2, 3, 4, 5.

(b) See if you can guess the values for $c[1]$, $c[2]$, $c[3]$, $c[4]$, in the $n = 4$ case, for all $f = 0, \ldots, 24$.

11. Simplify *DecodePermutation* by observing something about the value of $c[1]$.

Index